INDIA INFRASTRUCTURE REPORT 2012

INDIA INFRASTRUCTURE REPORT 2012

Private Sector in Education

IDFC FOUNDATION

Routledge
Taylor & Francis Group
LONDON NEW YORK NEW DELHI

First published 2013 in India
by Routledge
912 Tolstoy House, 15–17 Tolstoy Marg, Connaught Place, New Delhi 110 001

Simultaneously published in the UK
by Routledge
2 Park Square, Milton Park, Abingdon, OX14 4RN

Routledge is an imprint of the Taylor & Francis Group, an informa business

© 2013 IDFC Foundation

The views expressed in this report are those of the individual authors and not the institutions they are affiliated to, or IDFC Limited, or IDFC Foundation, or the Publisher.

Typeset by
Excellent Laser Typesetters
Pitampura, Delhi 110 034

British Library Cataloguing-in-Publication Data
A catalogue record of this book is available from the British Library

ISBN 978-0-415-83721-7

About IDFC Foundation

IDFC Limited (formerly Infrastructure Development Finance Company Limited) was incorporated in 1997 as India's first specialised infrastructure-financing intermediary in order to address the growing requirements of the various infrastructure sectors. IDFC's mandate is to lead private capital flows to commercially viable infrastructure projects. In keeping with its mission of 'being the leading knowledge-driven financial services platform, creating enduring value, promoting infrastructure and nation building, in India and beyond', IDFC has carved out its development agenda under the rubric of the IDFC Foundation. IDFC Foundation is a wholly-owned subsidiary of IDFC Limited and a not-for-profit company under Section 25 of the Companies Act, 1956. IDFC Foundation's activities, which are aimed at strengthening the delivery of public infrastructure services, include policy advocacy and research, programme support and advisory services, capacity-building and community engagement programmes.

India Infrastructure Report

India Infrastructure Report (IIR) is the result of the IDFC Foundation's collaborative approach towards providing a forum for free, frank and open exchange of views necessary to arrive at innovative and workable solutions across various infrastructure sectors that would find acceptance among various stakeholders. It is the outcome of the efforts of academics, researchers and experts, and is widely disseminated. The theme of *IIR* every year is carefully chosen to reflect a central contemporary issue in infrastructure development. The *Report* promotes discussion on various facets around the central theme and also suggests pragmatic solutions to overcome challenges. The *IIR*, considered extremely useful by policy-makers, receives wide publicity and provides an excellent forum for scholars and practitioners to share their views with decision-makers.

All the previous *IIRs* may be freely accessed from http://www.idfc.com/foundation/policy/india_infrastructure_report. htm.

OTHER IIR TITLES

India Infrastructure Report 2001
Issues in Regulation and Market Structure

India Infrastructure Report 2002
Governance Issues for Commercialization

India Infrastructure Report 2003
Public Expenditure Allocation and Accountability

India Infrastructure Report 2004
Ensuring Value for Money

India Infrastructure Report 2006
Urban Infrastructure

India Infrastructure Report 2007
Rural Infrastructure

India Infrastructure Report 2008
Business Models of the Future

India Infrastructure Report 2009
Land — A Critical Resource for Infrastructure

India Infrastructure Report 2010
Infrastructure Development in a Low Carbon Economy

India Infrastructure Report 2011
Water: Policy and Performance for Sustainable Development

Contents

Section III
Higher and Vocational Education

Section IV
Role of Teacher Training and ICT in Education

Section V
Review of Infrastructure Sector in India

Foreword

Nation-building rests on both physical and social infrastructure. This year, for the first time in our *India Infrastructure Report (IIR)* series, we turn to social infrastructure — in particular the educational system. Education is the cornerstone for social and economic transformation, for building a healthy, active citizenry participating in a just and democratic society.

After six decades, India has achieved near universal primary school enrolment. Increasingly, girls are going to school for basic education. While social inequalities persist, the gap has been narrowed in some areas. There are other advances too: school attendance has been rising and dropout rates have come down, though still unacceptably high. The demand for education has been growing rapidly as evidenced by the increasing number of parents sending their children to private schools in the rural areas. The private sector reaches 25 per cent of the children in elementary education, and more than 50 per cent of those in secondary and higher education.

Sadly, however, the quality of learning across all levels of the education system is abysmally low. All surveys and measurement tools unanimously point to one conclusion — extremely poor learning outcomes across-the-board. Urban schools are not significantly better than rural schools and the vast majority of private schools are not much better than government schools, after taking into account the advantage that children from wealthier, educated families have. About half of the primary school students are three classes below the levels they ought to be in reading and even more in arithmetic. These appalling outcomes continue or are even exacerbated at the secondary and higher levels. High school children do not have basic conceptual understanding. Students entering the workforce have very low employability. Clearly, *raising the quality of education is the biggest challenge in our educational system.*

After decades of neglect, education is being prioritised by policy-makers. Recent initiatives include the landmark Right of Children to Free and Compulsory Education Act (RTE), 2009, flagship schemes related to secondary and vocational education, and several Bills on higher education. The central government has also increased expenditure on education at all levels. Whilst there are positive features in all these efforts, there is a common theme that runs through them. It is more of the same: increased inputs, standardised norms and more finance in the same system. The RTE Act, though well-intentioned, could wreak further damage if it is implemented rigidly. It could aggravate the learning gap by automatic promotion to the next class. Further, thousands of schools may not be recognised under the new RTE norms and would have to close down, throwing millions of children out of school. It would kill innovation, experimentation and alternative schools; unless the states, that are bound by RTE, ensure that the rules in implementing the Act are flexible and focus on performance, not inputs.

This *IIR* makes a plea for a radically different approach. It is important to take on board the lessons from various experiments and try to apply them in a systemic way with much greater focus on assessment methods. At the school-level, the priorities should be a clear articulation of learning goals, organising children according to their learning abilities and not on the basis of their age, retaining students if they are not ready for the next class, and buttressed by professional teacher training and pedagogical reform. A major overhaul of the higher education system is also urgently needed with a view to going beyond minimum standards and enabling excellence. Along with mandatory accreditation by independent bodies, greater autonomy should be granted to institutions of higher learning that also allows them more flexibility to raise legitimate sources of financing to build endowments and provide scholarships. Further, there is a need for non-traditional approaches to regulate these institutions, relying more on internal and external evaluations and public disclosure of information.

Overall, a diversity of schools and higher educational institutions should be permitted as long as they are able to deliver quality outcomes. Greater partnership between the private sector and government is required to make all types of education, including vocational, more relevant to a rapidly growing economy and a more enlightened society.

This *IIR* brings together perspectives from experts deeply committed to the education sector. We present hotly debated alternative views and evidence to show what works and what does not. The underlying aim is to make suggestions for improving the quality of education in an inclusive way, keeping the child and the youth at the centre of the process. I hope that this *IIR* will contribute to the evolving literature on the education system, help raise public awareness and debate on the issue, and become an input to policy formulation. I would like to thank the authors, editors and all those who have contributed to the production of this *Report*.

RAJIV B. LALL
Vice Chairman and Managing Director
IDFC Limited

Acknowledgements

The *India Infrastructure Report* (IIR), for over a decade now, has taken up contemporary issues related to physical infrastructure. However, the writing on the wall is bold and clear — progress in social infrastructure, like education and health, should go hand-in-hand with advancement in physical infrastructure for sustainable development. Sadly, more often than not, the education sector in India is in the news headlines for all the wrong reasons. In this milieu, considering IDFC's commitment to nation building, Ritu Anand proposed that this year we should look into the concerns of the education sector.

First, I would like to express my deep gratitude to Ritu Anand for bestowing her faith in me to take up this important assignment. Her unwavering support, guidance and encouragement saw us through this publication.

We are deeply indebted to Geetha Nambissan, Madhav Chavan, Rukmini Banerji, Saumen Chattopadhyay, Anit N. Mukherjee, M. H. Suryanarayana, Raja Parthasarathy, Vikram Pant, Anand Sudarshan and Srinivas Rao for explaining to me the complexities of the sector, and for introducing us to other experts. The insightful discussions and diverse perspectives immensely helped us to define the contours of this *IIR*.

The lively and extremely valuable deliberations at the Writers' Workshop held at IDFC Foundation, New Delhi, on 30 and 31 March 2012 helped to shape the final report. We put on record our gratitude to all the workshop participants, including those who may not have contributed to the report as authors. In this regard, those who deserve special mention are Sumali Moitra, Srinivas Rao, Cherian Thomas, Ritu Anand, Ranesh Nair, Protiva Kundu, Jyoti Gujral, Chandrima Sinha, and Neeraj Agarwal. We would also like to express our appreciation to Babu Nambiar, Renu Mehtani and others from the IDFC Delhi Office for helping in organising the Writers' Workshop.

This report would not have been possible but for the authors, who made major contributions and despite their busy schedules cooperated with us throughout. Their patience, when dealing with our repeated editing requests and reminders, is deeply appreciated. We are grateful to all the contributors.

We would like to thank Rajiv B. Lall, Vice Chairman and Managing Director, IDFC Limited, for his unstinted support and encouragement to the publication of *IIR 2012*. We would also like to thank Cherian Thomas, CEO, IDFC Foundation and Animesh Kumar, Co-CEO, IDFC Foundation for their constant encouragement during the course of preparing the report.

In bringing out the *IIR 2012*, efforts and support have come from many more. First, we would like to deeply acknowledge the contribution of Bharati Sawant throughout the preparation of this report. Her versatility as well as keen eye for detail was indispensible. The competence with which she organised every event, coordinated with the authors on multiple tasks, assisted in editorial work and proofreading, interacted with Routledge, New Delhi, and tirelessly supported on many other tasks on the project is immensely appreciated. Our special thanks to Ranesh Nair, Megha Maniar and Satish M. K. for their editorial support. We would also like to thank Lavi D'Costa, Pritika Hingorani, Protiva Kundu, Tanvi Bhatkal, and Sourabh Ghosh for their help and encouragement at all times. We would also like to acknowledge our appreciation for the support extended by Santosh Parab, Lakshmi R. N., Rahul Samuel, Santosh Shinde, Arun Raste, Venkataraman K. V., and Mona Mohan.

Our special thanks are due also to Routledge, New Delhi, the publishers of this *IIR 2012*, who have been consistent in maintaining quality while accommodating sometimes exacting demands made on them.

Finally, we would like to thank all our colleagues at IDFC Limited and IDFC Foundation who provided us academic and practitioner perspectives on the issues. While we have taken care to include everyone who helped us in compiling the *IIR 2012*, any omissions are purely unintentional and we hope that they would be construed as such!

SAMBIT BASU

List of Tables, Figures and Boxes

Figures

BOXES

List of Abbreviations

AAI	Airport Authority of India
ABL	Activity-Based Learning
ADDIE	Analysis, Design, Development, Implementation and Evaluation
ADF	Airport Development Fee
AICTE	All India Council of Technical Education
AIE	Alternative and Innovative Education
APPEP	Andhra Pradesh Primary Education Project
ASEAN	Association of Southeast Asian Nations
ASER	Annual Status of Education Report
ASSOCHAM	Associated Chambers of Commerce and Industry of India
AT&C	Aggregate Technical and Commercial
AV	Audio-Visual
AWC	*Anganwadi* Centre
AWH	*Anganwadi* Helper
AWP&B	Annual Work Plan and Budget
AWW	*Anganwadi* Worker
BBNL	Bharat Broadband Network Ltd
BCG	Boston Consulting Group
BEd	Bachelor of Education
BElEd	Bachelor of Elementary Education (Programme)
BEO	Bihar Education Project
BGVS	Bharat Gyan Vigyan Samithi
BITE	Block Institute of Teacher Education
BITS	Birla Institute of Technology and Science
BOOT	Build–Own–Operate–Transfer
BPL	Below Poverty Line
BPO	Business Process Outsourcing
BRC	Block Resource Centre
BSNL	Bharat Sanchar Nigam Limited
BTSs	Base Transceiver Stations
BWA	Broadband Wireless Access
CABE	Central Advisory Board of Education
CAG	Comptroller Auditor General
CAMaL	Combined Activities for Maximised Learning
CAP	Comprehensive Turnaround Plan
CARE	Child and Adolescent Resources and Education
CAT	Common Admission Test
CBI	Central Bureau of Investigation
CBSE	Central Board of Secondary Education
CCE	Continuous and Comprehensive Evaluation
CCS	Centre for Civil Society

CDMA	Code Division Multiple Access
CERC	Central Electricity Regulatory Commission
CEO	Chief Executive Officer
CGPA	Cumulative Grade Point Average
CII	Confederation of Indian Industry
CIL	Coal India Limited
CIS	Commonwealth of Independent States
CISCE	Council for the Indian School Certificate Examination
CITI	Confederation of Indian Textile Industry
CLE	Council for Leather Exports
CM / SIS	Campus Management / Student Information System
CMS	Campus Management System
CRC	Cluster Resource Centre
CREDAI	Confederation of Real Estate Developers Associations of India
CRISIL	Credit Rating Information Services of India Limited
CRS	Crew Management System
CSR	Corporate Social Responsibility
CSS	Centrally Sponsored Scheme
CTE	College of Teacher Education
CTET	Central Teacher Eligibility Test
DDO	Drawing and Disbursement Officer
DEC	Distance Education Council
DEd	Diploma in Education
DGCA	Directorate General of Civil Aviation
DIAC	Dubai International Academic City
DIET	District Institute of Education and Training
DISE	District Information System for Education
DoT	Department of Telecommunications
DPEP	District Primary Education Programme
DWM	Drinking Water Mission
EAC	Engineering Accreditation Council
EDC	Education Development Centre
EduTech	Educational Technology
EGoM	Empowered Group of Ministers
EGS	Education Guarantee Scheme
EI	Education Initiatives
EPC	Engineering, Procurement and Construction
ERP	Enterprise Resource Planning
ESC	Educational Service Contracting
ESP	Educational Service Provider
EVS	Education Voucher System
EWS	Economically Weaker Section
FDI	Foreign Direct Investment
FICCI	Federation of Indian Chambers of Commerce and Industry
FIES	*Financiamento Estudantil*
FII	Foreign Institutional Investor
FOSS	Free Open Source Software
FRP	Financial Restructuring Plan
FSAs	Fuel Supply Agreements
GDP	Gross Domestic Product
GER	Gross Enrolment Ratio
GGV	Grey Ghosts Ventures

GJEPC	Gems and Jewellery Export Promotion Council
GMC	Grey Matter Capital
GoI	Government of India
GPI	Gender Parity Index
GSM	Global System for Mobile (Communications)
HER	Higher Education and Research
HNWI	High Net-Worth Individual
HR	Human Resource
HRD	Human Resource Development
IASE	Institute of Advanced Study in Education
ICF	Integral Coach Factory
ICRA	Internet Content Rating Association
ICSSR	Indian Council of Social Science Research
ICT	Information and Communication Technology
ID	Identity Document
IDMI	Scheme for Infrastructure Development in Minority Institute
IEDC	Integrated Education for Disabled Children
IEDSS	Inclusive Education for the Disabled at Secondary Stage
IEQA	Institutional Eligibility for Quality Assessment
IGC	India Growth Centre
IGCSE	International General Certificate of Secondary Education
IGNOU	Indira Gandhi National Open University
IHDS	India Human Development Survey
IHRDE	Institute of Human Resources Development in Electronics
IIM	Indian Institute of Management
IIT	Indian Institute of Technology
IL&FS	Infrastructure Leasing & Financial Services Limited
IL&FS ETS	IL&FS Education & Technology Services
IMaCS	ICRA Management Consulting Services Limited
IMF	International Monetary Fund
INQAAHE	International Network for Quality Assurance Agencies in Higher Education
IP	Intellectual Property
IP	Internet Protocol
IPAI	Institute of Public Auditors of India
IPv6	Internet Protocol version 6
IRAHE	Independent Regulatory Authority for Higher Education
IRI	Interactive Radio Instruction
ISFC	India School Finance Corporation
IT	Information Technology
ITC	Industrial Training Centre
ITI	Industrial Training Institute
IVRS	Interactive Voice Response System
JNNSM	Jawaharlal Nehru National Solar Mission
JNNURM	Jawaharlal Nehru National Urban Renewal Mission
JNPT	Jawaharlal Nehru Port Trust
J-PAL	Jamil-Poverty Action Lab
JSS	Jagadguru Sree Shivarathishwara
KVS	Kendriya Vidyalaya Sangathan
LFP	Low-Fee Private (school)
LHB	Linke Hofmann Bush
LJP	Lok Jumbish Project
LMIS	Labour Market Information System

LMS	Learning Management System
LNG	Liquefied Natural Gas
M&A	Merger and Acquisition
MA	Master of Arts
MACESE	Maulana Azad Centre for Elementary and Social Education
MaGE	Manipal Global Education (Services)
MDG	Millennium Development Goal
MDM	Mid-Day Meal
MFI	Mutual Funds Investment
MGNREGA	Mahatma Gandhi National Rural Employment Guarantee Act
MHRD	Ministry of Human Resource Development
MHUPA	Ministry of Housing and Poverty Alleviation
MI	Monitoring Institution
MIS	Management Information System
MIT	Massachusetts Institute of Technology
MLG	Millennium Learning Goal
mmscmd	million metric standard cubic metre per day
MNP	Mobile Number Portability
MNRE	Ministry of New and Renewable Energy
MoC	Memorandum of Cooperation
MOOC	Massive Open Online Course
MoP	Ministry of Power
MoR	Ministry of Railways
MoRTH	Ministry of Road Transport and Highways
MoS	Ministry of Shipping
MRTS	Mass Rapid Transit System
MS	Mahila Samakhya
MSE	Micro and Small Enterprise
MUD	Ministry of Urban Development
MV	M. Venkatarangaiya (Foundation)
NAA	National Accreditation Authority
NAAC	National Assessment and Accreditation Council
NAC	National Advisory Council
NARA	National Accreditation Regulatory Authority
NASSCOM	National Association of Software and Services Companies
NBFC	Non-Banking Finance Company
NCAER	National Council of Applied Economic Research
NCERT	National Council of Educational Research and Training
NCF	National Curriculum Framework
NCHER	National Commission of Higher Education and Research
NCHRH	National Commission for Human Resources for Health
NCLP	National Child Labour Project
NCPCR	National Commission for Protection of Child Rights
NCTE	National Council for Teacher Education
NCVT	National Council for Vocational Training
NEFC	National Education Finance Corporation
NEP	National Policy on Education
NER	North Eastern Region
NER	Net Enrolment Ratio
NET	National Eligibility Test
NFE	Non-Formal Education
NFSB	National Food Security Bill

NGO	Non-Governmental Organisation
NHAI	National Highways Authority of India
NHDP	National Highway Development Programme
NIOS	National Institute of Open Schooling
NIT	National Institute of Technology
NKC	National Knowledge Commission
NMMS	National Merit-cum-Means Scholarship
NOFN	National Optical Fibre Network
NOS	National Occupational Standard
NPE	National Policy on Education
NREGA	National Rural Employment Guarantee Act
NSDC	National Skill Development Corporation
NSDCB	National Skill Development Coordination Board
NSDF	National Skill Development Fund
NSDM	National Skill Development Mission
NSS	National Statistical Survey
NSSO	National Sample Survey Organisation
NTP	New Telecom Policy
NTPDC	National Transport Policy Development Committee
NUEPA	National University of Educational Planning and Administration
NVEQF	National Vocational Educational Qualification Framework
OBB	Operation Blackboard
OBC	Other Backward Class
OBE	Open Basic Education
OECD	Organisation for Economic Co-operation and Development
OMT	Operation, Maintenance and Transfer
PAB	Planning and Budgeting
PAISA	Planning, Allocations and Expenditures, Institutions: Studies in Accountability
PAT	Perform, Achieve and Trade
PI	Policy Innovations
PISA	Programme for International Student Assessment
PLF	Plant Load Factor
PLI	Postal Life Insurance
PMGSY	Pradhan Mantri Gram Sadak Yojana
PPP	Public–Private Partnership
ProUni	*Programa Universidade para Todos* — University for All
PSK	Prarambhik Shiksha Kosh
PTR	Pupil–Teacher Ratio
R&D	Research and Development
R-APDRP	Re-structured Accelerated Power Development & Reforms Programme
RAI	Retailers Association of India
RBI	Reserve Bank of India
RCT	Randomised Control Trial
REC	Renewable Energy Certificate
REPA	Right to Education Protection Authority
RGGVY	Rajiv Gandhi Grameen Vidyutikaran Yojana
RGI	Registrar General of India
RLDA	Rail Land Development Authority
RMSA	Rashtriya Madhyamik Shiksha Abhiyan
ROI	Return on Investment
RPOs	Renewable Power Obligations
RTE	Right to Education

RTI	Right to Information
RTO	Regional Transport Office
SAARC	South Asian Association for Regional Cooperation
SBD	Standard Bidding Document
SC	Scheduled Caste
SCERT	State Council of Educational Research and Training
SCPCR	State Commission for Protection of Child Rights
SCR	Student–Classroom Ratio
SCVT	State Council for Vocational Training
SD	Secure Digital
SDG	School Development Grant
SDP	School Development Plan
SEMIS	Secondary Education Management Information System
SERC	State Electricity Regulatory Commission
SIAM	Society of Indian Automobile Manufacturers
SIMS	Student Information Management System
SIS	State Implementation Societies
SJTU	Shanghai Jiao Tong University
SKP	Shiksha Karmi Project
SLS	Same Language Subtitling
SMC	School Management Committee
SMDC	School Management Development Committee
SMG	School Maintenance Grant
SMS	School Management System
SMS	Short Message Service
SMS	Student Management System
SPO	State Project Office
SPQEM	Scheme to Provide Quality Education in Madrassas
SPV	Special Purpose Vehicle
SRS	Student Records System
SSA	Sarva Shiksha Abhiyan
SSC	Sector Skill Council
ST	Scheduled Tribe
SWOT	Strengths, Weaknesses, Opportunities, and Threats
T4	Technology Tools for Teaching and Training
TAMP	Tariff Authority for Major Ports
TAN	Transnational Advocacy Network
TCS	Tata Consultancy Services
TEL	Technology Enabled Learning
TET	Teacher Eligibility Test
THES	Times Higher Education Supplement
TIMSS	Trends in International Mathematics and Science Survey
TISS	Tata Institute of Social Sciences
TLM	Teaching Learning Material (Grant)
TRAI	Telecom Regulatory Authority of India
TSC	Total Sanitation Campaign
TV	Television
UAE	United Arab Emirates
UAS	Unified Access Services
UEE	Universal Elementary Education
UEE	Universalisation of Elementary Education
UGC	University Grants Commission

UIDAI	Unique Identification Authority of India
UIDSSMT	Urban Infrastructure Development Scheme for Small and Medium Towns
UK	United Kingdom
ULB	Urban Local Body
UMPP	Ultra Mega Power Project
UNESCO	United Nations Educational, Scientific and Cultural Organization
UNICEF	United Nations Children's Fund
UPBEP	UP Basic Education Project
US	United States
USAID	United States Agency for International Development
USOF	Universal Service Obligation Fund
UTM	University of Technology, Mauritius
YES	Youth Employability Skill

Private Sector in Education: An Overview

Sambit Basu

Education holds the key to India's growth and socio-economic development. This has assumed greater importance over the last decade with India positioning itself as a knowledge economy in a fast globalising world. An educated population not only drives economic growth, but also has a positive impact on health and nutrition. Well-balanced education is also essential in building a just and democratic society. Thus, it is indeed critical for India, having a large young population and being low on human development indicators, to fast track access to quality education.

Realising the economic benefits of education, the political leadership set up several higher education institutions of excellence, like the Indian Institute of Technology (IIT), Indian Institute of Management (IIM), Indian Statistical Institute (ISI), and Indian Institute of Science (IISc) immediately after independence. For several decades the focus of central government policy was on higher education. School education, more specifically village-school education, was not given importance during the momentous nation-building period of the 1950s and the following decades. Although free and compulsory education for all children up to the age of 14 years was in the Directive Principles of State Policy in the Constitution, continued policy neglect was reflected in the number of illiterates rising from 294 million in 1951 to 376 million in 1971.

In 1976, education was transferred from the state to the concurrent list in the Constitution, making it the explicit responsibility of both central and state governments. But it was only in the 1980s that the political leadership saw the criticality of education in building 21ˢᵗ-century India. The New Policy on Education (NPE), which was introduced in 1986, and the National Curriculum Framework (NCF) ushered in education reforms and new institutions. The efforts were intensified in the 1990s through various schemes to improve school enrolment, reduce gender and other inequities as also dropout rates.

In 1993, the Supreme Court recognised that the right to education was a fundamental right as it was an inherent part of the right to life. The central government initiated the

Sarva Shiksha Abhiyan (SSA) in 2000, the most prominent centrally-sponsored scheme aimed towards enrolment of all children in school, bringing out-of-school children to school, retention of children at upper-primary level, and enhancement in learning achievement of students. Several other programmes outside the ambit of the Ministry of Human Resource Development (MHRD), including the Mid-day Meal Scheme (MDM) and pre-primary education under Integrated Child Development Services (ICDS), were introduced to support child education.

Taking cognisance of the Supreme Court declaration, the Constitution was amended in 2002 to provide for elementary education as a right of every child in the age group of 6–14 years. The fundamental right to education, enshrined in the Constitution, was followed by the Right of Children to Free and Compulsory Education (RTE) Act, 2009, which came into effect from 1 April 2010. The SSA norms were changed to align with the RTE Act, and SSA was made the primary implementation vehicle.

Presently, about 74 per cent of the country's population above 7 years of age is literate (i.e., able to both read and write) — a considerable improvement from 18 per cent in 1951 (see Chapters 1 and 3). There has been significant progress in enrolment of students at the elementary level with nearly universal enrolment, but it drops sharply at higher levels. The Gross Enrolment Ratio (GER) at elementary level is 119 per cent, at secondary level 63 per cent, higher secondary level 36 per cent, and in higher education 15 per cent.

Government initiatives have primarily been aimed at increasing access to education through capacity-creation, with equity and quality aspects largely remaining unaddressed. The sector continues to face many challenges such as poor quality of education at all levels, low quality of research, inadequate basic physical infrastructure, teacher apathy, low quality of training, and lack of autonomy and accountability.

The education sector in India is embedded in a restrictive regulatory environment. Although private participation is allowed in the education sector, but at all levels, these institutions have to function on a not-for-profit basis. The Supreme Court had ruled that educational institutions are permitted a 'reasonable surplus to meet the cost of expansion and augmentation of facilities' but they are prohibited from charging a capitation fee or profiteering.

This *India Infrastructure Report* looks at the challenges and opportunities of private sector participation in the sector. In this process, the report explores several questions, which include — is the government spending in the education sector being efficiently used? Enrolment is increasing, but are children learning? Is the private sector able to deliver better than the government? Are efforts socially inclusive? Is higher education over-regulated and under-governed? What is required to improve the employability of India's young population? How to overcome the problem of financing vocational education?

PUBLIC SPENDING IN THE EDUCATION SECTOR

Central government expenditure on education has increased significantly over the last decade during the 10th and 11th Plan periods (2002–12), particularly in the 11th Plan, driven by the consolidation and expansion of flagship schemes — the SSA and MDM, implementation of the RTE Act, establishment of the Rashtriya Madhyamik Shiksha Abhiyan (RMSA), a major initiative in secondary education, and enhanced expenditure on higher education. The budgetary allocation by the central government between 2007–08 and 2011–12 has nearly doubled in the case of elementary education, and has risen by more than three times for secondary education and higher education, at current prices. As a result, the proportion of expenditure on secondary and higher education increased, although over 52 per cent continues to be on elementary education. Most (two-thirds) of the increase has been funded by the education cess since 2004. India is unique among developing countries in its use of earmarked taxes for financing public expenditure on education.

Two distinct trends are observable in education spending. First, an increasing proportion of the resources is coming from the central government, making states more reliant on the centre. Second, even poor families are increasingly accessing private education services (Chapter 2).

ELEMENTARY EDUCATION

Progress in Universalisation of Elementary Education (UEE)

The RTE Act is a major initiative of the government, which aims at universalisation of education for all children (including children with disabilities) between 6 to 14 years. The primary focus of RTE is on the right to schooling and physical infrastructure. The Act provides for the establishment of neighbourhood schools within three years, school infrastructure with an all-weather building and basic facilities, and teachers as per the prescribed pupil–teacher ratio (PTR) of 30:1. It also mandates that all untrained teachers in the system must be trained within a period of five years from the date of enforcement of the Act. The fund sharing between centre and state is in the ratio of 65:35. All states have now notified state RTE Rules.

The result of these efforts is reflected in various indicators reported by the MHRD, such as expanding number of primary and upper primary schools, improvement in school infrastructure, higher Net Enrolment Ratio (NER) and fewer out-of-school children aged 6–14 years. The PTR though high has improved to 42.4 per cent in primary and 31.3 per cent in upper primary in 2010–11.

Although there has been notable improvement in the more quantifiable areas of infrastructure and other inputs, the MHRD does not report on any indicators of learning outcomes. Also, despite affirmative action by the government for several decades and efforts to reduce educational inequality, the gap still remains high.

Are Initiatives in UEE Able to Reduce Social Inequality?

Notwithstanding some narrowing of inequalities in basic literacy rates and school enrolments, disparities between social groups in educational experiences persist. The inequalities are in terms of: *(a)* enrolment and retention, and *(b)* learning skills. Sonalde Desai and Amit Thorat (Chapter 4) show that the social inequalities are greatest at early stages. The largest differences between forward castes and disadvantaged groups like Dalits, Adivasis and Muslims are in school entrances and before completing upper primary. Since the disadvantaged social groups are also poorer, it is assumed that their inability to pay for ancillary school expenses and the need for children to work and support family income may lead to lack of attendance and dropout. But equally important is the finding that even when children from a disadvantaged background attend school, their skill development seems to lag behind their peers. While parental income and therefore investment in children's education partly explain these differences (they are less likely to go to private schools and take private tuitions) it is not the only factor. Desai and Thorat suggest that teacher indifference or discrimination, school policies, medium of instruction, and excessive reliance on homework where parents are not educated and cannot provide an adequate support system perpetuate the disadvantage of low levels of skill development.

What are the implications of these findings on public policy? Until recently, public policies had been limited primarily to providing scholarships and other incentives to economically-disadvantaged families, and providing preferential admission to students in colleges and advanced professional programmes. According to Desai and Thorat, policy intervention, particularly in the highly controversial reservations or quotas in college admissions, comes at too late an educational stage. It should come at the primary education stage to have a long-lasting impact.

Desai and Thorat propose that inequalities in education could be reduced with remedial training before or after school hours. Further, there should be special programmes during school vacations for children who are slow learners or first-generation learners and are in danger of falling behind. For instance, Rayat Schools in Maharashtra has sub-schools attached to normal schools for children who have dropped out or fall behind. Teachers need training to be sensitive towards disadvantaged children and to be able to identify demotivating, discriminatory or exclusionary practices. Effective teaching techniques and curriculum to address the requirements of disadvantaged children have to be innovated or adapted from existing experiences from schools such as Navsarjan in Gujarat which has specially designed curricula for dalit children.

Recently, the government has moved to address social inequalities at an early stage of learning. One of the key features of the RTE Act is an attempt to redress social inequalities at the entry-level class (Nursery or Class I). The Act provides for 25 per cent reservation in private schools for disadvantaged groups, which include scheduled castes, scheduled tribes, low-income and other disadvantaged or weaker groups. This provision, challenged by private schools in the Supreme Court, was upheld by the court as constitutionally valid. The cost incurred by the school towards these reserved seats would be reimbursed by the government at the cost of government schooling or actual private tuition charged, whichever is lower. While this is a bold step taken by the government, it is not clear to what extent the learning levels of the disadvantaged children would improve. Given the research evidence cited by Desai and Thorat, the generational inequalities would be very large as such schools rely heavily on homework and parental inputs. Besides, categorisation of the needy is notoriously problematic in India, and subject to discretion, exclusions and patronage (Chapter 11).

Of course, much of the success of this provision would depend on its implementation. As Parth Shah and Luis Miranda (Chapter 7) discuss, all stakeholders would have concerns: ranging from how the seats are allotted, teacher sensitivity to learning needs of the disadvantaged, to uncovered costs of the private schools. The onus is on the government to design a transparent, fair and accountable method to implement this provision in private schools.

Shah and Miranda propose that the central government directly pay and include its contribution in the annual union budget as a separate line item. This would take away the problem of relying on the state governments to reimburse the schools in time. Another suggestion they make is that the centre create an independent Special Purpose Vehicle (SPV) to manage the reimbursement and to raise funds from corporate and other philanthropic entities. Shah and Miranda also propose that this 25 per cent reservation, which they call inclusion or opportunity seats, could evolve into a voucher programme, and states could put in place a mechanism to identify the qualified candidates and issue student cards, smart cards or vouchers. The state branches of the National Commission for the Protection of Child Rights (NCPCR) and affiliated non-governmental organisations (NGOs) could monitor the implementation. Those states that do not meet their targets could be charged a penalty that could go towards the SPV.

Children May be Going to School, But Are they Learning?

The objective of the RTE includes the provision of quality education to children but, as indicated earlier, the quality is associated with inputs instead of learning outcomes of school children. Even teachers' duties are only related to aspects such as punctuality and attendance, and not to learning achievements of their students. There is no norm in the RTE to ensure that a school provides a minimum *quality* of education.

Evidence from multiple surveys and research indicates the dismal quality of learning of school children. In fact, all the surveys are consistent in this regard. Observations from the Annual Survey of Education Report (ASER), 2011 (Chapter 11), which collects data from nearly 0.7 million rural children from almost all districts in rural India, shows that:

(a) At the all India level, 52 per cent of children in Class V cannot read a Class II text and 72 per cent cannot divide.

(b) While there is a lot of variation across states, none of the states are performing anywhere near a satisfactory level. Even for better performing states such as Himachal Pradesh (HP) and Kerala, 26 per cent in Class V cannot read a Class II text and 40 per cent and 67 per cent of children in Class V cannot divide respectively. Also states known for their success in terms of economic growth, including Andhra Pradesh, Gujarat and Tamil Nadu, have severely inadequate learning levels — Gujarat and Tamil Nadu are worse than Bihar, for example, in terms of basic learning.

(c) Urban schools are not much better than rural schools.

(d) Education Initiatives found that children in urban schools performed better at language and math levels but the difference was only 'meaningful' in terms of educational levels for language in Classes IV and VI.

The accumulating body of literature by researchers of international repute, using ASER and other data, points to extremely poor learning outcomes in elementary education, with no improvement in the past five years. That is, India seems to be in a 'big stuck' as far as basic learning is concerned. What is even more worrying is that the ASER 2011 data suggests a possible further decline in basic learning outcomes of children. Rukmini Banerji and Wilima Wadhwa (Chapter 5) report that Lant Pritchett et al. (2012) using ASER data from the past show further that the 'value added' for each subsequent year in school is very small.

Efficacy of Financing Elementary Education

There seems to be little link between the amount of funds allocated to elementary education and learning outcomes achieved, as observed by Accountability Initiative (2012) in a recent study (Chapter 6). The challenge of strengthening this link assumes greater importance in the context of the RTE, which guarantees 'age-appropriate mainstreaming' for all children, promising the acquisition of age-appropriate skills and knowledge by every child. Moreover, the RTE Act envisages a decentralised model for delivering the learning agenda that involves a key role for School Management Committees.

Financing of elementary education primarily comes from state governments, although the central government's share is increasing due to higher SSA allocations after the RTE Act. The centre's share has gone up to 23 per cent, up from 18 per cent in 2004–05. Most of the budget is focused on teachers' salaries and administrative expenses, and then on school infrastructure, with very little attention paid to quality-related aspects, innovation and learning enhancement. Moreover, when schools generally do not receive funds on time, their priority is to pay salaries, not incur other expenses. Schools receive limited funds over which they have direct control and have restrictions on its usage. Grants to schools for maintenance, development and teaching–learning materials are based on norms, which may not be aligned with the school requirement. Inefficiencies in expenditure management lead to delays in the release of funds, with unpredictability and bunching of fund release towards the end of the financial year. Further, the school principals or school management committees are often unaware of the purpose of the fund and so it remains unutilised or inappropriately spent.

Yamini Aiyar (Chapter 6) argues that the current financing system is extremely centralised, leaving little discretion and decision-making power at the school management level. Therefore, simply increasing financial allocations in the current system is unlikely to facilitate the decentralised implementation envisaged by the RTE. This would require a fundamental re-haul of the current financing, planning and budgeting system. Aiyar proposes untied block grants to school management committees, and the simplification of grant allocation and distribution to schools on a per-child basis rather than the present complex norms-based approach. She also indicates the need for a management information system to track fund flows in a transparent manner, and capacity building at all levels of decision-making and planning.

The reduction in public investment and inefficiency in public expenditure are often used to explain the rise of the private or non-state sector in elementary education.

Growing Importance of Private Sector in Elementary Education

Over the last two decades, there has been a significant increase in children receiving some form of private schooling, either through attendance in a private school or through private tutoring. The rapid rise in private schools has been driven by 'budget schools'. These broadly refer to unregulated private schools that are accessed by low-income families as they charge lower fees than regular private schools. Budget schools keep costs low by having minimum infrastructure and resources, and teachers on contract who are paid a fraction of the salaries of their counterparts in government schools.

Banerji and Wadhwa (Chapter 5) highlight two basic trends from the ASER: (a) the proportion of children not enrolled or out-of-school has dropped to under 4 per cent in 2011, and (b) the fraction of children in the age group 6 to 14 enrolled in rural private schools has risen by almost 7 percentage points in six years to reach 25.6 per cent in 2011.

There are some patterns across states. States that lie north and west of Delhi fall into a 'high' private-schooling region with one-third to half of all rural children enrolled in private schools, while in the eastern region private-school enrolment is very low. It is somewhat surprising that in Tamil Nadu, private-school enrolment is higher in early grades and growing, despite the state government investing heavily in government schools with quality enhancement programs like Activity-Based Learning (ABL).

Private supplemental help through tuition classes and coaching centres is widespread. Banerji and Wadhwa, using ASER data, observe that almost 25 per cent of all rural children access these kinds of supplemental inputs by Class VIII. More children are depending on private supplemental help, irrespective of whether they go to government or private schools. However, it is not clear whether parents are turning to the private sector because of lack of faith in government schools or because of their rising incomes and aspirations (Chapter 5).

With the increasing role of the private sector, the debate on private *versus* government school provisioning becomes louder. The proponents of private education advocate that the private sector should manage schools. For those who cannot afford to pay, the government should finance their education through scholarships, education vouchers and loans. As Shah and Miranda (Chapter 7) put it, the government stands as a guarantor of education, not by producing it but by financing it. This approach combines the efficiency of the private sector with the equity focus and independent supervision of the public sector (Chapter 7). Private schools should be treated at par with government schools and the licensing mechanism for a school to be recognised should be simplified. Also, for-profit private schools should be recognised and allowed to compete in the education space.

Shah and Miranda propose that parents should be empowered to influence the functioning and performance of schools, and be able to choose the right school for their children. The voucher is a tool to change the way government finances education, particularly for the poor, and also to give parents choice of school. In the present system of financing, schools are accountable to the government. The voucher system makes them accountable directly to the students and parents since parents pay the school of their choice through vouchers. Under the voucher system, 'the money follows the student, unlike the present system where the money follows the school' (Chapter 6, p. 76). Shah and Miranda argue that the voucher system enables equality of opportunity for children and creates competition among schools. Vouchers provide the missing ingredient that will change the incentive structure towards better performance of state schools.

Private Budget Schools?

Budget schools have mushroomed over the past decade but there is no reliable estimate of the number of such schools. Suzana Andrade Brinkmann (Chapter 10) indicates that though the official District Information System for Education (DISE) data records 26,377 unrecognised schools reaching out to 2.7 million students, this could be a gross underestimate — there are estimates as high as 40 million rural children (Chavan 2011).

Proponents of budget schools argue that these schools are more cost-effective than government schools (their per-pupil expenditure is only 40 per cent that of government schools). The low salaries they pay to contract teachers enable them to hire more teachers and have lower PTRs. As these schools charge low fees, the poor can access good quality education, often in English medium. Further, based on market principles of choice and competition, it is advocated that these schools are more accountable to parents and students. Studies by various international researchers in support of

budget private schools have highlighted their higher teacher attendance and activity. These schools are also conveniently located within poor settlements and hence are more easily accessible, especially to girls. Advocates of these schools therefore argue that low-cost or budget schools should be allowed to function free of regulations, and government funds should be directed towards these schools through the voucher mechanism.

Evidence in support of quality of education in low-cost budget schools is, however, not conclusive. Many researchers have strongly argued against the findings of the budget school supporters on conceptual and methodological grounds. Further, it is possible that these budget schools could have been 'preferred' since there was no government school available in the neighbourhood (as in some slums and many rural villages). Geetha B. Nambissan (Chapter 8) argues that a range of socio-cultural factors, together with commuting convenience, influence parental decision-making on schooling for their children. Although these schools may be projecting English medium education, often perceived by the poor as an indicator of quality education, the schools and teachers may not have the capacity to deliver. One of the fundamental problems highlighted for budget schools is para-skilling of teachers, which implies breaking down of curricular and pedagogical processes into simple routine and standardised tasks so that they can be handled by 'less-skilled but suitably-trained individuals' at low salaries.

Nambissan (Chapter 8) argues that much of the 'evidence' on low-cost schools is weak and the picture of this sector is still fragmentary. However, the available studies suggest that the drive toward profits and cutting down of costs in low-cost schools is likely to have detrimental implications for teachers, teaching and the very purpose of education (Chapters 8 and 20). Providers of low-cost shcools offer only a minimalistic education to children from low-income families. Yet, many of these players are simultaneously offering middle and elite sections of Indian society a qualitatively different package of education: Kindergarten to Class XII (K–12), well-resourced schools that will yield high profits. These trends are reflective of a democratic and ethical deficit in the spread of the new private schools. It is important that the rights of all children and especially of the poor are protected and serious research and policy attention be drawn to the unregulated school sector.

RTE and the Demise of Non-State Schools?

Going beyond the debate of private *versus* government, and recognised *versus* unrecognised non-state schools, it is imperative to understand the impact that provisions of the RTE Act would have on the unrecognised schools. By setting stringent requirements for schools on infrastructure, teacher qualifications and salaries, the RTE Act will force a large number of non-government schools to shut down if they fail to comply with the norms by April 2013. In effect, this means impending death for thousands of non-government schools around the country that do not meet these standards. Madhav Chavan (2011) estimates that nearly 40 million rural children will be affected if unrecognised private schools are closed down.

Andrade (Chapter 10) questions whether these RTE provisions are in the best interest of the children who attend non-state schools. The non-state schools cover:

(a) NGO or community schools for the poor (including charitable trusts, faith-based and community groups);
(b) Alternative schools (known for being innovative and experimental schools and catering to children who cannot fit into rigid mainstream schooling structures);
(c) Budget or low-cost schools;
(d) Non-formal schools (catering to deprived children, school dropouts, working children);
(e) Home-schooling.

It is ironic that most (95 per cent) government schools do not comply with the norms specified in the RTE Act, and that too even after a decade of intense efforts under the SSA, and two years post-RTE. Moreover, learning outcomes are as poor in government schools as in the unrecognised private schools. In fact, some studies have found that private schools provide moderately better education at lower cost than government schools. It is argued that if, despite the 'price advantage', better infrastructure and incentives in government schools, parents are still opting against them, the answer is to improve the system, not to eliminate alternatives.

One way of meeting the ultimate goal of the RTE Act, which is quality education, is to adopt flexibility in its implementation through the state-defined RTE rules. The recent Gujarat RTE Rules offer an approach towards recognition of existing private unaided schools. Instead of focusing only on input requirements specified in the Act like classroom size, playground, and PTR, the Gujarat RTE Rules put greater emphasis on learning outcomes of students in the recognition norms. In these rules, the criteria for unrecognised schools to meet RTE norms is a weighted average of student performance, students' improved performance over time, students' non-academic performance and parents' feedback, and teacher qualifications and infrastructure.

As long as children are learning, there should be a variety of schools from which parents can choose. Andrade (Chapter 10) advocates a more collaborative Public–Private Partnership (PPP) where the private sector views it as a joint venture and invests in strengthening the government system, while the government facilitates private participation.

The key issue is about ensuring quality education that is truly inclusive. The RTE Act, while intending to be inclusive and set quality standards, does the opposite by the norms it sets because it places systems over child. Further, just by defining a reservation of 25 per cent seats in private schools does not make the education policy inclusive. It is important to ensure an inclusive classroom where every child is getting an equitable quality education. As Annie Koshi (Chapter 9) points out, inclusive practices celebrate difference and require that the child be at the centre. A 'one size fits all' policy for elementary education cannot be inclusive. The education system should adapt itself to the requirement of the child and not the other way round. In order to ensure access, an inclusive school will work at removing the barriers that stand in the way of any child attending and continuing in school.

Koshi (Chapter 9) explains how non-state schools have sometimes adapted in fee structure, infrastructure, pedagogy, curriculum, assessment, and community engagement to suit the requirements of the neighbourhood community and child.

Thus, defining access, equity and quality through quantifiable standard norms is not going to achieve the objective of UEE. Emphasising the type of school that children should go to is also not going to help unless the children going to school are learning. It is important to recognise that while children in private schools or those receiving tuitions perform slightly better than children in government schools, the quality is still dismal.

Causes of Poor Learning Outcomes

There are various hypotheses on why the learning levels are low among children going to school (Chapter 11). First, more than 50 per cent of school children come from families whose parents have never been to any school (this is more so for children who go to government schools than private schools). So, for these first-generation students, their parents cannot identify or support them if they are not learning. On the other hand, children from wealthier homes have better educated parents and siblings and do better in school.

Second, although it is desirable that school facilities are of decent quality and the PTR is low, which also happens to be the thrust of the present RTE Act, it is not obvious that this will solve the quality problem. Thus, the government's focus on inputs — more expenditure on schools, teachers, training, textbooks and so on — is not yielding improvement in learning outcomes.

Third, although children are enrolled, they are not attending schools. Some are of the view that schemes such as mid-day meals would improve school attendance and also children's concentration. This, however, finds limited support in the fact that most of the school activities happen before lunch.

Fourth, since the RTE stresses age-grade learning and also specifies that the syllabus should be completed in a given time period, schools mainly focus on completing the curriculum rather than on delivering learning. As a result, many children never get a good foundation in basic learning in early school years. They learn much later than they should, with very little chance of ever catching up. With no one to identify children falling behind, and with no learning support, a large fraction of the children fall through the cracks.

Fifth, equally problematic is the automatic advancement irrespective of learning level. The policy of no detention up to Class V is already followed in some states. In the earlier examination system, the end-of-year exams functioned as mechanisms to filter out low performers, who were detained in their current class.

Sixth, teacher absenteeism in government schools is sometimes considered a major cause of children not learning. It is often argued that teachers in private schools lack tenure, and so face stronger incentives than government teachers to actually turn up and teach.

It is now evidently clear that learning outcomes should be put at the centre of any education strategy, and the views on the causes of low-learning outcomes should form the basis of exploration and experimentation to arrive at workable strategies.

What can Improve Learning Outcomes?

There are high levels of inequality in learning, with only a small proportion able to acquire good learning. Shobhini Mukerji and Michael Walton (Chapter 11), drawing upon several experiments and research studies, have identified a number of strategies that might work to improve learning outcomes. The promising strategies are:

(a) *Experiments on learning innovations, including remedial programmes:* alternative pedagogies can potentially yield substantial improvements in basic skills with existing resources, whether with volunteers, existing teachers or contract teachers. Designing appropriate class-level pedagogy, teacher training, use of supplemental help (including volunteers during off-school hours), and conducting summer camps as remedial programmes, all have played a positive role in improving learning outcomes. Pedagogy and teaching efforts tailored to the child can have significant impacts even with unpaid volunteers and low-paid teachers, provided this is the primary focus of their work. The failure of teachers to achieve results within the school year is consistent either with weak teacher motivation or an emphasis on delivering the curriculum rather than competencies.

(b) *Teacher incentives:* small financial incentives to teachers have been seen to lead to improvements in learning quality. A key lesson from the studies focusing on pedagogical innovations is the importance of the teacher's ability to understand the child's needs and adapt the teaching method accordingly. Although linking teachers' pay to attendance can increase student-learning, instituting teacher incentives within the government school structure will require considerable push and negotiation with the administration, especially where teacher unions are strong and active.

(c) *Teaching according to a child's ability:* reorganisation of children by ability and aligning the pedagogy to teaching by ability level rather than class level can lead to substantial gains especially when the teaching–learning activities focus on developing basic skills. The need is to overcome the challenge of an overambitious curriculum organised by class and age. Since, the textbook content is far above the level of most children at that class level and as the curriculum becomes more difficult, more children get left behind. Experiments have shown that when children are grouped by level rather than by class, and taught accordingly, their learning improves.

(d) *School choice:* for parents from a variety of schools provided through a new form of PPP, where the non-state agency, including the private sector, is seen as a partner in strengthening the arm of the government. The School Adoption programmes in Karnataka and Gujarat Government Rules to RTE are cases in point. Both of them allow the possibility of either state or non-state agencies taking over non-performing or unrecognised schools, rather than subjecting the school to sudden forced closure.

SECONDARY EDUCATION

The secondary (lower and higher) space is the weakest and most neglected so far in the education sector, despite being the key link between education and economic development. Rapid reform in secondary education is extremely critical for transitioning educated youth into higher education or to the join the workforce. The focus on elementary education policy and investment in the last five years, leading to higher enrolment rates and the automatic promotion under the Continuous Comprehensive Evaluation (CCE) scheme, have added pressure to an already stressed secondary education system. The demand for secondary education is also growing in view of the high returns from secondary education, which are even more than returns from higher education.

The key focus of the government is expanding access and equity, so as to improve enrolment and retention at the secondary level. Despite some improvements in the last few years, the GER is still low at 45.8 per cent. The enrolment levels vary considerably across states, with higher enrolment in wealthier states. This is not surprising since secondary education is not compulsory and the costs are higher at secondary than primary level. Dropout rates are also quite high within the secondary level, resulting in about 25 percentage points lower enrolment at the higher secondary level (Classes XI–XII) than the lower secondary level (Classes IX–X). Both gender and caste inequality is quite high at the secondary school level. The disparity in school attendance for boys is 15 per cent higher than the level for girls, in lower secondary and 20 per cent more in higher secondary. Similarly, while scheduled castes make up 21 per cent of the relevant age group, they only form 18 per cent of the same school-going age group.

The quality aspect at the secondary level is even more challenging for various reasons. The poor learning outcomes, coupled with no retention policy, at the elementary-school level leads to poor quality of students entering the secondary level. Another major reason for the varying quality is little uniformity in curriculum and standards between the state boards. Widely varying outcomes of state board-level examinations from one year to the other also raise doubts on their reliability.

Unlike for primary education, there is no national assessment of performance in secondary education. Assessments conducted in individual states, using internationally benchmarked assessments, suggest that student-learning is extremely low in India. The participation of Tamil Nadu and Himachal Pradesh in the Organisation for Economic Co-operation and Development (OECD) Programme for International Student Assessment (PISA) for 15-year olds showed deplorable results. In the assessment, both the states were ranked above only Kyrgyz Republic out of more than 70 participating countries. On average, 15-year old Indian students performed about four years behind the international average for OECD countries. Yet again, a test carried out using questions from the Trends in International Mathematics and Science Survey (TIMSS) assessment in mathematics on Class IX students in Odisha and Rajasthan found that Rajasthan was 47th out of 49 countries and Odisha 43rd. Studies have observed that there is no significant difference in the dismal performance between private and government schools, and hence there is no inherent advantage to private schools. Any better performance for students from private schools could be explained by the home environment and parental background of the students.

The government has recently started focusing on secondary education and launched the RMSA in 2009 with ambitious targets of providing universal access to secondary education by 2017. Besides improving access and equity, the RMSA aims to improve the quality of secondary education by making schools conform to prescribed norms, which include physical infrastructure, PTR, qualification of teachers, curriculum, focus on science subjects, teacher training, and Information and Communication Technology (ICT). However, the approach to quality improvement in the RMSA, like the RTE, is input-focused and not outcome-oriented.

The approach to quality improvement in the RMSA, like the RTE, is input-focused and not outcome-oriented. The learning achievement at the secondary level is poor, and the prevailing evaluation mechanism is not robust. The standards of state boards also vary considerably. Added to this is the confusion created by the introduction of the CCE. As also emphasised by Mukerji and Walton (Chapter 11), guidelines for implementation of the CCE mechanism are not well-defined and teachers are not well-trained to be able to use the assessments to map student outcome. Toby Linden (Chapter 12) emphasises the need to urgently put in place a robust evaluation and assessment mechanism, and also a strategy for different types of assessments to fit together. Besides continuous classroom-based evaluation, based on uniform and standard principles with sufficient flexibility for teachers to effectively define and use evaluation tools, there is need for end-of-stage (Classes X and XII) assessments. Further, there is a need to bring uniformity in standards across states and align assessment mechanisms for all states with the national level. States should together strengthen the technical quality of assessment. Evaluation should be based on the curriculum, which should be revised to ensure that students are evaluated on the basis of their conceptual understanding.

Besides the RMSA scheme, the government is also pursuing the Model School Scheme through the PPP mode to set up secondary schools and provide quality education to talented rural children through 6,000 model schools, of which 2,500 would be set up through the PPP route, as a benchmark of excellence at the block level at the rate of one school per block. More states are coming up with PPP policies for secondary school construction and management, including Andhra Pradesh (Residential Schools), Punjab (Adarsh Schools) and Rajasthan. The private partner manages the school while the costs are shared: land is provided by the state government free of cost or given on a 99-year lease. The capital cost is borne by the private partner or joint and operational costs are shared between the state and private partners. To ensure a more rapid roll-out of such PPP schemes all over the country, there is an urgent need to put in place a balanced comprehensive PPP policy, with measurable and quantifiable key performance indicators spelt out for the concessionaires (Chapter 12).

Currently, most states allow private schools to fix their own fees subject to certain restrictions (which includes getting the fee structure approved). The private school has to operate as a trust and can only earn reasonable surplus, which has to be ploughed back towards school development. However, as M. R. Madhavan and Kaushiki Sanyal (Chapter 1) point out that to bypass the requirement that trusts and societies have to plough back the surplus generated into the same school for its development, many operators have put in place a two-tier legal structure comprising a trust that runs the school and a company that owns the assets and provides services. This way the operator can easily repatriate a large portion of the surplus generated as profits of the company. It may, therefore, be better to allow for-profit schools mandating disclosure with regulatory oversight.

Some of the state governments spend a sizeable portion of their budget on aided private schools. While eight states assign more than 50 per cent of their budget on aided schools, an additional two states assign more than 90 per cent. However, as Linden (Chapter 12) observes, there is no direct relationship between the proportion of the secondary budget spent on non-government schools and the proportion of enrolments in these schools. This suggests that states should reconsider their allocation of funds to aided schools, possibly along the lines suggested here.

The direct and indirect cost of attending secondary school for a household is several times more than attending elementary school, and private secondary schools (aided and unaided) are more costly than government ones. In view of this, to ensure more equitable access to secondary schools and not compromise on efficiency and performance, the grants to school or financial support to students could be linked to attendance, retention of disadvantaged students and successful completion of a stage of education or performance of the students (Chapter 12). This requirement of efficient resource allocation is further strengthened by the fact that there is no direct relationship between the proportion of state public spending on non-state schools and the proportion of enrolment in these schools.

In order to maintain an acceptable PTR, large number of teachers need to be appointed to meet both the existing shortage and new requirements. Also, there is a huge shortage of teachers with subject-matter expertise. There is thus an urgency to focus on filling the vacuum in teacher training (an aspect also discussed by Poonam Batra in Chapter 20). Strengthening the capacity of the teachers would require greater support from the government and better regulation to govern the quality aspect of private teacher training institutes.

Vocationalisation of secondary education requires special thrust. Workplaces in a globalised economy are going through rapid technological changes. Every sector is going through change and thus the need for a skilled workforce has increased rapidly. The curriculum should include vocational training and schools should be provided with infrastructure. Appropriately trained teachers and linkage with industry is also required.

Finally, there is need for greater experimentation at the secondary level to generate more information so as to understand what works well, since the lessons from the initiatives at the primary and upper primary levels may not be replicable at the secondary level. For instance, the accountability framework at the primary level, wherein parents hold teachers and schools accountable under certain conditions, depends critically on features that are not present in secondary education, as Linden explains. Promoting and evaluating different approaches in secondary education is therefore important.

HIGHER EDUCATION

India boasts of the largest higher education system in the world. There are over 610 universities (including about 130 deemed universities) set up under central and state legislation, 33,000 colleges affiliated to universities, and a very large number of institutes of technical education; medical, legal, dental, nursing teaching; and polytechnics. By 2006, private institutes constituted 63 per cent of all higher education institutes and 52 per cent of the share of students. Private institutions are concentrated in select disciplines such as engineering, management, medicine, and Information Technology (IT). Private universities (including deemed) account for a lower share — about 30 per cent of the universities.

Indeed, much of the expansion in higher education has been driven by the private sector since the mid-1980s. The central and state governments' investment in higher and technical education is only 0.7 per cent of GDP as against a target of 1.5 per cent. The private sector accounts for more than 60 per cent of the total expenditure on higher education. Globally too, there was a surge of private sector in higher education since the 1990s, mostly in the developing countries. N. V. Varghese (Chapter 13) recounts the evolution of this development in different regions of the world, and suggests that the process of globalisation of economic activities also increased the economic returns to investments in higher education and, in turn, the demand for technical and professional education.

Challenges in Higher Education

For all the progress made in higher education, the sector is faced with many challenges even 65 years after independence. Enrolment is low and the inequalities at lower levels of education are exacerbated in higher education. India's GER is 15 per cent in higher education, which is much lower than the world average of 26 per cent (and of course, that of many advanced countries — over 50 per cent). Making matters worse, there is a wide disparity in GERs across states, urban and rural areas, gender, and communities. The enrolment ratio in urban areas is 24 per cent while in rural areas it's a poor 7.5 per cent; for women it is 10.5 per cent and for socially disadvantaged groups it is even lesser.

An equal, if not bigger problem is that the quality of higher education is mediocre at best. According to the National Accreditation and Assessment Council (NAAC), 90 per cent of the universities and 70 per cent of the colleges are of mediocre or poor quality (Chapter 15). In 2009, a review committee set up by the MHRD found 88 of the 130 deemed universities to be of inferior quality and identified problems such as control of management boards by nominees of the sponsoring trust or government functionaries, low quality of research, and improper practices in admissions process. These findings are reinforced by the very low employability of Indian graduates, as evidenced in studies and basic training institutes set up by corporates for fresh graduates.

Thus, the entry of private sector in higher education has done little to bring about improvements in curriculum, teaching methodology, research and development, and learning outcomes. This is not surprising considering the fact that higher education still remains one of the most tightly-regulated sectors in the economy, and could dissuade serious players from entering the field.

Over-Regulated and Under-Governed

The National Knowledge Commission (NKC) has aptly described the current regulatory environment in higher education as 'over-regulated and under-governed'. Multiple agencies, with overlapping functions, are regulating almost every aspect of functioning of a higher education institution. The University Grants Commission (UGC) and the All India Council of Technical Education (AICTE) have wide powers to regulate the sector: the UGC for universities and colleges teaching general subjects, and the AICTE for technical education. Beside the AICTE, there are 14 statutory professional councils that regulate courses related to areas such as medicine, law and nursing. The NAAC and the National Board of Accreditation (NBA) are autonomous bodies set up by UGC and AICTE, respectively that accredit institutions. But accreditation of institutions is currently voluntary.

The regulatory bodies have cumbersome procedures and complex and detailed rules, whose interpretation and implementation encourage rent-seeking. Anand Sudarshan and Sandhya Subramanian (Chapter 16) give examples of the kind of archaic 'license raj regulations' imposed that hamper the ability of genuine private education providers to grow over the long term, or innovate in technology, teaching methods and curriculum. Contrasted against the minutiae of rules on inputs, there is little to judge institutions on student-learning outcomes.

There are huge entry barriers for new universities. Each university needs to be separately legislated into existence, by parliament or state legislature, unless it is recognised as a 'deemed university' by the UGC. In order to be able to grant degrees, colleges and technical institutions have to 'affiliate' with existing universities, or else they can only award certificates or diplomas. The system of affiliation in its current form leads to excessive control by a university on the functioning of a college on virtually every aspect ranging from student intake, syllabus to faculty and examinations. On the other hand, the growing number of affiliated colleges to a university has become unwieldy and increased difficulty in monitoring affiliated institutions. Further, a state establishing a university has no legislative competence to set up campuses in other states. This means that the barriers to entry for a private university to set up a national institution with multiple campuses are formidable (Chapter 16). Presently, foreign institutions are allowed to operate in India through various modes, and Indian universities can grant degrees and diplomas in collaboration with foreign universities. However, foreign universities cannot set up branch campuses without an Indian partner (Chapter 1).

Higher education institutions have to be set up as a Trust or Society, on a non-profit basis, with returns ploughed back into the institution. Implicit disincentives in the current tax and trust laws provide very little incentive to raise resources. Trusts are required to spend 85 per cent of income streams from endowments in the same financial year, which prevents any meaningful endowment from being created, which in turn could be utilised for scholarships.

Fees are tightly controlled by the UGC and other statutory bodies, forcing universities to rely on UGC grants for meeting operating expenses, and leaving barely any funds for institutional growth and innovation. Yet, all these rules have not been able to prevent the commercialisation of education. Ironically, the non-profit status may even act as an incentive for unscrupulous players since such entities get tax exemptions, which makes it easier to launder money (Chapter 1). Madhavan and Sanyal (Chapter 1) highlight various Supreme Court judgments that have sought to curb profiteering by private institutions. Yet, according to the Yashpal Committee Report (MHRD 2009), charging capitation fees has not abated.

Since accreditation is not mandatory, monitoring private institutions is a major problem. A large number of private providers have been delivering sub-standard quality of education thereby reducing education to merely award of a certificate.

New Higher Education Bills

Government has introduced several new Bills in the Parliament. Some of the key Bills are:

(a) The Higher Education and Research (HER) Bill, 2011 to establish the National Commission for Higher Education and Research (NCHER);

(b) The National Commission for Human Resources for Health (NCHRH) Bill, 2011;

(c) The National Accreditation Regulatory Authority for Higher Educational Institutions Bill, 2010;

(d) The Educational Tribunals Bill, 2010;

(e) The Prohibition of Unfair Practices in Technical Educational Institutions, Medical Educational Institutions and Universities Bill, 2010;

(f) The Foreign Educational Institutions (Regulation of Entry and Operations) Bill, 2010.

The Bills largely focus on accountability through traditional regulatory approaches, by establishing new regulatory bodies, mandatory accreditation, dispute resolution, and penalising unfair practices including capitation fees. There is also a Bill to allow foreign institutions to set up campuses without an Indian partner.

Madhavan and Sanyal express doubts over whether these Bills will achieve their objectives. In many cases, there are already similar extant provisions but it is the enforcement that is currently lacking. The proposed new regulatory bodies, NCHER and NCHRH, are to set standards of education and research and promote autonomy, replacing the UGC, AICTE and various medical councils, but the powers of the new bodies are similar to those of the earlier regulatory entities. Amlanjyoti Goswami (Chapter 17) also questions whether the HER Bill will be enacted since there may be resistance to a new super-regulator and diminished powers of the special councils (like medical council and bar council). And it is only in the actual regulations of the Bill that the extent of autonomy that is enabled will be known.

The National Accreditation Bill only allows government-controlled non-profit agencies to register as accreditation agencies. The NKC had suggested that both public and private agencies be allowed to accredit educational institutions and the Yashpal Committee stated that accreditation agencies should be independent of the government. Capitation fee is already an offence, and the Prohibition of Unfair Practices Bill, 2010 does not provide a different system of enforcement and so is unlikely to make any difference on this score. The Bill does, however, require institutions to disclose certain information in their prospectus. The Foreign Educational Institutions Bill stipulates steep conditions, such as requiring foreign institutions to maintain a corpus fund of at least

₹500 million, have a track record of 20 years in the parent country, and prohibits repatriation of funds, which may deter top foreign institutions from coming to India.

Perhaps most importantly, Goswami (Chapter 17) argues that the Bills introduced by the government still leave the issue of autonomy largely unaddressed. As Goswami points out, curbing bad behaviour is important, but there should be serious reflection on how good performance needs further encouragement to become institutions of excellence. As he aptly says, the political economy of higher education seems to be guided by a premise that autonomy has to be the exception and that largely what is required is more regulation. Although the promise of autonomy lies in some portions of the HER Bill, there is no policy initiative yet on how to move beyond the 'over-regulation but under-governance' impasse or how regulatory principles can be better evolved that could help create more autonomous universities of excellence which are also privately funded.

Overcoming the Barriers

Higher education in India faces the triple challenge of 'expansion, inclusion, and excellence'. There will soon be huge demands on the system with universalisation of elementary and secondary education and the growing numbers of youth. Clearly, the government cannot meet all the needs and there is a role for non-state providers to play.

The higher education system needs a major overhaul — to provide greater autonomy with accountability and strengthening of governance as well as enforcement of regulation. The need is for more flexibility, diversity, different approaches and models.

Sudarshan and Subramanian (Chapter 16) suggest that multiple models should co-exist with a level playing field and strict checks and balances. In this context, for-profit institutions should also be allowed to attract serious education entrepreneurs to invest in the sector. This should be accompanied by strict public disclosure of information. Just as all companies are required by law to publish annual reports providing their financial details, every educational institution (whether public or private) should publish reports at regular intervals with details of infrastructure and facilities available, trustees and administrators, qualifications and experience of staff, courses offered, number of students, results of the examinations, amount of funds available to the university and sources of funding.

Funding is crucial if our institutions of higher learning are to be of high quality and for the long haul. For private universities, it is essential to build large endowments. Some of the measures proposed by Goswami (Chapter 17) are:

(a) Removal of disincentives in tax laws and trust laws by (i) allowing universities to invest in financial instruments of their choice; (ii) removing the restriction on trusts to spend 85 per cent of their income in the same year, so that they can build up a corpus; *(iii)* make exceptions in income tax laws to encourage the creation of large endowments;

(b) Diversification of sources of finance and exploration of innovative financial mechanisms;

(c) Contribution from every company towards an education fund as a Corporate Social Responsibility (CSR) initiative;

(d) Development of a comprehensive PPP Policy, with governance control left to a private board.

In addition, every institution must get itself rated by an independent and specialised accreditation agency and publicly announce its rating to prospective students. This will bring in transparency and accountability and generate healthy competition between various institutions. Given the importance of accreditation in quality assurance and the vast number of institutions that need to be evaluated, it would help if the private sector could be engaged with sufficient checks and balances to operate as accreditation agencies. Considering the importance of accreditation and ranking in quality assurance and the increasing global connect of Indian educational institutions, it is important to align the Indian quality assurance mechanism with the recognised global mechanisms (Chapter 15).

The focus of regulation should shift towards quality of outcomes. The most important reform is arguably to institute performance-based regulation. There should be greater discussion and debate in arriving at ways to judge an institution. Lessons can be drawn from several countries, such as Malaysia, which uses 'Programme Outcomes', i.e., statements that describe what students are expected to know and be able to perform or attain by the time of graduation. Or Brazil, where a two-tier mechanism is in place to conduct internal evaluation — by a council of students and faculty that analyses the performance of the institution — and external evaluation in which the Federal Council of Education names expert evaluators to analyse the curriculum and faculty performance. Goswami (Chapter 17) also proposes non-traditional regulatory approaches, through peer-driven processes and disclosure systems, which at the same time encourage academic innovation and diversity. Varghese (Chapter 13), drawing upon experiences in some countries, proposes a three-stage system to approve private universities, which would allow monitoring of facilities and quality of programmes before they are finally granted authority to award degrees.

The urgency is to arrive at a national policy in a holistic way, with a framework that would encourage private sector participation and go beyond ensuring minimum standards to advancing globally recognised standards of excellence. Goswami (Chapter 17) provides the elements of such a vision and accompanying principles of regulation. A vision of a liberal education, that encourages inquiry, pluralism of views, tolerance, humanism, is the backbone of a democracy.

VOCATIONAL EDUCATION

The shortage of a skilled workforce is possibly the biggest challenge that India faces in sustaining its growth and development. The source of the problems lies in the mismatch between demand and supply; most employment opportunities require vocational skills that are not provided by the current education system. It is estimated that 300 million youth will be entering the workforce by 2025 which may very well turn India's demographic dividend into a disaster.

Institutional Framework of Vocational Education

The current system of formal vocational education involves *(a)* vocational courses offered in professional colleges and polytechnics, *(b)* vocational courses offered at higher secondary level, *(c)* technical training institutions (Industrial Training Institutes [ITIs]/ Industrial Training Centres [ITCs]), and *(d)* apprenticeship training.

Government and government-aided schools offer vocational courses under a centrally-sponsored scheme, the 'Vocationalisation of Higher Secondary Education', which provides financial assistance to states to set up administrative structures, prepare the curriculum and offer training programmes for teachers. The scheme also provides financial assistance to NGOs to conduct short-term courses. The scheme was revised in 2011 to focus on industry and private-sector partnerships in vocational education, and build capacity in teachers.

Dilip Chenoy (Chapter 18) discusses the existing policies and institutions for vocational education. The National Policy on Skill Development lays down the framework within which skill-related training is to be conducted and specifies the roles different stakeholders will need to play for the creation of a skills ecosystem in India. The policy clearly specifies that skills-related training should be outcome focused. It calls for an effective assessment and credible certification framework, publicising training institution outcomes to ensure greater transparency, a greater role of state governments and the creation of infrastructure for on-the-job training and apprenticeships. Innovation in this area is encouraged, such as using school infrastructure for skills training after school hours, and employing more PPPs in the skills space.

The National Skill Development Mission was launched with the intent of skilling 150 million people by 2022 and to this effect the National Skill Development Corporation (NSDC) was set up in 2009 to enable skills-related training through its private sector partners, set up Sector Skill Councils, finance skill development, and create a supportive ecosystem for skill development.

Challenges in Skill Development

Many skill development initiatives are not focused on the needs of the potential employer, thereby resulting in low employability. Low enrolment in skilling centres could also be due to the negative perception that skill-training courses are for those who could not make it to the formal system. In some industries, the job remuneration is not sufficient to incentivise people to undergo skill-training. Financing skill development is another concern. While the poor are willing to pay for skill-training so long as there is a job guarantee, firms are not yet inclined to pay a placement fee for skilled persons. Companies are also not willing to pay for skill-training because of risks that the candidate is inadequately trained and/or leaves the job after joining. The current bank-financing model, with its emphasis on collaterals or guarantees, acts as a stumbling block. As of now, the Central Bank of India is the only public sector lender active in this space, but limited to partners of the NSDC. To motivate banks, the recently launched Credit Guarantee Fund (CGF), will compensate banks for providing credit to vocational training students.

Many argue that the Mahatma Gandhi National Rural Employment Guarantee Act (MGNREGA) has made rural people reliant on these guaranteed payments and discourages them from taking part in skill development programmes.

Overcoming the Challenges

Several suggestions have been offered by Chenoy (Chapter 18) and Manish Sabharwal and Neeti Sharma (Chapter 19). Most critically, the private sector cannot afford to play a passive role in the skill development process and must be involved in setting occupational standards, a sound accreditation system, and recognised certification.

Sabharwal and Sharma (Chapter 19) propose a reform agenda to improve the skill levels by matching the available labour supply to its demand, bringing about employability reform and reforming the education system to ensure learning for earning. To correct the mismatch in the labour market, they propose changes in the restrictive labour laws, and improvements in the infrastructure and responsibilities of employment exchanges that connect job-seekers to employers.

Chenoy (Chapter 18) argues that a clause should be introduced in the MGNREGA scheme so that persons who are employed under the scheme could use part of the funds to attain a skill that could, in the medium term, enable them to earn a livelihood and not be dependent on the scheme. Sabharwal and Sharma (Chapter 19) further suggest that beneficiaries of the MGNREGA scheme could be mandated to use a part of their compensation for skill development through skill vouchers, to obtain skills training from any accredited institute. Once the training is completed, the training institute can redeem the voucher for cash.

Many job-seekers are unable to pay for skill-training, so financing for skill development is most critical — specifically, who pays and how. The skill voucher system, which could be sponsored by the government, enables a transparent, cashless transaction between the trainee and the training organisation. Sabharwal and Sharma present other options of vocational financing, such as scholarships, compensating trainees through apprenticeship stipends, and reimbursing student fees following a suitable employment period.

The education system must incorporate practical training, relevant material and quality training facilities. The curriculum for skill development programmes cannot be designed unless the industry demand and skill requirements are taken into account and all industries define their own employability standards. Further, every skills development program should lead to an apprenticeship and/or a job, in addition to having the provisions of appropriate assessment, accreditation and certification standards. The curriculum should remain relevant and thus, should be developed and reviewed every two to three years, with inputs from academic and industry experts.

ROLE OF TEACHER TRAINING AND ICT IN EDUCATION

Teacher Training

The key challenge facing Indian school education is to institute a system to provide quality education. A good teacher is critical to the process of imparting quality education. It is widely acknowledged, and buttressed by empirical research and experiments, that teaching inputs, in the classroom as well as in the form of supplemental inputs, have a very big role in improving the learning outcome of students.

Currently, we are faced with a shortage of teachers, and inadequately qualified and poorly prepared teaching staff. Teacher recruitment in most states remained frozen for many years. Limited attention to teacher recruitment is evident in the proportion of single-teacher schools. Official estimates put the shortage of teachers in elementary government schools at over 1 million to meet RTE requirements and fill the current backlog of vacancies (National University of Educational Planning and Administration [NUEPA] and MHRD). Faced with the shortage of trained teachers and the huge demand created by the universalisation of education policy, schools have been resorting to hiring contract teachers and para-skilling of less qualified teachers. In many states, particularly central-eastern and north-eastern, the bulk of teachers are without professional qualifications.

Due to the lack of skilled teachers, many private initiatives are rolling out cost-effective standardised lesson plans to meet the curriculum requirements. Poonam Batra (Chapter 20) argues that the role of the teacher cannot be reduced to standardised 'lesson plans' since every child is special and the teacher has to understand the need of every student. Para-skilling cannot be a substitute for teacher training.

Limited attention has been given by the government to building institutions and institutional capacity to educate teachers, as Batra points out in Chapter 20. Over 80 per cent of teacher training institutes are in the poorly-regulated private sector and the remaining in public institutions that have outdated curricula and pedagogic approaches. The massive increase in private teacher training institutions is mostly in urban areas, leaving wide gaps in teacher education in the rural and remote areas. The ills that affect the state teacher training institutes, i.e., paucity of faculty, outdated curriculum and sub-standard reading materials, are also present in the private institutes.

Batra (Chapter 20) argues that the public system of training teachers needs to be strengthened with a concerted focus on quality. This can best be achieved by bringing the system of teacher education under the ambit of higher education. The Bachelor of Elementary Education (BElEd) Programme of the University of Delhi is a successful example of an inter-disciplinary pre-service education of elementary school teachers. There should be four-year integrated undergraduate programmes, two-year post-graduation university programmes and research-based programmes in centres of excellence. Under the 12th Plan, Schools of Education are proposed to be established which would undertake research in school education.

Existing institutions need to be restructured and strengthened, the content and pedagogy of teacher education programmes revamped along the lines suggested in National Curriculum Framework for Teacher Education (NCFTE), including the model syllabi, and new institutional arrangements established. Batra suggests that District Institutes of Education and Training (DIETs) could be upgraded to undergraduate colleges in a phased manner, along with guidelines and support for their implementation. More effective regulation of public and private teacher education services is also needed.

The availability of finances via the national educational cess and the commitment to increased rural employment opportunities provide a unique opportunity to create hundreds of thousands of jobs for adequately trained and motivated school teachers.

Information and Communication Technology (ICT)

Educational Technology can help realise the goal of delivering quality education across multiple tiers of education. But hitherto, the implementation of EduTech had taken the form of some computer labs with motley collections of software for students. EduTech could benefit all stakeholders, but the choice of appropriate technology, last-mile connectivity taking into account availability of infrastructure, cost of the technology as well as cost of connectivity have to be carefully factored into any solution.

The implementation of EduTech must shift from its narrow focus on systems used for teaching in the classroom and supplementary learning in 'labs', to a wider implementation, which involves teachers in curriculum content and policy-making, promotes the use of technology in improving education delivery and governance, and involves the collaboration of academic institutions, the government and the private industry for investment decisions. Manish Upadhyay and Amitava Maitra (Chapter 21) advocate an integrated implementation of EduTech within a framework that provides utility for all users — from education policy-makers and school administrators, to teachers, students and parents.

Upadhyay and Maitra (Chapter 21) suggest that a systems approach should be adopted while rolling out EduTech interventions, and propose the Analysis, Design, Development, Implementation and Evaluation model (ADDIE) model. There should be an emphasis on monitoring and evaluation (M&E), and the process should involve feedback mechanisms from multiple stakeholders to improve the effectiveness of the programmes. Alternative business models are also discussed for making technology-aided education delivery both cheap and high in quality. Additionally, effective regulation to address problems seen in the PPP and Build–Own–Operate–Transfer (BOOT) models implemented in EduTech is proposed. EduTech should be used to facilitate the learning of students in vocational streams, skill upgradation, and in facilitating the certification of educational courses. In certain content areas where hands-on experience is either relatively expensive to give or has safety concerns, the use of simulations, videos and other such e-assets creates a compelling case for the use of educational technology. The authors emphasise complete integration of ICT into the education policy framework, and ensuring its implementation and execution.

CONCLUSION AND RECOMMENDATIONS

Education is central to India's social and economic transformation, and the fulcrum of a more equitable, humane and democratic society. The over-riding concern echoed throughout this Report is the abysmally poor quality of learning of the vast majority of students reflected at all levels of education, starting from basic reading and numerical competency to conceptual knowledge, and creative and independent thinking. The private sector is pervasive at all levels of education, reaching about 25 per cent of elementary school children and more than 50 per cent of secondary and higher education students. But apart from a few elite schools and higher education institutions, the private sector has not achieved a significantly better performance than government educational institutions. The state of education in the country is one of policy failure, wrongly-focused regulation and poor governance. Year after year studies have shown that government actions are not yielding desired outcomes, but government policy focus remains steadfast on improving inputs.

It is urgent to radically overhaul the educational system in a holistic, not piece-meal way. At the school level, what is needed is overall pedagogical reform, clear articulation of learning goals, regrouping of children according to learning abilities, and all of this backed by professionally trained and motivated teachers. The regulatory framework needs to be flexible enough to encompass not just minimum standards but also enable educational excellence. Greater autonomy to innovate and produce cutting-edge research is needed. At the same time, it should be accompanied by greater accountability from internal and external evaluations and disclosure of information.

This section provides some key recommendations towards this vision. Two caveats: some of these are already being considered by the government and we urge their expeditious implementation. Some may be counter to the RTE Act provisions, but could be incorporated in a flexible way in the RTE rules notified by the states. Similarly, some of the suggestions may be considered while finalising the pending Bills on higher education.

Improving Learning Outcomes and Quality

(a) Key is to create properly-trained teachers — teacher education must be included as a full-fledged degree programme, with postgraduate degree and research avenues. There is a need for radical shifts in curriculum and pedagogic approaches to teacher preparation. Performance-based regulations are required to ensure that all teacher training institutes deliver skilled teachers. Teacher incentives can also make a difference in government schools.

(b) Classes should be organised according to learning abilities of children, not age–class-based. Grouping children according to their abilities and teaching by ability would help improve basic learning skills. This is particu-

larly important for children from a disadvantaged social background or first-generation learners.

(c) An annual assessment with a retention policy is highly recommended. The CCE is a good tool but there are no guidelines for evaluation and teachers have not been trained for it. In any case, continuous evaluation should be supplemented with a final examination to assess the student. Automatic promotion could make the learning-gap worse.

(d) In the short term, alternative pedagogies with volunteers, existing teachers or contract teachers could be considered along with remedial programmes after school hours, summer schools and so on.

(e) Curriculum reform, especially at higher primary and secondary levels, needs to be geared towards increasing conceptual understanding. Curriculum should be less ambitious and at secondary level should have a vocational component and while designing this component it should take into consideration the requirement of industry.

(f) Vocational training should be designed with the active involvement of industry to ensure skill development matches industry needs.

Assessment

(a) Regular information should be provided on school and student performance at both elementary and secondary levels. Independent bodies (like Pratham) can be empanelled to carry out surveys on learning achievements, based on an agreed approach and methodology. More experiments need to be undertaken to better understand what would work to improve learning outcomes and be scalable.

(b) Results should be published and report cards can be given to Village Education Committees to increase accountability.

(c) Assessment methods, especially for secondary education, need to be made more uniform across states so that evaluation is widely acceptable, comparable nationally, and over time, and also valued by college and universities.

(d) There should be mandatory accreditation of higher education by independent agencies. Principles of ranking should be evolved in order to introduce competition on quality and encourage accountability.

(e) Non-traditional regulatory approaches need to be introduced based on peer evaluation and public disclosure, using a variety of internal and external evaluation.

Enabling Environment and Regulation

(a) Criteria for recognition of schools should be based on learning outcomes, parent involvement and extra-curricular activities of children rather than infrastructure and input norms. For poorly performing schools, efforts should be made to improve their performance and even permit school adoption by credible non-state sector.

(b) Criteria for recognition of higher education institutions should be based on programme outcomes, defined in stages.

(c) A variety of schools and higher education institutions should be permitted, including for-profit. This should be accompanied by mandatory disclosure of information by the institutions on a regular basis.

(d) Non-profit institutions should be encouraged to grow by removing disincentives in trust laws to allow building an endowment; tax incentives could also be considered;

restrictions on courses and maximum student intake should be removed.

(e) Performance-based regulation should replace input-based regulation.

Financing

(a) Untied block grants should be given to schools.

(b) Grants should be linked to attendance and performance.

(c) Higher education institutions should be allowed to invest in diverse financial instruments, and universities allowed greater flexibility in offering courses to generate revenue.

(d) The industry must be willing to pay a premium for a skilled worker, and bear part of the training costs and/or take on board apprentices.

REFERENCES

Accountability Initiative. 2012. 'PAISA Report 2011'. http://www.accountabilityindia.in/article/state-report-cards/2475-paisa-reprt-2011 (accessed 30 October 2012).

Chavan, Madhav, 2011. 'The Unseen Change', in Annual Status of Education Report 2011. New Delhi: ASER Centre/Pratham.

Ministry of Human Resource Development (MHRD). 2009. 'Report of the Committee to Advise on Renovation and Rejuvenation of Higher Education'. http://www.academicsindia.com/Yashpal-committee-report.pdf (accessed 10 October 2012).

Pritchett, Lant and Amanda Beatty. 2012. 'The Negative Consequences of Overambitious Curricula in Developing Countries'. Working Paper, Harvard Kennedy School of Government.

Section I
EDUCATION LANDSCAPE IN INDIA

1

Regulations in the Education Sector

M.R. Madhavan and *Kaushiki Sanyal*

Ensuring access to quality education is crucial for India if it wants to take advantage of its demographic dividend. An educated population not only drives economic growth, but also has a positive impact on human development indicators such as life expectancy, birth and death rates, infant mortality rate, and nutrition levels of children (Chakrabarty 2011; GoI n.d., 2012). Presently, about 74 per cent of the country's total population above 7 years of age is literate (i.e., able to both read and write) — a considerable improvement from 18 per cent in 1951.[1] However, the sector faces many challenges such as poor quality of education at all levels, low quality of research, inadequate basic physical infrastructure, teacher apathy, low quality of training, and lack of autonomy and accountability.

The first section of this chapter gives a brief overview of the current system. This is followed by four sections that describe the regulatory framework at each level of education — i.e., elementary, secondary, higher and vocational education. In each section, some of the recent and proposed changes in the regulatory structure will also be discussed.

PRESENT STATUS

India's educational system broadly comprises school education (elementary, secondary and higher secondary), higher education (general and professional) and vocational education. The Ministry of Human Resource Development (MHRD) is the nodal ministry for the sector. The other bodies involved in regulating and maintaining standards in the sector include the National Council of Educational Research and Training (NCERT), the University Grants Commission (UGC), the All India Council of Technical Education (AICTE), and the National Council for Teacher Education (NCTE) at the central level. At the state level, the Department of Education and the State Council of Educational Research and Training (SCERT) have important roles to play.

The National Policy on Education (NEP), 1986 as modified in 1992 emphasised universal access and retention, correcting regional and social imbalances and education for women, Scheduled Castes/Scheduled Tribes (SC/STs) and minorities. It also set a goal of increasing expenditure on education to 6 per cent of the Gross Domestic Product (GDP). India spends about 11.5 per cent of its total annual budget on education (GoI 2012). The expenditure on education as percentage of GDP was 3.1 per cent in 2011–12.[2]

Private participation is allowed in all levels of the education sector. However, at all levels, these institutions have to function on a not-for-profit basis.[3] The Supreme Court has ruled that these institutions are permitted a 'reasonable surplus to meet the cost of expansion and augmentation of facilities'[4] but prohibited from charging capitation fee or profiteering (the judgement does not define 'reasonable surplus') (ibid.: 87).[5]

There has been significant progress in enrolment of students at the elementary level but it drops sharply at higher levels. The Gross Enrolment Ratio (GER) at elementary level is 102 per cent, at secondary level 63 per cent, 36 per cent at higher secondary level, and 15 per cent in higher education (MHRD 2011d).[6]

Recent legislative activity has focused on elementary and higher education, and not on secondary education. The Parliament has enacted the Right to Education (RTE) Act, 2009, which operationalises the fundamental right to elementary education up to Class VIII. It is currently considering a number of bills to reform the regulatory framework for higher education (at the university level).

ELEMENTARY EDUCATION

There are various types of schools providing elementary education:

(*a*) government and government-aided,

(b) schools run by autonomous organisations under the government (such as Kendriya Vidyalayas and Navodaya Vidyalayas),

(c) schools run by government departments directly (such as those run by defence and railways),

(d) schools run by public sector undertakings, and

(e) unaided schools (private).

Government schools are run by the the central, state or local governments. Aided schools are privately managed but receive grants-in-aid from central, state or local governments. Unaided schools (private) are non-profit entities established by trusts or as educational, charitable or religious societies registered under the Societies Registration Act, 1860, or State Acts.[7]

'Education' is a concurrent subject in the Constitution allowing both the centre and states to make laws. Prior to 2002, Article 45 of the Directive Principles of State Policy enjoined the state to 'provide within a period of 10 years from the commencement of [the] Constitution, for free and compulsory education for all children until they complete the age of fourteen years'.[8] Many states have enacted laws to make education free and compulsory. See, for example, the Delhi Primary Education Act, 1970; the Gujarat Compulsory Primary Education Act, 1961; and Tamil Nadu Compulsory Elementary Education Act, 1994 (Juneja 2003). Over the years enrolment rates improved but dropout rates were high. The GER of children between 6–14 years in 2002–03 was 82.5 per cent. The dropout rate of children at the primary level was 35 per cent (Planning Commission 2008a).

In 1993, the Supreme Court declared that the right to education was a fundamental right as it was an inherent part of the right to life. The Constitution was amended in 2002 to include this right and Article 21A was added, which requires the State to provide free and compulsory education to all children between the age of 6 and 14 years. The RTE Act, which became operational in April 2010, gives effect to this fundamental right.

The Right to Education Act, 2009

The Act seeks to implement the fundamental right to education for all children (including children with disabilities) between 6 to 14 years. The central RTE Rules were notified on 8 April 2010. Till date, 32 states, including Gujarat, Andhra Pradesh, Himachal Pradesh, Orissa, Rajasthan, Punjab, Haryana and Manipur have notified state RTE Rules (PIB 2012b). The government has committed ₹2.3 trillion for five years (2010–11 to 2014–15) to implement the Act. The fund sharing pattern between the centre and the state is in the ratio of 65:35 for five years (PIB 2011).

Key Features

(a) The Act states that every child has a right to free and compulsory education in a neighbourhood school. A school may be government-run or private (aided or unaided). (Note that private schools have to be run on a non-profit basis, which means that surplus money has to be ploughed back into the institution and no dividend can be distributed to the members of the entity that owns the school.)

(b) The Act makes it mandatory for all schools to meet certain minimum norms. Government schools have to meet the Pupil–Teacher Ratio (PTR). All other schools require a certificate of recognition (already established schools shall have three years to comply). Recognition shall be granted if the school satisfies certain norms such as PTR, infrastructure and qualification of teachers. Schools that do not meet these norms within the prescribed timeframe shall be shut down. In case the school violates this provision, it shall be liable to a fine.

(c) Government schools have to provide free and compulsory education to all admitted children. For aided schools, the extent of free education would be proportionate to the funding received, provided that a minimum of 25 per cent seats are reserved for disadvantaged students. All other schools (including unaided schools) have to reserve at least 25 per cent of seats for the students from SC, ST, low-income, and other disadvantaged or weaker groups (including children with disabilities). Unaided schools shall be reimbursed for either their tuition charge or the per-student expenditure in government schools, whichever is lower. If the per-student expenditure is higher than the government schools, the private school has to bear the cost.

(d) The Act prohibits physical punishment or mental harassment, screening procedures for admission of children, capitation fees, private tuitions by teachers,

---

Box 1.1
Legal Trajectory of Right to Education in the Supreme Court

Mohini Jain v. State of Karnataka (1992) SCR (3) 658: Every citizen has a 'right to education' under the constitution. Although it falls within the Directive Principles of State Policy, unless this right is made a reality, the fundamental rights will remain beyond the reach of a majority of the population. The State is under an obligation to provide this right through State-owned or recognised educational institutions.

Unnikrishnan J. P. v. State of Andhra Pradesh (1993) SCR (1) 594: The citizens have a fundamental right to education, which flows from Article 21 (right to life). But it is not an absolute right and applies only to children up to 14 years of age. Thereafter, this right to education is subject to limits of economic capacity and development of the state.

and running schools without recognition. It also prohibits children from being held back in class, expelled or the requirement to pass a board examination until the completion of elementary education.

Extent of Regulation of Various Schools

Since the Act covers all schools, it is important to understand the extent of regulation for various types of schools. It can be seen from Table 1.1 that the requirements differ for government schools and private schools. About 26 per cent of children between 6 and 14 years are enrolled in private schools (note that 7 per cent of primary schools and 13 per cent of upper primary schools are private [aided and unaided]) (GoI 2012; MHRD 2011d).

The only requirement for government schools is to meet the PTR norm. Also, there is no consequence for failing to meet this basic norm. However, private schools are subject to losing their recognition and shutting down if they do not comply with norms for PTR, infrastructure and teaching. The Act also only specifies penalties in case a school collects capitation fees or subjects the child to a screening procedure during admission. Furthermore, the Act places the onus on the government to ensure enrolment of all children, but does not identify which government agency will be responsible for this task.

Quality of Education

The primary focus of the Act is on the right to schooling and physical infrastructure. There is no norm to ensure that a school provides a minimum quality of education. Even teachers' duties are only related to punctuality, attendance, etc., and not on learning achievements of their students. Despite a number of government programmes, including the Sarva Shiksha Abhiyan, many students are performing well below their class levels (GoI 2012). Furthermore, mandating that no child shall be held back until completion of elementary education could result in children reaching Class VIII without achieving certain learning outcomes. In

fact, some studies show that despite a high pass rate of 95 per cent, the learning outcomes for children from Classes IV and V are much lower than the norm (NUEPA 2009). The Act does not address this problem nor does it require schools to provide any remedial training for students performing below their peer group. It also does not give parents and guardians the option of voluntarily holding their child back in school. The problem of shortage of trained teachers also remains an issue. Approximately 45 per cent of all elementary schools teachers do not have even a bachelor's degree (NUEPA 2010). In this context, some states have taken the lead to define norms on quality standards. For example, the RTE Rules notified by the state of Gujarat declare that schools need not meet infrastructure norms if they can demonstrate that they achieve certain learning outcomes, both in terms of absolute levels and as improvement from that of the previous years.[9]

In 2008, the National Knowledge Commission (NKC), chaired by Shri Sam Pitroda, recommended the setting up of a testing body at the national level for quality assessment of both government and private schools. The testing body would monitor schools on the basis of various types of indicators such as learning levels, enrolment and attendance (NKC 2007).

Reservation of Seats for Disadvantaged Groups

The Act requires private schools to reserve 25 per cent seats for disadvantaged groups. This provision was challenged in the Supreme Court by associations of private schools. However, the court ruled that the provision was constitutionally valid, except in case of unaided minority schools. It also asked the government to clarify whether the Act is applicable only to day scholars or extends to boarders.

While the court settled the issue of constitutional validity of the provision, other concerns still remain. Schools will be reimbursed only to the extent of the average per-child expenditure in state government schools. It remains to be seen whether this would result in increase of school fees for

TABLE 1.1 Comparison of Extent of Regulation for Various Schools

Government Schools	Other Schools (including Aided and Unaided)
All admitted students to be provided free education.	25 per cent seats to be reserved for disadvantaged students.
No recognition required. Have to meet the PTR norm.	Recognition is mandatory. Shall be granted if school meets norms such as PTR, infrastructure and qualification of teachers.
No provision.	If norms not met, schools to be shut down.
No provision.	In case a school operates without recognition, it shall be liable to a fine.
Constitute School Management Committee with representatives from parents and local authority. Shall prepare school development plan.	No provision for unaided schools. Other schools have to constitute the School Management Committee. Play an advisory role.

Source: PRS Legislative Research; Right to Education Act, 2009.

other students (who may cross-subsidise the students from disadvantaged groups). Some experts have also questioned the exemption of minority institutions from this requirement (Mehta 2012).

SECONDARY AND HIGHER SECONDARY EDUCATION

Secondary and higher secondary education (Classes IX–XII) is primarily the responsibility of the state governments. India has a much lower GER at this stage (49 per cent) as compared to countries in east Asia (70 per cent average) and Latin America (82 per cent average) (World Bank 2009). There are 190,643 institutions providing secondary education in the country.[10] The proportion of private schools (operating on a not-for-profit basis) at secondary level is 60 per cent (ibid.).

In order to give a boost to secondary education, in 2009, the central government launched the Rashtriya Madhyamik Shiksha Abhiyan. It seeks to achieve an enrolment rate of 75 per cent within five years, universal access by 2017 and universal retention by 2020. In order to achieve universalisation of access, the working group on secondary education has estimated that 19,946 additional secondary schools will be required to ensure 100 per cent GER by 2017.[11]

Regulation of Secondary Education

Schools are recognised by respective state departments of school education. Every recognised school which conducts a public examination at the end of Classes X and XII has to be affiliated with a board or council conducting such examinations. There are three central boards:
(a) Central Board of Secondary Education (CBSE),
(b) National Institute of Open Schooling; (NIOS) and
(c) Council for the Indian School Certificate Examination (CISCE).

Each state also has state boards such as the Andhra Pradesh Board of Secondary Education, Bihar School Examination Board and Maharashtra State Board of Secondary and Higher Secondary Education. The state boards are either statutory or under the state Department of Education. They vary considerably in terms of their quality, what they assess in terms of learning and how they are graded. The school boards set the syllabus and conduct the final evaluation (World Bank 2009).

Since 2010, the CBSE made the Class X Board examination optional for students studying in schools affiliated with the CBSE. It introduced the scheme of Continuous and Comprehensive Evaluation (CCE) to improve the quality of schools affiliated to it. If the students continue in the same school after Class X, they can be promoted either on the basis of CCE or the result of the Class X board examination. If the student wishes to leave the CBSE system after Class X he is required to appear in the Board examination conducted by the CBSE.[12] The CBSE scheme was presented to many state boards but it is yet to be implemented at the state level.

Fees: The central government does not regulate the fees charged from students by private schools. CISCE and CBSE's affiliation by-laws state that fees charged by schools affiliated to these Boards should be commensurate with the facilities provided by the schools. They also cannot charge capitation fees or accept donations to admit students.[13] Private schools under state boards have to follow regulations of their respective state governments. Currently, most states allow private schools to fix their own fees subject to certain restrictions (such as prohibiting charging of capitation fees and requiring private schools to get their fee structure approved by the government) (Ashar and Bhandary 2011; *Business Standard* 2012; *Deccan Chronicle* 2012).[14]

There is, however, evidence that some education providers have created new structures to bypass the requirement that trusts and societies have to plough back the surplus generated into the same school for its development. They operate through a two-tier legal structure: a trust that runs the school and a company that owns the assets (land, building) and provides services (management and technology). The school trust pays lease rentals and management fees to the company. In this way, the surplus of tuition fees over teacher salaries flows to the company which can then distribute it as dividends (Jayashankar 2010; Vora and Dewan 2009).

Various committees have recommended ways to strengthen the secondary education system. These include the NKC, the Central Advisory Board of Education (CABE) Committee's Report on Universalisation of Secondary Education and the Planning Commission's Working Group Report on Secondary and Vocational Education (12th Five-Year Plan). Some of the key recommendations are summarised in Table 1.2.

HIGHER EDUCATION

Education provided after completion of school education (Class XII) is known as higher education, which comprises education in general subjects, and professional and technical education. At present, India's GER is 15 per cent in higher education (MHRD 2011c), which is much lower than the world average of 23 per cent (Planning Commission 2008a). The aim is to increase the GER to 21 per cent by the end of the 12th Plan and 30 per cent by 2020 (MHRD 2011c). The number of unaided higher education institutions has increased over the years (currently 63 per cent of institutions are private) (Planning Commission 2008a). With about 50 per cent share in enrolment, private institutions have improved access. However, they are concentrated in a few select disciplines such as engineering, management, medicine, and information technology (IT). Also, the spread of private institutions is uneven, with some states witnessing more growth than others (ibid.).

Regulation of Higher, Professional and Technical Education

Both the centre and the states can enact laws related to education since it is in the Concurrent List of the Constitution. In addition, the centre has the power to determine standards for higher educational institutions while the states can incorporate, regulate and wind up universities.[15] The MHRD frames major policies related to higher education and provides grants to the UGC. The central government establishes central universities. The UGC may recognise institutions as deemed universities. The state governments are responsible for establishment of state universities and colleges, and they also provide grants for their development and maintenance (MHRD 2011b).[16]

Technical education is regulated by the AICTE, apart from which there are 14 statutory professional councils that regulate courses related to areas such as medicine, law and nursing (ibid.).[17]

Higher Education

The UGC (statutory body established in 1956) is the apex body that regulates universities and colleges teaching general subjects. It has the power to determine and maintain standards and disburse grants. Universities can be central, state, private, or deemed. The UGC stipulates that colleges that provide degree courses have to be affiliated with a university. The UGC provides minimum qualification of teachers, guidelines for award of various degrees and standards that private universities have to maintain. It can also regulate

TABLE 1.2   Key Recommendations of Committees on Secondary Education

National Knowledge Commission	CABE Committee Report	Planning Commission Report (12th Plan)
• Decentralisation of school management to local authorities such as panchayats as far as possible. • Transparent, norm-based procedures for the recognition of private schools, to reduce harassment and bureaucratic delay. • National evaluation body to monitor the quality of both government and private schools, using a results-based monitoring framework. • Need to revamp school inspection, provide training to teachers, reform curriculum and incorporate English into the curriculum. • Flexibility in disbursal of funds.	• Focus on universal access, equality, and relevance. • Flexible curriculum and scientifically designed student assessment system. • Develop a Secondary Education Management Information System to capture data on girls, SC/STs, minorities, etc. • Need for decentralised micro-level planning. • Allocation of 6 per cent of GDP for education. • Commercialisation of school education should be curbed.	• Extend Rashtriya Madhyamik Shiksha Abhiyan (RMSA) scheme to government-aided schools and to cover higher secondary education. • Provide for residential schools and hostels in existing schools to enhance access. • Civil construction work under RMSA should be carried out as per state schedule of rates since they vary from state to state. • Waive off financial ceiling on infrastructure support for existing secondary schools. Enhance school grant to ₹100,000 per school per annum from ₹50,000. These grants are used to pay electricity and water bills, books, periodicals, etc. • Provide untied fund of ₹10 million at the district level to improve quality in school.

Source: CABE (2005); Department of School Education and Literacy (2011); NKC (2009); PRS Legislative Research.

fees of universities if it is in the public interest to do so and prohibits such universities from taking any donations.[18]

Technical and Professional Education

Technical education is regulated by the AICTE and the subjects that fall under this include engineering, management, pharmacy, architecture. Technical institutions can provide degree programmes if they are affiliated with a university (this condition is waived for some institutions). Affiliation is not required if the institution runs only diploma programmes. The CABE, which includes representatives from the central and state governments and other experts, coordinates between the centre and the states. There are also 14 professional councils such as the Medical Council of India, the Dental Council of India, the Bar Council of India and the Council of Architecture that recognise courses, promote professional institutions and provide grants to undergraduate programmes.

Table 1.3 gives an overview of different types of institutions in higher education

The fees and the manner in which admission is granted in unaided institutions are regulated by the state-constituted Fee and Admission Regulatory Committee, which determines the fee that each private institution can charge and the student intake. The Supreme Court has ruled on this subject in a number of court cases (see Box 1.3).

Accreditation of institutions is currently voluntary. The National Assessment and Accreditation Council and the National Board of Accreditation are autonomous bodies that accredit institutions, set up by the UGC and the AICTE respectively. Presently, foreign institutions are allowed to operate in India through various modes. Indian universities can grant degrees and diplomas in collaboration with foreign universities. However, foreign universities cannot set up branch campuses without an Indian partner. The AICTE regulates foreign institutions, which provide technical education either directly or through collaboration with Indian partners (AICTE 2005).

There are many challenges facing higher education. Some of the key challenges are related to access, quality, governance and funding. There have also been several issues related to regulation of the private sector.

(a) *Access*: India's GER in higher education is about 15 per cent (MHRD 2011c). Other countries such as the United States (US) (81 per cent), the United Kingdom (UK) (54 per cent), Japan (49 per cent), and Malaysia (27 per cent) have much higher enrolment rates (NKC 2009).

(b) *Quality*: No Indian university is listed in the top 100 universities in the world and only two are listed in the top 200 (*Times Higher Education* 2012). In 2009, a review committee set up by the MHRD found 88 of the 130 deemed universities to be of poor quality and identified

TABLE 1.3   Regulatory Structure of Higher Education

Type of Institutions	Number of Institutions	Structure of Regulation
Universities	452	Set up by Act of Parliament or State legislatures (can be public or private).
Deemed to be Universities	129	Central government grants status on recommendation from UGC. Have autonomy to set their own syllabus, admission criteria and fees.
Colleges	33,023	Affiliation to a public university is mandatory (private universities cannot affiliate). Can be aided, unaided or autonomous.
Institutes of National Importance	39	Status granted by an Act of Parliament (IITs, NITs, etc.) to high-performing institutes. Can award degrees without affiliating with a university.
Institutions established under State Acts (Centres of Excellence)	5	Set up by a State Act. Includes Nizam's Institute of Medical Sciences, Hyderabad; Sri Venkateswara Institute of Medical Sciences, Tirupati; and Sher-e-Kashmir Institute of Medical Sciences, Srinagar.
Technical Education (Central or State Government-Funded and Self-Financed Institutions)	10,139	AICTE approves setting up of new institutions and introduction of new courses. Includes engineering, technology, management, architecture, town planning, and pharmacy.
Institutions offering Medical, Legal, Dental, Nursing, Teacher Education	—	Regulated by 14 professional councils such as the Medical Council of India, Bar Council of India, and Dental Council of India that can recognise courses and promote the institutions.
Polytechnics	3,716	Set up by state governments or by a private body with the approval of AICTE. Private polytechnics have to be set up through a sponsoring body: a society or a trust. Can offer only diploma or certificate courses.

Source: AICTE (2012); ICAI (2010); MHRD (n.d., 2011a, 2012); 'Monitoring of Technical/Professional Institutions', Starred Question no. 124, Lok Sabha, answered on 30 November 2011; 'Open and Deemed Universities', Unstarred Question no. 2554, Lok Sabha, answered on 17 August 2011; 'Setting up of New Polytechnics', Unstarred Question no. 316, Lok Sabha, 14 March 2012; 'Setting up Universities', Unstarred Question no. 1170, Lok Sabha, 21 March 2012.

> ## Box 1.3
> ### Key Supreme Court Judgements on Fees in Private Institutions
>
> *Mohini Jain v. State of Karnataka* (1992): Fees charged in private institutions in excess of tuition fees in government colleges is deemed to be capitation fees.
> *Unnikrishnan, J. P. v. State of Andhra Pradesh* (1993): Banned capitation fees and devised a scheme, which allotted 50 per cent seats in an unaided professional institution as free seats (fees same as a government institution) and 50 per cent as payment seats (fees higher than 'free seats' but have to be approved by a state-level committee).
> *T. M. A. Pai Foundation v. State of Karnataka* (2002): The decision regarding the fee to be charged must be left to the private institution that does not depend on any funds from the government. The object of an institution should not be to make profit. However, it can generate a reasonable revenue surplus, for the purpose of development of education and expansion of the institution.
> *Islamic Academy v. State of Karnataka* (2003): A committee in each state, headed by a retired High Court judge, should approve the fee structure, which shall be binding for three years.
> *P. A. Inamdar v. State of Maharashtra* (2005): The committees regulating admission and fee structure shall continue to exist, but only as a temporary measure until the central or state governments are able to devise a suitable mechanism for such regulation.

problems such as control of management boards by nominees of the sponsoring trust or government functionaries, low quality of research, and improper practices in admission process (MHRD 2009a). In 2005, the Supreme Court struck down a law in Chhattisgarh that allowed the state government to establish universities through a notification. Universities had been set up without adhering to UGC norms of infrastructure, teaching facility, financial resources, and teaching standards.[19] Shortage of quality faculty has contributed significantly to the problem (MHRD 2011b).

(c) *Funding*: Universities in India face financial constraints. Only 0.7 per cent of India's GDP is spent on higher education (NKC 2009), which is lower than countries such as the US (2.9 per cent), UK (1.3 per cent) and China (1.5 per cent) (NBS of China 2007; NCES 2010: 110–11). In general, about 75 per cent of maintenance expenditure is spent on salaries and pensions, and 15 per cent is absorbed by claims such as rents, electricity, telephones, and examinations (NKC 2009).

(d) *Governance*: India's National Policy on Education, 1986 emphasised the need for decentralisation, autonomy of educational institutions and the principle of accountability in managing educational institutions. However, the implementation fell short of the desired goals and principles. The regulatory bodies have a cumbersome procedure for granting recognition and there is large-scale corruption (GoI 2006; MHRD 2009a). Some issues that need to be resolved to promote autonomy, accountability and transparency are: government intervention, the large size of university councils, high entry barriers for new universities, and the system of affiliated colleges.

(e) *Regulation of Private Sector*: Various Supreme Court judgements have sought to curb profiteering by ordering varying degree of control on private institutions. States

such as Madhya Pradesh, Andhra Pradesh, Gujarat, Karnataka, and Orissa enacted laws to set up such committees to approve the fee structure in professional educational institutions.[20] However, according to the Yash Pal Committee report, the charging of capitation fees, which range from ₹0.1–1.2 million depending on the course, have not abated (MHRD 2009b). On the other hand, the private institutes claim that capitation fee is required to ensure financial viability of the institution. Some experts also contend that allowing only non-profit entities to operate in the education sector does not ensure quality, nor does it increase supply or curb charging of capitation fees (Basu 2009; Debroy 2008; Mehta 2005). The non-profit status may act as an incentive for unscrupulous players since such entities get tax exemptions, which makes it easier to launder money (Kapur and Mehta 2004).

(f) *Admission in Private Institutes*: This is also regulated by the government. A certain number of seats are earmarked as government seats where students pay the equivalent of the fee charged in government institutes. About 15 per cent of seats are categorised as management quota, where students pay the fee as mandated by the Fee Regulatory Committee. The 93rd Constitutional Amendment enables the Parliament or State Assemblies to enact laws reserving seats for SC/ST/OBC in private institutions.

In 2009, two high-level committees — the NKC and the Yash Pal Committee — suggested various ways to revamp the higher education sector. The main recommendations are summarised in Table 1.4.

Proposed Regulatory Structure for Higher Education

The government has introduced six Bills that would lead to significant changes in the regulatory structure for higher education:

TABLE 1.4   Key Recommendations of the NKC and Yash Pal Committee

National Knowledge Commission	Yash Pal Committee
Regulatory Structure	
• Establish an Independent Regulatory Authority for Higher Education (IRAHE) through an Act of Parliament to set standards and determine eligibility criteria for new institutions.	• Establish a National Commission of Higher Education and Research (NCHER) through a constitutional amendment, to replace UGC, AICTE, NCTE and Distance Education Council (DEC).
• It shall also settle disputes and monitor licensing of accreditation agencies (both public and private).	• Professional bodies such as Medical Council of India and Bar Council of India should conduct qualifying examinations.
• The UGC shall only disburse public funds. Abolish all professional bodies except the Medical Council of India and Bar Council of India who shall provide licences to those wishing to enter the profession.	• The NCHER shall create norms for accreditation and certify accrediting agencies, independent of the government.
	• Constitute a National Education Tribunal to adjudicate disputes.
Access	
• Expand the number of universities to 1,500 by establishing 50 National Universities and giving autonomy to individual colleges or clusters of colleges with proven track record.	• Regulatory mechanism should make rational and consistent rules for setting up institutions (both public and private). Education should be made affordable either through scholarships or loans.
• Give admission without taking into account a student's ability to pay. Have a National Scholarship Scheme and allow institutions to set their own fees if at least two banks are willing to give a loan without any collateral. Address disparities of income, gender, region by creating deprivation index.	• Allow only the top foreign universities to establish campuses.
	• The best colleges should be upgraded to university status. A number of colleges can be clubbed into clusters and be recognised as universities.
Quality	
• Existing universities: revise curricula, follow course credit system, promote research, performance incentives to faculty.	• Allow institutions to set their own targets and achieve those in a specified time frame. Reform the curricula based on principles of mobility and academic depth. Universities should have rich undergraduate programmes.
• Colleges: Replace affiliation system with autonomy to top colleges, remodel some into community colleges and establish a Central Board of Undergraduate Education.	• Optimise size of state universities. All private institutions have to be mandatorily accredited. Granting of deemed university status should be put on hold.
• Make disclosure norms for institutions stringent, including their accreditation level. Enhance quality through competition by allowing foreign institutions to operate in India.	• Competitive remuneration and improved infrastructure is required. Student feedback should be taken to identify poor performers.
Governance	
• Governance structures should preserve autonomy and ensure accountability of universities. Vice Chancellors should be appointed through a search process and peer judgement alone. The large size and composition of university courts, academic councils and executive are impediments. Decisions should be taken by standing committees of academic councils.	• Governance structure should preserve the autonomy of universities. Need to develop expertise in educational management and separate it from academic administration.
• Address the problem of politicisation of universities.	• Need for exclusion of politicians and limited representation of government in governance structures.
	• Teachers should have autonomy to frame their courses and assess the students.
Funding	
• Government funding should be 1.5 per cent of the GDP by 2012. Asset of universities such as land should be managed for revenue.	• Need to find supplementary sources of funding, including encouraging philanthropy. Alumni should be tapped as a source.
• Rationalise fees by requiring it to meet at least 20 per cent of the total expenditure. The UGC's grants-in-aid should not be reduced and disadvantaged students should have fees waived plus scholarships.	• Universities should hire professional fund raisers to attract funding from non-government sources.
• Encourage philanthropic contributions through incentives for universities and donors. Allow private investment in universities. Public–private partnerships to set up universities. Make efforts to attract international students.	• Give government funds as a block grant based on a plan.
	• Guaranteed students' loans for students who have the capacity to pay it back and free education for poor students should be implemented.

Source: MHRD (2009b); NKC (2009); PRS Legislative Research.

(a) *Higher Education and Research (HER) Bill, 2011*: It seeks to establish the National Commission for Higher Education and Research (NCHER) to facilitate determination and maintenance of standards of higher education and research in all areas except agricultural education. It shall replace the UGC, the AICTE and the NCTE.

(b) *National Commission for Human Resources for Health (NCHRH) Bill, 2011*: It aims at setting up a mechanism to determine and regulate the standard of health education in the country. It shall replace the Indian Nursing Council, the Pharmacy Council, the Dental Council, and the Medical Council.

(c) *Foreign Educational Institutions (Regulation of Entry and Operations) Bill, 2010*: It seeks to allow foreign institutions to set up campuses in India without an Indian partner subject to specific conditions.

(d) *National Accreditation Regulatory Authority (NARA) for Higher Educational Institutions Bill, 2010*: It is aimed at instituting an apparatus to accredit all higher educational institutions.

(e) *Educational Tribunals Bill, 2010*: Through this Bill, the government intends to set up national and state-level tribunals. Disputes related to institutions, students, faculty, and statutory authorities shall be adjudicated by these tribunals.

(f) *Prohibition of Unfair Practices in Technical Educational Institutions, Medical Educational Institutions and Universities Bill, 2010*: It seeks to penalise unfair practices of private educational institutions, which include charging of capitation fees, not giving receipts for payments made and publishing false advertisement.

The regulatory structure proposed by the six Bills states that the NCHER and NCHRH are the statutory authorities that will set standards and regulate higher educational institutions, including foreign educational institutions. The NARA shall licence agencies for accrediting institutions. Disputes between institutions, students and faculty shall be resolved through educational tribunals. Unfair practices such as capitation fees, donations, and false advertisements shall be penalised.

However, it is unclear whether each of these Bills will necessarily achieve their respective objectives. The HER Bill that establishes the NCHER (replacing the UGC and the AICTE) states that it seeks to maintain standards of higher education and promote autonomy. The NCHER has the power to specify requirements for award of degree or diploma; and norms for establishment and winding up of institutions, academic quality (includes physical infrastructure, faculty qualification) for accreditation and allocation of grants. It shall also maintain a directory of academics for leadership positions for appointment as Vice Chancellors. These powers are similar to the powers enjoyed by the UGC and the AICTE.

The National Accreditation Regulatory Authority Bill, 2010 makes accreditation mandatory for every educational institution and programme. However, the Bill only allows government-controlled non-profit agencies to register as accreditation agencies. This raises a number of issues:

(a) whether this will dilute the objective of creating a healthy competitive environment for quality rating of educational institutions;

(b) whether the time frame to get accredited is sufficient given that all educational institutions have to get accredited within three years (five years for medical institutes); and

(c) whether there is a need for a regulatory body (NARA) given the restriction on private sector participation. In countries such as the US, the UK and Germany, both

FIGURE 1.1   Proposed Regulatory Structure

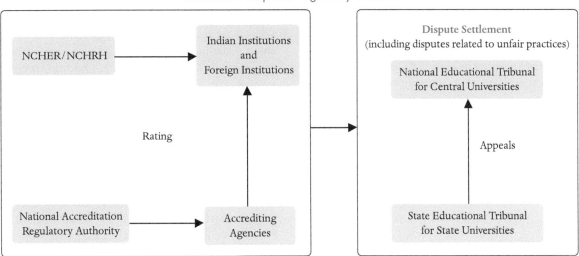

Source: Prepared by the authors.

public and private agencies are allowed to accredit educational institutions. Committees such as the NKC suggested that both public and private accreditation agencies should be allowed and the Yash Pal Committee stated that accreditation agencies should be independent of the government (MHRD 2009b; NKC 2009).

The Foreign Educational Institutions Bill, 2010 seeks to enable foreign universities to set up independent campuses in India. However, the Bill requires foreign institutions to maintain a corpus fund of at least ₹500 million, does not allow repatriation of funds and requires them to have a track record of 20 years in the parent country. Given such conditions, it is an open question whether top foreign institutions would choose to come to India. Experts are divided over whether foreign educational institutions should be allowed to operate in the country. Opponents argue that it would commercialise the sector and increase disparity in access (Chattopadhyay 2009; Chowdhury 2010; Rahman 2010). Proponents contend that it would increase choices for students, enhance competition in the sector with potential for qualitative improvement in the Indian educational institutions, provide technical skills for the job market, and retain some of the funds that flow overseas (*Indian Express* 2010; NKC 2009; Palit 2009; Schukoske 2006). The Standing Committee on HRD, which examined the Bill, recommended that it be passed with adequate safeguards for stakeholders. It suggested that: (a) an independent regulator should monitor, fee, curriculum, salary, etc; (b) approvals be given on a short-term basis first, which could be extended based on performance; and (c) the government devise incentives for foreign institutions to utilise their surplus funds in India (GoI 2011).

The Prohibition of Unfair Practices Bill, 2010 makes taking of capitation fees an offence. It also makes it mandatory for institutions to disclose certain information in the prospectus. However, some experts contend that capitation fee is prohibited even now (MHRD 2009b). Since the Bill does not provide a different system of enforcement of such regulations, the likelihood of such a law making a difference in unfair practices may not be high. Furthermore, if the core issues of shortage of seats and quality of institutions are addressed, this would automatically reduce capitation fees (Basu 2009; Debroy 2008; Mehta 2005). The Bill was examined by the Standing Committee on HRD. It recommended that excess of 10 per cent of tuition fee should be termed as capitation fees and the penalty for taking these increased (GoI 2011).

VOCATIONAL EDUCATION

In India, vocational education (training in a specific vocation or trade) is provided through two basic ways: formal and informal. The formal structure includes: (a) vocational courses offered in professional colleges and polytechnics, (b) vocational streams in schools at the higher secondary stage, (c) technical training in specialised institutions such as Industrial Training Institutes (ITIs)/Industrial Training Centres (ITCs), and (d) apprenticeship training. The informal structure includes training at the workplace and apprenticeships with family members (no certification is provided for such workers). There are 17 ministries of the government that impart vocational training (such as the ministries of HRD, labour, tourism, textiles, urban development, agriculture, and food processing industry) (PIB 2012a). Each ministry sets up training institutes in its subject of specialisation such as handloom, handicrafts, small industry, and tourism (Planning Commission 2008b).

Currently, only 2 per cent of the workforce in the age group of 15–29 years has undergone formal vocational training and 8 per cent have had non-formal vocational training. [Note that about 93 per cent of India's workforce is in the informal sector (Department of School Education and Literacy 2011)]. A large proportion of the workforce in the age group of 19–24 years has received vocational education in countries such as South Korea (96 per cent), Germany (75 per cent), Japan (80 per cent), and the UK (68 per cent) (Planning Commission 2008b). India has set a target of creating 500 million skilled workers by 2022 (PIB 2012a). Therefore, there is a dire need to increase capacity and capability of skill development programmes.

Regulation of Vocational Education

Government and government-aided schools offer vocational courses under a centrally-sponsored scheme termed Vocationalisation of Higher Secondary Education. The scheme, started in 1988, provides financial assistance to states to set up administrative structures, prepare curriculum and offer training programmes for teachers. It also provides financial assistance to NGOs to conduct short-term courses. Schools are selected by the state governments.[21] Since 1988, about 9,000 higher secondary schools have introduced the programme. There are about 150 vocational courses that schools may offer and students are awarded a certificate after completion.[22] In addition, the CBSE schools (including the National Open School) also offer vocational courses (Department of School Education and Literacy n.d.).[23]

Several types of educational institutions (colleges, polytechnics, ITIs/ITCs) offer vocational courses and training. Polytechnics offer three-year diploma courses in branches related to engineering, pharmacy and hotel management, and are regulated by the AICTE within the MHRD. The ITIs/ITCs conduct vocational training courses in 114 trades and are regulated by the Directorate General of Employment and Training, Ministry of Labour and Employment.

The duration of training courses varies from six months to three years and students with Classes VII to XII pass qualification can seek admission in these courses. These institutes can be started by the private sector provided they conform to the norms laid down by the Ministry (ibid.).[24] At present, there are 3,716 polytechnics and 9,480 ITIs/ITCs operating in the country (2,247 are government- and 7,233 are privately-managed).[25] The Apprentices Act, 1961 regulates training of apprentices in 94 vocational courses (apprentices include students who take up vocational courses in schools).

Key Government Schemes

National Vocational Educational Qualification Framework (NVEQF)

The government is in the process of preparing the NVEQF. The NVEQF would set common principles and guidelines for a nationally-recognised qualification system, covering schools, vocational education institutes and institutes of higher education. The aim is to enable stakeholders such as students and employers to objectively assess the level of competency gained through a vocational course. Furthermore, students will be able to opt for vocational courses from Class IX onwards, instead of Class XI (Department of School Education and Literacy 2011).

Centrally-Sponsored Scheme of Vocationalisation of Secondary Education

Launched in 1988, the scheme aims to enhance educational opportunities to enhance employability, reduce mismatch between demand and supply of skilled human resources and provide an alternative stream of education. The scheme offers two-year vocational courses in government and government-aided schools after Class X. The scheme provided financial assistance to states for running these courses. The existing scheme was revised in 2011 to (a) focus on partnerships with the industry in imparting vocational education in schools, (b) assist private schools under the Public–Private Partnership (PPP) model and (c) build capacity of vocational teachers (Department of School Education and Literacy n.d.).[26]

Sub-Mission on Polytechnics

Under the scheme, it is proposed to establish 1,000 polytechnics in the country:
(a) 300 polytechnics to be set up by the state governments/union territories with assistance from the central government in unserved districts;
(b) 300 polytechnics to be set up through PPP by the state governments and union territories (polytechnics will be selected in consultation with state governments,

and various industrial organisations such as Confederation of Indian Industry [CII], Federation of Indian Chambers of Commerce and Industry [FICCI], Associated Chambers of Commerce and Industry of India [ASSOCHAM], and PHD Chamber of Commerce, etc.); and
(c) facilitate the creation of 400 additional polytechnics by the private sector (Department of School Education and Literacy n.d.).

National Skill Development Mission (NSDM)

The NSDM was launched to create a pool of skilled personnel in line with the employment requirement across multiple sectors. Under the NSDM, the government set up three bodies:
(a) the National Skill Development Corporation (set up as a PPP to facilitate training for 150 million people);
(b) the Prime Minister's Council on Skill Development; and
(c) the National Skill Development Coordination Board. The basic purpose of this initiative is to bridge the skill-gap in the country and enhance employability of the workforce (Ministry of Labour and Employment 2011; PIB 2010).

Key Challenges

Vocational education and training in India faces a variety of challenges, which will be discussed in this section.
Access and Quality: The institutional spread of ITIs/ITCs shows acute disparity with over half of these institutes located in the southern states. The quality of the training provided is poor as the infrastructural facilities, tools, faculty, and curriculum are not of sufficient standard. The privately-run ITCs also have similar problems due to low-paying capacity of learners and absence of quality consciousness (Planning Commission 2008b).
Lack of Mobility: Vocational training is treated as distinct and separate from general education. Therefore, students opting for vocational courses in school are not able to gain further qualifications in general education. This creates two types of problems:
(a) people opting for such courses remain unprepared for the job market because a minimal level of both academic training and practical skills is required for any job, and
(b) since students have restricted access to higher qualification, these courses are considered as dead ends (Ministry of Labour and Employment 2011).
Industry and Job Linkages: The vocational training institutes do not have close linkages with employers hence the training provided is outdated and irrelevant. The curriculum often remains static for years, and facilities and laboratories are often outdated (ibid.).

Key Recommendations of Committees

In its 11th Five-Year Plan, the Planning Commission focused on upgrading existing infrastructure and setting up new institutes for vocational training (Planning Commission 2008b). The Working Group for Vocational Education for the 12th Five-Year Plan made certain recommendations (Ministry of Labour and Employment 2011):

(a) Assessment of human resource is essential for planning. Therefore, such estimates should be collected by Sector Skill Councils to be set up by the National Skill Development Corporation.

(b) The selection of schools and vocational electives should be based on assessment of skill needs, availability of required resources such as teachers/trainers, necessary raw material, electricity, water supply, and employment opportunities.

(c) Curriculum should be developed with inputs from academic and industry experts and should be reviewed and revised every two to three years or earlier.

(d) Teacher training courses should include a separate paper on vocational education.

(e) Schools should be provided with adequate tools, equipment and machinery for the development of soft and basic technical skills.

(f) Each school should have linkages with industry or business establishments. Specialised practical training can be arranged in these establishments.

(g) A separate management structure should be set up at the national, state and district levels for the implementation and monitoring of the NVEQF at various levels.

(h) The private sector should be engaged under a PPP model as academic and industrial partners along with NGOs and local government bodies.

The NKC also made certain recommendations related to vocational education (NKC 2009):

(a) Vocational education should be placed entirely under the MHRD (currently there is a fragmented management of the sector, i.e., it falls under different ministries).

(b) Retain aspects of general education within vocational education, which would enable students to return to mainstream education at a later stage.

(c) Students be permitted multiple entry and exit options in the vocational education stream.

(d) Links should be established between vocational education and school and higher education.

(e) Data should be collected periodically to assess the impact of training on employability.

(f) The government should aim to spend at least 10–15 per cent of its total public expenditure on vocational education.

(g) A massive increase in quantity of training is required to meet the need for skilled labour. The government may consider options such as PPPs, distance learning and computerised vocational training.

(h) Certain minimum standards should be introduced as a measure of quality, which should be followed by all public and private vocational institutions.

(i) Training options for unorganised and informal sectors should be enhanced.

(j) An independent regulatory agency should be established for vocational education and training. This body would license accreditation agencies and prescribe standards for certification.

(k) In order to ensure recognition of certification by employers, an electronic database of certified training providers as well as electronic identification for certified workers should be introduced.

CONCLUDING REMARKS

India is graduating to an economy where the bulk of its population will be in the relatively younger age group of 20–35 years. This 'demographic dividend' provides India great opportunities but also poses a great challenge. India will be able to reap the benefits of such a dividend only if its population is healthy, educated and appropriately skilled. This chapter focused on the regulation of the education sector and analysed the challenges that need to be overcome before India can have a world-class education system at all levels.

India's ability to emerge as a globally competitive country will substantially depend on its knowledge resources. Presently, there are a small number of institutions that provide high-quality education while the majority need significant improvement in terms of quality, access and equity. There have been some recent initiatives to reform the sector including the RTE Act, various bills to reform higher education regulation and schemes related to vocational education. However, many of these initiatives do not fully address issues related to quality and access of education and governance of the sector. They also do not encourage participation of the private sector in providing education. In order to bring about a systemic transformation, it is important to address many of the weaknesses and contradictions inherent in the regulatory structure of the education sector. The roadmap to reforming the sector needs to focus on enhancing access to knowledge, providing high quality of education, improving the delivery system, and re-shaping the research and development structures.

NOTES

1. *Census of India*, 2011.
2. Supreme Court cases such as the 1993 *Unnikrishnan* case, the 2002 *T. M. A. Pai Foundation* case, the 2003 *Islamic Academy of Education case*, and the 2005 *P. A. Inamdar* case.
3. *T. M. A. Pai Foundation & Ors v. State of Karnataka & Ors*, Writ Petitions (C) No. 317 of 1993, 25 November 2002.
4. *Islamic Academy of Education & Anr v. State of Karnataka & Ors* (2003) 6 SCC 697.
5. Supreme Court cases such as the 1993 *Unnikrishnan* case, the 2002 *T. M. A. Pai Foundation* case, the 2003 *Islamic Academy of Education* case, and the 2005 *P. A. Inamdar* case (see Agarwal 2006).
6. Also see 'Access to Higher Education', Unstarred Question no. 5404, Lok Sabha, answered on 9 May 2012.
7. Delhi Schools Education Act, 1973.
8. Article 45, Part IV, Directive Principles of State Policy. http://sec.up.nic.in/acts_rules/coi_english/Part_4.pdf (accessed 8 October 2012).
9. Rule 15, Gujarat Right of Children to Free and Compulsory Education Rules, 2012 (notified on 18 February 2012).
10. Unstarred Question no. 4479, Lok Sabha, answered on 21 December 2011.
11. Ibid.
12. Unstarred Question no. 5582, Lok Sabha, answered on 7 September 2011.
13. Starred Question no. 292, Lok Sabha, answered on 9 December 2009.
14. Unstarred Question no. 278, Lok Sabha, answered on 14 March 2012.
15. Seventh Schedule, Constitution of India.
16. UGC Act, 1956; AICTE Act, 1987.
17. Ibid.
18. Section 12A, University Grants Commission Act, 1956.
19. *Prof. Yash Pal v. State of Chhattisgarh & Ors*, Writ Petition (C) No. 19 of 2004.
20. *P. A. Inamdar & Ors v. State of Maharashtra & Ors*, Appeal (civil) 5041 of 2005, Supreme Court, 12 August 2005.
21. Unstarred Question no. 560, Lok Sabha, answered on 3 August 2011.
22. Unstarred Question no. 3999, Lok Sabha, answered on 19 December 2011.
23. Unstarred Question no. 1334, Lok Sabha, answered on 21 March 2012; Unstarred Question no. 1557, Lok Sabha, answered on 30 November 2011.
24. Unstarred Question no. 1557, Lok Sabha, answered on 30 November 2011.
25. Starred Question no. 364, Lok Sabha, answered on 2 May 2012; Unstarred Question no. 7217, Lok Sabha, answered on 21 May 2012.
26. Unstarred Question no. 1557, Lok Sabha, answered on 30 November 2011.

REFERENCES

Agarwal, Pawan. 2006. 'Higher Education in India: The Need for Change'. Working Paper no. 108, Indian Council for Research on International Economic Relations, June.

All India Council for Technical Education (AICTE). 2005. 'Regulations for Entry and Operation of Foreign Universities/Institutions Imparting Technical Education in India'. Notification, All India Council for Technical Education, 16 May.

—————. 2012. 'Approval Process Handbook 2012–2013'. All India Council for Technical Education.

Ashar, Sandeep and Shreya Bhandary. 2011. 'State Assembly Clears Bill on Fee Regulation'. *Times of India*, 4 August.

Basu, Kaushik. 2009. 'Report of the Committee to Advise on Renovation and Rejuvenation of Higher Education in India: A Note of Dissent'. 6 July. http://prayatna.typepad.com/education/2009/07/full-text-of-kaushik-basus-dissent-note-to-the-yashpal-committee-report.html (accessed 10 October 2012).

Business Standard. 2012. 'Raj Govt to Issue Ordinance on Fee Regulatory Commission', 30 May.

Central Advisory Board of Education (CABE). 2005. 'Universalisation of Secondary Education'. Report of the Central Advisory Board of Education Committee.

Chakrabarty, K. C. 2011. 'Indian Education System: Issues and Challenges'. Address, JRE.

School of Management, 5 August, Greater Noida. http://www.bis.org/review/r110809b.pdf (accessed 8 October 2012).

Chattopadhyay, Saumen. 2009. 'The Market in Higher Education: Concern for Equity and Quality', *Economic and Political Weekly*, 44(29): 53–61.

Chowdhury, Kavita. 2010. 'Foreign Univ Bill Divides Academics'. *India Today*, 18 May.

Debroy, Bibek. 2008. 'Higher Education in India: Ducking the Answers', *ISAS Insights*, 32, 16 May.

Deccan Chronicle. 2012. 'AP Plans to Adopt TN Model to Fix Fee', 5 March.

Department of School Education and Literacy. n.d. 'Vocational Education'. Department of School Education and Literacy, Ministry of Human Resource Development, Government of India. http://mhrd.gov.in/voc_eduu (accessed 11 October 2012).

—————. 2011. 'Working Group Report on Secondary and Vocational Education: 12th Five Year Plan (2012–2017)'. Department of School Education and Literacy, Ministry of Human Resource Development, Government of India, October.

Government of India (GoI). n.d. 'Sarva Shiksha Abhiyan … Education for All'. http://india.gov.in/spotlight/spotlight_archive.php?id=31 (accessed 12 October 2012).

—————. 2006. '172nd Report on University and Higher Education', Department-Related Parliamentary Standing Committee on Human Resource Development, May. http://164.100.47.5/newcommittee/reports/EnglishCommittees/Committee%20on%20HRD/172ndreport.htm (accessed 10 October 2012).

Government of India (GoI). 2011. '237th Report on the Foreign Educational Institutions (Regulation of Entry and Operations) Bill, 2010', Department-Related Parliamentary Standing Committee on Human Resource Development, August. http://www.prsindia.org/uploads/media/Foreign%20Educational%20Institutions%20Regulation/Foreign%20Universities%20Bill%20_SCR.pdf (accessed 10 October 2012).

—————. 2012. 'Human Development', in *Economic Survey 2011–12*, pp. 301–36. New Delhi: Oxford University Press.

Indian Express. 2010. 'Top Educational Institutions Hail Foreign Varsity Bill', 16 March.

Institute of Chartered Accountants of India (ICAI). 2010. *Technical Guide on Internal Audit of Educational Institutions*. New Delhi: Institute of Chartered Accountants of India.

Jayashankar, Mitu. 2010. 'The Business of Schools'. *Forbes India*, 8 April.

Juneja, Nalini. 2003. 'Constitutional Amendment to Make Education a Fundamental Right: Issues for a Follow-up Legislation'. Occasional Paper, National Institute of Education Planning and Administration, March.

Kapur, Devesh and Bhanu Pratap Mehta. 2004. 'Indian Higher Education Reform: From Half-Baked Socialism to Half-Baked Capitalism'. Working Paper no. 108, Centre for International Development, Harvard University, September.

Mehta, Pratap Bhanu. 2005. 'Regulating Higher Education'. *Indian Express*, 14 July.

—————. 2012. 'Classroom Struggle'. *Indian Express*, 18 April.

Ministry of Human Resource Development (MHRD). n.d. 'Institutions of National Importance'. http://mhrd.gov.in/instiutions_imp (accessed 12 October 2012).

—————. 2009a. 'Report of the Committee for Review of Existing Institutions Deemed to be Universities (2009)'. Ministry of Human Resource Development, Government of India, 19 October. http://mhrd.gov.in/sites/upload_files/mhrd/files/RepoRevCom-DmdUniv.pdf (accessed 10 October 2012).

—————. 2009b. 'Report of the Committee to Advise on Renovation and Rejuvenation of Higher Education'. http://www.academics-india.com/Yashpal-committee-report.pdf (accessed 10 October 2012).

—————. 2011a. 'All India Survey on Higher Education: Pilot Report'. Planning, Monitoring & Statistics Bureau, Department of Higher Education, Ministry of Human Resource Development, Government of India.

—————. 2011b. *Annual Report 2010–11*. New Delhi: Department of School Education & Literacy and Department of Higher Education, Ministry of Human Resource Development, Government of India.

—————. 2011c. 'Consolidated Working Group Report of the Department of Higher Education for XII Five Year Plan on Higher Education, Technical Education and Private Sector Participation including PPP in Higher Education'. Department of Higher Education, Ministry of Human Resource Development, Government of India.

—————. 2011d. 'Statistics of School Education, 2009–10 (Provisional)'. Bureau of Planning, Monitoring and Statistics, Ministry of Human Resource Development, Government of India.

—————. 2012. 'Report to the People on Education 2010–11'. Ministry of Human Resource Development, Government of India, March.

Ministry of Labour and Employment. 2011. 'Report of the Working Group on Skill Development and Training: 12th Five Year Plan (2012–2017)'. Ministry of Labour and Employment, Government of India.

National Bureau of Statistics (NBS) of China. 2007. *China Statistical Yearbook 2007*. Beijing: China Statistics Press.

National Center for Education Statistics (NCES). 2010. *The Condition of Education 2010*. Washington, DC: National Center for Education Statistics, Institute for Education Sciences, US Department of Education. http://nces.ed.gov/pubs2010/20100 28.pdf (accessed 10 October 2012).

National Knowledge Commission (NKC). 2007. *Recommendations on School Education*. New Delhi: National Knowledge Commission, Government of India.

—————. 2009. *Report to the Nation 2006–2009*. New Delhi: National Knowledge Commission, Government of India.

National University of Educational Planning and Administration (NUEPA). 2009. 'Elementary Education in India: Progress towards UEE — Flash Statistics 2007–08'. District Information System for Education, National University of Educational Planning and Administration.

—————. 2010. 'Teacher-Related Indicators', in *Elementary Education in India: Progress towards UEE*, pp. 151–90. New Delhi: National University of Educational Planning and Administration.

Palit, Amitendu. 2009. 'Let's Get Technical'. *Financial Express*, 26 December.

Planning Commission. 2008a. 'Education', in *Eleventh Five Year Plan (2007–2012): Social Sector*, pp. 1–40. New Delhi: Oxford University Press.

—————. 2008b. 'Skill Development and Training', in *Eleventh Five Year Plan (2007–2012): Inclusive Growth*, pp. 87–100. New Delhi: Oxford University Press.

Press Information Bureau (PIB). 2010. 'National Skill Development Mission'. Press Information Bureau, Ministry of Human Resource Development, Government of India, 16 August.

—————. 2011. 'The Right of Children to Free and Compulsory Education Act, 2009: Progress as on 1st April, 2011'. Press Information Bureau, Ministry of Human Resource Development, Government of India, 1 April.

—————. 2012a. 'National Policy on Skill Development'. Press Information Bureau, Ministry of Human Resource Development, Government of India, 21 March 2012. http://labour.nic.in/pib/PressRelease/RS/NationalPolocyonSkillDevelopment.pdf (accessed 12 October 2012).

—————. 2012b. 'Second Anniversary of RTE: Some Highlights'. Press Information Bureau, Ministry of Human Resource Development, Government of India, 2 April.

Rahman, Shafi. 2010. 'Degrees of Debate'. *India Today*, 1 May.

Schukoske, Jane E. 2006. 'Bringing Foreign Universities to India'. *Hindu*, 14 November.

Times Higher Education. 2012. 'Times Higher Education — QS World University Rankings 2011–12'. http://www.timeshighereducation.co.uk/world-university-rankings/2011-12/world-ranking (accessed 10 October 2012).

Vora, Nikhil and Shweta Dewan. 2009. 'Indian Education Sector: Long Way from Graduation'. Sector Report, IDFC-SSKI Securities Ltd, Mumbai, 16 January.

World Bank. 2009. *Secondary Education in India: Universalizing Opportunity*. Washington, DC: World Bank.

Public Expenditure on Education in India by the Union Government and Roadmap for the Future

Anit N. Mukherjee and *Satadru Sikdar*

India is undergoing a historic demographic transition where the majority of the population is below the age of 25. It is increasingly being recognised that education will play a major role in the country for reaping the expected 'demographic dividend' over the next decades. In this background, the 10th and 11th Plan periods corresponding to the last 10 years (2002–12) have witnessed a concerted effort to provide a thrust towards the universalisation of elementary education and significantly expanding access to secondary and higher education. This has mainly come about through the intervention of the central government in elementary education, which was traditionally in the domain of the states, having significant implications for the structure of financing the education sector in general, and the fiscal responsibilities between the centre and the states in particular. Comparatively, adult and technical education sectors have lacked a coherent strategy, although it is being recognised that they form an integral part of improving literacy among the general population and upgrading their skills (Mukherjee 2007). In 2009, the parliament passed the historic Right to Education (RTE) Act, which provides the framework for policy in the years to come.

The budget for the fiscal year 2011–12 was also the last budget for the 11th Plan, and the latest (2012–13) is the first one for the 12th Plan. This provides an opportunity to review the objectives of the Plan and how they have been translated into budgetary allocation by the Government of India over the last five years. The education budget of the government can be disaggregated into five broad components:

(a) elementary;
(b) secondary;
(c) university, higher and distance learning;
(d) technical education; and
(e) others, which includes adult education, promotion of language, etc.

This paper provides an analysis of the expenditure in the Department of School Education and Literacy and the Department of Higher Education, under the Ministry of Human Resource and Development (MHRD), which constitutes over 90 per cent of the total education budget of the Government of India.

The objective of this paper is to provide a comprehensive assessment of the allocations made by the Government of India through its budgetary provision in the education sector over the 11th Plan period. The initial (2007–08) and last years (2011–12) of the Plan have been compared and a trend analysis of the increase in union government expenditure on education provided. In the next stage, schemes have been categorised according to their purpose — administrative expenditure, increasing enrolment and reducing dropout, improving quality, ensuring equity, support to institutions of learning, etc. Then an analysis of the size of the schemes (above 5,000 million to less than 500 million) has been given, and their distribution, both within the education sub-sector (such as elementary education) and across the five sub-sectors explained earlier, has been tracked. Moreover, by classifying schemes in this manner a two-way analysis has been undertaken of the share of resources going to each sub-sector and the scheme category. The analysis, therefore, would provide a broad overview of the quantum, purpose and distribution of the expenditure on education by the Government of India through the MHRD. The paper concludes with some policy recommendations arising out of the analysis.

OBJECTIVES OF THE 11TH FIVE-YEAR PLAN AND ALLOCATIONS FOR EDUCATION

Among the 27 targets set by the 11th Five-Year Plan at the national level, those in education were:

(a) Reduction in the dropout rates of children at the elementary level from 52.2 per cent in 2003–04 to 20 per cent by 2011–12.

(b) Developing minimum standards of educational attainment in elementary schools, to ensure quality education.

(c) Increasing the literacy rate for persons of age 7 years or more to 85 per cent by 2011–12.

(d) Reducing the gender gap in literacy to 10 percentage points by 2011–12.

(e) Increasing the percentage of each cohort going to higher education from the present 10 per cent to 15 per cent by 2011–12 (Planning Commission 2008: 23).

While a comprehensive evaluation of these broad targets is not within the scope of this paper, the census data for 2011 indicate an increase in the literacy rate and reduction of the gender gap. However, the latest National Sample Survey Organisation (NSSO) data indicate that dropout rates are higher than 20 per cent in most states, and the percentage of each cohort going to higher education is also much less than the 11th Plan targets envisaged (Sikdar and Mukherjee 2012). The major developments during the 11th Plan period have been:

(a) expansion of Sarva Shiksha Abhiyan (SSA) as the vehicle of universal elementary education;

(b) extension of the Mid-Day Meal scheme (MDM) to all elementary schools;

(c) enactment of the RTE Act, 2009;

(d) establishment of the Rashtriya Madhyamik Shiksha Abhiyan (RMSA); and

(e) enhancement of allocation for higher education through the establishment of Indian Institutes of Technology (IITs), Indian Institutes of Management (IIMs) and National Institutes of Technology (NITs). The period also saw the initiation of reforms in higher education through the National Commission for Higher Education and Research (NCHER) Bill which is currently before the parliament.

Corresponding to these developments, the budgetary allocation and expenditure by the central government has increased significantly between 2007–08 and 2011–12. Budgetary allocation has doubled in the case of elementary education, and has risen by more than three times for secondary and higher education (Figure 2.1).

One major factor augmenting the resources available for elementary education in India is the revenue mobilised on account of the education cess. Initially levied at 2 per cent of all taxes collected by the central government, the education cess was increased to 3 per cent onwards with the extra 1 per cent earmarked for secondary and higher education

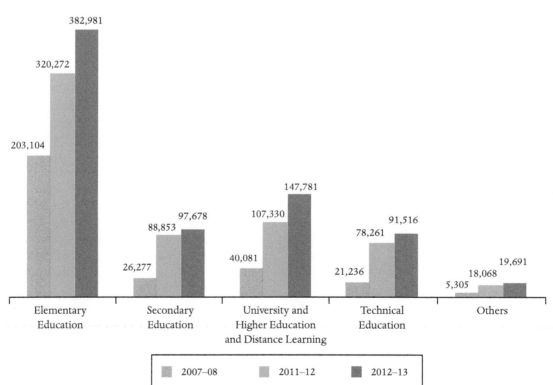

FIGURE 2.1   Central Expenditure in Education During the 11th Plan (₹in million)

Source: GoI (2011).

on all central taxes other than corporation and income tax. The last Plan period also saw a period of high growth, an economic slowdown on account of the global financial crisis, and recovery during the last two fiscal years. The initial years of the 11th Plan, therefore, saw rapid increase in tax collection, which translated into higher growth of revenues on account of education cess, while the rate of growth of cess collection slowed towards the end of the Plan. Table 2.1 provides a detailed report of the revenues collected through cess and its share in financing the different levels of education by the Government of India.

It has to be noted that the elementary education cess is earmarked for only two programmes — SSA and MDM. No such programme-wise earmarking is done for secondary and higher education cess, although most of the funds from the RMSA should be raised from that channel.

EXPENDITURE BY TYPE OF SCHEME

Almost the entire allocation in the budget for education by the central government is spent through different schemes. These range from large system-wide interventions, such as SSA, to particular organisations and institutions such as the Kendriya Vidyalaya Sangathan (KVS), to targeted scholarship schemes for girl students. Most schemes have a particular motivation, a funding structure and a delivery mechanism. These range from direct expenditure by the central government (funding for University Grants Commission [UGC], for example), expenditure through state governments, and pooling resources between centre and states (SSA and RMSA). The list is not exhaustive, and several intermediate arrangements also exist. The complete list of schemes is provided in Tables 2A and 2B.

Moreover, it is difficult to characterise the schemes into one type or the other — a scheme such as the SSA has several components and hence can be described as either increasing enrolment or improving quality. Similarly, a large scheme

such as the MDM has several externalities — although the scheme provides nutrition, it also has an impact on increasing enrolment and reducing dropout. Given these limitations, the expenditure of the central government has been categorised into five major groups according to their motivation: increasing enrolment, reducing dropout, improving quality, ensuring equity, institutional allowances and grants to north-eastern states (Table 2.2). Since all centrally-sponsored schemes have a north-east component, the allocations for the region have been separated to provide an estimate of the quantum of resources solely focused on improving education in the north-eastern states of India.

One implication of the data from Table 2.1 is the fact that the size of the schemes vary significantly. For example, there are six schemes to increase enrolment with a total outlay of over ₹200,000 million (of which SSA is the major recipient). On the other hand, there are 11 schemes with an equity focus with a total outlay of ₹11,670 million in 2011–12. Similarly, the number of funding schemes that have been earmarked for the north-east increased from 19 to 29 during the 11th Plan period.

Summary: During the 11th Plan, education financing by the central government has reflected the focus on increasing enrolment and reducing dropouts. Institutional grants for higher education, either directly or through the UGC, have shown significant increase in allocations.

DISTRIBUTION OF SCHEMES IN EXPENDITURE GROUPS

Multiplicity of schemes with similar objectives often suffers from inadequate administrative attention and capacity. Therefore, it is important to understand whether the plethora of schemes funded through the central government has shown any signs of consolidation. From a policy and financial management perspective, it is generally advisable to devote adequate resources to a particular scheme, rather

TABLE 2.1   Contribution of Education Cess to Elementary and Secondary/Higher Education Expenditure (₹in million)

	2007–08				2011–12			
	Expenditure	Cess[a]	Cess Going to SSA and MDM (per cent)	Expenditure Met by Cess (per cent)	Expenditure	Cess[a]	Cess Going to SSA and MDM (per cent)	Expenditure Met by Cess (per cent)
Sarva Shiksha Abhiyan	131,710	83,160	74.7	63.1	210,000	119,920	65.4	57.1
Mid-Day Meal	66,780	28,120	25.3	42.1	103,800	63,420	34.6	61.1
Secondary/Higher	92,900	27,160		29.2	292,510	42,920		14.7

Source: GoI (2011).
Note: [a] indicates allocation through Prarambhik Shiksha Kosh (PSK).

TABLE 2.2   Distribution of Government of India Education Expenditure, by Type

		2007–08 (RE)		2011–12 (RE)	
		Number of Schemes	Allocation (₹in million)	Number of Schemes	Allocation (₹in million)
Group I	Enrolment Increasing Scheme	7	122,382.2	6	213,930.0
Group II	Dropout Reducing Scheme	7	61,794.2	8	103,047.3
Group III	Quality Improving Scheme	19	7,356.2	17	20,314.6
Group IV	Equity in Education	8	3,103.0	11	11,678.9
Group V	Institutional Grant	40	76,501.3	43	212,943.7
Group Va	School Education	5	20,228.8	6	50,129.3
Group Vb	Higher Education	35	56,272.5	37	162,814.4
Group Vb(i)	University Grants Commission	1	35,819.4	1	89,274.1
Group Vb(ii)	Non-Technical Higher Education	16	4,236.6	15	16,140.7
Group Vb(iii)	Technical Higher Education	18	16,216.5	21	57,399.6
Group VI	Grant for North-East State	19	23,661.0	29	49,707.0
Group VII	Other Administrative Expenditure		844.1		2,029.9

Source: GoI (2007, 2011).

than introducing new schemes for the same objective, which lead to fragmentation and mismanagement.

In this analysis, schemes have been grouped together according to their allocation size for different sectors of education, with four groups for every sector. Group I contains schemes with allocation of ₹5,000 million or more, Group II comprises those between ₹1,000–5,000 million, Group III covers those between ₹500–1,000 million, and Group IV those below ₹500 million (Table 2.3). The complete list of schemes is provided in Table 2C.

Summary: Table 2.3 illustrates the within-group and across-group divergence in the size of the resource allocation. For all education sectors the number of schemes has increased in Group I (highest allocation category) and decreased in Group IV (lowest allocation category) from 2007–08 to 2011–12. This reflects a move towards consolidation of resources in 'flagship' schemes during the 11th Plan period, which is a welcome development.

Details of Allocation across Existing and New Schemes during 12th Plan

The policy objective of universal elementary education is primarily reflected in the consolidation of the large Centrally Sponsored Schemes (CSSs). In 2011–12, apart from

TABLE 2.3   Number of Schemes According to Scheme Sizes

Size of Scheme	Elementary Education		Secondary Education		University, Higher Education and Distance Learning		Technical Education		Others	
	2007–08 (RE)	2011–12 (RE)	2007–08 (RE)	2011–12 (RE)	2007–08 (RE)	2011–12 (RE)	2007–08 (RE)	2011–12 (RE)	2007–08 (RE)	2011–12 (RE)
Group I (Schemes above ₹5,000 million)	2	2	2	5	1	3	2	5	0	1
Group II (Schemes between ₹1,000 million to less than ₹5,000 million)	2	2	2	4	1	1	2	7	1	1
Group III (Schemes between ₹500 million to less than ₹1,000 million)	0	2	2	1	1	3	3	7	2	3
Group IV (Below ₹500 million)	3	1	8	6	15	10	22	14	20	21
Total	7	7	14	16	18	17	29	33	23	26

Source: GoI (2007, 2011).

the SSA) and the MDM, a new scheme — Strengthening of Teachers Training Institutions — has been introduced under the first group. The Scheme to Provide Quality Education in Madrassas (SPQEM) is the only scheme in Group II with an increased allocation in 2011–12. The SPQEM was launched in 2009–10, and the District Primary Education Programme (DPEP) was stopped in the same year. The Kasturba Gandhi Balika Vidyalaya, which was continuing from the 10th Plan as a separate scheme, was merged with the SSA after 2006–07. The Mahila Samakhya and the Scheme for Infrastructure Development in Minority Institute (IDMI), with ₹500 million allocation come under Group III. The 'National Bal Bhawan, New Delhi' is the only scheme in elementary education, whose allocation is less than ₹500 million.

For secondary education, five schemes come under Group I in 2011–12, instead of two schemes in 2007–08. The RMSA and the Model School Scheme are two new ones in the 11th Plan with a large allocation. Apart from these, allocation for Information and Communication Technology (ICT) in School scheme has been increased significantly in 2011–12 from what it had been in 2007–08. The KVS and the Navodaya Vidyalaya Samiti are two other schemes with an allocation of more than ₹5,000 million in the union budgets in both 2007–08 and 2011–12. The Scheme for Construction and Running of Girls' Hostels for Students of Secondary and Higher Secondary Schools, the National Council of Educational Research and Training (NCERT) and the Inclusive Education for the Disabled at Secondary Stage (IEDSS) are three schemes that come under Group II in the 2011–12 budget. IEDSS, which was earlier known as the Integrated Education for Disabled Children (IEDC), has become a new scheme from 2009–10. The National Merit-cum-Means Scholarship (NMMS) and the National Scheme of Incentive to Girls for Secondary Education are the two new schemes

of the 11th Plan that come under Group III in 2011–12. In Group IV, only one new scheme — Appointment of Language Teachers — was introduced in 2009–10 and the allocation is only ₹50 million in 2011–12 (Table 2.4). The lowest scheme in terms of allocation is Access and Equity with only ₹1 million in 2011–12.

For university and higher education and distance learning, four schemes come under Group I. These are due to high allocation for the UGC, which was necessitated by the revision in salary scales of university and college teachers. The educational loan interest subsidy, introduced in 2008–09, comes under Group I in 2011–12. The Scholarship for College and University Students was started in 2007–08 and it comes under Group II with an increased allocation. Apart from the Indira Gandhi National Open University (IGNOU), the Indian Council of Social Science Research (ICSSR) and the Establishment of Tribunals, Accreditation Authority, NCHER and National Finance Corporation come under Group III in 2011–12. The Group IV schemes in university and higher education and distance learning were more or less same in 2007–08 and 2011–12. The only change was that the Area Intensive and Madrassa Modernisation Programme was closed after 2008–09 and the Assistance to State Governments for Degree Colleges introduced in the Union Budget 2011–12 with an allocation of ₹100 million.

PROPORTION OF EXPENDITURE IN DIFFERENT SCHEME CATEGORIES

Analysis of group-wise expenditure in Table 2.5 indicates that there are increments in expenditure in the first three groups for every level of education (except Group II allocation in elementary education and Group III allocation in secondary

TABLE 2.4   Continuing and New Schemes — Comparison of 10th and 11th Plans

Scheme Size as of 2011–12	Continuing from 10th Plan	Introduced in 11th Plan	Schemes Withdrawn after 10th Plan
Over ₹5,000 million	Sarva Shiksha Abhiyan (SSA), National Programme of Mid-Day Meals in Schools, Navodaya Vidyalaya Samiti, Kendriya Vidyalaya Sangathan	Rashtriya Madhyamik Shiksha Abhiyan (RMSA); Scheme for Setting up of 6,000 Model Schools at Block-Level	
Between ₹1,000–5,000 million	Strengthening of Teachers Training Institutions; Information and Communication Technology in Schools	Scheme for Providing Quality Education in Madrassas (SPQEM)	District Primary Education Programme (DPEP), Kasturba Gandhi Balika Vidyalaya (included in SSA), Continuing Education for Neo-Literates
Between ₹500–1,000 million	Mahila Samakhya		
Below ₹500 million		Appointment of Language Teachers	National Council for Teacher Education (NCTE)

Source: Compiled by the authors from GoI (2007, 2011).

education) and decrease in expenditure in Group IV schemes (except at secondary and technical education levels).

The decrease in elementary education expenditure in Group II is due to two reasons. First, the Strengthening of Teachers Training Institutions scheme has been upgraded from Group II to Group I due to the increase in allocation to above ₹5,000 million in the Union Budget 2011–12. Second, the Kasturba Gandhi Balika Vidyalaya, which was started as a separate scheme during the 10th Plan, was merged with the SSA in 2007–08. The SPQEM is the only scheme in Group II of elementary education in Union Budget 2011–12 with an allocation of ₹1,500 million. Similarly, the NCERT and the ICT in schools were in Group III of secondary education in

2007–08, but had higher allowances in the 11th Plan and were upgraded to Group I.

Looking at the percentage distribution of expenditure within each categories of education in Table 2.6, we find that the proportion has increased in Group I and decreased in other groups, barring a slight increment in Group II for secondary education.

Summary: From the analysis carried out in this section, it is evident that the government has tended to focus on schemes with higher allocation. Calculating the percentage of allocation of each group out of the total education expenditure and adding up all sectors, it is clear that the government has increased expenditure through Group I

TABLE 2.5   Total Expenditure, by Group (₹in million)

Size of Scheme	Elementary Education		Secondary Education		University, Higher Education and Distance Learning		Technical Education		Others	
	2007–08 (RE)	2011–12 (RE)	2007–08 (RE)	2011–12 (RE)	2007–08 (RE)	2011–12 (RE)	2007–08 (RE)	2011–12 (RE)	2007–08 (RE)	2011–12 (RE)
Group I (Schemes above ₹5,000 million)	198,490.0	313,800.0	20,688.0	79,808.0	35,819.4	102,608.3	13,856.7	54,282.1	0.0	7,650.0
Group II (Schemes between ₹1,000 million to less than ₹5,000 million)	4,120.0	5,265.0	3,700.0	7,366.9	1,800.3	1,620.0	2,477.2	15,693.5	1,640.0	4,387.5
Group III (Schemes between ₹500 million to less than ₹1,000 million)	0.0	1,000.0	1,509.5	700.0	972.1	2,155.8	2,052.0	4,871.5	1,259.5	2,735.0
Group IV (Below ₹500 million)	494.0	206.5	379.3	978.0	1,489.0	946.1	2,849.8	3,414.0	1,848.7	3,295.7

Source: GoI (2007, 2011).

TABLE 2.6   Percentage of Expenditure within Education Group

Size of Scheme	Elementary Education		Secondary Education		University, Higher Education and Distance Learning		Technical Education		Others	
	2007–08 (RE)	2011–12 (RE)	2007–08 (RE)	2011–12 (RE)	2007–08 (RE)	2011–12 (RE)	2007–08 (RE)	2011–12 (RE)	2007–08 (RE)	2011–12 (RE)
Group I (Schemes above ₹5,000 million)	97.73	97.98	78.73	89.82	89.37	95.60	65.25	69.36	0.00	42.34
Group II (Schemes between ₹1,000 million to less than ₹5,000 million)	2.03	1.64	14.08	8.29	4.49	1.51	11.67	20.05	34.54	24.28
Group III (Schemes between ₹500 million to less than ₹1,000 million)	0.00	0.31	5.74	0.79	2.43	2.01	9.66	6.22	26.53	15.14
Group IV (Below ₹500 million)	0.24	0.06	1.44	1.10	3.71	0.88	13.42	4.36	38.93	18.24
Total	100.00	100.00	100.00	100.00	100.00	100.00	100.00	100.00	100.00	100.00

Source: Calculated from GoI (2007, 2011).

TABLE 2.7   Groupwise Percentage of Expenditure on Education

Size of Scheme	Elementary Education		Secondary Education		University, Higher Education and Distance Learning		Technical Education		Others		Total	
	2007–08 (RE)	2011–12 (RE)	2007–08 (RE)	2011–12 (RE)	2007–08 (RE)	2011–12 (RE)	2007–08 (RE)	2011–12 (RE)	2007–08 (RE)	2011–12 (RE)	2007–08 (RE)	2011–12 (RE)
Group I (Schemes above ₹5,000 million)	67.18	51.21	7.00	13.02	12.12	16.74	4.69	8.86	0.00	1.25	91.00	91.08
Group II (Schemes between ₹1,000 million to less than ₹5,000 million)	1.39	0.86	1.25	1.20	0.61	0.26	0.84	2.56	0.56	0.72	4.65	5.60
Group III (Schemes between ₹500 million to less than ₹1,000 million)	0.00	0.16	0.51	0.11	0.33	0.35	0.69	0.79	0.43	0.45	1.96	1.87
Group IV (Below ₹500 million)	0.17	0.03	0.13	0.16	0.50	0.15	0.96	0.56	0.63	0.54	2.39	1.44
Total	68.74	52.26	8.89	14.50	13.57	17.52	7.19	12.77	1.61	2.95	100.00	100.00

Source: GoI (2007, 2011).

schemes and reduced expenditure through other small-sized ones in other groups. This is particularly true of secondary education during the 11th Plan period. The proportion of expenditure on secondary education was 8.9 per cent of the total expenditure in 2007–08, and it has increased to 14.5 per cent of total expenditure in 2011–12.

SUMMARY: FUTURE DIRECTIONS IN FINANCING OF EDUCATION IN INDIA

Financing Responsibility of Union and State Governments

Education financing in India is at crossroads. As has been observed in the discussion in this chapter, the quantum of public expenditure on education by the union government has gone up significantly in the last decade. We have also analysed that the bulk of this expenditure is earmarked for a few key flagship programmes such as the SSA (the vehicle for implementation of the RTE), the MDM Scheme and the RMSA geared towards expansion of secondary education. Moreover, our study also points to the fact that a significant contribution to this increase in expenditure is through higher collection of the education cess, which now covers not only elementary education and MDM schemes, but also secondary and higher education. India is unique among other developing countries in its use of earmarked taxes for

financing public expenditure on education. It is extremely important, therefore, to see whether this increase in expenditure by the union government is 'crowding in' or 'crowding out' expenditure by the states or the private sector. Initial evidence seems to indicate that the state governments have not increased their education expenditure commensurately. They are becoming increasingly more reliant on the union government to augment their resource base for education. Consequently, education policy is increasingly being determined at the national, rather than the state level, as was originally envisaged in the Constitution. The implementation framework of the RTE and the proliferation of centrally-sponsored schemes would essentially guarantee the pre-eminence of the union government in the financing of education in the near future.

Increasing Privatisation of Education and Implications for Financing

The NSSO has conducted a survey on the participation and expenditure in education in 2007–08. The unit-level data gives some information about student participation in government, government-aided, private-aided and private unaided schools. In our study we have clubbed government, government-aided and private aided together as 'government-aided', keeping private unaided schools as the other category. Figure 2.2 depict that the participation in private school is increasing with income both in rural and urban areas, but in urban areas this increase is of a much higher order. In terms of private school enrolment in rural areas, the overall share is around 10 percent – most of them from the upper income strata. However, state-wise analysis figures from the unit level data (not presented here) indicates that in some states such as Himachal Pradesh and Uttar Pradesh, the proportion of children in rural areas from the lowest income quintile is over 25 per cent. This implies that parents of economically weaker sections are increasingly accessing private education services. This is a trend that is likely to continue, as incomes rise and the demand for quality education increases. The government system in many states might therefore suffer from over-capacity and under-utilisation. On the other hand, the problems faced by the higher education sector would be just the opposite. It is important therefore to take a pragmatic view of what would be the best use of public resources and provide innovative solutions to correct the imbalances both within and between sectors.

Public–Private Partnership for Education in India

One possible solution is to enhance the scale and scope of Public–Private Partnership (PPP) in the education sector in India. In one sense, the PPP model already exists in the form of 'government-aided' schools, which form the

highest proportion of schools in states like Kerala and West Bengal. There was also a proposal to build 'Model Schools' in the PPP mode in over 6,000 blocks of the country, which would then be a catalyst for other schools to perform as per the standards set by these institutions. PPP in education, however, is difficult to implement, not least due to the divergence in incentives between public and private schools.

A well-crafted PPP strategy is not only essential, but also can make best use of resources, technology and capacity of the education system to deliver the ultimate goal — universal and equitable access to high-quality education. The first step would be to recognise the fact that the demand for education at all levels would increase manifold in the medium term. Second, public provision is a necessary but not sufficient condition for increasing enrolments, reducing dropouts and upgrading knowledge and skills at elementary, secondary and tertiary levels. Third, it is essential to ensure standards of quality in education — otherwise parents would exercise their choice as consumers to move between public and private sectors, creating overcapacity and inefficiency in resource allocation.

The PPP strategy, therefore, is a combination of projecting demand for different levels of education, separation of public goods (equity, non-discrimination, knowledge creation, research and development, etc.) from private goods

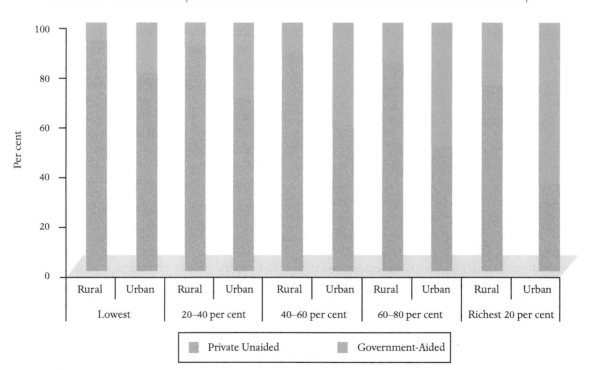

FIGURE 2.2   Student Participation in Government and Private Schools in Different Income Groups

Source: Calculated from NSSO 62nd Round data (2007–08).

(private school education, technical and professional courses, employment-oriented skill formation, etc.), and adhering to quality standards for both. The ensuing investment plan would take into account the existing stock of human and physical capital (students, teachers, schools, technical institutions, universities, etc.) and projected demand for each, filling the gaps in educational infrastructure over the next decade and beyond. That would be the most efficient way to harness our demographic dividend in the future Five-Year Plans.

REFERENCES

Planning Commission. 2008. *Eleventh Five Year Plan 2007–12: Inclusive Growth*. New Delhi: Oxford University Press.

Government of India (GoI). 2007. 'Expenditure Budget 2007–08', vol. 2, in 'Union Budget 2007–08', Ministry of Finance, Government of India. http://indiabudget.nic.in/ub2007-08/eb/vol2.htm (accessed 12 October 2012).

————. 2011. 'Expenditure Budget 2011–12', vol. 2, in 'Union Budget 2011–12', Ministry of Finance, Government of India. http://indiabudget.nic.in/budget2011-2012/vol2.asp (accessed 12 October 2012).

Mukherjee, Anit. 2007. 'Implications for Education', *Economic and Political Weekly*, 42(14): 1273–76.

Sikdar, Satadru and Anit Mukherjee. 2012. 'Enrolment and Dropout in School Education in India', *Economic and Political Weekly*, 47(1): 27–31.

TABLE 2A   List of Schemes of the Ministry of Human Resource Development, 2007–08

Elementary Education	1. Strengthening of Teachers Training Institutions 2. Mahila Samakhya 3. National Bal Bhawan, New Delhi 4. District Primary Education Programme 5. National Programme of Mid-Day Meals in Schools 6. Sarva Shiksha Abhiyan 7. National Council for Teacher Education
Secondary Education	1. National Council of Educational Research and Training 2. Kendriya Vidyalaya Sangathan 3. Navodaya Vidyalaya Samiti 4. Information and Communication Technology in Schools 5. Integrated Education for Disabled Children 6. National Institute of Open Schooling 7. Access and Equity 8. Central Tibetan Schools Administration 9. Vocationalisation of Education 10. National Scheme for Incentive to Girls for Secondary Education 11. Special Navodaya Vidyalayas 12. National Merit Scholarship Scheme 13. Upgrading 2,000 Kasturba Gandhi Balika Vidyalayas (Residential Schools, Hostels/Girls' Hostels) 14. Other Programmes
University, Higher Education and Distance Learning	1. University Grants Commission 2. Improvement in Salary Scale of University and College Teachers 3. Indian Council of Social Science Research 4. Indian Council of Historical Research 5. Rural Universities/National Council of Rural Institutes 6. Indian Institute of Advanced Study, Shimla, 7. Indian Council of Philosophical Research 8. Shastri Indo-Canadian Institute 9. Setting Up of a Refinance Corporation/Student Loan Scheme 10. National Institute of Studies in Sri Guru Granth Sahib 11. Area Intensive and Madrassa Modernisation Programme 12. Indira Gandhi National Open University 13. Commonwealth of Learning 14. Scholarship to Students from Non-Hindi Speaking States/Union Territories and Other Scholarships 15. Scholarship for College and University Students 16. Provision for University and Higher Education 17. Provision for Distance Learning (including Scholarships) 18. Other Programmes
Technical Education	1. Community Polytechnics 2. Indian Institutes of Technology 3. Scholarships/Apprenticeship Training 4. Indian Institutes of Management 5. Indian Institute of Science, Bangalore 6. All India Council for Technical Education (including National Institutes of Technology) 7. Polytechnics for Disabled Persons 8. Indian Institute of Information Technology, Gwalior 9. Indian Institute of Information Technology, Allahabad 10. Indian Institute of Information Technology, Jabalpur 11. Indian Institute of Information Technology, Design and Manufacturing, Kancheepuram 12. National Institute for Industrial Engineering, Mumbai 13. National Institute for Foundry and Forge Technology 14. School of Planning and Architecture, Delhi, 15. National Institutes of Technical Teachers' Training and Research 16. Sant Longowal Institute of Engineering and Technology 17. Indian School of Mines, Dhanbad 18. Board of Apprenticeship Training 19. Technical Education Quality Improvement Project of Government of India 20. Central Institute of Technology, Kokrajhar 21. New Indian Institutes of Information Technology 22. New Schools of Planning and Architecture 23. Indian National Digital Library in Engineering Science and Technology 24. Setting Up of New Indian Institutes of Technology (Erstwhile Setting Up of Three New Ones) 25. Indian Institutes of Science for Education and Research 26. Upgradation of Existing/Setting Up of New Polytechnics 27. North Eastern Regional Institute of Science and Technology, Itanagar 28. Provision for Technical Education 29. Other Programmes
Others	1. Directorate of Hindi, Commission for Scientific and Technical Terminology 2. Kendriya Hindi Shikshan Mandal 3. Appointment of Language Teachers 4. National Council for Promotion of Urdu Language 5. Central Institute of Indian Languages and Regional Language Centres 6. National Council for Promotion of Sindhi Language 8. Modern Indian Languages 9. Development of Tamil Language 10. Rashtriya Sanskrit Sansthan 11. Rashtriya Ved Vidya Pratisthan 12. Education in Human Values 13. Book Promotion 14. Indian National Commission/United Nations Educational, Scientific and Cultural Organization 15. Planning Norms 16. Administration 17. Provision for Development of Languages 18. Provision for Book Promotion 19. Adult Education and Skill Development Scheme 20. Support to Non-Governmental Organisations/Institutions/State Resource Centres for Adult Education and Skill Development 21. Directorate of Adult Education 22. National Literacy Mission Authority 23. Other Programmes

Source: GoI (2007).

TABLE 2B   List of Schemes of the Ministry of Human Resource Development, 2011–12

Elementary Education	1. National Programme of Mid-Day Meals in Schools 2. Sarva Shiksha Abhiyan 3. Strengthening of Teachers Training Institutions 4. Scheme for Providing Quality Education in Madrassas 5. Mahila Samakhya 6. Scheme for Infrastructure Development in Minority Institutions 7. National Bal Bhawan, New Delhi.
Secondary Education	1. Rashtriya Madhyamik Shiksha Abhiyan 2. Navodaya Vidyalaya Samiti 3. Kendriya Vidyalaya Sangathan 4. Scheme for Setting Up of 6,000 Model Schools at Block Level as Benchmark of Excellence 5. Information and Communication Technology in Schools 6. Scheme for Construction and Running of Girls' Hostels for Students of Secondary and Higher Secondary Schools 7. National Council of Educational Research and Training 8. Inclusive Education of the Disabled at Secondary Stage 9. National Merit-cum-Means Scholarship Scheme 10. National Scheme for Incentive to Girls for Secondary Education 11. Central Tibetan Schools Administration 12. Vocationalisation of Education 13. National Institute of Open Schooling 14. Access and Equity 15. Appointment of Language Teachers 16. Other Programmes
University, Higher Education and Distance Learning	1. University Grants Commission 2. Improvement in Salary Scale of University and College Teachers 3. Educational Loan Interest Subsidy 4. Provision for University and Higher Education (for the Benefit of North-Eastern Areas and Sikkim 5. Scholarship for College and University Students 6. Indira Gandhi National Open University 7. Indian Council of Social Science Research 8. Establishment of Tribunals, Accreditation Authority, National Commission of Higher Education and Research, and National Finance Corporation 9. Assistance to State Governments for Degree Colleges 10. Indian Council of Historical Research 11. Rural Universities/National Council of Rural Institutes 12. Indian Institute of Advanced Study, Shimla 13. Indian Council of Philosophical Research 14. Shastri Indo-Canadian Institute 15. Commonwealth of Learning 16. Scholarship to Students from Non-Hindi Speaking States/Union Territories and Other Scholarships 17. Provision for Distance Learning (including Scholarships) (for the Benefit of North-Eastern Areas and Sikkim 18. Other Programmes
Technical Education	1. Indian Institutes of Technology 2. National Institutes of Technology 3. Assistance to States for Upgradation of Existing/Setting Up of New Polytechnics 4. Indian Institutes of Science for Education and Research 5. Setting Up of New Indian Institutes of Technology (Erstwhile Setting Up of Three New Ones) 6. Provision for Technical Education (for the Benefit of North-Eastern Areas and Sikkim) 7. Indian Institute of Science, Bangalore 8. Technical Education Quality Improvement Project of Government of India 9. All India Council for Technical Education 10. Indian Institutes of Management 11. Community Polytechnics 12. Indian School of Mines, Dhanbad 13. Women's Hostels in Polytechnics 14. National Institutes of Technical Teachers' Training and Research 15. National Institute for Industrial Engineering, Mumbai 16. Indian Institute of Information Technology, Design and Manufacturing, Kancheepuram 17. Setting Up of New Indian Institutes of Management 18. Scholarships/Apprenticeship Training 19. Indian Institute of Information Technology, Allahabad 20. Polytechnics for Disabled Persons 21. Indian Institute of Information Technology, Gwalior 22. Indian Institute of Information Technology, Jabalpur 23. National for Foundry and Forge Technology 24. School of Planning and Architecture, Delhi 25. Sant Longowal Institute of Engineering and Technology 26. Board of Apprenticeship Training 27. Central Institute of Technology, Kokrajhar 28. New Indian Institutes of Information Technology 29. New Schools of Planning and Architecture 30. Indian National Digital Library in Engineering Science and Technology 31. Setting Up of New National Institutes of Technology 32. Training and Research in Frontier Areas 33. Expansion and Upgradation of State Engineering Institutions 34. Setting Up of Indian Institute of Engineering, Science and Technology 35. North Eastern Regional Institute of Science and Technology, Itanagar 36. Other Programmes.
Others	1. National Mission in Education through Information and Communication Technology 2. Adult Education and Skill Development Scheme 3. Support to Non-Governmental Organisations/Institutions/State Resource Centres for Adult Education and Skill Development 4. Provision for Information and Communication Technology (for the Benefit of North-Eastern Areas and Sikkim) 5. Rashtriya Sanskrit Sansthan 6. Directorate of Adult Education 7. National Literacy Mission Authority 8. Directorate of Hindi 9. Appointment of Language Teachers 10. Kendriya Hindi Shikshan Mandal 11. National Council for Promotion of Urdu Language 12. Central Institute of Indian Languages and Regional Language Centres 13. National Council for Promotion of Sindhi Language 14. Central Institute of Classical Tamil, Chennai 15. Rashtriya Ved Vidya Pratisthan 16. Provision for Development of Languages (for the Benefit of North-Eastern Areas and Sikkim) 17. Book Promotion 18. Indian National Commission/ United Nations Educational, Scientific and Cultural Organization 19. Planning Norms 20. Administration 21. Other Programmes

Source: GoI (2011).

TABLE 2C   List of Schemes of the Ministry of Human Resource Development, by Group

		2007–08	2011–12
Group I	Enrolment Increasing Scheme	1. National Bal Bhawan, New Delhi 2. District Primary Education Programme 3. Sarva Shiksha Abhiyan 4. National Institute of Open Schooling 5. Access and Equity 6. Scheme for Universal Access and Quality at the Secondary Stage 7. Indira Gandhi National Open University	1. National Bal Bhawan, New Delhi 2. Sarva Shiksha Abhiyan 3. Rashtriya Madhyamik Shiksha Abhiyan 4. National Institute of Open Schooling 5. Access and Equity 6. Indira Gandhi National Open University
Group II	Dropout Reducing Scheme	1. National Programme of Mid-Day Meals in Schools 2. National Merit Scholarship Scheme 3. Scholarship to Students from Non-Hindi Speaking States/Union Territories and Other Scholarships 4. Scholarship for College and University Students 5. Book Promotion 6. Scholarships/Apprenticeship Training 7. Setting Up of a Refinance Corporation/Student Loan Scheme	1. National Programme of Mid-Day Meals in Schools 2. National Merit-cum-Means Scholarship Scheme 3. Educational Loan Interest Subsidy 4. Commonwealth of Learning 5. Scholarship to Students from Non-Hindi Speaking States/Union Territories and Other Scholarships 6. Scholarship for College and University Students 7. Book Promotion 8. Scholarships/Apprenticeship Training
Group III	Quality Improving Scheme	1. Strengthening of Teachers Training Institutions 2. National Council for Teacher Education 3. National Council of Educational Research and Training 4. Information and Communication Technology in Schools 5. Vocationalisation of Education 6. Scheme for Universal Access and Quality at the Secondary Stage 7. National Mission in Education through Information and Communication Technology 8. Directorate of Hindi 9. Kendriya Hindi Shikshan Mandal 10. Appointment of Language Teachers 11. National Council for Promotion of Urdu Language 12. Central Institute of Indian Languages and Regional Language Centres 13. National Council for Promotion of Sindhi Language 14. Modern Indian Languages 15. Development of Tamil Language 16. Central Institute of Classical Tamil, Chennai 17. Rashtriya Sanskrit Sansthan 18. Rashtriya Ved Vidya Pratisthan 19. Education in Human Values	1. Strengthening of Teachers Training Institutions 2. National Council of Educational Research and Training 3. Information and Communication Technology in Schools 4. Vocationalisation of Education 5. Appointment of Language Teachers 6. National Mission on Teachers and Training 7. National Mission in Education through Information and Communication Technology 8. Directorate of Hindi 9. Commission for Scientific and Technical Terminology 10. Kendriya Hindi Shikshan Mandal 11. National Council for Promotion of Urdu Language 12. Central Institute of Indian Languages and Regional Language Centres 13. National Council for Promotion of Sindhi Language 14. Central Institute of Classical Tamil, Chennai 15. Rashtriya Sanskrit Sansthan 16. Rashtriya Ved Vidya Pratisthan 17. Education in Human Values
Group IV	Equity in Education	1. Mahila Samakhya 2. National Scheme for Incentive to Girls for Secondary Education 3. Integrated Education for Disabled Children 4. Polytechnics for Disabled Persons 5. Adult Education and Skill Development Scheme 6. Support to Non-Governmental Organisations/Institutions/State Resource Centres for Adult Education and Skill Development 7. National Literacy Mission Authority and 8. Other Programmes for Adult Education	1. Mahila Samakhya 2. National Scheme for Incentive to Girls for Secondary Education 3. Scheme for Construction and Running of Girls Hostels for Students of Secondary and Higher Secondary Schools 4. Women's Hostels in Polytechnics 5. Inclusive Education of the Disabled at Secondary Stage 6. Polytechnics for Disabled Persons 7. Adult Education 8. Adult Education and Skill Development Scheme 9. Support to Non-Governmental Organisations/Institutions/State Resource Centres for Adult Education and Skill Development 10. National Literacy Mission Authority 11. Other Programmes in Adult Education
Group V	Institutional Grant		

Group Va	School Education	1. Kendriya Vidyalaya Sangathan 2. Navodaya Vidyalaya Samiti 3. Central Tibetan Schools Administration 4. Special Navodaya Vidyalayas 5. Area Intensive and Madrassa Modernisation Programme	1. Scheme for Providing Quality Education in Madrassas 2. Scheme for Infrastructure Development in Minority Institutions 3. Kendriya Vidyalaya Sangathan 4. Navodaya Vidyalaya Samiti 5. Scheme for Setting Up of 6,000 Model Schools at Block Level as Benchmark of Excellence 6. Central Tibetan Schools Administration
Group Vb	Higher Education		
Group Vb(i)	University Grants Commission	University Grants Commission	University Grants Commission
Group Vb(ii)	Non-Technical Higher Education	1. Indian Council of Social Science Research 2. Indian Council of Historical Research 3. Rural Universities/National Council of Rural Institutes 4. Indian Institute of Advanced Study, Shimla 5. Indian Council of Philosophical Research 6. Shastri Indo-Canadian Institute 7. National Institute of Studies in Sri Guru Granth Sahib 8. Commonwealth of Learning 9. Indian National Commission/United Nations Educational, Scientific and Cultural Organization 10. Indian Institutes of Management 11. Indian Institute of Science, Bangalore 12. School of Planning and Architecture, Delhi 13. Indian School of Mines, Dhanbad 14. Board of Apprenticeship Training 15. New Schools of Planning and Architecture 16. Indian Institutes of Science for Education and Research	1. Indian Council of Social Science Research 2. Indian Council of Historical Research 3. Rural Universities/National Council of Rural Institutes 4. Indian Institute of Advanced Study, Shimla 5. Indian Council of Philosophical Research 6. Shastri Indo-Canadian Institute 7. Indian National Commission/United Nations Educational, Scientific and Cultural Organization 8. Indian Institutes of Management 9. Indian School of Mines, Dhanbad 10. Board of Apprenticeship Training 11. New Schools of Planning and Architecture 12. Setting Up of New Indian Institutes of Technology 13. Indian Institutes of Science for Education and Research 14. Setting Up of New Indian Institutes of Management 15. Training and Research in Frontier Areas
Group Vb(iii)	Technical Higher Education		1. Community Polytechnics 2. Indian Institutes of Technology 3. Indian Institute of Science, Bangalore 4. Indian Institute of Information Technology, Gwalior 5. Indian Institute of Information Technology, Allahabad 6. Indian Institute of Information Technology, Jabalpur 7. Indian Institute of Information Technology, Design and Manufacturing, Kancheepuram 8. National Institute for Industrial Engineering, Mumbai 9. National Institute for Foundry and Forge Technology 10. School of Planning and Architecture, Delhi 11. National Institutes of Technical Teachers' Training and Research 12. Sant Longowal Institute of Engineering and Technology 13. Technical Education Quality Improvement Project of Government of India 14. Central Institute of Technology, Kokrajhar 15. Indian National Digital Library in Engineering Science and Technology 16. Upgradation of Existing/Setting Up of New Polytechnics 17. Assistance to States for Upgradation of Existing/Setting Up of New Polytechnics 18. Setting Up of New National Institutes of Technology 19. All India Council for Technical Education 20. National Institutes of Technology 21. North Eastern Regional Institute of Science and Technology, Itanagar

Source: GoI (2007, 2011).

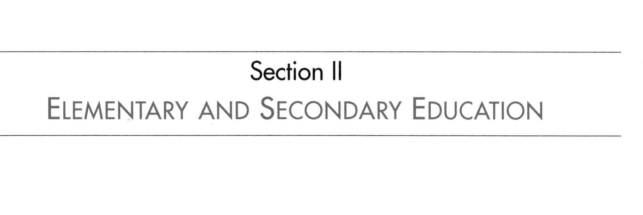

Section II

ELEMENTARY AND SECONDARY EDUCATION

3 | Right of Children to Free and Compulsory Education Act, 2009 and its Implementation

Chanchal Chand Sarkar*

The positive role of Universal Elementary Education (UEE) in strengthening the socio-economic base of a nation cannot be over-emphasised. Recognising the importance of it, the original Article 45 in the Directive Principles of State Policy in the Constitution mandated the State to endeavour to provide free and compulsory education to all children up to age 14 within a period of 10 years. The National Policy on Education (NPE), 1986/92, states:

In our national perception, education is essentially for all ... Education has an acculturating role. It refines sensitivities and perceptions that contribute to national cohesion, a scientific temper and independence of mind and spirit — thus furthering the goals of socialism, secularism and democracy enshrined in our Constitution.

Via the 86th Constitutional Amendment, a new Article 21A was added in Part I of the Constitution of India to make free and compulsory elementary education a fundamental right for children. The Right of Children to Free and Compulsory Education (or RTE) came into force in India with effect from 1 April 2010 (GoI 2009).

Even before the RTE came into force, the Government of India's (GoI's) efforts were towards universalisation of elementary education in the country. This paper describes the stages through which the RTE Act has come into effect and how, in the course of implementing the RTE Act, the existing system has been changed and aligned with a view to fulfil its objectives. It also discusses how various other important schemes of the central and state governments

play a crucial role in achieving the objectives of the RTE. Further, the actual implementation of the RTE-Sarva Shiksha Abhiyan (SSA) and its impact is presented. The concluding section of the chapter deliberates on future needs.

EVOLUTION OF THE RTE AND SSA

As a follow up to the NPE, a number of programmes were initiated in India with a view to achieving UEE. These efforts were intensified in the 1980s and 1990s through several interventions such as Operation Blackboard (OBB), the Shiksha Karmi Project (SKP), the Andhra Pradesh Primary Education Project (APPEP), the Bihar Education Project (BEP), the UP Basic Education Project (UPBEP), Mahila Samakhya (MS), the Lok Jumbish Project (LJP), and Teacher Education, which put in place a decentralised system of teacher support through District Institutes of Education and Training (DIETs) and the District Primary Education Programme (DPEP). The latest is the SSA, a centrally-sponsored scheme implemented in partnership with state governments for the UEE across the country.

Due to these initiatives, over the years there has been significant spatial and numerical expansion of elementary schools in the country. Today, access and enrolment at the primary stage of education have reached very close to universal levels. The number of out-of-school children at the elementary level has reduced significantly. The gender gap in elementary education has narrowed and the percentage of enrolled children belonging to scheduled castes and tribes has increased successively. Despite this, the goal of universal elementary education is yet to be achieved in the country. There remains the unfinished agenda of universal education at the upper primary stage. The number of children — particularly those from disadvantaged groups and weaker

* The author would like to thank all the officers of the Ministry of Human Resource Development (MHRD), Ministry of Women and Child Development and Ministry of Finance who provided important inputs/comments. Views expressed in the paper are strictly the author's own and not necessarily of the organisation/body to which he is affiliated.

sections — who drop out of school before completing upper primary education remains high. The quality of learning achievement is not always entirely satisfactory even in the case of children who complete elementary education. With a view to address these issues, the RTE has been introduced to directly counter the problems of illiteracy, poor quality infrastructure and learning level in the elementary education sector. However, the road to the RTE Act has not been easy. The exercise of consulting all stakeholders including the states and taking them on board has been time-consuming.

The main provisions in the RTE Act include the responsibilities of appropriate government and local authorities towards establishing neighbourhood schools; sharing of financial and other responsibilities between the central and state governments; prohibition of capitation fee and screening procedure for admission; prohibition of detention, expulsion and corporal punishment; specification of norms and standards for schools including those related to the infrastructure and teachers; laying down of teacher qualifications and their duties; prohibition of deployment of teachers for non-educational purposes; and ensuring that curriculum and evaluation is in accordance with the Constitution of India and as per child-centred principles and values. Children with disabilities and those belonging to minority communities are also covered under the Act.

As per the RTE Act, 2009, every child has the right to full-time elementary education of satisfactory and equitable quality in a formal school that satisfies certain essential norms and standards. The need to address inadequacies in retention, residual access, particularly of un-reached children, and the questions of quality are the most compelling reasons for the addition of Article 21A in the Constitution of India.

As has already been stated, even prior to the RTE, the GoI's efforts were towards universalisation of elementary education in the country. The SSA was the most prominent among all efforts initiated by the GoI before 2010 and was approved by the union cabinet in November 2000 as a centrally-sponsored scheme. The goals of the SSA are (a) enrolment of all children in schools, Education Guarantee Scheme (EGS) centres, alternate schools, 'back-to-school' camps, (b) retention of all children till the upper primary stage, (c) bridging of gender and social category gaps in enrolment, retention and learning, and (d) ensuring significant enhancement in the learning achievement levels of children at the primary and upper primary stages.

There is little difference between the objectives of the RTE and those under the SSA. Yet, there are fundamental variations between the two. While the provisions under the SSA were not part of the fundamental rights enshrined in the Indian Constitution, the RTE provisions form an integral part. Under the RTE, 'free education' has been defined, and

it states that no child, other than one who has been admitted by his or her parents to a school which is not supported by the appropriate government, shall be liable to pay any kind of fee or charges or expenses which may prevent him or her from pursuing and completing elementary education. 'Compulsory education' casts an obligation on the appropriate government and local authorities to provide and ensure admission, attendance and completion of elementary education by all children in the age group of 6–14 years. With this, India has moved forward to a rights-based framework under the RTE Act that casts a legal obligation on the central and state governments to implement this fundamental right.

The roadmap for universalising elementary education is derived from the definite timeframes mandated in the RTE Act; it prescribes a timeframe of three years for the establishment of neighbourhood schools, provision of school infrastructure with an all-weather building and basic facilities, and provision of teachers as per prescribed Pupil–Teacher Ratio (PTR) (30:1). Further, the RTE Act stipulates that all untrained teachers in the system must be trained within a period of five years from the date of enforcement of the Act. The rest of the provisions are required to be implemented with immediate effect.

The RTE Act has had considerable implications for the overall approach and implementation strategies of the SSA. With the enactment of the RTE, there was a need to review the interventions under the SSA and align its norms with the RTE mandate. Today, the SSA is the main implementation vehicle for the RTE Act, 2009: the Implementation Framework of the SSA has in fact been revised to coordinate with the provisions of the RTE Act. A comprehensive monitoring mechanism has also been put in place to ensure smooth implementation of the SSA.

The major changes in the SSA norms effected by the executive committee of the SSA in January 2010 are:

(a) School to be established/ensured within the limits of the neighbourhood as laid down by the state government pursuant to the RTE Act;

(b) All existing EGS centres that have been functioning for two years or more to be upgraded to regular schools, or closed down. No new EGS centres to be sanctioned from 2010–11 onwards;

(c) Special training to be carried out for age-appropriate enrolment of out-of-school and dropout children through residential and non-residential courses;

(d) School infrastructure norms to include libraries, including a one-time grant for books worth ₹3,000 for primary schools and ₹10,000 for upper primary schools;

(e) Ceiling on school repairs up to a maximum of 5 per cent of the existing schools for each district in a particular year, which inhibited the demand for repairs, removed;

(f) School grant to be utilised for play material and sports equipment, in addition to the existing provision for replacement of non-functional school equipment and other recurring costs such as consumables;

(g) Training norms to include training of resource persons, master trainers, and Block Resource Centre (BRC) and Cluster Resource Centre (CRC) coordinators for up to 10 days each year at ₹100 per person per day;

(h) Financial provisions for children with special needs increased from ₹1,200 to ₹3,000 per child per year, provided that at least ₹1,000 per child will be used for the engagement of resource teachers;

(i) Community mobilisation provisions strengthened by raising the number of training days for community personnel from two to six, comprising three-day residential and three-day non-residential training. Financial limits for training also hiked, from ₹30 to ₹100 per day per person for residential training and ₹50 per day per person for non-residential training;

(j) Management cost for districts with small annual plan and size increased from ₹2 million per district to ₹4 million subject to the overall ceiling of 6 per cent being maintained at the national level.

Further to the change in the SSA norms, the timeframes shown in Table 3.1, mandated by the RTE Act, become immediately applicable to the SSA:

TABLE 3.1   Activities and their Timeframes: Ministry of Human Resource Development

Activity	Timeframe
Establishment of neighbourhood schools • Provision of school infrastructure • All-weather school buildings • One-classroom-one-teacher • Office-cum-store-cum-head teacher room	3 years (by 31 March 2013)
• Toilets and drinking water facilities • Barrier-free access • Library • Playground • Fences/boundary walls	3 years (by 31 March 2013)
Provision of teachers as per prescribed PTR	3 years (by 31 March 2013)
Training of untrained teachers	5 years (by 31 March 2015)
All quality interventions and other provisions	With immediate effect

Source: GoI (2009, 2012).

Funding the RTE

An outlay of ₹2,312.3 billion has been sanctioned for implementation of the combined SSA programme under the RTE for the period 2010–11 to 2014–15. Out of this total amount, ₹1,836.4 billion (79 per cent) is recurring and ₹475.9 billion is non-recurring (21 per cent). The fund-sharing pattern between centre and state was originally approved under the SSA for the 11th Plan in a sliding scale, namely 65:35 in the first two years, 60:40 in the third year, 55:45 in the fourth year, and 50:50 in the fifth year. However, in view of the increased financial requirements, the need to revisit the ongoing funding pattern of the SSA is recognised and the sharing pattern has since been revised. The 13th Finance Commission award of ₹240.6 billion for elementary education has been made available to the states to implement the combined RTE-SSA programme. The balance requirement of ₹2,071.6 billion would be shared between the centre and the states in the ratio of 65:35 for all states/union territories for the period from 2010–11 to 2014–15. However, in the case of eight states in the North Eastern Region (NER), the existing sharing pattern of 90:10 will continue. Therefore, the provision of a central outlay is to the tune of ₹1,371 billion (out of which for the NER it would be ₹88.2 billion) over a five-year period from 2010–11 to 2014–15.

GOVERNMENT SCHEMES COMPLEMENTING RTE-SSA

There are a few other schemes that are being implemented simultaneously by various ministries/departments of the GoI. Some of the requirements mandated under the RTE also exist under certain other schemes of the Department of School Education and Literacy, such as Teacher Education and Mid-Day Meal (MDM) schemes. Certain other provisions of the RTE are sourced through convergence of agencies other than the MHRD, such as facilities of drinking water and toilets for existing schools. Therefore, these schemes directly and indirectly facilitate the attaining of the goal of UEE and fulfilling the mandate of the RTE. In this context, a few prominent schemes are

(a) the MDM Scheme of the Department of School Education and Literacy for providing a noon meal to children at the elementary stage of education;

(b) the Total Sanitation Campaign (TSC) and the Drinking Water Mission (DWM) under the Ministry of Rural Development for providing drinking water and toilets in schools;

(c) the National Child Labour Project (NCLP) of the Ministry of Labour to provide special schools for child labourers withdrawn from work;

(d) residential facilities for Scheduled Caste (SC) and Scheduled Tribe (ST) children by the Ministry of Social Justice and Empowerment and the Ministry of Tribal Affairs;

(e) pre-primary education under the Integrated Child Development Services (ICDS) scheme of the Ministry of Women and Child Development;

(f) the School Health Programme of the Ministry of Health and Family Welfare; and

(g) Teacher Education of the Department of Elementary and School Education.

A few of these major schemes are discussed in this section.

ICDS Scheme

One of the world's largest programmes for early childhood development called the ICDS scheme is being implemented through the *Anganwadi* system in India. The scheme was launched in 1975 with the objective:

(a) to improve the nutritional and health status of children in the age group of 0–6 years;

(b) to lay the foundation for proper psychological, physical and social development of the child;

(c) to reduce the incidence of mortality, morbidity, malnutrition, and school dropout;

(d) to achieve effective coordination of policy and implementation amongst the various departments to promote child development; and

(e) to enhance the capability of the mother to look after the normal health and nutritional needs of the child through proper nutrition and health education.

Keeping in view the importance of the ICDS, recommendations have been made to include the key provisions of this scheme in the proposed National Food Security Bill (NFSB). With the enactment of the NFSB, the services under ICDS would become legal entitlements.

'Pre-school non-formal education' is one of the six prominent services through which the ICDS objectives are to be fulfilled. This pre-school non-formal education plays a significant role in the smooth sailing of a child from pre-school to pre-primary school.

The ICDS scheme services are provided through *Anganwadi* centres (AWCs) in India. The total number of approved AWCs in the country is 1.4 million. As on January 2011, the total number of operational AWCs is 1.3 million and the number of *Anganwadi* Workers (AWWs) and *Anganwadi* Helpers (AWHs) is 1.2 million and 1.1 million respectively. The AWWs and AWHs are engaged to ensure uninterrupted services to the beneficiaries. Towards offering these services, the AWW and AWH are provided an honorarium of ₹3,000 and ₹1,500 per month respectively. The GoI has been making adequate budget provisions to carry out the activities under the ICDS, under which the total actual outlay during the 11th Five-Year Plan (up to December 2011) is reported to be ₹403 billion, and total likely expenditure till the end of the 11th Plan would be ₹438.2 billion as against the ₹444

billion originally approved/allocated for the ICDS during the 11th Plan.

Though studies have pointed out several shortcomings, including the challenge to bridge the gap between the policy intentions of the ICDS and its actual implementation, low priority accorded by state governments towards implementation of the ICDS, etc., the scheme has played a significant role in the areas of supplementary nutrition, immunisation as also in the realm of pre-school education. As per data provided by the Ministry of Women and Child Development, over time there has been an improvement in the number of children who attended pre-school. While 30 million children attended pre-school in 2010–11, the figure increased to 35.8 million in 2011–12. The evaluation of the ICDS by the Planning Commission, conducted through the National Council of Applied Economic Research (NCAER) in 2009, observed that the scheme has positively influenced formal school enrolment and contributed to reduction in early discontinuation among beneficiaries.

Mid-Day Meal Scheme

With a view to enhancing enrolment, retention and attendance and simultaneously improving nutritional levels among children, the GoI has been making adequate provision in the budget for the National Programme of Mid-Day Meal in Schools, popularly known as the MDM Scheme. The scheme has had a beneficial impact on school participation in terms of getting more children enrolled and encouraging regular pupil attendance. It acts as a regular source of 'supplementary nutrition' for children as well and can help spread egalitarian values. The MDM Scheme presently covers all children studying in Classes I–VIII of government, government-aided and local body schools; National Child Labour Project schools; and Education Guarantee Scheme (EGS) and Alternative and Innovative Education (AIE) centres, including *madrassas* and *maktabs* supported under the SSA.

As per the Ministry of Human Resource Development (MHRD), 84.1 million primary children and 3.36 million upper-primary children, i.e., a total of 117.7 million children were estimated to have benefited from the MDM Scheme during 2009–10. During 2010–11, 113.6 million children — i.e., 79.7 million children in primary and 33.9 million children in upper primary — are expected to be covered in 1.2 million institutions.

Studies have reviewed and observed the significant benefits of the MDM Scheme. As per the findings of T. Vijaya Kumar: 'The overall implementations of the programme in Primary schools are found to be satisfactory in all the six sample districts of Andhra Pradesh' (2011: xv). However, the report also mentions that '[a] lot of [effort still needs] to be put in for improvement of the programme implementation and [p]roper orientation [training is] to be conducted for functionaries and stakeholders like cooking agencies for effective implementation of the scheme' (ibid.). It further states that '[t]he mid-day meal programme has an impact on the enrolment and nutritional status of the children' (ibid.: xxxiv). The Indian Institute of Technology (IIT), Madras, in its MDM monitoring report on Theni and Kanyakumari districts has stated that '[t]he MDM is extremely beneficial to the children, especially the rural and urban poor. The scheme should be strengthened through allocation of more meals per school and should include *one fruit* and *one glass of milk* for every child every day' (IIT 2011: 31).

A provision of ₹37 billion has been made in the budget estimate for 2012–13 for the MDM Scheme as against ₹28.6 billion in the revised estimate 2011–12.

Teacher Education

The centrally-sponsored scheme of re-structuring and re-organisation of Teacher Education was initiated in 1987 pursuant to the formulation of the NPE, 1986, which emphasised the significance and need for a decentralised system for the professional preparation of teachers. It was in this context that DIETs, Colleges of Teacher Education (CTEs) and Institutes of Advanced Study in Education (IASEs) were established. At present, more than 555 DIETs are functional and 105 CTEs and 31 IASEs have been set up as resource institutions in the country. The DIETs run a pre-service Teacher Education Programme. About 60,000 innovative teachers are trained every year through the DIET's two-year diploma in Education. As per the evaluation report by the National Council of Educational Research and Training (NCERT 2009) these institutions have played a positive role in improving the quality of school and teacher education. The DIET programmes have given a platform towards undertaking research and experimentation among practising teachers. Almost all teachers who received training were found to be competent to conduct the action research and solve their own problems.

The NCERT evaluation report also suggested many changes based on the findings and inadequate performances with regard to certain aspects of the scheme (ibid.). The government has recently approved a revised Teacher Education scheme (mainly based on the NCERT's evaluation and felt need) with much emphasis on the needs arising due to the enactment of the RTE Act. The revised scheme aims to strengthen the teacher education system through qualitative and quantitative strengthening of the teacher education institutions so as to prepare an adequate number of qualified persons for the schools.

There are three salient components of the revised scheme:
(a) *Revision of existing norms*:
  (i) strengthening and upgradation of State Councils of Educational Research and Training and State Institutes of Education;
  (ii) strengthening of existing IASEs and improvement of departments of Education in universities into IASEs;
  (iii) strengthening of existing CTEs and establishment of new ones;
  (iv) strengthening of existing DIETs and extending their mandate for training of teachers at the secondary level.
(b) *Inclusion of new components*:
  (i) establishment of Block Institutes of Teacher Education (BITEs) in 196 identified SC/ST/minority concentration districts for undertaking elementary pre-service teacher education programmes;
  (ii) professional development of teacher educators;
  (iii) technology in teacher education
  (iv) Public–Private Partnership (PPP) in teacher education;
  (v) monitoring mechanism.
(c) *Revision of fund-sharing pattern between the centre and the state*: 75:25 ratio between centre and states (90:10 for the NER States including Sikkim) to ensure greater ownership by the states.

Modification of the scheme is also critical to meet the training requirements of teachers at the secondary level under the Rashtriya Madhyamik Shiksha Abhiyan.

To implement the revised centrally-sponsored scheme Restructuring and Reorganisation of Teacher Education, an estimated outlay of ₹6.4 billion for 2011–12 and of ₹63 billion for the 12th Plan has been approved by the Cabinet. A provision of ₹4.5 billion has been set aside for the scheme in 2012–13.

Thus, a number of important schemes with substantial budgetary provisions are in place contributing to improving school education. In fact, some of the existing and ongoing schemes are being re-structured/strengthened to overcome the weaknesses in realising the desired objectives.

IMPLEMENTING THE RTE ACT

Monitoring

One of the most crucial aspects of the RTE is a strong monitoring system. The central government has — via notification dated 29 March 2010 — constituted the National Advisory Council (NAC) under the RTE Act, 2009 (PIB 2010). The RTE Act provides for mechanisms for monitoring its implementation, including the following. *(a)* The National Commission for Protection of Child Rights (NCPCR) and the State Commissions for Protection of Child Rights (SCPCRs) have been empowered to protect and monitor the rights of children under the Act; *(b)* in States where the SCPCR is not constituted, the state government may constitute an authority to perform the functions of the SCPCR under the Act; *(c)* any person with any grievance relating to right of the child under the Act can make a written complaint to the local authority, which shall decide the matter within a period of three months; and *(d)* the School Management Committee (SMC) constituted under the Act is empowered to monitor the working of the school.

As per the RTE Act, 2009, every school other than an unaided private school shall constitute an SMC, which will perform various functions including preparation of the school development plan. At least three-fourths of the members of SMCs shall be parents or guardians, with a proportionate representation of parents and guardians of children belonging to disadvantaged groups and weaker sections, and 50 per cent of the members shall be women. The Model Rules prepared by the central government and circulated to all states and union territories for adoption/ adaption *inter alia* specify the manner of constituting the SMCs and the additional functions that they should perform. States and union territories have undertaken the process of constituting SMCs in schools. The SMC is likely to take care of local needs and act as a body ensuring checks and balances. This will also strengthen the efficiency of the scheme at the grassroot level.

In addition to this, 42 independent agencies of national repute have been engaged on a two-yearly basis to monitor the SSA programme. These Monitoring Institutions (MIs) submit reports every six months to the central authority. The half-yearly reports submitted by the MIs are shared with the concerned State Project Directors of the SSA of states and union territories for appropriate follow-ups and remedial action. The reports of the MIs are posted on the SSA website.[1] An independent agency, the Institute of Public Auditors of India (IPAI), has also been appointed for concurrent financial review to cover all the states and union territories. It submits reports to the Ministry annually which are further shared with the concerned states and union territories for taking necessary corrective action. The SSA also conducts third-party evaluation through independent agencies for civil work taken up in the states of Andhra Pradesh, Assam, Bihar, Chhattisgarh, Gujarat, Jammu and Kashmir, Madhya Pradesh, Maharashtra, Tamil Nadu, Uttar Pradesh and West Bengal.

The development of a sound information system is critical for successful monitoring and implementation of any programme, particularly in social sectors. The design of the school information system has, therefore, been accorded priority from the very beginning of the DPEP, as a result of which the District Information System for Education (DISE) was developed by the National University of Educational Planning and Administration (NUEPA), New Delhi. When the SSA was launched in 2001, not only was the coverage extended to all states and districts of the country, its scope was also expanded to include the entire elementary level of education including government-aided and private schools. Today, among various other sources, DISE data are used for evaluating the progress made so far as well as in framing policy initiatives.

Implementation

After enacting the RTE Act, 2009, the state governments have taken steps for implementing the same. All state and union territory governments have issued the RTE Rules, or adopted the Central RTE Rules, except for Goa and Karnataka, which are yet to notify the state RTE rules.

Several states have issued instructions/notifications for *(a)* banning capitation fees, corporal punishment, detention and expulsion, and private tuition by school teachers; *(b)* specifying working days/instructional hours; and *(c)* constituting the SCPCR or Right to Education Protection Authority (REPA). The central government has also taken several steps for implementation of the RTE Act. The National Council for Teacher Education (NCTE) and the NCERT have been notified as the academic authorities under Sections 23(1) and 29(1) of the RTE Act respectively. The NAC has been constituted under Section 33(1) of the Act. The NCTE has laid down the minimum qualifications for a person to be eligible for appointment as a teacher in schools.

The main challenges under the RTE Act include bringing out-of-school children into the schools, filling up the large vacancy of teacher posts, training of untrained teachers, and adherence by schools to the norms and standards specified in the Schedule of the RTE Act. The central government, along with the state governments, is taking several steps for addressing these issues, including resource allocation for meeting the infrastructural and manpower gaps as per the revised SSA norms.

Progress in Educational Indicators

A few of the indicators of progress made so far in terms of financial, physical and quality aspects are provided in Tables 3.2 and 3.3.

Financial Allocation

Table 3.2 shows a detailed list of funds that were given to states and union territories in 2010–11 and 2011–12 for the implementation of the revised SSA in keeping with the RTE Act.

TABLE 3.2   Details of Funds Released to States/Union Territories during 2010–11 and 2011–12 (Till 27 July 2011) for Implementation of Revised SSA (in ₹)

States/Union Territories (other than NER)	Amount Released (Central Share) during 2010–11 (in million)	Amount Released (Central Share) during 2011–12 (in million)
Andhra Pradesh	8,100	18,355.1
Bihar	20,478.9	18,510.8
Chhattisgarh	8,786.3	6,987.0
Goa	67.1	107.9
Gujarat	4,406.5	8,802.7
Haryana	3,278.6	4,046.1
Himachal Pradesh	1,378.6	1,419.2
Jammu and Kashmir	4,034.8	3,007.0
Jharkhand	8,956.2	5,790.3
Karnataka	6,690.3	6,278.8
Kerala	1,966.0	1,702.1
Madhya Pradesh	17,678.3	19,042.7
Maharashtra	8,553.7	11,796.2
Odisha	7,317.7	9,271.9
Punjab	3,961.2	4,811.2
Rajasthan	14,618.2	1,485.0
Tamil Nadu	6,906.8	6,814.1
Uttar Pradesh	31,046.2	26,368.2
Uttarakhand	2,579.3	2,089.2
West Bengal	17,470.3	17,765.2
Andaman and Nicobar Islands	35.7	90.7
Chandigarh	215.5	161.1
Dadra and Nagar Haveli	41.3	56.4
Daman and Diu	16.2	25.7
Delhi	355.2	378.3
Lakshadweep	12.7	12.7
Puducherry	48.5	75.7
National Component	78.0	347.9
Other Expenditure	346.5	561.2
Total (Non-NER)	179,424.6	189,534.8[a]

States/Union Territories (NER States)	Amount Released (Central Share) during 2010–11 (in million)	Amount Released (Central Share) during 2011–12 (in million)
Assam	7,685.4	10,692.1
Arunachal Pradesh	2,040.1	2,388.0
Manipur	1,325.3	394.0
Meghalaya	1,854.0	1,441.0
Mizoram	1,011.5	1,081.4
Nagaland	863.6	979.8
Sikkim	446.9	402.2
Tripura	1,712.1	1,749.3
Total NER	16,938.9	19,127.8
Grand Total	196,363.5	208,662.6[a]

Source: Ministry of Human Resource Development, Government of India.
Note: [a] The figures might not add up to the total as only major figures have been included.

TABLE 3.3 Status of Progress since 2006–07

	2006–07	2009–10	2010–11
Primary Schools (in million)	0.77	0.81	0.82
Upper Primary Schools (in million)	0.41	0.49	0.53
Primary Enrolment (in million)	132.00	133.00	135.00
Upper Primary Enrolment (in million)	47.50	54.50	57.80
Elementary Enrolment (in million)	180.00	188.00	192.80
GER[a] Primary (in per cent)	111.0	115.0	118.6
NER[a] Primary (in per cent)	93.0	98.0	99.8
GER Upper Primary (in per cent)	64.7	75.8	81.2
NER Upper Primary (in per cent)	48.4	58.3	61.8
Teachers in Government Schools (in million)	3.60	3.90	4.19
Out-of-School Children[b] (in million)	11.30	8.10	—

Source: Ministry of Human Resource Development.

Note: [a] GER and NER mean gross and net enrolment ratios respectively.

NER=Enrolled children in the official school age group/Total number of children in the official school age group.

GER=Enrolled children of all ages/Total number of children in the official school age group.

The primary school net enrolment ratio (NER) is the share of children of official primary school age that are enrolled in school; the NER cannot exceed 100 per cent. The gross enrolment ratio (GER) is the share of children of *any age* that are enrolled in primary school. In India, many children who are beyond primary level are still enrolled in the primary section and hence the GER exceeds 100 per cent.

[b] Figures are not available.

Enrolment

Efforts to universalise elementary education gained momentum during the last few years as indicated in Table 3.3.

Enrolment in government schools at elementary level increased from 126 million children in 2006–07 to 130 million in 2010–11. In addition, another 17 million were enrolled in government-aided schools, and 42 million were attending private unaided schools in 2010–11.

The GER at primary level is high at 118.6 per cent;[2] and NER has improved significantly from 92.7 per cent in 2006–07 to 99.8 per cent in 2010–11. The GER at upper primary level has shown considerable improvement of 11.8 percentage points in the four years between 2006 and 2009, and a further increase of 5.4 percentage points in 2010–11. With the RTE stipulations with regard to the entry level at age 6, no detention and expulsion, an eight-year elementary education cycle, and maintenance of record of children, it is expected that the GER at both primary and upper primary levels is going to improve in the years to come.

Schooling Facilities

The country has witnessed substantial increase in the number of primary and upper primary schools. Table 3.4 shows that in 2009–10 there was an increase of more than 9.1 per cent in the number of schools in the country as compared to 2006–07. This went up by another 4.5 per cent in 2010–11.

Enrolment – Gender

The percentage of girls out of the total number enrolled at primary and upper primary levels was 48 and 46.5 respectively in the year 2006–07; this increased to 48.4 and 48.3 at primary and upper primary levels respectively in 2010–11. The annual average growth rate of enrolment for girls is considerably higher as compared to boys (see Table 3.5).

Gender Parity Index (GPI) has also shown significant increase, particularly at the upper primary level. The primary-level GPI improved marginally from 0.93 in 2006–07 to 0.94 in 2010–11. However, GPI at upper primary level increased from 0.87 in 2006–07 to 0.94 in 2010–11. Year-wise details are given in Table 3.5.

Decline in the percentage of out-of-school children has taken place across gender and all social categories; nonetheless Muslim, SC and ST children need greater and more focused attention. The percentage of out-of-school children aged 6–14 years has decreased from 6.94 per cent in 2005 to 4.28 per cent in 2009. This decrease is sharper in rural areas, where it drops from 7.08 per cent to 4.53 per cent as compared to urban areas where it has moved from 4.34 per cent to 3.18 per cent only.

Teachers in Position

There has been a substantial increase in the availability of teachers at elementary level in the past few years. The total number of teachers in government schools increased

TABLE 3.4   Total Schools, by Category

Academic Year	Primary Only	Primary with Upper Primary	Primary with Upper Primary and Secondary/ Higher Secondary	Upper Primary Only	Upper Primary with Secondary/Higher Secondary	Total Schools
2006–07	779,482	210,014	29,312	108,095	67,601	1,194,504
2007–08	805,667	217,442	35,974	115,961	69,155	1,244,199
2008–09	809,108	234,345	39,440	125,169	77,225	1,285,287
2009–10	809,978	247,643	41,435	128,165	76,552	1,303,773
2010–11	827,244	258,803	48,135	136,423	91,719	1,362,324

Source: Ministry of Human Resource Development, Government of India.

TABLE 3.5   Sex-Wise Enrolment, by Stages (in million)

Academic Year	Primary (Classes I–V)			Upper Primary (Classes VI–VIII)			Elementary (Classes I–VIII)		
	Boys	Girls	Total	Boys	Girls	Total	Boys	Girls	Total
2006–07	68.4	63.4	131.8	25.4	22.1	47.5	93.8	85.5	179.3
2007–08	69.5	64.7	134.2	27.0	23.9	50.9	96.4	88.6	185.0
2008–09	69.4	65.0	134.4	28.0	25.4	53.4	97.3	90.4	187.7
2009–10	68.8	64.7	133.5	28.3	26.2	54.5	97.1	90.9	188.0
2010–11	69.8	65.5	135.3	29.9	28.0	57.9	99.6	93.4	193.0

Source: Ministry of Human Resource Development, Government of India.

from 3.6 million in 2006–07 to 3.9 million in 2009–10, and further to 4.19 million in 2010–11. This has resulted in the improvement of the PTR from 36:1 in 2006–07 to 32:1 n 2010–11 at the primary level and 29:1 at the upper primary level.

The norm prescribing 50 per cent of all teachers recruited under the SSA to be female has resulted in the increase in percentage of female teachers from 41.8 per cent in 2006–07 to 45.5 per cent in 2010–11.

The real challenge, however, lies in the imbalance in teacher deployment. The number of schools with adverse PTR remains high, though it has reduced from 46 per cent in primary and 34 per cent in upper primary schools in 2009–10 to 42.4 per cent and 31.3 per cent respectively in 2010–11. Even in states with an overall desirable PTR, there are many schools with adverse PTR. Moreover, 7.7 per cent single-teacher schools have an enrolment of more than 15 children functioning in the country. Although this is an improvement over 10.5 per cent single-teacher schools in 2006–07, there are large inter-state variations: Arunachal Pradesh (26.6 per cent), Assam (14.1 per cent), Madhya Pradesh (14.7 per cent), Manipur (10.1 per cent), Odisha (11.9 per cent), and Rajasthan (14.7 per cent). There is therefore an urgent need to fill up existing vacancies and rationalise teacher deployment.

Another challenge is the presence of teachers without professional qualifications notified by the NCTE as required under the RTE Act. As per the DISE 2010–11, there are about 0.8 million untrained teachers spread all over the country, but the majority are in the four states of Bihar (0.17 million), West Bengal (0.17 million), Uttar Pradesh (0.14 million), and Jharkhand (0.07 million), constituting about 68 per cent of total untrained teachers.

School Infrastructure

Under the SSA, the country has seen massive infrastructure development at the school level. Apart from opening over 0.3 million new schools, the SSA has also provided basic facilities in existing schools. The average student–classroom ratio (SCR) which was 36 in 2006–07 has come down to 31 in 2010–11. There has been a considerable rise in the availability of basic facilities in schools, including increase in percentage of schools having drinking water facility from 83.1 per cent in 2006–07 to 92.6 per cent in 2010–11. Girls' toilets are now available in 57 per cent of schools as against 42.5 per cent in 2006–07. The percentage of schools with ramps for the differently-abled has increased from 26.61 per cent in 2006–07 to 50 per cent in 2010–11. The details of improvement in school infrastructure are presented in Table 3.6.

With regard to opening of schools, provision of school infrastructure and drinking water facilities, the overall cumulative performance is more than 85 per cent.

An allocation of ₹255.55 billion has been provided for the RTE-SSA programme for 2012–13. The target for 2012–13

TABLE 3.6   School Infrastructure

Indicator	2006–07	2010–11
Average SCR	36.0	31.0
Schools with Drinking Water (in per cent)	84.0	93.0
Schools with Toilet Facilities (in per cent)	57.0	42.5
Schools with Ramps (in per cent)	26.6	50.0
School with Playground (in per cent)	—	55.0
School with Boundary Wall (in per cent)	—	55.0

Source: District Information System for Education, National University of Educational Planning and Administration, Government of India.

Note: '—' means data either not available or the classification/definition has undergone changes so that strict comparison is not possible.

is towards opening of 5,000 primary schools and 10,000 upper primary schools, recruiting 0.1 million teachers and construction of 0.1 million additional classrooms.

FUTURE NEEDS AND CONCLUSION

As mentioned previously, substantial spatial and numerical expansion of primary and upper primary schools has been achieved with access and enrolment at the primary stage of education reaching near universal levels, gender gap in enrolment being narrowed and the percentage of enrolled SC/ST children being proportionate to their population. Nonetheless, the agenda of universalising education at the upper primary stage remains unfinished. The number of children — particularly children from disadvantaged groups and weaker sections — who drop out of school before completing upper primary education remains high, and the quality of learning achievement is not satisfactory even in the case of children who complete elementary education.

Despite the fact that there has been a huge increase in the investment and levels of physical and infrastructural progress in elementary education in the SSA regime, and in the post-RTE regime in particular, the main objective of 'learning' is not satisfactory. It is therefore imperative to look beyond the provision of infrastructure alone in the pursuit of improved learning levels. While there is no denying the fact that school buildings and teachers are important, it is equally, if not more, important to achieve the desired quality of education and learning level of a child who completes primary education. So far, the existing structure has not yielded full results in terms of learning outcomes. It is thus imperative to do something more over and above what is already there today. It might lead us to approach the problem a little differently.

Learning level is directly and positively correlated to the quality of teaching. It also depends on a student's ability to understand and follow the teaching method, including the language and methodology of the teacher. A more personal approach rather than a generalised one would work better, and it may well be the case that the local teacher's personalised efforts even beyond school hours would yield better results. From the recent trends in the incidence of tuitions, it can be inferred that the rise in the number of private tuition is attributable to personalised efforts vis-à-vis the generalised approach in school. Teachers must also get requisite motivation through appropriate training on a continuous basis as well as financial incentives linked with the learning outcome of their students. To implement these practices there is a need to start a few pilots in select districts/blocks. Each pilot district/block could have a committee, flexible enough to experiment upon various policies including hiring local teachers (on need-basis). Depending upon need, this

TABLE 3.7   Cumulative Targets and Achievements, 2011–12

Items		Achievements (up to 30 September 2011)
Opening of Schools	Opened	333,458 (388,157)[a]
Construction of School Buildings	Completed and in Progress	267,209 (299,808)
Construction of Additional Classrooms	Completed and in Progress	1.41 million
Drinking Water Facilities	Completed and in Progress	212,233 (220,953)
Construction of Toilets	Completed and in Progress	477,263
Supply of Free Textbooks	Supplied	87.7 million
Teacher Appointment	Completed	1.22 million
Teacher Training (20 Days)	Completed	1.92 million

Source: Ministry of Human Resource Development, Government of India.

Note: [a] Targeted figures are in the parentheses and are given wherever available.

committee may advise and assist SMCs on the functioning of the school. This committee could remain directly responsible for the desired parameters including enrolment, learning outcomes, etc. In short, a model district/block needs to be developed for the purpose of achieving the objectives and mandates (with timelines) of the RTE. Once proven to be successful, the model districts may be replicated throughout the country.

Till date, children who are below 6 years and above 14 years of age are not covered by the Act. With the possible restructuring of the ICDS and making all its services part of the National Food Security Bill, children up to 6 years of age may be covered, which may be difficult under the existing ICDS infrastructure. It is also necessary to make efforts to universalise secondary and higher secondary education so that the GERs at these levels are ensured. Unless adequate initiatives are undertaken proactively towards addressing these issues, it may be difficult to gain the full benefit of RTE implementation in the country. Implementation of the RTE primarily depends on the states' effective participation. Under the federal structure each state would need to work, on priority, towards the common goal of achieving universalisation of primary education.

A lot has already been achieved in fulfilling the RTE mandates. However, there are still gaps between the RTE mandates/targets and the actual implementation/achievements. Available reports have pointed out a number of shortcomings and suggested various policy interventions. If these suggestions are examined and adopted wherever necessary, the gaps would soon disappear.

NOTES

1. http://www.ssa.nic.in/ (accessed 2 November 2012).
2. It may be noted that at primary level the GER is more than 100. This is due to the fact that many children who are not supposed to be admitted in the primary level as per the age criteria were enrolled in the same. Here, the NER may be a better indicator.

REFERENCES

Government of India (GoI). 2009. 'Right of Children to Free and Compulsory Education Act, 2009', *Gazette of India*, 27 August.

——————. 2012. 'Right of Children to Free and Compulsory Education Act, 2009: The 2nd Year'. Department of School Education and Literacy, Ministry of Human Resource Development, Government of India.

Indian Institute of Technology (IIT). 2011. 'State Wise Second Half Yearly MI Report (April 2011–October 2011)'. Indian Institute of Technology, Madras.

Kumar, T. Vijaya. 2011. '2nd Half Yearly Monitoring Report of Mid Day Meal Scheme for the State of Andhra Pradesh (Period 1st April 2011 to 30th September 2011)'. Centre for Equity and Social Development, National Institute of Rural Development, Ministry of Rural Development, Government of India.

Mehendale, Archana. 2010. 'Model Rules for the Right to Education Act', *Economic and Political Weekly*, 45(4): 9–12.

National Council of Educational Research and Training (NCERT). 2009. 'Comprehensive Evaluation of Centrally Sponsored Scheme on Restructuring and Reorganization of Teacher Education: A Report'. National Council of Educational Research and Training (NCERT), August.

National Council of Applied Economic Research (NCAER). 2001. *Concurrent Evaluation of ICDS*, vol. 1. New Delhi: National Council of Applied Economic Research.

——————. 2010. *Evaluation of ICDS*, vol.1 (Programme Evaluation Organisation). New Delhi: National Council of Applied Economic Research.

Press Information Bureau (PIB). 2010. 'National Advisory Council Constituted'. Press Information Bureau, Government of India, 29 March.

Teltumbde, Anand. 2012. 'RTE: A Symbolic Gesture', *Economic and Political Weekly*, 47(19): 10–11.

4 | Social Inequalities in Education

Sonalde Desai and *Amit Thorat*

Social stratification in India along the lines of caste, ethnicity and religion is also reflected in educational attainment with a vast quantity of literature documenting inequalities therein (GoI 2006; Govinda 2002; PROBE Team 1999; Thorat and Newman 2009). These inequalities have been a cause of concern to both the government and civil society. The government has put in place strong, affirmative action policies to redress many of the historical injustices. Some of these have received strong public support but others, particularly those regarding reservation of seats in colleges and universities, have led to resentment and protests from more privileged sections of the society (Mendelsohn and Vicziany 1998). Nonetheless, after more than 60 years of implementing policies aimed at restoring this imbalance, and some decline in educational inequalities, the gap still remains wide (Desai and Kulkarni 2008).

Educational imbalances in India deserve particular attention because traditional social disparities based on notions of pollution and impurity[1] that governed caste relations are rapidly being transformed into class inequalities through differential educational attainments. Although a number of studies describe various aspects of social distance and discrimination between different castes in diverse areas of life (Bayly 1999; Deshpande 2011; Mendelsohn and Vicziany 1998), economic disparities are perhaps the most pernicious, resulting in perpetuating the cycle of inequality across generations. While educational inequalities are not the sole determinants of economic status, they play an important role in creating disparities in earnings. Caste-based differences in education, income and other aspects of well-being have long been recognised. In recent years, similar religion-based imbalances have also been observed where Muslims are particularly vulnerable when compared with other religious groups such as Jains, Zoroastrians, Hindus, etc. (Basant and Shariff 2009; Desai and Kulkarni 2008; GoI 2006).

PUBLIC POLICY AND EDUCATIONAL INEQUALITIES

Public policies attempt to address these inequalities in two ways:

(a) by providing scholarships and other incentives to reduce financial stress on the family and to increase the motivation to continue education; and

(b) by providing preferential admission in colleges and advanced professional programmes through reservations or quotas. While some attempts at setting up special schools or hostels for children from marginalised communities have also been made, these have relatively been limited in scope.

Policy intervention, particularly in the case of the highly controversial reservations or quotas in college admissions, comes much too late in the educational path of students. Figures 4.1 and 4.2, charting school discontinuation rates circa 2005, provide interesting insights. Drawing on data from the India Human Development Survey (IHDS) conducted in 2004–05 by researchers from the University of Maryland and the National Council of Applied Economic Research (NCAER), it shows the rate of leaving school/college at a given education level for boys from different social backgrounds (Desai et al. 2010).

These figures show that the largest differences between forward caste Hindus and disadvantaged groups like dalits, adivasis and Muslims appear to lie primarily in school entrance and before completion of Class X. The differences decline on progression to the next level — on completion of Class X. Most minority students who have been able to pass the early hurdles have developed skills and may have intelligence, fortitude and motivation far exceeding their more privileged peers, which increases their chances of success and reduces the inequalities in educational outcomes. They may also belong to the more privileged sections of the dalit, adivasi, Other Backward Class (OBC),

FIGURE 4.1   Education Discontinuation Rates, by Educational Level and Social Background for Men

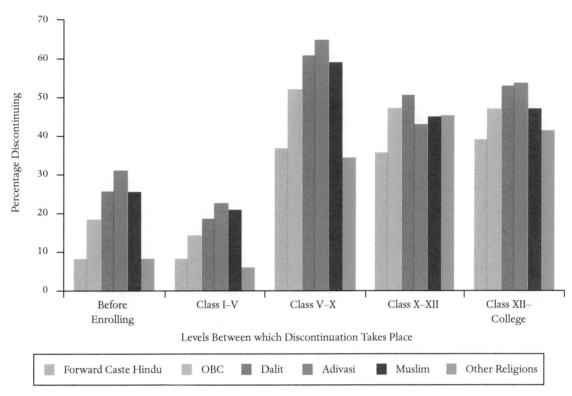

Source: Desai et al. (2010: 89).

FIGURE 4.2   Education Discontinuation Rates, by Educational Level and Social Background for Women

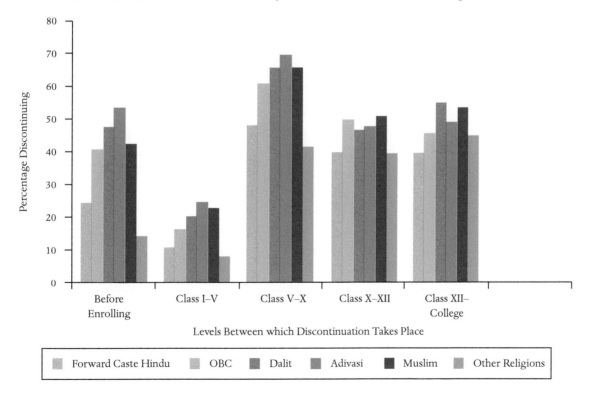

Source: Desai et al. (2010: 89).

or Muslim communities and may be less likely to be subject to prejudices and disadvantages faced by their less-privileged brothers and sisters.

These observations are consistent with the finding from international literature on comparative education (Raftery and Hout 1993; Shavit and Blossfeld 1993), which also notes greater inequalities in education at early stages. Unfortunately public policies, when it comes to addressing educational inequalities, tend to focus more on higher education instead of on early education, possibly because they are easier to address. In this paper, different dimensions of early educational experience will be examined in order to to understand the forces shaping educational inequalities.

GLASS HALF-FULL OR HALF-EMPTY?

The picture of educational inequalities in India is not uniformly bleak. Substantial narrowing in basic literacy rates has taken place. Statistics on rudimentary literacy are typically obtained by asking individuals or their family members whether they can read and write a sentence. In this, the IHDS, like the *Census of India* and other surveys,

documents the convergence between various social groups. To some extent this convergence is attributable to rising school enrolment among all sections of society, and to some extent is a statistical artefact generated by the higher education groups, forward caste Hindus and smaller religious groups such as Christians, Sikhs and Jains reaching near 100 per cent literacy rates (Figures 4.3 and 4.4).

More detailed studies also show that the gap is closing in some areas. An analysis of the National Sample Survey data between 1983 and 2000 states:

[These results suggest that holding] other factors [household income, place of residence and household size] at their mean values, for upper caste Hindu and other [Sikh, Jain and Christian] males, the probability of ever enrolling in school increased from .715 in 1983 to .858 in 1999–2000, an increase of about 14 percentage points. Over the same period, enrollment for dalit males increased by 20 percentage point in their probability of enrollment, and that for adivasi males increased by 21 percentage points. This has helped to narrow the disparities between high caste Hindus and dalits/adivasis ... Among females, the corresponding gain in primary enrollment for upper caste Hindus ... is 25 percentage points, compared with 33 percentage points for dalits and 35 percentage points for adivasis (Desai and Kulkarni 2008: 259).

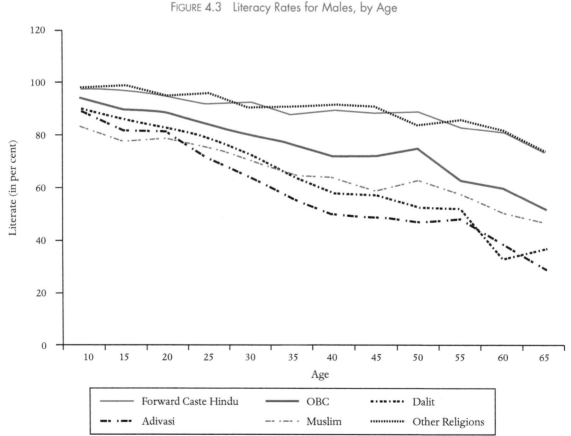

FIGURE 4.3   Literacy Rates for Males, by Age

Source: Desai et al. (2010: 77).

FIGURE 4.4   Literacy Rates for Females, by Age

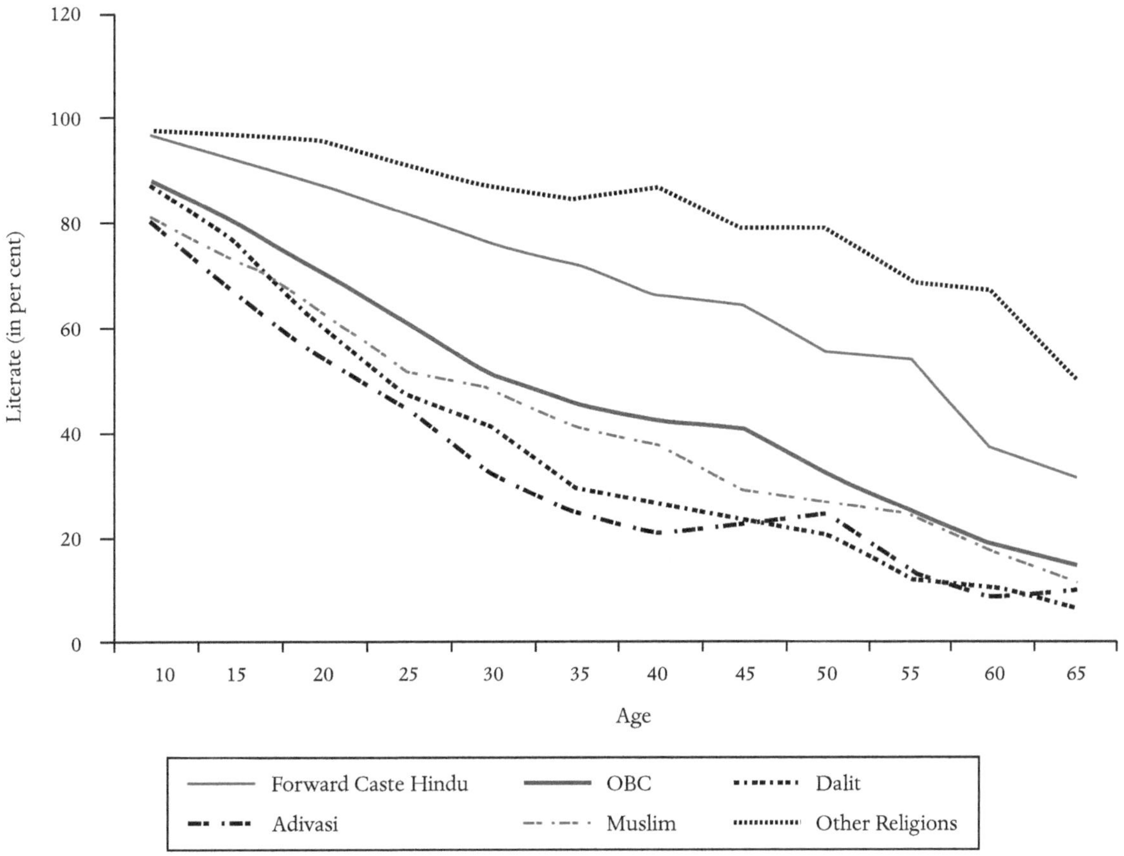

Source: Desai et al. (2010: 77).

However, in spite of this limited success, disparities in educational experiences of children between social groups persist. Table 4.1 shows differences in experiences of children aged 6 to 14 from various social groups documented by the IHDS. It is important to note that these data refer to the period before the Right to Education (RTE) Act was implemented and some of the parameters such as repeating or failing a class may be less relevant now.

Table 4.1 documents that dalit, adivasi and Muslim children fare far worse on all the mentioned indicators when compared to forward caste Hindus and other religious groups with OBCs falling somewhere in the middle. The disadvantages of Muslims are particularly noteworthy since their economic status is often at par with the OBCs (Desai et al. 2010), but when it comes to education, they are far behind OBCs and closer to dalits and adivasis.

INEQUALITIES IN SKILL DEVELOPMENT

Although inequalities in educational attainment are well recognised, there is a tendency to assume that these

inequalities are caused by differential poverty levels across social groups. Since dalits and adivasis, and to a lesser extent Muslims and OBCs, are poorer than the forward castes and other minority groups (ibid.), it is assumed that the need for children to work in order to support the family income instead of going to school, and inability to bear ancillary school costs such as for transportation or purchase of books may lead to lack of school attendance. Hence, the policy focus, such as the emphasis in the RTE Act, has been on increasing school attendance. Ensuring attendance is necessary but it is equally important to recognise the inequalities in learning outcomes.

Even when children from disadvantaged backgrounds attend school, their skill development seems to lag behind their peers. The IHDS administered short reading and arithmetic tests to children aged 8 to 11 years. These tests, designed by Pratham (2005) and extensively used in their *Annual Status of Education Report*, are very simple and measure the ability of children to read a short paragraph of two or three sentences in a language most comfortable to them and to subtract one two-digit number from another.

TABLE 4.1   Educational Experiences of Children (6 to 14 years), IHDS, 2004–05 (in per cent)

	Never Enrolled	Dropped Out	Now in School	Absent 6+ Days in Previous Month	Repeated or Failed a Class
All India	10	5	85	20	6
Forward Caste Hindu	3	3	94	15	5
OBC	9	4	87	21	5
Dalit	12	5	83	22	8
Adivasi	16	7	77	19	9
Muslim	17	8	76	21	5
Other Religions	2	2	96	4	4

Source: Desai et al. (2010: 91).

Only 54 per cent children could read this short paragraph (at Class-II level) and only 48 per cent could subtract. However, among forward castes this number was 71 per cent (for reading) and 63 per cent (for subtraction), while for dalits, adivasis and Muslims it was about 44 per cent each (see Figure 4.5).

At least some of these differences are attributable to differential parental investments in children's education. As Table 4.2 demonstrates, among the IHDS sample, forward caste children are far more likely to attend private schools, take private tuitions, and in general have greater access to a variety of financial inputs, such as textbooks.

However, it would be a mistake to attribute higher skill attainment of forward caste children and those belonging to minority religions as a sole function of greater parental investments. It is of no doubt that forward caste children are more likely to attend private schools and are associated with slightly higher skill attainment (Desai et al. 2009b), but even

FIGURE 4.5   Differences in Learning Outcomes, by Social Background for Children Aged 8–11

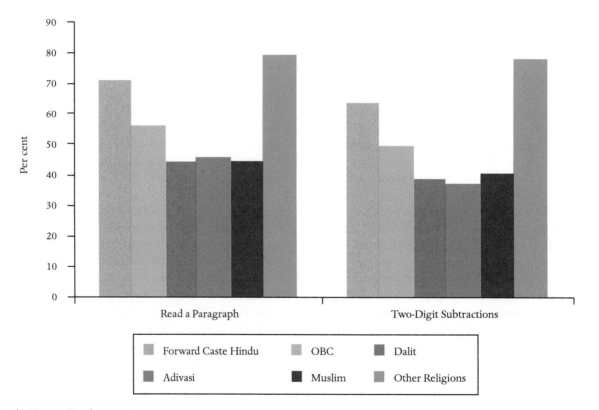

Source: India Human Development Survey, 2004–05.

TABLE 4.2   Social Inequalities in School Expenditure for Children (6 to 14 years), IHDS, 2004–05

	In Private School (in per cent)	In Private Tuition (in per cent)	Average Annual Expenditure (in ₹)			Total Expenditure (in ₹)
			School Fees	Books, Uniform and Transport	Private Tuition	
All India	28	20	481	606	178	1,265
Forward Caste Hindu	40	27	904	924	346	2,174
OBC	26	20	398	543	149	1,090
Dalit	17	18	271	471	134	876
Adivasi	15	9	203	392	73	669
Muslim	33	19	428	521	130	1,079
Other Religions	54	27	1,446	1,370	224	3,040

Source: Desai et al. (2010: 91).

when controlling for the type of school attended, children from dalit, adivasi and Muslim backgrounds show a lower ability to read and subtract. As Table 4.3 demonstrates, among children in private schools, 81 per cent of those from the forward caste can read a short paragraph as compared to 58 per cent of those from the dalit community. A similar difference has also been seen in government schools, i.e., 65 per cent as against 42 per cent.

Since parental education and income play an important role in shaping resources, access to private schools and tuitions, as well as a home environment that fosters learning, it is important to control for parental education in examining social differences in children's learning outcomes. However, even when controlling for income, parental education and family size, caste and religious differences in learning outcomes remain large (Desai et al. 2009a).

Given the limited research on what causes low levels of skill development among children from more vulnerable backgrounds, it is difficult to conclusively suggest remedies. However, the research that exists points to teacher indifference (towards) or outright discrimination (against

children from minority groups) as well as school policies, such as the medium of instruction being the state language rather than tribal languages or Urdu (Nambissan et al. 2002; PROBE Team 1999). Increasing reliance of schools on parental input may be another means through which generational disadvantage may persist. Parents with similar educational and economic backgrounds may still differ in their interpersonal, cultural and social skills of transferring educational and income gains onto to their children. This difference could lie between first-generation parents (dalits, Muslims, adivasis) with high income and education levels and, say, high-caste Hindu parents, with a tradition of good-quality education going back many generations in their families. No one can complain about the importance of involving parents in school governance. Parents are the best advocates for children and their involvement can only help children's education. However, there is a fine line between parental involvement in school governance and transferring some of the school responsibilities to the home. With the growing importance of homework in the Indian educational system, children who are first-generation learners are often

TABLE 4.3   Differences in Learning Outcomes, by School Type for Children Aged 8–11 Years (in per cent)

	Private Schools (Only Enrolled Children)		Government Schools (Only Enrolled Children)	
	Read	Subtract	Read	Subtract
All India	69	64	50	43
Forward Caste Hindu	81	78	65	55
OBC	69	64	53	45
Dalit	58	54	42	36
Adivasi	60	60	47	35
Muslim	55	49	41	38
Other Religions	82	81	76	76

Source: Desai et al. (2010: 93).

left without adequate support systems at home because parents themselves are not sufficiently educated to be able to help them. Since a vast proportion of first-generation learners are dalit, adivasi and Muslim children, excessive reliance on homework perpetuates this historic generational disadvantage.

PUBLIC POLICY IMPLICATIONS

It is well recognised by demographers that the largest improvements in life expectancy can be achieved by focusing on infant mortality rather than mortality reduction at older ages. Saving the life of one child adds about 70 years to his/her life, saving that of a 60-year-old may only add another 15. Similarly, reduction in educational inequality at the primary education stage can have a long-lasting impact and could be the most leveraged investment a society can make. However, Indian public policies are excessively focused on reducing inequalities in college education, possibly because interventions at younger ages are harder to identify and implement. Nonetheless, for a substantial reduction in educational inequality, we must focus on primary education. In order to do this, four types of activities are needed:

(a) *Ensuring that educational policies do not inadvertently exacerbate pre-existing inequalities*: It is important to ensure that the RTE is implemented in a way that reduces the reliance on parental inputs or resources and increases the role of schools in providing education. In systems where a great deal of reliance is placed on homework and/or private tuitions, children whose parents are unable to provide the required supervision are likely to be left behind. A couple of RTE provisions may well have such unintended effects. First, the RTE requires that newly-enrolled children be placed in classes appropriate to their age, regardless of their skill level. Second, children cannot be retained in Classes I–VIII. This places a tremendous burden on the teacher. When coupled with the fact that children who start school late are often from dalit, adivasi or Muslim backgrounds, this may lead to lower skill growth among those who start out later than their classmates. A number of studies have suggested that overambitious curricula without concomitant support to teachers lead to low levels of growth in learning outcomes (Pritchett and Beatty 2012) and inappropriate placement is likely to place too high a burden on teachers. One of the ways of dealing with this challenge may be to have remedial training before or after school hours.

(b) *Special programmes for children from disadvantaged groups*: Research suggests that children often lose ground during school vacations, particularly if they come from families where reading materials are not available. Having special programmes during summer vacations and other holidays for children who are in danger of falling behind or need remedial classes can help alleviate some of these problems. Rayat Schools, an interesting programme in Maharashtra, has sub-schools attached to normal ones for children who have dropped out or fall behind. Additionally, programmes designed to keep girls in school that involve cash payment to parents on completion of Class XII could be extended to dalit, adivasi and Muslim children.

(c) *Identifying specific problems faced by disadvantaged children in school*: Many studies are underway to identify the specific reasons for lower learning of disadvantaged children at school. Recent studies have shown that: (i) teachers are being indifferent to teaching these children and checking their class/homework; (ii) in case of shortages and even otherwise these children do not receive free books and uniforms like other children; (iii) other children in the class tease and trouble them discouraging them from attending school and teachers do not intervene most of the time; and (iv) these children are often made to sit separately in class, drink water from separate vessels or play in separate areas. Such discriminatory and exclusionary practices are highly demotivating and discouraging for the children and hence need to be identified and teachers and staff trained to not only be more sensitive but be pro-active in paying special attention to children from these groups.

(d) *Better monitoring of existing programmes*: A number of existing programmes (such as the Mid-Day Meal Scheme) fail to deliver the intended benefits and services. The food distribution is found to be discriminatory with food not given or served in separate utensils or with separate seating arrangements (Thorat and Lee 2005). Increasing the involvement of non-governmental organisations (NGOs) that focus on dalit, adivasi or Muslim issues in programme monitoring may ensure that benefits are appropriately distributed while raising the awareness level in the community about its educational needs.

(e) *Research on school performance and teaching techniques*: Very little attention has been directed towards classroom processes that put some students at a disadvantage, or effective teaching techniques that can reduce the gap. For example, we know little about whether schools for only children from minority communities can remedy the educational disparity. A number of innovative programmes already exist. For example, schools have been set up by Navsarjan in Gujarat with specially designed curricula for dalit children. Evaluation of these curricula and monitoring of outcome may help inform larger educational reforms.

Evidence suggests that there are clearly a set of factors specific to children from minority communities which unless explicitly understood, specified and made part of the educational reform process, would make this new initiative less effective in delivering to children from these groups and bridging the education, and eventually, income gap. In addition, the time and levels/standards at which these specific interventions are to be made is also important and need to be made part of the education reforms.

NOTE

1. The Hindu concept of 'purity and pollution' refers to the notion or idea that the lowest of castes are impure and any contact or association with them is polluting for the castes higher than them in the stratification, and hence they are termed 'untouchables'.

REFERENCES

Basant, Rakesh and Abusaleh Shariff (eds). 2009. *Oxford Handbook of Muslims in India: Empirical and Policy Perspectives*. New Delhi: Oxford University Press.

Bayly, Susan. 1999. *Caste, Society and Politics in India from the Eighteenth Century to the Modern Age*. Cambridge: Cambridge University Press.

Desai, Sonalde and Veena Kulkarni. 2008. 'Changing Educational Inequalities in India: In the Context of Affirmative Action', *Demography*, 45(2): 245–70.

Desai, Sonalde, Cecily Darden Adams and Amaresh Dubey. 2009a. 'Segmented Schooling: Inequalities in Primary Education', in Sukhdeo Thorat and Katherine S. Newman (eds), *Blocked by Caste: Discrimination and Social Exclusion in Modern India*, pp. 230–52. New Delhi: Oxford University Press.

Desai, Sonalde, Amaresh Dubey, Reeve Vanneman, and Rukmini Banerji. 2009b. 'Private Schooling in India: A New Educational Landscape', in Suman Bery, Barry Bosworth and Arvind Panagariya (eds), *India Policy Forum 2008–09*, pp. 1–58. New Delhi: Sage Publications.

Desai, Sonalde, Amaresh Dubey and Brij Lal Joshi. 2010. *Human Development in India: Challenges for a Society in Transition*. New Delhi: Oxford University Press.

Deshpande, Ashwini. 2011. *The Grammar of Caste: Economic Discrimination in Contemporary India*. New Delhi: Oxford University Press.

Govinda, R. 2002. *India Education Report*. New Delhi: Oxford University Press.

Government of India (GoI). 2006. *Social, Economic and Educational Status of the Muslim Community in India: A Report*. New Delhi: Government of India.

Mendelsohn, Oliver and Marika Vicziany. 1998. *The Untouchables: Subordination, Poverty and the State in Modern India*. Cambridge: Cambridge University Press.

Nambissan, Geetha B., Mona Sedwal and R. Govinda. 2002. *Education for All: The Situation of Dalit Children in India*. New Delhi: Oxford University Press.

Pratham. 2005. *Annual Status of Education Report*. New Delhi: Pratham Documentation Centre.

Pritchett, Lant and Amanda Beatty. 2012. 'The Negative Consequences of Overambitious Curricula in Developing Countries'. CGD Working Paper no. 293, Center for Global Development, Washington, DC.

Public Report on Basic Education (PROBE) Team. 1999. *Public Report on Basic Education in India*. New Delhi: Oxford University Press.

Raftery, Adrian E. and Michael Hout. 1993. 'Maximally Maintained Inequality: Expansion, Reform, and Opportunity in Irish Education, 1921–75', *Sociology of Education*, 66(1): 41–62.

Shavit, Yossi and Hans-Peter Blossfeld. 1993. *Persistent Inequality: Changing Educational Attainment in Thirteen Countries*. Boulder, Colorado: Westview Press.

Thorat, Sukhdeo and Joel Lee. 2005. 'Caste Discrimination and Food Security Programmes', *Economic and Political Weekly*, 40(39): 4198–201.

Thorat, Sukhdeo and Katherine S. Newman (eds). 2009. *Blocked by Caste: Economic Discrimination and Social Exclusion in Modern India*. New Delhi: Oxford University Press.

Every Child in School and Learning Well in India

Investigating the Implications of School Provision and Supplemental Help

Rukmini Banerji and *Wilima Wadhwa*

THE DEBATE

Much of the recent debate and discussion on schooling in India focuses on private and public provision of schooling. While there is consensus on the need for universal access to schooling, in India there are strong views on who receives it and how this provision is to be done. The commitment of the Indian government to provide access and reduce all gender and social gaps in enrolment has been strong and in place even before the Right of Children to Free and Compulsory Education or Right to Education (RTE) Act was passed into law in 2010. The RTE further strengthens this position. Not only should all children be in schools, but in schools with particular characteristics; taught by teachers with specific qualifications; and following a set of minimum procedures. The recent Supreme Court judgement on the RTE further focused the nation's attention on the issue of who goes to or is eligible to go to what kind of school.

Thus at one end of the spectrum are those who take a rights-based approach and believe in entitlements, where every child in India is entitled to schools and teachers who comply with the norms regarding inputs and processes laid down by the law. According to this viewpoint, every school in the country must have certain specific characteristics and education can be imparted in only such schools. At the other end are those who equally and strongly believe in freedom of enterprise and choice. This school of thought believes that parents should have the liberty and the option to send their child to a school of their choice, and that education can take place in government schools or in a variety of different types of private schools, with formal or non-formal education programmes.

While viewpoints and opinions may vary across people and over time, what does the available evidence suggest about who goes to what type of school in India? And, what are the outcomes and implications of the different patterns of school access? For the past seven years, for every rural district in India, the Annual Status of Education Report (ASER) has made available comparable data on school access and learning. This makes it possible to use empirical evidence to explore questions of school access and outcomes. This paper is primarily based on ASER data from 2006–11.[1]

Using ASER data, this paper sets out to explore three basic questions: First, what have been the trends in private schooling in rural India in the recent years? Second, are there other private educational inputs going into children's education such as tuition? How pervasive is the practice of tuition or coaching and what have been the trends in this over time? Third, what is the impact of private inputs — such as private schooling and private tuition on children's learning outcomes? The paper concludes with a discussion on the interpretation of the available evidence on effective strategies to ensure that every child is in school and learning well.

THE EVIDENCE: PROVISION OF SCHOOLING IN RURAL INDIA

How have Private School Enrolment Patterns been Changing in the Recent Years in Rural India?

This question can be answered in several ways. Table 5.1 focuses on the age group of 6–14-year-olds and examines national trends from 2006–11 for all rural districts put together.

Table 5.1 suggests two basic trends: first, the fraction of children in the age group 6–14 enrolled in private schools has risen considerably by almost 7 percentage points in six years to reach 25.6 per cent in 2011. At the same time,

TABLE 5.1   Percentage of Children Enrolled and not Enrolled in School: Rural India

Age Group 6–14	Government	Private	Other	Not Enrolled	Total
ASER 2006	73.3	18.7	1.2	7.6	100
ASER 2007	75.3	19.3	1.1	5.6	100
ASER 2008	71.8	22.6	1.3	4.9	100
ASER 2009	72.9	21.7	0.2	4.5	100
ASER 2010	71.8	23.7	0.2	3.5	100
ASER 2011	69.9	25.6	0.3	3.8	100

Source: ASER (2006–11).

the proportion of children not enrolled or out of school is declining, dropping to below 4 per cent in 2011.[2]

How do these enrolment patterns look when we disaggregate them according to age and sex? Figure 5.1 takes the all-India rural figures and divides the sample into two age groups by gender — boys and girls in the age groups of 7–10 and 11–14 for the 2006–11 period.

For each age group in every year, higher proportions of boys are enrolled in private school than girls. Although for some years the data suggests that older children were more likely to be in a private school than younger ones, by 2011 the differences between age groups in private school enrolment seemed to have narrowed considerably, but the differences in gender remained.

States vary substantially with respect to private school enrolment in rural areas. Table 5.2 summarises the private school enrolment in the major Indian states, using ASER 2011 data. Since ASER is a household survey, families are asked about the type of school that their children are enrolled in. While parents know whether their child goes to a government or private school, they often do not know if the private school is aided or unaided, recognised or unrecognised. Therefore, the data reported here is for all private schools clubbed together.[3]

FIGURE 5.1   Private School Enrolment, by Age and Gender

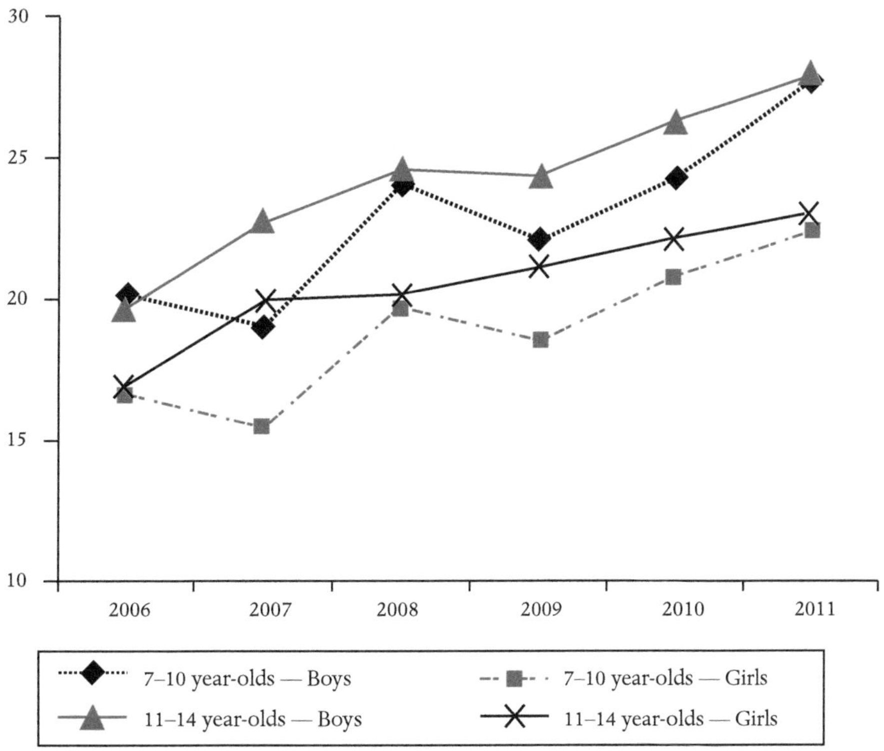

Source: ASER (2006–11).

TABLE 5.2   Percentage of Children Enrolled in Private Schools (age 6–14)

Percentage	States	Total Number of States
Above 50 per cent	Kerala, Manipur, Meghalaya	3
40–49 per cent	Haryana, Uttar Pradesh	2
30–39 per cent	Jammu and Kashmir, Punjab, Uttarakhand, Rajasthan, Maharashtra, Andhra Pradesh	6
20–29 per cent	Karnataka, Tamil Nadu, Himachal Pradesh	3
10–19 per cent	Madhya Pradesh, Chhattisgarh, Jharkhand, Assam, Gujarat, Arunachal Pradesh, Mizoram	7
Less than 10 per cent	Bihar, Odisha, West Bengal, Tripura	4
Total Number of States		25

Source: ASER (2011).

There are clear regional patterns in private school enrolment. The states north and west of Delhi, from Jammu & Kashmir in the north to Rajasthan in the west, as well as the large state of Uttar Pradesh fall into a 'high' private schooling region, where anywhere between half to a third of all rural children (in the age group 6–14) are enrolled in private schools. In the eastern region of India — West Bengal, Bihar and Odisha — private school enrolment is very low. The north-eastern states also provide contrasting cases: Manipur, Meghalaya and Nagaland have very high private school enrolment, whereas Tripura has extremely low levels.

Looking at the state-wise trends according to class levels over time is an even more interesting exercise (this section is based on the analysis laid out in Chavan 2011). Figures 5.2, 5.3 and 5.4 present three cases from three states to highlight the different regional trends across the country.

The three cases presented here highlight the need for a much deeper exploration of patterns of school provision and choice across states, over time and according to classes. So far, available research on this topic in India refers to general patterns and explanations across the country, rather than an investigation of the differences in geography, time and phases of education. These differences need to be explored more carefully. This is especially important since education is a concurrent federal and state subject in India, and state policies can and do differ significantly.

The Evidence: Incidence of 'Tuition'

Do children get any other educational supplements? The phenomenon of additional educational inputs through tuition classes and coaching centres is very widespread and visible in India especially in secondary and post-secondary education. For example, it is common to see signboards in many rural block and district headquarters as well as in state capitals for classes to prepare for college entrance and

FIGURE 5.2   Percentage of Children Enrolled in Private Schools, by Class and Year in Uttar Pradesh

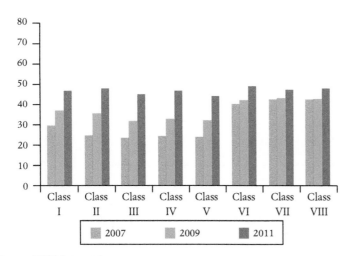

Uttar Pradesh: The ASER data suggest that a few years ago more children went to private schools in the middle-school years than the primary school. For example, in 2007, the proportion of children enrolled in private school in Class VI or VII was much higher than in Class II or III. However by 2011, it appears that close to 50 per cent of the children were going to private schools from Class I onwards. This fraction is high across all classes. Overall, the percentage of children (age 6–14) in private schools has increased from 29 per cent in 2007 to above 45 per cent in 2011.

Source: ASER (2007–11).

FIGURE 5.3   Percentage of Children Enrolled in Private Schools, by Class and Year in Tamil Nadu

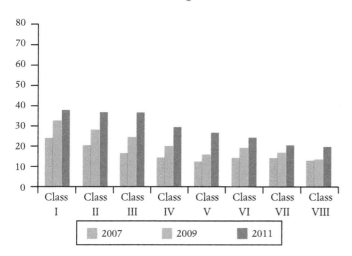

Tamil Nadu: The trends of private school enrolment by grade over time in Tamil Nadu show a different picture as compared to that of Uttar Pradesh. Private school enrolment is higher in early classes and is growing. For example, in 2011 the fraction of children enrolled in private schools in Class I was higher than that in 2007. This trend needs further analysis because it takes place against the backdrop of heavy investment by the Tamil Nadu Government in the early classes in government schools, with quality enhancement programmes such as Activity-Based Learning (ABL).

Source: ASER (2007–11).

FIGURE 5.4   Percentage of Children Enrolled in Private Schools, by Class and Year in Maharashtra

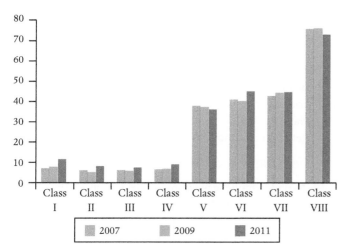

Maharashtra: The picture in the state looks relatively stable over time. Most children go to government schools (*zilla parishad* schools) in the primary years. Enrolment in private schools jumps in the post-primary years, with a substantial proportion of children going to private schools. These schools in Maharashtra are often government-aided.

Source: ASER (2007–11).

professional examinations (such as the civil service entrance examinations).

What does one know about the kind of supplemental inputs for students in elementary school? ASER asks families if their children are attending any paid classes outside school. Table 5.3 summarises the status of tuition in every class from Classes I to VIII for government and private school children in the sample. The 2011 ASER data shows that for rural India as a whole almost one-fourth of all children access these supplemental inputs by Class VIII.[4]

Table 5.4 uses ASER 2011 data for children in Class IV in different states and examines the incidence of tuition for those enrolled in government and private schools. It is clear that tuition patterns vary considerably across states even for the same class. For every state shown in Table 5.4, the incidence of tuition is substantially higher among private school children than government school children, ranging from double to four times higher in some states.

It is interesting to unpack the all-India patterns and look at the incidence of tuition across states. There are wide variations across states; among government school children we see almost no tuition in Rajasthan or Chhattisgarh, compared to nearly 75 per cent in West Bengal and Tripura.

The highest incidence of tuition is visible in states such as Bihar, West Bengal and Odisha, where private school enrolment is 10 per cent or below. ASER 2011 data for three selected classes in the three states has been shown in Table 5.5. The data shows that prevalence of tuition is very

TABLE 5.3   Percentage of Children taking Paid 'Tuition' Classes, by Class and Type of School

Type of School	Class I	Class II	Class III	Class IV	Class V	Class VI	Class VII	Class VIII	Total
Government	15.8	19.5	21.2	24.0	25.4	25.8	27.7	28.4	23.3
Private	18.9	21.1	23.2	23.3	23.1	21.6	22.2	22.4	21.8

Source: ASER (2011).

high even in classes as early as Class III and it rises even more by the time children reach higher classes such as Class VII.

Putting it all together, the tuition data from ASER suggests three broad patterns: first, even in rural areas, states vary substantially from each other in terms of the proportion of

TABLE 5.4   Percentage of Children in Class IV taking Paid Tuition Classes, by School Type

States	Government	Private
Jammu and Kashmir	6.9	22.7
Himachal Pradesh	3.6	18.6
Punjab	9.0	26.4
Uttarakhand	5.9	36.3
Haryana	10.1	23.3
Rajasthan	1.5	8.6
Uttar Pradesh	5.8	14.8
Bihar	48.2	60.5
Jharkhand	23.8	42.1
West Bengal	72.7	79.4
Odisha	48.6	61.2
Maharashtra	5.5	23.7
Gujarat	11.3	46.3
Madhya Pradesh	5.8	11.9
Chhattisgarh	1.2	2.4
Andhra Pradesh	16.2	29.0
Karnataka	6.7	27.0
Kerala	32.2	31.6
Tamil Nadu	16.3	24.4
Arunachal Pradesh	10.0	21.9
Assam	15.2	31.5
Manipur	12.5	51.3
Meghalaya	10.9	23.3
Mizoram	0.9	17.2
Tripura	73.9	45.5
Nagaland	13.0	39.0

Source: ASER (2011).

TABLE 5.5   Percentage of Children in Government Schools taking Tuition, 2011

States	Class III	Class V	Class VII
Bihar	42	51	59
Odisha	44	46	52
West Bengal	67	77	82

Source: ASER (2011).

children who avail of tuitions. Second, even though all-India numbers show little difference in this regard between private and government schools (Table 5.3), in many states, even as early as in Class IV, private school children are more likely to take tuition classes (Table 5.4). Third, in the high tuition-low private school states in eastern India (Odisha, West Bengal and Bihar), the percentage of students who take tuition classes is high even in primary classes and rises as children get older and move to higher classes.

Case Study of a Village from West Bengal

To understand the phenomenon of tuition in a high incidence state, a case study was done in a village in Mohammad Bazar block, Birbhum district, West Bengal. The village has approximately 350 households living in four separate habitations (*paras*). The government primary school here has 135 children enrolled in Classes I to IV. A quick survey of the village revealed that there were five tutors who taught primary school children, and an additional two volunteers working with children in Classes III and IV who were lagging behind.[5] Table 5.6 gives details about tuition in the village.

Table 5.6 shows that 51 children get tuition from paid tutors. Besides, an additional 40 children are taught by Pratham volunteers (who are unpaid). So, of the 135 children enrolled in school close to 100 are also getting supplemental help outside school. According to the villagers, the monthly payment for tuition for primary classes ranges from ₹30–50.

This village also has two tutors who teach at the post-primary level and are very well known in the area. The tutors draw children from a catchment area of five–six surrounding villages. Table 5.7 shows that fees are higher for higher classes.

TABLE 5.6 Tuition for Primary School Children in a Village in West Bengal

Tutor	Location of Tuition Class in the Village	Age of Tutor	Educational Qualifications of Tutor	Class of Children	Class-wise fees (₹per month)	Number of Children Enrolled	Number of Years the Tutor has been giving Tuition
Tutor 1	Sarkarpara	20	High Secondary	I	30	2	1 year
				II	30	2	
				III	30	4	
				IV	40	4	
Tutor 2	Dangalpara	22	Secondary	I	30	4	4 years
				II	30	3	
				III	30	3	
				IV	30	3	
Tutor 3	Dangalpara	17	Secondary	I	40	1	2 month
				II	40	1	
				III	40	1	
				IV	0	0	
Tutor 4	Dangalpara	17	Secondary	I	30	5	2 years
				II	30	4	
				III	30	2	
				IV	50	7	
Tutor 5	Moral *Para*	37	Secondary	I	50	2	10 years
				II	50	1	
				IV	50	2	
				Total Students with Tutors		51	

Source: Data collected by Pratham, West Bengal team, March 2012.

TABLE 5.7 Details of Tutors who Teach at Post-Primary Level

Name of Tutor	Age	Qualification	Subjects Taught	Class of Students	Monthly Fees (in ₹)	Number of Children Enrolled	Experience as Tutor	Catchment Area
Tutor 1	52	Bachelors in Commerce	All	V	50	10	28 years	From Six Neighbouring Villages + own Village
				VI	50	15		
				VII	60	20		
				VIII	60	30		
				IX	75	40		
				X	100	50		
				XI	100	25		
				XII	100	30		
				Total Students		220		
Tutor 2	40	Bachelors in Electrical Engineering	All	V	50	20	12 years	From Seven Neighbouring Villages + own Village
				VI	50	20		
				VII	50	20		
				VIII	50	20		
				IX	100	25		
				X	100	15		
				XI	100	15		
				XII	100	35		
				B.A	150	10		
				Total Students		180		

Source: Data collected by Pratham, West Bengal team, March 2012.

Each of these surveyed tutors makes well above ₹14,000 per month as income from tuition. This case study provides evidence for the fact that there is a substantial teaching activity in a village outside the school or the formal education system. Even this medium-sized village and its surrounding areas can support a significant 'market' for additional teaching. The case study illustrates that by ignoring this large and active unorganised sector in education, any discussion of school provision and educational inputs is incomplete. For trying to understand the educational landscape in India, the incidence and the 'value added' of these supplemental inputs need to be understood properly.

THE EVIDENCE: PULLING TOGETHER ALL PRIVATE INPUTS INTO SCHOOLING

Much of the debate on provision of schooling revolves around private and government schools, but putting the private schooling, tuition data and the trends together we see that the educational landscape in the primary and upper primary stages is much more diverse. There are at least four scenarios that are possible for children in the 6–14 age group who are enrolled in school as indicated in Table 5.8.

TABLE 5.8   Percentage of Children (6–14 age group) and the Type of School

Type of School and Tuition	Percentage
Government school + No Tuition	54.8
Government School + Tuition	17.6
Private School + No Tuition	21.4
Private School + Tuition	6.3
Total (ASER Rural)	100.0

Source: ASER (2011).

The ASER 2011 data suggests that close to half of all school-going children in rural India get some form of paid private input or supplement in their 'education portfolio'; this spans across children who are attending both private and government formal schools.[6] ASER data allows us to look back over the last half a dozen years in a consistent manner. However, lack of annual national data for previous years means that one does not know if the incidence of tuition has increased, decreased or stayed the same over time.

In India, in other sectors such as manufacturing or services, the importance and extensive spread of the un-organised sector is well documented. It is clear from the evidence presented here that there is immense activity in the 'unorganised' sector in education. This phenomenon needs to be better documented, researched and analysed. Some questions also need to be answered: where, how and

why is formal schooling supplemented with inputs from the unorganised sector? What are its impact and implications?

THE EVIDENCE: BASIC LEARNING LEVELS OF CHILDREN

Implications and impact of school provision and other inputs on educational outcomes can be explored in many ways. For the purposes of this paper, only one kind of educational outcome will be examined — children's learning outcomes in basic reading and arithmetic.

With well over 95 per cent of 6–14-year-olds enrolled in school, India is very close to universal enrolment. But, what about children's learning? The evidence shows that children are enrolled in schools, but are they actually learning? Are they learning well? Children learn in school. Children learn at home. Children learn from variety of other sources. As India's elementary school enrolment increases, the focus needs to move to thinking about the 'value added' for each year spent in school. The underlying assumption is that this 'value' accumulates over time; years of schooling are a proxy for this.

What is the evidence? The last six years' data from ASER indicates that by Class V close to 50 per cent of all enrolled children are not yet able to read Class II-level text fluently. The arithmetic findings are even less satisfactory. Further, although India seems to have been in a 'big stuck' as far as basic learning is concerned, the ASER 2011 data suggests a possible additional decline. Using ASER data from the past, Lant Pritchett and Amanda Beatty (2012) go further to show that not only are learning levels low, the 'value added' for each subsequent year in school is very small.[7]

In this context, the debate on private and public schooling becomes louder. First, in some quarters, there is widespread perception that government schools do not function well or deliver quality education. Therefore parents are turning to private options. Second, it is also possible that rising private enrolment and supplementation may also be correlated with rising aspirations, better information about schools and their characteristics and rising incomes. These 'demand'-side considerations have been discussed in several recent research papers, for example Karthik Muralidharan and Michael Kremer (2006), recent work in India by S. Pal (2010), and Amita Chudgar (2012); Tahir Andrabi, Jishnu Das and Asim Ijaz Khwaja (2008) point to factors on the 'supply' side in Pakistan.[8]

ASER data from 2006 onwards provides annual measurement of basic reading and arithmetic outcomes. Table 5.9 presents basic reading level (ability to read Class II-level text fluently) of Class V children across states by school type and tuition.

TABLE 5.9 Class V Children who can Read Class II-Level Text (in per cent)

ASER 2010	READING LEVELS					Private School	TUITION	
	Private School Enrollment + Tuition 2010	Private School Enrollment + No Tuition 2010	Government School Enrollment + Tuition 2010	Government School Enrollment + No Tuition 2010	All Children Enrolled in Class V (Government + Private) 2010	Children in Class V Enrolled in Private Schools 2010	Government School Children Attending Tuitions in Class V 2010	Private School Children Attending Tuitions in Class V 2010
Himachal Pradesh	81.8	81.7	72.0	76.0	77.4	23.5	8.5	22.4
Punjab	74.9	73.7	78.3	68.1	69.7	33.6	10.5	31.0
Uttarakhand	79.9	70.1	66.4	64.1	65.8	23.8	7.5	26.1
Haryana	75.2	79.1	55.6	59.7	67.5	39.1	12.8	25.0
Rajasthan	76.3	64.5	62.1	43.4	51.1	33.4	4.6	12.9
Madhya Pradesh	76.9	62.2	68.7	54.4	NA	14.1	NA	NA
Chhattisgarh	81.8	68.9	67.8	60.9	61.6	7.8	1.9	9.4
Uttar Pradesh	73.4	55.1	56.9	34.3	44.1	36.1	7.6	16.8
Bihar	71.8	66.3	62.7	54.7	58.3	4.0	55.5	63.7
Jharkhand	68.2	61.0	57.0	46.2	49.7	7.0	30.2	45.3
Odisha	61.3	63.9	58.2	37.3	46.0	3.5	49.9	78.3
West Bengal	42.5	68.6	59.5	39.1	53.9	2.5	75.6	65.4
Assam	76.3	49.2	55.5	41.0	45.4	17.6	17.8	28.7
Maharashtra	82.2	76.2	74.1	70.8	73.1	33.1	8.0	12.9
Gujarat	66.6	63.1	65.3	41.3	45.5	9.9	9.5	40.8
Andhra Pradesh	64.1	67.0	67.0	55.9	60.3	34.4	12.6	26.4
Karnataka	45.4	55.4	49.4	42.4	45.0	18.1	6.9	22.6
Kerala	81.6	75.9	79.3	71.9	76.1	54.7	44.3	44.1
Tamil Nadu	44.9	25.5	34.9	32.3	30.6	23.1	19.8	30.3
All India (Rural)	71.0	62.3	60.7	48.2	53.4	22.1	26.9	23.9

Source: ASER (2010).

Note: NA = Not Applicable.

At first glance private schools, even in rural areas, seem to be producing children who do somewhat better in school (at least in terms of basic reading ability). However, as soon as the data is disaggregated by school type and tuition, the picture is no longer as clear.[9] Several important implications emerge from the ASER 2010 data (summarised in Table 5.9).[10] Here, the ability of Class V children to read Class II-level matter is taken as a learning indicator (similar arguments can be made for arithmetic as well from ASER data).

This section discusses the implications. First, the data raises questions. Is the self-selection of 'advantaged' children into private schools further reinforced by additional supplemental inputs such as tuition?[11] If it is 'dissatisfaction' with government schools that led parents to send their children to private schools, then why is it that parents of children going to private schools send their children to tuition as well. Is this trend fuelled by high aspirations or low faith in schools?

Second, even in the best performing states, such as Himachal Pradesh, Kerala or Maharashtra, among those who are going to private schools and for tuition classes, there are about 20 per cent children who are in Class V but unable to read a Class II-level text fluently.[12] Whether looking at their households or their schools, this is the strongest evidence for the biggest challenge faced by elementary education in India today. Despite the flagship programmes for universalising education, regardless of the RTE Law which emphasises 'age-grade mainstreaming', despite parental expenditures on education in private schools and for supplemental help, as a country India is unable to ensure that about half of all children who have spent five years in a school are able to read Class II-level text. This means that 50 per cent of all children are at least three class years behind.

Third, in terms of relative performance, children in private schools who take tuition seem significantly ahead of those going to government schools and taking no tuition; the difference in reading levels between private school children without tuition and government school children with tuition is narrow. In fact, in Madhya Pradesh, Uttar Pradesh, Assam, Gujarat, Kerala, and Tamil Nadu, more children in government schools who take tuitions are reading well as compared to their counterparts in private schools who do not get supplemental coaching.

Fourth, there are significant differences across states in the ability of government schools to impart basic learning. Taking the example of two contiguous states, Table 5.10 provides some cases for discussion.

In Case 1, if language or distance were not an issue, parents in Gujarat who are sending their children to private schools and for tuitions would be better off if their children attended government schools in the neighbouring district in Maharashtra. In Case 2, it is seen that the reading levels of Class V children in government schools in Bihar are very similar to that of Class V children in private schools in Uttar Pradesh. In fact the performance of children in Bihar, who are enrolled in government schools but also take tuitions, is the best among these three categories.

Several researchers have explored these issues; deeper analysis indicates that controlling for other factors the private school advantage in terms of children's learning may not be as sharp as the raw numbers indicate. For example, Shobhini Mukerji and Wilima Wadhwa (2011) use the nationally representative ASER 2009 dataset and find that while private schools seem to have a significant advantage in learning outcomes, a lot of this advantage gets vitiated once other factors are controlled for. They state that the 'wide variations in learning across states indicate there is more beyond the type of village, type of school or type of family that determines the educational destiny of the child'. Other works by Wilima Wadhwa (2009) and Chudgar (2012) point to similar results.

So Where Do We Go From Here? What 'Works'?

The available evidence discussed earlier suggests three main points: First, the data shows that while there are variations over time and across classes, a trend has been seen in many states towards increasing private school enrolment. Second, there is strong evidence of the incidence of supplemental help in children's education across many states and among private school children. Third, supplemental help does matter in terms of learning outcomes; those who get it are more likely to have higher basic learning levels.

In India, we are at a unique point in history. Due to rising demand from parents and rapid provisions by governments, children are now in schools. But more than 50 per cent of

TABLE 5.10 Reading Levels of Class V Children in Different States

Comparisons and Choices	State	Schooling and Tuition Inputs	Percentage of Children in Class V able to Read Class II-Level Text
Case 1	Maharashtra	Government School + No Tuition	70.8
	Gujarat	Private School + Tuition	66.5
Case 2	Uttar Pradesh	Private School + No Tuition	55.2
	Bihar	Government School + No Tuition	54.7
	Bihar	Government School + Tuition	62.7

Source: ASER (2010).

the children who are in schools in India come from families where parents have no schooling. This is more so for children who go to government schools rather than private ones. So, families cannot identify or support their children who are not learning. Indian schools focus on completing curriculum rather than on delivering learning. As a result, many children never get a good foundation of basic learning in the early years of school. They learn but much later than they actually should, with very little chance of ever catching up. With no one to identify, children who are not moving forward and are falling behind, with no learning support at home or in school, a large fraction of Indian children fall through the cracks. Parents have high aspirations for children. Those who can afford it spend money on more inputs, such as tuitions and private schools. Like parents, the government is also input-focused; more expenditures on more schools, teachers, training, textbooks, and so on. The ultimate result is that large numbers of children continue to be 'stuck' in a low-learning situation with not much value being added in terms of learning as they move through the primary classes.

Apart from ASER and other evidence on basic learning outcomes in India, the last five years have seen accumulation of considerably well done research and impact evaluation studies on 'what works' in elementary education in India, especially for improving children's basic levels in reading and arithmetic (in particular, see Banerjee and Duflo 2011; Muralidharan et al. 2012; Pritchett and Beatty 2012). Some of this research has been synthesised and discussed in another chapter in this volume (see Chapter 11); so is not be discussed in detail here. However, some key elements from this body of literature have been pulled out to help in interpreting the evidence presented here, in understanding why children's learning levels are low and suggesting what can be done about it.

Two interconnected and clear messages emerge from the recent body of empirical research. The first is that countries such as India suffer from an 'overambitious curriculum' (Pritchett and Beatty 2012). In India, as in many other countries, schools are organised by classes and in turn classes are mainly anchored by age. So a typical 8-year-old in India is supposed to be in Class III or IV depending on when he/she entered school in Class I. Each year the textbook content grows in difficulty often in a linear fashion and assumes that children who have entered, say, in Class III have mastered the content and skills expected of them in Class II. So the teacher in Class III proceeds to use the Class-III textbook and teach from there. The reality is that the textbook content is far above the level of most children at that class level and as the curriculum becomes more difficult, more and more children get left behind.

The ASER data from 2005–11 has been able to pinpoint this phenomenon very clearly in empirical terms. For example, Table 5.11 shows Class IV reading data at the all-India (rural) level from ASER 2011.

TABLE 5.11   All-India (Rural): Reading Level of Children in Different Classes (in per cent)

Class	Nothing	Letter	Word	Level 1 (Class I Text)	Level 2 (Class II Text)	Total
I	38.4	39.4	15.3	3.9	3.0	100
II	16.6	34.6	28.3	11.8	8.7	100
III	8.5	22.9	28.4	21.5	18.8	100
IV	4.7	14.4	21.2	25.7	34.2	100
V	3.5	9.7	14.6	24.1	48.2	100

How to read this table: Each cell shows the highest level of reading achieved by a child. For example, in Class III, 8.5 per cent children cannot even read letters, 22.9 per cent can read letters but not more, 28.4 per cent can read words but not Class-I texts or higher, 21.5 per cent can read Class-I texts but not Class-II level texts, and 18.8 per cent can read Class-II level texts. In sum, for each class, the total of all these exclusive categories is 100 per cent.
Source: ASER (2011).

Table 5.11 lays out the following reality: in Class IV, 34 per cent children can read at Class II level (some of these children may be able to read at higher levels too, but ASER administers a 'floor' test and it is not possible to assess whether these children are at Class IV level). 25.7 per cent children can read Class I-level text but not higher. The remaining fraction of children — almost 40 per cent — cannot read even a sentence. However, the Class IV language textbook in any state in India has difficult and long content, which according to the ASER results would be well beyond the reach of a large majority of all children.

Once this problem becomes visible and is accepted, solutions can be designed. For example, an impact evaluation study by Abdul Jamil Poverty Action Lab (JPAL), in a programme run jointly by Pratham and Bihar government, finds that the gains in learning during the school year were very minimal (see Banerjee and Duflo 2011). But, when the same teachers taught in a special summer camp, the learning gains for the targeted children were significant (see ibid.: 94). The summer camp organised under the programme was designed for children in Classes III–V who were not yet at Class II level of reading and arithmetic (the special one-month summer programme was launched by the Bihar government in 2008). The teaching–learning package (developed by Pratham) focused on teaching children at the level they were, enabling them to become fluent readers and become proficient in basic number knowledge and operations. This suggests that when children are grouped by levels rather than by classes and taught accordingly, their learning improves.[13] This is a major and serious recommendation that has been generated by recent experience and evidence.

The second message from recent research has to do with the role of supplemental help. Since 2000, Massachusetts Institute of Technology (MIT)'s Poverty Action Lab has been evaluating different aspects of Pratham's work using randomised control trials (See Banerjee et al. 2007, 2010; Banerjee and Duflo 2011). In over 10 years, and across several impact evaluations of Pratham's work in different parts of India, the one significant influence on children's learning that comes across as strong and consistent is the role of village volunteers.

Having figured out which children need extra help, Pratham provides a set of straightforward solutions that have been implemented on scale in India. The organisation recognises that children learn not only in schools but also outside the schools. And both in school and at home or in the community, children who need extra help need to be given time. As described earlier, teachers need to be oriented to work with these children and schools are required to be organised differently to make this happen. Pratham via its Read India Programme has participated in many large-scale partnerships with state governments to jointly implement learning programmes. In addition, it is very important that in the community people need to be catalysed to give children the extra help that they need. In the peak period of the Read India Programme, village volunteers (who were not paid) worked with children in half of all villages in India. Simple and effective methods of teaching were used to accelerate learning. Affordable and appropriate materials were given to children. Simple measurement was used to track children's progress. This basic package of methods, materials and measurement forms the core of Pratham's Read India Programme.[14] New and innovative strategies both in teaching–learning methods and materials and in organising people have to be devised on scale. 'More of the same' will not lead to sustained results. In addition to energising schools, engagement of communities on scale is needed to change the learning status of India's children.

Thus, in thinking ahead, to help children 'catch up' and bridge the 'learning gap' the focus needs to be on the two real challenges of improving educational outcomes. One, the challenge is not to continue to debate how schooling is provided, instead it is to think of how schools, whether private or government, can be organised differently so that children can be taught from the level where they are today and enabled to reach where they need to be. Two, instead of focusing only on the school as the location of learning, one should think about integrating and maximising the impact of additional supplemental help that children need and get.

NOTES

1. ASER is a household survey usually conducted in October and November every year, which is the middle of a school year in most states of India. The sample size ranges from 500,000– 700,000 children in the 3–16 age group. Every child, who is 5 years old or above, is asked to answer a set of simple questions about his or her enrolment status and the type of school they go to; each child is also given basic reading and arithmetic tasks that are carried out on a one-on-one basis. ASER provides a unique opportunity to look back over the last seven years and track the trends in schooling and learning in India. Since 2006, each year ASER has surveyed a representative sample of children (age 3–16) from every rural district in the country.

2. Other sources of data also document the rapid increase of private schooling in India. For example, the India Human Development Survey (IHDS) published in 2010 collected data from a nationally representative sample of almost 42,000 rural and urban households in 2004–5. The report states that 'one of the most striking things about the educational panorama in the last decade has been explosion of the private sector in the educational field' (Desai et al. 2010: 82). The report notes that the Fifth All India Education Survey had recorded a 'bare 2 [per cent] attendance in private schools in 1986' (ibid.). The IHDS data shows that 21 per cent of rural and 51 per cent of urban children are enrolled in private schools. A previous round of the same IHDS survey conducted in 1994 had found only 10 per cent children from rural households enrolled in private schools.

3. Government of India's District Information System for Education (DISE) data provides numbers of aided and unaided schools in each state.

    IHDS 2004–5 attempted to collect more refined information from households for type of school than has been attempted in ASER. See Table 6.1 (Desai et al. 2010: 82). According to this data, 72 per cent children are enrolled in government schools and 28 per cent in private schools. Broken down further, for the age group 6–14, 67 per cent children go to government schools, 5 per cent to government-aided schools, 24 per cent to privately managed schools, 5 per cent to *madrassas*, convents or other types of schools.

4. Data on 'tuition' was collected for the first time in ASER (2007). The data suggests that for Classes I–VIII, 20 per cent of government school children and 24 per cent of private school children in rural India took 'tuition'.

    IHDS 2004–5 finds that across their rural and urban sample, 20 per cent of children in the 6–14 age group received some form of private tutoring in the year before the survey (Desai et al. 2010: 82).

    Rohini Somanathan and Michael Walton (2012) are working on this issue as well. They presented a paper at the India Growth Centre (IGC) conference in Bihar in early 2012.

5. This village is covered under Pratham's Read India Programme in which youth volunteers work in each village with children who are lagging behind academically. These volunteers do not

get any financial remuneration for their time. However, an integral part of the programme is a component called Education for Education — anyone who gives time for children in the village will be eligible for a learning opportunity. In the case of Pratham's work in West Bengal, youth volunteers get a course in basic digital literacy and spoken English.

6. IHDS 2004–5 finds that in their sample of 6–14-year-olds (rural and urban) about 40 per cent participated in private sector education, either through enrolment in private school, through private tuition or both (Desai et al. 2010).

7. The term 'big stuck' has been coined by Lant Pritchett. His position regarding shallow learning curves has been laid out in Pritchett and Beatty (2012) and also in ASER 2011 national report.

8. The supply-side factors influencing the emergence of the private school option in rural areas include the availability of educated young women in labour force in the local area, government infrastructure, road connectivity, etc. Chudgar (2012) uses ASER 2009 data and looks at a variety of village-level correlates to construct a broader landscape in which the private and government school differences in learning outcomes can be studied.

9. Table 5.3 summarises the national situation. The data in the table refers to the percentage of children getting tuition within each category — government school children and private school children. The national aggregate table hides state-level variations. Table 5.4 gives variations by state and uses a class (Class IV) as an example. Here too the data refers to percentages within each category of children (government and private). Table 5.8 also summarises the national situation but in a different way to that in other tables. Here the denominator is all children and therefore government school children dominate.

10. ASER 2010 data has been used here rather than 2011, mainly because the trends for the past few years held steady around this year. Up until 2010, the learning profiles in most states, although low and shallow, were quite unchanging over time. The ASER 2011 data shows a downward trend in learning levels across many states especially in government schools. The reasons for this learning loss is yet to be understood; This visible 'learning loss' and its reasons have to be understood better — is it a one year drop or the beginning of a secular decline? Only data from ASER 2012 will be able to provide clues. So, for now, Table 5.9 uses ASER 2010 data to lay out the differences between the kinds of schools and tuition patterns.

11. Here 'advantaged' refers to a combination of household education, income and aspirations. In addition, given that private schools can be selective for admission, the self selection into private schools may have an ability bias as well.

12. In ASER, the most difficult reading task that a child is asked to do is read a paragraph Class II-level of difficulty. So, when it is stated that 50 per cent of Class V children in a state are reading at Class II level, one is not sure what proportion of these children are reading at Class V level.

13. In this context, does something happen in private schools that is different from government schools? There is very little data investigating such issues for private schools but we can conjecture that apart from the issue of self-selection and parental advantage that private school children have, it is possible that class repetition is more likely in private schools as is the possibility that children who are not performing well academically are not encouraged to continue in the school.

14. Currently Pratham's Read India Programme is active in 250 districts across India in blocks of 100 villages each. It is estimated that approximately 40,000 village volunteers work with close to a million children on a daily basis.

References

Andrabi, Tahir, Jishnu Das and Asim Ijaz Khwaja. 2008. 'A Dime a Day: The Possibilities and Limits of Private Schooling in Pakistan'. *Comparative Education Review*, 52(3): 329–55.

Annual Status of Education Report (ASER). 2005–11. *Annual Status of Education Report*. New Delhi: ASER Centre/Pratham. http://www.asercentre.org (accessed 18 October 2012)

Banerjee, Abhijit and Esther Duflo. 2011. *Poor Economics*. New York: Public Affairs.

Banerjee, Abhijit, Shawn Cole, Esther Duflo, and Leigh Linden. 2007. 'Remedying Education: Evidence from Two Randomized Experiments in India', *Quarterly Journal of Economics*, 122(3): 1235–64.

Banerjee, Abhijit, Rukmini Banerji, Esther Duflo, Rachel Glennerster, and Stuti Khemani. 2010. 'Pitfalls of Participatory Progress: Evidence from a Randomized Evaluation in Education in India', *American Economic Journal: Economic Policy*, February, 2(1): 1–30.

Chavan, Madhav. 2011. 'The Unseen Change', in *Annual Status of Education Report 2011*. New Delhi: ASER Centre/Pratham.

Chudgar, Amita. 2012. 'Variation in Private School Performance: The Importance of Village Context', *Economic and Political Weekly*. 12 March, XLVII(11): 52–59.

Desai, Sonalde, Amaresh Dubey, Brij Lal Joshi, Mitali Sen, Abusaleh Shariff, and Reeve Vanneman. 2010. *Human Development in India*. New Delhi: Oxford University Press.

Mukerji, Shobhini and Wilima Wadhwa. 2011. 'Do Private Schools Perform better than Public Schools? Evidence from Rural India'. Working Paper, ASER Centre/Pratham, New Delhi.

Muralidharan, Karthik. 2012. 'Priorities for Primary Education Policy in India's 12th Five Year Plan'. Paper presented at the 'India Policy Forum', National Council of Applied Economic Research (NCAER)-Brookings Institution, 17–18 July, New Delhi.

Muralidharan, Karthik and Michael Kremer. 2006. 'Public and Private Schools in Rural India'. Working Paper, Massachusetts Institute of Technology, Cambridge, MA.

Pal, S. 2010. 'Public Infrastructure, Location of Private Schools and Primary School Attainment in an Emerging Economy', *Economics of Education Review*, 29(3): 783–94.

Pritchett, Lant and Amanda Beatty. 2012. 'The Negative Consequences of Overambitious Curricula in Developing Countries'. Working Paper, Harvard Kennedy School of Government.

Somanathan, Rohini and Michael Walton. 2012. Presentation in IGC Conference, Patna, Bihar.

Wadhwa, Wilima. 2009. 'Private Schools: Do They Provide Higher Quality Education?', *Annual Status of Education Report*. New Delhi: Pratham Resource Centre and ASER Centre.

6 | From the Right to Schooling to the Right to Learning

Towards a New Frontier for Governing Elementary Education Finances in India

Yamini Aiyar

SETTING THE CONTEXT

In the last few years, the Indian government has substantially increased its financial allocations to elementary education. According to latest figures available from the Ministry of Human Resource Development (MHRD), between 2007–8 and 2009–10, India's elementary education budget increased from ₹687,100 million to ₹972,550 million in 2009–10. With the launch of the Right to Education (RTE) in April 2010, the elementary education budget has increased further. Allocations for Sarva Shiksha Abhiyan (SSA) alone have more than doubled since 2009–10, from ₹26,169 to ₹55,746 in 2011–12.[1] While this increased expenditure has resulted in improved inputs, India has now reached near universal enrolment and basic school infrastructure has been built (almost every habitation in the country now has a school building), learning levels remain low.[2] In fact, there seems to be a weak link between the quantum of finances allocated to elementary education and learning outcomes achieved. A recent study on elementary education finances compared per-child budgetary allocations across seven states in India, with the ability of Class V children in these states to read a Class II textbook, and found absolutely no link between budgetary allocations and learning levels.[3] In 2010–11, Maharashtra, for instance, allocated ₹12,075 per child, while Andhra Pradesh allocated ₹8,390. However, learning levels for both states were somewhat similar — 64 per cent Class V children in Maharashtra, and 60 per cent in Andhra Pradesh, could read a Class II textbook. The story remains unchanged even among poorer states in India. Rajasthan, for instance, allocated ₹9,192 per child in 2010–11 while Bihar allocated ₹4,705 per child. However, Bihar's learning levels are significantly better than Rajasthan's — 50 per cent children in Class V were able to read a Class II textbook in Bihar compared with 43 per cent in Rajasthan.

These statistics clearly point to India's greatest challenge — strengthening the link between increased outlays and improved learning outcomes to build an education system that is accountable for learning. Addressing this challenge is all the more urgent in the context of the RTE Act, 2009. At the heart of the law is a guarantee to ensure 'age-appropriate mainstreaming' for all children. In other words, the Act is a guarantee that every child in India acquires skills and knowledge appropriate for her age. Thus, a Class V student should be able to read a Class V textbook. Therefore, by guaranteeing age-appropriate learning, the RTE has shifted the goalpost away from input provision to learning achievement.[4] The challenge lies in meeting this goal.

Now as efforts to deliver on this guarantee gain ground and financial allocations are on the rise, the question that needs to be asked is this: can the current system for financing elementary education in India deliver on the RTE promise? The RTE envisages a decentralised model for delivering the learning agenda. According to the MHRD's (2011b) framework for implementing SSA, the RTE requires

[the] creation of capacity within the education system and the school for addressing the diversified learning needs of different groups of children who are now in the schooling system ... planning and implementation for universal access in the rights-based approach would require an understanding of community needs and circumstances as well as decentralized decision-making for meeting the diversified needs of children (ibid.).

To facilitate this decentralised decision-making, the Act mandates the creation of School Management Committees (SMCs) tasked with monitoring school functioning and developing annual school development plans (SDPs). Can the current system of planning and budgeting for SSA support this transition envisaged in RTE? In other words, can a decentralised system evolve by pouring more finances into the current system? If not, how should education resources be channelised in order that decentralised planning can be facilitated?

The first step to answering this question is to understand the status quo. This paper draws on findings from the Planning, Allocations and Expenditures, Institutions: Studies in Accountability (PAISA) district studies (Accountability Initiative 2011) to analyse the current financing system. These studies are based on a detailed analysis of Government of India (GoI) and state government planning and budgeting documents in seven states (Andhra Pradesh, Bihar, Himachal Pradesh, Madhya Pradesh, Maharashtra, Rajasthan, and West Bengal) of the country as well as a district-wise school-level sample survey undertaken in nine districts of these seven states.[5] Through the PAISA findings, this paper argues that the current system for financing elementary education is extremely centralised leaving little discretion and decision-making power at the school management level. Therefore, simply increasing financial allocations in the system is unlikely to facilitate the decentralised implementation envisaged by the RTE. This would require a fundamental re-hauling of the current financing, planning and budgeting system. The paper ends with a brief set of recommendations pointing to reforms that could facilitate this re-haul.

At the outset it is important to state that this paper does not attempt to pass judgement on whether decentralisation or greater autonomy at the school level is the only or even the appropriate mechanism for strengthening the link between financial outlays and learning outcomes.[6] The starting point of this paper is the RTE's mandate to decentralise education delivery through SMCs. Given this mandate, this paper is an effort to answer the question of how best to implement this decentralised model for the RTE.

THE PLANNING AND BUDGETING SYSTEM

Before unpacking the current status of education finance it is important to first understand the institutional arrangements and processes that have been put in place for planning and budgeting for elementary education. This section briefly sketches the key features of the planning and budgeting system for elementary education in India.

Budgetary Allocations

Elementary education is primarily financed by state government revenues channelled through state education line departments.[7] The bulk of the state budget is used to fund salaries and administrative expenses. On average, in the seven PAISA states, between 2009–11, teacher salaries accounted for 75–80 per cent of state governments' financial contribution to elementary education.

The GoI's financial contribution to elementary education is through the SSA, the current programmatic vehicle for implementing RTE. The SSA is a centrally sponsored scheme and is structured such that both GoI and state governments contribute to its financial pool. At present, GoI's expected contribution is 65 per cent, while state governments are expected to contribute the remaining 35 per cent. In addition, state governments draw on funds from the special component plan for Scheduled Castes (SCs) and the Tribal Sub-Plan to finance elementary education-related activities targeted at specific beneficiary groups. State budgetary expenditure also includes statutory transfers determined by the 13th Finance Commission which awarded ₹240,000 million to support implementation of RTE between 2010–15.

The Fund-Flow Structure

State government finances are transferred directly from the state treasury account to the education line department for state-level expenditure. All district expenses are transferred to designated officers at the district level (Drawing and Disbursement Officers or DDOs) who are responsible for incurring relevant expenditures. Allocations are determined through the annual state budgetary process.

The fund-flow system for SSA is more complex. The funds do not flow through the state treasury (see Figure 6.1). At the state level, SSA is administered and implemented through specifically created State Implementation Societies (SIS) whose bank accounts fall outside the state treasury. Once budgets are approved, the MHRD instructs the Reserve Bank of India (RBI) to transfer the agreed amount to the respective SIS. The entire process ought to take a minimum of 15 days to be completed. State governments are also expected to transfer their share of funds to the SIS immediately.

Funds are transferred in two instalments. The first instalment — known as an ad hoc grant — is expected to be released in April, at the start of the financial year. The quantum of money released is based on various factors, including state expenditure performance in the previous year. It amounts to approximately 25 per cent of the total SSA budget for the state in a given year. The second instalment is released in September; it depends on the fulfilment of the following two conditions:

(a) Transfer of the state government share to the SIS. This is to be made within 30 days of receipt of the GoI share; and

(b) 60 per cent utilisation of funds.

Once funds arrive at the district bank account from the SIS, the district is expected to transfer funds to schools (based on school-specific entitlements) within 15 days of receipt.

Funds can reach school bank accounts in two ways:

(a) Direct Transfers: From the SIS to school bank accounts (common in states with good banking facilities).

(b) Through the District and Block: This process tends to be manual and funds are transferred using cheques (though some states have shifted to the system of electronic transfers).

The Planning Process

To enable this financial system, the SSA has put in place an annual plan process (also referred to as the Annual Work Plan and Budget or AWP&B). In its intent, this plan process is aimed at facilitating decentralised decision-making. According to SSA guidelines, the AWP&B process begins at the habitation level, with SMCs preparing an SDP. Plans made at this level are compiled by the planning team at the block level. The block-level plans are sent to the district level where they are consolidated and appraised by the district planning team into a district-level AWP&B. These district AWP&Bs are then sent to the state level for the formulation of the state AWP&B (SSA 2010). The state-level AWP&B is an aggregation of the district Annual Work Plan (AWP) and is expected to provide an overview of the state's vision, interventions in different functional areas and the strategy of state's support to the district.

To ensure that the planning process is completed before the end of the financial year, SSA guidelines prescribe a timetable for the preparation of the state AWP&B. In accordance with the calendar, the visioning exercise and planning of activities at the district level are required to be completed by 1 January every year. The state-level AWP&Bs are to be prepared and submitted to the MHRD. At the MHRD, states' plans are appraised through a Planning and Budgeting (PAB) negotiation process. This process begins in February and ends in May every year. Final budgets allocated to states are based on the outcome of the PAB process.

UNPACKING EDUCATION FINANCE: AN OVERVIEW OF PAISA FINDINGS

As the brief overview of the financing and planning process indicates, the SSA is designed to facilitate decentralised

FIGURE 6.1   The Financing Structure

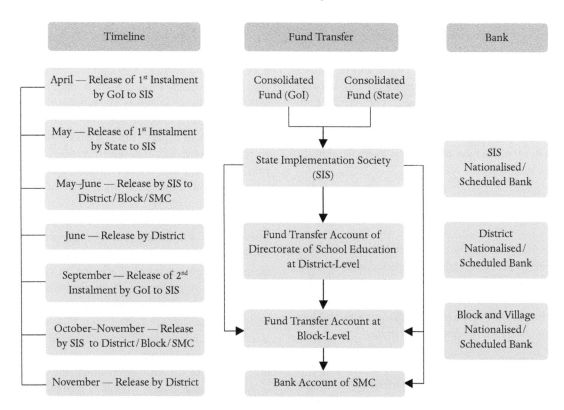

Source: Prepared by the author.

planning and decision-making. In this section, we draw on PAISA findings that have been used to examine ground realities and understand how this design works in practice (Accountability Initiative 2011).

Resource Allocation

As mentioned in the previous section, the state government funds the bulk of the elementary education budget. However, in the long run, we may see a shift in this trend with SSA becoming the dominant financier of elementary education. This is on account of the increased allocations to SSA, consequent to RTE. PAISA analysis highlights that between 2009–10 and 2010–11 SSA's contribution as a proportion of the total education budget of a state (including the state budget) increased by 9 percentage points from 31 per cent in 2009–10 to 40 per cent in 2010–11. Given that the GoI contributes to as much as 65 per cent of the SSA, increased financing through the programme could, in the long run, result in curbing state discretion by reflecting GoI priorities over state government priorities. A close reading of the PAB meeting minutes points in this direction. The case of Bihar's PAB negotiation for 2010–11 illustrates this best. In 2005, Bihar initiated a number of direct entitlement schemes, such as uniform provision, scholarships and cycles to encourage enrolment and reduce dropout rates. With the launch of the RTE, in 2010 SSA too introduced a number of such schemes each with its own budget. Given that Bihar was already implementing these schemes, when the state made its proposed budget for 2010, it chose not to allocate much money to children's entitlement schemes. In the final negotiation however, because of specific requirements in the RTE, which had a budget for entitlements that needed to be spent, the GoI increased the state's entitlement budget by a whopping 210 per cent over what was proposed. Unsurprisingly, much of this went unspent.

Resource Prioritisation

How are elementary education finances prioritised across different activities? To answer this question, PAISA 2011 analysed the entire elementary budget (including both state government and SSA contributions) across key education activities for 2009–10 and 2010–11. Broadly, PAISA found that on average, 77 per cent of the education budget is invested in teachers and management costs. Following this, the next largest investment is on the creation of school infrastructure — 15 per cent of the budget. The quantum of money going to infrastructure has increased substantively post the RTE. Interventions aimed directly at children, such as the provision of free textbooks and uniforms and addressing the problem of out-of-school children, account for 7 per cent of the total investment. Quality-related activities, specifically the innovation and learning enhancement programme under SSA, account for 1 per cent of the total investment.

Resource availability in schools: Schools receive relatively little by way of an annual budget over which they have direct expenditure control. Under SSA, all schools across the country are entitled to three annual school grants: *(a)* Maintenance Grant (SMG); *(b)* Development Grant (SDG); and *(c)* Teaching Learning Material Grant (TLM). In 2010–11, these grants accounted for 5 per cent of the SSA budget.

However, even though schools have expenditure control over these funds, these grants arrive in schools with very clear expenditure guidelines set by the GoI. The SMG is for infrastructure upkeep, the SDG is meant for operation and administration and TLM for extra instructional aids. These guidelines are so rigid that if a school wants to set its own priorities, for instance, to invest more in improving children's reading capabilities by dipping in to its maintenance fund — it cannot. The quantum of money provided to schools is also based on norms determined by GoI. This, inevitably, results in a mismatch between school conditions and needs and the funds received. To illustrate the point, an old school with significant maintenance needs and a student population of over 1,000 students is entitled to just about three times the grant amount that a school constructed in 2007 with 100 students and relatively fewer maintenance needs receives (for a detailed description of the problem, see Accountability Initiative 2009).

In addition to grants, schools also receive funds for infrastructure work. However, they have no decision-making control over these expenditures. For instance, infrastructure monies arrive in schools for specific construction purposes (such as boundary wall or new classrooms). Schools have the authority to 'demand' infrastructure. But the final decision on the nature of infrastructure work to be undertaken and the amount of money that ought to be devolved lies with the district. The district, in turn, decides on the basis of fund availability and priorities set by the state government. The SMC is expected to contribute to the actual construction process — key responsibilities include procurement of materials and provision of labour.

How do Funds Flow to Schools?

How do budgetary allocations translate into action on the ground? The first step to answering this question is to track the processes through which funds flow from their point of origin to their final destination — schools. This section draws on PAISA 2011 findings to examine fund-flows. Owing to paucity of data on state budgets, the focus of the analysis is on SSA funds.

Significant Gap between Funds Allocated and Funds Released

No state in the PAISA sample received its entire share of funds in 2009–10 and 2010–11 (see Table 6.1). The quantum of funds received varies widely across states. Himachal Pradesh and Rajasthan received the largest proportion of their allocation while Bihar received the least.

TABLE 6.1   Percentage of Allocated Funds Released (State)

State	2009–10	2010–11
Andhra Pradesh	42	64
Bihar	49	53
Himachal Pradesh	84	91
Madhya Pradesh	81	73
Rajasthan	86	83
Maharashtra	68	63

Source: Right to Information (RTI) applications filed by PAISA team. See Accountability Initiative (2011).

Inefficiencies in expenditure management are the primary reason for this gap. As mentioned, both GoI and state governments contribute to SSA funds. Apart from the ad hoc grant, GoI releases are contingent upon state governments' releasing their share of the SSA allocation. In most states, we find that state governments have been slow to release their share of SSA funds. In fact, the gap between the total amount of finances that the state government ought to release and the actual share of finances released is much larger than the gap between the total GoI contribution and actual amount released. Interestingly, this trend reversed in 2010–11, as state governments began to put in a greater share while the GoI share declined. Bihar is an important exception where the state government has consistently released a greater proportion of its funds than GoI. In 2010, for instance, the Bihar state government released 65 per cent of its share while GoI released only 46 per cent.

Gaps in fund receipt at the state level have a knock-on effect on the quantum of money received at the district level (see Table 6.2). Between 2009–10 and 2010–11, only three districts — Kangra, Himachal Pradesh, and Jaipur and Udaipur, Rajasthan — received close to 90 per cent or more of their allocations. All other districts received half or less.

One reason for low release is that state governments often incur expenditures on behalf of districts. Consequently, funds, although allocated to the district, are never actually transferred to the district account. To explain, in Sagar district, Madhya Pradesh, for instance, close to 60 per cent of the total district expenditure is booked under an expenditure head called State Project Office or SPO (the state name for the SSA society). Analysis of this expenditure head reveals

that the bulk of these funds are allocated to teacher salaries and civil works. The civil works monies account for 50 per cent of the district civil works budget. Civil works funds are directly released by the state society to *panchayat* accounts, thereby bypassing the district. Teacher salaries are also directly deposited into teacher accounts. Arguably, this appropriation of district funds by the state suggests that the district has limited flexibility or decision-making power over key activities.

TABLE 6.2   Percentage of Allocated Funds Released (District)

District	2009–10	2010–11
Medak	47	66
Nalanda	43	45
Purnea	50	51
Kangra	90	84
Sagar	NA	35
Satara	60	72
Jaipur	99	92
Udaipur	89	88
Jalpaiguri	66	52

Source: RTIs filed by PAISA team. See PAISA (2011).

Bunching of Fund Transfers to the End of the Financial Year

While fund-flows from GoI and the state are meant to be released to the state society in two instalments between the first and third quarters of the financial year, in practice, the bulk of the money is released towards the end of the financial year.[8] As highlighted in Table 6.3, in 2009, states such as Andhra Pradesh, Bihar and Maharashtra received half or just under half of their finances for the year in the last quarter, between January and March. Fund-flows improved significantly in 2010. Unsurprisingly, delays in fund transfers at the state level also result in delays at the district level.

Gaps and Delays in Grant Receipts at the School Level

Data collected through the school survey points out that on average, 76 per cent of schools received their annual school grants. However, a school is not guaranteed to receive a grant every year. To illustrate, 27 per cent schools received the TLM grant in only one of the two years under consideration. Similarly, 28 per cent and 27 per cent schools received the SDG and SMG grants in only one of the two years respectively.

The survey also points to significant delays in fund-flows at the school level. On average, schools received their grants by the end of September or early October in both years — a good six months after the school year begins.

TABLE 6.3 Fund Transfers till Quarters 3 and 4 as Percentage of Total Allocation

| States | Funds Transferred till Quarter 3 (in per cent) | | | | Funds Transferred till Quarter 4 (in per cent) | | | |
| | 2009–10 | | 2010–11 | | 2009–10 | | 2010–11 | |
	GoI	State	GoI	State	GoI	State	GoI	State
Andhra Pradesh	19	19	38	80	55	23	55	80
Bihar	17	47	46	36	47	52	46	65
Madhya Pradesh	73	38	61	58	84	77	69	82
Rajasthan	83	63	66	79	94	74	71	105
Maharashtra	66	0	37	57	78	54	63	63
Himachal Pradesh	78	37	40	42	78	96	83	96

Source: RTIs filed by Accountability Initiative.

Headmasters cope with these delays in various ways. They either use leftover funds from previous years or those received from community contributions to purchase essential items. In one school in Jaipur district, the teachers pooled their TLM funds from the previous year to meet daily expenditures till the year's funds arrived. On occasion, headmasters use their own money to purchase essential supplies. Once funds arrive, schools reimburse themselves and adjust the books accordingly. Such practices, while they enable schools to get by till they receive their funds, do result in serious accountability problems that contribute to the accountability deficit at the school level.

Expenditures: Do Schools Spend their Money?

Significant Under-Spending and Bunching of Expenditures at the District Level

Overall, across districts spending varies widely from 50 per cent to 100 per cent (see Table 6.4). When monies are spent, it usually occurs at the end of the financial year. This is largely a consequence of delays in fund release to the district.

TABLE 6.4 District-Level Expenditures

District	Percentage Spent Out of Allocation (2009–10)	Percentage Spent Out of Allocation (2010–11)
Medak	84	NA
Kangra	88	80
Satara	96	86
Sagar	69	100
Nalanda	53	50
Purnea	50	55
Jaipur	99	93
Udaipur	86	84
Jalpaigudi	NA	77

Source: Monthly expenditure statements obtained from the respective district.

Expenditure trends reveal a clear prioritisation of expenditures on administrative (teacher salaries) and infrastructure-related activities. Much of the under-spending can be found in line items related to training, provision of entitlements to children and quality-specific activities.

There is an important caveat to district-level expenditures on infrastructure. As mentioned previously, the district is not responsible for actual expenditures on infrastructure creation. This is the responsibility of the SMC. The district, therefore, releases infrastructure monies to school bank accounts and books them in its monthly reports as expenditures.

In practice, schools are slow to undertake infrastructure activities. This is partly a consequence of the cumbersome procedures involved in spending infrastructure monies — works need to be sanctioned and approved from authorities outside the Department of Education, such as the State Public Works Department; issues such as land access need to be negotiated; and finally, competent authorities need to provide a certificate of approval. All this requires coordination between multiple administrative authorities causing delays in getting works started. In fact, the PAISA school survey reveals that despite high expenditures on infrastructure at the district level for 2009–10 and 2010–11, most schools had not started construction activities in 2010–11.

From the school's point of view, these procedures can be intimidating and even when approvals are given, act as a disincentive for spending. One headmaster in Medak district, Andhra Pradesh, informed PAISA surveyors that headmasters lack a proper understanding of the procedures involved in spending infrastructure monies and thus prefer to whitewash walls rather than spend large amounts on big infrastructure construction. Empirical data suggests that this is the case in most schools in India. The PAISA National Survey (Accountability Initiative 2012) reveals that as many as 68 per cent schools across the country whitewashed their walls in 2011![9]

Delays in Spending School Grants at the School Level

Expenditures in schools are slow. At minimum there is a 60-day time lag between the day a school receives a grant and the day it starts spending its money. But once spending begins, schools utilise the bulk of the money they receive: 90 per cent schools that received their grants report spending all their money in both financial years tracked.

Analysis of spending patterns, however, highlights that schools have limited discretion over how they spend their grants. Anecdotal evidence collected during the PAISA survey reveals that schools are given formal and informal orders from higher authorities on how to spend their money. In Jaipur, for instance, an official directive was issued requesting all schools to use the SDG (also known as School Facility Grant) to purchase furniture. The school in question had no requirement for furniture but was told by local officials to do so because of the directive. Schools in Purnea, Bihar, reported similar stories. In one instance, the district approved a request from some schools to use their development grant to purchase a storage cupboard. This was interpreted at the frontline as an order for all schools and regardless of need schools were made to spend their grant buying the cupboard. In another case, schools were made to buy fire safety equipment, even schools that had yet to receive their school building grant! These anecdotes point to a systemic problem — the absence of discretion creates a complete disconnect between school-articulated need and actual expenditures. Schools can thus legitimately claim that they have no responsibility over meeting school needs, thereby significantly compromising accountability.

Summary and Conclusions

One broad conclusion that can be drawn from the PAISA 2011 analysis is that elementary education financing is designed such that despite the intent to decentralise, in practice, planning and expenditure decision-making authority rests with higher levels of government resulting in a centralised rather than decentralised system. As discussed, schools and SMCs have expenditure control over relatively small amounts of money and even for these funds, de facto, decisions tend to be taken by block- and district-level authorities. This is the anti-thesis of decentralisation.

With the increased role of SSA in financing elementary education, this centralised system runs into the danger of curbing State government discretion in planning and decision-making over elementary education finances. PAISA 2011 analysis of PAB minutes points to this trend. But a second consequence of this increased SSA financing is that state plan funds for elementary education are now increasingly being used to finance the state share component of SSA,

leaving them with little money to plan and design schemes suited to the state's own socio-political needs.

This trend towards centralisation is further exacerbated by governance deficits in implementation and expenditure management. PAISA 2011 is a story of delays and gaps in fund-flows across all levels of government. These delays create a lot of unpredictability in the funding cycle rendering decentralised planning ineffective. Worryingly, delays in fund flows also create pressures to spend, resulting in a last minute rush that further serves to delink plans from expenditures.

Given this scenario, if the RTE mandate to decentralise planning and decision-making is to be implemented then the current financing system will have to undergo a radical overhaul. The challenge lies in designing a financing system that is aligned to a decentralised delivery system.

CONCLUSION: TOWARDS A NEW FRAMEWORK FOR GOVERNING EDUCATION FINANCES

Proponents of decentralisation in India argue that a well-designed decentralisation system is premised on the alignment of 'three Fs': Funds, Functions and Functionaries. In essence, this means that every level of government must have a clearly delegated set of responsibilities or functions. This process of delegation must be based on the principle of subsidiarity which holds that 'functions shall be carried out closest to citizens at the smallest unit of governance possible and delegated upwards only when the local unit cannot perform the task'. Second, funds must follow functions. However, these funds must be devolved in a manner that allows enough flexibility to local bodies to align expenditures to expressed needs and preferences. Third, functionaries (or the actual service providers) must be accountable to the body responsible for delivering that function (see, for instance, GoI 2007; Rao 2007; World Bank 2006).

How can this alignment of the three Fs be achieved in the context of elementary education? There is remarkably little by way of academic or policy research that directly addresses this question, with only one exception — Lant Pritchett and Varad Pande's work (2006), which draws on first principles of public finance and accountability to design a decentralised model for elementary education delivery that allocates functional responsibility across levels of government such that accountability and efficiency are optimised. Pritchett and Pande argue that effective decentralisation requires more than simply devolving an entire sector to a lower tier of government. Rather, each sector needs to be unbundled into its sub-components or functions. Once unbundled, functions ought to be assigned to different levels of government guided by first principles of public finance and accountability.

The first step in their analysis therefore is to unbundle elementary education into distinct activities. Accordingly, education activities fall into the following five categories: standard setting (curriculum design and setting learning goals); planning; asset creation; operations (asset maintenance, enrolment, and teachers); and monitoring and evaluation. When first principles are applied, standard setting and monitoring and evaluation emerge as the primary responsibilities of the central and state governments. Functions such as planning, asset creation and day-to-day control of school operations ought to be the responsibility of local governments. In particular, they argue that control over school operations, including recurrent expenditures, teacher management (assignment, performance evaluation), monitoring school-level performance, should be handed over directly to the lowest level of government (the *gram panchayat* or an SMC). Accountability can be enhanced by creating clear performance measures, monitoring of which remains in the control of the respective state and the central government. With the state government freed from any day-to-day responsibility of running schools, monitoring and evaluation become their main responsibility. Pritchett and Pande argue that this focus on monitoring and evaluation is essential if decentralisation is to yield improvements in outcomes. In this framing, the districts' primary functional responsibilities are planning, coordination of asset creation, and providing technical and pedagogical support to teachers.[10]

Through their work, Pritchett and Pande provide a useful starting point for designing a financing system that is aligned to functional responsibilities. Their framework clearly indicates the set of activities that ought to be performed at the school level. This could act as the guide for determining the quantum of money that ought to be devolved to SMCs. Crucial to ensuring effective decentralisation is the process through which finances are transferred to lower levels of government. As mentioned, autonomy and flexibility are the two essential features of a well-designed, decentralised financial structure. Transparency is the third feature, which is essential, first, because it can ensure that all levels of government understand their financial entitlements and therefore safeguard against funds being re-appropriated by higher levels. Second, transparency can ensure effective monitoring both by higher levels of government and, perhaps more important, by citizens. Four key reform steps emerge from these principles.[11]

Providing Untied Block Grants to School Management Committees

As revealed by the PAISA 2011 study, the current system of financial transfers to schools is based on specific guidelines

that curb flexibility at the school level. The first reform needed is to redesign the transfer system away from this line-item-based devolution to an untied block grant system. The district could identify broad areas of expenditure (for instance, infrastructure, maintenance) but schools must be given the flexibility to spend on activities prioritised by them. Interestingly, the need for freeing school grants from the current norm-based approach has been well-recognised. In 2011, the MHRD's Joint Review Mission (MHRD's monitoring committee for SSA) recommended that the government move away from the current system, which they described as a 'one size fits all' method of determining grant allocations to a system that '…reflect(s) the student strength of the school rather than providing the same grant for all schools, a scale or "slab" system could be devised which would provide larger school grants for larger schools' (MHRD 2011a).

Simplify the Transfer System and Distribute Grants to Schools on a Per-Child Basis

Rather than transfer funds on complex criterion, such as the number of rooms in a school or teachers appointed, finances to schools should be devolved on a per-child enrolled basis. This would ensure simplicity in the transfer system and thereby facilitate greater transparency. Moreover, it would guarantee a greater correspondence with school needs than the current system enables. Finally, a simplified transaction system will also smoothen process-related inefficiencies that are often the cause of delays in fund-flows.

Building a Real-Time Management Information System that Tracks Expenditures

A real-time management information system (MIS) is critical to enabling transparency. Such a system could be modelled on the current MIS for the Mahatma Gandhi National Rural Employment Guarantee Act (MGNREGA) that enables detailed fund tracking all the way to the *gram panchayat*. Transparency will ensure that both district and local bodies have access to data on timing of fund-flows (thereby enhancing predictability), and also enable higher authorities to track the flow of funds regularly to identify and unlock process bottlenecks in real-time. This can go a long way in ensuring predictability in fund-flows. Crucially, this MIS system must be made publically accessible, so that citizens and SMCs are informed of financial processes and can succeed in enhancing transparency and accountability.

Predictability in Fund-Flows

Apart from measures already described, predictability in grant flows can be enhanced by building in a reward- and sanction-based incentive structure for fund transfers at the state and district level. This could include penalising sub-national governments that delay fund transfers by requiring them to pay schools an interest on delays.

Capacity-Building for Planning

The problem of weak capacity is one of the most frequently offered arguments against greater financial and functional devolution to local governments and SMCs. There is little argument that in their current form, SMCs have almost no planning skill and capacity. In fact, many studies on village education committees (the pre-RTE avatar of SMCs) point out that most often members are not even aware of their membership in these bodies. However, this is a chicken and egg argument; capacity cannot be built in a vacuum. In fact, with the absence of finances and powers there are no incentives for SMC members to participate in meetings and make plans. After all, why participate and plan if there is no authority to ensure implementation? Arguably, therefore, effective decentralisation is the first step to capacity-building. However, this needs to be accompanied by a concerted effort by higher levels of government to train and mobilise SMCs and, perhaps most importantly, facilitate them in making plans. Consequent to the RTE, every district now has a large financial allocation for community training and mobilisation. However, this line item is given very low priority and for the most part goes unspent. Placing a greater emphasis and priority on spending these funds and organising well-designed training for SMCs will be an important first step in addressing this capacity deficit.

To conclude, this paper examines the day-to-day implementation of SSA planning and budgeting systems. This analysis points to an increased trend towards centralisation of expenditure powers and decision-making, despite the RTE mandate for decentralised planning. Drawing on current experience, this paper makes the case that if the RTE mandate for decentralisation is to be achieved, the current planning and budgeting system for the SSA will require a radical overhaul. The reform proposals suggested here are one step in this direction.

Will greater and more effective decentralisation of elementary education lead to improved learning outcomes? No doubt, improving outcomes requires significant investments in many different aspects of the education system that extend beyond decentralisation. However, what a decentralised school management can ensure is increased parent engagement and ownership with the school, which in turn can encourage accountability to parents. This is the first critical step.

NOTES

1. The figures have been obtained from Government of India (GoI) planning and budgeting documents, available on http://ssa.nic.in/ (last accessed 30 October 2012). Allocation figures for 2011–12 are based on proposed allocations obtained from the Annual Work Plan and budget documents. The actual approved allocations were not publically available when this paper was written. For more details on SSA allocations, see Accountability Initiative (2012); Kapur and Chowdhury (2012).

2. In recent years there has been a slew of research studies ranging from the annual ASER survey, which has been tracking learning outcomes since 2005, to the recently released Programme for International Student Assessment (PISA 2009) all of which point to this problem of low learning achievement.

3. The learning outcomes data has been drawn from Annual Status of Education Report (ASER 2011).

4. Ironically, although the RTE sets age-appropriate learning as the goal, its prescription for meeting this goal is largely input-driven and most of its key provisions are aimed at meeting infrastructure goals rather than learning goals.

5. The PAISA district studies are undertaken annually by Accountability Initiative. For more details, see www.accountabilityindia.in (last accessed 30 October 2012). Study districts include: Medak, Andhra Pradesh; Nalanda and Purnea, Bihar; Kangra, Himachal Pradesh; Sagar, Madhya Pradesh; Sattara, Maharashtra; Jaipur and Udaipur, Rajasthan; and Jalpaigudi, West Bengal.

6. This is an important question but it is best answered in a separate research piece altogether.

7. State governments contribute a substantive 74 per cent to the total education budget (2009–10 estimates). For details see Kapur (2011).

8. The financial year in India is broken up into four quarters: Quarter 1: April–June; Quarter 2: July–September; Quarter 3: October–December; Quarter 4: January–March. The release is determined on the basis of the SSA financial manual.

9. The PAISA National report, reports on the annual PAISA survey the covers over 14,000 primary and upper primary schools across the country (Accountability Initiative 2012).

10. This distribution of functional responsibility has been adopted by the Administrative Reforms Commission in its recommendations for strengthening local government in India.

11. The focus of these reform suggestions are on fiscal transfers to local governments. However, as described in Pritchett and Pande's formulation, the district and block play an important role in planning, co-ordinating and most crucially supporting schools in making effective expenditure decisions. Thus, financial reforms are required to be undertaken at the district level as well. For paucity of space this has not been elaborated in this paper. However, broadly the same principles would apply to fiscal decentralisation at the district level.

REFERENCES

Annual Status of Education Report (ASER). 2011. 'Annual Survey of Education (Rural)'. http://www.asercentre.org/ngo-education-india.php?p=Spotlight%3A+ASER+2011 (accessed 5 November 2012).

Accountability Initiative. 2009. 'PAISA Briefs: A Tale of Two Schools: Untying Tied-Grants in SSA'. http://www.accountabilityindia.in/article/paisa-project-reports/794-paisa-briefs-tale-two-schools-untying-tied-grants-ssa (accessed 5 November 2012).

————. 2011. 'PAISA District Studies'. http://www.accountabilityindia.in/paisa_states (accessed 30 October 2012).

————. 2012. 'PAISA Report 2011'. http://www.accountabilityindia.in/article/state-report-cards/2475-paisa-report-2011 (accessed 30 October 2012).

Government of India (GoI). 2007. 'Local Governance'. Second Administrative Reforms Commission, October. http://arc.gov.in/6-1.pdf (accessed 5 November 2012).

Kapur, Avani. 2011. 'Analysis of State Budgets: Elementary Education'. Accountability Initiative and Azim Premji Foundation, Budget Briefs series. http://www.accountabilityindia.in/sites/default/files/budget-education/apf_-_study_of_state_budgets_brief_mar_7_yamain.pdf (accessed 5 November 2012).

Kapur, Avani and Anirvan Chowdhury. 2012. 'Budget Briefs: Sarva Shikha Abhayan, GOI 2012–13'. http://www.accountabilityindia.in/sites/default/files/sarva_shiksha_abhiyan_2012-13.pdf (accessed 30 October 2012).

Ministry of Human Resource Development (MHRD). 2011a. '14th Joint Review Mission'. http://ssa.nic.in/monitoring/joint-review-mission-ssa-1/joint-review-mission-ssa (accessed 30 October 2012).

————. 2011b. 'Sarva Shiksha Abhiyan: Framework of Implementation'. http://www.opepa.in/Download/ssa_framework_Contents.pdf (accessed 17 February 2012).

Programme for International Study Assessment (PISA). 2009. 'OECD Programme for International Study Assessment: PISA 2009 Key Findings. http://www.oecd.org/pisa/pisaproducts/pisa2009/pisa2009keyfindings.htm (accessed 5 November 2012).

Pritchett, Lant and Varad Pande. 2006. 'Making Primary Education Work for India's Rural Poor: A Proposal for Effective Decentralization'. Paper no. 95, *Social Development Papers*, South Asia Series, World Bank.

Rao, Govinda M. 2007. 'Rural Fiscal Decentralization in India: Problems and Reform Issues', in Satyajit Singh and Pradeep K. Sharma (eds), *Decentralization: Institutions and Politics in Rural India*, pp. 135–153. New Delhi: Oxford University Press.

Sarva Shikha Abhayan (SSA). 2010. 'Manual for Financial Management and Procurement Unit', pp. 5–50. http://ssa.nic.in/financial-management/manual-on-financial-management-and-procurement/manual-on-financial-management-and-procurement-unit/ (accessed 30 October 2012).

World Bank. 2006. 'India: Development Policy Review'. http://web.worldbank.org/WBSITE/EXTERNAL/COUNTRIES/SOUTHASIAEXT 0,,contentMDK:20980493~pagePK:146736~piPK:146830~theSitePK:223547,00.html (accessed 5 November 2012).

Private Initiative in India's Education Miracle

Parth J. Shah and *Luis Miranda**

India saw the largest increase in literacy rate in the decade of 1991–2001 — from about 52 per cent to 65 per cent. From 2001 to 2011, the literacy rate increased by 9 per cent to 74 per cent (Planning Commission 2011). The 13 per cent increase in 1991–2001 has been the largest for any 10-year period in the history of the country. How was this jump in the literacy rate achieved? The foreign exchange crisis of 1991 had led to the Structural Adjustment Program, imposed by the International Monetary Fund (IMF) and the World Bank, forcing the Indian government to cut back on spending. The central government's education budget kept going down through much of the 1990s. It was only around 1998 that the expenditure on education went back to the pre-crisis level. Therefore, during the decade in which we saw the largest increase in literacy rate, the government spending on education was on the decline.

What explains this education miracle? Private investments and the emergence of budget private schools! As parents began to earn more in the post-reform era, they began to invest in their children. As better employment opportunities arose, the value of education became more apparent to parents. This increased demand for education was met by a rapid expansion of budget private schools — schools that charge ₹50–300 per month which came up or 'mushroomed' in slums and shanty towns around the country. The biggest success story of literacy in India has been written with private initiative — parents' willingness to pay and the edupreneur innovation of an affordable school.

If there were any doubts regarding what parents and edupreneurial innovation could do for education in a poor country, India has given the answer. In the first decade of reforms, India achieved an economic miracle, which is well-known, but it also achieved an equally significant education miracle, not as known or appreciated.

This chapter builds on this insight and experience of India and speculates what would be necessary to develop a 21st-century education ecosystem. It traverses apparently disparate themes but hopes that a patient reader would see a coherent narrative of principles, policies and practices. First, a new role of the state so that it can effectively balance the equity and efficiency concerns in the provision of education is argued for. Second, the importance and modalities of empowering parents through school vouchers is examined, including a brief description of a school voucher pilot in Delhi. Third, there is a discussion on the Right to Education (RTE) Act, particularly the 25 per cent reservation in private schools for economically weaker and disadvantaged groups, a form of school voucher scheme, and the negative impact of the input-focused school recognition norms along with innovations in the Gujarat RTE Rules. Finally we attempt to link the ideas and policies discussed so far into a set of suggestions for a broader education ecosystem reform.

EQUITY AND EFFICIENCY IN ECONOMIC AND SOCIAL GOODS

In post-liberalisation India, the importance of the private sector in economic growth is well understood and appreciated. Not even die-hard socialists argue that the state should occupy 'the commanding heights' of the economy any more. For economic growth, the state's role is primarily to enable the private sector as a facilitator, prudent regulator, impartial enforcer of contracts, and at times as a financier (say, through Public–Private Partnerships [PPPs]).

Despite the recognised primacy of the private initiative in the production of economic goods, it is commonly assumed that the state must occupy 'the commanding heights' in the production of social goods like education and healthcare. The justification is that inequality in access to economic goods may be tolerated but in the access to social goods, equality must be the norm. However, in terms of efficiency,

* The discussion in this paper is based on the experiences of the School Choice Campaign: 'Fund Students, Not Schools!'. http://www.schoolchoice.in/ (accessed 17 October 2012).

it is very hard to make a cogent case that the state is a more efficient producer of social goods than the market. It would mean arguing that an agency that is inefficient in producing bicycles and bread is somehow efficient in producing education and healthcare.

Why is the government commonly seen as incapable of cultivating farms or running factories? The answer exists in various forms. One is what we call the 'Dialectics of Three "I"s' — Interest, Incentives and Information. The (self-) interest of government employees, like everyone else's, is to look after themselves. Individuals do not suddenly behave differently just because they work in a government school as opposed to a private one. The conflict between public interest and the interest of the government needs no further proof than the drama around the Sixth Pay Commission. The salaries were supposed to be increased in exchange for performance guarantees and administrative reforms. Salaries went up immediately but no one remembers anything about performance.

Incentives for efficiency are also weak. Government employees have little incentive to minimise costs, find and correct mistakes, innovate, and acquire necessary information about resources and consumer demand. The high teacher absenteeism in government schools is just one indicator of poor incentives. The information on which government decisions are based is normally as reliable as the statistics on poverty levels or balance of payments or industrial production index. The 'Dialectics of Three "I"s' is what provides a systemic explanation of why governments are normally less efficient than markets in the production of economic goods.

If the government is inefficient in producing food — cultivating land — then how could it become efficient in producing education — cultivating the mind? Tilling land is certainly a far simpler task than training the young. If government monopoly and controls play havoc in the production of simple economic goods, how could they be expected to offer opposite results in the production of rather complex social goods like education?

The equity concern requires that social goods cannot be completely left to the market; the state must play a role. The efficiency concern suggests that the state role should not be to produce social goods; it would be as inefficient in producing social goods as it is in producing economic goods. What role then should the state play that would balance the equity as well as the efficiency concern?

Broadly, the state should make the following three mindset changes:

- from controller to facilitator
- from producer to financier
- from inspector to informer

What has been done for the economy needs to be done for the education system — delicense, depoliticise, decentralise. High prices in terms of tuition fees, donations and long queues for admissions are signs of the shortage of quality educational institutions. The same paucity of supply existed for consumer goods before the 1991 liberalisation. The license-permit-quota raj still exists in our education system. Schools and colleges need to be made accountable not to education bureaucrats (licensors) but to parents and students (customers). The government policy should be to increase choice and competition in education as it has been done in many areas of the economy — facilitate, not control.

The core competency of the private and public sectors should be combined. The private sector should be allowed to produce education — manage schools and colleges — and provide it to all who can afford to pay. For those who cannot afford to pay, the government should finance their education through scholarships, education vouchers and loans. The government stands as a guarantor of education not by producing it but by financing it. Instead of focusing on the inputs to education, the government ensures the output — meaningful, high quality learning. This approach combines the efficiency and accountability of the private sector with the equity and independent supervision of the public sector.

The role of the government is to liberate the supply side, fund the demand of the poor and monitor the access and quality of education. Let the private initiative and entrepreneurship — for profit and non-profit — govern our schools and colleges. Scholarships, education vouchers and loans would offer the same freedom of choice to the poor as the rich enjoy today. Governments and Non-Governmental Organisations (NGOs) should evaluate schools and colleges and publish the results so that parents can make informed decisions.

Ideally the state role should change from controller to facilitator, from producer to financier, from inspector to informer. One idea that effectively captures this new role of the state is school vouchers.

SCHOOL VOUCHERS: MAKING SCHOOLS ACCOUNTABLE TO PARENTS

India is not the only country where state schools perform poorly. Most of the people are unhappy with the performance of state schools in their countries. The United States (US) spends one of the highest amounts per student in the world but the quality of education usually ranks as the second major issue of concern after the economy among the citizens. In a typical Western country, a vast majority of students go to state schools (almost 90 per cent in the US).

What are these countries doing to reform their education systems?

Each national education system is unique and each one tries to fix its problems in its own way. However, one common theme underlying many of the reforms around the world is the empowerment of parents, giving them more voice in the education system.[1] State schools are commonly accountable to the education department or ministry. One key goal of global reformers is to increase the accountability of schools towards parents — restructure the system so that schools are at least as much accountable to parents as they are to the education officials. There are many ways to achieve this goal: put parents on school boards or district education councils, give powers to parent-teacher associations, create something like our village education committees. One new idea in this bucket is that of school vouchers. Several countries have undertaken pilot projects. Sweden has actually converted to a universal voucher system where every child, irrespective of parental income, gets a voucher.

The voucher is a tool to change the way governments finance education, particularly of the poor. It is a coupon offered by the government that covers full or partial cost of education at the school of the student's choice. The schools collect vouchers from the students, deposit them in their bank accounts and the banks then credit the school accounts with equivalent money while debiting the account of the government. No money actually changes hands, only the voucher moves from the student to the school, and back to the government. This process could easily be digitised so that no physical voucher is necessary; smart ID cards would perform even better.

In the present system, the schools are accountable to the government. The voucher system makes them accountable directly to the students and parents since they pay for their education through vouchers. If the parent does not like the school, she can take the voucher to another school. Under the voucher system, the money follows the student. In the present system, the money follows the school.

The school voucher provides:[2]

(a) *Choice for students*: The voucher empowers poor students so that they can attend a school of their choice. If the school does not meet their expectations, they have the power to change the school.

(b) *Equality of opportunity*: The scheme satisfies the basic human right that all children are treated equally and equal opportunity for education is provided to all irrespective of cash, caste or creed.

(c) *Competition among schools*: Today private Indian schools only compete for students with money. With vouchers, not only private schools, but also government ones will compete for all students, rich and poor.

(d) *Performance-based payment*: The revenue of a school depends on the number of students it has, both those who pay directly and those who pay through vouchers. Schools therefore have an automatic incentive to improve quality that will increase enrolments and retain students.

(e) *Win-win outcome*: Those government school students who get a voucher are able to change schools and do better for themselves. Evidence suggests that even those students who stay in government schools perform better. First, the Pupil–Teacher Ratio (PTR) improves and second, schools become more attentive to stopping student numbers from going down further. All students are likely to achieve better learning outcomes.

In a voucher system, instead of funding schools, the government funds students. The resultant choice and competition working together provides universal access along with constantly improving the quality of education.

Delhi Voucher Project[3]

This is a privately-funded pilot or proof-of-concept programme in Delhi. In 2007, school vouchers worth up to ₹3,600 per year were awarded to 408 students in 68 wards of Delhi (Plate 7.1).

In these 68 wards, more than 50 School Choice activists reached out to more than 1.2 million parents. All students in government primary schools qualified for the programme. Over 125,000 parents applied for a voucher for their child.

As a fair and transparent method of selecting students from the large number of applicants, a public lottery was held in each ward where the local Ward Councillor picked 12 students — six winners and six for a waiting list, in case some of the students in the first list had eligibility or acceptance problems.

Those who did not win the lottery submitted a petition to their Ward Councillor asking for school vouchers from the government. In the all-India campaign, more than 250,000 parents submitted voucher demands to their elected representatives.

The vouchers were awarded to winners in the presence of the Chief Minister of Delhi Sheila Dikshit and the Education Minister Arvinder Singh Lovely. In the assessment of the project, the voucher children performed better in reading and mathematics.[4] The biggest gain was the change in the attitude, belief and aspirations of the parents of the voucher students. In the first week of school, many principals complained of voucher students not coming on time, showing up without taking a bath, combing their hair or wearing proper uniforms, and many did not bring lunch and often resorted to 'forced sharing' of lunch from others. After a couple of meetings with parents, the situation slowly improved, which meant that both the students and parents

PLATE 7.1   Voucher Award Function with the Delhi Chief Minister and Education Minister

Source: Centre for Civil Society, 2007.

became more punctual, improved their hygiene and took extra effort to prepare for the school with proper lunch and a full school bag. More importantly, after two years of the programme, the aspirations of parents changed. At the beginning of the programme, they had said that they expected their children to study until Classes V or VIII; after seeing the changes in their children, they said they would like them to study until Classes X or XII and a few even hoped that their children would go to college. This transformation also probably demonstrates that several parents spent more on their children's education after winning the voucher than they had done before. This 'crowding in' of investment is very powerful — when the parents find more responsive schools because of others' investment (through vouchers), they also begin to invest more. These attitudinal and aspirational changes are far more important in the long run, not just for the education of the voucher child but for all the other siblings in the family.

PAHAL in Uttarakhand[5]

This is the first government-sponsored school voucher programme in India. It is billed as a PPP initiative that provides school vouchers worth ₹3,000 per student per year to children (6–14 yrs) who are rag-pickers, scavengers, snake-charmers, or orphans. The eligibility criterion is that the child should have been a drop-out for at least a year or never enrolled and that there is no government school/Education Guarantee Scheme (EGS) centre within a kilometre of their habitation. The scheme was started in 2007 in the city of Dehradun and based on its success, a year later, was expanded to Nainital and Udham Singh Nagar with a total of 651 children.

Alternative Voucher Schemes

Vouchers are a very flexible instrument and can be easily adapted to address specific challenges of a particular population group or geographical area.

(a) There should be targeted vouchers for specific underserved groups such as migrant, out-of-school or street children; girls; ST/SC/OBC, Muslim or differently-abled children; those from poor families or living in peri-urban areas (e.g., resettlement colonies); children of refugees, prisoners or migrating tribes; and orphans.

(b) Vouchers could be used to reward performance of government schools. When a government school attracts voucher students who could also go to a private school, the voucher amount could be given to the school/teachers as an incentive.

(c) Mobile schools for children of migrants could be supported by vouchers where educated members of the community run schools and get paid through the vouchers from students. This would ensure that children of such communities receive education throughout the year.

(d) To encourage establishment of community schools, vouchers could be introduced specially in areas where there are no or very few government schools.

(e) School vouchers could be used to provide opportunity to enterprising government school principals/teachers to compete with the rest of the schools. Such principals and teachers could opt for more managerial and financial autonomy with 100 per cent funding through vouchers and no direct state grant.

(f) A city or state could decide that all new government schools would be funded through vouchers. The government would fix the voucher amount per student and the school would get money depending on the number of students it attracts and retains. A part of the payment could be tied to learning achievements of students.

(g) Universal vouchers can be given to all children in urban slums where there are no government schools and no space to open a school.

Vouchers don't annihilate state schools; they make them more accountable to parents and compel them to compete with other schools to attract and retain students. Most government schools are better equipped than the budget private schools that the poor use in terms of infrastructure of libraries, labs and playgrounds; the amount of funds they have per student; and qualification, training and salaries of the teachers. On head-to-head competition, government schools should out-perform budget private schools. That does not happen currently, but vouchers provide the missing ingredient that will change the incentive structure towards better performance of state schools.

The recent RTE Act builds on the idea of government funds empowering poor parents to choose private schools.

THE RIGHT TO EDUCATION ACT: 25 PER CENT OPPORTUNITY SEATS

Section 12 of the RTE requires private unaided schools to reserve 25 per cent seats in the entry-level class (nursery or Class I) for socially disadvantaged and economically weaker sections. The government would provide private schools with reimbursements equal to their fees or the per student cost in government schools, whichever is lower. Various associations of private schools had challenged this compulsion in the Supreme Court. The Supreme Court in a 2–1 judgement upheld the constitutionality of the 25 per cent reservation. When fully implemented, Clause 12 would create the world's largest school voucher programme — public funds would support students to go to private schools of their choice.

The onus is now on the government to design a transparent, fair and accountable method to implement this in private schools.[6] Instead of '25 per cent reservation', it is perhaps better to call the initiative '25 per cent inclusion seats' or '25 per cent opportunity seats'. A general estimate is that anywhere between 2.5 to 7 million poor students would benefit in the first year of full implementation. And this number would double every year thereafter for eight years. The future of a large number of underprivileged children is at stake in proper implementation of the 25 per cent opportunity seats.

Different stakeholders — parents, schools and the government — have their own concerns and problems, and we need to understand these clearly and triangulate them well in order to create an effective model of implementation.

The underprivileged parents are concerned whether those who really qualify would get seats in the elite private schools or the seats would get auctioned off to the 'connected' ones or the highest bidders. Even after getting admission, what other costs would the schools pass on, either directly or indirectly? How hard would schools and teachers work to make it easier for their children to adjust to this new challenging environment?

The schools need to ensure that it is easy for parents to get application forms, provide them with the required supporting documents and run a credible lottery process for the final selection. They need to get their teaching and non-teaching staff aligned to the inclusion objective and train them in understanding and sensitivity. The schools are particularly worried whether the promised reimbursement by the government would come at all or in time. Many schools in Delhi admitted children under the 25 per cent system last year but are yet to see any payment from the Delhi government even after the year is over. The government has not yet even outlined the process of reimbursement clearly in a mutually acceptable manner. The high-fee private schools are worried about the reimbursement amount that would be far less than the fees they charge. The Ministry of Human Resource Development (MHRD) minister has recently suggested that the government is considering ways to bridge this gap in the 12th Five-Year Plan.

The government has to make sure that the qualified students are admitted under the 25 per cent opportunity seats and its own officers do not abuse this provision to seek admission for their preferred students. It needs to supervise as well as help schools to achieve full-hearted social integration and holistic learning, and design an efficient process of timely reimbursement, along with finding ways to bridge the gap between reimbursement amount and the actual cost of private schools as far as possible.

This admittedly is not an exhaustive list of issues and problems but is a good indication of the challenges that must be immediately addressed to make this historic provision well accepted and implemented. From the multitude of consultations and discussions that have happened over the last two years on the 25 per cent provision, there are certain clear ideas that should help fulfil this promise of inclusive education.

First, the central government must directly pay for the 25 per cent opportunity seats instead of relying on state governments to reimburse schools on a state-by-state basis. State governments have already been pointing out that the Sarva Shiksha Abhiyan (SSA) funding they receive from the Centre does not include the cost of the 25 per cent seats in private schools. Instead of including this cost in the SSA budget, which would vary widely from state to state, it is far more convenient and straightforward for the Centre to take this responsibility directly. The amount to be paid should be decided by state governments as per the costs incurred in providing education in state schools, and this would vary by state. The payment however should be directly from the central government.

The central government should adopt a uniform criterion for adjusting the reimbursement amount from year to year. The current state RTE rules differ widely in re-calculating the amount for future years. Some states offer to re-look at state expenditures every two years and re-calculate the reimbursement amount, while some others suggest adjusting the first year's amount by the rate of inflation for all future years. It is better to have a uniform national rule about re-calculating the reimbursement amount.

Second, the centre should create an independent special purpose vehicle (SPV) to manage the reimbursement, which may be called the India Inclusive Education Fund or the India Education Opportunity Fund. The central government would deposit all its contributions to the Fund. The Fund would also raise extra money from corporates (under Corporate Social Responsibility [CSR] or otherwise), foundations and individuals. These non-government funds could be used to incentivise schools to do a better job of social and educational inclusion of the poorer students under the 25 per cent opportunity seats. The private schools would be free to raise their own funds to bridge the gap through donations, or charity events like music concerts, cultural fairs, annual events, but they could also get support from the Fund. The Fund could also offer 'inclusion awards' to schools that do well in social integration and holistic learning of the 25 per cent students. These awards could help cover a part of the gap for private schools as well as incentivise them to take the challenge of inclusion more seriously.

To assure schools that they would be reimbursed on time and in full as per the process outlined by the Fund, the Centre should include its contribution in the annual central education budget as a separate line item. The Centre should calculate its liability as equal to the amount paid out by the Fund in the previous year and deposit that amount on 1 April in the Fund's account. The adjustment of the reimbursement amount for the current year should be made by August and the Centre should then deposit the corresponding amount on 1 September to meet its full obligations for the academic year.

Third, the definition and identification of qualified candidates under the 25 per cent should be left to state governments. Some states have suggested that they would issue 'Student Cards' to those who qualify and this Student Card would then be used by schools to determine eligibility for the 25 per cent seats. Some states may issue 'smart coupons' or vouchers or biometric cards. There is certainly a need for experimentation to discover better methods of identification. After some years of experience, we may evolve a commonly accepted method across the states.

The verification of the qualified candidates should be done by the National Commission for the Protection of Child Rights (NCPCR), its state branches and affiliated NGOs. The NCPCR should have the powers to take action against states that have significantly high rates of identification errors of omission and commission (Type 1 and Type 2 errors) in order to keep the pressure on the states to improve their identification processes and technologies. The NCPCR may require that the failing states contribute to the Fund in proportion to the degree of their failure.

Many more details and processes need to be worked out for effective implementation of the 25 per cent education opportunity seats but the above three ideas form the foundation of a structure that will help fulfil the historic promise.

School Recognition Norms under the RTE: Demise of Private Budget Schools

On the one hand Clause 12 of the RTE Act opens up opportunities for underprivileged children to access private schools through a de facto voucher programme, and on the other the strict school recognition norms would shut down a majority of the private schools that the poor can afford to use. Out of the underprivileged, 25 per cent would benefit from the Act but the remaining 75 per cent would lose whatever little choice they had for their children's education.

The RTE Rules of Gujarat offer an innovative approach towards recognition of existing private unaided schools.[7] The Committee in charge of drafting the rules in Gujarat, headed by the former Chief Secretary Sudhir Mankad, has broken new ground in understanding the policy issues faced in the realm of education in India today.

Instead of focusing only on input requirements specified in the Act like classroom size, playground, and PTR, the Gujarat RTE Rules put greater emphasis on learning outcomes of students in the recognition norms. Appendix 1 of the Gujarat Rules is one that has a path-breaking formulation for recognition of a school, a weighted average of four measures:

(a) *Student learning outcomes (absolute levels): weight 30 per cent*

Using standardised tests, student learning levels focusing on learning (not just rote) will be measured through an independent assessment.

(b) *Student learning outcomes (improvement compared to the school's past performance): weight 40 per cent*

This component is introduced to ensure that schools do not show a better result in 'absolute levels' simply by not admitting weak students. The effect of school performance looking good simply because of students coming from well-to-do backgrounds is also automatically addressed by this measure. This measure will not be available in the first year, in which case the weightage will be distributed among the other parameters.

(c) *Inputs (including facilities, teacher qualifications): weight 15 per cent*

(d) *Student non-academic outcomes (co-curricular and sports, personality and values) and parent feedback: weight 15 per cent*

Student outcomes in non-academic areas as well as feedback from a random sample of parents should be used to determine this parameter. Standardised survey tools giving weightage to cultural activities, sports and art should be developed. The parent feedback should cover a random sample of at least 20 parents across classes and be compiled.

This is one of the first times that education policy in the country has focused on children and parents rather than the public sector producers of education services.

Furthermore, the Gujarat RTE Rules have taken a more nuanced and flexible approach in other areas too. For instance, both class size and PTR have been defined not in absolute terms, but in relative terms. The required classroom size is 300 sq. feet, but in case the classrooms are smaller, then instead of re-building them, the rules allow for a way to accommodate that with a different PTR. The formula is:

$$PTR=(Area\ of\ the\ classroom\ in\ sq.\ feet-60)/8$$

This approach not only allows smaller classrooms to exist but also gives schools a more efficient way to manage physical infrastructure.

If a private school is unable to meet recognition norms, then the RTE Act de-recognises the school and forces it to close down. This sudden forced closure would create serious problems for students and parents who would have to find a new school in the neighbourhood. The Gujarat RTE Rules allow for the state to take-over the school or transfer

management to a third party. This creates a possibility for the school to continue and meet the norms. This, once again, demonstrates the focus upon the interests of students and parents.

This approach is significantly better than that of the other states where recognition norms are based solely on input requirements, which are also rigid (like playground, classroom size and PTR). The Gujarat approach recognises the substantial contribution made by budget private schools in urban and semi-urban areas where land and buildings are very expensive. The other states need to re-look at their rules and use the approach taken by Gujarat to assure quality education to the poor.

SOME IDEAS FOR EDUCATION ECOSYSTEM REFORM

Just as in economic reforms, the list of education reform ideas could be quite long. This paper suggests that two principles should be the focus of reforms in the education ecosystem — efficient use of public funds and the promotion of equity and quality through choice and competition.

Achieve Efficient Use of Public Funds

(a) Fund students, not schools (school vouchers, charter schools, conditional cash transfers);
(b) Convert state funding to per student basis and link it to performance;
(c) Pedagogical and operational autonomy to state schools;
(d) Give poorly performing state schools to private parties on learning outcome contracts;
(e) Hire teachers at the school level, not at the state level;
(f) Put all budget and expenditure data in digital form in the public domain.

Promote Equity and Quality through Choice and Competition

(a) Learning outcomes as the central focus of regulation:
  (i) Apply the same standards to both private as well as government schools;
  (ii) Annual independent learning outcome assessment across all schools;
  (iii) Decentralise and depoliticise syllabi and textbooks;
  (iv) Open Central Board of Secondary Education (CBSE) and state board exams to all students, not only for students who study in CBSE or state board affiliated schools.
(b) Encourage edupreneurs
  (i) Remove the license raj;
  (ii) Declare education an 'industry' for easier access to credit and venture capital fund;

(iii) Offer schools (and colleges) the choice to be non-profit or for-profit and treat for-profit ones as companies for disclosure and taxation norms.

Most of these ideas are quite self-explanatory so this paper elaborates only on a select few.

Fund Students, Not Schools

The current model of guaranteeing education for the poor is for the government to give grants to government schools, which then provide education for free. This system of financing education has created a situation in which government schools have become a monopoly provider of education for the underprivileged. The poor have only one place to go — the government school. Like any monopoly, these don't deliver good education and are less responsive and accountable to their customers.

This monopoly must be broken by changing the way the education of the poor is financed. Instead of giving grants to schools, the money should be given to poor parents through a school voucher. The parent would take this voucher and go to any school of their choice. The school collects the voucher, deposits it in a bank, and the government transfers the equivalent money into the school's bank account. School vouchers are a special scholarship that empowers the underprivileged with the choice that the richer parents enjoy.

Conditional cash transfers go one step further — they not only cover the cost of education (like the voucher) but also provide cash incentives if the child stays in school and achieves specified attendance and learning targets. The cash incentive compensates for the lost earnings from the children or lowers the opportunity cost of going to school instead of work. Typically the cash is transferred directly into the bank account of the mother.[8]

Charter schools are fully funded by the government (just as government schools) but the management is with a private body that is given the 'charter'. The students do not pay any fees; the entire cost is born by the charter school. Managerial autonomy and often extra funding from philanthropists allow charter schools to stand out among state schools. The American experience in charter schools provides a very good case study. India needs to pass a 'charter law' to open this option.[9]

Fund Government Schools through a Per-Student Formula

Wide differences in state funding to government schools with the same number of students are very common. This inequity in funding is inhumane and unjust. This archaic mode of funding must be changed; schools must be funded based on the number of students they have. It would obviously not be a simple multiplication but would require a somewhat complex formula, which would have to take into account the fixed costs, variable cost per student, location of the school, composition of the student body (more challenged students would get higher amount), and other pertinent factors.[10] The per student funding approach would provide strong incentives to schools to work hard to attract and retain students.

Currently there is no link between the performance of government schools and the grant they receive. There is no incentive for better performance; whether student learning achievements are good or bad, the schools get the same funds. It is critical to link the grant amount to performance.

One way to start the process is to link increments in the grant to schools to performance — that is, increments in per student funding would depend on increments in learning outcomes or specified performance parameters. The current grant amount can continue if the performance is below par but the next increment could be tied to performance. If the school consistently fails to improve, it can be given to the community or a third party for management.

Grant Managerial and Financial Autonomy to Schools, Principals and Teachers

The government schools are minutely controlled by education departments. The schools hardly have any autonomy to manage their affairs. They are closest to their customers and should have the necessary freedom to adjust their functioning to be better able to meet the changing needs of students and parents. The principals should be education leaders and role models, not just bureaucrats. They and the teachers must be empowered and given the freedom that their private school counterparts enjoy. The schools should hire teachers directly, not through the state education department. The teachers would enjoy the same salaries and perks as they currently do but hiring and performance assessment would be done at the school level. This would also help principals to be genuine leaders of their schools, with all the staff accountable to them.

Give the Worst Performing Government Schools on Learning Achievement Contracts

A group of worst performing government schools should be selected and handed over to other interested and qualified parties to manage them. There are many ways to identify such parties. One could be through tenders, based not on the amount of money the parties would charge, but the degree of improvements they promise in student learning. The government can promise to pay the same amount per student to the new managers as it currently spends. The parties then compete on the degree and type of progress they promise to achieve every year during the period of the contract.

Apply the Same Standards to Private and Government Schools

Private schools have to meet stringent standards set by the government to be recognised. However, the government exempts itself by not requiring government schools to go through the process of recognition. Therefore, under the law, the government school must meet the same norms but in practice it may or may not, since no one would close down a government school for failing to do so. This means that for a richer child going to a private school, the government guarantees that the school would meet all its requirements while for a poor child going to a government school, there is no guarantee that the situation would be the same. The government treats the children of the poor like second-class citizens. This inequity must end; government schools must meet the same standards of quality. Every government school should be required to follow the same application process for recognition as private schools and must be formally recognised by the education department. It would be even better if government schools actually exceeded the standards and became a role model for private schools to emulate.

Establish Independent Learning Outcome Evaluation Agencies

Except for board examinations, there is no objective information to judge the quality of schools in India. We need to develop more meaningful systems of evaluation other than high-stakes annual exams, and implement them at regular intervals. These evaluations should be made public so that parents can make informed decisions. Given the size and diversity of the education market in India, we should have several competing independent agencies to perform this task. Recently, financial rating agencies have started rating maritime training institutes under the initiative of the Directorate General of Shipping. They are a good case study for understanding the mechanisms of school rating.

Remove the License Raj

It takes anywhere between 15 to 36 licenses to open a school (Wadhwa 2001). Some states require that the proposed school must first demonstrate that it is 'essential' in the area in which it will be opened. Given the difficulties in acquiring licenses, we suffer from adverse selection. Those who are not so good in providing education but very proficient at getting licenses enter and dominate the sector. Why else would politicians dominate the education scene in India?

Shed the Hypocrisy of Only Non-Profits in Education

As most people suspect, private schools in India earn a handsome 'surplus'. Under the current law they have to find discreet methods to distribute the surplus among founders and managers. What do we gain by forcing schools to be dishonest?[11]

Historically education has been a cherished philanthropic activity, with some of the best schools and colleges of the world being based on charity. There is no reason to believe that philanthropy in education is going to subside. However there is nothing to lose by allowing for-profit entities to also compete in the education space. Let the non-profit, for-profit and government-funded institutions compete on a level-playing field. This could start with higher education institutions and depending on the experience a decision made whether to open up school education as well.

Conclusion

Let us remember the 1948 United Nations (UN) Declaration of Human Rights, which also forms the basis of the current Millennium Development Goals (MDGs). Article 26 of the Declaration says:

(a) Everyone has the right to education. Education shall be free, at least in the elementary and fundamental stages. Elementary education shall be compulsory. Technical and professional education shall be made generally available and higher education shall be equally accessible to all on the basis of merit.

(b) Education shall be directed to the full development of the human personality and to the strengthening of respect for human rights and fundamental freedoms. It shall promote understanding, tolerance and friendship among all nations, racial or religious groups, and shall further the activities of the United Nations for the maintenance of peace.

(c) Parents have a prior right to choose the kind of education that shall be given to their children.[12]

The Right to Education enshrined in the first two clauses becomes meaningful only when it addresses the third clause, that is, when it becomes the Right to Education of Choice!

NOTES

1. See Hoxby (2003) for the larger theme of school choice and school competition. For debates on vouchers in the US, see Greene and Marcus (2008); Forster (2009).

2. These are authors' inferences from a large number of studies on vouchers and from the first principles of choice and competition. Success of any voucher programme depends on several factors and so whether to assign the failure of any particular voucher programme to the idea itself or to any part of the design or implementation is always a judgment call. There is a vast literature on vouchers; see Shah and Braun-Munzinger (2006) for a review of global voucher programmes and Shah (2009) for specific challenges from an Indian context. Muralidharan (2006) suggests various types of PPP models for India, including school vouchers. The counter arguments are not dealt with directly since the canvass in this chapter is much broader than just vouchers.

3. The project is managed by Centre for Civil Society (CCS) as part of their School Choice Campaign: 'Fund Students, Not Schools!' In 2009, CCS also launched another voucher pilot with 400 Muslim girls.

4. The details of the assessment are provided in CCS (2009).

5. Mahapatra (2011); Yasmeen et al. (2009).

6. The discussion in this section is based on Shah (2012).

7. For the Gujarat RTE rules, see Government of Gujarat (2012).

8. 'As of 2010, all but two countries in Latin America and over 15 countries in Asia and Africa had a CCT [conditional cash transfer] program as part of their social protection systems . . . CCT average effect sizes on enrollment, attendance and dropout are all positive and statistically significant and larger in magnitude for secondary than for primary schooling' (Saavedra and Garcia 2012: 2–3).

9. Some of the summary studies of charter schools are Bulkley and Fisler (2012); CREDO (2009); Toma and Zimmer (2012).

10. See Snell (2006) for various formulas used in the US to calculate per student funding by the state.

11. For a broader discussion of private *vs* state and for-profit *vs* non-profit education, see Coulson (2008).

12. http://www.un.org/en/documents/udhr/index.shtml (accessed 23 October 2012).

REFERENCES

Bulkley, Katrina and Jennifer Fisler. 2002. 'A Decade of Charter Schools: From Theory to Practice'. CPRE Working Paper no. RB-35, Consortium for Policy Research in Education, University of Pennsylvania.

Center for Research on Education Outcomes (CREDO). 2009. 'Multiple Choice: Charter School Performance in 16 States'. Center for Research on Education Outcomes, Stanford University, June. http://credo.stanford.edu/reports/MULTIPLE_CHOICE_CREDO.pdf (accessed 17 October 2012).

Centre for Civil Society (CCS). 2009. 'Delhi Voucher Project: First Assessment Report'. New Delhi.

Coulson, Andrew J. 2008. 'Markets vs. Monopolies in Education: A Global Review of the Evidence'. Policy Analysis no. 620, Cato Institute, 10 September. http://www.cato.org/pubs/pas/pa620.pdf (accessed 17 October 2012).

Forster, Greg. 2009. 'A Win-Win Solution: The Empirical Evidence on How Vouchers Affect Public Schools'. *School Choice: Issues in Depth*, Friedman Foundation for Educational Choice, February.

Government of Gujarat. 2012. 'Rules and Orders (Other than those Published in Part I, I-A and I-L) made by the Government of Gujarat under the Gujarat Acts'. *Gujarat Government Gazette*, 18 February. http://gujarat-education.gov.in/education/Portal/News/159_1_MODEL%20RULES%2029.2.12.PDF (accessed 23 October 2012).

Greene, Jay P. and Marcus A. Winters. 2008. 'The Effect of Special Education Vouchers on Public School Achievement: Evidence From Florida's McKay Scholarship Program'. Civic Report no. 52, Manhattan Institute for Policy Research, April.

Hoxby, Caroline M. 2003. 'School Choice and School Competition: Evidence from the United States', *Swedish Economic Policy Review*, 10(2): 9–66.

Mahapatra, Richard. 2011. 'Kind to Cash'. *Down to Earth*, 15 February. http://www.downtoearth.org.in/content/kind-cash (accessed 25 June 2012).

Muralidharan, Karthik. 2006. 'Public-Private Partnerships for Quality Education in India', *Seminar*, 565.

Planning Commission. 2011. 'Health', in *Faster, Sustainable and More Inclusive Growth: An Approach to the Twelfth Five Year Plan (2012–17)*, pp. 87–95. New Delhi: Planning Commision, Government of India.

Saavedra, Juan Esteban and Sandra Garcia. 2012. 'Impacts of Conditional Cash Transfer Programs on Educational Outcomes in Developing Countries: A Meta-Analysis'. Working Paper no. WR-921-1, RAND Corporation, February.

Shah, Parth J. 2009. 'School Choice: Assuring Quality Education to All', *Vikalpa*, 34(2): 70–74.

—————. 2012. 'How to Fulfil the RTE Promise'. *Indian Express*, 23 April.

Shah, Parth J. and Corinna Braun-Munzinger. 2006. 'Education Vouchers: Global Experience and India's Promise'. Policy Review no. 1, Centre for Civil Society, February.

Snell, Lisa. 2006. 'The Agony of American Education: How Per-Student Funding can Revolutionize Public Schools', *Reason*, 37(11): 22–27.

Toma, Eugenia and Ron Zimmer. 2012. 'Two Decades of Charter Schools: Expectations, Reality, and the Future', *Economics of Education Review*, 31(2): 209–12.

Wadhwa, Mayank. 2001. 'Licenses to Open a School: It's All about Money'. Working Paper no. 1, Centre for Civil Society. http://www.ccs.in/RP01_1.asp (accessed 25 June 2012).

Yasmeen, Summiya, Prachi Guron, Autar Nehru, Neha Ghosh, Natasha Pathak, and Hemalatha Raghupathi. 2009. 'The Charter School Alternative'. *EducationWorld*, 5 October. http://www.educationworldonline.net/index.php/page-article-choice-more-id-1966 (accessed 25 June 2012).

| 8 | # Low-Cost Private Schools for the Poor in India |

Low-Cost Private Schools for the Poor in India
Some Reflections*

Geetha B. Nambissan

A key feature of elementary education in India post-2000 is the rapid spread of private unregulated/unrecognised schools. What has been particularly significant, especially since the last decade, is the advocacy for private schools for the poor and the 'edu-business' that is riding on it. These are schools referred to as 'budget' or Low-Fee Private (LFP) schools[1] that are projected as responding to the growing demand of poor families for 'good quality' private English-medium education. In this chapter, the evidence and claims about budget/low-cost/LFP schools in India have been examined. It has been pointed out that while the picture one has of this sector is fragmentary and requires systematic study, the low-cost private schools being advocated for the poor and the emerging edu-business around it have serious implications for the right to education of their children.

THE LOW-COST PRIVATE SECTOR IN ELEMENTARY EDUCATION

There has been a significant growth of the private sector in elementary education in India especially in the last two decades.[2] From around 10 per cent of enrolment in the 6–14 years' age group in private unaided schools in 1996,[3] the proportion increased to as much as 28 per cent in 2005. According to the Indian Human Development Survey (IHDS) carried out in 2005, as many as 51 per cent of children in urban areas and 21 per cent in rural areas were enrolled in private unaided schools.[4] There are also variations across states, with Punjab, Haryana and Uttar Pradesh having a high proportion of enrolment in private schools as compared to Assam and Himachal Pradesh (Desai et al. 2010).

Though unrecognised (unregulated) private schools that cater to low income families are seen to have increased rapidly, there are as yet no reliable estimates of how many such schools there are today. A. C. Mehta (2005) provides information on the number of unrecognised schools in seven districts of Punjab. He reports that around 86 per cent of the 3,058 elementary schools in these districts were un-recognised in 2005 (cited in Juneja 2010). Majority of these unrecognised schools appear to have mushroomed after the mid-1990s and especially after 2000. It was found that of the 2,640 unrecognised private schools identified in the Punjab districts in 2005, 'only 16.4 per cent of them were established before 1986. 26 per cent were established between the years 1996–2000, almost 30 per cent were established between 2001 and 2005' (ibid. 18–19).

The IHDS does not make a distinction between private schools according to 'recognition' status. However, since it is a household survey, families accessing the low-cost school sector also come under its purview. This is reflected in the data on access to private unaided schools by different income quartiles. Among the economically weakest sections, as well as in households that have little or no schooling, and among socially vulnerable sections (with considerable overlap among all three), there was a small but significant proportion of children who were accessing private unaided schooling in 2005. The IHDS reports that 15 per cent of enrolment of children aged 6–14 years in the lowest income quartile, as compared to 52 per cent in the top quintile, is in private unaided schools.[5] Also mentioned is that as many as 13–15 per cent of children in these schools came from families where members had no schooling or had not completed primary level of education. Who are these families, what quality of schooling do their children receive, how do they perform? In the following section some of the findings from studies conducted on low-cost private schools have been brought together to try and build a picture of this

---

* This chapter, based on the available research studies, as well as websites where discussions, comments and articles about these schools feature, is a revised and edited version of Nambissan (2012).

sector and the contexts in which families that access budget/unrecognised schools make their choices.

LOW-COST SCHOOLS: A PROFILE

The available research on the low-cost private unregulated sector is fragmentary. The most publicised study is the one carried out by James Tooley et al. (2007, 2010. See also Tooley 2009) in Hyderabad from 2003–05. The findings that emerged from the research have been used as a reference point by others who have studied and commented on budget schools. The main results can be summarised as follows: Private unregulated budget schools were run at a low cost—with minimum infrastructure and resources, and teachers on contract who were paid a fraction of the salaries their counterparts received in government schools. These schools charged low tuition fees (less than $2/₹100 a month) (Tooley et al. 2007: 548). They were hence seen to meet the demand from poorest of families for private, good quality education in the medium of English at a low fee. Per pupil costs were shown as higher in government as compared to private schools, with teacher salary comprising a major component of cost in the former. Using standardised tests on a 'random sample' of schools and children, Tooley et al. claimed that their research provided 'evidence' to show that budget schools were 'better performing' than state schools at a far lower cost, and hence were cost-efficient (Tooley et al. 2010: 134–35). Market principles that informed these schools — choice and competition — were seen to lead to greater accountability as well.

Tooley et al.'s research (ibid.) has been followed up by Ross Baird (2009), Shruti Joshi (2008) and others who have reiterated his findings, especially in relation to the preference of the poor for low-cost schools as against government primary schools. Studies in villages by Prachi Srivastava (2007) and Joanna Harma (2011) have also pointed to the 'universal preference'/'popular choice' by poor and disadvantaged households for 'low fee private schools'. Karthik Muralidharan and Michael Kremer (2008), in a survey of rural schools in some states, have highlighted higher teacher attendance and greater teacher activity in private as compared to government classrooms as indicators of better quality of teaching in the former. It is also said that as low-cost schools provide 'free places' to those who cannot afford to pay the fees, and are conveniently located within poor settlements and hence are more easily accessible especially to girls, they score on equity considerations as well (Nambissan and Ball 2011: 177). It is argued that in the light of the poor performance of government schools and the 'evidence' made available regarding low-cost private schools, the latter should be allowed to function free of

regulations. Further, government funds should be directed through vouchers to parents to enable them to exercise choice in relation to their children's education. Equally highlighted is that budget schools are presently making modest profits. With the necessary financial support, low-cost teaching technology, creating school brands and chains and so on, they can be a good business proposition for private investors. Budget school advocates emphasise that there is a fortune to be made from schooling for the poor — as C. K. Prahlad (2005) says, at the 'bottom of the pyramid' (see Nambissan and Ball 2011).

Studies by advocates of schooling for the poor, particularly Tooley and his associates, have been the basis for building the school choice discourse in India as well as advocacy for the promise of edu-business from this sector. However, scholars have raised conceptual and methodological issues that suggest that the evidence from Tooley et al.'s research may be less robust than is claimed (Ross and Dyer 2008; Sarangapani and Winch 2010). One major criticism is that there is a failure to factor in the heterogeneity within government and private schools, particularly in relation to the levels of education (primary/upper primary/secondary classes) offered by the school as well as its age (when it was established). P. M. Sarangapani and C. Winch underscore that:

[a]mong the most important determinants of the role that... education providers could play in the education market are their 'stability' as indicated by their age, their 'scope' or the level of education that they offer, and their medium of instruction. Segregated tabulated data of all schools surveyed (by age, level and medium, in addition to management type) are very necessary in order to understand the complexities of their existence and functioning (2010: 506–7).

Given that the rapid spread of unrecognised schools is a post-2000 phenomenon, the age of the school needs to be factored in as this bears upon infrastructure and resources made available as well as the kind of teachers recruited.

However J. Tooley et al. (2010) compare the performance of students across broad management categories of schools — government, government-aided, private unaided recognised, and private unrecognised schools. Their analysis shows that 'pupils in private unrecognised and recognised schools, when controlled for age, pupil's IQ, and class average IQ, achieve higher scores in mathematics and English than equivalent pupils in government schools' (ibid.:117). However, they fail to control for the diversity within these broad categories of schools in relation to the level of education (primary, upper primary or secondary classes) offered by the school. More than 80 per cent of government schools in their study offer only five years of primary education. This is true of a much smaller proportion of unrecognised schools (60.8 per cent that provide nursery sections as well) and a minority

(25.5 per cent) of recognised private schools (Tooley et al. 2007: 546). In other words, only 17.2 per cent of government schools offered up to secondary schooling as compared to 39.2 per cent of unrecognised schools and as many are 74.3 per cent of recognised private schools (ibid.). Composite government schools that offer primary and secondary classes are preferred, including by poor parents, as they provide continuity in their children's education (Juneja 2010; Nambissan 2003). Primary students in these schools also have better access to facilities and resources as compared to those that offer only primary classes (Nambissan 2003). How do Class IV students from low-income families in government secondary schools perform as compared to children from similar backgrounds enrolled in private recognised and unrecognised schools offering the same level of education? Or, how do Class IV students perform in schools that offer only Classes I–V across different management categories? However, Tooley et al. (2010) do not make such comparisons. Their results are hence misleading.

P. Rose and C. Dyer observe that Tooley's research 'lacks any attempt to define what is meant by the "poor"', and further that '[i]t is extremely unlikely that those attending even these low-budget private schools are among the chronically poor' (2008: 23). Indeed Tooley's 'poor' appear to be largely from lower middle class fractions, who are self-employed and own petty businesses, organised sector workers, and those with relatively regular sources of income rather than families in extreme poverty. Contrary to what is claimed by Tooley and others, majority of those who are actually at the lowest end of the economic hierarchy are more likely to enrol their children only in government schools as they charge no tuition fee and provide free textbooks and other essentials as well as mid-day meals. Rose and Dyer's scepticism about whether it is the poorest that are largely accessing low-cost schools is borne out in Jyotsna Lall's study of 'small fee' schools in Jaipur city (2000). Parents accessing the lowest fee schools (under ₹100 per month) for their children were mainly peons, vegetable vendors, factory workers and auto-rickshaw drivers. Where schools charged a higher fee (even between ₹100 and ₹300 per month), parents were either from lower middle class or middle class backgrounds (Lall 2000: 25). Harma's (2011) study of LFP schools in Uttar Pradesh focused on whether these schools were 'pro poor and equitable' as was being claimed by budget school advocates.[6] Harma also found that the proportion of Muslim and lower caste children (30 per cent) enrolled in LFP schools was far lower than non-scheduled caste Hindu children (68 per cent). Further, she observed that 'less than one third of the children of unskilled workers attend LFP schools, while 55 per cent of farmers' children and over three quarters of skilled workers children do so' (ibid.: 352–53). This indicates that affordability of school fees is a key factor influencing enrolment in LFP schools, and though Harma had categorised these schools as 'low fee' the fees were obviously not low enough at least from the perspective of a large section of the families studied.

Contexts of Choice

Larger institutional and social contexts appear to shape the choices and decisions that low income families make about schooling and how they allocate resources and opportunities among children. Broad generalisations about the 'poor' that appear in the research on the low-cost school sector must hence be viewed with caution. The availability of government schools and their perceived quality are highlighted as reasons why low income parents aspire to private schooling for their children. Baird (2009) observes that the lack of availability of government schools in urban 'slums' led the parents to low-cost schools. In north Mumbai slums the 'poor' had access to only private schools as the nearest government school was often over two hours away from students' homes. Private schools were within a kilometre of their homes (ibid.: 12). In a number of studies 'distance' has been posed as a factor in the choice of schools, especially for very young children and girls (Harma 2011; Srivastava 2007).

A range of socio-cultural factors together with mobility strategies influence parental decision-making on schooling for their children. The aspiration for English-medium instruction among low income parents has been highlighted by pro-LFP school proponents as a key factor that drives the demand for low-cost schooling. This is largely because of the linkages they draw between the knowledge of English, middle-class jobs, social distinction, and elite status. The fact that government schools impart education in the regional language makes them less attractive than private schools that advertise themselves as 'English medium'. Baird observes that 'the vast majority of low income parents I interviewed believed that if their child can speak English, he or she would be guaranteed a middle-class job' (2009: 21). However, the fact that teachers in these schools often do not know English themselves makes the quality of instruction suspect as well as belie parental aspirations that their children will learn the English language.

Sarangapani and Winch (2010) dwell at length on the specific context of schooling in Andhra Pradesh as well as of Muslims in Hyderabad among whom Tooley et al. (2010) have done their research. This does not allow for generalisation of the latter's findings to all 'poor'. Sarangapani and Wench note that Andhra Pradesh is an educationally backward state, but the market plays a key role in the education sector, as seen in private schools and colleges and a large 'shadow school industry' in the state (ibid.: 512–13). By 2000 neoliberal policies had clearly entered different spheres of the state sector. Hyderabad has been called the cyber city and has become a major Information Technology (IT) hub. Within the state Sarangapani and Winch point to the minority status of the Muslims in relation to their religion and language, and the complex historical and social factors as well as neglect by the state that have led to their alienation from government schooling (2010). A closer reading of Tooley (2009) shows that the early unrecognised schools in the Charminar area (that formed the site of the Hyderabad study) were established by school managers not merely with business interests in mind, but more importantly with a sense of doing good to members of the community in tune with what their religion expected of them. The schools that Tooley first visited (vividly described in the first chapter of his book, see ibid.) were established in the mid-1970s and 1980s. By 2000 these were secondary/high schools that imparted education in English. Their teachers were well-educated young women and men (who failed to get regular employment) and were committed to teaching other members of their community (ibid.).

Religion is seen as a factor 'propelling private school enrolment', and hence one of the factors underlying choice. Referring to his Hyderabad study, Baird observes that,

Several schools visited in the case studies had optional subjects in Arabic, separate rooms set aside for prayer time, and facilities (such as pre-prayer washrooms) to accommodate Muslim children. Also, religion can also be highly tied to other factors that explain parental choice: for example, Muslim parents in Hyderabad speak Urdu, and most schools in Andhra Pradesh are Telugu-medium (2009: 22–23).

This specific context of schooling cannot be generalised as typical of the 'poor' (Sarangapani and Winch 2010).

The failure to enforce and monitor the regulatory framework within which private schools are to function has left the educational landscape open to corrupt practice and manipulation. While there is a formal institutional framework within which recognised schools function, Srivastava points to the existence of a 'shadow institutional framework' that is used by private unrecognised schools (2008: 452). She elaborates that this is a 'codified yet informal set of norms and procedures' used to 'manipulate and mediate the formal policy and regulatory framework for their benefit, and forms part of the de facto LFP sector, a sub-sector of the greater private unaided sector' (ibid.). She observes:

Fundamentally, the most detrimental consequence of playing by the shadow rules is that it fuels and is fuelled by perverse incentives. This can contribute to an even greater culture of bribery and corruption in the education sector, decaying the greater institutional environment for education provision (ibid.: 471–72).

Low-income families are extremely vulnerable in such a situation. Harma's study schools appear to have been established after 2000 and are primary-level schools. She mentions that

since the fieldwork for this study was carried out in winter 2005–06, four out of 16 sample LFP schools have closed down, with the continued existence of another 2–3 schools found to be financially precarious, as reported by the schools' owners in a follow-up visit (Harma 2011: 351).

A study of 'small fee'-charging private schools for the less privileged was carried out by A. De et al. (2002) in six urban and rural locations in educationally disadvantaged districts of Haryana, Uttar Pradesh and Rajasthan in 1999. Their observations were:

We came across a schooling situation of great fluidity: entrepreneurs wooing poor parents, schools breaking up or closing down because of manipulation among this group or because of oversupply. In rural areas the prospect of opening a private school is exciting for the local notables including the sarpanch (ibid.: 5234).

Pointing to what they characterised as a 'government retreat' through the absence of schools and their poor quality, they find that the educational terrain is left to private entrepreneurs who are able to flout norms and negotiate 'quality' of schooling offered so that it is only marginally better than that offered in the government school in the vicinity. Low-income parents who are unhappy with government schools find that the choice is between 'low quality and no quality at primary level — and the enrolment in the new schools (low-cost schools) is mainly at this level' (ibid.). They go on to say that though

Parents often helplessly observe while their child struggles through government primary school it is only fair to point out that there were also cases where parents were disillusioned with private schools and moved helplessly from one to the other and even went back to the government school (ibid.).

THE BUSINESS OF LOW-COST SCHOOLING[7]

Today, there is powerful advocacy for the spread of low-cost schools in India that is enmeshed in transnational networks and linked to local pro choice organisations (Nambissan and Ball 2011). The transnational roots of advocacy for school choice and educational markets for the poor in India can be traced back to United Kingdom (UK) and United States (US), to foundations, think tanks and organisations that propagate a free market philosophy. There are also important links with businesses and business philanthropists (ibid.). In India, organisations such as the Centre for Civil Society, Liberty Institute and Educate Trust are also part of these networks and have been key actors in the campaign for school vouchers and parental choice; school choice/private schooling advocacy networks also include investment companies and venture capitalists looking to new markets in India (Nambissan and Ball [2011] for details).

The major focus till around 2008 was the building of Transnational Advocacy Networks (TANs) of organisations and individuals towards advocacy of parental choice and vouchers. The objective appears largely the creation of policy climate favourable to legalising unregulated schools and to direct state funds through vouchers to 'budget schools'. The de-regulation of low-cost private schools was a major thrust of advocacy efforts in India. Efforts were also directed to creating a market for schools through school chains that were expected to yield profit from the low-income market segment. Investment companies, microcredit organisations and banks were encouraged to provide finance for existing and new schools (Tooley 2009). In 2007, the Singapore-based billionaire Richard Chandler from Oriental Global created a $100 million education fund with Tooley as its president. The education fund was set up (a) to target the market for private schooling for low-income families, (b) for research and development for chains of budget schools and extending grants to private schools, and (c) to explore appropriate technology for schooling. Microfinance organisations such as SKS Microfinance and Basix stepped in to offer loans to educational entrepreneurs who were now being referred to as 'edupreneurs' (Nambissan and Ball 2011). Grey Ghosts Ventures (GGV) also set up the India School Finance Corporation (ISFC) to provide funds to creditworthy low-cost schools. In 2008 it was reported that ISFC along with Deutsche Bank and Budget International Academies had 'committed $80,00,000 in investment to develop scalable systems that use new capital to strengthen local expertise and delivery systems that will eventually provide millions of poor children in the developing world with *high quality education*'(emphasis mine).[8] It must be remembered that this was also the time when elementary education was made a fundamental right (RTE 2009). Whether the low-cost scalable systems and standardisation of quality advocated for poor children would provide them an education of equitable quality is the moot question. Some of the evidence has been examined in the next section.

Around 2009–10 we see signs of corporate players beginning to establish schools/school chains and build brands to 'sell' low-cost schools in India. Their entry appears to be based on research by their advocates that showed that budget schools were a profitable venture but required specific marketing strategies. Richard Chandler came in to establish the Rumi budget schools in 2008 along with Tooley and his associate Mohammed Anwar. Career Launcher, well known for setting up the high end 'coaching' or preparatory

institutes for entry to elite institutions, established the Indus Budget Academies. The SKS Microfinance group set up the Bodhi schools, while Reddy Labs had their Pudami schools. All these were mainly primary-level schools, some with pre-school and early middle-school classes. Interestingly, all of these were set up in Hyderabad/rural Andhra Pradesh. About the same time Policy Innovations (PI) and Grey Matter Capital (GMC) sponsored a study in Hyderabad (the city where Tooley did his research) to study the leading role that GMC could play in the low-cost school market (PI and GMC 2010). They also explored the possibility of parental demand for GMC ratings of what were now being called 'Affordable Private Schools'(APS) — schools that charged a tuition fee of up to ₹800 per month. Business prospects for new 'market entrants' in educational services were also studied (ibid.). Educational services that have been listed as top priority (based on a survey of APS 'shoppers'/parent 'consumers') are: private tuition classes, computer classes and computers. Computer classes were flagged as the 'new English' by PI and GMC, meaning that these services were most in demand by a parent (ibid.: 63–64). By 2011 the promise of the low-cost budget school market bubble appeared to have burst. The poor quality of teaching in low-cost schools, problems of sustainability and scalability were proving to be costly for the companies in edu-business in this sector. Career Launcher closed down its Indus Budget Academies in less than two years of its establishment. Nupur Garg (2011) has quoted the project director explaining why the organisation was forced to close its 'budget' schools:

Indus Budget Academy had struggled to reach financial sufficiency. Based out of Delhi they could not establish relationships with local communities. Their enrolment rates continue to remain low (10–30 enrolments in a year) and at a monthly fee of $4, Career Launcher lost a fair amount of money before they exited (ibid.: 29).

More recently there appears to be an effort by some players in the low-cost market to rework strategies and look for greener educational pastures — the buzz words being Affordable Private Schools and Educational Service Providers (ESPs). Garg observes that

Education Service Providers have become an increasingly important part of the Indian education eco system and this segment has been seeing rising private sector interest. ESPs offer a range of services including teacher and management trainings/workshops, curriculum management and teaching activities and methodologies. They target improved educational experience for students through improved teaching methods and teacher trainings (ibid.: 35).

Chandler for instance has now entered the APS market to provide educational services (as Rumi Schools of Excellence)

to schools that cater to the upper segment of the low-cost private education market — 'the middle of the pyramid'. Tooley (as discussed later) has also entered the market for educational services.

Corporate players appear to be looking towards higher-fee school markets that are likely to yield greater profits than budget schools catering to the near bottom of the economic pyramid. For instance, after its Indus Budget school fiasco, Career Launcher is now 'planning their second phase involvement in rural schools, though this time, they intend to charge a fee in the range of $10–12 per month' (Garg 2011: 29). There are also international players who are investing/co-investing in chains of schools in the higher-fee/affordable (though still referred to as 'low fee') private school sector. These include SONG Investment Advisors (Song), Omdiyar Network, Google and Clinton Global Initiative. Some (including Tooley) are involved in similar for-profit school chains (Omega schools) in Africa as well. Career Launcher, Omdiyar and Song are also targeting middle-class parents. For instance, Career Launcher has its K-12 Indus World Schools in two-tier cities. Song advisors have invested in Gowtham (low-cost schools) as well as Chaitanya schools for the elite. It is important that all these corporate groups strongly advocate a more conducive regulatory environment for the private school sector (ibid.).[9]

The movement of low-cost school players in and out of segments of the private school market is likely to have serious implications for the education of children, especially from low-income families. It is surprising that the voices of parents who enrolled their children in these new schools with aspirations of quality education at relatively low cost (though the tuition fee in most schools appears to be well over ₹250/₹300 per month, likely to be unaffordable even for the near poor) are not heard in any of the reports, studies or websites.

THE QUALITY OF EDUCATION

The most critical issue in schooling today is that of quality. As has been highlighted by budget school advocacy, it is because of aspirations for 'quality' education variously perceived by different social classes that there has been a shift from government to private schooling. English-medium schooling is often equated with 'good education' by low-income parents, a fact exploited by players in the private sector who are advocating low-cost schools for them. There have been scattered references in the literature to fluidity of enrolment across the state and low-cost private sector schools (De et al. 2002). Low-income parents are seen to move their children between schools in search of good education for them and are constrained by its availability, cost and sustainability.

Studies are silent about the quality of the teaching–learning process in the low-cost schools. The teacher, the target of budget school advocacy and of making such schools cost-efficient, has also received inadequate attention and there are few references to their perceptions and experiences or career pathways. De et al. (ibid.) speak of educated youth being brought to these schools to teach and willing to work for a pittance. Teachers in Lall's study were mainly young women for whom teaching was a 'time pass' activity, a stepping stone to some other vocation and not a career in itself. While teachers were mainly graduates, there were some who had passed secondary school. Very few were trained teachers. They were paid very low monthly salaries, ranging from ₹400–2,000, the latter likely in higher classes, and for teaching specific subjects (Lall 2000: 19).

The nature of curriculum transactions and classroom processes in low-cost schools are yet to become the focus of research, and reports on what happens in these schools is usually anecdotal. The schools that Tooley visited in 2000, which form the basis of his advocacy for budget schools are secondary and high schools that were already part of the 'Federation of Private Schools Management', which was lobbying for a more 'conducive' regulatory framework (2009). Descriptions of these schools in his book give us a glimpse of the perspective of school managers and their concern with the quality of the teaching and learning process. He tells us that Peace High School was founded by the present manager's mother in 1973. She motivated the manager to help his community saying that he should consider the 'less blessed people in the slums, and that his highest ambition should be to help them, as befitting his Muslim faith' (ibid.: 8). The school offered kindergarten to Class X and the fees ranged from ₹60–100 per month. Tooley describes the morning assembly, which like any regular private school had announcements, readings from newspapers, demonstrations of interesting activities by students, and so on. These schools made a modest profit, but Tooley was told by the manager that 'profit wasn't a great issue for them, but certainly they viewed themselves as businesspeople, as well as people who served the poor' (ibid.: 9). Another school founded in 1982 had a school manager who taught mathematics and also trained his teachers before they began teaching in his school. Tooley's description of one such teacher (who had a master's degree in organic chemistry) is reflective of the older schools in the community:

She was clear, lively, animated, and engaged her class throughout. There was nothing labored about her approach; the whole lesson moved forward smoothly. She taught without notes and seemed completely on top of her subject. At the end she summarised the lesson, expertly managing the class so that all seemed to have understood, and set a three-part homework assignment (ibid.: 11).

Tooley's associate, Anwar, also had a high school and was holding a 'science fair' for other schools at the time of the former's visit. It was these teachers that Tooley was impressed by in early 2000. Unfortunately the budget school advocacy in which he has played a key role is based on a different kind of teacher: minimally qualified, low-skilled and easily replaceable. This has serious implications for the quality of education on offer.

Lall (2000) observed primary classrooms in the 10 'small fee' private schools that she studied in Jaipur city in 2000. Her report provides some descriptions of curriculum transactions and teacher–student relations in these schools. Unlike what Tooley has described, in none of the schools was the pedagogy anything more than reading from the text and copying of answers by children from the textbook into their notebooks with copious amounts of unfinished lessons given as homework. Teachers in these schools lacked training and as mentioned did not see teaching as a career, but a temporary activity. Teachers who were not equipped to teach first and second generation of school goers and were not competent in the English language had to meet the high expectations of school managers who were competing for students and parents who wanted to see some signs of learning and speaking English in their children. Working under pressure, it is not surprising that corporal punishment was reportedly frequent when children did not meet their teachers' expectations:

The approach to teaching all the subjects is the same — the syllabus should be completed and the children prepared to perform in the examinations…Very rarely were children asked to participate, even in the rote learning by giving examples. Their participation was limited to repeating a few definitions when asked for and copy things from the blackboard. Activity based teaching was an unheard of concept. Most of the children are quite conditioned in schooling, understand the code quite well, and behave accordingly. They also know the result of not conforming … We have observed children being slapped hard right across their faces for doing some extra worksheets in their workbook, for asking sometimes innocuous questions. (ibid.: 35).

From available reports, the quality of education in the post-2000 low-cost schools that offer largely primary-level education is likely to be a serious concern. Teachers are largely untrained, an increasing number whose basic educational qualifications are barely beyond secondary/higher secondary school. They are on contract and their salary is linked to classroom presence. Market surveys/credit ratings by corporate players have also voiced scepticism about the quality of instruction in budget schools (Chandrasekaran 2012; Joshi 2008). In 2003 Tooley had observed that teachers who were paid a fraction of the salary received by regular government school teachers were doing a better job at teaching than the

latter. In 2010 Tooley himself admits to shoddy teaching and rapid turnover of teachers — who leave these schools for a mere raise of ₹100/200 (Chandrasekaran 2012). His associate Anwar acknowledges that 'in some low cost schools (not his) teachers are so under qualified, that they cannot speak in English let alone teach in English one of the biggest attractions for parents in the lower income segment' (Garg 2011: 31).

What are the solutions offered by the new players in the low-cost school sector to address the key concern of improving teacher performance in terms of pedagogy and classroom transactions? Tooley, now a player in the low-cost education market himself, says that he is 'hoping to treat two primary ailments without stretching his purse: shoddy instruction and teacher attrition' (Chandrasekaran 2012: 1). He along with Anwar has set up Empathy Systems to provide educational services to a chain of low-cost schools to improve their quality. Chandrasekaran notes that '[a]t Empathy schools, detailed lesson plans are used to combat higher teacher turnover, so that new teachers can immediately fill in the shoes of their predecessors'. As Tooley explains: '[a] low-cost teacher training model ensures that you are not investing in instructors so much that the whole system collapses when they leave' (ibid.). His company Empathy Systems provides low-cost tools to teachers to improve the 'quality' of their teaching. The model seen as particularly relevant for low-cost education markets is 'para skilling', defined as 'disaggregating complex processes into simple, routine and standardised tasks. These can then be undertaken by less skilled workers, with the desired reduction in costs and a simultaneous increase of volume and output'. In schools this effectively means breaking down of curricular and pedagogical processes into simple routine and standardised tasks so that they can be handled by 'less skilled' but suitably trained individuals' at low salaries (Karamchandani et al. 2009: 57–58). Rather than ensuring that teachers in these schools are professionally trained and equipped to teach children from poor and disadvantaged families, the effort appears to be to reduce teaching to simple standardised set of tasks that can be handled by anyone who is 'suitably trained'. In other words, the effort appears to be to cut costs and 'teacher proof' the schools so that the teacher herself does not matter.

Given the value that parents place on private schooling (good education), the ethics of advocating low-cost schools as providing 'high quality education' must be questioned. Baird recalls that:

[a]cross Hyderabad and Mumbai, parents repeatedly cited the overwhelming importance of education as a reason why they would spend large proportions of their income to send their children to private school—if they felt that private education was

providing their children with the best available educational needs, they would make financial sacrifices to do so. Poor families spend up to one third of their income sending their children to private school because they value education so highly. Many parents that I spoke with have sold, pawned, or mortgaged comforts to send their children to private school, if it meant that the child's education would be substantially better (and some families I spoke with sold land that had been in their family village for generations). This variable is difficult to operationalise in a model, though. Individual level data about the value of education, such as state-wise public opinion surveys, are not available (Baird 2009: 37).

Unfortunately low-cost private school advocates who use that variable (parental aspirations) to advocate such schools have turned a blind eye to these aspirations as they look for ways to maximise profits through low-cost schooling. There is also a systematic attempt to denigrate public systems of education that overwhelmingly cater to most vulnerable and disadvantaged families who have never been factored into the budget school advocacy.

CONCLUSION

The foregoing discussion draws attention to the unregulated private school sector in India. Over the last decade this sector that has been the target of advocacy groups that are projecting the low-cost school market as a cost-efficient, high quality and equitable solution to the education of the poor. It is also showcased as a site for viable business options. The advocacy is driven by powerful financial and political (pro-market) interests that are linked together through transnational networks, and is couched within a neoliberal discourse of school markets for the poor through school choice and voucher programmes. These are programmes that are yet to show reliable research evidence of having worked elsewhere in the world.

As highlighted, much of the 'evidence' on low-cost schools is weak and the picture we have is very fragmentary. However, the available studies suggest that the drive toward profits and cutting down of costs have detrimental implications for teachers, curriculum transactions and the very purpose of education. 'Para skilling', that is being acclaimed as a model for training of teachers in low-cost schools, is merely the 'drilling' of young people to perform the role

of 'less skilled workers' who will transact a narrow set of skills — standardised, homogenised and mechanical skills that do not provide a meaningful and holistic education for children. The fact that private and corporate players are content largely with offering only minimalistic primary-level schooling with a promise to poor parents that their children will have access to good quality English-medium education is a clear case of discrimination against these families. Further, many of the corporate players in the low-cost school sector are simultaneously offering middle and elite sections of Indian society a qualitatively different package of education: K-12, well-resourced schools that will yield high profits. These trends are reflective of a democratic and ethical deficit in the spread of the new unregulated private schools.

The non-state sector has played a critical role in the spread of elementary education in India. The history of schooling, especially in the colonial period and early post-Independence decades, bears witness to these efforts. Today the RTE Act (2009) provides a framework within which the private sector can meaningfully participate in the education of children. In fact it shows the way ahead for the corporate players who wish to provide 'high quality' education to children of the poor and thereby carry out their social responsibility. However, the Act requires that all schools meet basic norms that have been laid down in relation to indictors of quality and commitment to social justice. Not surprisingly the private school advocates and new players in the market are leading the efforts to lobby to see that they are not covered by the RTE (2009).[10]

As discussed, there are powerful financial interests involved in the private school sector in India, recently estimated to be a $70 billion recession-proof industry (Jhingan and Mohanty 2008). Hence we are likely to see well-organised efforts to influence policy-makers to create more 'conducive' regulatory environments to enable profits to be made from the private education sector across the board. In this context, low-income parents aspiring to private education for their children are likely to be most seriously affected. The framing of education as a fundamental right has brought the education of children within the perspective of judiciable rights and non-discrimination back on the agenda. It is important that the rights of all children and especially of the poor are protected and serious research and policy attention be drawn to the unregulated school sector.

NOTES

1. 'Budget'/Low-fee schools are terms that have emerged in the literature on private schools for the poor. These are not clearly defined but broadly refer to unregulated private schools that are accessed by low-income families as they charge what are

seen as lower fees than regular private schools. Budget schools were identified as those that charged less than around $2 (less than around ₹100) a month. Gradually the term 'low fee' private school was used. Studies using this term do not make clear how 'low' is 'low fee' and who decides this. The term 'low cost'/ 'budget' has been used to underscore that these schools are run at minimal costs.

2. Data from the District Information System for Education (DISE 2009–10) shows that in 2009, around 20 per cent of recognised schools in India were under private managements. Of these 14 per cent were unaided schools (NUEPA 2011). The number of private unaided schools does not include unregulated/unrecognised schools.

3. As is well known, there are private schools that receive financial assistance from the state. In 2005 these schools accounted for 5 per cent of enrolment in the school-going age group (Desai et al. 2010).

4. The IHDS (2005) covered 41,500 households in urban and rural areas across India and focused on indicators to assess human development. For details, see De et al. (2010).

5. In the light of the popular assumption that the middle classes were no longer accessing government educational institutions, it must be emphasised that IHDS reports that in 2005 a fairly large section of children from relatively better-of families in the fourth (67 per cent) and top (48 per cent) income quintiles continued to send their children to government-run/aided elementary schools (see ibid.).

6. Harma's study was carried out in 2005–06 in a 13-village cluster in western Uttar Pradesh. Her sample comprised 250 households randomly selected from the primarily agricultural village with the majority 'farmers or landless day labourers'. Sixteen LFP schools in the villages were included in the study (2011).

7. The discussion on private low-cost schools and the players in this market draws on information from Garg (2011) as well as relevant websites: http://www.guardian.co.uk/global-development/2012/jul/03/pearson-invest-private-education-africa-asia; http://www.sedfny.org/portfolio/success-stories/song-success-story.html; and http://www.indusworldschool.com/ (accessed 12 April 2010).

8. http://www.clintonglobalinitiative.org/commitments/commitments_search.asp?Section=Commitments&PageTitle=Browse%20and%20Search%20Commitments&id=304699 (accessed 20 May 2012).

9. See also the following websites: http://www.guardian.co.uk/global-development/2012/jul/03/pearson-invest-private-education-africa-asia; http://www.sedfny.org/portfolio/success-stories/song-success-story.html; and http://www.indusworldschool.com/ (accessed 12 April 2010).

10. See http://schoolchoice.in/blog/?cat=12 (accessed 25 June 2012).

REFERENCES

Baird, Ross. 2009. 'Private Schools for the Poor Development, Provision, and Choice in India: A Report for Gray Matters Capital'. http://www.dise.in/Downloads/Use%20of%20Dise%20Data/Ross%20Baird.pdf (accessed 22 October 2012).

Chandrasekaran, A. 2012. 'Law Threatens Low-Cost Private', *livemint.com*. http://www.livemint.com/2010/06/24233124/Law-threatens-lowcost-private.html. (accessed 30 April 2012).

De, A., M. Samson and C. Noronha. 2002. 'Private Schools for Less Privileged: Some Insights from a Case Study', *Economic and Political Weekly*, 28 December, 37(52): 5230–36.

Desai, Sonalde, A. Dubey, B. L. Joshi, M. Sen, A. Sharif, and R. Vanneman. 2010. *Human Development in India. Challenges for a Society in Transition.* New Delhi: Oxford University Press.

Garg, Nupur. 2011. 'Low Cost Private Education in India: Challenges and Way Forward'. Dissertation, MIT Sloan School of Management.

Harma, Joanna. 2011. 'Low Cost Private Schooling in India: Is it Pro-poor and Equitable?', *International Journal of Educational Development*, 31: 350–56.

Jhingan, Seema and Dimpy Mohanty. 2008. 'India's Education Sector — Back to School'. http://ezinearticles.com/?Indias-Education-Sector—Back-to-School&id=1654398 (accessed 27 February 2010).

Joshi, Shruti. 2008. 'Private Budget Schools in Hyderabad City, India, a Reconnaissance Study'. http://www.greymatterscap.com (accessed 20 February 2012).

Juneja, Nalini. 2010. 'Access to What? Access, Diversity and Participation in India's Schools', CREATE Pathways to Access, Research Monograph, no. 32. http://www.create-rpc.org/pdf_documents/PTA32.pdf (accessed 4 April 2012).

Karamchandani, A., M. Kubzansky and P. Frandano. 2009. 'Market-based Solutions to the Challenges of Global Poverty', http:// www.bdsknowledge.org/dyn/bds/docs/752/Emerging%20Mkts%20Full.pdf (accessed 27 February 2010).

Lall, Jyotsna. 2000. *Schools for Thought: A Study of Small Private Schools in Jaipur.* Jaipur: Bodh Shiksha Samiti.

Mehta, A. C. 2005. *Elementary Education in Unrecognised Schools in India – A Study of Punjab Based on DISE 2005 Data.* New Delhi: National Institute of Education Planning and Administration (NIEPA).

Muralidharan, Karthik and Michael Kremer. 2008. 'Public and Private Schools in Rural India'. http://www.economics.harvard.edu/faculty/kremer/files/Public%20and%20private%20schools%20in%20rural%20india%20%28Final%20Pre-Publication%29.pdf (accessed 28 May 2012).

Nambissan, Geetha. 2003. 'Educational Deprivation and Primary School Provision – A Study of Providers in the City of Calcutta', IDS Working Paper no. 187. Brighton: Institute of Development Studies.

———. 2012. 'Private Schools for the Poor: Business as Usual? *Economic and Political Weekly*, 47(41): 51–58.

Nambissan, Geetha B. and S. J. Ball. 2011. 'Advocacy Networks, Choice and Private Schooling of the Poor in India', in Lall Marie and Geetha B. Nambissan (eds), *Education and Social Justice in the Era of Globalisation — Perspectives from India and the UK*, pp. 161–86. New Delhi: Routledge.

National University of Educational Planning and Administration (NUEPA). 2011. 'Elementary Education in India: Progress towards Universal Elementary Education', DISE, 2009–10, *Flash Statistics*. New Delhi: NUEPA.

Policy Innovations and Gray Matters Capital (PI and GMC). 2010. 'Consumers of Affordable Private Schools: A Study of Parents in Low-Income Communities in Hyderabad, India'. https://graymatterscap.box.net/shared/16sv06u95y (accessed 20 January 2012).

Prahlad, C. K. 2005. *The Fortune at the Bottom of the Pyramid: Eradicating Poverty through Profits*. New Delhi: Pearson Education.

Right to Education (RTE). 2009. 'Right of Children to Free and Compulsory Education Act, 2009', *Gazette of India*, 27 August. Ministry of Law and Justice. http://ssa.nic.in (accessed 5 April 2012).

Rose, P. and C. Dyer. 2008. 'Chronic Poverty and Education: A Review of Literature'. Working Paper no. 131. Manchester: Chronic Poverty Research Centre. http://www.chronicpoverty.org/uploads/publication_files/WP131_Rose_and_Dyer.pdf (accessed 27 February 2012).

Sarangapani, P. M. and C. Winch. 2010. 'Tooley, Dixon and Gomathi on Private Education in Hyderabad: A Reply', *Oxford Review of Education*, 36(4): 499–515.

Srivastava, Prachi. 2007. 'Neither Voice nor Loyalty: School Choice and the Low-Fee Private Sector in India'. http://www.ncspe.org/publications_files/OP134.pdf (accessed 15 April 2012).

————. 2008. 'The Shadow Institutional Framework: Towards a New Institutional Understanding of an Emerging Private School Sector in India', *Research Papers in Education*, 23(4): 451–75.

Tooley, J. 2009. *The Beautiful Tree: A Personal Journey into how the World's Poorest People are Educating Themselves*. New Delhi: Penguin.

Tooley, J., P. Dixon and S. V. Gomathi. 2007. 'Private Schools and the Millennium Development Goal of Universal Primary Education: A Census and Comparative Survey in Hyderabad, India', *Oxford Review of Education*, 33(5): 539–60.

Tooley, J., P. Dixon, Y. Shamsan and I. Schagen. 2010. 'The Relative Quality and Cost-effectiveness of Private and Public Schools for Low-income Families: A Case Study in a Developing Country', *School Effectiveness and School Improvement*, 21(2): 117–44.

9 | The Idea of Quality in Inclusive Schools

Annie Koshi

THE CHALLENGE OF DEFINING 'QUALITY' EDUCATION

The rationale of reserving 25 per cent seats for the economically weaker section (EWS) in schools run by the non-state sector and the ongoing debate on it contributes interestingly to the definition of a 'quality' education as envisaged in the Right to Education (RTE) Act, 2009. The RTE has used the word 'quality' to define what the state envisages as a meaningful and relevant education and in the process has succumbed to the need of modern times to quantify, prioritise and compare. While setting quality standards is not something to be rundown, the effort becomes particularly problematic in an area like education, where the quality that requires to be quantified is something so delicate a product, as the core or character of education. When we attempt to further define this character by such tangibles as a school building, pupil–teacher ratio (PTR) and timelines for curriculum completion and outcomes, we are stepping into neoliberal ideas of system and management, which are strongly influenced by economic policies. In *A Pedagogue's Romance* (2008), Krishna Kumar explains that the romance and adventure of education lies in the fact that children, like stem cells, have the ability to transform themselves to something far beyond their predicted outcomes, that there is no guarantee that a particular input will produce a specific result. It is in such a situation that this paper looks at the words 'access', 'equity' and 'quality'. These are words synonymous with the RTE. Each of these terms while seemingly simple to understand and deal with, have scaffolding meanings and consequent transactions in different contexts. This paper will explore the meanings and implications of these three interconnected words specifically in the context of inclusion, with special references to the practices of two private, unaided schools — Loreto Day School, Sealdah, Kolkata and St Mary's School, Safdarjung Enclave, New Delhi.

PRACTISING 'INCLUSION' IN SCHOOLS

Inclusive practices celebrate difference and require first and foremost that the child be set at centre stage. All systems are changed to accommodate the child while in other more typical setups the child is required to adapt in order to fit into an inviolate system. Adventure and romance, as is argued here, lies at the core of such an education.

In order to ensure access, an inclusive school will work at removing the barriers that stand in the way of any child attending and continuing in school. The attitude of teachers and their understanding of a child's ability, teaching methodology in classroom, homogeneous assessment practices and high fees, while an integral part of all schools, can become insurmountable barriers to a child with disability (Booth and Ainscow 2000).

In the case of the just mentioned schools, both have reduced, removed or redistributed fees to ensure that they have a representative population from their neighbourhood. For instance, while some children pay half the fees there are others who pay their own and an extra half voluntarily. There is also a category of students who do not pay any fee at all. The community — comprising teacher, student, parent, and immediate neighbourhood — and its empowerment to think beyond conventional understandings form a strong component of all programmes in the schools. This in turn results in changing attitudes and creating welcoming communities.

One visually challenged child was enough to prove in St Mary's that most classroom methodologies in the school catered to a homogeneous group. As attitudes changed and became more welcoming of difference and as a diverse student population entered the school, modifications in pedagogy and curriculum became a daily feature. Each special child brought with him/her new opportunities for the school as well as for the teacher to grow, leading to the introduction of a comprehensive and continuous, child-centred and child-driven method of assessment. Soon this diverse classroom transaction and assessment patterns was extended to include all children. The modification of classroom transactions, curriculum and evaluation practices is an extremely important part of ensuring an equitable quality education for all children, since a homogeneous curriculum and evaluation cannot be considered equitable unless it is matched with differentiated instruction that suits the needs of every child.

When approached from a rights-based model (and not through a medical or charity model), inclusion has the ability to transform teaching methodologies and assessment practices. It is a great way to enhance a teacher's repertoire of classroom transactions. For in the teacher's quest to reach the child, he/she reaches into him-/herself for new ideas and reservoirs of understanding; as a result, teacher empowerment is an important outcome of the ongoing journey of inclusion. It is a journey that requires each group — parents, teachers and children — to examine itself and to change coordinates in order to fit into each other better.

Working with inclusion requires focused and committed Heads who are prepared for the long haul. Committed Heads hold themselves accountable for their teachers' performances and levels of commitment. The teacher then in turn holds him-/herself accountable to the child. It is only this continued focus, on what matters, that changes attitudes that are stuck in socio-cultural understandings of disability. This melting of hardened attitudes and prejudices continues to be the major focus in all programmes of the mentioned two schools.

It was in trying to understand and implement inclusion in every sense of the word that St Mary's School first modified infrastructure. Ramps were built where possible and a lift was also installed to enable children with special needs to access every floor. Furniture was modified to individual needs and toilets were equipped with supporting bars. Loreto School, Sealdah has proved that the idea of quality and equity does not lie in giving all children similar infrastructure, but in the will of a school and all its inmates to adapt itself to the needs of its children. In Loreto, the use of the building was changed to include a residential space for street children in danger of abuse and violence. St Mary's opened a centre for the Open School so as to allow children studying in mainstream classes an alternative school leaving certificate.

Loreto, Sealdah, in response to the needs of the neighbourhood, held flexi-time classes. They used students to teach their peers. The logic of using peers is that children understand better where the gap in their colleague's learning is and they are best equipped to appropriately address the problem. Thus, both teacher and student benefit and grow in the relationship. Alternative solutions will be required to address new problems; examples of which can be seen.

Tillonia, Rajasthan runs a night school and Deepalya has schools in slums, all of which will have to be closed down if the norms of the RTE (discussed in the next section) are strictly implemented. Access to quality education for all requires that we consider Basil B. Bernstein's statement that 'the right to be included may also require a right to be separate' (2000: xx).

RTE AND INCLUSION

The emerging educational paradigm currently envisaged by the RTE demands greater access and integration of children to help create a more equitable social milieu for access to opportunities. The RTE while wanting to be inclusive and to set quality standards does the opposite by setting norms and standards in class strength, PTR and curriculum and evaluation procedures because it places systems over child and in the process removes the adventure from education by negating difference.

The idea of access as envisaged by the RTE looks at providing 'special training' to differently-abled children, which will presumably enable them to 'be at par with other children' (MHRD 2011: 15) and familiarise them with the new, changed educational transactional mode enabling them to cope with an age appropriate class (GoI 2009). The focus on age appropriate admission, when combined with 'complet[ing the] entire curriculum within the specified time' (ibid.: 8), 'all round development of the child' and 'comprehensive and continuous evaluation of child's understanding of knowledge and his ability to apply the same' (ibid.: 9), raises concerns regarding accessibility of children with special needs. Rather than enabling children to learn at their own pace and providing the space to do so the *Framework for Implementation* (2011) sends out the message that all children can do the same thing. It specifically states that 'the same curriculum be followed for children with and without special needs' (MHRD 2011: 49). In its effort to give access to an equitable quality education to all, the RTE has attempted to plug the loopholes through which schools exclude children by making illegal interviews, admission tests and other such discriminatory practices. But the RTE has denied retention and continued presence by not acknowledging that there are children who are not typical, that there will always be some children who benefit with an early assessment and intervention, while there will be others who will not.

RTE AND RESERVATION

The RTE seeks to reserve 25 per cent of the seats for the EWS, in the very same private schools that have publicly and sadly stated that admitting children from this category will reduce the quality of their schools. Private unaided schools have taken legal action against the government on this issue. If in spite of this the government insists that these reluctant institutions admit the 'disadvantaged category', one can only conclude that it must be because they believe that admission to an unaided private school guarantees the child quality education. The question that rises then is how will the State guarantee the same quality of education to the remaining 75 per cent of 'out-of-private-school' children. The discrimination in the design seems to indicate that it is right of the state to provide quality education to some and let the others, who also happen to be the majority of students, remain in state schools with constraints.

But more importantly, by indiscriminately seeking placement of 25 per cent in every private unaided school the RTE has indicated that all private unaided schools are quality schools. This is obviously not true. Just like there are good and bad state schools, there are also good and bad private schools. While minimum norms are desirable, the ongoing debate has shown that quality education will be impossible unless schools are also welcoming communities. While infrastructure is important, quality schools would first and foremost have to be inclusive schools, i.e., *(a)* schools that are open to change and adaptable; *(b)* schools that are defined by the attitudes and participation of not just the students and staff, but also the community around it; and *(c)* schools that while redefining themselves also give time for consolidation and research, or what Peter M. Senge (2000) calls 'moving schools' are those that will personify and hopefully redefine quality for all of us.

'Quality' as defined by a 'moving school' and by the RTE has two different parameters. The RTE tends to define a quality education in its narrowest terms of infrastructure, curriculum and evaluation. By creating invisible children who require a differentiated or individualised curriculum and evaluation, the RTE has celebrated a curriculum that is discriminatory. The RTE and the *Framework for Implementation* (2011) have given legal standing to this perspective by conspicuously omitting any reference to co-curricular activities or even to essential parts of education such as physical fitness and sports. It is in this context that this paper argues that there is a need to extend the ambit of education in the RTE to include its ancillary services such as nutrition, care, physical fitness, and community participation if we are to accept the concept of education as one that is more than just schooling.

Conclusion

If the government expenditure is to create long-term solutions and not just dependence, the quality of State-run schools needs to be urgently and consistently addressed. The RTE needs to acknowledge that every child is different from the other and that one story will not fit all. The SSA *Framework of Implementation*, which states that '[i]t provides for children's right to an education of equitable quality, based on principles of equity and non discrimination' (MHRD 2011: 3), needs to clearly acknowledge the need, as well as provide for, a diverse transactional framework and alternate assessment patterns in order to prove that it is serious about delivering an education that is truly inclusive and non-discriminatory. The RTE and the Framework need to accept the value of physical education as well as the arts and crafts in its curriculum. It needs to look closely at infrastructural requirements and state these in appropriately sensitive terminology. It also needs to be clarified that the best infrastructure and parameters in evaluation and curriculum may still fall short of delivering an ideal education if our teachers falter and our understandings fail. Consequently, the RTE should most importantly emphasise and implement a strong teacher education programme focused on the vision of an inclusive classroom and where every child is getting an equitable, quality education.

References

Bernstein, Basil B. 2000. *Pedagogy, Symbolic Control and Identity*. Oxford: Rowman & Littlefield.

Government of India (GoI). 2009. 'The Right of Children to Free and Compulsory Education'. *Gazette of India*, 27 August.

Kumar, Krishna. 2008. *A Pedagogue's Romance: Reflections on Schooling*. New Delhi: Oxford University Press.

Ministry of Human Resource Development (MHRD). 2011. *Framework for Implementation: Based on the Right of Children to Free and Compulsory Education Act, 2009*. New Delhi: Department of School Education and Literacy, Ministry of Human Resource and Development, Government of India.

Senge, Peter M. 2000. *Schools That Learn: A Fifth Discipline Field Book for Educators, Parents, and Everyone Who Cares About Education*. New York: Doubleday.

10 Thinking Outside the Government Box

The Role of the Non-Government Sector in Achieving Quality Education for All

Suzana Andrade Brinkmann

Discussions about the role of the private sector in education have become increasingly polarised between those who feel its contribution should be expanded, and others who believe the opposite. But what can sometimes get lost in these heated debates are the repercussions of these decisions for children themselves.

On one hand, the government's 11th Five-Year Plan speaks repeatedly of the benefits of public–private partnership (PPP) in education, and strongly encourages PPP models through private investment (Planning Commission 2008). In 2009, the Ministry of Human Resource Development (MHRD) released a note on PPP that highlighted several advantages of private schools: cost-effectiveness, better quality and greater accountability through incentives and competition. Others have argued similarly about the merits of the private sector *vs* the inefficiency of the government system (Das 2010; Shah 2010) with Pankaj Jain and Ravindra Dholakia (2009) proposing that the only practical way to achieve universal education is for the government to outsource the bulk of primary education to the private sector. Such proposals have incited vociferous objections from academics, who argue that assumptions regarding the superiority of private schools are unsubstantiated, that it is unacceptable to relinquish the government's responsibility in providing education, and that greater private involvement will only create a more stratified and inequitable school system (Kumar 2008; Ramachandran 2009; Rampal et al. 2009; Sarangapani 2009). The difficulty with these debates is that often the issue gets so bogged down in theoretical positions, ideological prejudices and mistrust of the other side, that it becomes difficult for either side to truly pay attention to valid points being raised by the other, look objectively at the scale of the problem, and agree on a workable way forward based on what's best for children.

Faced with the problem of over 220 million children receiving education of dubious quality, the ultimate goal for both sides is the same: to provide quality education to every child. The question is how best to achieve the goal. This goal is now upheld constitutionally by the 'Right to Education' (RTE) Act, 2009, which is highly commendable. However, what still remains in question is whether the strategy laid out by the Act is indeed the best way to achieve the desired goal. The RTE was intended to promote an inclusive approach to providing quality education for all, yet its provisions will end up excluding a diverse set of stakeholders from helping achieve this gargantuan task. By setting stringent requirements for schools focusing on infrastructure, teacher qualifications and salaries rather than on learning processes and outcomes, the Act will force a large number of non-government schools to shut down. The norms laid down by the Act are well-intentioned, but the question remains whether they will help or hinder us in achieving the desired goal of providing quality education to every child.

This paper argues that these RTE provisions are not ultimately in the best interest of children since they exclude five key non-state education providers and thereby eliminate schooling options for millions of children. It examines some of the key arguments advocated by those supporting this move, and ultimately calls for a shift from a competitive to a collaborative PPP model to enable us to achieve our common goals.

RTE's Consequences for Non-State Schools

In the attempt to ensure quality education for all children, the RTE lays down certain norms that all schools (government and private) must comply with by April 2013 (see Table 10.1). Any private school that fails to obtain government recognition based on meeting these norms by then will be forced to shut down. Anyone who continues to run an unrecognised private school shall be fined ₹100,000 plus an additional ₹10,000 per day. In effect, the Act means impending death for thousands of non-government schools around the country that do not meet these standards and are unlikely to be able to. Sure enough, the crackdown has already begun. Education officials in Visakhapatnam and Chennai have already closed down hundreds of unrecognised schools, threatening to impose fines, seal premises, launch criminal proceedings, and even imprison errant school managements (Kumar 2011; Manikandan 2012). The ironic part is that most government schools themselves have been unable to meet these norms, even after a decade of intense efforts under the Sarva Shiksha Abhiyan (SSA), and after two years of the RTE being in place. A recent review of the RTE's implementation by the civil society-led RTE Forum reveals that 95.2 per cent of government schools are not compliant with RTE (*First Post* 2012). However, it is not clear whether there will be any consequences for government schools that do not meet the April 2013 deadline — in fact there are already attempts by the government to simply extend this deadline (Chopra 2012).

WHO IS BEING EXCLUDED BY THE ACT?

There are five non-state educational providers in particular that will largely be forced to close down as a result of the Act. This section will look more closely at each of these groups.

NGO or Community Schools for the Poor

India's education sector has had a rich history of participation by voluntary non-state organisations (charitable trusts, NGOs, faith-based, community groups) that have provided quality education to the poor at very low costs. Although their number is difficult to assess, NGOs have played a significant role in complementing, and at times making up for the lack of state initiative or capacity in providing access to primary education (Blum 2009; Kumar 2008; Sarangapani 2009). The idea and history of mass education in India traces back to the very first schools for lower caste and girl children set up by missionaries in the 19th century (Kumar and Oesterheld 2007). NGOs have been particularly effective in penetrating remote or difficult areas or groups where cultural, social or geographical barriers keep children away from attending school. NGO-run schools have often sought to promote strong school-community links in curriculum and teaching, and community participation in school management and support, such as the schools run by Bharat Gyan Vigyan Samithi (BGVS) (see Box 10.1).

While some NGOs have remained small-scale, others have expanded and also sought to strengthen the government system. As Krishna Kumar (2008) points out, 'there now exists a small but significant number of NGOs who have made a valuable contribution in augmenting the state system's meagre capacity to innovate' (ibid.: 9). Shanti Jagannathan (2001) conducted a study of six such prominent NGOs: M. Venkatarangaiya (MV) Foundation, Pratham, Bodh Shiksha Samiti, Rishi Valley Rural Education Centre, Eklavya, and Centre for Educational Management and Development. She found that their work was catalytic in

---

Box 10.1
BGVS Community-Owned Schools

Bharat Gyan Vigyan Samithi (BGVS) was set up in 1989 to promote mass literacy campaigns and universalisation of quality education across the country. Originally set up at the Indian government's request by the All India People's Science Network based on their positive experience in Kerala, BGVS's general council includes activists, government representatives, educationists, and social workers from across India. BGVS has worked in various community development initiatives in 20 states with nearly 400,000 volunteers. In 2005 it began partnering with communities to open 1,200 'Gyan Vigyan Vidyalayas' in nine states — schools owned and supported by the community without government or outside funds. The idea was to avoid dependency, become sustainable and retain freedom in teaching-learning processes. Teaching methods are child-centred and fear-free, based on activities, exploration, creativity, critical pedagogy, and children's socio-cultural contexts (many of the features promoted by the RTE). The schools foster democratic secular values through songs, stories and activities promoting equality, peace and respect for diversity. Schools also act as community centres with a village library, children's activity centre, mothers' self-help group, and primary health centre. All schools are non-profit, and while they may charge minimal fees, no poor children are denied admission. Schools are managed by School Management Committees (with strong representation from women and marginalised groups), who mobilise community resources of approximately ₹200,000 per school for infrastructure, and an average of ₹1,000 per teacher for honorariums. In the first two years, the BGVS spent about ₹15 million on material preparation, residential trainings and monitoring of over 4,000 teachers, while communities invested almost ₹222 million in start-up costs and ₹100 million in salaries for the 1,200 schools. However, most of these schools will have to close after the RTE, although about 70 have said they will try to raise community funds to meet the RTE norms (BGVS n.d.).

TABLE 10.1   RTE Requirements and their Implications for Various Types of Schools

RTE Requirements

1. *Infrastructure*: All-weather building, separate classrooms for each teacher, Head-Teacher's office, playground, boundary wall, library, separate boys' and girls' toilets, drinking water, kitchen for mid-day meals, ramp access, teaching-learning equipment, play material and sports equipment.
2. *Maximum pupil–teacher ratio (PTR)*: 30:1 at primary, 35:1 at upper primary. Separate Head-Teacher and part-time art, physical and work education teachers for schools with over 100 children.
3. *Minimum teacher qualifications*: Typically Diploma in Education (DEd) or Bachelor of Education (BEd), plus passing the national Teacher Eligibility Test.
4. *Teacher salaries and service conditions*: As per prescribed State norms (Sixth Pay Commission followed in most states; e.g. in Uttar Pradesh, monthly salaries range from ₹17,996 to ₹22,955 for regular primary teachers [Kingdon 2010]).
5. Schools must follow a standardised time-bound syllabus prescribed by state/central boards.
6. Out-of-school children must enrol directly in formal schools at age-appropriate class, and receive supplementary 'special training' at the school itself for prescribed time-periods.
7. All children must enrol in a recognised formal school as defined in section 2(n) (UNICEF 2011).
8. National Institute of Open Schooling's (NIOS's) 'Open Basic Education' (OBE) programme, which hitherto certified children in home-schooling or non-formal centres through exams in Classes III, V and VIII, will now be discontinued, since all must enrol in formal schools (Sinha 2010).

School Type	Implications of RTE
Government Schools	• As per the RTE Forum report (cited in *First Post* 2012), only 4.8 per cent government schools were compliant with the RTE in 2009–10. • As per the MHRD (2012), 20 per cent government teachers (nearly 800,000) lack qualifications; 43 per cent primary and 33 per cent upper primary government schools have PTR higher than the RTE norms. • However, no clear penalty exists if government schools fail to meet RTE norms by April 2013.
Non-Governmental Organisation (NGO) Schools	• Many serve the poor, charging minimal fees, and cannot meet the RTE infrastructure, qualification and salary norms, and thus will have to close. • Many NGOs are now focusing instead on enrolling children in government schools, as the RTE suggests (Sengupta 2011).
Alternative Schools	• Many founded by concerned individuals on minimal budgets and fees, thus unable to meet norms. • Schools' philosophy based on moving beyond textbooks and designing flexible self-paced curriculum with experiential materials, no longer admissible under the RTE. • Some have appointed unqualified community youth as teachers and designed their own high-quality but uncertified training programmes. Several educators have been teaching at SSA teacher trainings and prestigious masters programmes (e.g., Tata Institute of Social Sciences [TISS] Master of Arts [MA] in Elementary Education), but do not have the government prescribed qualifications, and thus are no longer qualified to teach children (Alternative Schools 2010).
Private Budget Schools	• Mostly cater to the poor, charging monthly fees of ₹70–150 (rural) and ₹350 (urban) (De et al. 2006; Shah 2010). • Kartik Misra (2012) estimates that to meet the RTE norms, they would need to raise monthly fees to ₹1,370–4,426, which most parents cannot afford. Thus, most would have to close. • Many have *kaccha* structures (De et al. 2006). In densely-populated urban areas or slums, it is impossible to build RTE-mandated playgrounds and classrooms • Teacher salaries are typically less than one-fifth of government salaries — sometimes even one-tenth (Muralidharan 2006).
Non-Formal Schools	• No non-formal schools are permitted under the RTE. • The Act makes little mention of what will happen to thousands of children (34 per cent) that drop out of formal primary schools annually (UNESCO 2010) — hitherto being reached by non-formal schools. Thus, thousands of children will have to return to the very schools that were unable to retain them.
Home-Schooling	• When Delhi homeschooler Shreya Sahai was denied permission to take the OBE exam because of the RTE, she filed a case with the Delhi High Court arguing that the RTE infringes on parents' freedom, which has dragged on for two years (Dore 2011, 2012). • The MHRD's stance has been ambiguous: at the last court hearing it released an affidavit on 16 July 2012 that said that parents who voluntarily opt for home-schooling may continue to do so. However, in October 2012 the MHRD reversed this stand saying that the RTE is indeed against home-schooling, seeking more time to clarify the issue. The next hearing is scheduled for 19 December 2012 (*Deccan Herald* 2012; Garg 2012).

Source: Compiled by the author from the RTE Act and RTE Model Rules, 2010.

strengthening the accountability, quality and effectiveness of the government system. Jagannathan postulated a growing and strategic role for NGOs at the macro level, in supporting and enriching the government's efforts to provide quality education. However, in the wake of the RTE, the space for community schools run by small NGOs is rapidly shrinking. As educationist Meena Shrinivasan argues, 'while NGOs that cheat parents and children will be tackled by RTE, the "ones doing good work, especially in tribal areas, will also be elbowed out"' (Sengupta 2011).

Alternative Schools

One distinct category of NGO-run schools is 'alternative schools', also known as innovative or experimental schools. While many of these have also targeted marginalised children, their distinctive feature is their focus on experimenting with progressive or holistic philosophies of education. Their attempt is to cater to children who do not fit into rigid mainstream schooling structures. Their approach involves non-competitive learning environments with a flexible learning pace, enriched curriculum and child-centred pedagogy, non-threatening continuous assessment, and welcoming of different learners' uniqueness and mother-tongues (Alternative Schools 2010). By innovating in their own alternative settings, many have also been able to play a key role in supporting innovation in government schools, developing good classroom working models, and extending the national education discourse. Many of their founders have been involved in developing national educational policies such as the National Curriculum Framework, 2005, and in government teacher training, curriculum and material development processes. Thus, alternative schools have enabled the government to achieve its own educational goals by nurturing the seedbeds where educational innovations can grow and ultimately catalyse shifts in the mainstream system. This is perhaps best exemplified in the work of Rishi Valley, described in Box 10.2.

However, many alternative schools are now uncertain about their future in light of the RTE. On 14 July 2010, a National Consultation on the impact of the RTE on alternative/innovative schools was organised in Pune by Dr Maxine Bernstein, who runs an innovative school in rural Maharashtra. The group of alternative educators thereafter drafted a document titled 'A Space for Alternative Schools' (Alternative Schools 2010) which was submitted to the MHRD, advocating preserving their existence despite the RTE. The document was signed by about 35 prominent institutions like Digantar (Jaipur), Loreto School (Kolkata), Sita School, Suvidya, Asha for Education, Taleemnet (Karnataka), Centre for Learning, Rishi Valley, and others. However the fate of these schools is still unknown.

Non-Formal Education

Another significant area of NGO involvement has been non-formal education (NFE). The National Policy on Education, 1986 initiated a large systematic NFE programme for deprived children, school drop-outs, children from habitations without formal schools, working children, etc. After reaching Class V children were expected to move to formal schools. Under the SSA, a special component called Education Guarantee Scheme (EGS) and Alternative and Innovative Education (AIE) was set up to provide diversified non-formal strategies for bridging out-of-school children into the educational system. EGS centres are set up in remote areas with at least 15–25 children and no nearby formal school. AIE centres are intended for very deprived children who do not fit into the rigid formal system, e.g., street-children, migrating or working children, sex-workers' children, and older out-of-school children, transitioning them to school through back-to-school camps or bridge courses.

The SSA strongly encouraged NGOs to run non-formal education centres, acknowledging their useful role in advocacy and ensuring accountability of SSA initiatives. In fact government funding for NGOs in the education sector has

---

Box 10.2
Rishi Valley's 'School-in-a-Box'

Rishi Valley Rural Education Centre (Andhra Pradesh) began by setting up 16 one-room multi-grade 'satellite' schools in remote villages without schooling access. In 1993 it developed the 'School-in-a-Box' kit with an accompanying teacher-training programme, which it began trialling in interested government schools. The approach breaks up the syllabus into small 'milestones', arranged in the form of a 'learning ladder' with a series of activities and learning cards for each milestone, including self-assessment cards. Each child tracks their own level, and independently carries out a series of activities at their own pace with the help of teachers and peers, using a variety of learning materials. Groups of government teachers visited these schools from Karnataka (1995) and Tamil Nadu (2003), and were inspired to adapt this approach to their own government schools. Based on their success, today this 'Activity-Based Learning' approach has been upscaled to all government schools in both these states, as well as in pilots in 11 other states, reaching an estimated 10 million children in over 250,000 primary schools across the country (UNICEF 2012).

been predominantly for running NFE courses (Jagannathan 2001). For example, the MV Foundation (Andhra Pradesh) has helped mainstream thousands of rural marginalised children into government schools. However, the NFE system in India has been criticised for not getting children successfully absorbed into formal schools, or for providing sub-par education quality to underprivileged segments of the child population (where quality is defined particularly in terms of school facilities and qualified teachers). However, when quality is seen in terms of learning outcomes, not all NFE initiatives have been of poor quality, as can be seen in the example of Gyanshala schools which have produced learning outcomes comparable or higher than government schools (see Box 10.3). Moreover, NFE centres have been meeting a critical gap in reaching children that have been unable to enrol or be retained in mainstream schools. Regardless, all such non-formal education centres are now outlawed by the RTE.

Private Budget Schools

Low-cost or unrecognised private schools have been rising rapidly across the country: while official DISE data records 26,377 unrecognised schools reaching 2.67 million students, *the Annual Status of Education Report (ASER) 2011* (ASER Centre 2012) estimates that nearly 40 million rural children will be affected if budget private schools are closed down by the RTE. Many suggest official figures are grossly underestimated; for example, while official DISE 2011 data records

14 recognised and three unrecognised private schools in all of Bihar, Rangaraju et al. (2012) found 1,224 private schools in Patna alone (78 per cent of Patna's total schools), out of which 69 per cent are unrecognised. Parents typically choose these schools out of desire to learn English, and dissatisfaction with teacher attendance and performance in government schools (Das 2010; De et al. 2006, 2008; Kingdon 2008; Ohara 2012). While some have labelled these schools 'sub-standard teaching shops' that exploit children and teachers with low infrastructure and salaries (Ohara 2012; Ramachandran 2009), others argue that they are more accountable and significantly more cost-effective than government schools (their per-pupil expenditure is only 41 per cent that of government schools [Kingdon 2008]), which also enables them to hire more teachers, have lower PTR and reduce multi-grade teaching (Jain and Dholakia 2009; Kingdon 2008; Muralidharan 2006). Concerned about the RTE's ultimatum, 21 budget private schools from eight states have formed a National Independent Schools Alliance to improve their learning outcomes and convince the MHRD to allow their continuation (Singh 2012).

The quality of budget private schools has been debated, and findings remain inconclusive. In terms of learning outcomes, several studies have found that private schools perform better at both primary and upper-primary levels (ASER 2012; De et al. 2006; Goyal and Pandey 2009; Mehta 2005), with some finding this even after controlling for family and school characteristics (Desai et al. 2008; Kingdon 2008; Muralidharan 2006; Wadhwa 2008). For example, Sangeeta Goyal and Priyanka Pandey (2009) found that students of Classes IV–V from Uttar Pradesh and Madhya Pradesh perform better in language and maths in private than government schools, and in private-unrecognised than private-recognised schools, although overall learning levels were found to be low in all three school-types. Sonalde Desai et al. (2008) found that among 12,000 8–11-year-olds tested, children in private schools have higher reading and arithmetic skills than in government schools after controlling for family factors. Wilima Wadhwa (2008) uses ASER 2008 data to also show that after controlling for family-income-related factors, Class V private schools still have a learning advantage of 9 per cent over government schools, although the effect varies considerably across states. Geeta Kingdon (2008) reviews various studies from the past two decades conducted at different class levels in various states (Uttar Pradesh, Tamil Nadu, Madhya Pradesh, Andhra Pradesh), and finds that all, including her own, share the common conclusion that private schools outperform government schools in imparting learning, even after controlling for student intake. In terms of non-academic quality indicators, several studies have found that unrecognised private schools outperform government schools in terms of

---

Box 10.3
Gyanshalas

The Ahmedabad-based NGO Gyanshala, started in 1999 by Pankaj Jain, has set up over 350 low-cost non-formal schools for poor children in Classes I to III. Classes are held three hours per day in slum or village residences so that young children can easily walk to them. Costs are kept low by hiring local teachers who have passed Class XII and are willing to work for ₹2,000–2,500 per month. Gyanshala's design team studied top schools in India and the United Kingdom (UK) and put together its own curriculum with a detailed schedule of daily lesson plans and small-group activities, which teachers follow strictly and are closely monitored for. Studies have found that after three years children can read, write and perform basic maths better than their government-school counterparts. Since 2006 the Gujarat government has been supporting 70 per cent of project costs under the SSA's AIE scheme. Currently Gyanshala plans to expand to Bihar and Uttar Pradesh as well. Though critiqued for their low infrastructure and teacher salaries, Gyanshala argues that it is able to provide effective basic education at ₹1,500 per child annually — roughly one-tenth the cost incurred by government schools in the same city (Vachani and Smith 2008).

PTR, teaching activity, teacher attendance, and infrastructural inputs (Bajpai et al. 2005, 2006, 2008 cited in Jain and Dholakia 2010; Rangaraju et al. 2012; Tooley and Dixon 2007; Tooley et al. 2007). Others have shown similar findings, in addition to aspects such as having less single-teacher and single-classroom schools, higher levels of teaching activity, higher school-level accountability, and higher teacher and student attendance (Goyal and Pandey 2009; Mehta 2005; Muralidharan 2006; PROBE Team 1999).

Critics of budget private schools such as Padma Sarangapani (2009) and Vimala Ramachandran (2009) have argued that the findings of Pankaj Jain and Ravindra Dholakia (2009) and James Tooley et al. (2007) are 'seriously flawed' (Sarangapani 2009: 68) and their proxies of school quality narrowly selected, and they claim there is 'no credible evidence' (ibid.: 69) that the quality of budget private schools is better, suggesting that the problem of low learning is all-pervasive across government and private schools. However, neither of them address the studies cited above, or cite any research that proves that private schools are any worse than government schools; the only support cited by Sarangapani (2009) is a second-hand opinion shared in an e-group debate. Overall, there does not appear to be much rigorous research indicating that private schools are worse than government schools. While many suggest that further research is needed, most show that the performance of private schools is at least at par if not better than government schools.

Home-Schooling

There are a small but growing number of Indian parents opting for home-schooling, often because they are dissatisfied with the mainstream system, or feel that rigid school structures don't allow their children to pursue other interests. The modern-day home-schooling movement gained prominence in the 1960s in America, particularly with educationists like Ivan Illich, John Holt and others, with 1.5 million children in the US now being homeschooled (Planty et al. 2009). It is common in many other countries like the UK, Australia, France, Poland, and Austria, typically due to dissatisfaction with government schools and high-cost private schools, religious beliefs, or wanting to cater to gifted or learning-disabled children (Gross 2003). In India, home-schooling currently does not require any registration or regulation, and on reaching Class X a homeschooler can sit privately for examinations in Classes III, V and VIII through the NIOS's OBE programme, and for Class 10 exams with NIOS or International General Certificate of Secondary Education (IGCSE). There is no specified syllabus, and parents use the CBSE, government syllabi, or alternative methods such as Montessori or Waldorf. Homeschoolers argue that home-schooling allows children to excel in their natural talents and interests, and lets them learn from a more flexible open-ended set of experiences rather than being confined to a classroom. Examples include Sahal Kaushik who become the youngest topper of Delhi's Indian Institute of Technology (IIT) entrance exam at the age of 14, or Shreya Sahai who had her first solo painting and photography exhibitions, and became a Hindustani classical violinist, all before age 11 (Sinha 2010). In recent years, Indian home-schooling parents have increasingly connected through social networking media like Yahoo groups, Facebook, blogs, etc. Many of them are facing considerable anxiety due to the RTE and because of the resulting discontinuation of the NIOS OBE scheme.

TO KEEP OR NOT TO KEEP THE PRIVATE SECTOR: WHAT'S BEST FOR CHILDREN?

Notwithstanding the divergent ideological positions on whether the private sector must be promoted or relegated in the sphere of education, the question remains: will closing down thousands of NGO-run, alternative, non-formal, and private schools ultimately benefit children, and will it for that matter benefit the government's efforts to provide quality education for all? The answers should be sought in the arguments extended in favour of closing these schools. This section examines key assumptions underlying arguments in support of the RTE's provisions and argues that the strategy adopted by the RTE will not ultimately benefit children or help achieve its own goal.

Assumption 1: It's the *Government's* Job to Provide Education; What's the Need for Involving Others?

Key RTE proponent Vinod Raina has argued that it is the government's responsibility to provide schools for all children, and if unrecognised schools — negligible in number according to him — are forced to close, the government will simply step in to meet the gap (Mukherjee 2012). The assumption is that education is a public service, and that privatisation is an ideology that seeks to 'dislodge the government from its status as the major player in educational provision' (Kumar 2008: 8; Ramachandran 2009). This paper by no means wishes to exempt the government from its primary role in universalising quality education. However it is simply unrealistic to expect the government to achieve this on its own. After decades of attempts, the goal remains a distant dream, and it certainly will not be achieved by April 2013 — the date when thousands of unrecognised schools will be shut down. Pankaj Jain and Ravindra Dholakia (2009) have demonstrated that even a proposed allocation of 6 per cent of government GDP on elementary education (current spending is less than 4 per cent) would be insufficient for achieving universal education as per current RTE norms. In order to be able to pay all teachers according to the Sixth Pay Commission, the education budget would have to be over 15 per cent of the GDP, which is simply not feasible.

If all unrecognised schools close in April 2013, nearly 40 million children will be ousted from their schools and will have to enrol in government schools, which are already short of a million trained teachers just to cater to those currently enrolled. Meeting such a vast intake would require government schools to flout RTE norms themselves either by appointing untrained teachers, or by exceeding the mandated PTR. Either way, the quality of education would suffer until more schools can be built and teachers hired to accommodate these children. Additionally, many slum or remote areas currently served by unrecognised non-state schools do not even have government schools nearby, which raises the question of what would happen to these children if their schools were to suddenly close down. By emphasising rigid norms, the RTE may end up reducing access to education for millions.

Assumption 2: Since Many of these Schools have Low Quality, Allowing them to Continue Denies Children's Right to Quality Education

Some argue that budget private schools should not be endorsed since there is no credible evidence that their quality is better than government schools, and studies show that both private and government schools struggle with poor learning (Sarangapani 2009; Ramachandran 2009). The concern of this group, according to Venu Narayan (2010), is that 'profit-driven private provisioning will lead to exploitation of the poor who are too ignorant and apathetic to make informed choices' (ibid.: 25). Ultimately, it's a question of upholding children's right to quality education, rather than fighting for the right of individual schools to survive, argues Vinod Raina (Mukherjee 2012); if it's the child's right to have schools with proper infrastructure, playgrounds, etc., then all schools must meet these obligations.

First, as mentioned earlier, many studies indicate private schools do provide better or at least comparable quality to government schools; so far none have indicated they are any worse. Even if the evidence is not yet conclusive, the answer is not to eliminate them entirely but to conduct further research, and not punish those who may be performing better. Until the government can itself meet its own norms and offer the quantity and quality of education mandated by the Act, would it not be a greater denial of poor children's right to education to force closure of all alternate options that offer comparable or better quality education? The government does not need to shut down other schools in order to fulfil its obligation to provide quality education

to all children. If government schools improve their own quality, parents themselves will willingly choose to send their children to government schools, as happens in most Western countries. Research suggests most parents' first choice would indeed be to send their children to well-functioning government schools rather than private schools (Ohara 2012).

If despite the 'price advantage', better infrastructure and incentives in government schools, parents are still opting out, the answer is to improve the system, not to eliminate alternatives. The right to education should also mean that children or their guardians have the right to choose the type of education they feel is better — whether private, alternative or home-schooling — rather than the state dictating the form it should take. The right to freedom is as much enshrined by our Constitution as the right to education. Part of the problem is that we don't trust the poor to make wise choices; we think they are being fooled and exploited by budget private schools. We ignore the fact that parents intrinsically want the best for their children. It seems unfair that only the rich (including the policymakers and officials implementing the Act) should have the freedom to send their children to high-fee private schools able to meet RTE norms, while the poor will not have a similar choice. One could argue that this rule is also promoting inequality and stratification: while the Act opens the door to private schools for a few from economically weaker sections (25 per cent), it in effect closes the door for the rest (Das 2010; Shah 2010).

Assumption 3: Quality Education Requires High Infrastructure, Teacher Qualifications and Salaries

A more fundamental issue is how the Act defines quality education. Section 8(g) of the RTE Act states that the government's obligation is to 'ensure good quality elementary education conforming to the standards and norms specified in the Schedule' (GoI 2009: 4) — a Schedule that talks almost entirely of infrastructure, numbers and inputs but mentions nothing about learning processes or outcomes for children. While the rest of the Act does talk about learning processes, these are not the criteria used to determine whether schools obtain recognition. Things like rooms, floor-space, toilets, etc., may be easier to monitor, but these are the requirements for a good building, not for a good education. At its essence, quality education is one that enables students to learn with understanding, to learn how to learn, to think for themselves, to realise their full potential, and to develop an open mind committed to values of equality, freedom and service. As many of India's greatest educational philosophers have argued, such things do not require a formal school building. In fact, many have argued that our present-day schools are having negative effects on children's individual and social well-being. The Act guarantees a right to schooling rather than a right to education. If followed to its entirety, it will produce a schooled population, but not necessarily an educated citizenry.

There is little proof that having bigger buildings and teachers with higher degrees will result in better quality education. Studies have demonstrated that when the US in the early 20th century moved towards universal government formal schools with bigger infrastructure and more qualified teachers, learning levels actually decreased (Gatto 2009). Similarly, Bhattacharjea et al. (2011) found that teachers' qualifications did not make a significant difference in their ability to teach well. This is substantiated by the fact that 93 per cent of trained teachers who appeared for the 2011 Teacher Eligibility Test did not even pass (*First Post* 2012). Neither does having standardised textbooks and syllabi ensure quality education — many alternative schools are able to cater to individualised students' needs better with contextualised learning materials. And as Gurcharan Das (2010) points out, high teacher salaries are good in principle, but only if accompanied by improved performance.

Assumption 4: The Private Sector is Driven by Profit Motives and will Invariably Deepen Inequality and Exploitation

This argument is partly driven by an ideological mistrust of the capacity of markets and the private sector to contribute to any larger societal good. First, as highlighted above, one must acknowledge that the private sector is much larger than profit-driven private schools, and there are a myriad NGO-run, alternative, non-formal, and even private school initiatives that have aimed at benefiting the poor (e.g., Loreto Day School [Kolkata], Aksharnandan and Gyanankur [Pune] are three examples of quality private schools that have opened their doors to the poorest). Venu Narayan (2010) argues that while there has indeed been an upsurge of private schools that are driven by capitalist entrepreneurship, rather than pointing to an inevitable phenomenon of failed markets, this upsurge could well be seen as the product of failed regulation. The government's tendency of trying to prevent profiteering by choking supply through regulatory overkill has often promoted greater corruption and lower quality, when groups with political leverage manage to capture licenses. Sure enough, the RTE's long list of recognition criteria has already generated an increase in corrupt inspectors demanding bribes in exchange for not closing down schools, or of schools maintaining false records with inflated fee and salary figures (Das 2010; Rao 2010).

On the other hand, if diversity, competition and choice are encouraged, but regulated through monitoring of quality, this could actually help to trigger a virtuous cycle of competitive improvement and accountability. If dissatisfied parents have no alternative of transferring their children elsewhere, government schools will have little incentive to improve. Sectors such as telecommunications and transport have shown that opening up private opportunities can have a positive effect on the public sector's willingness for reform, and that the government can indeed deliver results when faced with consumer choice and competition. This can be seen even in the education sector in Kerala, which has a unique model of choice and competition with among the highest percentage of private schools in the country, and also among the highest quality government schools.

WAY FORWARD: A NEW KIND OF 'PARTNERSHIP'

While the RTE's goals are laudable, it is not clear whether its means are the best to achieve these goals. To increase access to quality education, what's best for children is to have a variety of schools that parents can choose from — both well-functioning government schools and non-government options. But this calls for a new approach to 'public–private partnership' — beyond the narrow traditional models of 'supply-side' PPP (e.g., private-aided schools which are government-funded but often not of much better quality) or 'demand-side' PPP (e.g., government-funded vouchers that allow parents to choose any school, but which may be difficult to implement in India) (Narayan 2010). A more sustainable model is a collaborative approach to PPP where the private sector views it as a partnership and invests in strengthening the government system, while the government also views it as a partnership and allows other players to contribute. This requires encouraging greater choice and diversity in the system, but with a stronger quality benchmarking process for both private and government schools, and greater faith in parents' capacity to make intelligent choices when provided with more information. Some suggestions are offered in this section.

Partnership in Strengthening the Public Sector, Not Replacing It

Kumar (2008) rightly critiques the current 'partnership' model for being more of a roadmap for territorial division than a true sharing of responsibility aiming to improve government efficiency through joint engagement. The focus of private partners has been more on running parallel schools than on investing in systemic institution-building and structural reforms, particularly in neglected areas such as teacher education. Conversely, even NGOs that have invested in strengthening the system have not been viewed by the government as full-fledged partners, and collaboration has remained fragmented and ad hoc, with no enduring institutional mechanism for civil society partnerships (Chauhan 2011; Jagannathan 2001). Vinod Raina has suggested setting up of a Council for People's Partnership to institutionalise Government–NGO partnerships (Chauhan 2011), while Alternative School advocates have suggested that these be recognised as Resource Centres to support or even help run nearby government schools. Some seeds of hope lie in examples like the Goa Unaided Schools Association, which recently approached the state government to adopt neighbouring government schools to help improve their quality or in the Karnataka government's School Adoption Programme, described in Box 10.4.

Strong Monitoring Based on Outcomes not Inputs

If our goal is to guarantee children's rights, not just to schooling but to quality education, we must place greater emphasis on outcomes. Gujarat offers a hopeful example of moving towards performance-based public policy that focuses on children and parents (*Financial Express* 2012). In its recently-notified RTE rules, the criteria for unrecognised schools to meet RTE norms places 30 per cent weightage on student performance (through independent standardised assessments focusing on learning, not just rote); 30 per cent on the students' improved performance over time (so that results are traceable to school's efforts, not just to admitting 'brighter' students); 15 per cent on students' non-academic performance and parents' feedback; and only 15 per cent on

Box 10.4
Karnataka's School Adoption Programme

The Karnataka government in 2001–02 initiated a School Adoption Programme that invites donors, NGOs and corporates to get involved in improving the quality of government schools. Partners select any school and prepare a time-bound 'programme of action' for its overall development or specific interventions, ranging from infrastructure development, teacher training, students' educational tours, after-school or weekend remedial classes taught by local corporate employees, etc. About 900 schools in Bangalore and across Karnataka have been adopted by foundations such as Azim Premji, Infosys, Akshara, Shikshana, and Dream School Foundation. For example, Shikshana has adopted 120 schools, providing teaching aids, library books, extra materials, assessments, and scholarships. Despite some drawbacks like low monitoring and accountability, the programme has been a success. As one participating government teacher explains, 'Everyone says government schools are bad. Instead of blaming each other, if people in society — parents, corporates and NGOs — work together, we'll get there faster and our children are the ones who'll benefit' (Ravi 2008).

inputs like teacher qualifications and infrastructure. This is a tremendous step forward in facilitating schools that offer quality despite not having huge financial resources, while penalising schools that are not performing despite having high infrastructure and funding.

To curb corruption by officials in the evaluation process, parents should be closely involved, since they have the biggest stake in schools functioning well and thus the least incentive to mis-report, and are unpaid, which leaves less room for pocketing bribes. Increasing community accountability of schools is indeed one of the goals of the RTE and of the Panchayati Raj Institutions (PRI) Act. Another option is a graded recognition system that evaluates schools through independent agencies, such as Gray Matters Capital in Hyderabad, which has evolved a rating system for low-cost private schools based on student performance, teacher attention and essential safety and comfort features (Dixon 2010). This would promote transparency, which helps parents exercise informed choice, while also incentivising schools to acquire higher ratings by improving their quality. Monitoring of alternative, non-formal and home-schools could be done either by a Council of Alternative/Innovative Education established for this purpose, or help could be sought from the NIOS which already has an accreditation system in place.

Freedom, Flexibility and Facilitation for Private Partners, Not Over-Regulation

Once a strong monitoring mechanism can identify which schools are performing reasonably well, there needs to be a shift from a suspicion-based regulatory approach seeking to close schools down, to a facilitative approach based on freedom, trust and public vigilance that aims to help these schools improve. Instead of being closed, unrecognised schools could be allowed to develop an Improvement Plan and then be assessed on its adherence to the plan over a period of time. Raina's suggestion that NGO/budget schools should raise funds from corporates to meet RTE requirements (Mukherjee 2012) is not very realistic or sympathetic, given that many of them have little resources or expertise required to engage in successful fundraising. Second, compared to the cost of closing down existing unrecognised schools and building entirely new government schools to replace them (not to mention the consequences for children who are left temporarily without a school), it seems much more simple and cost-effective for the government to give grants to help these schools improve their infrastructure and teachers, or in the case of poorly-performing schools, to transfer management to the government or a third party (which has been Gujarat's approach). Flexibility for infrastructure norms may also be needed depending on the location and context of the school, without compromising on the essential needs of children. For example, aspects like toilets, drinking water, light, ventilation, and some open space can be prioritised, while others like square-footage or playgrounds could be treated more flexibly for urban or tribal locations where these may not be feasible. In Gujarat's pragmatic approach, as previously mentioned, if a classroom doesn't meet the minimum square-footage, instead of needing it rebuilt, the PTR can be altered so that at least each student has adequate space.

Similar flexibility could be given to teacher qualification norms, by allowing alternative modes of school-based certification programmes for teachers, perhaps drawing from innovative training programmes developed by alternative schools. A well-designed test could also be developed to assess working teachers' subject-related and pedagogic competence, whereby those who pass the test and have significant experience may be exempted from the qualification requirement (Alternative Schools 2010). Moreover, schools could be allowed to pay teachers based on the fees they charge, and to move beyond the state-prescribed textbooks and syllabi as long as they uphold larger curriculum objectives and quality standards (which could be assessed from students' learning outcomes). Finally, the NIOS OBE scheme must be permitted to continue to allow freedom and flexibility to alternative, non-formal or home schools that meet quality benchmarks to offer diverse curricula and still be recognised by the formal system.

CONCLUSION

Ironically, the RTE's strategy, rather than facilitating quality education for more children, will end up closing educational options for millions of children. To truly uphold every child's right to quality education, the strategy we need is to have a variety of schools that all children can choose from, both well-functioning government schools and non-government options. But this requires a shift from the current competitive PPP model, where each player sees the other as a rival whose role should be minimised, to a collaborative PPP model, one of true partnership between public and private sectors. On one side, the government needs to amend the RTE to provide flexibility to private partners rather than seeking to exclude them, and to help ensure they deliver quality as defined by outcomes, not just inputs. On the other side, private players must invest in strengthening the government system rather than just running parallel initiatives. Such a diverse system will in the short term increase parents' freedom to choose what they see as best for their children, and in the long term put pressure on both government and non-government schools to improve quality for India's 220 million children — a task which neither side can achieve on its own.

REFERENCES

Aggarwal, Yash. 2000. 'Public And Private Partnership in Primary Education In India: A Study of Unrecognised Schools in Haryana'. National Institute of Educational Planning and Administration, New Delhi.

Alternative Schools. 2010. 'A Space for Alternate Schools: Note on Behalf of "Alternative Schools" with Regard to Certain Provisions of the RTE Act 2009'. *Teacher Plus*, 18 February. http://www.teacherplus.org/moot-point/marks-or-grades-whats-your-choice (accessed 3 May 2012).

Annual Status of Education Report (ASER) Centre. 2012. *Annual Status of Education Report (Rural) 2011*. New Delhi: Annual Status of Education Report Centre.

Bajpai, Nirupam, Ravindra Dholakia and Jeffery D. Sachs. 2005. 'Scaling Up Primary Education Services in Rural India'. Working Paper no. 28, Center on Globalization and Sustainable Development, The Earth Institute, Columbia University.

———. 2006. 'Scaling Up Primary Education Services in Rural Rajasthan'. Working Paper no. 31, Center on Globalization and Sustainable Development, The Earth Institute, Columbia University.

———. 2008. 'Scaling Up Primary Education Services in Rural India, Case Studies of Andhra Pradesh and Karnataka'. Working Paper no. 28, Center on Globalization and Sustainable Development, The Earth Institute, Columbia University.

Behar, Anurag. 2012. 'Alike in Incompetence'. *Mint*, 25 January. http://www.livemint.com/2012/01/25213645/Alike-in-incompetence.html (accessed 20 June 2012).

Bharat Gyan Vigyan Samiti (BGVS). n.d. http://www.bgvs.org/ (accessed 20 June 2012).

Bhattacharjea, Suman, Wilima Wadhwa and Rukmini Banerji. 2011. *Inside Primary Schools: Teaching and Learning in Rural India*. New Delhi: Annual Status of Education Report Centre.

Blum, Nicole. 2009. 'Small NGO Schools in India: Implications for Access and Innovation', *Compare*, 39(2): 235–48.

Chauhan, Chetan. 2011. 'A New Fund for Corporate and Individuals to Invest in Education'. *Hindustan Times*, 19 September.

Chopra, Ritika. 2012. 'Govt. Mulls over Extension of Right to Education Deadline'. *Mail Today*, 7 October.

Das, Gurcharan. 2010. 'It's Criminal to Close Schools that Teach the Poor'. *Times of India*, 19 September. http://blogs.timesofindia.indiatimes.com/men-and-ideas/entry/it-is-criminal-to-close-schools-for-the-poor (accessed 3 May 2012).

De, Anuradha, Reetika Khera, Meera Samson, and A. K. Shiva Kumar. 2006. *PROBE Revisited: A Report on Elementary Education in India*. New Delhi: Oxford University Press.

Deccan Herald. 2012. 'Home Schooling Affidavit Incorrect', 12 October. http://www.deccanherald.com/content/286674/home-schooling-affidavit-incorrect.html (accessed 26 October 2012).

Desai, Sonalde, Amaresh Dubey, Reeve Vanneman, and Rukmini Banerji. 2008. 'Private Schooling in India: A New Educational Landscape'. Working Paper no. 11, India Human Development Survey.

Dixon, Pauline. 2010. 'RTE Act & Private School Regulation'. Policy Review no. 4, Centre for Civil Society.

Dore, Bhavya. 2011. 'Home-Schooling Faces Test in Delhi High Court'. *Hindustan Times*, 3 August. http://www.hindustantimes.com/News-Feed/mumbai/Home-schooling-faces-test-in-Delhi-high-court/Article1-728730.aspx (accessed 1 May 2012).

————. 2012. 'Fate of Open Schools, Home Schooling Students Unclear'. *Hindustan Times*, 19 April. http://www.hindustantimes.com/India-news/Mumbai/Fate-of-open-schools-home-schooling-students-unclear/Article1-842783.aspx (accessed 2 May 2012).

Financial Express. 2012. 'Learning vs Buildings', 19 April. http://www.financialexpress.com/news/fe-editorial-learning-vs-buildings/938702/0 (accessed 26 April 2012).

First Post. 2012. 'No Water, No Toilet: 95% Schools in India Lack RTE Infrastructure', 8 April. http://www.firstpost.com/india/no-water-no-toilet-95-schools-in-india-lack-rte-infrastructure-269363.html (accessed 8 May 2012).

Garg, Abhinav. 2012. 'RTE does not Allow Home Schooling'. *Times of India*, 23 October. http://articles.timesofindia.indiatimes.com/2012-10-23/news/34679696_1_alternative-schools-rte-act-formal-school (accessed 26 October 2012).

Gatto, John Taylor. 2009. *Weapons of Mass Instruction: A Schoolteacher's Journey Through the Dark World of Compulsory Schooling*. Gabriola Islands: New Society Publishers.

Government of India (GoI). 2009. 'The Right of Children to Free and Compulsory Education'. *Gazette of India*, 27 August.

Goyal, Sangeeta and Priyanka Pandey. 2009. 'How do Government and Private Schools Differ? Findings from Two Large Indian States'. Report no. 30, South Asia Human Development, World Bank. http://www-wds.worldbank.org/external/default/WDSContentServer/WDSP/IB/2010/01/11/000333038_20100111004939/Rendered/PDF/526340NWP0publ10box345574B01PUBLIC1.pdf (accessed 18 October 2012).

Gross, Jane. 2003. 'Unhappy in Class, More are Learning at Home'. *New York Times*, 10 November. http://www.nytimes.com/2003/11/10/nyregion/10SCHO.html?ei=5070&en=d107a4da9198dcef&ex=1070254800&pagewanted=print&position= (accessed 3 May 2012).

Jagannathan, Shanti 2001. 'The Role of Nongovernmental Organizations in Primary Education: A Study of Six NGOs in India'. Policy Research Working Paper no. 2530, World Bank.

Jain, Pankaj and Ravindra Dholakia. 2009. 'Feasibility of Implementation of Right to Education Act', *Economic and Political Weekly*, 44(25): 38–43.

————. 2010. 'Right to Education Act and Public–Private Partnership', *Economic and Political Weekly*, 45(8): 78–80.

Kingdon, Geeta. 2008. 'School-Sector Effects on Student Achievement in India', in Rajashri Chakrabarti and Paul E. Peterson (eds), *School Choice International: Exploring Public–Private Partnerships*, pp. 111–40. Cambridge: MIT Press.

————. 2010. 'The Impact of the Sixth Pay Commission on Teacher Salaries: Assessing Equity and Efficiency Effects'. RECOUP Working Paper no. 29, Centre for Education and International Development, University of Cambridge.

Kumar, Krishna. 2008. 'Partners in Education?' *Economic and Political Weekly*, 43(3): 8–11.

Kumar, Krishna and Joachim Oesterheld (eds). 2007. *Education and Social Change in South Asia*. New Delhi: Orient Longman.

Kumar, M. Sagar. 2011. 'Act Against 'Unrecognised' Schools, HC tells Govt'. *Times of India*, 26 April. http://articles.timesofindia.indiatimes.com/2011-04-26/hyderabad/29474625_1_unrecognised-schools-private-school-school-managements (accessed 1 May 2012).

Manikandan, K. 2012. 'Spotlight on Unrecognised Schools'. *Hindu*, 30 January. http://www.thehindu.com/news/cities/chennai/article2843041.ece (accessed 26 April 2012).

Mehta, Arun C. 2005. *Elementary Education in Unrecognised Schools in India: A Study of Punjab Based on DISE 2005 Data*. New Delhi: National Institute of Educational Planning and Administration. http://www.dise.in/Downloads/Reports&Studies/UnRecPunjab05.pdf. (accessed 24 April 2012).

Ministry of Human Resource Development (MHRD). 2010. 'Model Rules under the Right of Children to Free and Compulsory Education Act, 2009'. Ministry of Human Resource Development, New Delhi.

————. 2012. 'RTE 2009: The 2nd Second Year'. http://ssa.nic.in (accessed 20 June 2012).

Misra, Kartik. 2012. 'How the RTE can Make the Budget Performing Schools Extinct'. *School Choice*, 18 April. http://schoolchoice.in/blog/?p=5544 (accessed 1 May 2012).

Mukherjee, Anahita. 2012. 'Right to Education will Take the Fear Out of Learning'. *Times of India*, 21 April. http://epaper.timesofindia.com/Default/Client.asp?Daily=TCRM&Enter=true&Skin=CREST&AW=1334988226552 (accessed 26 April 2012).

Muralidharan, Karthik. 2006. 'Public-Private Partnerships for Quality Education in India', *Seminar*, 565.

Narayan, Venu. 2010. 'The Private and the Public in School Education', *Economic and Political Weekly*, 45(6): 23–26.

National University of Educational Planning and Administration (NUEPA). 2012. 'Elementary Education in India: Progress towards UEE — Flash Statistics 2010–11'. District Information System for Education, National University of Educational Planning and Administration.

Ohara, Yuki. 2012. 'Examining the Legitimacy of Unrecognised Low-Fee Private Schools in India: Comparing Different Perspectives', *Compare*, 42(1): 69–90.

Planning Commission. 2008. *Eleventh Five Year Plan 2007–12: Social Sector*. New Delhi: Oxford University Press.

Planty, Michael, William Hussar, Thomas Snyder, Grace Kena, Angelina KewalRamani, Jana Kemp, Kevin Bianco, and Rachel Dinkes. 2009. *The Condition of Education 2009*. Washington, DC: National Center for Education Statistics, Institute of Education Sciences, US Department of Education. http://nces.ed.gov/pubsearch/pubsinfo.asp?pubid=2009081. (accessed 24 October 2012).

Public Report on Basic Education (PROBE) Team. 1999. *Public Report on Basic Education in India*. New Delhi: Oxford University Press.

Ramachandran, Vimala. 2009. 'Right to Education Act: A Comment', *Economic and Political Weekly*, 44(28): 155–57.

Rampal, Anita, Geetha Nambissan, Gurumurthy, Naimur Rahman, and Padma Sarangapani. 2009. 'Response from Consultation at NCERT as an Input to MHRD on the "PPP in School Education" Document'. 5 November. http://www.

azimpremjifoundation org/pdf/comprehensive-report.pdf (accessed 2 May 2012).

Rangaraju, Baladevan, James Tooley and Pauline Dixon. 2012. *The Private School Revolution in Bihar: Findings from a Survey in Patna Urban.* New Delhi: India Institute.

Rao, Jan S. 2010. 'RTE's Budget Schools Blindspot'. *Education World*, 6 September. http://educationworldonline.net/index.php/page-article-choice-more-id-2365 (accessed 26 April 2012).

Ravi, Padmalatha. 2008. 'City's Government Schools Get a Hand'. *Citizen Matters*, 24 April. http://bangalore.citizenmatters.in/articles/view/137-education-government-citys-government-schools-get-a-hand-education (accessed 2 May 2012).

Sarangapani, Padma. 2009. 'Quality, Feasibility and Desirability of Low-Cost Private Schooling', *Economic and Political Weekly*, 44(43): 67–69.

Sengupta, Nandita. 2011. 'It's Tricky to Stay on the Right Path'. *Times of India*, 23 June. http://articles.timesofindia.indiatimes.com/2011-06-23/education/29694379_1_ngos-mainstream-schooling-government-school (accessed 20 June 2012).

Shah, Parth J. 2010. 'Opening School Doors to India's Poor'. *Wall Street Journal*, 31 March. http://online.wsj.com/article/SB10001424052702304739104575154582256397118.html?mod=googlenews_wsj (accessed 2 May 2012).

Singh, Abhimanyu. 2012. 'Budget Private Schools Oppose RTE Act'. *Sunday Guardian*, 2 May. http://www.sunday-guardian.com/news/budget-private-schools-oppose-rte-act-2 (accessed 2 May 2012).

Sinha, Chinki. 2010. 'Plea Dismissed, but Homeschooling Still a Grey Area'. *Indian Express*, 31 May. http://www.indianexpress.com/news/plea-dismissed-but-homeschooling-still-a-grey-area/627581/0 (accessed 3 May 2012).

Tooley, James and Pauline Dixon. 2007. 'Private Schooling for Low-Income Families: A Census and Comparative Survey in East Delhi, India', *International Journal of Educational Development*, 27(2): 205–19.

Tooley, James, Pauline Dixon and S. V. Gomathi. 2007. 'Private Schools and the Millennium Development Goal of Universal Primary Education: A Census and Comparative Survey in Hyderabad, India', *Oxford Review of Education*, 33(5): 539–60.

United Nations Educational, Scientific and Cultural Organization (UNESCO). 2010. *Education for All Global Monitoring Report: Reaching the Marginalized.* Paris: United Nations Educational, Scientific and Cultural Organization.

United Nations Children's Education Fund (UNICEF). 2011. 'Frequently Asked Questions on the "Right of Children to Free and Compulsory Education" Act 2009'. United Nations Children's Fund.

——————. Forthcoming. 'Activity-Based Learning in India: Overview, Strengths and Challenges'. Unpublished Draft.

Vachani, Sushil and N. Craig Smith. 2008. 'Socially Responsible Distribution: Distribution Strategies for Reaching the Bottom of the Pyramid'. Faculty and Research Working Paper no. 2008/21/ISIC, Social Innovation Centre, INSEAD.

Wadhwa, Wilima. 2008. 'Private Schools: Do They Provide Better Education?' in Annual Status of Education Report Centre, *Annual Status of Education Report 2008*, pp. 21–23. New Delhi: Annual Status of Education Report Centre.

Learning the Right Lessons

Measurement, Experimentation and the Need to Turn India's Right to Education Act Upside-Down

Shobhini Mukerji and Michael Walton

India has almost achieved universal enrolment in primary schools. This is an important achievement, albeit one that has arrived too late for the many young men and women who missed out in recent decades. They are already of working age now and have children themselves.

The government is now focusing its attention on retaining children and ensuring that they complete secondary schooling. This is fine and needed. However, getting children enrolled in schools has turned out to be radically insufficient for the real task of providing children with the skills they need for their future lives as workers, citizens and parents. All evidence shows that the bulk of India's basic education system is dismally failing in this task. With minor exceptions, the quality of learning varies from average to poor across all states — for both government and the vast majority of private schools. Even worse, this limited evidence, over time, has effectively found no progress in levels of quality since the mid-2000s. There is a huge risk that, despite schooling, another generation of Indian schoolchildren will enter the workforce and adult citizenship with grossly inadequate skills. This will be a drag on growth and a source of rising inequality. The few with high skills and access to capital will continue to benefit from growth, while the unskilled products of India's education system will face weak job prospects in an increasingly globalised world.

Can the quality problem be tackled? This depends on a proper diagnosis. There is little evidence that the issue lies with demand. Parents, including those who did not have schooling themselves, almost universally want their sons and daughters to complete schooling. The rapid growth of private schooling and tuition throughout India, even in poor rural areas, is a direct expression of this demand. But parents typically have little idea of what goes on in schools;

even though they pay the fees they have less influence in the affairs of the school, in spite of a formal existence of parent committees in government schools and in most private schools.

There are sharply differing views on what the problem is on the supply side, and thus what the remedy should be. Some see this as an issue of inadequate 'inputs'— poor facilities, shortage of teachers, lack of teacher-training and so on. These are the cornerstones of the Right to Free and Compulsory Education Act (Right to Education or RTE) that came into force on 1 April 2010.[1] A different view sees the issue as a lack of incentives for teachers to put effort into genuine teaching. Within this perspective some argue that further expansion of private schooling is *the* answer, whether through use of vouchers or other means. Others advocate sharper incentives for those teaching within government schools, for example in the form of rewards for quality of learning outcomes, or greater use of contract teachers (who are typically lower-paid and younger, but lack job security). Or, some argue, non-financial incentives could come from providing better information to parents, who could then put pressure on schools. Yet another view emphasises the fundamental issue of a misaligned pedagogy: teachers are indeed teaching something, but not what the children need; besides, they are also required to keep pushing through a set curriculum, with the consequence that most children continue to fall further behind and never really learn. These interpretations have hugely different implications for policy design.

Fortunately, it is possible to inform the debate with careful analysis. In the past few years, there has been a range of careful studies involving rigorous analysis and interpretations of what does and does not work in Indian schools.

Many of these have been conducted in collaboration with leading international academics (including from the Massachusetts Institute of Technology [MIT], Harvard and Stanford universities, in association with the Indian Government and non-government institutions) and are being published in peer-reviewed journals. Some have been carried out in Non-Governmental Organisation or NGO-run schools, but most involve actual experiments within the government schooling system. For example, MIT economists Abhijit Banerjee and Esther Duflo (2011) have devoted a chapter in their publication reviewing evidence from across the world on what works in education policy — from increasing the demand for schooling to improving student learning. This type of work is complemented by extensive analysis of patterns from large-scale, nationally-representative surveys that actually measure quality of learning.

While much more is needed, these analyses have important implications. This paper consolidates recent rigorous evidence into an assessment of what is known and not known. It then suggests implications for the future of education design and experimentation over what does and does not work in India.

The studies reviewed here find a mixed picture. There are several important examples of success in improving outcomes. Research involving children attending government schools in rural Bihar and Uttar Pradesh found that both pedagogy and teaching capacity available have a substantial impact on basic learning levels in the subjects of reading and mathematics. This was found in the case of unpaid volunteers working outside school (in both the states), and in a summer learning camp with government teachers in Bihar. In rural Andhra Pradesh, innovations linked to learning that provided incentives — both group-based and individual — for government teachers have borne fruit in the form of better outcomes. Adding contract teachers also improved learning in the state, despite the fact that these teachers were being paid a fifth of the salary of regular teachers (while teachers in private schools were paid even less). All these studies were based on comparisons with control groups (through randomised control trials or RCTs; see the next section for a discussion on design details).

However, what is *not* known is how to effect systemic change within state education systems. The large quantity of central and state government resources that has gone into the primary education sector across the country, notably under the Sarva Shiksha Abhiyan (SSA, the 'Education for All' movement), has apparently supported in getting children to schools. There have been some striking successes in increased enrolment in states such as Bihar. But these efforts have failed to achieve anywhere near satisfactory attendance or learning levels. In experimental studies in government schools in Bihar and Uttarakhand, attempts to introduce the same pedagogy within the school system in the regular school year had little or no impact in either state (in contrast to successes in Bihar outside the regular school context). It is unclear whether the incentive-based or contract-teacher innovations in Andhra Pradesh could be replicated state-wide — on financial or political economy grounds. A study in Uttar Pradesh also explored whether Village Education Committees (VECs), which are mandated under the SSA, could be mobilised to make a difference, but this had no impact; indeed, many VEC members did not even know that they had been appointed to the committee!

There is no conclusive evidence that private schooling is a panacea to shortfalls in education. Both private schooling and tutoring are extensive, with private schools accounting for a majority of enrolment in most urban areas, and about a quarter of rural children between the ages of 6 and 16. Over a fifth of children in both government and private schools receive private tutoring; therefore, in total over 40 per cent of all rural children have some form of private education, from schools or tutors (with substantial variation across states). Children who attend private schools or receive extra tutoring do have better learning levels, but are still way below the desired standard. Indeed, after keeping household characteristics as a control, the difference between children in private and government schools is small, except in the level of English language that many private schools offer. Besides, there is a contrast in the economic cost (as opposed to the household expenditure) of the schools — most private schools have much lower total costs, especially because of the much lower salaries that the teachers receive.

These results have a major implication. There is an urgent need to foster a process of exploration and experimentation within the government and private schooling systems, with systematic monitoring and analysis of results in actual learning levels. Effecting systemic change is difficult. Within the government system, it requires the alignment of reasonable commitment levels of government actors, all the way down from the State education services to district-, block- and cluster-level administrative structures, and of course into the drivers of behaviour of teachers themselves. The evidence indicates that large effects can *potentially* be attained with existing resources, and do not (necessarily) require radical shifts in inputs, the introduction of vouchers, etc. This will, however, almost certainly involve providing the incentive, curriculum and information base for teachers to teach according to the children's specific needs. This can involve various routes — adjusting the curriculum, streaming or organising of children according to learning levels, providing effective pedagogies to private schools and tutors, using volunteers or contract teachers, and so on. These are all different ways of getting at the same problem, but one simply does not know how this can be done at the state level, in a politically supportable and administratively feasible way. The very lack of consensus implies that analysis and informed debate is of utmost importance. And this can only be done if there is systematic measurement of inputs, incentives, processes and, fundamentally, of actual learning levels.

Is this approach in line with the RTE? Not as it is currently framed and generally interpreted. In particular, the RTE, rather than emphasising how schools should be made to deliver a certain minimum level of learning to every child, stresses upon a standardised, input-oriented approach to both government and private schools, imposes government terms of service on private teachers, and supports automatic advancement of children without allowing an independent measurement of learning at each class. These features could damage experimentation, render the low-cost private schooling movement financially unviable (even with the public transfers for the 25 per cent quota for disadvantaged students) and stop systematic exploration and discovery of what does and does not work. How the RTE will be implemented at the state-level is unknown, and at least in the spirit of the Act there is attention to quality (see Mehta 2012). This only underscores the importance of public debate now, both at the Centre and, even more importantly, in the states.

The remainder of the paper is organised as follows. The first section briefly summarises the evidence on the quality of education and the divergent views on what can be done about it. Then it provides a review of recent research on attempts to make a difference, and interprets the results. Finally, the paper discusses the implications for public action and how the RTE can be made to work better.

THE DISMAL QUALITY OF LEARNING IN INDIAN SCHOOLS

Dismal Quality of Basic Learning

The evidence for the dismal quality of learning is overwhelming. It comes from multiple sources. These include the Annual Status of Education Reports (ASER), coordinated by Pratham and the ASER Centre, that have been conducted in rural areas every year from 2005–11; they cover some 700,000 children and are statistically representative of almost all districts in India. Education Initiatives (EI) surveyed rural and urban schools in 2009, covering 160,000 children in 18 states (2010). The nationally-representative National Council of Applied Economic Research (NCAER) India Human Development Survey (IHDS) for 2004–05 included both rural and urban areas (Desai et al. 2011). Himachal Pradesh and Tamil Nadu were included in the internationally comparable Programme for International Student Assess-

ment (PISA) under the Organisation for Economic Cooperation and Development (OECD) in 2009 (see OECD 2010). Moreover, in-depth surveys were undertaken as part of research projects in specific states, including Andhra Pradesh, Bihar, Odisha, Rajasthan, Uttarakhand, and Uttar Pradesh.

These surveys used a variety of testing techniques and instruments, and yet the results were strikingly consistent. Both the ASER and NCAER surveys use the test instrument that Pratham/ASER Centre has developed and extensively piloted over many years, which allows a rapid categorisation of children into different reading, mathematics and comprehension levels. These tests are administered to children in a random selection of households in order to provide a statistically representative assessment of learning levels in the rural population. The ASER tests all children in a household between the ages of 5 and 16. For the purpose of understanding the state of learning among children in the country, this household-based testing is greatly superior to the school-based one. It covers children in government and private schools (whether or not the latter are registered), and, of particular importance, children who are not in school on the day of testing (survey data finds that many enrolled children are not in attendance on the day of a school visit).

The ASER instrument is designed for rapid assessment, so it is important to compare it with other testing instruments. The Bihar and Uttarakhand surveys, conducted by J-PAL South Asia,[2] did exactly this, comparing the ASER test instrument with two other tools — a 'fluency battery test' in Hindi adapted from Early Grade Reading Assessment used in United States (US) and many developing countries, and extensive Hindi and mathematics written tests, also developed with some items from international tests (Vagh 2009). These were administered to the same children, allowing comparison between the various test instruments. Analysis of the results found that *all* tests had desirable testing properties, provided consistent results across tests, and had different relative powers in terms of discrimination across learning levels (the ASER tests, and even more the fluency battery, are relatively strong at basic levels of learning, while the written test was designed to also discriminate across higher reading and mathematics levels).

Among other surveys, the EI's research involved development of a sophisticated testing instrument that was administered to Classes IV, VI and VIII in both urban and rural areas' schools. EI also developed the test instrument used for a different research study in Andhra Pradesh (Andhra Pradesh Randomised Evaluation Study or APRESt). These instruments were full-length tests and included multiple-choice and free-response questions involving written answers and oral reading. PISA is an internationally designed test administered to 15–16-year-olds who have had at least six years of formal schooling (since it seeks to assess the effects of schools). While the ASER survey and the older NCAER survey provide a good picture of learning levels in the overall population of children covered, the EI and PISA surveys are designed to assess the quality of actual learning in schools. A final example is a 2005 survey, analysed by Jishnu Das and Tristan Zajonc (2010), which took items from the Trends in International Mathematics and Science Study (TIMMS) mathematics test and tested 6,000 children in public and private, urban and rural, secondary schools in Odisha and Rajasthan.

Main Findings of All Surveys

First, while there is substantial variation across states, *none* of the states' performance is anywhere near the satisfactory level. Table 11.1 provides some illustrative results from the 2011 ASER survey of rural children. Even in relatively better-performing states in terms of learning outcome, such as Himachal Pradesh and Kerala, the quality is severely inadequate for the bulk of students. Moreover, states known for their success in terms of economic growth, including Andhra Pradesh, Gujarat and Tamil Nadu, all have severely inadequate learning levels (and Gujarat and Tamil Nadu are even worse than Bihar in terms of basic learning).[3] To the extent that growth in these fast-growing states required skills, this was likely due to the very small minority of workers who managed to get access to elite educational institutions such as the Indian Institutes of Technology (IITs).

TABLE 11.1   Indicators of Learning Deprivation in Rural Areas across Indian States, 2011

State	Children in Class V who Cannot Read Class II Text (in per cent)	Children in Class V who Cannot Divide (in per cent)
India	52	72
Andhra Pradesh	40	62
Bihar	50	63
Gujarat	51	77
Himachal Pradesh	26	40
Kerala	26	67
Tamil Nadu	68	86

Source: Pratham–ASER Centre (2011).

Second, the variety of survey results indicates the depth as well as the breadth of the problem. ASER and other tests vividly show how most children are far below the learning levels expected in Class II. This finding also highlights the mismatch between curriculum (expected learning levels) and actual learning levels of children — an issue discussed later in the paper. Figure 11.1 illustrates dismal trends across Classes in Andhra Pradesh.

The PISA results show how India's children are ranked way below than those of other countries. In international rankings, Himachal Pradesh and Tamil Nadu came last, but only above Kyrgyzstan. As Lant Pritchett (2012) has commented, the average child in these two states is at the same level as the *worst* OECD or American student (those in the 5th percentile), and it is even worse when compared with children in Hong Kong, Korea and Singapore (this might be considered aspirational levels for an emerging market country such as India). The *best* students in Himachal Pradesh and Tamil Nadu are 24 points (a quarter of a standard deviation) behind the *average* 15-year-old American. The American education system is notorious for its weak quality when measured according to the standards of an advanced country. Furthermore, 58 per cent of 15-year-olds in schools in Himachal Pradesh and 44 per cent in Tamil Nadu cannot be distinguished from those not having learned any science at all — 10 times as many as those in US. More than 80 per cent in both states are below a level that, according to PISA, equips them with the science competencies that will enable them to participate actively in life situations related to science and technology (ibid.). This is consistent with the earlier work of Das and Zajonc (2010) that found a mean test score of over *three* standard deviations below the OECD mean for secondary school students in Odisha and Rajasthan (OECD 2010). And all these results only apply to children in schools — according to ASER (Pratham–ASER Centre 2011), 6 per cent of 15–16-year-olds rural children were out of school in Tamil Nadu, and 2 per cent in Himachal Pradesh.

Figure 11.1 illustrates the learning levels of school children in primary classes indicating the proportion of children who can solve a class-appropriate competency-based question in mathematics. The figure demonstrates that only a minority of children learn basic addition skills between Classes II and V. The y-axis represents the proportion of children who got the particular competency (question) correct. For example, by Class II, the proportion of children who could do the double-digit vertical addition correctly — which is an appropriate competency for Class II students — is just above 40 per cent. Almost no child could make the quite simple conceptual adjustment needed to undertake horizontal addition even at Class V.

Third, urban schools are better than rural schools, but not substantially. For example, EI found that children in urban schools performed better at most language and mathematics levels, in terms of statistical significance, but the difference was only 'meaningful' in terms of educational Levels for Language in Classes IV and VI (there were no meaningful differences in language in Class VIII or in mathematics for Classes IV, VI or VIII).

Fourth, any strategy on learning in India has to take private schooling into account. As noted earlier, there has been

FIGURE 11.1   Basic Addition Skills of Children between Classes II and V, Andhra Pradesh
(Proportion of Children at Different Learning Levels)

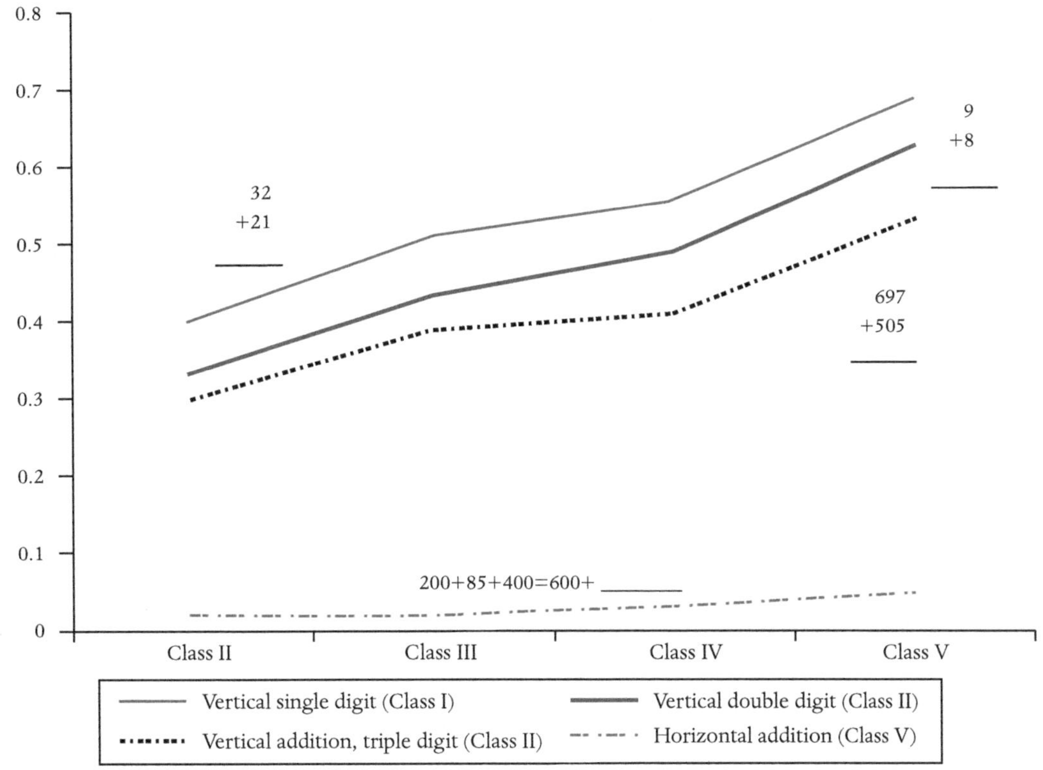

Source: Pritchett and Beatty (2012) based on APRESt data provided by Karthik Muralidharan.

a significant increase in the number of children receiving some form of private training, either through attendance in a private school or through private tutoring. While there are some elite, expensive private schools, the bulk of schools are low-cost, have low fees and cater to middle-class groups in urban and rural population. Some (for example, Tooley and Dixon 2005) have argued that the low-cost private schooling movement is central to any progress in education in India. It surely has a major role, but the survey results also show that while children in private schools or those receiving tutoring perform slightly better than children in government schools, the quality remains dismal. Moreover, in all the statistical analyses, a good part of the difference is attributable to some children coming from wealthier homes with more educated parents (Chugdar and Quin 2012; Desai et al. 2009; Mukerji and Wadhwa 2012). The typical apparent gain is actually less than the differences across government schools in India's states.

Fifth, it might be asked how this awful overall quality can be consistent with India's apparent global success in producing high quality engineers and other talents. Some have left the country — the US Silicon Valley, one of the innovation capitals of the world, is buzzing with Indian names (Luce

2012). But many, of course, remained in India and helped power the economic dynamism of recent decades, in the iconic sectors of Information Technology (IT) and pharmacy, and also in many other industries. There are two answers to this. There is the well-known story of the elite IITs (and a few other elite establishments), but this applies to only a tiny group of Indians. Then, there are the sheer numbers of Indians combined with high levels of learning inequality. Das and Zajonc (2000) found the inequality of learning in Odisha and Rajasthan to be only exceeded by South Africa from among countries with TIMMS data. This meant that both statements that follow were consistent with the data: 'for every ten top performers in the United States there are four in India' and 'for every ten low performers in the United States there are two hundred in India' (ibid.: 1).

NO CONSENSUS ON CAUSE AND TREATMENT

Policy design would be easier if there was agreement on the sources of the problem. When the issue is that children are not enrolling in schools, the challenge is clear, at least at face value. And there has been great success in getting children, especially girls, enrolled, notably in the most lagging or disadvantaged states. A big part of this seemed to be an issue of having a supply of accessible schools: as far back as the late 1990s, the Public Report on Basic Education (PROBE) of northern Indian states found substantial demand for school among poor rural households (PROBE Team 1999). Bihar's big push to get children into school, under the first administration of the Chief Minister Nitish Kumar, was in part driven by an enormous expansion and upgrading of schools, with about a three-fold rise in the number of teachers in government schools.

But on the question of what can be done to improve children's learning, there are diverse and sometimes opposing views. Some of the main views have been briefly outlined as follows.

Household conditions and behaviour: One of the major regularities in international research on learning is the correlation between the socio-economic status of the home and learning outcomes. Children from wealthier homes with well-educated parents and siblings perform better in school. This also appears to be true of India, based on the survey evidence. How much of this is causal is unclear. It could be that homes of 'better' socio-economic status live in better neighbourhoods, and send their children to better schools, or parents put more pressure on teachers. The home environment may play a direct causal role in learning via direct inputs, placing lower demands for child 'labour', or instilling effort and aspirations in the children. This would take policy in the direction of expanding economic opportunity, engaging with parents, providing transfers linked to education, or compensatory action for the children from more education-poor homes.

School infrastructure and other inputs: A very popular diagnosis of why quality of education is poor or why children's learning is low focuses on lack of school inputs: it *seems* obvious that effective teaching and learning require reasonable pupil–teacher ratios (PTRs), well-trained teachers, decent infrastructure (classrooms, toilets, etc.), and teaching materials (textbooks, exercise books, blackboards, and so on). This is a major thrust of the newly-passed RTE Law which mandates minimum input norms for both government and private schools. There is, however, surprisingly little evidence from international literature or from research in India to support this position: PTRs, infrastructure or measures of teachers' qualifications are typically unrelated to learning outcomes (see Hanushek [2010] for a review of developed country evidence, and Kremer and Holla [2009] for a review of evidence from developing countries). While there have been very few experiments that carefully analyse effects of increasing inputs in an Indian context, children who attend schools with better infrastructure did not seem to perform better in terms of quality. It is desirable that

school facilities are of decent quality and teachers do not have to face huge classes, but it is not obvious that this will solve the quality problem.

Mid-day meals: A very different argument concerns the importance of having mid-day meals in schools. This can make a difference in terms of incentivising children to actually go to school. There is indeed a large difference between enrolment and attendance in many schools: in one research project, it was found that the ratio of attendance to enrolment on the day of a surprise visit was only about a quarter of enrolled children in Classes II and IV in rural schools in Bihar, and less than 60 per cent in Uttarakhand (Banerjee et al. 2011). (Moreover, these were schools that were offering mid-day meals.) A different argument is that mid-day meals could potentially make a difference to concentration levels and thereby, impact learning of school children; however, for most schools, the bulk of the school day takes place before lunch.

Incentives: There is growing interest, especially among economists, on the role of incentives in schooling. Arguments are made about the 'incentive properties' of private schooling — school managers are effectively selling a product (at least, for fee-paying private schools; the so-called 'government-aided' private schools are effectively run on the same terms as government schools). They need to convince parents that it is worth sending their children to their schools. Parents often say school quality is the reason they choose private schools over government schools, though English language teaching is at least as important a reason. Another argument is that teachers in private schools lack tenure, and so face stronger incentives than government teachers to actually turn up and teach. This has led some observers to argue for supporting a large-scale shift into private schooling by tolerating their growth, through vouchers or other means (see, for example, Tooley and Dixon 2005).

Incentives as a major issue within government schools: It is well-known that there is both a major absenteeism problem in much of India, and that teachers who are at school are often not teaching. The PROBE Team report (1999) found that in only 53 per cent of government schools across four states any teaching activity was going on — in half of the sample schools, there was none at all during the investigator's visit. Michael Kremer et al. (2006) found, in a survey of 3,700 primary schools across 20 states, that 25 per cent teachers were absent from school on a given day. Among the teachers found present, only about half were observed engaging in teaching activity. A common interpretation is that teachers have low incentives to actually turn up and teach, since they have security of tenure, receive few rewards for putting effort into teaching let alone improve learning, and are often required by officials or politicians to work on other matters.

This diagnosis leads to a range of policy recommendations. One alternative is to engage teachers on term contracts (whether or not they are considered regular teachers, albeit on lower pay), on the principle that they will be incentivised to teach or lose their job. Another is providing additional rewards to teachers if learning levels improve. Yet one more involves creating a career path for teachers linked to performance in learning outcomes (Pritchett and Murgai 2006). A different kind of measure concerns empowering parents: having VECs (typically required under the SSA, and now part of the RTE) on the principle that they will put pressure on heads and other teachers to turn up and teach.

Curriculum design: Another argument is regarding the failure of curriculum design. The RTE education stresses age–class learning and also specifies that the syllabus should be completed in a given time period. This assumes a linear progression from year to year with children mastering the content/curriculum of each year before moving up to the next class-level. The reality is quite different: there is a lot of evidence that the level of learning of most children is typically way below the requirements of the curriculum. Yet teachers are required to complete the syllabus.

Systemic issues:

(a) *Administration*: what happens in schools, both government and private, is influenced by the layers of administrative structures that lie above the school itself. This includes cluster- and state-level school administrators, inspectors of private schools, state-level bureaucracies and, not least, the central government that provides funding with requirements (as in the SSA) and passes federal laws (as in the RTE). Systems can change if everything is aligned, from top to bottom, to achieve goals that are clearly articulated, and leadership is in place.

(b) *Political economy*: a complementary argument focuses on political economy issues. In India, as in many countries, teaching is a valued source of employment, and government teaching is especially valued since it pays substantially above alternative jobs (both private teaching and other private sector jobs) (Pritchett and Murgai 2006). Teachers are also one of the largest groups of public employees and can become both an important area for patronage and a political force. There is evidence that this is salient in India: there are mutually reinforcing relations between teachers, politicians and officials, with both political influence and threats of incentives, and disincentives being linked to patterns of absenteeism and placement in better and worse teaching positions, in the form of discretionary transfers (Béteille 2009). Further, while teacher associations and unions have been able to exert influence to demand (and receive) better pay

scales, job security and other benefits, this has not led to much progress in improving education quality (Kingdon and Muzammil 2008).

Each of these major diagnoses suggests a different strategy or path as solution and therefore these interpretations have hugely different implications for policy design. This is precisely why measurement and analysis and informed debate based on empirical evidence are of utmost importance.

RESULTS FROM THE RIGOROUS ANALYSIS OF ACTUAL EXPERIENCES

Fortunately, in the past few years, there has been a variety of careful studies and interpretations of what does and does not work. These include a number of RCTs[4] of programmes that aim to address some of the problems discussed earlier, and point to solutions that work. This is by no means the only source of evidence of value, but has advantages in assessing causality for the specific innovation analysed. By contrast it is hard to design RCTs to test systemic issues. Sometimes this leads to discovery of small innovations that can have large gains; in other cases they provide insights into systemic or structural issues. There is a steep learning curve with every piece of research contributing to a larger body of evidence that could be used by practitioners and policy-makers alike in designing programmes for effective learning outcomes. This section reviews and presents evidence that measures the impact of inputs on the schooling process, the effect of remedial learning measures and teacher-level incentives on student learning outcomes, giving a brief overview of why certain measures have worked while others had no effect. The evidence presented here is by no means exhaustive and conclusive. The focus is especially on RCTs undertaken in India with selected results from other relevant studies. These provide carefully researched, evidenced-based results. But this is still a partial account of what would be needed on the scale of a state, in a politically supportable and administratively feasible way. This can only be assessed with systematic measurement of inputs, incentives, processes and, fundamentally, of actual learning levels.

Increasing School Inputs under the RTE Provisions

There have been several initiatives in India and elsewhere to improve enrolment and learning by providing inputs such as additional teachers, free textbooks and reading material, uniforms, scholarships, schools meals, etc. The large quantity of central government and state resources that has gone into the primary education sector across the country, notably under the SSA, has apparently supported in getting children into schools. Increased enrolment has been striking, for example in Bihar. But these efforts have failed to achieve anywhere near satisfactory attendance or learning levels. The issue now is not enrolment, but there is a strong case for new research on determinants of daily attendance, that is ill-understood. Mid-day meals have been considered effective in getting children into schools, but much more careful analysis is needed to determine if it has been successful in impacting attendance positively.

There is considerable mention under the RTE framework of what inputs schools should have. As noted earlier, it may seem commonsense to assume that in a country such as India with low levels of inputs, any additional inputs provided in the form of teachers, textbooks, stationery and materials, school meals, etc. will have a positive impact. However, the general consensus from research is that most inputs often do not have any effect. While we might find an increase in enrolment in some cases, this has *not* generally led to higher learning outcomes. This illustrates the gains from careful research. It is a process of learning, and evaluation teaches which inputs could provide more returns on the investment. Thus, while much more is needed, some general lessons can be drawn from the empirical evidence that is currently available.

Teaching–Learning Materials

There is mixed evidence on the impact of instructional inputs such as reading materials and flipcharts on children's learning outcomes. In rural India, an evaluation of specially designed, colourful reading and mathematics materials did not show an impact on children's learning outcomes, when used by school teachers without any training and additional support (Banerjee et al. 2011). These materials were specially designed as part of a larger evaluation of a learning enhancement programme, aimed at imparting basic skills to children who were behind their peers in achieving class-appropriate competencies. A proportion of schools were randomly allocated to receive these reading materials, and it was hypothesised that teachers would be motivated to use them to enhance children's learning. However, only when materials were combined with appropriate training to use them, *and* teachers were provided with additional volunteer support, that there was an impact on basic mathematics and reading skills of the children. In Kenya too, use of flipcharts showed no impact on test scores (Glewwe et al. 2004). In rural primary schools of Kenya, a group of randomly selected schools were given flipcharts (schools without flipcharts were used as comparison schools). There was no impact on test scores in schools using flipcharts vis-à-vis schools that were not given any.

However, inputs sometimes have been found to have some effect. Providing free textbooks to a randomly selected group of primary and middle schools in Kenya increased the scores of the best students, that is, those with high pre-test scores, as compared to schools that did not receive them (Glewwe et al. 2009). However, there was almost no impact on test scores of the weaker students. From Andhra Pradesh, there are interesting results that suggest that investments in specific additional inputs may have an impact on learning; however, this disappears as soon as parents, in anticipation of the free inputs, substitute for their own investments into their child's education (Muralidharan et al. 2010). This particular piece of research on material inputs comes from a series of experiments that involved a mix of input- and incentive-based policies for teachers and schools, designed to test different hypotheses. A group of schools in Andhra Pradesh were provided block (cash) grants for inputs over two years. Results indicated that nearly half of the grant allocation was spent on stationery (notebooks, chalks, slates) and close to another 40 per cent was spent on classroom materials (such as charts and toys) and practice books. As a result of spending on classroom-level inputs, student learning improved in the first year. However, these gains were insignificant in the second year of the experiment. Interestingly, at the same time, household expenditure on these specific school inputs fell significantly in the second year of the allocation, indicating that households were changing their spending in response to the anticipated school expenses in the second year. An interpretation is that schools spent money on material goods such as child stationery and practice books that parents are likely to buy for their children in the absence of school provision. This led to substitution, allowing households to reduce their own spending on the same.

This highlights that the type of inputs matters. For example, in Kenyan rural schools the uniforms that are usually paid for by parents of school children, when distributed for free did lead to a significant reduction in absenteeism and improved test scores (Kremer and Holla 2009). The premise behind evaluating the provision of free school uniforms was that this would reduce part of the financial barrier to access to education. This was an experiment in which a proportion of students were randomly chosen by lottery to receive free uniforms and results were compared a year later with students who did not get them. The results showed that the provision of free uniforms reduced school absenteeism by 44 per cent for the average students and by 62 per cent for students who previously did not own a uniform (in the treatment group). There was a substantial impact in test scores (that improved by a significant 0.25 standard deviation).

Increasing Supply of Teachers, Reducing Class Size

Large class sizes, teacher absenteeism and heterogeneous classes are commonly cited as sources of low quality. Results from several studies done in other developing countries suggest that there is little or no impact on learning from reduced PTRs. This is particularly striking since, in contrast to developed countries, the starting point in poor countries is typically of high PTRs. An initial intuition would be that when inputs are low, marginal gains are high.

A series of experiments have systematically evaluated the effects of reducing class sizes by recruiting extra (contract) teachers in schools (Duflo et al. 2008), as well as by adding civil service teachers (Banerjee et al. 2005; Muralidharan 2010).[5] This model is especially important, given that state governments are increasingly hiring teachers on temporary contracts to meet the pressures from the large-scale expansion of primary education. Typically, contract teachers are younger with less formal training than regular teachers, are paid much less, and are more likely to be from the same village as the school where they teach. There is a concern that contract teachers will not impact children's learning because of lower qualifications. This paper has reviewed the studies that have systematically tested the impact on learning by reducing class sizes by hiring extra teachers, as well as a more focused approach whereby extra teachers are specifically assigned to lower performers within classes. The following section presents two key pieces of evidence that evaluate the impacts of extra contract teachers on government primary schools.

As part of a series of experiments from Andhra Pradesh (APRESt), a group of schools were provided with an additional teacher on contract (this cadre is similar to the *panchayat* teachers in Bihar, and perform a similar role to the *balsakhi*, community-based tutor, in Vadodara or the intended role of volunteers in Uttarakhand, discussed subsequently in this paper). In the APRESt intervention design, a group of 100 schools got an extra contract teacher who was assigned to a school (and not a particular class or a subset of students based on initial achievement). Overall, contract teachers were found to be more effective with students, who significantly outperformed those in comparison schools with no contract teachers (0.13 standard deviation improvement in learning over two years for children with a contract teacher). In addition, the extra contract teacher was particularly beneficial for students in Class I, although overall, all students across all classes gained from the programmes. Contract teachers were also significantly less likely to be absent from school than regular government school teachers. Thus, a key policy message from this study is to hire local teachers on fixed-term renewable contracts and have them focus on children who need help in early schooling years, adding to the critical mass of evidence supporting the effectiveness of this type of programme. It is a highly cost-effective model, as contract teachers cost much less than regular teachers, and have large gains for children's learning improvement.

The results from Andhra Pradesh also find resonance in a study in rural Kenya, where in a randomly selected group of schools, children in Class I were split by ability and grouped as per initial achievement (based on a pre-test), while in a comparable cluster of schools, the students were divided into two groups within the class with no predetermined criteria (Duflo et al. 2006). Both groups of schools got an extra teacher, either a government or a contract teacher (the latter was lower paid and did not have tenure). These schools were compared with each other, as well as with a control group of schools which had no extra teacher. The researchers were trying to disentangle the effects of reduction in class size on learning levels (and in part, the effects of dividing classes by ability). Results indicated that merely reducing class size by adding an extra teacher had no effect on the test scores of students. In fact, in the schools which had extra contract teachers, the regular (government) teachers showed even less effort in teaching, as observed through random visits to the school. (There is some evidence of similar responses in Indian studies as well.) Only when a group of schools with extra government teachers (with reduced class size) were monitored by the school management committee members, did this lead to the teachers exerting more effort to teach; however the higher teaching activity did not substantially reduce the learning impact gap between contract and regular teachers.

Thus far the evidence has focused on inputs: a few studies find some impact in specific contexts, but there is no general support for the view that further investments in school-level inputs will improve learning (however desirable it may be on other grounds). Yet, that is not the entire spectrum of the issue. Children are clearly lagging behind and need additional help. Some view additional inputs as the solution, while others argue that it is the curriculum that is at the base of the learning issue and thus needs to be addressed. The current debate brings pedagogy and teaching practices to the fore, with a growing body of research suggesting the need to employ remedial measures for children to cope with the curriculum, and teaching practices to be adapted to the child's level.

Specific Pedagogy Aligned with Children's Needs

The evidence available also raises the important issue of *curriculum design*. The RTE stresses age–class learning and also specifies that the syllabus should be completed in a given time period. This assumes a linear progression from year to year with children mastering the content/curriculum of each year before moving up to the next level. The reality is very different.

The Problem of Curriculum Design

In review of the current patterns of achievement mentioned earlier, it has been seen that most children in Indian schools have learning levels that are way below expectations of the curriculum or levels expected of them at their current class level. Using data from studies in South Asia and Africa, Lant Pritchett and Amanda Beatty (2012) analyse the risks of an 'overambitious curricula' and find that a majority of students spend years in schooling with very little progress in learning. Low level of learning is in part the result of the curriculum moving faster than the students' learning pace, creating a *growing* gap between student skills and instructional material. Pritchett and Beatty observe that

Of children lacking the ability to answer simple curricular-based questions going into a typical grade, only 1 in 8 children demonstrate that skill after an additional year of schooling. This means that seven out of eight children made no progress on a typical item after an entire year of schooling (ibid.: 7).

The consequences of the problem are illustrated with simulations illustrating the pernicious effects of such a *curricular gap* with actual learning levels. Even if children start at the same initial level of learning, a higher curricular gap can lead to worse cumulative learning achievement. They demonstrate that the combined effect of lower initial-skill levels with an inappropriately accelerated curriculum is much larger than the student arriving with the low-skill level alone. A 'slower' curriculum, adapted to the learning levels of children, can paradoxically lead to substantially faster learning.

The problem of a curricular gap is consistent with the experimental results discussed earlier. Getting incentives right for teachers has to be embedded in a curricular approach that is aligned with a child's needs; otherwise, increased effort will have no effect. This also may explain the inefficacy of higher inputs in many studies — since increased teaching inputs will have no effect if the 'required' action in the classroom is inconsistent with what children need.

To explore whether textbooks aligned with the curriculum only matter for the best performing children, Paul Glewwe and others conducted a randomised evaluation of providing free textbooks to government school children studying in Classes III–VIII in rural Kenya (Glewwe et al. 2009). Providing textbooks increased the scores of the best students (those with high pre-test scores) but had little effect on other students — and almost no impact on test scores of the weaker students. Over the four years of the programme, it was found that the gap between textbook schools and comparison schools (who were not supplied the free government textbooks) actually narrowed considerably over time. This is consistent with the hypothesis that textbooks help only strong students who can already read fluently and are thus designed such that they are out of reach of the understanding of an average child in class. Further, the general issues of high teacher and student absence rates and inability to keep

pace with the curriculum only compounded the problem in this case. There was no evidence to suggest a positive impact on class repetition, dropout and student absence rates.

In addition to thinking about children's abilities, there is also the question of teachers' capabilities. Several studies provide estimates of teachers' capability to teach — which raises critical questions about the preparation and support to teachers for teaching (Atherton and Kingdon 2010; Bhattacharjea et al. 2011). In fact, a recent study finds that a large proportion of teachers have difficulties in doing simple traditional tasks such as summarising a basic text, explaining word meanings in simple language or step by step laying out word problems even at Class-IV level (Bhattacharjea et al. 2011).

The RTE mandates that there be no external board examinations, no automatic promotion and the prescribed curriculum should be completed (by the teacher) in each class, thus leaving very little room for adjusting teaching to a very heterogeneous group of children. By contrast, the results cited earlier strongly suggest the need to go beyond inputs and look more closely at classroom practices and class organisation to understand actual influences on learning. The next section discusses a growing body of research from India that has evaluated key interventions that improve reading, including structured reading instruction and training teachers to teach at the child's level, and greater parental and community engagement to effect change in schools.

Evidence on Teaching at the Level of the Child

Several large-scale interventions have been carried out in different parts of the world that focus on teaching children by ability rather than by class. Impact evaluations of such programmes have systematically found significant effects on learning levels of children. There is evidence for an effective pedagogy that can work for children who need remedial help as well as those in higher levels, and can be imparted by both government teachers and volunteers — but it is effective only if the pedagogy is aligned with the task at hand for teachers.

An evaluation of a remedial education programme that was undertaken in government schools in Vadodara and Mumbai in 2001 found a substantial improvement in learning for low-performing students, who received remedial tutoring by a *balsakhi*, hired at a fraction of the cost of a government school teacher and placed in all schools during school hours to work with children who had fallen behind their peers in basic reading and mathematics (Banerjee et al. 2005). Typically, the *balsakhis* were females with no formal teacher training, and were younger and less educated than government teachers. They usually belonged to the neighbourhood of the local primary school. They taught for two hours a day, and alternated between Classes III and IV in government schools. The class was split into two groups, with the lower performing (bottom 20 students) of the class assigned to the *balsakhi* and the remaining children with the regular teachers. Scores on the post-treatment test showed gains over both years for all the children at the bottom in both language and mathematics, especially in higher mathematics competencies. The proportion of children at the bottom of the class, who could pass basic competencies, increased by 8 per cent. This was interpreted as being a result of the *balsakhi* tailoring instruction to suit the needs of the lower performing students and focusing on basic skills (rather than the general reduction in class size that was responsible for the programme's gains).

As discussed, merely reducing class size by hiring extra teachers does not have an impact, whereas splitting a class by students' initial achievement on test and assigning extra teachers to work with them has found to be effective in improving learning outcomes measured through test scores. The extra teacher project in rural Kenyan primary schools, that was evaluated through an experimental design, assigned extra teachers on renewable contracts to classrooms that were split by ability (on initial achievement on test for Class I students — the 'tracking schools'). These were compared to schools where students in Class I were grouped at random and not based on any test or criteria ('non-tracking schools'). This design allowed researchers to disentangle the effects of merely decreasing class size by grouping class according to ability and tracking students' learning outcomes through a focused approach (Duflo et al. 2006). As noted earlier, simply reducing class size by adding an extra teacher (in this case, it reduced from 82 to 44 students in a class) had no effect on the test scores of students for classes that were not streamed by initial achievement levels. By contrast, in classes where students had been grouped by ability, test scores increased for all students — both low and high performers. Substantial increases in test scores in tracking schools were observed after 18 months, and a further year later. Low-performing students benefited more from instruction at a more appropriate level than they did from having high performing peers in the same class.

The earlier discussion shows that it is indeed possible that lower paid, less-trained and often less-qualified teachers on renewable contracts can have positive impacts on children's learning within government schools. What about unpaid volunteers from the community? In 2005, J-PAL researchers evaluated a model that was being implemented by Pratham[6] in rural Uttar Pradesh, which recruited and trained village volunteers to teach basic reading and mathematics skills to children lagging behind to 'catch up' with their peers once they are back in class (Banerjee et al. 2010). Three interventions were tried with the aim of improving learning outcomes for children and evaluated through RCTs. The first

two interventions explored the influence of information and community participation on improving the quality of education. It involved sharing information about low learning levels in the community through a participatory process by developing 'village education report cards' for learning levels. The last intervention supplemented these discussions with an action component: unpaid village volunteers were recruited and trained to conduct after-school community-based reading camps that supplemented the usual primary school teaching.

Just providing information to parents and community members had no effect; VEC members were not even aware of their appointment to the committees; as a result, the school system was left untouched. However, the volunteer programmes of supplemental teaching proved to be highly effective. In the community-based after-school reading camps, the average child who attended the reading programmes and could decipher letters, but not words in the baseline, was 26 percentage points more likely to be able to read and understand a story than a comparable child in the control villages. Combined with the natural progress of children over the course of a year, these results implied that among the children who attended the camp, those who could not read at all were able to decipher letters, and the 35 per cent who could read letters were able to read and understand a short story. Though information to parents, including around the Village Education Committees, failed to have an impact on government schooling, the basic reading and maths pedagogy ('Learning to Read') developed by Pratham was effective when delivered by unpaid volunteers trained by Pratham workers in villages; volunteers taught children out of school hours (ibid.).

Remedial Education Interventions in School

The major learning from these reading camps in Uttar Pradesh led to a series of innovations to test whether the pedagogy could be embedded in the normal functioning of a government school during regular school days, so that more children could be reached, using existing teachers and supplemented by volunteers (Banerjee et al. 2011). This was Pratham's flagship 'Read India' programme, which has reached 35 million children in over 350,000 villages in 19 states across India since 2007. Under this programme, Pratham extended its pedagogy to cover all primary schools till Class-V level. A set of materials for use in schools and training was developed. In the resulting pedagogy (Combined Activities for Maximised Learning or CAMaL), activities included focusing on a specific target group of children, articulating clear learning goals, using appropriate teaching–learning activities and materials, and organising children into groups by ability level. Ongoing measurement of children's ability to read, write, comprehend, and do basic arithmetic and solve problems was used to assess progress.

The basic programme in schools (in selected blocks of Bihar and Uttarakhand) included alternative combinations of three main elements: first, training and monitoring of teachers to teach more effectively the specially designed class-level material during the normal school hours; second, supplemental teaching through volunteers working to help lagging behind children (this was similar to the Uttar Pradesh programme by the same NGO) and third, distribution of the teaching–learning materials and books to schools without extra training and support of teachers (in Bihar). A final treatment (in Bihar) involved a month-long summer learning camp, targeted at lagging children in Classes III–V, using specific learning materials. In Bihar, the volunteers worked after school hours, while in Uttarakhand they worked inside the schools alongside teachers. Villages were randomly selected to receive one model or the other and the programme was evaluated over a period of two school years. The results confirm the effectiveness of the programme when implemented by volunteers in the communities (overall, learning levels increased by 0.1 standard deviation in an average of all tests). For this particular intervention group (only implemented in Bihar for volunteers in the community), results significantly improved on all tests relative to the control group, including for the advanced competencies. Children benefited at both very low and higher levels of baseline competency.

The study, however, also confirms that mainstreaming the programmes through the regular school system, even with the explicit collaboration of the states' education departments, proved to be difficult. In both states of Bihar and Uttarakhand, the programmes which focused on training teachers for implementing the pedagogy during the school year, without adding volunteers to support government teachers, had very small effects, and gains were concentrated among kids who could read letters, or words/ sentences; children at the bottom and at the top did not benefit at all. Government teachers continued to teach in age-class groupings using the usual textbook and curriculum. In Uttarakhand where the volunteers were embedded in the school system that had the responsibility to monitor them, the programme including teacher training, volunteers and materials had no effect whatsoever. Thus, bringing volunteers to the schools in Uttarakhand, which had been effective in other contexts, failed in this case possibly because the volunteers just substituted for teachers (who could then work less), or were directed to non-teaching activities.

These results are aligned with the earlier studies in Kenya by Esther Duflo, Pascaline Dupas and Michael Kremer, referred to earlier, where they found an increase in teacher absence when an extra teacher was provided to the school,

except when school committees were explicitly instructed to monitor the programmes (Duflo et al. 2008). In the study of *balsakhis* in Vadodara and Mumbai, Pratham's staff exerted constant monitoring of the school, whereas in the Bihar and Uttarakhand studies it was largely the school's responsibility to ensure that the volunteers and teachers were present and did their work, with Pratham staff visiting less frequently.

Summer learning camps:

A first interpretation of the weak in-school results could be that teachers do not exert effort, are not motivated to teach, or are too set in their ways to implement the innovative pedagogy. However, a very different result was found in the gains in learning among children who attended summer camps in Bihar. J-PAL researchers had conducted a randomised evaluation of this pilot 'summer learning camp' that was implemented by the Bihar government and Pratham teachers in government schools, who were paid their salary for the extra month. These camps were taught by the same teachers who taught in the regular school year, supported by a volunteer in the classroom. The summer camp was aimed at children in Classes III, IV and V who were not yet reading or doing arithmetic of Class-II level. The classes took place in government school buildings. The evaluation found significant learning gains in reading and mathematics, with significant persistence even after two school years. Overall, there was a significant, but modest, impact on overall reading levels in the villages with the camps. Virtually all the learning gains were found among children with low levels of initial learning, indicating that the pedagogy was well-designed for this group. Fourteen per cent of children moved up one level in reading, on an average, in the treatment villages in comparison to control. For those who actually attended, the gains were much larger (for example, a child gained 0.56 of a level, indicating that half the class moved up one level if they regularly attended the summer camp). This impact was mainly driven by larger gains for the children who could only read letters at the baseline before the camp. As already emphasised, these learning gains occurred with existing government school teachers. Perhaps their work in the summer was much more effective because they too were freed from the grip of age-class curriculum and could work in a focused manner with the children left behind. During the school year, teachers are compelled to teach by class and are busy completing curriculum as required by law.

An interpretation of the mixed results from the Read India evaluation throws up questions on how to integrate innovation within a government framework; it also highlights some important lessons: *Pedagogy and teaching effort tailored to the child's need can have significant impacts even with unpaid volunteers and low-paid teachers, provided this is the primary focus of their work.* The failure of teachers to achieve results within the school year is consistent either with weak teacher motivation or an emphasis on delivering the curriculum rather than competencies.

School and Teacher-Level Incentives

A key lesson from the studies focusing on pedagogical innovations is that teaching behaviour seems to be an important channel through which learning happens for students. This raises the question of the incentives that teachers recieve when actually in the classroom. A number of studies have tested alternative interventions, providing incentives to schools or teachers, or using contract teachers, who may be incentivised to teach since they could otherwise lose their job. These questions are systematically studied in a series of randomised evaluations in India under the APRESt and helps inform us better on what worked in a particular context (Muralidharan and Sundararaman 2011). As discussed before, earlier studies found that the effort of government school teachers in India is a serious problem, as reflected in high rates of teacher absenteeism or being present but not teaching (Muralidharan and Kremer 2008; PROBE Team 1999).

The APRESt explored several interventions, with a mix of input- and incentive-based policies for teachers, hiring additional contract teachers, and material inputs designed to test different hypotheses. It was carried out in five districts of Andhra Pradesh. Overall, the interventions with contract teachers were found to be *more* effective than the regular teacher, with students significantly outperforming in schools with extra contract teachers, than in comparison schools. This is a highly cost-effective model, as contract teachers cost much less than regular teachers and have large gains for children's learning improvement. Testing the hypothesis that teachers do not know how to help students and thus feedback and better information can help them address the specific needs of students, existing regular teachers in a selected set of schools were provided with detailed feedback on students and were subject to minimal, low stakes monitoring. Results indicated that teaching activity of the teachers in feedback schools seemed to be higher relative to the comparison group with no feedback and monitoring. They were found to be actively teaching, reading from textbooks, using the blackboard more and assigning more homework as compared to the comparison school teachers (a significant effect of 0.1 standard deviation higher teaching activity in treatment schools relative to comparison schools). However, while teaching activity improved under observation, this did not translate into any learning gains for children. The lack of impact on test scores of students, despite enhanced teaching activity, suggests that teachers temporarily changed behaviour when observed, but did not actively use the feedback reports in their teaching, or that their teaching activities were not suited to the children's needs.

Performance-Pay Incentives for Teachers

The debate around performance-based pay to increase teacher output has received much attention. A common criticism of financial incentives is the reduction of intrinsic motivation, and the danger of the teacher teaching to the test in order to gain the desired learning outcomes from the child. In a key set of interventions that gave additional rewards to teachers — linked to financial bonus based on student improvements — the hypotheses were that pay could incentivise performance on learning outcomes, or contract teachers could be as or more effective as regular teachers (APRESt, see Muralidharan and Sundararaman 2011). The study explored whether teacher performance-pay can improve test scores, whether teachers change behaviour and if there are negative consequences. In the randomised experiment design, there were two variants of the financial bonus. One, where individual teachers received bonus pay based on average test score gains made by their students. In the other, all teachers in a school received the bonus based on average test score gains for the entire school (group incentive). In addition, in order to estimate long-term effects, half the schools in each of the treatment groups were randomly allocated to continue receiving the performance bonuses for a period of five years. The student test was designed to check conceptual knowledge that required a deeper understanding of basic concepts, in order to reduce the problems of teaching to the test, and language and mathematics were chosen as the focus subjects. Further, the bonus was estimated as a function of the average improvement of all students in a class, to counter teachers being incentivised to focus only on students near some target (for example, the low-performing students).

There were three significant results of the experiment: First, the bonus (incentive) schools did better in major sub-groups (individual and group incentives) and in all classes (Classes I–V) relative to the comparison schools which did not receive a bonus. This was found in both mathematics and language, and at all levels of question difficulty. These students performed better on conceptual (and not just mechanical) questions, and did significantly well even in subjects for which there were no incentives (scoring 0.5 and 0.3 standard deviations higher than students in comparison schools on tests in science and social studies). Second, individual incentive schools outperformed the group incentive schools on student outcomes at the end of the programme, though they were equally effective in the first year of the experiment. Third, students who had completed five years of primary schooling under the programme scored an overall 0.5 standard deviation higher in language and 0.35 standard deviations higher in mathematics as compared to the comparison schools. The impact of individual teacher incentives on performance and student learning was significant over the entire duration of the five-year programmes. However, neither of these interventions reduced teacher absenteeism; instead, only increased teachers' efforts while at school, leading to the supposition that the main mechanism for the improved outcomes in incentive schools is teaching activity conditional on presence.

Figure 11.2 shows that among all the programmes tested under the umbrella of the APRESt study (contract teachers, grants to buy additional classroom stationery and materials, feedback and monitoring of teachers, and performance-pay incentives), the individual and group bonuses that comprised the performance-pay incentives had the largest impact and were more cost-effective relative to the gains on student outcomes.

Though it is clear that financial incentives for existing government school teachers, linked to actual outcomes in skills, led to substantial improvements, it is unclear if this was a pure incentive effect on effort, or a means of having teachers focus on actual learning outcomes. Further, although linking teachers' pay to attendance can increase student learning, instituting teacher incentives within the government school structure will require considerable push and negotiation with the administration, especially where teacher unions are strong and active.

GUARANTEEING THE RIGHT TO EDUCATION AND LEARNING FOR ALL

In the speech marking the introduction of the Right to Free and Compulsory Act into law, Prime Minister Manmohan Singh said: 'We are committed to ensuring that all children, irrespective of gender and social category, have access to education. An education that enables them to acquire the skills, knowledge, values and attitudes necessary to become responsible and active citizens of India.'[7]

This is a superb aspiration. But it is not at all clear that it is consistent with current government policy or the provisions of the RTE itself. This concluding section summarises what the lessons from evidence imply for an approach to education policy, compares this with the RTE, as currently interpreted, and then suggests a way forward.

What does the review of evidence here imply regarding achieving the aspiration mentioned earlier? The following has been seen — there is a huge quality problem in rural and urban schools; there are high levels of inequality in learning, with only a small proportion able to acquire good learning; and there is a steady shift from government to private schooling, supplemented by use of private tutors. This shift almost certainly affects all children of elites, but also extends to over half of urban children in urban areas, and about a quarter of rural children. Outside the very small number of elite schools, private schooling is associated with only slightly higher quality (at least in English), but at much lower economic cost. This is especially because the market wage for private teachers is way below the salaries for regular government teachers.

Against this background, there have been a range of carefully conducted and assessed research studies and RCTs on a variety of efforts in India that are trying to improve learning outcomes.

FIGURE 11.2   Combined Impact of APRESt Interventions

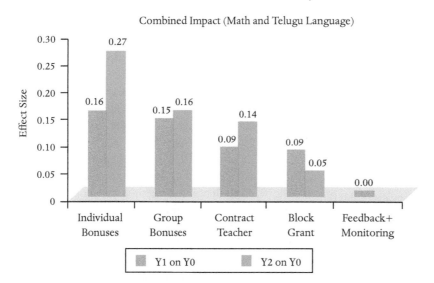

In summary, comparison of all the interventions indicates that performance-pay was twice as cost-effective as an extra contract teacher, and a contract teacher is five times more cost-effective than a regular teacher. This suggests that expanding a performance-pay programme would be 10 times more cost-effective than a business of usual expansion of spending.

Source: Muralidharan (2011).

The review discussed earlier of the current empirical literature on 'what works' points to several promising directions:

(a) *Experiments in learning innovations*: substantial improvements in basic skills can *potentially* be had through alternative pedagogies with current resources, whether with volunteers, existing or contract teachers. These gains can come about in government schools as the system now works, but they rarely occur and only seem to work with strong monitoring and enforcing mechanisms to ensure effective implementation.

(b) *Teacher incentives*: small financial incentives to teachers have been seen to lead to improvements in learning quality, and *can* also make a difference within the government school system. These were not achieved with increases in inputs — indeed there is little, though mixed, evidence that changing inputs will have much of an effect at all on learning levels (both from the Indian and international evidence). Therefore while inputs may be needed in schools for other reasons, policies should not rely on these to guarantee learning.

(c) *Teaching to a child's ability level*: reorganisation of children and aligning the pedagogy to teaching by ability level rather than class level can lead to substantial gains, especially when the teaching–learning activities focus on developing basic skills rather than delivering content from textbooks.

The big question is how to change conditions in schools and classroom practices so that all children can learn effectively. Basic skills are fundamental building blocks for everything else, including conceptual ability, creativity and critical thinking. This implies urgently focusing on these skills in the early schooling years across India. It is also critical to recognise that motivated teachers are integral part of the effort and pedagogies have to be adapted to the needs of children. There is a need to acknowledge the huge backlog of children who are already in school and need remedial help. The evidence is that this *can* be done effectively with relatively straightforward basic training, at least in lower classes. There are potentially large learning gains to be reaped from setting realistic goals for teachers and children and from reorganising curricula and regrouping children to allow them to learn at a reasonable pace. These processes need to be initiated in both government and private schools, and supported by supplemental learning, and in some cases private tutoring and perhaps even parental involvement.

These directions for action flow from the results of careful experimentation of innovative ideas and systematic and independent empirical research and impact evaluation. However, an equally important result is that teaching innovations often fail if they are just added on to the existing system of incentives, processes, pedagogies, and curriculum requirements. How to change the overall government (and private) system to effect large improvements in learning is still unknown. This implies that it will be necessary to design a process of exploration and experimentation within the government and private schooling systems, with systematic monitoring and analysis of results in actual learning levels. Effecting systemic change is difficult, and is likely to require leadership from the top of state education systems, and experiments in pedagogical, administration and teacher incentives all the way down the government system. Outreach to the private system and exploration of learning successes and failures is also needed. This is an urgent need, given the breadth and depth of the learning deficit, if the current generation of students are not to miss out on the learning they need and deserve.

How does the RTE relate to this approach? At first sight, RTE provisions appear to go in exactly the wrong direction. It is strongly input-focused, specifying norms for facilities, including infrastructure and PTRs, which will apply to both government and private schools. Children will automatically advance through the classes, whatever their ability, and board exams are prohibited — though teachers are supposed to continuously assess quality. Teachers are not allowed to tutor outside school. Private schools have to be recognised to be allowed to practice, and will be fined if they continue without it. They are given three years to meet the new norms. All private schools, with the exception of unaided minority schools, are required to reserve 25 per cent of their places for children from weak disadvantaged backgrounds — with the cost reimbursed by the government at a rate based on the cost of government schooling or of actual private tuition charged, whichever is lower. (This provision was challenged as unconstitutional, but the Supreme Court, in a 2–1 ruling on 12 April 2012, declared that it was consistent with the constitution, see PRS India [2012] for a discussion).

Now, actual rules are being drafted at the level of states, so specific mechanisms for implementation could vary substantially. As Pratap Bhanu Mehta (2012) has commented that at present it is still not known how the RTE will be implemented in practice. That, of course, is precisely why public debate is so important. Here are some issues that will be central to the success or failure of RTE's implementation in relation to the quality issue.

Norms on infrastructure inputs and PTRs are desirable for the working conditions of teachers and the comfort of pupils, and it makes sense to implement these in government schools. However, as already noted, there is little or no evidence that these will have an impact on learning levels. It is thus crucial that the focus on inputs not divert attention from the measurement and tracking of actual learning, and discovery of what does make a difference.

Potentially much more problematic is the requirement that private schools satisfy the norms if they are to be recognised. Especially if this is linked to setting private teacher salaries at the level of regular government school teachers, this could drastically affect the low-cost schooling movement — either through forcing productive schools to close or providing an incentive to bribe education inspectors (that, anecdotally, is already of significance.) RTE currently specifies that all teachers in private schools have to meet formal training requirements, but salary levels are (at least implicitly) to be determined by the states. As seen before, learning outcomes are only moderately better in private than in government schools (but this is being achieved at a much lower cost) to a significant extent because private schools are paying market salary levels, and often to teachers without the formal teacher qualifications specified in the Act.

A comparable consideration applies to terms of employment within government schools. A common diagnosis has been that teachers face weak incentives to actually teach. They are also paid way above the market wage for similar skills. Experiments with contract teachers have led to better, not worse, results in quality, owing to the stronger incentives. It may be possible to get similar results through shifting work and career incentives (financial or non-financial) within the regular teaching service, but this is still to be explored — the political economy of teachers is likely to resist this. Further, as seen while reviewing the series of impact evaluations of Pratham programmes, Pratham-trained volunteers (who are unpaid) often can bring about large improvements in learning levels too. This is an area where *more,* not less flexibility and experimentation is required.

Profoundly missing from the RTE are mechanisms to get relevant information on learning performance of children, classes and schools. Until now, student evaluations have focused almost exclusively on academic subjects, with an end-of-year high stakes examinations (National Curriculum Framework 2005). The RTE Act of 2009 mandated the introduction of a system of Continuous and Comprehensive Evaluation (CCE) to address endemic issues arising from traditional methods of evaluation and broaden the scope to include non-academic aspects to promote the holistic development of children. CCE is meant to allow for regular flow of information regarding student learning (collected by teachers) which enables tracking their progress and tailoring of lessons and teaching practices to student capabilities. Therefore, CCE establishes an intensive school-based evaluation system wherein external examinations, such as board exams, are absent.

However, the move to CCE has been met with confusion due to the lack of guidelines for implementing this effectively at the school level. In many states, the CCE activity is anchored in the current age-class curriculum (the very element that is holding children back). In several states, the actual assessment activity has also been made cumbersome and complicated, thereby further reducing the possibility that each teacher will make an effort to understand where the child stands and what needs to be done to help him or her move forward. The teachers are not well-trained to be able to use the assessments to map students' outcomes, both scholastic and non-scholastic. So while CCE in principle may have been a good thing, in practice it is likely to totally miss the boat, the effects of which will only be visible when students take the Class IX exams or competitive exams.

The RTE clearly states that the syllabus must be completed in a specified time and that children cannot be held back. At its core the RTE relies on inputs and age-class organisation of children as the main classifying principle of school education in India. Equally problematic is the automatic advancement irrespective of learning level. The policy of no detention up to Class V is already followed in government schools of some states (for e.g., Haryana). As observed earlier, there is a dramatic difference between the learning levels of most children and the current curriculum. In the traditional examination system, the end-of-year exams functioned as mechanisms to filter out low-performers, who were detained in their current class. Aligning pedagogies with the needs of children — and exploring alternative ways of doing this — has to be part of the solution. Some of this is about 'remedial' education, supplemental learning support or in fact 'special training' (that is referred to in RTE). But the divergence between learning levels and the curriculum is so extensive that this goes way beyond the typical notion of remedial needs for limited numbers of children. It is about getting overall pedagogical alignment, regrouping of children, clear articulation of learning goals, and all of this backed by support to teachers motivating them to teach, for large proportions of the elementary school population. A no-detention policy could make learning worse, if it means no evaluation and a rising gap between learning levels and curriculum requirements, especially for the weakest.

One of the more intriguing parts of the Act is the provision that 25 per cent of seats in private schools have to be allocated to children from 'weaker sections and disadvantaged groups' from scheduled castes, scheduled tribes, low-income, and other disadvantaged or weaker groups. Again, much will depend on implementation. It could evolve into a voucher scheme for 'qualified' children or could become embedded in local influence. In either case the effects on learning quality are unclear. It has been observed that learning levels in private schools are slightly above those of government schools, but some of this difference is explained by socio-economic background. There is no clear evidence from India on what would be the effects on the targeted students who do gain access. There is some international evidence that access to private schooling via a voucher programme can improve schooling outcomes for students (see Angrist et al. [2002], for example, for a programme involving secondary schooling in Colombia). But this may be context-specific, and the net impact on the whole schooling system is unclear since effects on government schooling are ambiguous. And a further concern is over the vagueness of the criteria: categorisation of the needy is notoriously problematic in India, and subject to discretion, exclusions and patronage. This is another area which requires, more than anything, experimentation.

Is this, then, a time to be pessimistic or optimistic for the future of learning in India? This review suggests a decidedly mixed picture. The problem is huge; there can surely be no question on the need to put questions of learning *outcomes* at the centre of any education strategy. Indian households clearly want education. The RTE is an important step, at least in symbolic terms. There is a lot of evidence on what does and does not work. Some of this evidence is encouraging: existing pedagogies can make a substantial difference to children with existing resources, but none of the evidence provides a clear pathway to a transformative solution. For that, the only coherent way forward is to encourage widespread exploration of alternatives, working within the government and private systems, and including private tutoring. On the other hand, the RTE has some major flaws — omission and commission. However, real implementation will depend primarily on the actual rules and practices at state level. This constitutes an immense opportunity for exploration and experimentation, but one that will depend, fundamentally, on putting measurement, assessment and public debate at the very centre of the process of discovery of what does and does not work. This could make the difference between providing India's children with 'the skills, knowledge, values and attitudes necessary to become responsible and active citizens of India' and a profound failing in terms of what the country *could* offer to this generation, with deep consequences for poverty, inequality and the condition of Indian society and economy.

NOTES

1. The Right of Children to Free and Compulsory Education Act or Right to Education (RTE) Act, which was passed by the Indian parliament on 4 August 2009, describes the modalities of the provision of free and compulsory education for children between 6 and 14 in India, under Article 21A of the Indian Constitution.
2. The Abdul Latif Jameel Poverty Action Lab (J-PAL) in South Asia (based at the Institute for Financial Management and Research, IFMR) is the regional branch of the Massachusetts Institute of Technology.
3. A similar result was found in the NCERT survey of 2010 for Class V students, which shows that Uttar Pradesh is doing better than Gujarat, West Bengal, Jharkhand, and Tripura. The survey tested over 0.1 million students across 31 states in both rural and urban schools, in language, mathematics and environmental studies.
4. RCTs are a type of Impact Evaluation that uses random assignment to allocate resources, run programmes, or apply policies as part of the study design. The main purpose of an RCT is to determine whether a programme has an impact, and more specifically, to quantify *how large* that impact is. Impact evaluations measure a programme's effectiveness typically by comparing outcomes of those (individuals, communities, schools, etc.) who received the programme against those who did not. Though there are many methods of doing this, but randomised evaluations are generally considered the most rigorous and, all else equal, produce the most accurate (i.e., unbiased) results, see http://www.povertyactionlab.org/methodology (accessed 19 November 2012).
5. See also Urquiola and Verhoogen (2009) for the lack of impact of PTRs in Chilean schools.
6. Pratham is a nationwide NGO and has been implementing large-scale programmes that deliver basic reading and mathematics skills to rural and urban children. Pratham's programmes seek to partner with village communities and government school systems to bring about a significant improvement in basic learning levels across the country. Pratham's strength lies in participative organisational strategies combined with practical pedagogies that can be implemented at scale with existing teaching resources and volunteers.
7. Prime Minister's address to the nation on 1 April 2010, http://www.pib.nic.in/newsite/erelease.aspx?relid=60001 (accessed 18 May 2012). For the gazetted version of RTE, see GoI (2009).

REFERENCES

Angrist, Joshua D., Eric Bettinger, Erik Bloom, Elizabeth King, and Michael Kremer. 2002. 'Vouchers for Private Schooling in Colombia: Evidence from a Randomised Natural Experiment', *The American Economic Review*, December, 92(5): 1535–58.

Atherton, Paul and Geeta Kingdon. 2010. 'The Relative Effectiveness and Costs of Contract and Regular Teachers in India'. Centre for the Study of African Economies (CSAE) Working Paper Series 2010–15, University of Oxford.

Banerjee, Abhijit, Shawn Cole, Esther Duflo, and Leigh Lindon. 2005. 'Remedying Education: Evidence from Two Randomised Experiments in India', *Quarterly Journal of Economics*, 122(3): 1235–64.

Banerjee, Abhijit, Rukmini Banerji, Esther Duflo, Rachel Glennerster, and Stuti Khemani. 2010. 'Pitfalls of Participatory Programmes: Evidence from a Randomised Evaluation in Education in India', *American Economic Journal: Economic Policy*, 2(1): 1–30.

Banerjee, Abhijit, Rukmini Banerji, Esther Duflo, and Michael Walton. 2011. 'Effective Pedagogies and a Resistant Education System: Experimental Evidence on Interventions to Improve Basic Skills in Rural India'. Cambridge and New Delhi: Jameel Poverty Action Lab.

Banerjee, Abhijit and Esther Duflo. 2011. *Poor Economics*. New York: Public Affairs.

Béteille, Tara. 2009. 'Absenteeism, Transfers and Patronage: The Political Economy of Teacher Labor Markets in India'. D.Phil. dissertation, Stanford University.

Bhattacharjea, Suman, Wilima Wadhwa and Rukmini Banerji. 2011. *Inside Primary Schools*. New Delhi: Annual Status of Education Report (ASER) Centre.

Chudgar, Amita and Elizabeth Quin. 2012. 'Relationship between Private Schooling and Achievement: Results from Rural and Urban India', *Economics of Education Review*, 31: 376–90.

Das, Jishnu and Tristan Zajonc. 2010. 'India Shining and Bharat Drowning: Comparing Two Indian States to the Worldwide Distribution in Mathematics Achievement', *Journal of Development Economics*, 92(2): 175–87.

Desai, Sonalde, Amaresh Dubey, Reeve Vanneman, and Rukmini Banerji. 2009. 'Private Schooling in India: A New Landscape', in Suman Bery, Barry Bosworth and Arvind Panagariya (eds), *India Policy Forum 5*, pp. 1–58. New Delhi: Sage Publications.

Desai, Sonalde, Amaresh Dubey, Brij Lal Joshi, Mitali Sen, Abusaleh Sharif, and Reeve Vanneman. 2011. *Human Development in India: Challenges for a Society in Transition*. New Delhi: Oxford University Press.

Duflo, Esther, Pascaline Dupas and Michael Kremer. 2008. 'Peer Effects and the Impact of Tracking: Evidence from a Randomised Evaluation in Kenya', *American Economic Review*, 101(5): 1739–74.

Education Initiatives. 2010. *Student Learning Study: Status of Student Learning in 18 States in Urban and Rural Schools*. Ahmedabad: Education Initiatives.

Glewwe Paul, Michael Kremer, Sylvie Moulin, and Eric Zitzewitz. 2004. 'Retrospective vs. Prospective Analyses of School Inputs: The Case of Flipcharts in Kenya', *Journal of Development Economics*, 74(1): 251–68.

Glewwe Paul, Michael Kremer and Sylvie Moulin. 2009. 'Many Children Left Behind? Textbooks and Test Scores in Kenya', *American Economic Journal: Applied Economics*, 1(1): 112–35.

Government of India (GoI). 2009. 'Right of Children to Free and Compulsory Education Act, 2009', *Gazette of India*, 27 August.

Hanushek, Eric A. 2010. 'Education Production Functions: Developed Country Evidence', in Dominic J. Brewer and Patrick J. McEwan (eds), *Economics of Education*, pp. 132–36. Amsterdam: Elsevier.

Kremer, Michael, Nazmul Chaudhury, Karthik Muralidharan, Halsey F. Rogers, and Jeffrey Hammer. 2006. 'Teacher Absence in India: A Snapshot', *Journal of the European Economic Association*, 20(1): 91–116.

Kingdon, Geeta and Mohd. Muzammil. 2008. 'A Political Economy of Education in India: The Case of Uttar Pradesh', *Oxford Development Studies*, June, 37(2): 123–44.

Kremer, Michael and Alaka Holla. 2009. 'Improving Education in the Developing World: What have we Learned from Randomised

Evaluations?', in Kenneth J. Arrow and Timothy F. Bresnahan (eds), *Annual Review of Economics*, vol. 1. Palo Alto, California: Annual Reviews.

Luce, Edward. 2012. *Time to Start Thinking*. New York: Atlantic Monthly Press.

Mehta, Pratap Bhanu. 2012. 'Classroom Struggle', *The Indian Express*, 18 April. http://www.indianexpress.com/news/classroom-struggle/937982/ (accessed 1 June 2012).

Mukerji, Shobhini and Wilima Wadhwa. 2012. 'Do Private Schools Perform better than Public Schools? Evidence from Rural India'. Working Paper, Annual Status of Education Report (ASER) Centre.

Muralidharan, Karthik. 2011. 'Lessons from the Andhra Pradesh Randomised Evaluation Studies (APRESt)'. Paper presented to Cabinet Secretariat, Government of India, 18 July.

Muralidharan, Karthik and Venkatesh Sundararaman. 2010. 'Contract Teachers: Experimental Evidence from India'. Working Paper. http://econ.ucsd.edu/~kamurali/research.html (accessed 8 November 2012).

—————. 2011. 'Teacher Performance Pay: Experimental Evidence from India', *Journal of Political Economy*, 119(1): 39–77.

National Council of Educational Research and Training (NCERT). 2005. *National Curriculum Framework 2005*. New Delhi: National Council of Educational Research and Training.

Organisation for Economic Co-operation and Development (OECD). 2010. *PISA 2009 Results: What Students Know and Can do: Performance in Reading, Mathematics and Science*, vol. 1. Paris: OECD.

PRS India. 2012. 'Supreme Court Upholds 25% Reservation in Private Schools', PRS Legislative Research, New Delhi. http://www.prsindia.org/theprsblog/2012/04/14/supreme-court-upholds-25-reservation-in-private-schools/ (accessed 1 June 2012).

Pratham–Annual Status of Education Report (ASER) Centre. 2005–11. *Annual Status of Education Report (Rural)*. New Delhi: ASER Centre.

Pritchett, Lant. 2012. 'The First PISA Results for India: The End of the Beginning'. http://ajayshahblog.blogspot.com/2012/01/first-pisa-results-for-india-end-of.html (accessed 20 May 2012).

Pritchett, Lant and Rinku Murgai. 2006. 'Teacher Compensation: Can Decentralisation to Local Bodies Take India from the Perfect Storm Through Troubled Waters to Clear Sailing?', *India Policy Forum*, Global Economy and Development Programmes, The Brookings Institution, 3(1): 123–77.

Pritchett, Lant and Amanda Beatty. 2012. 'The Negative Consequences of Over-Ambitious Curricular in Developing Countries'. Working Paper no. 293. Washington, DC: Center for Global Development.

PROBE Team and Delhi School of Economics. 1999. *Public Report on Basic Education in India*, Centre for Development Economics. New Delhi and Oxford: Oxford University Press.

Tooley, James and Pauline Dixon. 2005. 'Private Schools Serving the Poor', Working Paper, A Study from Delhi, India. New Delhi: Centre for Civil Society.

Urquiola, Miguel and Eric Verhoogen. 2009. 'Class Size Caps, Sorting, And The Regression Discontinuity Design', *American Economic Review*, 99(1): 179–215.

Vagh, Shaher Banu. 2009. *Evaluating the Reliability and Validity of the ASER Testing Tools*. New Delhi: ASER Centre.

12

Secondary Education

*Toby Linden**

Responsibility for the provision and financing of secondary education is — like other aspects of education — a shared responsibility between union and state governments. However, until the last five years or so, both levels of government had given priority to policy development and financial investments in elementary education. This chapter therefore will not provide a historical overview, but it is worth noting that the policy and programmatic landscape is changing quickly; which also offers opportunities to identify good practice and implement effective reforms. The recent focus on secondary education was generated by the 2005 Central Advisory Board of Education (CABE) Report (2005).

This pattern of investment has been common in many countries. Whether through domestic pressures or the pursuit of the Millennium Development Goals, countries have devoted time, effort and resources to elementary education; and higher education has long received generous (per pupil) funding but remained small and elite (World Bank 2005). Secondary education in this context has served to filter out those who would not go on to higher education. The expansion in enrolments in elementary education has changed the context for secondary education, though, to date, it has done little to change the structures, curriculum or organisation. It is the contention of this chapter that secondary education is not simply an extension of primary education, in particular given the more significant presence of the private sector. Keeping in mind the particular features of secondary education, it will identify relevant and effective reforms.

This chapter will look at the access to, and equity and quality in, lower and higher secondary education[1] (Classes IX–XII) in India and examine some ideas for improvements in each.

* The findings, interpretations and conclusions expressed herein are those of the author and do not necessarily reflect the views of the executive directors of the International Bank for Reconstruction and Development/World Bank or the governments they represent.

CHALLENGES IN SECONDARY EDUCATION: ACCESS

There are 44.8 million children in secondary education in India, which translates into a gross enrolment ratio (GER)[2] of 45.81 per cent in Classes IX–XII.[3] Most of these 44.8 million children are in lower secondary education — 28.4 million — while the remainder are in higher secondary education. While the overall GER in Classes IX–XII is 45.81, the GER is much higher in lower secondary (at 58.15 per cent) than in higher secondary (33.48 per cent).

The number of children in secondary education is expected to continue to rise due to both supply and demand factors. On the supply side, the GER in primary education is over 100 per cent and is approaching that figure in upper primary (Figure 12.1). The proportion of children completing primary and upper primary education continues to rise, albeit slowly — from 73.7 per cent to 75 per cent between 2004–05 and 2010–11 — as does the transition rate from elementary to lower secondary. Moreover, the size of the young age cohorts is expected to increase for a couple more decades. The total number of people aged 15–19 is expected to continue to rise until 2025, at which point it will be 4 million more than it is today; and it will not be until after 2035 that the cohort size falls below the current level (Table 12.1).

On the demand side, the returns to education for individuals indicate that there is still labour market demand for secondary education graduates despite the increasing number of them in the working age population. Over the last decade, returns for lower secondary and higher secondary education have been the highest returns for any level of education, even greater than for higher education; with the latest returns being a wage premium of 36 per cent for someone completing lower secondary education compared to someone completing primary education, and 43 per cent for someone completing higher secondary as against completing lower secondary education (Figure 12.2). These

FIGURE 12.1   Gross Enrolment Ratio

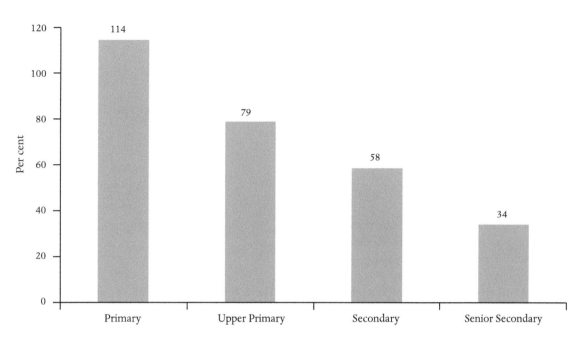

Source: Adapted from Sankar (2011).

TABLE 12.1   Population of Males and Females 15–19 years of Age, 2010–50

	2010	2015	2020	2025	2030	2035	2040	2045	2050
Males	60,150	60,838	61,202	62,301	62,048	61,175	59,758	58,230	56,644
Females	54,943	55,677	56,069	57,162	57,035	56,317	55,071	53,704	52,267
Total	115,093	116,515	117,271	119,463	119,083	117,492	114,829	111,934	108,911
Year-on-Year Change (in per cent)		101.2	100.6	101.9	99.7	98.7	97.7	97.5	97.3
Cumulative Change (in per cent)		101.2	101.9	103.8	103.5	102.1	99.8	97.3	94.6

Source: Author's calculations based on data from World Bank (n.d.).

increasing returns have occurred even while the proportion of people with secondary education in each succeeding cohort has also risen (Figure 12.3).

These national averages, however, conceal considerable variation at the state level in terms of access to secondary education. The richer states like Tamil Nadu and Himachal Pradesh have the highest rates for both primary completion and for Class IX gross intake (both these states have rates at 100 per cent or more);[4] while poorer states like Bihar and Jharkhand have the lowest, with, for example, Bihar's overall primary completion rate at around 40 per cent and its Class IX gross intake at about 35 per cent (Figure 12.4) This is the expected pattern since secondary education is not compulsory and the direct and indirect costs of attending school are significantly greater than in primary education.

CHALLENGES IN SECONDARY EDUCATION: EQUITY

Not surprisingly, there are gaps in enrolment rates for several sub-populations. For example, in lower secondary education, a slight majority (51 per cent) of children aged 14–15 attend school in urban areas; while of the same-aged children in rural areas, less than 40 per cent attend school (Table 12.2). It is noteworthy that a significant proportion of children in both rural and urban areas are over-age in secondary education. The scheduled tribe (ST), scheduled caste (SC) and Muslim minority students are underrepresented, in proportion to their shares in the population: for example, SCs constitute about 20.6 per cent of the general

FIGURE 12.2   Wage Premiums in India, by Level of Education

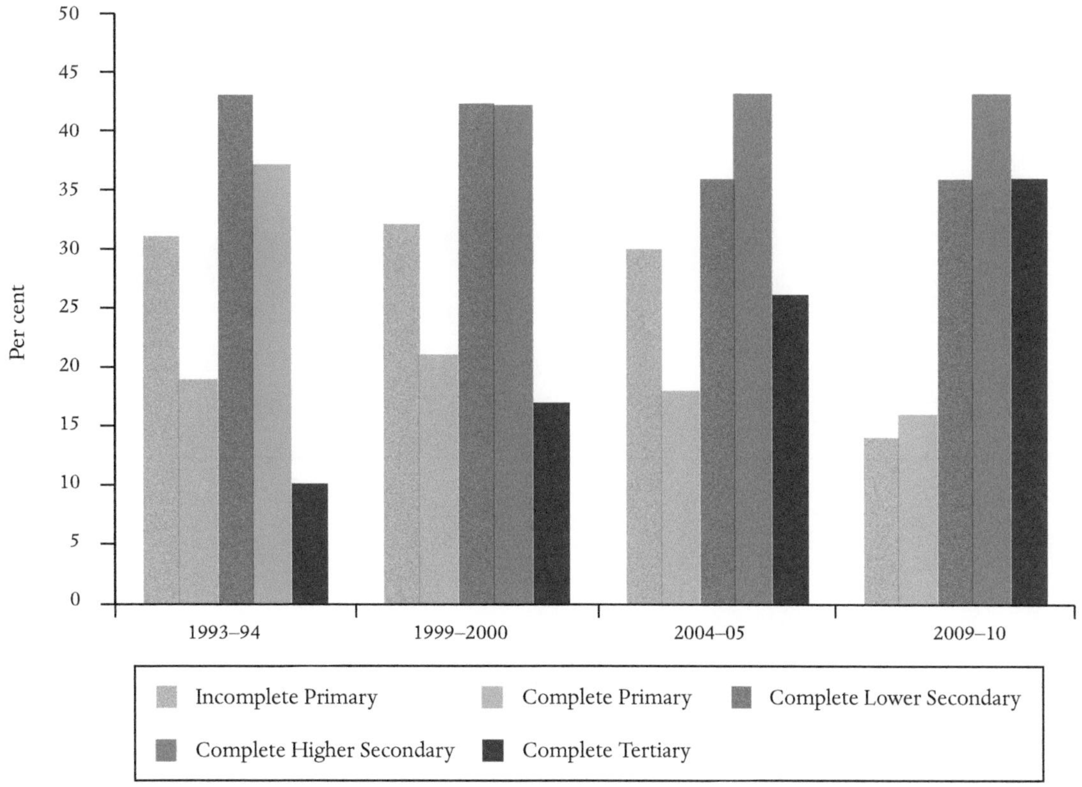

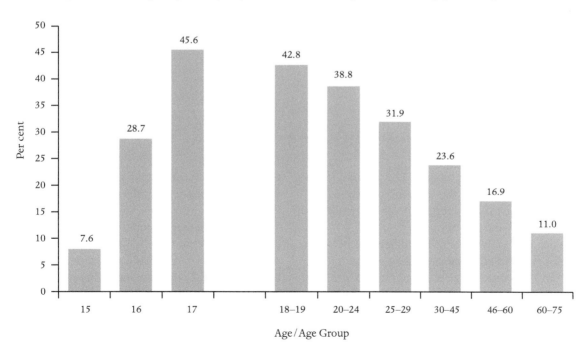

Source: World Bank (2011a).

FIGURE 12.3   Proportion of the Age/Age Group Population that has Completed Secondary (or Above) Education, 2007–08

Source: Sankar (2011).

FIGURE 12.4   State-Wise Gap between Class VIII Gross Completion Rate (2007) and Class IX Gross Intake Rate (2008)

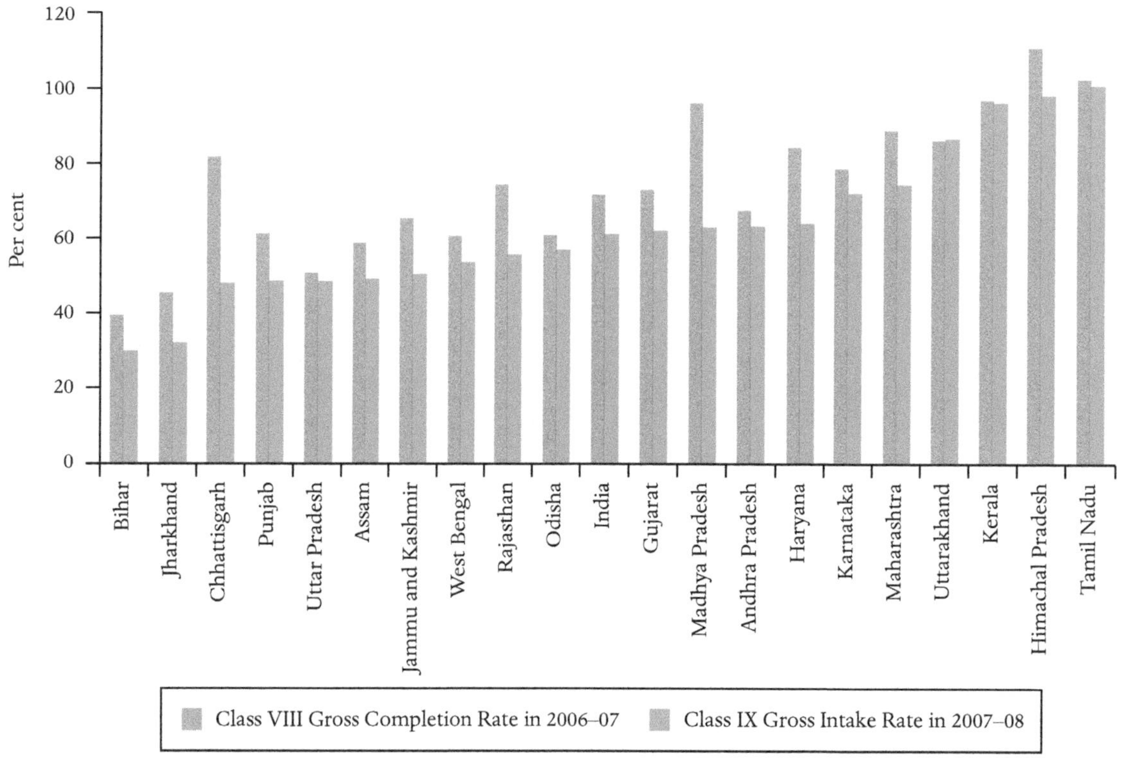

Source: MHRD (2006, 2007); Registrar General of India (RGI) single-age population projections.

TABLE 12.2   School Participation, by Location and Age Group and by Stage of Education

Age Group	Out of School (in per cent)		Attending Classes IX–X (in per cent)		Attending Classes XI–XII (in per cent)	
	RURAL	URBAN	RURAL	URBAN	RURAL	URBAN
11–13	14.7	10.8	3.9	7.4	0.0	0.0
14–15	30.9	21.2	37.7	51.3	2.5	6.2
16–17	51.5	39.2	20.9	17.9	22.7	39.7
18+	95.7	95.8	1.1	0.7	3.0	3.4

Source: Sankar (2011).

Note: Age-appropriate enrolment for Classes IX–X is 14–15 and for Classes XI–XII is 16–17.

population of the relevant age but only 17.9 per cent in the school population. However, the differences between minority groups and the majority population are generally less than the rural–urban and girl–boy gaps.

The gender gap is significant. The difference between boys and girls in terms of enrolment is 15 per cent in lower secondary (42.5 per cent for girls as against 57.5 per cent for boys) and almost 20 per cent in higher secondary (40.3 per cent as against 59.7 per cent) (Sankar 2011). These gaps are also replicated at the state level, though interestingly there are a few states that have better participation rates for girls at the lower secondary level (Kerala, Mizoram,

Goa, Puducherry, Karnataka and Delhi — and it should be noted that these are generally states with high overall rates) (Figure 12.5).

However, there is an equity dimension to the enrolment in different types of schools. In general, private schools have significantly lower proportions of students from ST and SC backgrounds, in both lower and higher secondary education. The share is especially low in private unaided schools; for example, while 7.9 per cent of government-school children are from ST backgrounds, this number is 3.5 per cent in unaided and 4.3 per cent in aided schools (Table 12.3). This is perhaps not surprising given that these sub-groups are on

FIGURE 12.5   Gross Attendance/Participation Rates at Lower Secondary (Classes IX–X), by Gender and State

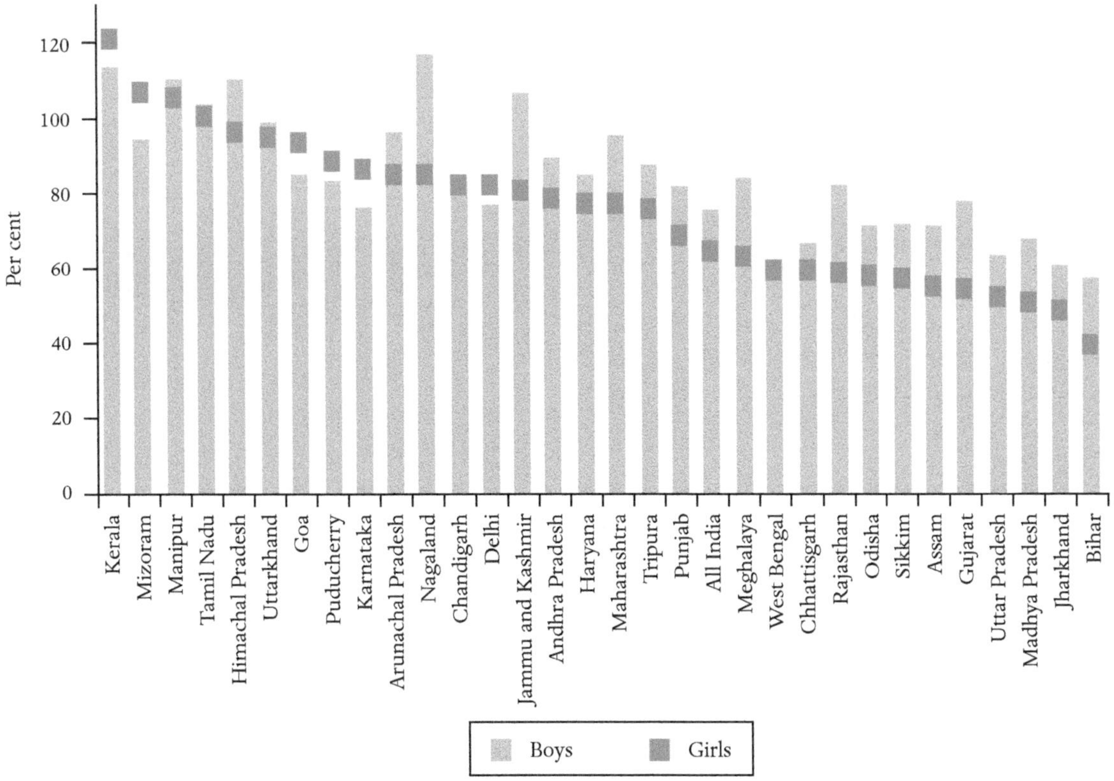

Source: Sankar (2011).

TABLE 12.3   Enrolment in Lower and Higher Secondary Education, by Social Category, 2008 (in per cent)

| | Lower Secondary | | | | | Higher Secondary | | | | |
	ST	SC	OBC	Others	Total	ST	SC	OBC	Others	Total
Government + Local Body	7.9	20.2	44.1	27.9	100.0	6.5	17.8	42.8	33.0	100.0
Private Aided	4.3	15.9	43.2	36.6	100.0	4.4	14.3	39.5	41.8	100.0
Private Unaided	3.5	11.8	42.1	42.5	100.0	2.9	10.7	44.2	42.2	100.0
Other	3.8	18.6	49.8	27.7	100.0	1.1	20.9	48.4	29.6	100.0

Source: Author's calculations from NSS data, 64th round.

average poorer and so are less likely to be able to afford the fees associated with private schools. These schools are also generally located in urban areas.

CHALLENGES IN SECONDARY EDUCATION: QUALITY

Good data on the quality of education is scarce and, importantly, there is no national assessment of performance in secondary education. There are about 30 state examination boards that prepare examinations for students at the end of lower secondary and higher secondary education,

with schools in some states also participating in examinations set by a national board. However, the pass rates across states are not comparable as they vary considerably (Table 12.4). Moreover, pass rates are not comparable across time within one state: for example, there are five state Boards in which the pass rate fluctuated by more than 5 percentage points between 2007 and 2008, and a further six Boards in which the difference was more than 10 percentage points.[5] If an examination is reliable, one would expect examination results from one year to the next to vary only by a small degree. This is because the abilities of students do not vary greatly and they have had very similar educational experiences over consecutive years. The wide variations in Indian

TABLE 12.4   Number of State Board Examinations in Different Pass Percentage Rate Brackets, 2008

Pass Rates (in per cent)	Number of States					
	40–49	50–59	60–69	70–79	80–89	90–99
Lower Secondary (High School)	1	8	6	5	6	4
Higher Secondary	1	3	7	9	8	3

Source: Author's calculations based on data from MHRD (2006, 2007).

examinations indicate a lack of technical reliability in the examinations, and no comparisons across states can be considered absolute. Therefore, there is no national picture of the quality of secondary education, as measured by the skills and knowledge acquired by students at the end of this stage of education.

Some assessments conducted in individual states, using internationally benchmarked assessments, suggest student learning is very low in India. The most recent one was the participation of two Indian states (Tamil Nadu and Himachal Pradesh) in the Organisation for Economic Co-operation and Development (OECD) Programme for International Student Assessment (PISA) in the 2009+ round.[6] PISA is an assessment of 15-year-olds in reading, mathematics and science. It focuses on the ability of students to analyse material and apply knowledge and concepts in new contexts. In the assessment, the two Indian states were ranked above only one country (Kyrgyz Republic) of the more than 70 countries and economies participating (Walker 2011). On average, 15-year-old Indian students performed about four *years* behind the international average for OECD countries. The average of the top 5 per cent of Indian students was close to the OECD average, which indicates what is achievable for Indian students. It is also worth noting that, when controlling for socio-economic factors, there were no significant differences between the performance of public and private schools in India. This is a pattern found in most other countries and suggests that there is no inherent advantage to private schools; their better performance is mostly explained by the family background of the students attending those schools.

A second study (Das and Zajonc 2010) used data from a test carried out using questions from the Trends in International Mathematics and Science Survey (TIMSS) assessment in mathematics on Class IX children in Odisha and Rajasthan. Overall, when compared with countries that took the regular TIMSS assessment, Rajasthan was ranked 47th out of 49 countries and territories, and Odisha 43rd. Just above Odisha was Egypt, while just below Rajasthan was Philippines. The study estimated that the Indian average is about three standard deviations below the OECD country mean.[7]

ADDRESSING THE CHALLENGES

Any strategy to address these challenges in secondary education must start from understanding the institutional landscape in the sector: a landscape that is very different from that in primary education.

More than half of students in secondary education study in privately-managed schools. These take two forms:
(a) private-aided schools, which receive recurrent funding from state governments, usually through paying teachers' salaries and some other costs, but where the school management is responsible for capital costs and investments; and
(b) unaided schools, which receive no public funds. Overall, in Classes IX and X in 2007–08, 45.6 per cent of children were enrolled in government schools, 28.6 per cent in aided schools and the remaining 25.8 per cent in private unaided schools (Sankar 2011).[8]

Patterns of school management of secondary education are complex and vary considerably across states, and even within states between lower and higher secondary. It seems that there is no comprehensive study of the reasons behind these variations. Figure 12.6 shows the situation in higher secondary education. For example, almost all enrolment in West Bengal is in aided schools, while there are none such schools in Manipur; and, in Chhattisgarh there are almost equal numbers of government and private unaided schools.

Moreover, *within* many states, the share of student enrolment between government, government aided and unaided schools varies between lower secondary and higher secondary schools. Sometimes the shift in management structure between lower and higher secondary is between aided and unaided schools (for example, in Kerala). In other states the shift is between government and either private-aided schools or unaided schools (Figure 12.7).

This presence of private-aided schools is reflected in the public education budget allocations at the state level. There are eight states that assign more than half of their budgets to aided schools, and an additional two states that allocate more than 90 per cent of their respective budgets to

FIGURE 12.6   Management of Higher Secondary Education by State, 2006–07

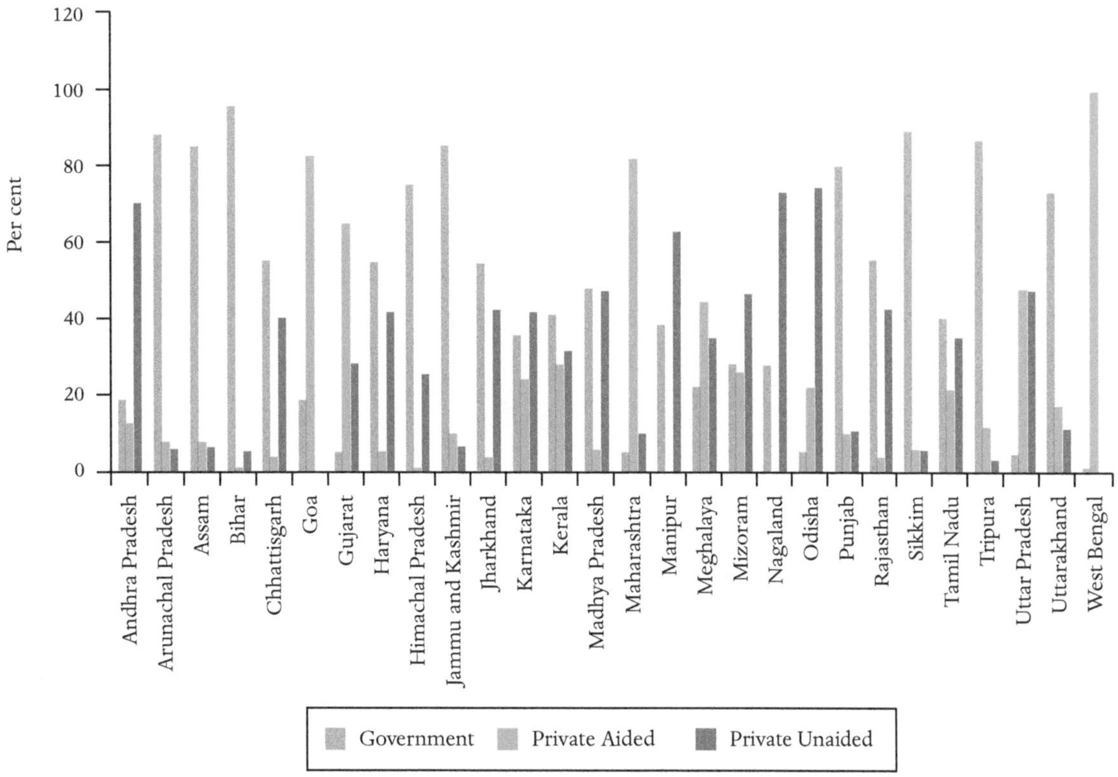

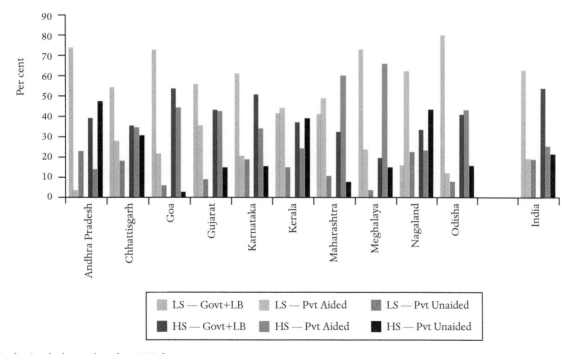

Source: Author's calculations based on data from MHRD (2007).

FIGURE 12.7   Relative Proportions of Enrolments by Management Types in Lower and Higher Secondary Education, Selected States, 2007–08

Source: Author's calculations based on NSS data.
Note: Govt=Government; HS=Higher Secondary; LB=Local Body; LS=Lower Secondary; Pvt=Private.

these schools (MHRD 2007). However, it is important but curious to note that there is no direct relationship between the proportion of the secondary education budget spent on non-government schools and the proportion of enrolments in these schools (Table 12.5). These figures suggest that there is considerable scope for states to take another look at the way they fund aided schools.

Addressing the Access Challenge

Expanding access will require both public and private investments, given the needs and the distribution of management types. The Government of India launched a major programme in 2009 — the Rashtriya Madhyamik Shiksha Abhiyan (RMSA) — to improve access, quality and equity in lower secondary education (though not as yet higher

TABLE 12.5   State Public Spending on Secondary Education by Category, as a Percentage of Total Expenditures, Actuals, 2006–07

	Government and Local Body			Non-Government		
	Secondary Education Budget (in per cent)	Enrolment (in per cent)	Difference	Secondary Education Budget (in per cent)	Enrolment (in per cent)	Difference
	1	2	(1)–(2)	1	2	(1)–(2)
Andhra Pradesh	77.1	60.1	17.0	14.1	39.9	−25.8
Arunachal Pradesh	84.1	93.9	−9.7	1.1	6.1	−5.0
Assam	2.8	88.6	−85.7	91.4	11.4	80.0
Bihar	61.6	90.3	−28.7	2.1	9.7	−7.5
Chhattisgarh	89.0	81.3	7.6	7.5	18.7	−11.2
Goa	8.4	63.9	−55.5	61.0	36.1	24.9
Gujarat	8.2	51.2	−43.0	89.8	48.8	41.0
Haryana	88.0	79.4	8.6	4.9	20.6	−15.7
Himachal Pradesh	95.5	52.6	42.9	1.2	47.4	−46.2
Jammu and Kashmir	0.0	83.4	−83.4	0.0	16.6	−16.6
Jharkhand	100.0	78.5	21.5	0.0	21.5	−21.5
Karnataka	87.4	56.3	31.1	8.9	43.7	−34.8
Kerala	32.4	39.3	−6.9	58.9	60.7	−1.9
Madhya Pradesh	86.4	69.7	16.8	10.4	30.3	−19.9
Maharashtra	6.1	37.6	−31.5	92.3	62.4	29.9
Manipur	86.6	51.4	35.2	4.8	48.6	−43.8
Meghalaya	16.6	59.6	−43.0	64.9	40.4	24.6
Mizoram	69.2	82.4	−13.2	15.2	17.6	−2.4
Nagaland	57.3	23.0	34.2	0.4	77.0	−76.5
Odisha	83.1	68.7	14.4	11.0	31.3	−20.3
Punjab	90.6	49.7	40.9	8.0	50.3	−42.3
Rajasthan	88.7	55.6	33.1	2.9	44.4	−41.5
Sikkim	89.1	92.7	−3.6	1.0	7.3	−6.3
Tamil Nadu	59.7	64.8	−5.1	35.4	35.2	0.2
Tripura	0.2	95.5	−95.3	8.0	4.5	3.6
Uttarakhand	75.8	43.8	32.0	18.5	56.2	−37.7
Uttar Pradesh	7.0	69.3	−62.3	67.2	30.7	36.6
West Bengal	1.3	89.2	−88.0	95.3	10.8	84.5
India	35.6	0.0	35.6	51.2	100.0	−48.8

Source: Author's calculations based on data from MHRD (2007).

secondary education). The aim is to achieve an enrolment rate of 75 per cent from 52.26 per cent in 2005–06 at secondary stage within five years by providing a secondary school within a reasonable distance of any habitation. The other objectives include improving quality of education by making all secondary schools conform to prescribed norms; removing gender, socio-economic and disability barriers; providing universal access to secondary level education by 2017, i.e., by the end of 12th Five-Year Plan; and achieving universal retention by 2020. Broad physical targets include providing facilities for an estimated additional enrolment of more than 3.2 million students by 2011–12 through the strengthening of about 44,000 existing secondary schools, opening around 11,000 new secondary schools and the appointment of additional teachers to improve the Pupil–Teacher Ratio (PTR), and the construction of more than 80,000 additional classrooms (MHRD n.d.). States are required to meet 25 per cent of the costs (10 per cent for north-east states). Total programme costs over the next five years could be as high as $12 billion (₹600 billion). In 2010–11, the following were sanctioned: 1,257 new schools; 7,435 schools to be strengthened, i.e., infrastructure improvements to increase the years of schooling available at the school; and 8,511 additional classrooms.

Public expenditure on secondary education has risen rapidly in real terms and, for the past four years, in per student terms (Figure 12.8). Per pupil expenditure is significantly higher in government and government-aided schools, driven by the much higher teacher salaries. However, very little money is spent on capital expenditures — less than 2 per cent of public funding in 2008–09 (World Bank 2012).

Families make a significant contribution to spending in secondary education. While 74 per cent of those in government schools did not pay any fees, 54 per cent of those in aided schools and 94 per cent of those enrolled in private unaided schools reportedly paid fees for lower secondary school. Of those who paid fees, the average fee in a government school was about ₹650 compared to around ₹1,750 in an aided school and ₹3,375 in a private unaided school. Overall, on average, total household expenditure was ₹2,158 for a student attending secondary education in a government school compared to ₹3,874 in an aided school and ₹7,542 in a private unaided school in a year (World Bank 2012).[9]

The supply of private schools is also likely to increase in India. Given the rapidly expanding demand for secondary education and the historical patterns of school management, parents are likely to continue to seek private schools at the secondary level. However, it should be noted that internationally, as countries get richer they tend to have more students in government schools: for example, in lower secondary education, the average for OECD countries as a whole is 85.8 per cent of pupils studying in government schools, 10.7 per cent studying in government-dependent private schools and the remaining 3.5 per cent in independent private schools. Only five countries — Australia, Belgium, Chile, Denmark, and Spain — have more than 25

FIGURE 12.8   Public Expenditure on Secondary Education in India (in Constant 2004–05 Rupees)

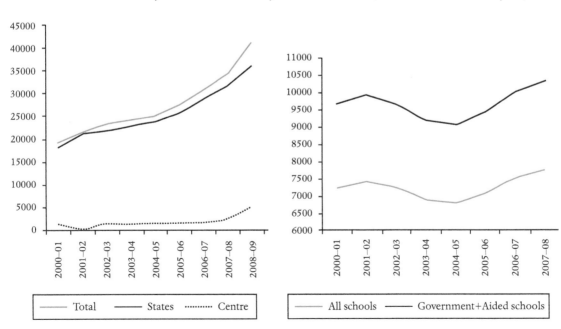

Source: Sankar (2011).

per cent of enrolments in non-government schools. The figures are similar in higher secondary education.

Both the national and state governments are using Public–Private Partnerships (PPPs) to expand access. A major Government of India scheme for expanding access for secondary schools, this time on a PPP approach, is the Model Schools Scheme. The scheme aims to provide quality education to talented rural children through setting up of 6,000 model schools as a benchmark of excellence at block level at the rate of one school per block, with 2,500 of these schools to be set up under PPP mode in blocks that are not educationally backward. A call for expressions of interest for the PPP element was launched in March 2012. More and more states are also pursuing PPPs for school construction and management to help meet the huge infrastructure costs (Table 12.6).[10]

Addressing the Equity Challenge

Many of the equity gaps will be closed over time merely due to the expansion of secondary education. The differences across sub-populations in terms of access are almost non-existent at the primary level and in states where overall participation rates are high (Sankar 2011). This is not surprising given the near universal access to primary education. This suggests that continued expansion of secondary education will reduce these gaps. However, it may not be automatic in some cases; for example, the rural–urban difference may require specific measures to address because the distances to

a secondary school are always likely to remain larger than the distance to primary schools, even with higher levels of enrolment. This also implies that a disproportionate investment will need to be made in rural areas. More generally, the direct and indirect costs of attending secondary schools for families are significantly higher than attending primary schools, so the poorer sections of the community will very likely need some kind of assistance to ensure they attend secondary schools. Some of the direct costs, such as transportation or books, could be met by in-kind assistance; however, the lost potential income from attending school rather than working will need to be met by cash transfers. There is good experience internationally in conditioning those transfers on school attendance and achievement, an option which is likely to make a difference in India too (Carlson 2009).

Addressing the Quality Challenge

Improving the quality of education and raising the learning outcomes of students is perhaps the key challenge for both public and private schools. In terms of PPPs in capacity-building initiatives, there are a number of possibilities ranging from curriculum and pedagogical support to management and administrative training; textbook provision; teacher training; and the development of support networks, professional partnerships and linkages (World Bank 2011b). The Government of India's RMSA programme includes specific guidance on quality improvements (Box 12.1). International assessments in secondary schools tend to show that private

TABLE 12.6   Existing or Proposed PPP Models in the States

Activity	Finance: Expenditure	Finance: Revenue	Provision and Monitoring
Residential Schools in Andhra Pradesh	• Land is provided free of cost by the state government on a long-term lease. • Private partner bears the entire non-recurring cost of construction and the schools buildings and facilities.	• 75 per cent of the seats in the school would be reserved for students to be sponsored by the state government for which the state would pay the recurring costs. The remaining 25 per cent of the student strength would be filled up with the management quota seats.	• Private partner appoints and manages teaching and non-teaching staff.
Adarsh Schools in Punjab	• The land would be given on a 99-year lease by the government to the private partner. • 50 per cent of the capital cost would also be provided by the state government.	• The operational cost of the school would be shared on 70:30 basis between the state government and the private partner.	• There would be a two-tier management structure at state and school level.
Schools in Rajasthan	• The private partner will bear the entire capital cost upfront. • State government would provide a capital incentive in instalments.	• The state reimburses a part of the recurring cost for the sponsored students through vouchers. • 50 per cent of each school would be reserved for students sponsored by the state government.	

Source: Adapted from World Bank (2011b).

Box 12.1
Draft Vision Document for the Improvement of Quality of Secondary Education

The document is designed to deal with the following quality components embedding equity within that to guide the states/union territories for each of these components providing essential and indicative norms in terms of modalities as well as finance:

(a) *Curriculum Reform*: A major quality aspect of secondary education which includes:

    (i) Revision of state syllabi and textbooks at secondary stage in accordance with the National Curriculum Framework-2005 (NCF-2005).

    (ii) Improving classroom processes and school management to implement the curricular and pedagogic shift for enhancing participation in learning process and providing success experience to all learners.

    (iii) Assessment and examination in consonance with the emerging perspectives on Continuous and Comprehensive Evaluation (CCE) as well as examination reform at secondary stage.

(b) *Teacher Preparation*: Another quality imperative which deals with setting up of mechanisms for continuous in-service professional development of secondary stage teachers in each state/union territory.

(c) *Researches and Monitoring for Quality*: As important quality interventions, which is not only helpful in ensuring quality but also improving modalities for quality inputs as and when required.

(d) *Information and Communication Technology*: A quality component that is infused in each of the quality initiatives such as curriculum reform, teacher preparation, research and monitoring.

(e) *Quality Indicators*: Monitoring quality interventions require concrete measurable and observable indicators for various aspects such as curriculum, pedagogy, assessment, etc.

(f) *Roles of Various National-/State-/District-Level Agencies*: Each state/union territory has various structures to deal with the planning and implementation of the programme. For quality secondary education it is imperative to bring clarity on the roles of these institutions to further increase synergy among them.

(g) *Multi-Layer Strategic Guidelines and Indicative Financial Norms*: Each of the aforesaid quality aspects requires guidelines and norms for stakeholders operating at different levels under the RMSA for the effective implementation of the programme. In the context of quality components, the guidelines and norms need to be specific with the main objective to improve real school-classroom setting and learning of students.

Source: MHRD (n.d.).

and public schools perform equally well when the socio-economic backgrounds of children are taken into account (in other words, private schools tend to attract children of wealthier families, and this accounts for most of the better results of private school children) (OECD 2011).

There are a number of challenges in this area. First, like elementary education, there is a shortage of teachers in secondary education. For example, only 30 per cent of schools (Classes IX and X) have a sufficient number of teachers in all five core subjects (World Bank 2012). The particular challenge in secondary education is that teachers are subject specialists so the demand for and deployment of teachers is much more complex. Second, the professional development of secondary education teachers is also made harder by the subject specialisations; understanding how to teach mathematics is different from understanding how to teach history, since the things children don't understand are derived from the nature of the mathematical concepts or topics being studied. The institutional structures to help teachers in government schools are sorely lacking, in addition to the problem of lack of coordination across primary, secondary and teacher education programmes. Little is known about how private schools get support for professional development.

There is a need for a more reliable system of assessment of student learning outcomes in secondary education. The role of assessment, testing and examination is undergoing reform in elementary education, under the provision of the Right to Education Act, 2009, which abolishes testing in that phase of education. These mechanisms have not yet been replaced by alternative methods of Continuous and Comprehensive Evaluation (CCE) that teachers understand and are able to use to keep track of students' progress and achievements. The situation is more complex in secondary education given the presence of high-stakes examinations and the multiple need for measuring achievement, providing a basis for entry into higher education, and giving students relevant certification for entry into the labour market. In India, universities set examinations for entry, though there are moves to increase the role of performance in Board examinations. As shown in this section, there is an urgent need to improve the technical quality of State Board examinations, so they can provide a reliable picture of student achievement.

A strategy for how different types of assessment work and fit together is needed. Such a strategy would need to include different elements. First, classroom-level mechanisms, which teachers can use on a regular basis to identify the strengths and weaknesses of children's grasp of the material so that teaching can be adjusted accordingly. Some of these mechanisms could be common across multiple schools and provided by the private sector; others individual teachers might develop themselves. Second, there is a need for end-of-stage assessments. These summative assessments of individual student achievement would be curriculum-based and could be either at the state or national level. Many countries around the world have changed their examinations — in line with revised curricula — to ensure that students are assessed as to whether they have a conceptual understanding of the subject and can apply these concepts and principles to new problems and in new contexts. The examinations therefore are not about factual recall. This change in examination and curriculum approach would require a consequent change in the way teachers teach. It would be helpful if states collaborated not only to improve the technical quality of the assessment but also to develop some common elements which would allow cross-state comparisons. Third, there is a place for a national assessment. Assuming multiple State Board examinations continue, a sample-based national assessment would enable a reliable picture to emerge. The government's commitment to establishing Class X assessments is an important step. This national assessment would allow India to identify key system issues amenable to policy or programmatic intervention. For example, the assessment could identify where the teaching of a particular subject is strong or weak, to guide teacher professional development and materials; or the particular challenges that large or small schools face to help school managers become more effective. Fourth and finally, India should continue to participate in international assessments so that it can assess its progress in the globalised world.

Aided schools are a significant opportunity to bring change. The substantial resources that state governments give to aided schools offer the opportunity to leverage change. Unfortunately, at the moment, grants-in-aid are provided on an input-driven basis (essentially, the state governments pay some portion of (or all) teacher salaries). An opportunity exists for this funding to be adjusted so that it is provided on the basis of outcomes or results, such as enrolment and retention of disadvantaged groups (access and equity concerns) and the successful completion of a stage of education or student performance on assessments (quality concerns). Given the size of the private-aided sector, providing private management with different incentives could offer a major opportunity to address some of the outstanding issues in secondary education.

Concluding Remarks

Any policy or programme that seeks to make improvements in the access, quality and equity of secondary education needs to recognise two complexities: the differences between elementary and secondary education, and the various models of school governance. First, there are significant differences between elementary and secondary schools, so it cannot be assumed that lessons learnt in one sub-sector can be applied to the other. There are differences between elementary and secondary schools in terms of size, organisation, relationship to their communities/parents, and ways of assessing quality. So one should not assume that patterns in elementary education will work in secondary schools; for example, there is a lot of evidence that parents can hold elementary teachers and schools accountable, under certain conditions. These conditions are reasonably well-understood: for instance, parents are informed about their rights and responsibilities, they are given the information they need to hold the schools accountable in an accessible form, that information is readily understandable and easily measured, and there are some consequences for parental action (Bruns et al. 2011). But this accountability framework that produces positive results in primary education depends critically on certain features that are not present in secondary schools: *(a)* parents can understand measures of quality (such as basic reading and mathematical skills), *(b)* parents form a reasonably coherent community because the primary school draws its students from a single village or residential area, and *(c)* the social distance between parents and the teachers is not too great. These features do not hold in secondary education. School Management Development Committees (SMDCs) have been introduced in secondary schools following the broadly positive experience of such committees in primary education. However, considerable work will be needed to help them become effective instruments of school accountability. Second, as already noted, the management arrangements in secondary education are significantly different from those in elementary education with different combinations of government, aided and unaided schools across states and within states across lower and higher secondary education. Any policy or programme should take account of these differences.

This indicates the importance of promoting and evaluating different approaches. Given these complexities, a single solution that will be relevant and applicable to the whole of the secondary education sector and across different states is highly unlikely. Thus, there should be attempts to encourage innovation and experimentation, within a strong monitoring and evaluation framework. The government is explicitly encouraging this in the case of the RMSA programme, having created innovation activities through which local actors and states can develop their own ideas about how to improve access, equity and quality. The lessons from these ideas will also then seed the development of the RMSA programme itself.

NOTES

1. The usual Indian practice is to refer to Classes IX and X as 'secondary education'. However, in this paper, I will use the term 'lower secondary' to refer to these and 'higher secondary' to refer to Classes XI and XII. In this way, I reserve the term 'secondary education' to refer to both lower and higher secondary education collectively (i.e., Classes IX to XII).

2. The GER is calculated by taking the number of children in secondary education and dividing it by the number of children in the relevant age category (in this case 14–17 years of age). Due to the presence of over- (and, more rarely, under-) age children in secondary education, this ratio can be greater than 100 per cent. See Sankar (2011) for a fuller description of different types of ratios relevant for measuring access to secondary education.

3. These figures, for the school year 2007–08, are the latest official figures from the Ministry of Human Resource Development (MHRD 2007) based on administrative data. Different sources of data give different numbers of those students in secondary education. For example, Sankar (2011), using National Statistical Survey (NSS) data, calculates the figure to be 50.6 million in secondary and higher secondary education. While the variation according to the sources is noted, the general trends discussed in this paper hold using any data source. Recently, the National University for Educational Planning and Administration (NUEPA) has rolled out the Secondary Education Management Information System (SEMIS) which has started to improve significantly the accuracy and timeliness of secondary education data. At present, this data covers mainly government and government-aided schools, but is expanding each year to include more private unaided schools, which is crucial to enable a more comprehensive picture of the system to be obtained.

4. The gross intake rate is calculated by taking the total number of children (of all ages) enrolling in Class IX and dividing it by the number of children of the appropriate age (i.e., 14–15). So if there are significant numbers of over-age children, then the gross intake rate can be higher than 100 per cent.

5. Author's calculations based on MHRD (2006, 2007).

6. The 2009+ round included 10 states or countries, all of which were non-OECD. The assessment was actually conducted in 2010 (hence the 'plus'), but the assessment instrument used allowed direct comparison with the main survey, which was conducted in more than 60 countries and economies in 2009. For more details see Walker (2011).

7. The results in this and the previous paragraph should be treated as giving a general sense of the relative performance of Indian states but the particular rankings should be seen as indicative rather than definitive. First, PISA and TIMSS only test children who are in school, so in those countries like India that have high levels of children of the relevant age not in school, the average performance across the whole 15-year-old population would very likely be even lower (on the reasonable assumption that those not in schools would score lower). This means that the Indian averages for the entire 15-year-old population are even further below the OECD means. However, the ranking in these circumstances is much harder to assess since the countries with rankings close to Indian state rankings also have significant out-of-school populations. Second, it is also worth noting that the assessment survey carried out in Rajasthan and Odisha was only on a subset of TIMSS questions, not the full TIMSS test administered to the other countries.

8. However, private schools tend to be smaller than government schools, so private-aided and unaided schools represent two-thirds of all *schools* (author's calculations based on data from MHRD [2007]). In addition, it should also be noted that there were as small number of students — about 343,000 — studying lower or higher secondary education outside of formal schooling through the National Institute of Open Schooling (NIOS) (ibid.).

9. These figures are for the school year 2007–08.

10. This chapter has not directly discussed a large private element in secondary education, which is private tutoring. India is no different than other countries in this respect and its widespread prevalence in all different kinds of countries suggests that it will not be readily eliminated.

REFERENCES

Bruns, Barbara, Deon Filmer and Harry Anthony Patrinos. 2011. *Making Schools Work: New Evidence on Accountability Reforms*. Washington, DC: World Bank.

Carlson, Samuel. 2009. *Secondary Education in India: Universalizing Opportunity*. Washington, DC: Human Development Unit, South Asia Region, World Bank.

Central Advisory Board of Education (CABE). 2005. 'Universalisation of Secondary Education'. Report of the Central Advisory Board of Education Committee.

Das, Jishnu and Tristan Zajonc. 2010. 'India Shining and Bharat Drowning: Comparing Two Indian States to the Worldwide Distribution in Mathematics Achievement', *Journal of Development Economics*, 92(2): 175–87.

Ministry of Human Resource Development (MHRD). n.d. 'Rashtriya Madhyamik Shiksha Abhiyan'. Department of School Education and Literacy, Ministry of Human Resource Development, Government of India. http://mhrd.gov.in/rashtriya_madhyamik_shiksha_abhiyan (accessed 29 March 2012).

———. 2006. 'Statistics of School Education 2006–07'. Bureau of Planning, Monitoring and Statistics, Ministry of Human Resource Development, Government of India.

———. 2007. 'Statistics of School Education 2007–08'. Bureau of Planning, Monitoring and Statistics, Ministry of Human Resource Development, Government of India.

Organisation for Economic Co-operation and Development (OECD). 2011. *Private Schools: Who Benefits?* Paris: Organisation for Economic Co-operation and Development Publishing.

Patrinos, Harry Anthony, Felipe Barrera-Osorio and Juliana Guáqueta. 2009. *The Role and Impact of Public–Private Partnerships in Education*. Washington, DC: World Bank.

Sankar, Deepa. 2011. 'Participation in India: An Analysis of the NSS 64th Round Data'. Report No. 33, Discussion Paper Series, South Asia Human Development Unit, World Bank.

Walker, Maurice. 2011. *PISA 2009 Plus Results: Performance of 15-Year-Olds in Reading, Mathematics and Science for 10 Additional Partici-pants*. Camberwell, Victoria: Australian Council for Educational Research (ACER) Press.

World Bank. n.d. 'Population Projections Tables by Country and Group'. Health, Nutrition and Population (HNP) Statistics Database, World Bank. http://go.worldbank.org/KZHE1CQFA0 (accessed 31 March 2012).

———. 2005. *Expanding Opportunities and Building Competencies for Young People: A New Agenda for Secondary Education*. Washington, DC: World Bank.

———. 2011a. *More and Better Jobs in South Asia*. Washington, DC: World Bank.

———. 2011b. *Public Private Partnerships in Secondary School Education in India*. Washington, DC: World Bank.

———. 2012. 'India — Secondary Education Project'. Project Appraisal Document, Education Unit, Human Development Department, South Asia Region, World Bank.

TABLE 12A   Examples of Different Types of Public–Private Partnerships (PPP) in Education

PPP Initiative	Examples
1. Private Sector Philanthropy	• Philanthropic Foundations (United States [US], Philippines) • Academies Programme (United Kingdom [UK]) • Philanthropic Venture Funds (US) • World Education Forum's Global Education Initiative (Jordan, Egypt, India, Palestinian Authority)
2. School Management	• Contract schools (US) • Charter schools (US and Alberta [Canada]) • Concession Schools (Bogotá [Colombia]) • Independent Schools (Qatar) • Private Management of Railways Schools (Pakistan) • Alternative Education (New Zealand) • Quality Education for All (Pakistan) • Management of Government Schools (Lahore [Pakistan])
3. Purchase of Educational Services from Private Schools	• Government sponsorship of Students in Private Schools (Cote d'Ivoire), Educational Service Contracting (ESC)/Education Voucher System (EVS) (The Philippines) • *Fe y Alegría* (South America, Spain) • Financial Assistance on Per Child Enrolled Basis (Punjab [India], Pakistan) • Universal Post-Primary Education and Training (Uganda) • Venezuelan Association of Catholic Education (Venezuela)
4. Vouchers	• *Programa de Ampliación de Cobertura de la Educación Secundaria* (Colombia) • School Funding System (The Netherlands) • Targeted Individual Entitlement and Independent School Subsidies (New Zealand) • Milwaukee Parental Choice Program (Milwaukee [US]) • Urban Girls' Fellowship Program and Rural Girls' Fellowship Program (Baluchistan [Pakistan]) • Education Voucher Scheme (Punjab [India], Pakistan)
5. Capacity-Building	• Cluster-Based Training of Teachers Through PPP (Punjab [India], Pakistan) • Quality Assurance Resource Centre (Sindh [Pakistan]) • Quality Advancement and Institutional Development (Sindh [Pakistan]) • Teaching in Clusters by Subject Specialists (Punjab [India], Pakistan)
6. School Infrastructure	• Private Finance Initiative (UK) • New Schools' Private Finance Project (New South Wales [Australia]) • New Schools Public Private Partnership Project (South Australia [Australia]) • PPP for New Schools (Egypt) • Public–Private Partnerships for Educational Infrastructure (Nova Scotia [Canada]) • Offenbach Schools Project and Cologne Schools Project (Germany) • Montaigne Lyceum (The Hague [The Netherlands]) • Leasing of Public School Buildings to Private Operators (Punjab [India], Pakistan)

Source: Patrinos et al. (2009).

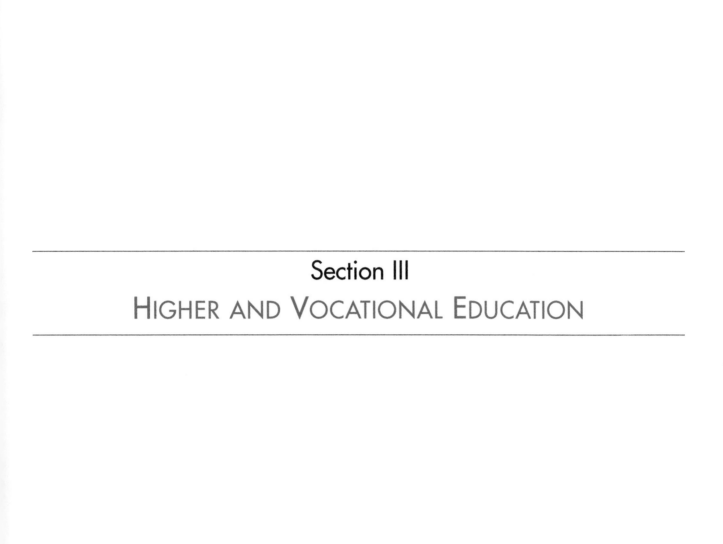

Section III
HIGHER AND VOCATIONAL EDUCATION

13

Private Higher Education
The Global Surge and Indian Concerns

*N. V. Varghese**

The emergence of the knowledge economy signifies an increase in the knowledge intensity of economic activities. Knowledge has become the driver of economic growth underlining the central role of human capital and technology in development (OECD 1996). This recognition increased the awareness regarding the economic value of institutions engaged in knowledge production and dissemination. Higher education institutions and their graduates became dearer to policy-makers and to corporate leaders. In many of the fast-growing emerging economies, the tertiary-level educated workforce has become a constraint for sustaining their growth rates and is investing more on higher education. The share of budgetary resources allocated to higher education increased in the developed countries in the 1990s and in many of the developing countries in this millennium. Consequently, the expansion of higher education became a global phenomenon experienced by all countries. Higher education is almost universalised in the developed countries, 'massified' in most of the middle-income countries, and growing at high rates in the less-developed countries.

While the expansion of higher education depended heavily on public investment in the previous century, it relies considerably on non-public sources of funding in its current phase of expansion. The process of globalisation of economic activities necessitated an expanded codification of knowledge, digitalisation of information and its commodification (Houghton and Sheehan 2000); and it increased the economic returns to investments in higher education. At present, there is a near unanimity on the need for enhanced investment in higher education even when opinions vary on sharing the financial responsibilities among public, private and household sectors. A common trend experienced in

many countries is a shifting of the financial burden of seeking higher education from public to private sources.

The private sector has grown in many countries and has certainly increased its role in higher education in a majority of the countries. This paper analyses the move towards the private sector globally and in India. It is interesting to note that matured market economies have relied less on the market process to meet the expanding social demand for higher education than the developing countries where markets are poorly or less developed. Countries such as India follow a dual policy of relying on the public universities in core areas of research and development and on private institutions to meet the expanding social demand for higher education, especially in market-friendly study programmes such as technical and professional education. This results in an enhanced public investment and an increasing private share in higher education contributing to faster growth of the sector.

The next section discusses the rationale for public investment in higher education followed by an analysis of the emerging typology of private higher education institutions. The fourth section examines the global surge and spread of private higher education with the subsequent one looking at the evolution of different categories of private education in India. The sixth section highlights some of the issues arising out of the functioning of private higher education institutions and their effect on the quality of private higher education in India. The chapter concludes by underlining the need for regulatory measures and mechanisms.

PUBLIC GOOD AND PUBLIC INVESTMENT IN HIGHER EDUCATION

The debate on who should finance higher education stems from the characterisation of higher education as a public

---

* The opinions and views expressed in this paper are of the author and hence should not necessarily be attributed to the institution where he is employed.

or a private good. Some economists consider knowledge as a public good (Samuelson 1954) or as a global public good (Stiglitz 1999). The higher education sector, which produces and transmits knowledge, is also treated as a public good. A public good has two critical properties — non-rivalrous consumption and non-excludability. The non-rivalrous consumption implies that consumption by one does not diminish that by others while non-excludability implies that its distribution cannot be restricted to a few selected people.

The higher education sector can exclude those who do not pay for it when it is priced or restrict access when the government relies on a policy of limited expansion. However, if more people receive higher education it does not diminish its value to society, so it is a non-rivalrous good. Higher education has externalities since the benefits from it are not confined to students seeking higher education but also extend to society at large. Higher education is a merit good and the advantages from higher education are neither all public nor all private. The development of new knowledge, training of highly-qualified personnel, provision of service to society, ethical function and social criticism, etc. are public good functions carried out by the sector (Cemmell 2002).

Although higher education may not be a pure public good, it has the characteristics of one. In the absence of state investment, it will be under-produced and under-supplied since profits cannot be a criterion to decide the optimum amount of investment (Tilak 2008) and markets will not have incentives to produce it to optimum levels. Therefore, the public good character of higher education justifies continued public investment in the sector. In reality, as noted in a letter to President Obama from the President of the University of Michigan in 2010, 'higher education is a public good currently lacking public support' (Woodhouse 2011).

The State played a dominant role in development during the post-World War II reconstruction phase in Europe and nation-building phase following national independence in the developing countries. Most countries invested in higher education during this phase, recognising the importance of qualified and trained manpower in nation-building. There was, in a sense, a period of 'state monopoly on tertiary education' (World Bank 2002: 69) and public universities became the dominant feature of the development of higher education. This tradition continues and public universities continue to dominate in all regions except Latin America and East Asia.

The State-led model of development came under attack in the 1980s. The neoliberal thinking, structural adjustment programmes of the 1980s and the political changes in eastern Europe questioned the role of the State in development and the rationale for continued State investment in higher education. The argument was for a reduced public investment in education in general, and a diversion of public investment from higher to primary education in developing countries in particular (Banya and Elu 2001; Psacharopoulos 1986). Consequently, developed and developing countries reduced, if not withdrew, subsidies on higher education and introduced cost-recovery measures, cost-sharing strategies and income-generating activities in public higher education institutions.

This period also experienced the emergence of the private sector in higher education, especially in many of the developing countries which did not have a tradition of any private higher education institutions. The private returns from investing in higher education continue to be substantial and therefore households are willing to invest in educating their children. The capacity and willingness of the households to pay contributed to the privatisation of public institutions and the expansion of private higher education institutions.

PRIVATISATION AND THE PRIVATE SECTOR

The ascendancy of the market in higher education decision-making promoted a view that higher education is less of a public good and can be served privately. Further, it was felt that even a public good can be better served by being less public. This view leads to a situation of public higher education losing its 'publicness' (Longaneckar 2005) and public funding. The other view was that higher education gives more private gains and thus should be financed primarily by the direct beneficiaries rather than by the public exchequer. Both views supported a move away from the State for financial support for the growth and expansion of the higher education sector and led to two phenomena: the privatisation of public institutions and the promotion of the private sector.

Privatisation implies applying market principles to the functioning of public institutions of higher education. While the ownership and management of the institutions remain with the public authorities, the services provided by the institutions are priced (Varghese 2004). The price levied (for example, student fees) may be equivalent to the full cost or full cost-plus-profit in some instances. Privatisation was very often facilitated by transferring the governance to public institutions (autonomy), with many of them becoming public enterprises venturing into cost-recovery, income-generating and for-profit activities in public universities (Kezar et al. 2005).

The private sector, on the other hand, implies the non-State sector in higher education. The institutions are owned and operated by private individuals or agencies. In most cases, this sector does not receive funding from the government and, in any case, it does not rely on State funding for its growth and expansion, although at times they receive partial public funding support in some countries (Varghese 2004). Private higher education institutions can be universities or non-university institutions offering professional training courses. Private universities offer courses leading to a degree, while courses offered in other types of private higher education institutions very often lead to a certificate or a diploma.

One of the earliest and most commonly used classifications of private higher education institutions is categorising them into: *(a)* elite, *(b)* religious and *(c)* demand-absorbing (Levy 1986). A more recent and modified categorisation by Daniel C. Levy is in terms of: *(a)* elite and semi-elite, *(b)* religious/ cultural and *(c)* non-elite and demand-absorbing (Bjarnason et al. 2009). Most of the top ranking universities in the United States (US) are, in a sense, elite private institutions. As per the QS world ranking of universities 2011, six US universities were listed in the top-10 category.[1] All of them (Harvard, Massachusetts Institute of Technology [MIT], Yale, Pennsylvania, Chicago, and Columbia) are private institutions. The top-ranking universities in other countries, very often, are public institutions.

Many of the private higher education institutions are religion-based. While the Catholic Church dominated in the provision of private higher education in Latin America, Evangelical and Islamic faiths are common in Africa (Levy 2006). Religious institutions are the fastest growing type of private higher education institution in almost every African country perhaps, with the exception of South Africa (Karram 2011; Varghese 2006). This is partly due to the fact that most of the religious-based private higher education institutions are not-for-profit, especially in Africa, and at times they not only levy low fees, but also provide financial support to students (Varghese 2008).

The non-elite and demand-absorbing private institutions are the largest and the fastest growing segment. Many of them are in the non-university sector and they help expand access to higher education. The study programmes are vocational in nature and the duration of courses in these non-university sector institutions is short.

Most of the private institutions are self-financing, relying on student fees as the major source of income. However, some are for-profit while others are not-for-profit institutions. In the case of for-profit institutions, the main motivation for starting these may be profits rather than educational objectives. The for-profit institutions are at times labelled as 'pseudo universities' since they do education business (Altbach 2005: 23). It is also true that many private higher education institutions maintain a formal non-profit legal status while functioning like for-profit entities. Some of the

for-profit institutions in the US also receive public funding support. According to a recent US Senate report (Moodie 2011), for-profit schools receive 23 per cent of all federal student financial aid (around US$24 billion) in the 2008–09 academic year.

Universities like Phoenix, DeVry and Kaplan have helped turn the for-profit sector into a massive revenue generator and the engine for higher education growth. From 1998 to 2008, for-profit enrolment in the US grew by 225 per cent. For-profit colleges have experienced a boom in business even during the recession period; however, this situation is changing now in the US. Due to the federal rules against certain forms of recruitment, the federal support to for-profit institutions has declined and consequently enrolment decreased by 14.1 per cent in most high profile institutions — DeVry University experienced an enrolment fall by 25.6 per cent and Corinthian by 21.5 per cent (ibid.).

At times the private institutions are also an easy route for the entry of cross-border institutions. This is a very common trend in most countries in Latin America, the Commonwealth of Independent States (CIS) region and Africa. In some cases the domestic private institutions are affiliated to a foreign institution. In some of the countries such as Oman, affiliation to a foreign institution is a necessary condition for approval (Martin 2007) and in some instances it is used as a convenient mechanism to levy high fees.

In some instances foreign universities establish their branch campuses in these countries. Malaysia, Singapore, Hong Kong, Dubai, Doha, etc. are good examples of this trend. Universities in Australia, the UK, the US, and other countries open branch campuses in many developing countries. Malaysia has branch campuses of universities including that of Nottingham University in the UK, Monash University, Curtin University in Australia, etc. Singapore has branch campuses of John Hopkins, the University of Chicago, INSEAD, etc. Bond University and Monash University in Australia have branch campuses in many Asian and African countries and are developed in the form of education hubs. Foreign universities such as Ave Maria, Florida State University, Columbus University, and IPADE Business School are opening franchises in Nicaragua, Panama and Costa Rica (Long 2011).

The trend is similar in CIS countries, in Asia and in Africa (Varghese 2004, 2006). Some of the cross-border institutions are public ones in the country of origin and operate like private institutions in the host country. According to the Observatory of Borderless Higher Education, there were 200 branch campuses around the world in 2011. The largest flow of cross-border institutional mobility (branch campuses) used to be from the US to Gulf countries; now more and more branch campuses are opened in East and South Asia (Lawton and Katsomitros 2012).

THE GLOBAL SURGE AND SPREAD OF PRIVATE HIGHER EDUCATION

The process of privatisation and expansion of the private sector have been on the increase globally. One of the interesting features of these developments is that private higher education institutions emerged and expanded in countries that have less-developed markets while countries with developed and matured markets relied on their public institutions to expand higher education. For example, contrary to general belief, the private sector surge is experienced mostly in the developing countries and privatisation efforts are seen more in the Organisation for Economic Co-operation and Development (OECD) countries. The introduction of cost-recovery measures and indirect mode of financing public higher education through student loans and student-aid programmes from the late 1980s onwards contributed to an increased share of private funding in public institutions in many OECD countries (Kärkkäinen 2006). In fact, OECD countries relied more on public institutions and privatisation measures than private higher education institutions to massify, and later to universalise, higher education.

The public universities in western Europe have become more entrepreneurial and have diversified their sources of funding, but remained public institutions. Private institutions are not very common in most of the developed countries. The exceptions to this general rule are Japan, Portugal, the US, etc. Japan has a major share of its students (77 per cent) enrolled in private higher education institutions; the US and Portugal have more than one-fourth of their students; while other countries in that league have a limited share of students in the same category. Many of the private higher education institutions in these countries are in the not-for-profit category and receive financial support from the State.

Among the developing countries, the East Asian region has the largest concentration of countries with the majority of students enrolled in private higher education institutions. Indonesia (72 per cent), Philippines (65 per cent) and Malaysia (51 per cent) are examples of such countries. Similarly, private higher education is widespread in Latin American countries (Bjarnason et al. 2009). There were virtually no private universities in Latin America 30 years ago and today there are more than 151, and every year more emerge (Long 2011). In many of the Latin American countries (such as Brazil, Chile, Costa Rica, El Salvador, Peru, etc.) the share of private higher education in enrolment is more than 50 per cent, with the share being more than three-fourths in some of them (Chile and Brazil).

The 'private revolution' in central and eastern Europe started after the fall of the Soviet Union. Although there was a spurt in private enrolment, the enrolment shares still continue to be less than one-third of the total even in the most privatised countries such as Estonia, Georgia, Latvia, and Poland (Slantcheva and Levy 2007). In some countries, such as Ukraine, there is a fear of private higher education institutions being closed down due to shortage of students (Siwinska 2011).

Sub-Saharan Africa shows that despite fast expansion in the number of institutions, private higher education enrolment accounts for less than one-third of the total enrolments in most countries, except in Gabon where it is close to half (Bjarnason et al. 2009). Private higher education is an emerging sector in the Arab world. Often the governments in the Arab world are pro-active in facilitating the establishment of private universities. Since the early 1990s, 14 out of 22 Arab countries have officially opted for private higher education and started licensing private universities, which have been set up by either local investors or foreign universities. Two-thirds (around 70) of the new universities founded in the Arab states since 1993 are private, and at least 50 of them are branches of western, mostly American, universities.

As noted earlier, not-for-profit and for-profit private institutions co-exist in many countries. Experience shows that both of them surged ahead and in the process 'private non-profit institutions became much more entrepreneurial in many respects like for-profit institutions' (Levy 2005: 35). Another phenomenon in the surge of private higher education provisions is the growth of bogus 'degree/diploma mills', which very often offer online courses that are sub-standard or degrees on payment. Private colleges marketing to overseas students at times are also in collusion with diploma mills. For example, Manchester College of Professional Studies, Irish International University, Columbia Commonwealth University, International University of America located in London, etc. are examples of diploma mills and fraudulent practices (Cohen and Winch 2011).

It is estimated that more than 2,500 bogus institutions (diploma mills) operate globally. The US (with 1,008 institutions) continues to hold the dubious distinction of the most popular destination for diploma-mill providers. The state of California leads the league and is followed by Hawaii, Washington and Florida. Europe ranks second (after the US) hosting a total of 603 diploma mills. More than half (339) of the European diploma mills are located in the UK. The principality of Sorboga in Italy hosts a disproportionally large number of diploma mills (Head 2011).

A related issue is the multiplication of accreditation mills — a bogus accrediting agency that is not recognised by the authority responsible for governing education provision in a country. What is interesting is that 'accreditation mills are often fabricated by the owners of diploma mills' (Cohen and Winch 2011: 6). The best evidence is that many of the university websites and accreditation agency websites are linked to a single Internet Protocol (IP) address hosted on the same server operated by the same person or group of people.

The fast expansion of the for-profit institutions and commercialisation of the sector have, especially in the cross border segment, led to some undesirable influences, fraudulent practices and negative effects in higher education. Many of these providers are fake offering a credential for payment and lack legal authority to operate, offer study programmes and award degrees. In some instances, concerns are raised about the link between international student recruitment in these institutions and a potential route to illegal migration (Middlehurst and Fielden 2011).

The discussions in this section indicate that the financial burden of expansion of higher education has systematically been shifted from public to individual shoulders either through privatisation measures in public institutions or through private institutions and providers. While matured market economies relied more on public institutions, the less-developed countries with poorly-developed markets saw fast growth of private institutions. Many of the private higher education institutions are not-for-profit while some are for-profit institutions. The unregulated growth, especially of the for-profit institutions, has led to commercialisation and many undesirable practices. Therefore, countries are developing regulations for the growth and expansion of the private sector in higher education.

EVOLUTION OF THE PRIVATE SECTOR IN HIGHER EDUCATION IN INDIA

The number of universities proliferated and the number of students multiplied during the period after independence in 1947 — the total number of universities increased by nearly 18 times between 1950 and 2010. More interestingly, the increase was rather fast in this millennium. While it took 50 years to add 227 universities between 1950 and 2000, it took only 10 years to add the next 210 universities. The universities in India include central universities established by an Act of the national parliament, state universities and private universities, which are established by an Act of the state legislature. The student enrolment in higher education increased from 0.17 million in 1950 to 20.7 million in 2009 (MHRD 2011).

The Indian policy response to private higher education has gone through a process of evolution from a reliance on public institutions to promoting private higher education institutions to expand the system. The evolution of the policy shows that India, like many other countries in the world,

adopted privatisation measures and also encouraged the private sector in higher education.

In the initial years following independence, the ideological orientation emphasised on a State-dominated model of development. India promoted the public sector in all spheres of activity including education. The country nationalised many private institutions of higher education since the policy was to provide higher education through public universities. This also implied transforming the then-existing private higher education institutions into public institutions (Gnanam 2008). This was a stage of 'publicisation' of private institutions.

Most of the higher education institutions established in India in the 1950s and 1960s were public institutions. India seems to have followed a dual strategy of attaining self-reliance and global standards through public institutions. The establishment of high-quality institutions in the areas of engineering, medical and management studies — the Indian Institutes of Technology (IITs), medical institutions (All India Institute of Medical Science [AIIMS]), the Indian Institutes of Management (IIMs), and regional engineering colleges (now National Institutes of Technology or NITs) exemplify the dual motives of self-reliance and global standards.

Public Universities and Private-Aided Colleges

The situation seemed to be that India had public universities and private colleges that received financial support from the state. The public financial support covered a major share of the expenditure incurred by the private colleges. The affiliated system of higher education helped to promote this process of establishing public universities and affiliated colleges that were mostly private. This was perhaps a stage of publicly supported/sponsored private growth in higher education.

More than 80 per cent of the higher education enrolment in India used to be in private affiliated colleges which mostly followed the same study programmes, offered the same courses and students appeared for the same examinations conducted by the university to which these institutions were affiliated. The student fees in these private colleges were also fixed by the state governments. These colleges in general were functioning more like public institutions than for-profit private higher education institutions.

Privatisation of Public Institutions

This trend changed in the 1970s and 1980s when self-financing courses were offered in public institutions. This was more a stage of privatisation of public institutions of higher education since the ownership of the institutions remained with the public authorities even though some of the courses were self-financing. The committees appointed by the University Grants Commission (UGC) and the

All India Council of Technical Education (AICTE) also recommended privatisation rather than the promotion of private higher education. For example, the Punnayya Committee (1992–93) set up by the UGC suggested cost recovery and income generation to a level of 15 to 25 per cent of the annual recurrent expenditure of a university. The Dr Swaminathan Panel (1992) set up by the AICTE also suggested cost recovery from students and the introduction of an education cess from industries.

Some of the state governments went ahead with establishing self-financing courses in public institutions and self-financing public institutions. The fee-levels in these instances were decided by the state governments or the university to which the institution was affiliated. A. Gnanam (2008) notes that the policy of the government to empower public universities and colleges to offer 'self-financing courses' concurrently with public-funded programmes leaves one to wonder whether there are any more truly public institutions in the country. For example, to meet the growing demand for technical education and to arrest the outflow of students to other states seeking higher technical education, the government of Kerala decided to open institutions on a cost-recovery mode. The Institute of Human Resources Development in Electronics (IHRDE) is a case in point. The success of the IHRDE led to the opening of self-financing public colleges supported by the government and later many such colleges were established by the private sector (Varughese 2006).

For-Profit Self-Financing Private Institutions

The 1980s and 1990s witnessed the establishment and fast expansion of self-financing private higher education institutions. The self-financing colleges, which are commonly known as capitation fee colleges (Tilak 1994), are mostly for-profit private institutions. Most of these self-financing institutions were colleges established in the subject areas of engineering, medicine and management (Agarwal 2007). The southern states of Andhra Pradesh, Karnataka and Tamil Nadu and the western state of Maharashtra led the private higher education (self-financing colleges) revolution in India. Although these for-profit, private self-financing institutions (capitation fee colleges) were concentrated in a few states, students from all parts and regions of India sought and got admission into these colleges. It seems money power, rather than any other influences, ensured admission in these institutions. A major part of India's private higher education surge came from the proliferation of private self-financing colleges mostly in the technical and professional subject areas. This is in contrast to the developments in many other countries where private institutions were established in areas which required less investment unlike engineering and medical colleges.

From Self-Financing Private Colleges to Private Universities

India had private colleges but not private universities. In the 1990s many private providers felt that the rules and regulations by the public authorities were very strict and severe. To escape from this and to attain the authority to award degrees, they sought deemed-to-be university status to private institutions and many private institutions became deemed universities (Agarwal 2007). The next stage in the evolution was the establishment of private universities.

A Private Universities Establishment and Regulations Bill was introduced in the Rajya Sabha in August 1995 with a view to providing for the establishment of self-financing private universities. The bill was referred to the Standing Committee to get views on the subject. The private providers were not happy with some of the provisions in the bill, especially those pertaining to endowment funds, regulation by government bodies and subsidised education for nearly one-third of the intake. Although the bill was not passed, discussions on the need for a private universities bill continued. In 2000, the Prime Minister's Council on Trade and Industry set up a committee (Birla–Ambani Committee 2000–01) that recommended entrusting higher education provision to the private sector, promulgation of a private university bill, cost recovery from students, and loans and grants to economically and socially weaker sections.

Since 2002, several state governments have passed private university Acts. Chhattisgarh took the lead in enacting a private universities Act and it has the distinction of having set up the first officially-established private university in India (Sri Rawatpura Sakar International University) in 2002. The state of Chhattisgarh established 97 private universities in that same year. This was followed by many state governments — Assam, Haryana, Himachal Pradesh, Gujarat, Odisha, Punjab, Uttar Pradesh, Uttarakhand, etc.

The private universities need to be established within the regulations stipulated by UGC (UGC 2003a). These regulations stipulate that each private university should be established by a separate Act and should conform to the provisions of the UGC Act of 1956. The private universities will be unitary in structure but permitted to operate off-campus and off-shore campuses. The student admission procedures and fixation of fees shall be in accordance with the norms/guidelines prescribed by the UGC and other concerned statutory bodies. Some states established private universities before these regulations came into effect and in some cases before the private universities Act was passed.

Some private universities seem to be attracting a good number of students. The Symbiosis International University in Pune has 11,000 full-time students from 75 countries in campuses across four cities. The Amity University in

Noida, has 80,000 students up to PhD level, 3,500 academics, four universities in India and six international campuses in Dubai, Mauritius, Singapore, the US, and the UK (Mishra 2011).

The pattern seems to be that some private colleges were deregulated by granting them an autonomous status. Some of them graduated to deemed-to-be universities status and further to private universities in later years (UGC 2003b). Others were new institutions established as private universities from the beginning.

To sum up, an anatomy of institutions in India shows that the traditional pattern of mostly public universities and private colleges still continues, although the private share in both categories of institutions has increased. Some of the colleges are public, many of them receive aid and others do not receive any financial support from the government. The most common form of private higher education in India is self-financing institutions, which do not receive any financial support from the government. They are owned and operated by private enterprises or individuals and for the purposes of funding they rely on the fees levied from students.

There is another type of private institution where the university is public but it has privately-managed affiliated institutions. These affiliated institutions have free seats and payment seats. Fees for the free seats are decided by the university while that for the payment seats is decided by the affiliated institution. The Guru Gobind Singh Indraprastha University belongs to this category of private higher education institutions. It has several self-financing courses in its affiliated institutions (Singh and Mishra 2008). There are also non-university private institutions such as the NIIT and APTECH group of institutions. Although they cannot grant degrees, a certification from these institutions is accepted by employers. Another type of private institutions is coaching centres, which do not issue any certificate (Gnanam 2008).

The degrees do not necessarily signal/reflect the competencies acquired by the graduates and hence they are subjected to further tests for job selection. The best example is the replacement of university performance and certificate with competitive examinations for further studies and jobs (Kapur and Mehta 2004). It is interesting to see that even to select an academic faculty in the university, the performance of the candidate in the university examinations in not relied upon. The public authorities insist on eligibility test certificates — National Eligibility Test (NET) for national and others for state-level institutions of higher education.

Coaching for all competitive tests (for entrance to higher education institutions and jobs) has become very common in India. Parents and children willingly invest more money and time in coaching institutions for entrance examinations and competitive tests for jobs than what they pay as student

fees in public institutions. Preparations for entrance examinations for engineering, medical and management studies are very demanding and that for bank tests, Indian civil services and other jobs too have become very competitive, which are taken advantage of by this segment of private higher education.

Cross-Border Institutions

India has a tradition of collaborating with foreign institutions. The IITs and IIMs were established in collaboration with foreign education institutions. This, again, was an effort to acquire and maintain global standards in education. In the recent past, many private higher education institutions are seeking cross-border collaboration mostly with institutions located in the UK and the US (Bhushan 2005). Collaboration with foreign universities and institutions helps domestic ones to obtain academic credibility, quality appeal and also permits them to levy high fees. Since India is one of the top sending countries of cross-border students, this is a lucrative market for many of the foreign institutions. Several high-level delegations are visiting India to establish institutions as branch campuses or for collaborations with Indian institutions. In an effort to facilitate the establishment of cross-border institutions, the government presented a bill in the Parliament to permit entry and operation of foreign education institutions in India. The monsoon session of the Parliament in 2012 was expected to discuss and decide on the bill. However, recent reports (*Economic Times* 2012) indicate that this bill may not be taken up for discussion in the forthcoming session of the Parliament. The establishment of foreign education institutions and expansion of cross-border education in India depends on the passage of the bill and the resulting regulations stipulated for the operation of foreign education institutions in India.

India can also take advantage of the globalisation process in higher education. Many institutions in India have international standing and credibility. India is becoming an attractive destination for foreign students, especially from the developing countries. Many institutions have established foreign students cells and applications are invited online. The Government of India has also liberalised visa rules for foreign students.

Some of the prestigious Indian institutions plan to establish overseas branches. The Government of India is planning to open branch campuses of IITs and IIMs abroad. The Human Resource Development (HRD) Minister reiterated recently that India is 'keen to take IITs abroad' (*Deccan Herald* 2012) and as an initial step may establish campuses soon in Qatar and Singapore. The Pune University has established its campus in the United Arab Emirates (UAE). A similar proposal to establish IIMs abroad too is active. Some of the private institutions have already established campuses overseas. Prestigious private institutions such as Birla Institute of Technology and Science (BITS), Pilani have already established branch campuses in Dubai. The Jagadguru Sree Shivarathishwara (JSS) Academy of Technical Education was set up in Mauritius in 2006; the D. Y. Patil Post-Graduate School of Medicine in 2009 at Quatre-Bornes, in partnership with the University of Technology, Mauritius (UTM); and the Jawaharlal Nehru Hospital for clinical training. The Amity University has established international campuses in six countries.

FUZZY RULES, MESSY DEALS AND QUALITY OF PRIVATE HIGHER EDUCATION

The Approach Paper to the 12th Five-Year Plan recognises that the higher educated are critical to sustain, if not increase the high rate of economic growth. It notes that 'education is the single most important instrument for social and economic transformation' (Planning Commission 2011: 96). The National Knowledge Commission strongly recommended the expansion of quality higher education to improve national production and competitiveness. The Approach Paper envisages an additional enrolment of 10 million students during the plan period (2012–17) to bring the Gross Enrolment Ratio (GER) close to the global average (which was 26 per cent in 2010). It predicts that India is likely to develop into 'a global hub for higher education' (ibid.: 103) and encourages centres of excellence to enter into a collaborative partnership with the best universities abroad.

The public investment in higher education went up in the 11th Five-Year Plan. However, it is being increasingly realised that public institutions alone will not be in a position to facilitate the required expansion. The reforms in higher education may be dominated by neoliberal thinking and encourage expanded operation of the private sector (Rizvi and Gorur 2011). It is evident that the government is envisaging a reliance on private institutions to expand the sector. The question is to what extent the country can depend on the private sector without compromising on equity, relevance and quality considerations.

Private higher education in India has expanded fast both in terms of institutions and student enrolment. The number of students enrolled in private higher education institutions is also large, although precise estimates are not readily available. The 52nd National Statistical Survey (NSS) round estimated the share of private enrolment in total enrolment in higher education for 1995–96 to be 8 per cent. The share of private enrolment in engineering education is estimated to be around 20 per cent, which was projected to increase by 60 per cent within a decade. Some of the recent estimates show that the enrolment share of private providers increased from a third of all enrolments in 2001 to just over half in 2006 (Mishra 2011). According to the most recent estimate as per the Approach Paper to the 12th Five-Year Plan (Planning Commission 2011), private higher education accounts for about four-fifths of the enrolment in professional higher education and one-third of the total enrolment in higher education. If the enrolments in self-financing courses in public higher education institutions are added, the share of private higher education in total enrolment would be much higher. Further, the 12th Plan also foresees an increase in the share and contribution of private higher education in India.

A closer analysis of expansion will indicate that the private share of universities is small while the private share of enrolment in non-university institutions is high in India. The fast expansion of the non-university sector in the private surge is a global trend that can be noticed in India as well. The establishment of these for-profit private colleges and institutions, very often, was not based on clearly defined policies or plans to develop higher education in the country. Such unplanned growth has led to many issues related to equity, relevance and quality of education provided by the private providers in India.

Some actions of the private self-financing colleges were challenged in the courts of law. The self-financing or capitation fee colleges in the state of Karnataka followed a discriminatory pricing policy whereby students from outside the state were expected to pay a higher level of fees than those paid by the students from within. This was challenged in court (*Mohini Jain v. State of Karnataka* [1992]) and the Supreme Court banned the capitation fee as it did not agree with the discriminatory fee structure, and declared the state notification to be null and void (Gupta 2005). The court however allowed paid seats up to 50 per cent in private professional colleges, which contributed to the proliferation of self-financing colleges in India.

In another case — *Unnikrishnan J. P. v. State of Andhra Pradesh* (1993) — the Supreme Court came out strongly against for-profit higher education institutions and noted that 'they are poisonous weeds in the fields of education and are financial adventurers without morals and scruples and characterised them as pirates in high seas of education' (quoted in Gupta 2008: 250). The Supreme Court laid down a formula to bring about partnership between the public and private sectors and allowed state governments to administer and regulate admissions of private professional institutions. However, in other cases, the Supreme Court rulings were in favour of self-financing colleges. For example, in the case of *Inamdar v. State of Maharashtra* (2002), the Supreme Court ruled that professional colleges would enjoy full autonomy in admitting students. In another case (*T. M. A Pai v. State of Karnataka* [2002]), the Supreme Court granted the right to establish private higher education institutions, hitherto confined to minorities, to all citizens.

Self-financing colleges are the most visible form of for-profit private higher education in India. Some of the recent evidences implicate that a reckless growth of self-financing private colleges has resulted in the establishment of institutions of questionable quality. Many private higher education institutions have very poor infrastructure, insufficient and unqualified faculty, and levy exorbitant fees from students. Doubts have been raised about the process and consideration based on which approval was granted to such institutions by the AICTE. Further investigations showed that the process of granting permission to open and operate these institutions was not transparent and found that the AICTE officials, including the former chairman, were guilty. One of the former AICTE chairmen was suspended in 2009 for demanding and accepting bribes to approve new technical private colleges (Mishra 2011).

In another instance, a court judgement in a case in 2005 (*Yashpal Sharma and others v. State of Chhattisgarh*) the Supreme Court ruled all colleges established by the state of Chhattisgarh under the Private Universities Act of 2002 as null and void since they did not follow the regulations stipulated by the UGC in 2003. This judgement implied the closing down of 117 private universities established by the state of Chhattisgarh between 2002 and 2005. These instances indicate the need for a more regulated and credible private sector in higher education in India.

Quality is becoming a major concern affecting enrolments in private institutions. Enrolments in management education declined from 260,000 to 200,000 in the last three years; a similar situation was seen in the applications for the Common Admission Test (CAT). According to the AICTE, around 30 per cent (60,000 seats) of the seats in management institutions remained vacant in 2010. This trend is more visible in the low-rung business schools and the top-level institutes are mostly insulated from the decline in enrolments (Umarji 2011). This is an indication of quality determining quantity in private institutions and shows the need for regulations by the state and commitment from the private institutions to invest in facilities promoting quality. In the absence of improving quality in provision, many private institutions may be forced to exit the scene by the very same market forces that brought them to the scene.

NEED FOR REGULATING PRIVATE HIGHER EDUCATION

While such a growth is an example of public–private partnership (PPP) and might have helped reduce the financial burden of the government to expand the sector, it is impor-tant to discuss the desirability of this model of expansion of higher education in India. There are some good and credible private higher education institutions, but a majority of them operate in poor conditions. Despite the interventions by the Supreme Court, regulations stipulated by the UGC and the AICTE do not seem to be very effective in regulating the private providers. The mechanisms to enforce these limited regulations seem to be absent or weak in India.

International experience shows that unregulated growth of private higher education leads to its unhealthy growth and expansion. Studies (Hallak and Poisson 2007) show that fraudulent practices such as relaxed admission rules, distorted evaluation processes and faked examination results and degrees are prevalent in the sector. If a university is opened, many ill-informed potential students desperate for higher education may register for courses without knowing its credentials and quality. Strict regulations to establish private institutions are necessary for protecting the students. The aim therefore is to ensure that an effective regulatory system is in place to prevent under-qualified or fraudulent providers from trading as universities and issuing worthless qualifications.

Some countries have strictly applied a three-phase system of regulations (Varghese 2006) to approve the establishment of a private university:

(a) letters of interim authority — temporary recognition;
(b) registered universities — recognition of existence of institutions with no authority to grant degrees; and
(c) full accreditation — when universities are permitted to award degrees. This has helped to monitor facilities and the quality of programmes before they are finally granted the authority to award degrees. In some countries the national commissions on higher education publish the details on their website, which can guide students on the status of an institution.

In some countries, the applicants for establishing private institutions are required to provide a financial bond or deposit as an indication of their financial strength to run an institution. This measure is also intended to protect students' interests by reducing the chances of closing an institution when profit levels decline. In most cases there is a process of regular review of financial and operational performance mainly through professionally audited reports and annual reports. Such auditing of financial status is a necessary step in avoiding financial irregularities.

There are countries where regulations are stipulated for the type of courses offered by a private university. There is a need to take prior approval for the courses from the appropriate bodies. The quality of the programmes offered by the private institutions is questionable in many instances. There is a need for accreditation agencies to be more active, especially in the initial stages to ensure that standards and quality are maintained. In South Africa, the regulation stipulates that private institutions maintain standards that are not inferior to standards at comparable public higher education institutions and that they comply with the requirements of the appropriate quality assurance body and with any other reasonable requirement prescribed by the ministry.

Many private institutions do not have a high share of regular staff. They rely heavily on guest lecturers and temporary academic staff. There is a need for regulations to ensure the share of regular academic staff expected in a private institution. Similarly, there is a need for strictly adhering to the qualification levels of the staff, their working conditions and salary levels.

Some countries try to regulate the amount of fees that can be levied. A permission to alter the fees in private institutions in China needs to be obtained from the Ministry of Education. This may be a concern more for for-profit institutions than for non-profit institutions. In some countries, for-profit institutions are requested to register under a company's (corporation) acts and they are expected to pay taxes on profits generated. The most difficult issue is the mechanism to ascertain the amount of money collected by some of the private institutions since some of them may provide reports that may not reflect the actual amount collected.

The government is very often criticised for the lack of adequate regulatory measures to facilitate growth and expansion of the private sector in higher education in India. There is a need to look into the adequacy of the existing regulatory measures with a view to develop a foolproof regulatory mechanism. Equally worrying is the fact that the existing regulations have not been enforced and that the penalty that exists for defaulters is inadequate. The cases discussed in this paper indicate that there are incentives not to enforce these regulations.

The private higher education segment in India is growing and acted as a safety valve to absorb the unsatiated demand for higher education especially in professional and technical education. In the absence of regulations and their implementations, these institutions have also contributed to many undesirable practices. A clear policy, guidelines and regulations, and mechanisms of authority to enforce them effectively are necessary to help the sector to grow in a legitimate and balanced manner.

There is need for developing guidelines and mechanisms to strictly comply with issues related to establishment and operation of private higher education institutions in India. The rules regarding the granting of permission to establish a private institution are a very basic requirement. It is important to ensure that the institutions have adequate facilities before permission is granted for opening a private institution. In many countries, a visiting team or an expert group visits and certifies the adequacy of facilities before permission to open and operate an institution is given. The multi-staged process to grant full authorisation to award degrees discussed in this section of the paper may be one of the ways to make institutions adhere to the regulations.

Student admission is an area where regulations can play an important and positive role. The minimum requirements for student admissions need to be strictly followed by the institutions. Although selecting less-qualified students with better paying capacity may be an incentive for many private institutions, it may not be a desirable feature from the point of view of both equity and quality. As discussed previously, relaxed admission rules, distorted evaluation processes and faked examination results are at times prevalent in the sector. Therefore, a control on the quality of the intake may be essential and helpful.

Staff recruitment is an important area that needs strict regulations. There is a need to clearly stipulate qualification requirements for academic staff and these requirements need to be adhered to when academic staff members are recruited. This is an objectively verifiable criterion and defaulters can be identified without difficulty.

India has a well-established accreditation agency — the National Assessment and Accreditation Council (NAAC). Accreditation by the national accreditation agency may be made a compulsory requirement for all private higher education institutions. At times private institutions introduce courses and study programmes without prior approval from the regulatory bodies. Seeking prior permission to introduce new courses must be made a necessary condition. This will give an opportunity to assess the academic readiness of an institution to offer the proposed course.

The level of fees levied by private education institutions are at times very high, leading to disparity in access to these institutions. While institutions need to mobilise resources for self-financing, it is important to put a limit on the maximum amount of student fees that can be levied for a course. Further, the ministry or regulatory body would need to be consulted regarding any changes in the fee-level before it is announced to the students.

Some of these measures may help in developing regulations for establishing private higher education institutions that may not seriously dilute or distort equity and quality concerns. The country already has regulations related to many of these aspects. However, mechanisms to enforce these regulations seem to be weak in India. In the absence of appropriate enforcement mechanisms, the regulations may not serve the desired purpose. Introduction of regular monitoring and periodic auditing of activities of private institutions may be necessary to ensure compliance and accountability of these institutions to the regulatory bodies and students.

NOTE

1. http://www.topuniversities.com/university-rankings/world-university-rankings/2011 (accessed 16 November 2012).

REFERENCES

Agarwal, Pawan. 2007. 'Higher Education in India: Growth, Concerns and Change Agenda', *Higher Education Quarterly*, 61(2): 197–207.

Altbach, Philip G. 2005. 'The Rise of the Pseudouniversity', in Philip G. Altbach and Daniel C. Levy (eds), *Private Higher Education: A Global Revolution*, pp. 23–27. Rotterdam: Sense Publishers.

Bhushan, Sudhanshu. 2005. 'Foreign Universities in India: Market-Driven New Directions', *International Higher Education*, 41: 4–5.

Banya, Kingsley and Juliet Elu. 2001. 'The World Bank and Financing Higher Education in Sub-Saharan Africa', *Higher Education*, 42(1): 1–34.

Bjarnason, Svaja, Kai-Ming Cheng, John Fielden, Maria-Jose Lemaitre, Daniel Levy, and N. V. Varghese. 2009. *A New Dynamic: Private Higher Education*. Paris: United Nations Educational, Scientific and Cultural Organization.

Cohen, Eyal Ben and Rachel Winch. 2011. *Diploma and Accreditation Mills: New Trends in Credential Abuse*. Bedford: Verifile Accredibase.

Cemmell, James. 2002. 'Public vs. Private Higher Education: Public Good, Equity Access — Is Higher Education a Public Good?'. Paper presented at the First Global Forum on International Quality Assurance, Accreditation and the Recognition of Quality in Higher Education, United Nations Educational, Scientific and Cultural Organization, 17–18 October, Paris.

Deccan Herald. 2012. 'Centre to set up IIT Campuses Abroad', 16 August.

Economic Times. 2012. 'HRD Ministry not to Push for Foreign Educational Institutions Bill in the Monsoon Session of Parliament', 8 August.

Gnanam, A. 2008. 'Private Higher Education in the Current Indian Context', in Asha Gupta, Daniel C. Levy and K. B. Powar (eds), *Private Higher Education Global Trends and Indian Perspectives*, pp. 104–14. New Delhi: Shipra Publications.

Gupta, Asha. 2005. 'International Trends in Private Higher Education and the Indian Scenario'. Research and Occasional Paper no. CSHE.11.05, Center for Studies in Higher Education, University of California, Berkley.

———. 2008. 'Judicial Interventions and Private Higher Education in India', in Asha Gupta, Daniel C. Levy and K. B. Powar (eds), *Private Higher Education Global Trends and Indian Perspectives*, pp. 239–52. New Delhi: Shipra Publications.

Hallak, Jacques and Muriel Poisson. 2007. *Corrupt Schools, Corrupt Universities: What can be done?* Paris: International Institute for Educational Planning and United Nations Educational, Scientific and Cultural Organization.

Head, Sarah King. 2011. 'Global: Degree Mills Tarnish Private Higher Education'. *University World News*, issue no. 197, 13 November.

Houghton, John W. and Peter Sheehan. 2000. *A Primer on the Knowledge Economy*. Melbourne: Centre for Strategic Economic Studies, Victoria University.

Kapur, Devesh and Pratap Bhanu Mehta. 2004. 'Indian Higher Education Reform: From Half-Baked Socialism to Half-Baked Capitalism'. CID Working Paper no. 108, Center for International Development, Harvard University.

Karram, Grace. 2011. 'Africa: Rapid Growth in Private Religious Universities'. *University World News*, issue no. 197, 13 November.

Kärkkäinen, Kiira. 2006. *Emergence of Private Higher Education Funding within the OECD Area*. Paris: Centre for Educational Research and Innovation, Organisation for Economic Co-operation and Development.

Kezar, Adriana J., Tony C. Chambers and John C. Burkhardt. 2005. *Higher Education for Public Good: Emerging Voices from a National Movement*. San Francisco: Jossey-Bass.

Lawton, William and Alex Katsomitros. 2012. *International Branch Campuses: Data and Development*. The Observatory on Borderless Higher Education.

Levy, Daniel C. 1986. *Higher Education and the State in Latin America: Private Challenges to Public Dominance*. Chicago: University of Chicago Press.

———. 2005. 'Private Higher Education's Surprise Roles', in Philip G. Altbach and Daniel C. Levy (eds), *Private Higher Education: A Global Revolution*, pp. 33–36. Rotterdam: Sense Publishers.

———. 2006. 'The Unanticipated Explosion: Private Higher Education's Global Surge', *Comparative Education Review*, 50(2): 217–40.

Long, Chrissie. 2011. 'Central America: Private Higher Education Booming'. *University World News*, issue no. 197, 13 November.

Longaneckar, David. 2005. 'State Governance and the Public Good', in Adriana J Kezar, Tony C. Chambers and John C. Burkhardt (eds), *Higher Education for Public Good: Emerging Voices from a National Movement*, pp. 56–70. San Francisco: Jossey-Bass.

Martin, Michaela (ed.). 2007. *Cross-Border Higher Education: Regulation, Quality Assurance and Impact*. Paris: International Institute for Educational Planning and United Nations Educational, Scientific and Cultural Organization.

Middlehurst, Robin and John Fielden. 2011. *Private Providers in UK Higher Education: Some Policy Options*. Oxford: Higher Education Policy Institute.

Ministry of Human Resource Development (MHRD). 2011. 'Selected Educational Statistics'. Ministry of Human Resources Development, New Delhi.

Mishra, Alya. 2011. 'India: Regulation Lags Private Higher Education Growth'. *University World News*, issue no: 197, 13 November.

Moodie, Alison. 2011. 'US: For-Profits Controversial but Driving Growth'. *University World News*, issue no: 197, 13 November.

Organisation for Economic Co-operation and Development (OECD). 1996. *The Knowledge-Based Economy*. Paris: Organisation for Economic Co-operation and Development.

Planning Commission. 2011. *Faster, Sustainable and More Inclusive Growth: An Approach to the Twelfth Five Year Plan*. New Delhi: Planning Commission, Government of India.

Psacharopoulos, George, Jee-Peng Tan, Emmanuel Jimenez, and the Research Division of the World Bank's Education and Training Department. 1986. *Financing Education in Developing Countries: An Exploration of Policy Options*. Washington, DC: World Bank.

Rizvi, Fazal and Radhika Gorur. 2011. 'Challenges Facing Indian Higher Education'. The Fearless Nadia Occasional Papers on India–Australia Relations, Australia India Institute, Melbourne.

Samuelson, Paul A. 1954. 'The Pure Theory of Public Expenditure', *Review of Economics and Statistics*, 36(4): 387–89.

Slantcheva, Snejana and Daniel C. Levy (eds). 2007. *Private Higher Education in Post-Communist Europe: In Search of Legitimacy*. New York: Palgrave-Macmillan.

Stiglitz, Joseph E. 1999. 'Knowledge as a Global Public Good', in Inge Kaul, Isabelle Grunberg and Marc A. Stern (eds), *Global Public Goods: International Cooperation in the 21st Century,* pp. 308–32. New York: Oxford University Press.

Singh, L. C. and Sudarshan Misra. 2008. 'Self-Financing Higher Education: Issues and Concerns', in Asha Gupta, Daniel C. Levy and K. B. Powar (eds), *Private Higher Education Global Trends and Indian Perspectives*, pp. 126–33. New Delhi: Shipra Publishers.

Siwinska, Bianka. 2011. 'Europe: Tired Pioneers in Eastern and Central Europe'. *University World News*, issue no. 197, 13 November.

Tilak, Jandhyala B. G. 1994. 'The Pests are here to Stay: Capitation Fee in Disguise', *Economic and Political Weekly*, 29(7): 348–50.

————. 2008. 'Higher Education: A Public Good or a Commodity for Trade? Commitment to Higher Education or Commitment of Higher Education to Trade', *Prospects*, 38(4), 449–66.

Umarji, Vinay. 2011. 'B-Schools Fail to Write Off Empty Classroom Worries'. *Business Standard*, 23 July.

University Grants Commission (UGC). 2003a. 'Higher Education in India: Issues, Concerns and New Directions'. Recommendations of UGC Golden Jubilee Seminars-2003 held at Eleven Universities in India, University Grants Commission, New Delhi.

————. 2003b. 'UGC (Establishment of and Maintenance of Standards in Private Universities) Regulations, 2003'. University Grants Commission, New Delhi.

Varghese, N. V. (ed.). 2004. *Private Higher Education: Country Experiences*. Paris: International Institute for Educational Planning.

————. (ed.). 2006. *Growth and Expansion of Private Higher Education in Africa*. Paris: International Institute for Educational Planning and United Nations Educational, Scientific and Cultural Organization.

————. 2008. 'Private Sector as a Partner in Higher Education Development in Africa'. IIEP-ADEA-AAU Policy Brief, International Institute for Educational Planning, Association for the Development of Education in Africa, Association of African Universities and United Nations Educational, Scientific and Cultural Organization.

Varughese, Rajan. 2006. 'Privatisation of Public Assets in Higher Education: Emerging Trends in Private Aided Colleges in Kerala', *Journal of Educational Planning and Administration*, 20(3): 313–20.

Woodhouse, Kellie. 2011. 'Coleman to Obama: "Higher Education is a Public Good Currently Lacking Public Support"'. *AnnArbor. com*, 16 December. http://www.annarbor.com/news/coleman-to-obama-higher-education-is-a-public-good-currently-lacking-public-support/ (accessed 16 November 2012).

World Bank. 2002. *Constructing Knowledge Societies: New Challenges for Tertiary Education*. Washington, DC: World Bank.

14 | The Emerging Market for Higher Education

Rationalising Regulation to Address Equity and Quality Concern

Saumen Chattopadhyay

The Indian higher education sector is faced with the daunting challenge of ensuring inclusive and quality education to all in an emerging regime of constrained budgetary allocation for higher education, particularly by state governments, coupled with increasing private sector participation. Further, even though increasing globalisation has opened up opportunities in the higher education space, it has also compounded the severity of these challenges. Overcoming these challenges is also critical to ensure that India attains a sharper competitive edge in the emerging global knowledge economy. However, there is a considerable degree of overlap among the set of identified challenges, i.e., expansion, inclusion and excellence, which need to be studied in a holistic manner.[1] A market for higher education is gradually evolving, and recent policy initiatives by the government could be viewed as attempts towards regulating the market. World over, education reform is guided by a pro-market rationale, which involves exposing the sector to competition resulting in improved efficiency and quality. This paper discusses how the market for education, and in particular higher education, is different and hence needs to be treated with caution in the context of the prevailing socio-economic situation in India. In this context, the paper highlights how delicately the government has to intervene in the market to reconcile the two conflicting issues — education for masses and education for profit.

UNIQUE FEATURES OF THE MARKET FOR EDUCATION

Education policy world over is increasingly being positioned within the framework of neoliberal approach in which the State steers the market through regulations and rules, and only if required plays an active role. Effectively the neoliberals argue in favour of setting up a regulated market. It is imperative, therefore, to understand the specific features of an education market in a developing economy to better define the role of government and the rules and regulations thereof. The role of the government would differ with respect to the levels of education. Primary education, being ubiquitously considered a merit good, has to be primarily provided by the government. However, higher education is recognised as a quasi-public good with a blend of both 'publicness' and 'privateness'.[2] The extent of government intervention would determine the extent of 'publicness' higher education produces. This is because the government-supported provision of education would make it affordable and therefore, help the sector to cater to the rising social demand. Greater the extent of subsidisation, larger would be the extent of inclusiveness of such an expansion. This massification of education would also maximise the positive externalities generated by education. This is a policy decision as the extent of subsidisation as reflected in the budgetary provision would be determined politically. There are two aspects of such an expansion. If it entails lowering the cut-off for admission-seekers and arguably, compromise with quality as it is often popularly understood, then possibly we would be failing to adopt a broader approach to understand the notion of quality in the Indian context. In view of low educational attainment at the school-level, the focus should be on inclusion to maximise the hunt for talent and foster social mobility rather than being unduly obsessed with myopic and narrow vision of quality. Expansion is mainly being driven by the rising demand for the professional education. Since the expected return on a professional degree is higher than the general stream, there is an attempt to recover cost from the student even in government-supported institutions such as Indian

Institutes of Technology (IITs) and Indian Institutes of Management (IIMs). Though education loans are being promoted by the government to help those who have the merit but not the means, it is possibly not a good option particularly for those who genuinely need it.[3] Hence, considering the role of education in nation-building, framing an appropriate higher education policy is critical to balance the public good concept with the private good concept of higher education. From the perspective of economic theory the government should define the rules for private provisioning of higher education, and also ensure equal opportunities for all to foster social mobility.[4]

The market for higher education may fail on various counts to guarantee an efficient allocation of resources. Not only is the market imperfect because of the possible delivery of diverse quality of education, but higher education being a quasi-public good generates positive externalities, often internalised as higher remuneration, leading to an educational requirement that is suboptimal resulting in misuse of societal resources. Unequal distribution of resources puts to question any advocacy for market-driven higher education on efficiency considerations. Education leads to social mobility and social cohesion, the provision of which should be guided by social demand rather than by market demand, which is essentially determined by the private returns on education and also income distribution. From a broader perspective, market failure provides a rationale for the government to intervene by reducing the price of education through subsidisation.[5] But the scope for government intervention need not remain restricted to the direct subsidisation of cost of education. The reformers argue in favour of changing the mode of funding from input-based approach to client-based approach. In the latter, financial help would be given directly to the students instead of institutions, which would nurture competition and help in constructing a competitive market.[6] But in either approach, blanket provisioning of subsidies could be restricted by raising the cost recovery from those who can afford to pay. However, given the high cost of education, the extent of cost recovery must remain limited. Knowledge being in the nature of public good, the government can play a vital role in funding Research and Development (R&D) in Higher Education Institutions (HEIs) and research organisations. The mode of subsidisation is undergoing a change world over as there is an increasing tendency to ensure that subsidies accrue directly to the intended beneficiaries. Subsidies can be given directly to the institutions to lower the fees or to the students in the form of vouchers (or even scholarships). Since education is an 'experience good' (Teixeira et al. 2004), in the sense that quality of education could be assessed only through consumption, it becomes difficult for the students to ascertain the value of an institution while they seek admission in it

— their decisions to choose courses and institutions would remain imperfect as they suffer from information asymmetry.[7] Not only does limited freedom of students alter their choices, as and when they want to, making choices is also expensive in terms of time and money. Scope for exercising consumer sovereignty is further limited by the fact that merit comes first in the admission process and not ability to pay, unless seats are up for sale (Chattopadhyay 2009). Limited scope for exit by the providers restricts the scope for competition.

Further, the nature of competition in the market for education is characterised by S-competition (selection-based) rather than E-competition (efficiency-based) (Glennerster 1991: 1270). Under E-competition, the inputs are passive and homogenous and the competition takes place in the realm of transforming the inputs to outputs. A firm competes when at a given price the quality is superior compared to others; when for a certain quality the given price is less; or a combination of these two. In S-competition the critical inputs, i.e., the students and the teachers are neither passive nor homogenous. This is because institutions choose their students and teachers to produce good quality education in the presence of competition, just as the good students (and parents) and the worthy teachers choose an institution for its academic engagement.[8] Competition does not therefore take place in a fair manner, as the best of the institutions are reputed with high credibility and financially well-endowed to attract the best of the minds. It takes years before an institution gains credibility and earns fame. This leads to an accentuation of hierarchy in ranking of the institutions, as the best ones are adequately funded to produce quality output and remain at the top of the ranking table (Winston 1999). This weakens the efficacy of competition to achieve the goal of imparting quality education as opposed to the desirability of competition to achieve efficiency and quality in a typical consumption goods market. However, if a new entrant enters the higher education sector with a large endowment fund, it is possible to negate the nature of S-competition over time. In India, there are a few credible initiatives from the private sector where the institutions, though pretty young, have established their credibility. The apparent dominance of mainline economics among the policy-makers and the thinkers, as evident in the neoliberal approach to education reform, makes the reform measures seem to be guided by the market logic. The following section discusses some of the policy measures being mooted and some that are in the process of being implemented in India.

In general, imparting education is viewed as an exchange in a market for education, and therefore an analysis of delivery of education could be subject to the economic logic as it is applied to the study of market of any other consumable good or service. Commodification of education (particularly in case of higher education) in economic theory has led the neoliberal policy-makers to repose faith on market and its ability to achieve efficiency and quality through competition at the economy level and that of the institute through governance reform.[9] This argument is further bolstered by the economic logic of allowing the consumers (students) and the producers (the institutions) to enjoy sovereignty to the extent possible in the sphere of market. The question is how much freedom can be given to the students to choose the courses and the institutions of their choice and the education providers to determine its pricing in a highly unequal world for a 'commodity' with a difference.

QUASI-MARKET FOR HIGHER EDUCATION

Since the market for higher education is imperfect, as discussed earlier, the government needs to intervene. It needs to regulate the quasi-market and should intervene in crucial areas to address wider social goals (Jongbloed 2004: 91). The overall approach for the government should be to foster competition wherever possible and regulate otherwise (ibid.). Designing a proper mode of funding higher education is one important way of achieving a balance between competition and regulation (Jongbloed 2007). One major way is to assume the responsibility of provisioning through the subsidisation of the cost of education by directly channelling subsidies to government-owned institutions. But these institutions in the majority of cases have failed to deliver quality education. This is not really unexpected as government-owned institutions suffer from what the economists call 'government failure'. The privately-owned institutions similarly have failed to deliver quality education albeit for a different reason — commercialisation. The other way is to regulate the market with the broader objectives of ensuring quality and addressing the equity concerns. In an emerging regime of greater private sector participation in provisioning education, subsidies may be directly channelled to the students, thereby empowering them to make a choice. Thus, the market can be developed by strengthening the students' ability to exercise their sovereignty. Also, institutional reform is an imperative to ensure efficient managerial practices in the market for higher education. The extent of intervention required may be determined in terms of freedoms that could be bestowed on the two parties — the consumers (students) and the providers (institutions). Since a perfect market cannot be created and managed, the policy-makers seek to simulate a market-like situation or what is called a quasi-market.

Four Freedoms of Consumers

This section explores how and to what extent freedoms to the students and the providers can be realised in a higher education market. In the process, it seeks to understand the nature of the quasi-market in higher education.

Freedom to Choose Provider

The neoliberals would argue that this freedom is a necessary condition for developing a quasi-market-like situation. But for higher education in particular, merit comes first, followed by the ability to pay to exercise the choice. Getting admission into the top institutions is highly competitive as only 2 to 4 per cent of the candidates who apply and appear in the entrance tests qualify for getting into the top-ranking institutions, such as the IITs and the IIMs. If the ability to pay gets priority while choosing an institution, merit will be bypassed and education will be degraded to a mere consumption good (or service to be precise). A majority of the institutions follow certain criteria to offer admissions to ensure uniformity and avoid discrimination. The controversy about capitation fees in some of the states is a case to drive home the point that the exercise of this freedom may degrade education (Thomas 2012). The transfer of credit being considered by the University Grants Commission (UGC) and the concept of a meta-university will enable the students to exercise more freedom in their choices of both courses as well as institutions.[10]

Freedom to Choose Product

The freedom to choose a course or discipline to pursue higher studies is constrained by the limited number of seats in the best institutions and high demand for the coveted courses. When students appear in the admission tests, if required, they can express their willingness to study a particular course or stream. But since choice of a course requires fulfilment of certain eligibility criteria, the liberty to choose is limited. However, the freedoms to select a product and a provider may not be entirely independent. If the institutions have high brand value, the students may choose the institution first and then the subjects. It can be the other way round if the subject or stream is in high demand in the job market.

Adequate Information on Prices and Quality

Since the students often do not have adequate information about the institutions and the courses they choose before taking admission, making a choice might be fraught with mistakes. Corrupt providers could mislead the applicants primarily by hiding information on quality of infrastructure and education. The ministry concerned has made it compulsory for privately-funded colleges and universities to upload relevant information on their respective websites. Of course some scope for cheating would still remain either by way of arbitrarily raising the fees or cutting costs. Moreover, the qualifications of the faculty and the lab facilities are rarely revealed to the candidates.

Direct and Cost-Covering Prices

On account of subsidisation, the tuition fees charged would only be a fraction of the cost incurred by the institution per student. Some universities, mostly the State universities have sought to garner more resources through self-financing courses which are generally market-oriented professional courses. Since the fee structure in centrally-funded institutions has remained virtually stagnant, compared to the cost of education, there has been a growing pressure to offer self-financing courses and explore other alternative sources to mobilise more revenue. Rising demand for educational loans indicates substantial cost recovery being made by the universities, which is tantamount to financial privatisation of public institutions of higher education (Tilak 2008). If government support for education ceases, the latter will become incapable of serving the larger interests of the people (Patnaik 2007: 7).

Though the government has expressed interest to institutionalise a gradual rise in the fee structure, the fees should not be linked in any way to the institution-specific cost structure. This is because in higher education, cost and quality are positively related, as good quality education requires better infrastructure. Thus, efficiency gains in terms of cost minimisation cannot be reaped in the absence of a well-specified production function (Majumdar 1983). This implies that the value attached to a degree or certificate would depend on how much the student had to pay for the education.[11]

Given the salient role of education in ensuring social mobility and social cohesiveness, allowing the market to solely determine the price of education would, therefore, not only relegate talent and erode India's edge in knowledge economy but also pave the way for social disaster.

Four Freedoms of Providers

The sovereignty of the education providers could also be discussed in terms of four freedoms. The degree of these freedoms would determine the competitiveness of the higher education market. The extent and nature of the regulation specified by the government for curbing the freedoms of the providers would reflect how the government balances the autonomy of the private sector and the concern for equity and quality in the delivery of education.

Freedom of Entry

For a perfectly competitive market, free entry and exit are necessary to generate competition. For a sector such as education, the credibility of the investors would matter a great deal and that is why the freedom of entry should ideally be regulated. If entry is free and unregulated, then corrupt education providers could 'create an illusion of learning' (Pathak 2009: 153).[12] Unfortunately, this is true for the majority of private operators today (Altbach 2009; Jayaram 2006; Vaiydanathan 2009). This is also what appears to be believed by the Ministry of Human Resource Development (MHRD) from their decision to set up an overarching regulatory body, subsuming the UGC, All India Council for Technical Education (AICTE) and other bodies, obliquely referring to the failure of the UGC and AICTE to maintain academic standard while granting affiliations. Though there are not yet too many private universities, private sector participation has witnessed a very high growth in the market for professional courses (Tilak 2008). Universities can be established under the State Legislation but are required to get permission from the UGC, which has become almost automatic.[13] Regulated entry is what is desirable for both domestic and foreign players in the higher education market. However, even if there is a regulatory authority, compliance with the requirements does not necessarily guarantee good quality education. It may be possible for the private providers to circumvent the specified requirements in an unfair manner.

Freedom to Specify and Offer Product

In the government-aided segment of the market, there is autonomy to offer courses but with the approval of the state governments or the UGC. This is because additional funding is often required to start a new course, unless it is a self-financing one. Private unaided educational institutes also have the freedom to decide courses and its content, but with the approval of the relevant regulatory authority, UGC or AICTE, as the case may be. To facilitate introduction of specialised courses, the UGC has been proactive to grant deemed-to-be university status to research institutions with established reputation and credibility so that they can offer degrees. However, there are restrictions on them to diversify into new areas lest it dilutes their specialisation which, in the first place, earned them their status.

As argued by Avijit Pathak, marketisation could blight the quest for fundamental knowledge as market-oriented courses assume prominence at the expense of the fundamental disciplines such as physics and history (2009: 155–56). It can even lead to a sort of hierarchy of knowledge, as what sells less in the market place becomes irrelevant for the students who look for courses to facilitate their professional career.

In India, the market for professional courses is increasingly being dominated by the private institutes and there is evidence that the competition is also getting stiffer. The private institutions are also affiliating with foreign universities to develop brand loyalty and offer courses which have relevance and acceptability in the global job market. However, the foreign counterparts, though they may be the mediocre in their countries of origin, continue to evoke respect and hope among the aspiring Indian students.[14]

Freedom to Use Available Resources

This section distinguishes between the institutions which receive grants-in-aid and those that do not. In case of support from the UGC, the freedom to use resources as per the discretion of the institutions is rather limited as the release of grants is linked to specific heads and it is subject to submission of utilisation certificates. Within a particular 'head', there is autonomy with regard to the use of resources, of course subject to audit. Maintenance cost, inclusive of salary, as a percentage of total cost has been large, resulting in a reduction of the discretionary part of the expenditure. This has hampered development-related expenditure. However, the departments can compete for funds under several assistance schemes of the UGC or apply for project-/plan-based assistance. Possibly there is a need for freedom to use resources by the institutions as financial independence is a precursor to autonomy in the broader sense. Though the privately-owned institutions are not supposed to make profit, they are allowed to make 'reasonable surplus' which can be reinvested to further the growth of the institutions.[15] In reality, private institutions often maintain two sets of accounts or produce fabricated accounts as they would prefer to enjoy the freedom to use available resources. At the same time, essential expenditure to deliver education is curtailed which leads to the dilution of quality of education. Arbitrary reduction in expenditure and choice of any input combination is feasible as there is no well-defined production function for an educational institution (Majumdar 1983).[16] For the government institutions, it is often debated that the lack of freedom is stifling functioning and innovation. The argument is tenable if it can be ensured that there is no corruption. Since the system suffers from poor governance and malpractices, financial autonomy requires the institution to behave responsibly and respect autonomy. Striking a balance is critical.

Freedom to Determine Prices

If the privately-owned institutions are given the freedom to determine prices, there may be a tendency to keep these at cost-recovery level. Education then loses its relevance for the society and the economy. Fees are often periodically revised upwards and the overall fee structure is loaded with hidden and unjustified demands. This has the potential to render education as a commercially exploitable commodity. The prevalence of a capitation fee has detrimental effect on access despite the quota regime. It is not, therefore, desirable that the private providers should have the discretion over the fee structure even in higher education in the interest of the larger section of the society. Raising fees in the name of easy

availability of loans does not help as there are many short-comings of even interest-free education loans for a country such as India. Sudhanshu Bhushan argues that it is generally expected that owing to competition in a market setup there should be convergence towards a uniform fee structure (2010: 185). However, as the market is imperfectly competitive, as quality of the same product varies across the institutions, convergence towards single price is not expected.

MARKET-ORIENTED REFORMS

The concepts of competition, efficiency and quality are rather untenable for arguing in favour of a market for education. A degree certificate, which is often degraded to a mere piece of paper, cannot reflect true quality if the providers resort to unfair means covertly or overtly. Education in terms of skill and values goes much beyond 'credentialism'. However, what is quality and how to assess it remain debatable issues. A majority of the private providers, mostly of poor repute, have abused the absence of a production function in the delivery of education and have ended up delivering substandard quality of education, thereby reducing it to merely awarding of a certificate (Chattopadhyay 2009).[17]

The market-driven privatised higher education sector has other concerns. Being driven entirely by the market would demand marketable outputs from education that is quantifiable. Disciplines that create greater job opportunities and are easily quantifiable in terms of monetary returns from education would assume greater importance. However, subjects such as humanities and arts, the returns of which are not easily quantifiable but contribute substantially to preserving and shaping the character of democracy, get cut off in the race for competitive profit-oriented market for education. Thus, as Sybil Thomas suggests (see Box 14.1), it is important to put appropriate policies and commitment in place so that not only education adds to the improvement of economic wealth of the nation but also continues to richly contribute towards preserving and evolving the democratic fabric of the society.

ECONOMIC RATIONALE BEHIND RECENT POLICY INITIATIVES IN EDUCATION

The rationale behind several policy initiatives, which are in the process of implementation in the Indian context, is based on the neoliberal approach to education reform, despite a substantial increase in budgetary allocation for higher education in the recent years. Some of the major reforms include encouraging entry of the private providers, setting up of a regulatory authority, quality assurance mechanism, promotion of public–private partnership (PPP) in new ventures, infusing competition in publicly funded institutions such as outsourcing and privatisation of non-core activities, and application of 'performativity' principle in guiding institutional reform, which is tantamount to the application of corporate managerial practices in governing the publicly-funded institutions to enhance responsiveness to the need of the consumers (i.e., the students). In this emerging regime where market principle gains prominence, it is essential to set up a regulatory authority, along with a tribunal for grievance redressal, and encourage participation of foreign education providers, make accreditation mandatory and promote ranking of HEIs, explore alternative modes of funding and even an alternative mechanism for subsidisation such as through the voucher scheme, so as to simulate a market-like situation (Chattopadhyay 2007).

The underlying principle behind PPP is basically based on two arguments. First, the private sector is considered to be more efficient in the use of resources and delivery of quality education than the public sector and, second, fiscal stringency would not permit the government to budget for adequate resources necessary for quality expansion of the sector. The belief that through proper policy measures efficiency and quality can be achieved is based on an understanding that input–output relationship is tenable and applicable for an educational institution. Supporting private sector and PPP in professional education is often justified on the grounds that scarce fiscal resources could be deployed in non-professional education which would otherwise not be supported by the market. There can be many different forms of PPP and the outcome of such a blend would depend on the kind of partnership arrangement they enter into and the nature of ownership and objective of the private sector. To allow profit-making in the absence of a substantial cost reduction through efficiency would either raise the pricing of education or would entail an increase in the government financial support or a mixture of the two (Chattopadhyay 2012: 247). However, this is different from the unbridled growth of the private sector with poor credibility. It is now well recognised that the private sector may not be interested in investment in education on a large scale unless they are allowed to make reasonable amount of profit. The challenge before the policy-makers today is to judiciously manage the private and the public sector in education without compromising with the three objectives envisaged in the 11th Five-Year Plan — expansion, inclusion and exclusion.[18]

The government is considering setting up a regulatory authority in the form of National Council for Higher Education and Research (NCHER) to develop a regulated market for the higher education sector.[19] This would help overcome the problem of multiple regulatory authorities with overlapping functions, ensure transparency and uniformity, regulate standards, and hopefully reduce political interference. However, the problems associated with the marketisation of higher education would largely remain unaddressed. Setting up a tribunal in higher education will seek to address the grievances of the students studying primarily in privately funded institutions. The need arises because the education market lacks intense competition due to restricted mobility of the students, and education is an 'experience good' which makes students suffer from information asymmetry at the time of choice of courses and institutions (as discussed earlier).[20] The institutions are now to be accredited compulsorily even within the country to facilitate informed choice-making which is central to sovereignty and competition (Bill on Accreditation). However, the concept of quality of education as used in the process of accreditation and ranking may not address the university-specific mandate to serve the society or, in other words, the university–society linkages. This would also interfere with the autonomy of the institution to pursue its objectives if it participates in ranking.[21] In effect, a highly discriminatory market for education is being created, which would in turn lead to a differentiated and hierarchical society. It is possible that the market elements would continue to gain strength which may deter imparting of value-based inclusive education; as teaching–learning process becomes more like exchange in a market, the students become investors and the teachers become merely service providers.

INDIA IN THE GLOBAL KNOWLEDGE ECONOMY

The question now is whether India will be well-equipped to participate in the global knowledge economy. In some sense, the country is already a part of it, if one goes by the number of students who leave the country to study abroad, the contribution of the non-resident Indians in knowledge production overseas and engagement of some universities and research institutes in global collaborations. However, in the realm of innovation, R&D and the reputation of the research institutions and universities, there is nothing much that India can take pride in even in the context of the Asia–Pacific nations.[22]

One way to build up research capacity is to increase global connectedness. Research universities are generally more networked than other HEIs. The growth in such collaborations, student and faculty exchanges have risen in the recent years. Meaningful, effective and long-term participation in the global knowledge economy entails development of research capacity, without which India will be dependent on knowledge flows from outside and will not be able to

Box 14.1
Silent Crisis in Higher Education

Education is that process by which thought is opened out of the soul, and is associated with outward things, is reflected back on itself, and thus made conscious of their reality and shape.

—Bronson Alcott, Massachusetts educator, c.1850

India is in the midst of a crisis of massive proportions and grave global significance. It is not the global economic crisis that began in 2008. At least everyone knew that a crisis was at hand and world leaders worked quickly and desperately to find solutions. This section refers to the crisis that goes largely unnoticed, a crisis that is likely to be, in the long run, far more dangerous to the future of a democratic society: a world crisis in education. The reference here is to higher education, though some of the problems are also common to elementary and secondary education as discussed in other papers.

Radical changes are taking place in the way society is reaching out to young minds. However, these changes are directed by social and economic policies of the society. Education is now looked at as a commodity that can be traded in the global market. India has adopted a model of development where education is being considered for 'economic growth'. Hence, given that economic growth is so easily sought by society at the macro level as well as by individuals at the day-to-day level, too few questions have been posed about the direction of education as well as that of democratic society itself!

The section begins by acknowledging the fact stated that publicly funded higher education systems are in need of overhaul, and private-run agenda driven by markets and profits raise some issues and implications that need to be addressed (see Chapter 8). The profit motive suggests that education for economic growth needs basic skills, literacy and numeracy. It also needs people who have more advanced skills in computer science and technology. States such as Gujarat and Andhra Pradesh have seen increased Gross National Product (GNP) per capita through the education of the technical elite that make the states attractive to foreign investors. There is no problem with good scientific technical education; it cannot even be suggested that education should not be driven by profit. The concern here lies in the fact that when market forces motivated by profit alone determine the kind of education to be imparted, a declining trend is experienced in investment as well as interest in humanities and liberal arts. The abilities associated with humanities and arts are: to think critically, to transcend local loyalties, to approach world problems as a 'citizen of the world', and finally to imagine sympathetically the predicament of another person.

To some extent these changes are being externally imposed but a line of caution is also that the university system too have taken shortcuts — by teaching large courses without critical engagements, which has made it easy for the system to succumb to external social and economic pressures. Drew Gilpin Faust (2009) concludes in his ringing defence of the role of liberal arts in a democratic society:

Higher learning can offer individuals and societies a depth and breadth of vision absent from the inevitable myopic present. Human beings need meaning, understanding, as well as jobs. The question should not be whether we can afford to believe in such purposes in these times, but whether we can afford not to.

Therefore, the policies and commitment need to be looked at to see that these abilities that can be developed through humanities and arts are not cut off in the fury of a competitive profit-oriented market.

For India as a nation aspiring to get a greater share of the global market as well as create job opportunities through education for the young people, imagination and critical faculties seem to look like paraphernalia. Private- and public-funded higher education institutions today compete in a global market. The key driving factor that determines the competitive edge for an institution is still the quantitative progress indicated by the marks acquired by a student along with the economic returns that the student is able to get after investing in the system of higher education. Though these may be easy indicators of quality, here again the concern that is reiterated is that of the curriculum, which needs to be built around humanistic elements, and the pedagogy that needs to be revisited. Even in higher education, the focus of the content has shifted away from text that focuses on enlivening imagination and training the critical faculties towards material that is directly relevant to test preparation. Along with this is an even more baneful shift in pedagogy. Socrates proclaimed that 'the unexamined life is not worth living for a human being'. However, in an educational world that is driven by maximising economic growth alone, the implication could be that people would consider Socratic pedagogy as dispensable. A society that is motivated by market forces would demand marketable outputs from education which are quantifiable. Though today people still maintain that they like democracy and self governance, but distracted with the pursuit of wealth they cut costs and prune away just those parts of the educational endeavour that are crucial for preserving a healthy democratic society.

Looking at the challenges in higher education in a privatised educational world, what is required is not only monetary investments (though money is good), but also committed people and strong policies for promoting the abilities and skills that humanities discipline can promote with sound content and pedagogy. One needs to pause and ask questions on the direction of education and society if this trend continues. Democracies have great rational imaginative powers. It also has some flaws in reasoning besides parochialism, sloppiness, selfishness, and narrowness of spirit. Education based purely on economic growth magnifies these deficiencies, producing a technically trained docility that could threaten every strand in the fabric of democracy.

SYBIL THOMAS
Department of Education
University of Mumbai

contribute to the development of global science and culture. R&D spending in India was 1.03 per cent of Gross Domestic Product (GDP) in 2006 (Agarwal 2009: 252) compared to 3.44 in Japan, 1.49 in China, 3.47 in South Korea, 2.01 in Australia, and 1.2 in New Zealand. Research in Asian universities is lower than in US (13.3 per cent in US compared to 8.3 per cent in China). It is beyond doubt that India does not have a promising research university sector. Almost 80 per cent of all R&D is in the public sector with a high share for the government research agencies. The share of the university is minor and basic research is only 17.8 per cent (ibid.: 253). In terms of growth in scientific papers (science and engineering) during 1995–2007, China witnessed an annual growth of 16.5 per cent as compared to India's at 5.7 per cent (Marginson 2010). Dissemination of technology would depend on adult literacy and quality of education, among other factors. The adult literacy rate in China was 93.3 per cent compared to 66 per cent in India (ibid.). As argued by Altbach, despite English being the main academic language and the availability of bright and well-trained scholars, India is unlikely to have competitive research universities in the coming several decades whereas China is likely to join the league of top-ranking universities in the world (2009: 200). Marginson (2010) rightly remarked that though India talks about knowledge economy, it underperforms relative to its reputation as an emerging economic giant.

India is yet to develop a coherent national strategy and has weak national-level coordination. With 32 per cent population in the age group of 0–14 years, the country is likely to see a rise in demand for higher education. Thus there is enormous scope to provide a larger pool of productive labour to generate national wealth. The challenge however is one of creating capacity for quality education to make that expansion relevant in the domestic economy and achieve excellence in the global arena.

The quality of education in India, in general with regard to school as well as higher education, by any measure is poor as indicated by various studies. The quality of education imparted in the private schools is hardly better. With regard to higher education, the employability of the graduates is low as claimed by some studies (NASSCOM–McKinsey Report 2005). It is an irony that the Indian HEIs do not even feature in the ranking of the top 100 in the world despite the fact that IITs and IIMs are generally regarded as institutions par excellence,[23] and also considering that India has the third or fourth largest skilled manpower in the world and the largest number of institutions. With very few universities of excellence, the research base is rather limited. State-funded universities somehow maintain the day-to-day functioning as the state governments do not raise the budgetary allocations. The quality of infrastructure for supporting research activity is somehow better in the central universities, IITs and IIMs

and some select government-funded institutions. In the aggregate sense, in a country with 400 plus universities the production of knowledge is inadequate by any international standard.

For a meaningful integration with the emerging knowledge economy, the higher education sector is confronted with many challenges. The government has of late emphasised the salience of knowledge and development of human resources, and initiated many policy measures to overhaul the system. The question is how good are these measures in the context of the prevailing system and effectiveness of implementing the programmes. The problem is aggravated by the stagnancy in the budgetary allocations by the governments; the existing ones are suffering from poor governance.[24]

The issue is why even the private sector institutions are failing to impart good quality education when the advocates of market and the private sector dominate policy-making; though privatisation has helped in major expansion of technical education.

Concluding Remarks: Looking Beyond 'Commodification'

Commodification of education in mainstream economic theory has informed policy-making in education even in the context of a developing country such as India. However, in view of the fact that higher education is a quasi-public good, the government has to play a crucial role in its provision so as to maximise its 'publicness'. Ideally, to ensure access to all, even in professional education, the government-funded institutions could play a larger role. However, at this juncture where the private sector occupies nearly half of the higher education sector and continues to cater to the rising demand for professional education, the role of this sector has to be thought through pragmatically. It is true that both the public-funded as well as the private sector have failed to deliver good quality education. The reasons behind this lack of excellence are however different (Chattopadhyay 2012). Mushrooming of private institutions with the over-riding objective of maximising 'reasonable surplus' in the absence of strong regulation have led to poor quality education. The government institutions typically suffer from 'government failure'. In view of this, what is needed is investment from private sector with commitment to quality and societal responsibility. The character and the motive of such investment are of utmost importance. Advocating the role of private sector in the name of efficiency and equity is somewhat misleading. While the concept of efficiency in education is weak and irrelevant, absence of subsidies in its provisioning is bound to mitigate access. The clamour for autonomy is justifiable, one has to safeguard with concern and care that this autonomy is not abused. Marketisation for a change cannot ensure excellence. Students are not only poorly informed about the decisions they make but also the quality they assess. What is more important is the quality produced in the classrooms with committed participation from the teachers and the students and not by the teachers alone. Education is such a sector, mere compliance with the regulatory norms is not good enough. And therefore what is needed is genuineness and sincerity when it comes to the delivery of education to the society, be it public or private.

NOTES

1. The fourth one which is often added is relevance of education.
2. Higher education does not conform strictly to the definition of a public good as given by Samuelson (1954). A public good is characterised by non-rivalry in consumption and non-excludability. Non-rivalry means that the benefits of higher education accrue to all and those who do not want to pay for the benefits cannot be excluded from their appropriation. But higher education is not a typical public good as the benefits which accrue primarily to those who pursue higher studies in the form of higher incomes are different from those who do not pursue higher studies. What the others gain is called externalities which are not easily quantifiable in the absence of markets. Externalities would assume the role of good citizenry, functioning of democratic institutions, inculcation of moral and ethical values which are required for nation-building. While 'publicness' would refer to the externalities generated and inclusiveness, 'privateness' denotes monetary benefits and the status higher education confers on an individual.
3. There are instances of discrimination by the banks with respect to region, gender and caste while sanctioning loans.
4. Since primary education has been argued to be a merit good, the concept of market for primary education does not need to be invoked. Higher education being a quasi-public good, the neoliberals advocate for a regulated market. The important question is that of the extent of intervention.
5. Market failure occurs when one or more of the assumptions underlying a perfectly competitive market are not satisfied. The assumptions include absence of information asymmetry, externalities and product heterogeneity. Apart from a large number of buyers, there should be a large number of sellers as well.
6. This latter approach is called voucher system. Though theoretically it appeals to mainstream economic logic of efficiency and competition in the realm of market, but application of this logic is not tenable for education particularly in the context of a developing country.
7. Quality and usefulness of education are experienced as the students go through the process of education, and even much after the formal completion of their studies. Technically, this is often referred to as information asymmetry as it is difficult to ascertain the true quality of education when the students take admission in an institution.
8. This is different from a typical textbook concept of competition. Both the inputs — students and the teachers and the institutions — earn credibility of being associated with each other. A university department is known for its faculty and the students produced.
9. Adjusting for quality and efficiency can be defined as the ratio between outputs to inputs (Massy 2004: 21).
10. This includes the mobility of students across universities, within two Indian universities, as well as between Indian and foreign universities. See Prakash (2011).
11. This is not to deny that there is no scope for reorganisation of the institution to raise efficiency and better use of resources. Corruption often leads to gross mis-utilisation of resources. Before it is sought to raise cost recovery, achieving good governance is essential.
12. Since education is a concurrent subject under the Indian Constitution, some states such as Chhattisgarh enacted private university acts on their own, which led to mushrooming of private universities in the state.
13. The proliferation of the deemed universities has become a contentious issue after the change in the leadership in MHRD.
14. India does not yet have a legislation in place to regulate foreign collaborations. Varying jurisdiction between the central and the state governments and the changing policy perspectives are the major hurdles (Altbach 2009: 44).
15. In the case of *T. M. A. Pai Foundation v. State of Karnataka* (2002), the Court ruled, 'the government can provide regulations that will ensure excellence while forbidding capitation fees … there can be however, be reasonable revenue surplus which may be generated'. It was further clarified in another judgement in 2003 (*Islamic Academy of Education v. State of Karnataka*) fee should correspond to cost, surplus to be used for investment, and no profiteering be allowed.
16. Inputs and outputs are not only well-defined, but there are many combinations of inputs to produce output as the concept of quality remains vague and arbitrary.
17. In the absence of a well-defined production function between the inputs and output and substitutability among the inputs, if the objective is to make profit or reasonable surplus, there will be a tendency to cut costs, which can adversely affect quality and fleece students, as they do not have the option to exit. For education, quality requires better quality inputs, i.e., infrastructure and faculty.
18. It is often argued whether all the three objectives can be pursued together or there exists a trade-off among them. Privatisation of any kind will compromise with inclusiveness. There is a big question mark whether excellence in education can be achieved through increasing private participation.
19. The National Knowledge Commission (NKC) also advocated for a regulatory authority (Independent Regulatory Authority for Higher Education or IRAHE). The rationale given by the Yash Pal Committee Report in favour of NCHER is somewhat different.
20. This leads to failure of students in anticipating the quality of education, and in the process they often get duped being forced to succumb to arbitrary hiking of fees and other unscrupulous measures leading to a fall in the quality of education (Chattopadhyay 2009).
21. The extent of funding, both from the government as well as private sources, may also depend on accreditation and ranking.

22. Not a single Indian university has been included in the top 100 universities across the world. In comparison, universities from China are doing particularly well in view of their late entry into the global high-ranking HEIs.
23. The IITs and the IIMs are not full-fledged universities, and therefore, in terms of the criteria for ranking, they fail to qualify. As noted by Simon Marginson (2010), India has only one institution in the top 100.

24. Generally it is argued that because of the principal-agent problem, the quality of service delivery in the government sector is poor, as self-interest dominates the conduct of the employees. The neoliberals advocate for a public choice approach to reform the governance structure.

REFERENCES

Agarwal, Pawan. 2009. *Indian Higher Education: Envisioning the Future*. New Delhi: Sage Publications.

Altbach, Philip G. 2009. 'The Giants Awake: The Present and Future of Higher Education System in China and India', in *Higher Education to 2030, Vol. 2, Globalisation*, pp. 179–203. Centre for Educational Research and Innovation: Organisation for Economic Co-operation and Development (OECD).

Bhushan, Sudhanshu. 2010. *Public Financing and Deregulated Fees in Indian Higher Education*. New Delhi: Bookwell.

Chattopadhyay, S. 2007. 'Exploring Alternative Sources of Financing Higher Education in India', *Economic and Political Weekly*, 20 October: 4251–59.

————. 2009. 'The Market in Higher Education: Concern for Equity and Quality', *Economic and Political Weekly*, 18 July: 53–61.

————. 2012. *Education and Economics: Disciplinary Evolution and Disciplinary Discourse*. New Delhi: Oxford University Press.

Faust, Drew Gilpin. 2009. 'The University's Crisis of Purpose', *The New York Times*, 1 September. http://www.nytimes.com/2009/09/06/books/review/Faust-t.html?pagewanted=all&_r=0 (accessed 19 November 2012).

Glennerster, Howard. 1991. 'Quasi-markets for Education?', *Economic Journal*, September, 101(408): 1268–76.

Jayaram, N. 2006. 'India', in James J. F. Forest and Phillip G. Altbach (eds), *International Handbook of Higher Education, Part Two: Regions and Countries*, pp. 747–67. Dordrecht: Springer.

Jongbloed, Ben. 2004. 'Regulation and Competition in Higher Education', in Pedro Teixeira, Ben Jongbloed, David Dill and Alberto Amaral (eds), *Markets in Higher Education: Rhetoric or Reality?*, pp. 87–111. Dordrecht: Kluwer Academic Publishers.

————. 2007. 'Creating Public-Private Dynamics in Higher Education Funding: A Discussion of Three Options', in J. Enders and B. Jongbloed (eds), *Public-Private Dynamics in Higher Education: Expectations, Developments and Outcomes*, pp. 113–38. New Brunswick, US: Transcript, Transaction Publishers.

Majumdar, Tapas. 1983. *Investments in Education and Social Choice*. Cambridge: Cambridge University Press.

Marginson, Simon. 1997. 'Subjects and Subjugation: The Economics of Education as Power-Knowledge', *Discourse: Studies in the Cultural Politics of Education*, August, 18(2): 215–27. (Reprinted in James Marshall and Michael Peters [eds]. 1999. *Education Policy, An Elgar Reference Collection*. Cheltenham: Edward Elgar Publishing Limited.)

————. 2007. 'Five Somersaults in Enschede: Rethinking Public/Private in Higher Education for the Global Era', in J. Enders and B. Jongbloed (eds), *Public-Private Dynamics in Higher Education: Expectations, Developments and Outcomes*, pp. 187–219. New Brunswick: Transcript, Transaction Publishers.

————. 2010. 'The Asia–Pacific Region of Higher Education: National Funding and Global Influence'. Paper presented at '*Universitas* 21 Symposium', University of Delhi, 29 April, New Delhi.

Massy, William F. 2004. 'Markets in Higher Education: Do they Promote Internal Efficiency?', in Pedro Texeira, Ben Jongbloed, David Dill, and Alberto Amarel (eds), *Markets in Higher Education: Rhetoric and Reality?*, pp. 13–35. Dordrecht: Kluwer Academic Publishers.

National Association of Software and Service Companies (NASSCOM)–McKinsey Report. 2005. 'Extending India's Leadership of the Global IT and BPO Industries'. http://www.mckinsey.com/locations/india/mckinseyonindia/pdf/nasscom_mckinsey_report_2005.pdf (accessed 19 November 2012).

Pathak, Avijit. 2009. *Recalling the Forgotten: Education and Moral Quest*. New Delhi: Aakar Books.

Patnaik, Prabhat. 2007. 'Alternative Perspectives on Higher Education', *Social Scientist*, November–December, 35(11–12): 3–14.

Pedro Teixeira, Ben Jongbloed, David Dill, and Alberto Amaral (eds). 2004. *Markets in Higher Education: Rhetoric or Reality?* Dordrecht: Kluwer Academic Publishers.

Plato. 1999. 'The Apology', Section 38(a) (trans. John Smith). New York: Classic Books. http://classics.mit.edu/Plato/apology.html (accessed 24 December 2011).

Prakash, Ved (ed.) 2011. *University and Society: Issues and Challenges*. New Delhi: University Grants Commission.

Samuelson, Paul. 1954. 'The Pure Theory of Public Expenditure', *Review of Economics and Statistics*, 36(4): 387–89.

Thomas, Shibu. 2012. 'Future of 81 Students at Stake as Ex-couple Spars'. *The Times of India*, Mumbai, 6 November. http://articles.timesofindia.indiatimes.com/2012-11-06/mumbai/34947152_1_high-court-vaishali-city-students (accessed 19 November 2012).

Tilak, Jandhyala B. G. 2008. 'Transition from Higher Education as a Public Good to Higher Education as a Private Good: The Saga of Indian Experience', *Journal of Asian Public Policy*, July, 1(2): 220–34.

Vaidyanathan, A. 2007. 'Private Sector in Education: Trends, Causes and Consequences'. C. D. Deshmukh Memorial Lecture delivered at Council for Social Development, Hyderabad.

Winston, Gordon C. 1999. 'Subsidies, Hierarchy and Peers: The Awkward Economics of Higher Education', *The Journal of Economic Perspectives*, 13(1): 13–36.

15 | Quality, Accreditation and Global University Ranking

Issues before Indian Higher Education

Emon Nandi and *Saumen Chattopadhyay*

Since the last couple of years, there has been much hue and cry about quality in Indian higher education. Not only the students and the academicians but also media, politicians and the policy-makers have all expressed concern about the poor quality of education in higher education sector. The bills which are being considered by the government, almost all of them, talk about quality directly or indirectly.[1] The approach paper to the 12th Five-Year Plan clearly argues that the focus should not only be on increased enrolment in higher education, but also on the improved quality of the expansion in higher education (Planning Commission 2011). Poor quality, arguably, is often exemplified by the fact that no Indian university figures in the top-100 list of popular global university rankings.[2] Even in the national context, according to the National Accreditation and Assessment Council (NAAC), 90 per cent Indian universities and 70 per cent colleges are of mediocre or poor quality (Agarwal 2009). Various studies have also indicated low degree of employability of Indian graduates, which is a matter of serious concern both for the planners as well as the industry.[3] In this situation, improvement in quality is an imperative and quality assurance is the first step in this direction.

Rankings and accreditation are two different forms of quality assurance or measurement. They provide information to students, employers, policy-makers, educationalists, and concerned individuals, as information asymmetry poses hindrance in assessing quality. National accreditation agencies such as the NAAC and the National Board of Accreditation (NBA) play an important role in monitoring quality in the Indian higher education sector, but this system presently suffers from various problems. Such issues are sought to be addressed in the pending National Accreditation Regulatory Authority for Higher Educational Institutions Bill, 2010 (GoI 2010). University ranking is also gaining importance. Universities are ranked on the basis of comparable performance indicators and the league tables point to a university's relative position vis-à-vis others. Thus, the measures of quality — accreditation and ranking — are also critical for developing a global market for higher education.

This paper seeks to understand the mechanism of accreditation and ranking done by specific parameters and distribution of their weights, and analyse the scope, significance and limitations of this system. In the face of ongoing reform in the Indian higher education sector and increasing participation of the private sector, this chapter examines the role and scope of national quality assurance agencies in the emerging global context.

THE CONCEPT OF QUALITY IN EDUCATION

Assessing the quality of education is an extremely difficult and delicate exercise. Education is a service that is not a one-shot affair. Delivery of education is a process and lasts over a period of time. In terms of learning, education is a continuous process. Primarily, the level of motivation of the teachers along with the infrastructure, governance of the institutions and course curriculum determine the quality. Before embarking on policy issues, it is important to know how difficult it is to assess quality and what makes education different. By definition, quality should be the intrinsic feature of any education system. If education is the assimilation of gathered knowledge, then one has to think whether education devoid of quality can be called education at all (Kumar 2010). In case of goods and services, the general definitions of quality (Garvin 1988), as mentioned in NAAC reports (Mishra 2006), can be listed as follows:

(a) Product-based definition (objective and measurable).
(b) User-based definition (customer satisfaction oriented).
(c) Manufacturing-based definition (subject to fixed input requirements and specifications).
(d) Value-based definitions (in relation to cost).
(e) Transcendent definition (subjective, personal and beyond measurement).

In the case of education, the first four types of definitions cannot be applied at all. This is obvious, since education is not a 'product' that can be explained with a production function and fixed input–output relationship (Majumdar 1983; Winch 2010). In a market of commodities, consumers can buy any good if they can afford it, but in the education sector, its customers — i.e., students — cannot join any course or university even if they can afford the tuition fees unless they satisfy the merit-based selection process. Customer-based definition of quality is also problematic in this case as students' satisfaction cannot shape the features of the higher education sector in a nation. For example, an institute may have a lenient grading system and students may be very happy with their high grades, but this practice should not be continued as it might lower the overall quality of higher education in the country. In a market of commodities, customers can very easily switch from one good to another if they are not satisfied with the quality, but in the education sector a student can spend his or her whole life to understand whether the education received in the university was worthwhile. Therefore, the only definition of quality that can be applied in the case of education is the transcendent definition which considers quality as an attribute that cannot be strictly measured but largely perceived.

Krishna Kumar and Padma M. Sarangapani (Kumar 2010; Kumar and Sarangapani 2004; Sarangapani 2010) have made an attempt to deconstruct the notion of quality and identify the possible contributory factors with reference to school education. Imparting good quality education depends on several aspects including the teachers' sense of commitment, compassion and care. These attributes are not necessarily measurable and the focus on 'performativity'[4] would fail to do justice to the delivery of quality education. During the evolution of ideas of 'total quality management' theories by W. Edwards Deming (1986), 'quality control' and 'assurance' became common terms in an attempt to ensure maximum efficiency and standards in manufactured goods. In the same line, from 1960 onwards, these terms started becoming familiar in the field of education as well. Over time, quality assurance gained importance because assessment of quality was considered the first step for chalking out designs for future improvement. There lies an urgent need to monitor the performance of higher educational institutes as many of

them are engaged in subversion of norms and duties. The risk with the transcendent definition is that it gives scope to do away with the accountability as there is no perfect standard of quality. In case of education, the problem is serious because unfair practices and poor quality in many educational institutions have the potential to not only ruin the career prospects of the students, but also adversely affect the families and the societies and dent productivity and competitiveness of a nation. In view of this, many countries have adopted external quality assurance mechanisms in higher education.

CONCEPTUALISING QUALITY ASSURANCE, ACCREDITATION AND RANKING

To avoid internal biases and stakeholders' influences, generally an external agency, which is supposed to be independent and credible, is entrusted with the responsibility of assessing the quality of an educational institute. The term 'External Quality Assurance' refers to all forms of external quality monitoring, evaluation or review and may be defined as a process of establishing stakeholder confidence that the provision (input, processes and outcomes) fulfils expectations or measures up to the minimum requirements (Martin and Stella 2007). Accreditation and ranking are different forms of quality assurance mechanisms that are expected to enable a higher education system to maintain its quality. Ranking, done by independent agencies, particularly helps in realising the position of an institution according to its performance in comparison to others, whereas accreditation assigns a particular grade to an institution if it qualifies for it. The main difference is that rankings *rank* a Higher Education Institution (HEI) with respect to others but accreditation agencies *rate* HEIs independent of others. The following section gives the three main purposes they claim to serve.

Providing 'Information' about Quality to Stakeholders

The important role of quality assurance agencies as the provider of information about quality of education has immense significance since the market for higher education is often characterised as one with information asymmetry and imperfect information (Arrow 1973). This is because of the following reasons:

(a) First, education is an 'experience good' and none, except the student, can judge the quality of education provided in a university.[5]
(b) Second, the producers, or the authorities of universities may have an idea about the quality of education provided in their institutions, but not all of them would be interested in making the information public.

(c) Third, unlike in a market for normal goods, price here fails to reveal information about quality since the provision of education is largely subsidised.⁶ As the price of education is not market-determined, quality fails to be captured through price.

It is in this context that quality assurance agencies play the key role of assessing the quality of an educational institution and making it accessible to the students, employers and the authorities.

Fostering Competition among HEIs

Another important objective that the global ranking mechanism ends up achieving is fostering competition among the universities across the nations for attracting the best minds, thereby ensuring quality. Students being rational consumers will choose the best possible institutions for themselves given their budget constraint, and only the best universities will draw good students. Not-so-good universities will try their level-best to achieve the 'best' stamp, and those who ultimately fail to perform well will automatically go out of business. Thus, in a competitive environment every university will try to improve their quality for their own benefit, which ultimately leads to an enhancement of the overall higher education sector.

Helping HEIs to Take Steps to Improve Quality

Before embarking on a path of improvement in quality, an institution must know where it stands and what its strengths and weaknesses are. Only when the problems are identified can a solution be found. Although an institution can undertake a self-assessment procedure to judge its functioning, an unbiased and well-informed external agency can serve the role of a 'mirror' to an institution (Goel and Goel 2010). Along with self-assessment, an external quality agency can help in undertaking a Strengths, Weaknesses, Opportunities, and Threats (SWOT) analysis of an institution and rate it on a pre-defined scale.

ACCREDITATION AND QUALITY ASSESSMENT: THE INDIAN CONTEXT

In India, there is a wide variety in terms of quality across higher educational institutes. On the one hand, there are 'Centres of Excellence' such as Indian Institutes of Technology (IITs), and on the other are the institutes that have failed to maintain even a minimum standard of quality. Not only is there a wide gap between the world and Indian averages of quality, but there also exists a vast disparity between the institutions across India. The reasons for this low quality are multifaceted and interlinked — poor governance being the main reason. Resource constraints and poor infrastructure further worsen the situation. Many private institutes, especially in the field of professional education, provide low-quality education as they are mostly interested in cutting cost and making profits (Chattopadhyay 2009). A corrupt and ineffective regulatory system aggravates the problem as many educational institutes are engaged in subversion of duties and in maximising the benefits that accrue to the authorities without any effort to improve the quality of education. Also, there has been an age-long trade-off between excellence and inclusion (Velaskar 2010). Since the quality of education largely depends on that of the students and teachers, an institution may choose to be extremely selective and only offer seats to brainy people in order to maintain its quality. This selective competition may make HEIs more hierarchical and exclusive (Clotfelter 1996; Winston 1999). While we consider the fact that in India only 15 per cent in the age group of 18–23 years enter into a college, 'excellence' appears to be an 'elite' term. However, maintaining a minimum quality in all the HEIs is imperative. The problem is to appropriately define and quantify for effective monitoring and enforcement of minimum quality of education. This is critical because unfair practices and poor quality of education can ruin the entire life of students and affect their families, societies and the nation. Keeping this problem in mind, quality assurance mechanisms in higher education were adopted in India and at present the popular agencies are:

(a) National Assessment and Accreditation Council (NAAC) under the University Grants Commission (UGC);

(b) National Board of Accreditation (NBA) under the All India Council of Technical Education (AICTE);

(c) Accreditation Board under the Indian Council of Agricultural Research (ICAR).

Among these, the two most popular accreditation agencies are the NAAC and the NBA.

National Assessment and Accreditation Council (NAAC)

The Council was established in 1994 under the UGC following the recommendations of the National Policy on Education (1986). The NAAC generally deals with universities recognised by the UGC and its affiliated colleges and autonomous institutes that have a minimum experience of functioning. For accreditation and assessment, the NAAC follows a two-step process in which HEIs first have to get Institutional Eligibility for Quality Assessment (IEQA) status and then send a filled-up format to the council. Institutions that have already gained IEQA status can directly send a letter of intent to the NAAC. After receiving a self-study report from the HEIs, a team of NAAC members and experts visit them and a final decision is taken by the NAAC executive members. Based on indicators and assigned measures, a cumulative grade point average (CGPA) is calculated for the institution and the implication of the grades are as follows:

TABLE 15.1   NAAC Grades, CGPA and Performance Descriptor

Range of Institutional Cumulative Grade Point Average (CGPA)	Letter Grade	Performance Descriptor
3.01–4.00	A	Very Good (Accredited)
2.01–3.00	B	Good (Accredited)
1.51–2.00	C	Satisfactory (Accredited)

Source: NAAC (2007: 20).

According to the NAAC, the major role of an HEI is to promote the values inherent in education. These core values as specified for the Indian higher education system are:
(a) contributing to national development,
(b) fostering global competence among students,
(c) inculcating a value system among students,
(d) promoting use of technology, and
(e) quest for excellence. Table 15.2 gives the criteria, indicators and weights specified by the NAAC.

Although the NAAC had started doing the accreditation and assessment in 1998, it was only after 2002–03 that it gained momentum, and by October 2006 it had accredited 129 universities and 2,956 colleges (only 13 per cent of higher educational institutes). This was mainly because of the voluntary accreditation process that was recently made compulsory in India.[7] Among the HEIs accredited by the NAAC, most are public- or government-run, and mainly public universities and public colleges. Private universities and private colleges perhaps showed less interest in getting accredited by the NAAC.

National Board of Accreditation

The NBA (under the AICTE) offers accreditation to all institutions or programmes that are approved by the AICTE, provided at least two batches have passed out of the programme or institution. Under the provisions of the AICTE Act of 1987, all diploma, degree and postgraduate programmes coming under certain disciplines (Engineering and Technology, Management, Architecture, Pharmacy, Hotel Management and Catering Technology, Town and Country Planning, Applied Arts and Crafts) are covered under accreditation by the NBA. Institutions interested in being accredited by the NBA need to fill up a form with necessary details about their

TABLE 15.2   NAAC — Criteria, Indicators and Weights

	Criteria	Indicators	Weights (in per cent)		
			University	Autonomous Colleges	Affiliated Colleges
1	Curricular Aspects	Curricular design and development, academic flexibility, feedback on curriculum, curriculum update, best practices in curricular aspects	15	10	5
2	Teaching, Learning and Evaluation	Admission process and student profile, catering to diverse needs, teaching–learning process, teacher quality, evaluation process and reforms, best practices in teaching, learning and evaluation	25	35	45
3	Research, Consultancy and Evaluation	Promotion of research, research and publication output, consultancy, extension activities, collaborations, best practices in research, consultancy and extension	20	15	10
4	Infrastructure and Learning Resources	Physical facilities, maintenance of infrastructure, library as a learning resource, ICT as learning resources, other facilities, best practices in the development of infrastructure and learning resources	10	10	10
5	Student Support and Progression	Student progression, student support, student activities, best practices in student support and progression	10	10	10
6	Governance and Leadership	Institutional vision and leadership, organisational arrangements, strategy development and deployment, human resource management, financial management and resource mobilisation, best practices in governance and leadership	15	15	15
7	Innovative Practices	Internal quality assurance system, inclusive practices, stakeholder relationships	5	5	5
	Total		100	100	100

Source: NAAC (2007).

institution or programmes. A team comprising the chairperson and programme experts is then constituted which visits the institution and verifies the facts. The team carries out physical authentication of infrastructure facilities, records, interviews faculty, staff, students, alumni, industry, and any other activity deemed necessary, and ensures transparency. The parameters on which accreditation is done and their respective weights are shown in Table 15.3. These eight criteria carry a sum total of 1,000 points, with a minimum of 600 points required to qualify for accreditation. The accreditation is 'yes' or 'no' type. Any institution scoring a sum total greater than 600 points but less than 750 gets a provisional accreditation valid only for two years. If the institution or the programme gets 750 or more and meets all qualifying criteria mentioned in the table, then it gets an accreditation for five years from NBA.

The NBA accreditation is voluntary for institutions, and in May 2009 only 3,274 out of 6,040 eligible undergraduate engineering programmes got accredited.

Issues of Concern for the Indian Accreditation System

Recently the UGC has made it compulsory for all institutes to go for NAAC accreditation and have at least a 'B' grade to get the benefit of additional funding. Such a move can be expected to generate a 'quality culture' among universities and colleges which would help in improving the quality of the sector. However, there are other concerns with the present accreditation system for HEIs in India:

(a) Lack of functional autonomy and co-ordination between different government regulatory bodies is a concern. Multiple entities, such as central and state governments, regulatory bodies, and government quality assuring agencies, are involved in accreditation of the HEIs.

(b) There is scope of subversion of norms and the objectivity of the peer-team report is not beyond doubts and questions (Stella 2002).

(c) Criteria of assessment are subjective and impressionistic.

Further, with rise in global competition for attracting international students, Indian HEIs will try to gain international recognition. There are some international agencies such as the International Network for Quality Assurance Agencies in Higher Education (INQAAHE) or the Washington Accord, which accredit many institutes across nations. If Indian quality assurance agencies join these international agencies or if Indian HEIs begin to be accredited by them, the institutions will get global reputation. But at the same time the applicability of uniform norms and standards across a diverse world is also questionable. In December 2005, the United Nations Educational, Scientific and Cultural Organization (UNESCO) and the Organisation for Economic Co-operation and Development (OECD) jointly issued non-binding guidelines on Quality Provision in Cross-Border Higher Education (OECD and UNESCO 2005). If Indian quality assurance agencies follow these, then the country may emerge as a favoured global knowledge destination for international students. But the accreditation agency must not neglect the local value judgements and needs of the specific society before evaluating performance of an HEI. Norms and standards should not be rigid but flexible, depending upon the need of the hour and that of the society. Further, India is at the threshold of opening the doors to foreign education providers if the Foreign Education Bill is approved. Since the concept of quality education can vary across countries, the implications of globalisation of higher education system can be contentious and debatable depending on the type of courses, reputation of the foreign providers, nature of collaboration with foreign institutes, etc. (Chattopadhyay 2012).

Some of the concerns with quality assurance mechanism in Indian higher education have been addressed in The National Accreditation Regulatory Authority for Higher Educational Institutions Bill, 2010.

TABLE 15.3   Parameters and Weights used by NBA

Parameters	Weights for Undergraduate College (per cent)	Weights for Diploma (per cent)
Organisation and Governance	8	3
Financial Resources, Allocation and Utilisation	7	7
Physical Resources	5	5
Human Resources including Faculty and Staff	20	20
Human Resource of Students	10	10
Teaching–Learning Process	35	45
Supplementary Processes	5	5
Research, Development and International Efforts	10	5

Source: www.nba-aicte.ernet.in/parameter.doc (accessed 18 March 2012).

The National Accreditation Regulatory Authority for Higher Educational Institutions Bill, 2010

The National Accreditation Regulatory Authority for Higher Educational Institutions Bill, 2010 seeks to

make provisions for assessment of academic quality of higher educational institutions, programmes conducted therein and their infrastructure through mandatory accreditation by independent accreditation agencies and to establish a statutory Authority for the said purpose (GoI 2010: 1).

The Bill mentions that the purview of academic quality includes

teaching, learning and research and their contribution to enhancement of knowledge. The assessment would include physical infrastructure, human resources (including faculty), administration, course curricula, admission and assessment procedures, governance structures including infrastructure and governance structures of the institution (ibid.: 20–21).

The salient features of the Bill include the following:
(a) Accreditation is mandatory for an HEI of more than 12 years of age.
(b) Independent quality assurance agencies (non-profit professional bodies) will certify quality assurance and the agencies would be regulated, audited and monitored by the National Accreditation Authority (NAA).
(c) Criteria will be determined by the UGC or its successor body. Such criteria will include teaching, learning, research, governance, administration, admission, course curricula, infrastructure (physical and human), placement.
(d) The NAA will also monitor a code of ethics, conflicts of interest, disclosure of information, and ensure transparency.
(e) The National Educational Tribunal would adjudicate disputes between HEIs and accreditation agencies. The accreditation agency shall be liable to pay compensation to an HEI in case of any wilful wrong accreditation.
(f) The Bill also argues that HEIs should help in student and teacher mobility across national and global institutions. Collaborations across the border will be encouraged and the national accreditation system should be a part of the global one.

The Bill allows independent private assurance agencies under the purview of the NAA to assess quality of HEIs in India. Independent registered accreditation agencies are supposed to carry out the task of quality assurance in a credible, fair and transparent manner. The Bill also proposes following the global system of quality assurance, and is expected to facilitate informed choice-making by the stakeholders,

particularly by students to foster mobility across the institutions, both within the national boundary as well as at the global level. In addition, teacher mobility and global level cooperations would be encouraged. However, in view of the rapid globalisation of higher education, ensuring conformity among quality assurance agencies across nations is a pre-requisite so that comparison among HEIs across nations is meaningful and globally accepted. The Bill thus also seeks to set the stage for making the Indian higher education system internationally acceptable and considered comparable to those in other countries.

GLOBAL UNIVERSITY RANKINGS

Over time, the ranking of global universities has become so popular all over the world that it has started influencing national policy-making in the case of education. In the case of India, experts, academicians and policy-makers have often expressed serious concern that no Indian university figures in the top list of these rankings. After preparing the draft Bill on quality assurance, discussed earlier, the need is felt to tune the national accreditation system so as to figure in the scheme of global ranking. The most popular global university rankings are Shanghai Jiao Tong University (SJTU) or Academic Ranking of World Universities (ARWU) ranking, Times Higher Education Supplement (THES) World University Ranking and QS World University Ranking.
(a) *SJTU or ARWU Ranking*: The SJTU or ARWU ranking is the most popular in the case of universities that are mainly engaged in research. In four broad categories — Quality of Education, Quality of Faculty, Research Output, and Per Capita Performance — several indicators are chosen and definite weights are assigned to each of them. The SJTU ranking is mainly considered as pertinent for a research university as it assigns 40 per cent weight to research output.
(b) *The THES Ranking*: The Times ranking of world universities assigns equal weights to teaching and research — 30 per cent each. Citations carry another 30 per cent while international outlook of a university and industry income have 7.5 per cent and 2.5 per cent weight respectively (*Times Higher Education* n.d.).
(c) *QS World University Ranking*: The QS World University Ranking currently considers over 2,000 universities and evaluates over 700 universities in the world, focusing on ranking for the top 400. This ranking is mainly reputation-based as academic reputation from global survey has 40 per cent weight and employer reputation 10 per cent. Half of the total points are thus based on the reputation of the universities and the rest are distributed among citations (20 per cent), faculty–student

ratio (20 per cent), and proportion of international students and staff (10 per cent). The comparative Table 15.4 illustrates the basis for popular ranking.

These ranking agencies do a good job in providing information about educational quality in worldwide HEIs. The parameters, weights and process of assessment are made public through their respective websites, which can be accessible to anyone easily. Rankings indeed give us some idea about the performance of the universities across the world. But this information needs to be used with great care and caution as the system has some inherent bias and preferences. Some of these issues are discussed in the next section.

Issues of Concern for Global University Rankings

(a) *Reputational Ranking*: Most of these rankings are based on popular perception of reputation. Thus, the survey tends to have an inherent bias for universities that have already gained academic reputation and have an influential position in the global market (Altbach 2006).

(b) *Teaching versus Research*: Not all the global university rankings provide a holistic assessment of a university. The ranking methods vary in terms of weights assigned as select parameters are given more importance as compared to others. Due to this, any ranking process would fail to capture the overall measure of quality which in turn may result in incomplete, misleading or bad decision-making by the stakeholders and those concerned (Marginson 2006). For example, the SJTU ranking is basically a research university ranking and a national university meant for teaching would not figure anywhere in this ranking.

(c) *Bias in Favour of Science Streams and English-Speaking Nations*: These rankings have an automatic bias in favour of researchers who write in English because most research work is published in that language (Marginson 2007a). Excessive emphasis on research in English may discourage research in native languages. Since English is the dominant language in the academic sphere, the citations that good quality researches get are unevenly spread across the world with a bias in favour of countries where English is the predominant medium of education. In social sciences there are different paradigms of research mainly due to ideological differences, which not only infuses favouritism in the selection of papers for publication in some of the reputed journals but also in the grant of awards like the Nobel Prize (Patnaik 2011).

(d) *International Outlook*: These rankings often assign a large weight to the proportion of international students and staff. But this proportion would depend on the vision, mission and goal of a university and may unduly penalise universities with a more social mission of being inclusive.

(e) *Threat of Losing Diversity in World Education System*: Rankings emphasise vertical differences between institutions and between nations, differences of power and authority and obscure horizontal differences, and those of purpose and type (Marginson 2006, 2007b). Every university in this world was established with a certain goal, mission, vision, and objective that are supposed to shape the nature of activities they are involved in. Rankings undermine these characteristics. As universities are not universal in nature — rather they are very much 'organic' — the quality of education they provide cannot be homogeneous and measurable through universal yardsticks (Patnaik 2007).

Although no Indian university (except for some such as the IITs and the Indian Institutes of Science) has so

TABLE 15.4 Basic Parameters and their Weights used in Global University Rankings (in per cent)

Times Ranking	QS Ranking	Shanghai Jiao Tong
Teaching: 30	Academic Reputation from Global Survey: 40	Alumni of an Institution Winning Nobel Prizes and Field Medals: 10
Research: 30	Employers' Reputation from Global Survey: 10	Staff of an Institution Winning Nobel Prizes and Field Medals: 2
Citation: 30	Citations per Faculty: 20	Highly-Cited Researchers in 21 Broad Subject Categories: 20
Industry Income: 2.5	Faculty–Student Ratio: 20	Papers published in Nature and Science: 20
International Outlook: 7.5	Proportion of International Students: 5	Papers Indexed in Science Citation Index-Expanded and Social Science Citation Index: 20
	Proportion of International Faculty: 5	Per Capita Academic Performance of an Institution: 10

Source: Compiled from ARWU (n.d.-a); *Times Higher Education* (n.d.).

TABLE 15.5 Academic Ranking of World Universities' Top 100 List: Selected Country- and Faculty-Wise Statistics

Country	Natural Sciences and Mathematics Top 100	Engineering/Technology and Computer Sciences Top 100	Life and Agricultural Sciences Top 100	Clinical Medicine and Pharmacy Top 100	Social Sciences Top 100	Total Top 500
United States (US)	52	46	57	54	71	280
United Kingdom (UK)	8	4	10	11	8	43
Canada	2	4	4	5	8	23
Germany	8	1	5	7	0	21
Japan	7	5	3	2	0	17
China	1	13	0	0	1	15
Australia	1	5	4	3	1	14
South Korea	1	2	0	0	0	3
Brazil	0	0	0	1	0	1
India	0	1	0	0	0	1

Source: Compiled from ARWU (n.d.-b).

far figured at the top of the lists of university rankings, yet the significance and impact of these rankings cannot be neglected in the globalised era. The draft bill on the national accreditation regulatory mechanism, as discussed previously, also mentions following the global practice of quality assurance. In this context, it is important to examine the ranking system more carefully and to be aware of its strengths, weaknesses and threats before addressing the reforms measures in the Indian quality assurance system.

QUALITY ASSURANCE AND GOVERNANCE REFORM: IMPLICATIONS FOR NATIONAL POLICY-MAKING

In an increasingly globalised world, institutions now cater to diverse clientele and so greater diversity in the institutions is appreciated. At the same time, as generation and dissemination of knowledge have assumed greater importance in facilitating growth and overcoming spatial inequalities, the expectations from higher education institutions have also gone up. As the global higher education market is evolving, there is a tendency towards vertical stratification rather than a horizontal one (Wende 2008), as the high ranking institutions get differentiated from the low ranking ones in the ranking list, which is inimical to equalise access to good quality education and accrual of equal benefits arising out of education to the society as a whole. This is undesirable from the public good character of education. Both accreditation and ranking follow a pre-determined set of criteria. There would always be a tendency for the HEIs to satisfy these pre-determined requirements for the purpose of being awarded high ranking. In the process, there remains the possibility of compromising with autonomy and dilution of the mission of the HEIs.

In this context, the linkage between quality management and the reform in governance in HEIs should be analysed more carefully. In view of globalisation of higher education, the international comparative measures of performance have become a global aspect of corporate type governance (New Public Management). It is necessary for embracing the global economy and participation in global market for higher education and research. The new governance emphasises on performance, reconceptualises education policy in economic terms, and production of human capital as necessary for global competitiveness. These numbers are new forms of assessing mutual accountability. The performative policy is closely aligned to 'audit culture' with emphasis on efficiency and effectiveness (value for money). This cultural shift in evaluative practices is also a reflection of the tilting of balance in favour of the market and away from the state (Rizvi and Lingard 2010). Promotion of corporate type governance and audit culture in education will see an institution as a corporate entity, a student as a customer and a teacher as a worker, which can be harmful in case of an educational institute, unless regulated, as it generates externalities for the society.

It cannot be denied that assessment of quality is extremely important for designing the future trajectory of improvement for any HEI. Quality assurance can play a very important role in pointing out the strengths and weaknesses of any institution. It is an important step towards achieving an improved higher education sector. It raises awareness, popularises quality concerns and helps in developing an internal quality assessment mechanism. However, a single frame of reference may interfere with the autonomy of the institutions. While it helps to compare across the HEIs, diversity and autonomy need to be promoted. Also a quality assurance agency should understand the basic reasons for poor quality in HEIs and unless it does so, meagre statistics or numbers would not help in improving quality in education.[8] The root of the problems in private and government-funded institutions is commercialisation and poor governance respectively (Chattopadhyay 2010). While the problems need to be tackled differently, a single standardised solution may not ensure improvement in quality across HEIs (Altbach and Chitnis 1993).

Any quality assurance mechanism should not ignore the fact that education generates externalities. The true quality of education should be assessed by its ability to foster citizenship and social cohesiveness, and inculcate moral and ethical values. But this very aspect of quality education goes beyond the contour of the course curriculum and the actual teaching–learning process that takes place inside the classroom. The quality of a university depends on that of the students and faculty. It has been observed in the US that in order to rank higher up the ladder, the universities compromised with the student selection policy and preferred merit-based aid over need-based. Accreditation and ranking is critical for ensuring quality, but overemphasising on quality may compromise the broader mission of the university. Further, higher education transforms an individual into a responsible human being with social, moral and ethical values embedded in him or her (Patnaik 2007) apart from making them more productive (Schultz 1961). Thus, the assurance and accreditation mechanism should acknowledge the transformative role of education in a broader sense and facilitate in widening the horizons of Indian higher education system. The discussion in the chapter can be summarised as follows:

(a) Quality assurance agencies should understand that quality in education is different from that of other goods and services and is an intrinsic feature of education, without which, it has no meaning at all.

(b) Despite adopting some rigid and strict universal parameters to assess quality, it may be noted that the assurance system measures quality in a holistic manner because some crucial determinants of quality education like teachers' motivation cannot be measured and hence get ignored in the process.

(c) Quality assurance agencies should not treat quality as a homogeneous substance across nations, as it is also associated with societal and cultural value systems. They should maintain diversity in global education systems.

(d) In the name of improving 'efficiency' in HEIs, the quality assurance system should be cautious while advocating corporate-type management in education so as not to undermine the transformative role of higher education.

(e) An effective quality assurance mechanism should understand the varied reasons of poor quality, judge the performance of an HEI in accordance with the objectives, missions, visions, and goals with which it was established.

Concluding Remarks

Accreditation and ranking help in assuring quality of an education system and they serve two main purposes. In view of the fact that when students make informed choices about courses and institutions they suffer from what the economists would like to describe as 'information asymmetry' — with education being in the nature of an 'experience good', it is difficult for the students to assess quality fully before they take admission — what accreditation does is to assure the clients that quality of education being imparted by an institution conforms to the well-defined standards set by the regulatory authority. Ranking also provides information about the performance of HEIs within a competitive set up. Further, the quality assurance mechanism helps the students choose courses and institutions on the basis of grades or ranks they have obtained. Since education is an 'experience good' and its true quality can only be meaningfully assessed over time, the students use the accreditation to gather requisite information for making informed choices about the courses and the institutions. From the perspective of the institutions, in the absence of any measurement of output, it is important that the higher education institutions are intimated how they fare and help them in identifying gaps in their delivery mechanism. It encourages the HEIs to put in an extra effort and improve their ranking. On the down side, the output-centric quality assurance mechanism based on certain criteria may compromise a broader mission of the institution. It, therefore, has the potential to interfere with the specific objectives of the higher education institutions for which they were set up. However, as Richard Lewis (2009) argues, the trend is towards greater intervention by the government towards maintenance of quality with a move towards the inspectorate model. The government has to reconcile its pursuit for enhancement of quality with 'massification' of the higher education system in India. Since good-quality education depends on good-quality inputs in the form of students and teachers, it will take years for a newly-set up IIT and Indian Institute of Management (IIM) to reproduce the quality that IITs and IIMs stand for.

However, from a methodological point of view, both national accreditation agencies and global university rankings have been subject to some valid criticisms. Assessing the quality of a university based on some predetermined indicators would never be an easy job given the multiple products a university produces, which are often not measurable. Quality assurance, in case of higher education, will only be meaningful if it understands that education is very different from other marketable products, as it does not have a production function, fixed input–output relationship and quantifiable characteristics. It should recognise that education imparts value to the society (Tilak 2004) and

therefore quality assurance should appropriately reflect the same. Since quality is not homogeneous across institutions and nations, the mechanism should consider the different societal contexts and the diverse missions, visions, goals, and objectives of different universities in assessing the quality of education.

Notes

1. Some of the recent Bills are the National Commission of Higher Education and Research Bill, 2010 (NCHER); the Foreign Educational Institutions (Regulation of Entry and Operations, Maintenance of Quality and Prevention of Commercialisation) Bill, 2010; the Unfair Practices in Technical, Medical Educational Institutions and Universities Bill, 2010; and the National Accreditation Regulatory Authority for Higher Educational Institutions Bill, 2010.
2. Performance of Indian universities is really poor in rankings done by Shanghai Jiao Tong University, Times Higher Education Supplement and the QS group (ARWU n.d.-a; *Times Higher Education* n.d.).
3. According to the widely quoted report by the National Association of Software and Services Companies (NASSCOM) and McKinsey in 2005, only 25 per cent of the engineering education graduates are employable by a multinational company (NASSCOM 2005: 16).
4. The practice of measuring teachers' 'performativity' in terms of a points-system has been adopted in our country also. The system assigns points to teachers based on the number of hours spent in the classroom, the number of research papers published, the number of doctoral candidates trained under him/her, etc. Though it claims to help in avoiding the arbitrariness associated with teachers' performance, it actually fails in assessing 'quality'

as none of the indicators can indicate the true 'quality' of teaching or research.
5. Even the students may not assess the true quality as benchmarking would be difficult in view of lack of exposure of curriculum and pedagogy of other reputed quality institutions.
6. In the private sector, to an extent, the cost of education imposed on the students may reflect the cost of its provision but not quality of education, truly speaking. Quality is co-produced in the classroom as the students are also required to put in effort with a high level of motivation to help produce and experience quality education.
7. Until recently, the NAAC accreditation process was voluntary for HEIs in India. A college or university had to first apply for accreditation, and then subject to some basic qualifying criteria the NAAC would initiate its accreditation process.
8. For example, suppose Institution A and Institution B, both do not have a library and lose points on this ground. Now, if Institution A is run by the government and Institution B by a private institution, the causes of not having a library will be different. For A, it might be the resource constraints faced by the government, while for B, it might be the profit motive that has led them to cut costs in this head and increase profits. On the basis of this analysis, suggestions have to be made by the agency and consequently, the regulatory mechanism has to be re-designed.

References

Academic Ranking of World Universities (ARWU). n.d.-a. http://www.arwu.org/ (accessed 17 November 2012).
————. n.d.-b. 'Statistics by Country'. http://www.shanghai-ranking.com/ARWU-FIELD-Statistics-2011.html#3 (accessed 18 March 2012).
Agarwal, Pawan. 2009. *Indian Higher Education: Envisioning the Future.* New Delhi: Sage Publications.
Altbach, Phillip G. 2006. 'The Dilemmas of Ranking', *International Higher Education*, 42(2–3): 2–3.
Altbach, Phillip G. and Suma Chitnis. 1993. 'The Dilemma of Change in Indian Higher Education', in *Higher Education: Perspectives on Higher Education in India*, 26(1): 3–20.
Arrow, K. J. 1973. 'Higher Education as a Filter', *Journal of Public Economics*, 2(3): 193–216.
Chattopadhyay, Saumen. 2009. 'The Market in Higher Education: Concern for Equity and Quality', *Economic and Political Weekly*, 44(29): 53–61.

————. 2010. 'An Elitist and Flawed Approach towards Higher Education', *Economic and Political Weekly*, 45(18): 15–17.
————. 2012. *Education and Economics: Disciplinary Evolution and Policy Discourse*. New Delhi: Oxford University Press.
Clotfelter, Charles T. 1996. *Buying the Best: Cost Evaluation in Elite Higher Education*. Princeton: Princeton University Press.
Deming, W. Edwards. 1986, *Out of the Crisis*. Cambridge, MA: MIT Centre for Advanced Engineering Study.
Goel, Aruna and S. L. Goel. 2010. *Quality and Excellence in Higher Education*. New Delhi: Deep and Deep Publications Pvt. Ltd.
Government of India (GoI). 2010. 'The National Accreditation Regulatory Authority for Higher Educational Institutions Bill, 2010'. Bill No 54/2010. http://www.prsindia.org/uploads/media/National%20Accreditation%20Regulatory%20Authority/National%20Accreditation%20Regulatory%20Authority%20for%20Higher%20Educational%20Institutions%20Bill%20%202010.pdf (accessed 18 March 2012).

Kumar, Krishna. 2010. 'Quality in Education: Competing Concepts', *Contemporary Education Dialogue*, 7(1): 7–18.

Kumar, Krishna and Padma M. Sarangapani. 2004. 'History of the Quality Debate', *Contemporary Education Dialogue*, 2(1): 30–52.

Lewis, Richard. 2009. 'Quality Assurance in Higher Education — Its Global Future', *Higher Education to 2030: Globalisation*, vol. 2. Centre for Educational Research and Innovation: Organisation for Economic Co-operation and Development.

Marginson, Simon. 2006. 'Global University Rankings at the End of 2006: Is This the Hierarchy we have to have?' Paper presented at a workshop 'Institutional Diversity: Rankings and Typologies in Higher Education', organised by OECD/IMHE & Hochschulrektorkonferenz, Bonn.

—————. 2007a. 'Dynamics of National and Global Competition in Higher Education', *Higher Education*, 52(1): 1–39.

—————. 2007b. 'Global University Rankings: Where to from Here?'. Paper presented at 'Ranking Systems: University of Choice', organised by Asia–Pacific Association for International Education, National University of Singapore, 7–9 March.

Martin, Michaela and Antony Stella. 2007, *External Quality Assurance in Higher Education: Making Choices*. Paris: United Nations Educational, Scientific and Cultural Organization and International Institute of Educational Planning.

Mishra, Sanjaya. 2006. *Quality Assurance in Higher Education: An Introduction*. Bangalore: National Assessment and Accreditation Council, and Canada: Commonwealth of Learning.

National Assessment and Accreditation Council (NAAC). n.d. http://www.naac.gov.in/ (accessed 18 March 2012).

—————. 2007. 'Frequently Asked Questions (FAQs) on Assessment and Accreditation (2007)'. National Assessment and Accreditation Council, Government of India.

National Association of Software and Service Companies (NASSCOM), 2005. *Extending India's Leadership of the Global IT and BPO Industries: NASSCOM-McKinsey Report 2005*. New Delhi: National Association of Software and Service Companies and McKinsey & Company Inc. http://www.mckinsey.com/locations/india/mckinseyonindia/pdf/nasscom_mckinsey_report_2005.pdf (accessed 19 November 2012).

Organisation for Economic Co-operation and Development (OECD) and United Nations Educational, Scientific and Cultural Organization (UNESCO). 2005. *Quality Provision in Cross-Border Higher Education*. Paris: Organisation for Economic Co-operation and Development and United Nations Educational, Scientific and Cultural Organization.

Patnaik, Prabhat. 2007. 'Alternative Perspectives on Higher Education in the Context of Globalization'. Lecture delivered at National University of Education Planning and Administration (NUEPA) Foundation Day, 11 August.

—————. 2011. 'Their Rankings and Ours — Academic Quality is not a Uniform Substance'. *Telegraph*, 2 November.

Planning Commission. 2011. *Faster, Sustainable and More Inclusive Growth: An Approach to the Twelfth Five Year Plan*. New Delhi: Planning Commission, Government of India.

Rizvi, Fazal and Bob Lingard. 2010. *Globalizing Education Policy*. New York: Routledge.

Sarangapani, Padma M. 2010. 'Quality Concerns: National and Extra-National Dimensions', *Contemporary Education Dialogue*, 7(1): 41–57.

Schultz, Theodore W. 1961. 'Investment in Human Capital', *American Economic Review*, March, 51(1): 1–17.

Stella, Anthony. 2002. *External Quality Assurance in Indian Higher Education: Case Study of the National Assessment and Accreditation Council (NAAC)*. Paris: International Institute for Educational Planning.

Tilak, J. B. G. 2004. 'Absence of Policy and Perspective in Higher Education', *Economic and Political Weekly*, 39(21): 2159–64.

Times Higher Education. n.d. 'Top 400 Universities'. http://www.timeshighereducation.co.uk/world-university-rankings/ (accessed 17 November 2012)

Velaskar, Padma. 2010. 'Quality and Inequality in Indian Education: Some Critical Policy Concerns', *Contemporary Education Dialogue*, 7(1): 58–93.

Wende, Marjik van der. 2008. 'Rankings and Classifications in Higher Education: A European Perspective', in John C. Smart (ed.), *Higher Education: Handbook of Theory and Research*, vol. 23. London: Springer.

Winch, Christopher. 2010. 'Search for Educational Quality: The Dialectic of Inputs and Outputs', *Contemporary Education Dialogue*, 7(1): 19–40.

Winston, Gordon C. 1999. 'Subsidies, Hierarchy and Peers: The Awkward Economics of Higher Education', *Journal of Economic Perspectives*, 13(1): 13–36.

16 | Private Sector's Role in Indian Higher Education

Anand Sudarshan and *Sandhya Subramanian*

'Our progress as a nation can be no swifter than our progress in education. The human mind is our fundamental resource'.[1]
– John. F. Kennedy

For the first 50 years since India became a republic, its education sector has been traditionally built on the core principle that it is the State's responsibility to educate its citizens. Towards this purpose, a significant aspect of policy-focus over the last two decades has been on capacity creation. Government has continued to invest in creating new capacities as well as enhancing them in existing institutions. Progress has been made — India has certainly come a long way from 28 universities and 578 colleges in 1950–51 to over 500 universities and more than 25,000 colleges at present. Today, the country has the largest number of higher education institutions in the world and close to 20 million students enrolled.

The present approach towards higher education is governed by the National Policy on Education (NPE) of 1986 and Programme of Action of 1992. Two landmark reports, Radhakrishnan Commission Report (1948–49) and Kothari Commission Report (1964–66), in fact laid down the basic framework for the National Policy on Higher Education in the country. The NPE document acknowledges the fact that 'higher education has to become dynamic as never before' and to this effect outlines a series of steps including encouraging autonomy, specialisation, vocationalisation, emphasis on research and development.

CHALLENGES BEFORE INDIAN HIGHER EDUCATION

For all the progress made, even 62 years after India's independence, higher education faces challenges in the critical areas of Access, Equity and Quality.

Access

Presently the 15–35 years age bracket has a population of more than 350 million, which is expected to peak at about 485 million in 2030 (Altbach and Jayaram 2010). Providing affordable, good quality, globally relevant higher education to such huge numbers remains one of the biggest problems facing this nation. Unless it is able to get its act together and put in place a wide range of mechanisms, India will be staring at a tsunami of young people approaching higher education and the system will not have the capacity to meet the demand. Such a situation, in the words of Narendra Jadhav, member of Planning Commission of India, would lead to a 'demographic disaster, just adding mouths to feed, not hands that can work' (this statement was made at a Penn State University meeting, see Lane and Kinser 2011).

Equity

Making matters worse, there is a wide disparity in higher education Gross Enrolment Ratios (GERs) across states, urban and rural areas, gender, and communities. According to Ernst & Young–FICCI (2011), the GER in urban areas is 23.8 per cent while in rural areas it is a poor 7.5 per cent. Delhi has a GER of 31.9 per cent whereas Assam lags behind at 8.3 per cent. India is already reeling under the rich–poor and rural–urban divide. Education can perhaps be the best tool to bridge the gap between the haves and the have-nots. Yet, as these statistics show, there are glaring inequalities in access to education which only further accentuates the divisions in the society.

Quality

Reports put out by National Assessment and Accreditation Council (NAAC) have time and again emphasised that most of the higher education institutions face an acute problem in terms of shortage of academic and physical infrastructure. Lack of innovation, redundant curriculum, an over-emphasis on theory, less importance to research and social sciences, de-motivated teachers and researchers, and no quality monitoring in the education system are prime reasons for such a dismal state of affairs. Hence, it was not at all surprising when a National Association of Software and Services Companies (NASSCOM)–McKinsey Report (2005) found out that a mere 25 per cent of technical and 10 per cent of non-technical graduates are actually employable. The fact that most companies have to spend huge amounts of time and money training fresh graduates can be seen as an indicator of the skill-set gap between what industry wants and quality of output emerging from the higher education institutions. All these years, governments have focused primarily on capacity-building. The NPE document, perhaps acknowledging the fact that quality of existing institutions needs to be focused upon in a greater way, proposes that 'in the near future, the main emphasis will be on the consolidation of, and expansion of facilities in, the existing institutions' (NCERT 1986: 18).

Indian higher education unquestionably faces huge challenges. While on one hand there is a need to bring as many young people as possible into the higher education fold, on the other it is required to significantly focus on building quality and global competitiveness. Quality of education has a wide-ranging impact on employability and labour productivity. According to official data, India's labour force, which was 472 million in 2006, is expected to be around 653 million in 2031 (Altbach and Jayaram 2010).

India's growth story is primarily driven by its services sector which in turn derives strength from skilled labour force. Unless the country has a nimble-footed dynamic higher education system, it faces the danger of losing its competitive advantage not just to China and Brazil but also smaller nations such as Philippines and Malaysia.

GOVERNMENT HAS LIMITATIONS

The government cannot provide all the solutions to India's higher education challenges. India's public expenditure on higher education as a percentage of Gross Domestic Product (GDP) is 0.6 per cent (Ernst & Young–FICCI 2009), which is less than what other nations such as United States (US), United Kingdom (UK) and China spend on a per-student basis. Most of the public expenditure on higher education is used up on salaries and maintenance of existing institutions. Majority of central government's spending on higher education is allocated to the University Grants Commission (UGC) (around 40 per cent), which in turn assists colleges, mainly in the form of grants for their maintenance and development. Very little is spent on curriculum, research and technology. Only a few institutions, such as Indian Institutes of Technology (IITs) and Indian Institutes of Management (IIMs), stand as beacons of excellence amidst a sea of mediocrity. Entrance to these institutions is characterised by a mad rush leading to extreme stress among the aspirants.

INCREASING PRIVATISATION OF HIGHER EDUCATION

Over last two decades, a rapidly growing Indian economy has led to a huge demand for an educated and skilled labour force. To meet the manpower needs of a dynamic economy, not surprisingly, private enterprises have cropped up to complement public educational institutions, plagued as they are by capacity constraints. In fact, over the past few decades, it has been the private sector that has really driven capacity-creation in Indian higher education. Private presence in higher education got a fillip starting the mid-1980s, coinciding with the reducing investment by Government of India (GoI) and the states. In 2001, when private unaided institutes made up 42.6 per cent of all higher education institutes, 32.8 per cent of Indian students studied there. By 2006, the share of private institutes went up to 63.2 per cent and their student share went up to 51.5 per cent.

Privatisation of higher education is especially noticeable in higher education professional courses such as engineering and Master of Business Administration (MBA), where majority of the institutions offering such programmes have been established by the private sector. So much so, the share of private institutes in the field of pharmacy and engineering is more than 90 per cent. These statistics show that private education players are the norm rather than exception and that privatisation of higher education is now an irreversible trend in India. Critics who argue that education is a social good and should remain exclusively in the hands of the government will find it hard to disagree that given the scale and complexity of Indian higher education challenges, the government on its own cannot single-handedly tackle all the issues.

This is not to say that privatisation is the panacea to all of India's higher education problems. In fact, this phenomenon has brought about its own set of issues and challenges. Yet, the fact that India has a burgeoning youth population that sees education as a ticket to prosperity, coupled with declining education spending by the government, translates into a great demand for private higher education.

PRIVATISATION OF HIGHER EDUCATION REMAINS A COMPLICATED STORY

Despite the huge demand for higher education, especially professional education, Manipal Global Education (MaGE) Services has taken a conscious decision to eschew going down the traditional brick and mortar campus model followed in India. Instead they have decided to focus on building an education services business here. This business presently spans almost the entire education services ecosystem ranging from university services to assessments, placements and vocational training. It may puzzle many as to why MaGE as a corporate entity is not setting up educational campuses in India, in spite of the fact that the company promoters have the distinction of having set up one of the first and finest private universities in the country — Manipal University.

Answers to this conundrum would become easier to understand once the nature of privatisation happening in Indian higher education sector is examined. What is being witnessed is, to a large extent, ad hoc privatisation — myriad institutes continuing to come up without, perhaps, adequate checks and balances. Definitely, the burgeoning privatisation has reduced pressure on public colleges, but even their most ardent supporters will find it hard to claim that private institutions have brought about great improvements in curriculum, teaching methodology, research and development, and learning outcomes. This is not surprising considering the fact that higher education still remains one of the most tightly regulated sectors in the economy. Privatisation in higher education is a convoluted story with some arguing that Indian higher education has moved from 'half-baked socialism to half-baked capitalism' (Kapur and Mehta 2004).

The role played by private enterprise in transforming sectors, such as Information Technology and Information Technology Enabled Services (IT and ITES), telecom, banking, etc., is evident. Today, IT's growth story has put India on the global economic map. These sectors are shining examples of the progress that can be made when private enterprise is allowed to function in a free and encouraging manner. Unfortunately, the higher education operating environment provides certain challenges which dissuade serious players from entering the field. In the following sections, issues that need to be resolved for a dynamic, thriving private enterprise in higher education have been highlighted.

NOT-FOR-PROFIT STRUCTURE

A higher education institution in India can only be set up by a Trust or a Society. Policy-makers are opposed to setting up of higher educational institutions as for-profit corporate entities, ostensibly because education is a public good and hence should be outside the purview of commerce. As observed earlier, all policies by Ministry of Human Resource Development (MHRD) are based on NPE of 1986. Given the socialist structure of the polity, NPE 1986 has strong underpinnings of social good; not surprisingly, profit-making is a strict no.

However, many of India's colleges and universities — both private and public — face acute shortages of faculty,

ill-equipped libraries, outdated curricula, and poor infrastructure. Building a good educational institution requires great physical and soft infrastructure, i.e., infrastructure, faculty and research. In an era of soaring market-driven salaries in other sectors, how can there be hope to attract and retain talent if competitive compensation is not paid? All these require great deal of financial resources. Soaring land rates make it even more difficult to recoup investments. Hence, it is imperative that educational enterprises have access to fungible capital, which becomes well-nigh impossible given the 'Not-For-Profit' structure of the sector. The need of the hour is to make every possible effort to attract serious players with institutional funding who can enter the sector and build transparent and high-quality institutions.

No doubt the intentions behind having a 'Not-For-Profit' structure might be noble, yet the question one needs to ask is whether this is serving the desired purpose. The fact, that everybody including law-makers know but fail to acknowledge, is that commercialisation of education can happen even in educational bodies set up by a Society or a Trust. In addition, it is now 26 years since NPE was written in 1986 (the previous version was in 1968), and a lot has happened in these two and a half decades. NPE is due for a thorough overhaul, including actively considering allowing for-profit entities. The visceral dislike by some policy-makers and bureaucrats towards for-profit education needs to be addressed and allayed.

The government must not equate 'profiteering' with the 'for-profit' legal structure of an organisation to deliver education. On the contrary, it may actually be better for it to allow legitimate profits in higher education and derive revenues from service tax on tuition incomes and income tax on surpluses made by the institutions. The income made from these corporate education entities can then be ploughed back into education. As it is, the government is applying an 'education cess' on everybody.

The for-profit motive will also allow fungible capital to move into the higher education space to create different models for different needs. The present structure in fact dissuades serious entrepreneurs from putting their equity into this sector. This means, the only recourse is debt which increases pressure and in a way creates entry barriers.

On the other hand, there are enough loopholes that allow rampant profiteering to take place. It is indeed ironical that all the regulations have not really managed to keep out players who view education merely as a business with potential high returns. Nobody is surprised when confronted by facts such as many of the private universities and colleges are run by the dubious section of the political class in this country.

Question is, instead of making it mandatory for an educational institute to be set up as a Trust or a Society only, why cannot alternate models be allowed? These could be borrowed from the corporate sector. Just as all companies are required by law to publish annual reports providing their financial details — specifying their assets, liabilities, profits and losses, the profiles of the board of directors and the management, and various other financial information — every educational institution (whether public or private) should publish such reports at regular intervals, with details of the infrastructure and facilities available, profiles of the trustees and the administrators, the academic qualifications and experience of the staff, the courses offered, the number of students, the results of the examinations, the amount of funds available to the university and the sources of funding, and so on. In addition, every educational institution must get itself rated by an independent and specialised accreditation agency, such as Credit Rating Information Services of India Limited (CRISIL), Internet Content Rating Association (ICRA) or Child and Adolescent Resources and Education (CARE), and publicly announce its rating to prospective students to enable them to choose the institution they want to enrol in.

At one stroke, this will bring in transparency and ensure that every educational institution, whether public or private, is accountable not only to those students who are studying in the institution, but to prospective students and the public at large. Public announcements of the financial and educational records of the institutions as well as their ratings by independent rating agencies will generate healthy competition between the various institutions. In fact, a public company/corporate entity is a lot more accountable to the many constituencies it serves as against a Trust. Whatever is the regime there should be accountability, which is presently not there in the case of Trusts.

It is somewhat gratifying to note that the 12th Five-Year Plan document of the Planning Commission clearly moves the focus from exclusive attention to building capacity, to a more nuanced thrust which puts quality right up front. This change will allow granular movement of the very best of Indian higher education entities — both public and private — to start aligning themselves with global standards over a period of time, while creating clear pressures at multiple levels for institutions to improve continuously. The plan document is only an announcement of intent (besides its primary role of being the funds allotment plan for the government), policy changes — including allowing for-profit ventures in a gradual fashion perhaps — will have to be brought in to effect true transformation.

HIGHER EDUCATION — AN OVER-REGULATED SECTOR

Multiple regulatory agencies with overlap of functions and mandates govern almost every aspect of functioning of a higher education institution. Setting up a private university requires parliamentary approval. Unless one sets up a private/deemed university, in order to be able to grant degrees, colleges will have to 'affiliate' with existing universities and follow the existing norms. The system of affiliation in its current form leads to excessive control by a university on the individual functioning of a college. The affiliated college has to toe the university line on virtually every aspect, ranging from intake and syllabus to faculty and examinations. As a result, very little original work or innovation happens in private colleges. Colleges have little incentive to differentiate themselves in the market (Khemani and Narayan 2006).

In the higher education sector, 'inputs' are the students that enter the institute, admission procedures, infrastructure, faculty members, etc. The 'processes' refer to the teaching and delivery mechanisms, the curriculum, etc. The 'output' is the total number of graduates, and the 'outcome' is the quality of these graduates. Following is an example of how All India Council of Technical Education (AICTE) regulations impact the inputs and processes but have little to say on outcomes.

(a) The AICTE norms state the maximum number of students that can be admitted per 'division' and maximum number of 'divisions' allowed in an institution. For example, Engineering & Technology Department can admit 60 students per division and can have a maximum of five divisions, that is, a maximum intake of 300 students in a year. There are similar norms for other areas such as pharmacy, architecture, applied arts, etc. While the intention behind such norms might be to ensure that colleges do not just keep recruiting more and more students, putting restrictions on capacity-intake acts as a big deterrent to private education providers. No genuine long-term private player would want to enter a sector where there are restrictions on growth. Every institution should have the autonomy to decide for itself as to what should be the ideal number of seats it can offer, provided it can prove that it has the requisite infrastructure to do so.

(b) A new technical programme shall not be started in existing technical campus without prior approval of the Council. When universities in other nations are talking about cutting edge research and open source courseware, the very notion that here even things as basic as introduction of new courses or for that matter curriculum changes need approvals seems archaic and counterproductive.

(c) Again, there are norms specifying a mandatory list of courses from which a prescribed minimum number of courses have to be offered. Regulatory control over academic processes hampers the ability of an institution to respond to changing market demands and student needs. In fact, many academicians have called for the system of compulsory grouping of subjects to be replaced by a credit system, which would give flexibility to the students to choose combinations that they want. Having an outdated curriculum means graduates from some of the best colleges enter the job market armed with theoretical knowledge but little idea on up-to-date practices in the marketplace. Employers such as Tata Consultancy, Wipro, Infosys, Hindustan Lever, Reliance, ITC, etc., have no choice but to run training programmes to train college graduates who should ideally require only minimal preparation before becoming productive. For any higher education system to be truly useful and productive, it is imperative that the system is in sync with market trends by constantly innovating in technology, teaching methods and curriculum. For education and industry to be in sync with each other, educational institutions must have autonomy over their curriculum.

(d) Again, there are specific regulations governing the institution: right from land requirements, building plan and needs of instructional, administrative and amenities' area, to computers, software and even subscription of e-journals. In fact, the norms even prescribe how much area should be allotted for staircases, entrance lobby, and so on.

These are a few examples of how every aspect of higher education in this country is tightly governed. Not surprisingly, such license raj regulations give scope for corruption allegations. While nobody can deny the importance of having rules and regulations in place, it appears that presently almost all rules seek to control the inputs and processes of an educational institution while there are very few that measure student learning outcomes. A lot more debate needs to take place on ways to judge institutions based on parameters such as quality of student outcomes. While minimum requirements need to be prescribed for the setting up and functioning of an institute, a lot more discussion needs to take place on why there should be limits especially in cases of capacity-intake or increase in seats.

WHY MANIPAL GLOBAL EDUCATION SERVICES CHOSE TO GO ABROAD

Given a complex operating and regulatory environment in India, MaGE has taken a conscious decision to set up campuses abroad. MaGE's journey of international campuses started in 1994 when it affiliated itself with a local private university in Nepal. At a time when the ratio between the doctors in Nepal and its population was 1:25000, the collaboration between MaGE and Kathmandu University was one of the first private education ventures catering to South Asian Association for Regional Cooperation (SAARC) nations. Through all these years of political turmoil MaGE has stayed committed to medical education in Nepal and today enrol 150+ students each year.

Apart from Nepal, MaGE has top-notch campuses in various regions of the world: from Dubai in Middle East to Malaysia in Association of Southeast Asian Nations (ASEAN) and Antigua in the Americas. Besides strong business reasons for the organisation's presence in each of these regions, they have also been encouraged by the facilitative environment provided by these countries.

Dubai — keen to sell itself as a great investment destination — is a very easy place to structure an education company. For a corporate enterprise such as MaGE, Dubai not only serves as a hub for students from the Middle East and North Africa (MENA) region but also offers ease of business and very transparent rules regarding issues such as repatriation. Not surprisingly, Dubai has the largest number of branch campuses in the world — 27 branch campuses offering 400 degrees. Today, MaGE has a state-of-the-art multi-disciplinary campus in Dubai International Academic City (DIAC), the world's only Free Zone dedicated to Higher Education.

The latest international foray of MaGE has come in Malaysia where the institution is, on the invitation of the Malaysian Government, in the midst of setting up a comprehensive multi-disciplinary university — Manipal International University. Over one-sixth of medical doctors in Malaysia are alumni of Manipal University (through Melaka-Manipal Medical College, as well as Kasturba Medical Colleges at Manipal and Mangalore). The Melaka-Manipal Medical College was set up by MaGE over a decade ago in partnership with certain distinguished Malaysian entities, including the Melaka Government. Having decided to transform itself into a regional education hub, the Malaysian authorities have been taking a series of steps to facilitate the entry of foreign universities into the country. As in Dubai, it is easy to structure a private education company to run a university in Malaysia. Here, there is a single regulatory window — Malaysian Quality Authority — which handles all approvals, accreditation process, etc. In 1995, the Malaysian Government was faced with a situation where 20 per cent of Malaysian students studied abroad. This cost the country an estimated $800 million, nearly 12 per cent of the country's current account deficit. To tackle this, previous regulations that prevented the private sector and foreign universities from conferring degrees were dismantled and new regulatory frameworks were put in place. Malaysia's efforts in trying to become a regional hub have started to pay off: 5 years back, the total number of non-Malaysians studying there was less than 30,000. This year, it is expected to cross 100,000 (Blessinger and Sengupta 2012).

In the earlier sections of this paper, some examples of regulations governing technical education were provided. In order to draw out a contrast with the governance of technical education in India, the engineering education as regulated by Engineering Accreditation Council (EAC) in Malaysia has been examined. The EAC clearly lays out 'Programme Outcomes' — statements that describe what students are expected to know and be able to perform or attain by the time of graduation. While there are broad indicative guidelines, the underlying approach is to ensure that the curriculum, the educational content and the teaching learning and assessment methods are consistent with and support the attainment of the Programme Outcomes. This is in stark contrast to the way regulations are framed in Indian higher education, where almost all focus in on specifying inputs rather than student outcomes.

Again, Brazil's higher education system offers interesting parallels. Based on Ministry of Education, Brazil, *Instituto Nacional de Estudos e Pesquisas Educacionais Anísio Teixeira* (MEC/INEP) Education Census figures of 2010, post-secondary education (undergraduate and graduate programmes) in Brazil comprised 5.45 million enrolments in 2010, up from approximately 1.4 million in 1998 (Estacio 2012). The private sector has grown at Compound Annual Growth Rate or CAGR of 9.7 per cent between 1997 and 2010, while the public sector grew at the rate of 5.1 per cent per year during the same period. As a result, the private sector share of the market increased from 61 per cent in 1997 to 73.3 per cent in 2010, while the public sector experienced a decline from 39 per cent to 26.8 per cent (ibid.). Such a growth has come about due to the fact that public institutions in Brazil are highly selective; in fact, some would argue 'elitist'. They offer limited capacity-intake and the competition to enter them is intense. Mainly, students from well-off families who have access to required training facilities ace the entrance exams. 'The Brazilian Basic Framework Law for National Education', or LDB, was passed in December 1996 which encouraged private-sector participation in higher education by loosening several regulatory constraints and paved way for education institutions to be organised as for-profit institutions. While government-funded public institutions focus on being centres of research and excellence, the private sector is increasing access to higher education among all strata of Brazilian society, thus serving the country's rapidly growing economy. The government has in fact taken a number of steps to support financing for students in private institutions by launching programmes such as *Programa Universidade para Todos* (ProUni) — 'University for All' and *Financiamento Estudantil* (FIES) that provide scholar-

ships and low-interest loans. To counter criticisms regarding quality of education being provided in private institutions, the authorities have put in place a new two-tiered evaluation system: internal evaluation — a council of students, faculty and employees analyses the performance of an institution; external evaluation — the Federal Council of Education names expert evaluators who analyse the curriculum and faculty performance of each institution (Holzhacker et al. 2009). So while there is an effort to push privatisation, there is also a system of quality control in place. For example, the government has mandated that 30 per cent of faculty in an institution must hold doctoral degrees. The government response to critics of education privatisation is that implementation of a strong, sophisticated quality assurance system can ensure even low-income students in private institutions to attain good quality education.

Providing good quality education at an affordable price to millions is a difficult challenge for any nation. If rising aspirations and rapidly growing manpower needs are fuelling higher education demand in developing nations, then large well-known public universities are facing funding cuts and shrinking revenues in deficit-afflicted developed economies. In such a scenario, a favourable regulatory environment that allows multiple education models to flourish should be encouraged. The focus of regulations must be to ensure a level playing field for all entities and a strong system of checks and balances that enforces adequate supervision on quality of output. Beyond that, the consumers (parents and students) should be allowed to decide. In the last two years, several low-quality private colleges have been forced to shut down due to dwindling students. Thus, it is evident that excess capacity is being weeded out on its own by forces of demand and supply.

MaGE as a corporate enterprise is responsible to its investors which include some of the marquee names in private equity. The organisation is hence naturally drawn to nations that have transparent regulatory regimes and enable it to scale up quickly, i.e., few constraints on growth. One should be able to start and close an institution in a much easier way (of course, in a measured and regulated manner). Similarly, individual institutions should have the freedom to decide what and how to teach, and how to fix the fees and manage costs. Most importantly, one does not want to be castigated for aspiring to build world-class large-scale educational institutions, and in the process of delivering a superior product make money as well. Education market like any other market in India is not homogeneous. Those at the lower end of the economic spectrum of course need to be supported through scholarships, student grants, loans, education vouchers, etc. On the other hand, there are these large numbers who are migrating abroad each year to countries such as US, UK, Australia, and others. The system needs to be able to serve the entire cross-section of education aspirations.

Conclusion

In India, it seems to be a case of one step forward and two steps back. While the government has introduced various bills in the Parliament, each of these seems to be stuck at various levels. Bills, such as National Commission for Higher Education and Research, National Accreditation Regulatory Authority for Higher Educational Institutions, and Foreign Educational Institutions, if passed can bring much needed structural changes. There is an urgent need to debate these bills and ensure that they are passed. Most importantly, a change in mindset is required. Perhaps, time has come to remove the stigma associated with profits in the education sector so that legitimate private enterprises can have access to capital and set up world-class institutions that the country needs so badly. A lot of debate has taken place on 'affiliation', 'accountability', 'autonomy', and so on. Everyone seems to agree that a radical overhaul of the higher education system is much needed. Time has now come to walk the talk. Or else India's youth will be left behind in the global race.

Note

1. John F. Kennedy in a special message to the Congress on Education, 20 February 1961, http://www.presidency.ucsb.edu/ws/index.php?pid=8433 (accessed 8 November 2012).

References

Altbach, Philip G. and N. Jayaram. 2010. 'Can India Garner The Demographic Dividend'. *The Hindu*, 1 December. http://www.thehindu.com/opinion/lead/article924112.ece?homepage=true (accessed 21 October 2012).

Blessinger, Patrick and Enakshi Sengupta. 2012. 'Is Malaysia the Regional Leader in International Higher Education?' *The Guardian*, 2 July. http://www.guardian.co.uk/higher-education-network/blog/2012/jul/02/higher-education-in-malaysia (accessed 21 October 2012).

Ernst & Young–FICCI. 2009. 'Making The Indian Higher Education System Future Ready'. Paper presented at 'FICCI Higher Education Summit', 6–7 November, New Delhi.

——————. 2011. 'Private Sector Participation in Indian Higher Education'. Paper presented at 'FICCI Higher Education Summit', 11–12 November, New Delhi.

Estacio. 2012. 'Education Market, Industry Overview'. Estacio Company website, 27 January. http://www.estacioparticipacoes.com.br/estacio2010/web/conteudo_en.asp?idioma=1&tipo=30243&conta=44 (accessed 21 October 2012).

Holzhacker, Denilde, Olena Chornoivan, Demet Yazilitas, and Khishibbuyan Dayan-Ochir. 2009. 'Privatization in Higher Education: Cross-Country Analysis of Trends, Policies, Problems and Solutions', Institute for Higher Education Policy. http://www.ihep.org/assets/files/publications/m-r/(Issue_Brief)_Privatization_in_Higher_Education-Cross_Country_Analysis_of_Trends__Policies__Problems__and_Solutions.pdf (accessed 21 October 2012).

Kapur, Devesh and Pratap Bhanu Mehta. 2004. 'Indian Higher Education Reform: From Half-Baked Socialism to Half-Baked Capitalism'. CID Working Paper no. 108, September. Center for International Development at Harvard University.

Khemani, Tulika and Jayaprakash Narayan. 2006. 'Higher Education Sector in India: Opportunities & Reforms'. Foundation for Democratic Reforms/Lok Satta. http://www.fdrindia.org/publications/HigherEducationInIndia_PR.pdf. March (accessed 21 October 2012).

Lane, Jason and Kevin Kinser. 2011. 'Building Capacity in India: What Role for Cross-Border Higher Education'. The Chronicle, 1 November. http://chronicle.com/blogs/worldwise/building-capacity-in-india-what-role-for-cross-border-higher-education/28857 (accessed 8 November 2012).

National Association of Software and Services Companies (NASSCOM)–McKinsey Report. 2005. 'Extending India's Leadership of the Global IT and BPO Industries'. http://www.mckinsey.com/locations/india/mckinseyonindia/pdf/nasscom_mckinsey_report_2005.pdf (accessed 8 November 2012).

National Council of Educational Research and Training (NCERT). 1986. 'National Policy on Education'. http://www.ncert.nic.in/oth_anoun/npe86.pdf (accessed 8 November 2012).

Higher Education Law and Privately-Funded University Education in India

Towards a Vision?

*Amlanjyoti Goswami**

BACKGROUND

The role of the private sector in university education in India is a matter of debate. At one extreme of the ideological frontier are votaries for 'for-profit' educational institutions. On the other is opposition to any role for the private sector in higher education. Between the binaries of public–private, market–State, regulation or no-regulation lie complex shades whose visions, principles and goals need more meaningful exploration and articulation.

The numbers seem to indicate that the higher education sector is poised for expansion to meet new demand. This demand will inevitably arise from increasing thrust on universalisation of primary education (as constitutionally mandated by the Right to Education) and later, on secondary education. Only 0.7 per cent of the Gross Domestic Product (GDP) is being spent on higher and technical education (as against a target of 1.5 per cent of GDP) (MHRD 2011).[1] Even a spending of 1 per cent is only 19 per cent of the total expenditure on education. Much of the remaining spending will deservedly go to elementary, primary and secondary education. Student enrolment in higher education has already increased from 8.4 million in 2000–01 to 14.6 million in 2009–10 (Planning Commission 2012). The demand is expected to increase at a compounded rate of 11–12 per cent till 2022 and will require another 26 million seats (ibid.). This requires more investment — public and private. While the Working Group on Higher and Technical Education has pointed to a need for ₹4,133.68 billion for the 12th Plan, it is unlikely that the current fiscal environment will allow such

allocations. The Gross Enrolment Ratio (GER) target of 21 per cent by end of the 12th Plan and 30 per cent by year 2020 cannot be achieved by the public sector alone (ibid.). The GER estimates are currently around 17 per cent though there is a debate on exact figures (UGC 2011). This means more private investment will be needed. The critical issues pertain to the vision behind such investment, the enabling regulatory framework and critically, the perspectives regarding the nature of learning expected in institutions funded through such investment.

Mere expansion is of little use without efforts to improve quality or reach standards of excellence. The demographic impact of higher education will only be visible when it is also inclusive — one that provides opportunities for the historically marginalised. According to the 11th Plan, the GER lagged behind for rural areas (7.5 per cent), women (10.5 per cent), SCs (6.5 per cent), STs (6.52 per cent), OBCs (8.7 per cent), and Muslims (9 per cent) along with regional variations (Planning Commission 2008: 22). While attention has also been drawn to the role of private investment in higher education to create a globally competitive workforce in India, the sheer magnitude of national challenges will also require it to engage with critical development goals, including affirming basic liberal constitutional and democratic values, furthering environmental sustainability and ensuring social inclusion. To imagine more possibilities for private-funded university education, which reaches out to larger constituencies and also impacts areas not otherwise immediately remunerative but nevertheless essential to the life of a nation, is also at its heart, a question of vision.

Jawaharlal Nehru, in his famous convocation address to the University of Allahabad in 1947, extolled the role of a university thus: 'A university stands for humanism, for

---

* Views expressed are personal. The usual disclaimers apply.

tolerance, for reason, for the adventure of ideas and the search for truth … If the universities discharge their duties adequately, then all is well with the nation and the people' (NCERT 1970: 553; see also MHRD 2009). The Kothari Commission, dwelling on this role for universities, had stated that the principal object of a university is 'to deepen man's understanding of the universe and of himself-in body, mind and spirit, to disseminate this understanding throughout society and apply it for the service of mankind' (ibid.).

It is in keeping with this larger vision of learning that the role of private investment in higher education and in particular, university education, also needs to be explored. Since universities have historically been the sites of learning, between the State, the community and the individual, the role of the private sector in contributing to, or even detracting from, such a vision needs better understanding. Of around 611 universities in India, there are around 94 private universities under state legislation and about 90 private deemed universities (out of around 130 deemed universities) (UGC 2011: 9). In other words, private universities account for about 30 per cent of the universities in India, which will see an increase over the next few years. This dynamic renders such appreciation all the more necessary.

This paper focuses on the private sector specifically in university education (as different from those without the university umbrella, whether as 'technical institutions' or in other forms of professional education). This is a particular segment that seems likely to grow, and requires a transparent and enabling policy framework within which to locate its ambitions. Within the larger political economy, given the heterogeneous needs of this country, allowing more private involvement in higher education within an appropriate regulatory framework would signal the State's willingness to accommodate newer and more diverse entities in a manner that can enable excellence and at the same time curb fraudulent practice (Salmi 2010). It is also critical, in the same breath, to ensure a regulatory framework that does not stymie excellence and innovation in the name of curbing fraudulent practice. On the other hand, some of the disquiet regarding private participation in university education also stems from a perception that the private sector needs more comprehensive envisioning of its goals and much better application.

REGULATORY ENVIRONMENT

The regulatory environment in higher education is a curious one — which the National Knowledge Commission (NKC) had succinctly described as 'over-regulated and under-governed' (2009: 62). Higher education regulation controls supply, building from an unarticulated underlying premise that such control is somehow a means of ensuring quality, even in the face of significantly increasing demand. Quality control lies largely in attempting to ensure a basic minimum 'floor', designed along inputs, with a standardised formula across various parameters applicable in a largely homogenous manner with little incentive to innovate.

Before getting into regulatory specifics, it is therefore necessary to allay some legal misconceptions regarding the role and nature of education (and higher education) itself. These misconceptions play a role in the competing ideological debates on private participation in higher education. To the detractors of private entities, the very notion of such entities in higher education is itself an anathema, where 'privatisation' and 'commercialisation' are tarred with the same brush. On the other hand, to the votaries of 'for-profit' education, education is like any other private good or service, where the profit motive and the market logic impels competitiveness, which in turn enables better returns and quality. Both visions are somewhat inadequate in understanding the nature of education (and learning and knowledge) itself, and both are similar in displaying an incomplete understanding of the constitutional position in India.

The Supreme Court of India has clearly stated that education (and higher education) is a non-profit activity. The fundamental right to establish and administer educational institutions has been held by the Supreme Court to be an 'occupation' rather than a trade/business or profession. No 'profiteering' or capitation fee is allowed. There is an 'obligation to maintain requisite standards of professional excellence by giving admissions based on merit and making it equally accessible to eligible students through a fair and transparent admission procedure and based on *reasonable fee structure*', based on merit and non-exploitation, with greater autonomy for 'unaided' professional institutions in admissions and fees.[2]

Subject to supervision and determination on what is 'reasonable', the court has held that unaided professional institutions can devise their own fee structures, but fees can be regulated to prevent profiteering and capitation fee since education is not trade or business. 'Capitation Fees' is further made illegal by the pending Bill in Parliament on Prevention of Unfair Practices.[3]

A 'reasonable surplus' is however allowed, for future expansion, where determination of reasonableness is on the basis of the following:[4]

(a) infrastructure and facilities available;
(b) investments made;
(c) salaries paid to teachers and staff;
(d) future plans for expansion and betterment.

The notion of 'reasonable surplus' allows returns to be ploughed back into the institution, while keeping intact the overall non-profit nature of education. It also makes room for particular needs, investments and expansion plans of a specific institution.

The State controls fees tightly. For example, the UGC (Institutions Deemed to be Universities) Regulations 2010, states that 'the fee structure for various programmes of study in the deemed to be universities shall also be fixed in accordance with the Fee Regulations framed by the Government or the UGC [University Grants Commission] in this behalf from time to time' (UGC 2010: 71). Fees must however have a reasonable relation to the cost of running the course. As per the UGC's Regulation for Private Universities under State Route (2003), fixation of fees has to be in accordance with norms/guidelines prescribed by the UGC and other statutory bodies. The underlying motive behind these regulations is one that seeks to prevent what is perceived as 'commercialisation'. If poorer students are left out, the inclusion agenda is derailed.

There is clearly a need to provide an adequate balance between the rising costs of providing quality education in a manner that encourages universities to create more endowments and raise resources. The NKC, for example, had stated that

fees constitute less than 10 per cent of total expenditure in our universities … The problem has been compounded by the UGC method of providing grants-in-aid to bridge the difference between income and expenditure. Consequently, there is no incentive for universities or colleges to raise income through higher fees as that sum would be deducted from their UGC (or [state] government) grants … It is for universities to decide the level of fees but, as a norm, fees should meet at least 20 per cent of the total expenditure in universities … This rationalisation of fees should be subject to two conditions: first, needy students should be provided with a fee waiver plus scholarships to meet their costs; second, universities should not be penalised by the UGC for the resources raised from higher fees through matching deductions from their grants-in-aid (2009: 72–73).

Resource allocation is also skewed. The NKC had pointed out that nearly 65 per cent of the UGC budget is used for meeting the operating expenses of the central universities and University of Delhi colleges, leaving only 35 per cent for the rest of the universities in the country. Within the ambit of whatever resources are available, more than 90 per cent of the grants goes towards meeting operating expenses, leaving very little for institutional growth and capital assets.

If there is limited money for institutional growth and innovation, educational quality visibly suffers. Efforts at providing opportunities to the very needy also need a much better and buoyant financial base, especially in endowments. The clear imperative for providing scholarships to the needy and for exploring possibilities for 'needs-blind' admission)

cannot be disputed. Yet, implicit disincentives in the current tax and trust laws provide very little motivation to raise resources. Trusts are required to spend 85 per cent of income streams from endowments in the same financial year, which prevents any meaningful endowment from being created that in turn could be utilised for scholarships (Planning Commission 2012; see also NKC 2009).

If financial sources are limited, there is a need to diversify such sources in a manner that creates better balance between the financial needs of the institution (including its capital and recurring operational expenditures), its learning goals, its aspirations to excellence, as well as its aims to ensure inclusion through meaningful access to opportunity (Agarwal 2009: 39–114). These sources could be found in better macro policy encouragement to private philanthropy, enhanced asset management of endowments, as well as in the ability of the university to generate 'plough-back' revenues through advisory services and other revenue sources such as Intellectual Property (IP), etc. Enabling loan conditions and improved scholarship schemes for the needy can be initiated when the university has sufficient financial resources, which in turn can be increased over the long run. This 'chicken–egg' dilemma is at the heart of the 'triple bind' of ensuring 'expansion, inclusion and excellence', all at the same time. And yet, universities funded by the private sector will also have to grapple with the challenge of ensuring expansion, inclusion and equity (with more than just lip service) if they have to remain strategic and relevant to the greater needs of the country.

General Powers of Coordination and Regulation

As per the current law, the UGC (and the All India Council of Technical Education [AICTE]) enjoys very wide powers to 'coordinate and determine standards' of higher education. This power is often interpreted as 'harmonisation', which is aimed at ensuring 'uniformity', operating in a predominantly centralised framework. Laws made under Entry 66[5] of the Union List of the Constitution (such as the UGC Act read with its Regulations and the AICTE Act read with its Regulations) will override those made by states under Entry 25[6] of the Concurrent List.[7] 'Coordination' is understood as not just evaluation or making grants. 'It means harmonisation with a view to forge a uniform pattern for concerted action according to a certain design, scheme or plan of development. It, therefore, includes action not only for removal of disparities but also for preventing the occurring of such disparities'.[8]

This notion of an imposed 'uniformity' includes nitty-gritties on complex details such as curriculum, teaching, examination, evaluation and research qualification, admission, pupil–teacher ratio, practical examination, equipment and many more, all driven by a centralised regulator.[9] Doubts persist as to whether these measures actually ensure any minimum 'floor' or whether such complex and specific detailed rules encourage the raising of the quality 'ceiling' at all. Where supply is already constrained by regulatory barriers, complex and non-transparent procedures within the interpretation and implementation of the minutiae of rules (and by multiple authorities) in turn encourage information asymmetries, patronage and rent-seeking. Such a paternalistic centralised system leads to 'over-regulation and under-governance' and prevents meaningful utilisation of the rich diversity of approaches in a country as large and heterogeneous as India. It is also distrustful of private initiative. An enabling regulatory environment should encourage rather than prevent academic innovation and diversity, and that can be done through better use of peer-driven processes involving academia at its heart and through disclosure systems that are rigorously followed and open for public review.

It is important to highlight that federal issues remain politically significant here, even as incorporation of 'universities' is a legislative head in the Concurrent List.[10] A particular state can establish and incorporate universities under Entry 25 of the Concurrent List, but wherever the matter pertains to Entry 66 of the Union List, the central legislation will override the State legislation to the extent of inconsistency between the two. Any provision of an enactment made by the state legislature concerning higher education that is in conflict with the central enactment/ regulations would be *ultra vires* to that extent.

High Barriers to Entry

According to Section 2 (f) of the UGC Act, 1956,

'University' means a University established or incorporated by or under a Central Act, a Provincial Act or a State Act, and includes any such institution, as may, in consultation with the University concerned, be recognised by the Commission [UGC] in accordance with the regulations made in this behalf under this Act [e.g., deemed universities under Section 3, UGC Act] (UGC 2002: 6).

This means that, other than the deemed university route, universities need to be legislated into existence, by Parliament or state legislature. Starting an institution through parliamentary or state legislation is a very uphill task because of various political vagaries. There is no clear policy or direction on how to reduce such high barriers for new universities.

The deemed university route originally allowed reputed institutions such as the Indian Institute of Science (IISc) and the Tata Institute of Fundamental Research (TIFR) among others to be incorporated as universities, directly through notifications from the Ministry of Human Resource Devel-

opment (MHRD). In fact, the Kothari Commission report had highlighted that the bringing of 'high-level institutions such as the Indian Agricultural Research Institute at Delhi, the Indian Institute of Science at Bangalore' into the university system 'by deeming them as universities under Section 3 of the UGC Act' was a 'welcome development' (NCERT 1970: 626). It had added that

[t]here is in our educational system a need for institutions having the academic status and privileges which ordinarily belong to a university, but with more specific and limited functions and scope. While such institutions in their limited field should maintain the highest standard of teaching and research, their organizational set-up need not be the replica of a university ... We would like to stress that, in deeming institutions as universities under the UGC Act, *the most careful attention should be paid to the question of educational standards. This provision under the Act gives scope for experimentation and innovation, but it should not become a cheap side- or back-door to university status* (ibid.; emphasis added).

The Kothari Commission report displayed uncanny prescience. In a case currently *sub judice* before the Supreme Court (*Viplav Sharma v. Union of India*) 46 years later, the deemed university route and the operation of 44 specific deemed universities are themselves under the scanner for low quality. This has created a situation where clearly the wheat and the chaff need separation. Institutions of repute such as TIFR, IISc, Tata Institute of Social Sciences (TISS), Birla Institute of Technology and Sciences (BITS) among others, are incorporated under the deemed university route while there are others of dubious quality whose recognition and functioning are being questioned. This has resulted in a curious political economy where, according to reports, no new deemed university has been recognised by the MHRD in 2010 and 2011 (Chopra 2011). In any case, the recognition of any new deemed university will be understandably under a very strict bureaucratic scanner, especially where there are political stakes involved and governing regimes change.

In the Yashpal case, the Supreme Court clamped down on a number of universities that were established in Chhattisgarh without having the necessary infrastructure or facilities. The Supreme Court clarified that a university cannot be set up without necessary infrastructure and simply on the basis of a detailed project report.

In order to establish a University, there must be adequate land on which the campus may be made and necessary infrastructural facilities provided. No University can come into existence without a proper campus which requires land ... what is necessary is actual establishment of institutions having all the infrastructural facilities and qualified teachers to teach.[11]

Further, as per the Supreme Court, universities can establish study centres only within their territorial jurisdiction. A state establishing a university has no legislative competence to set up campuses in other states. This is a Constitutional bar on legislative competence, which requires universities to approach multiple state governments for setting up universities in respective states or attempt at affiliating campuses with established public state universities in such states, thereby increasing transaction costs and multiple inefficiencies.[12] This means that the barriers to entry for a private university to set up a national institution with multiple campuses are formidable, if not insurmountable.

High entry barriers to setting up new universities (argued in the name of ensuring quality) have therefore also resulted in a complex affiliated college system within universities, where colleges are 'affiliated' to existing public universities. These universities have grown to near unmanageable sizes,[13] with unwieldy administrative and decision-making structures, limited scope for innovation and increased difficulty in monitoring affiliated institutions — all of which often adversely impacts quality, which was ironically the very basis for keeping entry barriers high. Currently there are more than 31,000 affiliated colleges in the country. As per the UGC (Establishment of and Maintenance of Standards in Private Universities) Regulations, set up under state legislation route, such universities are expected to be 'unitary' universities (UGC 2003). Further, as per the relevant regulations, a deemed university also has to be unitary. This means the public universities have to bear the disproportionate share of the burden of managing affiliated colleges. Sometimes, this is too difficult a burden to bear.

Internal Governance

As per the Supreme Court, the fundamental right to establish and administer educational institutions (subject to reasonable restrictions) entails:

  (a) admitting students;
  (b) setting up a reasonable fee structure;
  (c) constituting a governing body;
  (d) appointing staff (teaching and non-teaching);
  (e) taking action if dereliction of duty on part of employees is proved.[14]

The right also includes the duty to maintain standards of excellence.[15] 'Non-aided' institutions have greater autonomy.

As per the UGC (Establishment of and Maintenance of Standards in Private Universities) Regulations, private universities under state legislation also need to conform to relevant centralised UGC provisions from time to time (UGC 2003).[16] The Deemed University Regulations prescribe the authorities and the constitution/memberships within each body. There is therefore a clear need for autonomy in internal governance, where appointments of vice chancellors are not subject to political or governmental controls.

Degree

As per the law, only a university can grant degrees.

Mere conferment of degree is not enough ... what is necessary is that the degree should be recognized ... 'degree' means any such degree as may, with the previous approval of the Central Government, be specified in this behalf by the Commission [the UGC] by notification in the Official Gazette.[17]

Further, in the Yashpal case, the Supreme Court quoting the UGC (Establishment of and Maintenance of Standards in Private Universities) Regulations, 2003 also stated that '[f]ailure to comply with this requirement, shall render any degree/diploma awarded by a private university as unspecified in terms of Section 22(3) of the UGC Act and shall invite penalty under Section 24 of the UGC Act' (UGC 2003). These provisions are intended to prevent the awarding of 'fake degrees'. At the same time, it is potentially possible for such penal measures to also indirectly prevent any innovative disciplinary or new interdisciplinary development. New disciplines arrive at interstitial spaces or from contestation within existing disciplines. Interdisciplinary ideas involve a variety of approaches, including those stemming from the margins or unanswered questions or even within disciplines, including those arising out of the inadequacy of a particular discipline to address or comprehend particular issues. Some of the new interdisciplinary developments fall outside conventional disciplinary compartments where 'degrees' could be specified. Where knowledge is constantly growing, the generation of new knowledge and its acknowledgment is best done by peers (whether such peers work within the mainstream or the margins of particular disciplines, or still further, outside either). Innovation in knowledge needs more encouragement and better-enabling frameworks, and the regulatory structure needs to be flexible enough to accommodate new knowledge domains. Without such understanding or comprehension, it is possible that genuine innovative endeavours could also get stymied ostensibly in the name of curbing fraudulent practice. This is a serious question that impacts new and emerging areas of human knowledge, where the law often cannot keep up with the dynamic nature of knowledge. No one disputes the need to limit deceitful undertakings. But what is in question is the potential of the same regulatory tendency to label otherwise genuine and innovative knowledge activity as 'fraudulent'. This is the double-edged nature of the regulatory approach itself, especially one which is directed at preventing 'harm' and interpreting 'good outcomes' largely on the basis of prevention of 'harm' rather than encouraging the evolution of peer-driven benchmarks as ideas to anchor the pursuit of excellence.

New Bills in Parliament

Besieged by perceptions regarding quality assurance and questions of malpractices in higher education in the private sector, most of the MHRD's Bills in Parliament are about ensuring 'accountability' using traditional regulatory approaches. These approaches are aimed at curbing bad behaviour. Yet, there is need for serious reflection on how good performance needs further encouragement, to become institutions of excellence. Curbing malpractices may be a necessary but certainly not a sufficient condition in ensuring quality or excellence.

As far as the basic floor is concerned, the Prevention of Unfair Practices Bill, to its credit, seeks to create a transparent disclosure system while making capitation fees and other unfair practices illegal. It explicitly clarifies the not-for-profit nature of education, with surplus revenues to be ploughed back for growth and development of institutions. It also makes a clear statement that while '[t]here has been unprecedented growth in higher education in recent years', largely through private participation, '[t]here is public concern' regarding 'unfair practices', such as

charging of capitation fee and demanding donations for admitting students, not issuing receipts in respect of payments made by or on behalf of students, admission to professional programmes of study through non-transparent and questionable admission processes, low quality delivery of education services and false claims of quality of such services through misleading advertisements, engagement of unqualified or ineligible teaching faculty, forcible withholding of certificates and other documents of students (GoI 2010d).

The Mandatory Accreditation Bill similarly seeks to create a regime of compulsory accreditation through a new national accreditation authority (GoI 2010c). This is a worthwhile measure, but only if guided by regulatory approaches on accreditation that actually enable the development of better institutions and incentivise quality. The Educational Tribunals Bill similarly seeks to create a specialised dispute resolution mechanism within higher education (GoI 2010a). The Foreign Education Providers Bill seeks to create a framework for foreign providers to operate, provided they fulfil all the requirements (with a detailed bureaucratic apparatus) to oversee their functioning (GoI 2010b). It seeks to confer autonomy by way of exception, where exceptional institutions of 'international standing and repute' could be allowed to frame their own rules, so long as a committee of experts deems fit.

The political economy of higher education seems to be guided by a premise that autonomy has to be the exception, and that largely, what is required is more regulation.

Regulation is being understood as an 'all-or-nothing' approach. There is no debate or policy initiative yet on how to move beyond this 'over-regulation but under-governance' impasse or how regulatory principles can be better evolved that could help create more autonomous universities of excellence that are also privately funded. The Universities for Research and Innovation Bill however shows some promise (GoI 2012). Intended to set up new public, private as well as Public–Private Partnership (PPP) universities, and develop ecosystems of quality, aspiring to reach internationally competitive standards, the Bill does allow such universities, once established, autonomy on critical parameters of administration, finance and academic matters. However, the fine print remains to be seen as to whether such universities at all have autonomy in their respective documents of incorporation or whether the Bill will at all pass muster in Parliament.

The promise of autonomy also lies in some portions of the new Higher Education and Research (HER) Bill that seeks to create a new regulatory authority, called the National Commission of Higher Education and Research (NCHER) (GoI 2011). This Bill is of importance since it seeks to replace or absorb the various existing regulatory agencies, including the UGC, with the proposed NCHER. It remains to be seen whether this Bill will at all be enacted, given the existing authorities and the plethora of regulations that are already in operation and the understandable resistance to allowing a new super-regulator to subsume existing agencies. The HER Bill does have language that indicates that the proposed NCHER can take measures 'to promote autonomy', which, it adds, are not 'obligatory' but only to serve as points of 'reference' (ibid.: 9).

However, in the same breath, it is only in the actual Regulations of the HER Bill — also to 'determine [and] coordinate … standards' (same as the UGC) — that it will finally be determined how much autonomy is really enabled. It is yet unclear as to whether the many UGC Regulations could in turn be 'retrofitted' into the new authority or whether 'measures' to promote 'autonomy' (as mentioned in the Bill) may in any way be different from the specific regulations to coordinate and determine standards. Specific regulations could still be intrusive even with a new regulator without a clearer enunciation of what regulatory principles should govern regulatory behaviour.

Regulatory Principles

A clearer policy on the role of the private sector in higher education, one that is holistic and comprehensive, encompassing its many dimensions and sectors, has become necessary. All the legalese needs to be anchored in some basic regulatory principles in order to be effective in creating an enabling environment for high-quality universities in India, including those funded by the private sector. There has to be a premise that steps to ensuring a basic floor are different from those to encourage quality or create ecosystems of excellence.

The strategies discussed in this section could become a part of a national policy and serve as guiding posts for detailing the fine print of specific rules and regulations. They are necessary to provide a clearer vision of how best to achieve a comprehensive and holistic regulatory environment, in the absence of which a definite direction would be difficult to achieve.

Regulatory Simplification

Rules and processes need to be eased and the establishment and smooth operation of universities facilitated through a set of transparent, responsive and easily implementable regulations and guidelines — as a significant departure from the current maze of rules and regulation that encourage rent-seeking.

'Autonomy' and 'Accountability'

Transparent e-information-based/disclosure systems need to be ensured. Networks of open-ended communities could facilitate peer review, coordinated by an independent quality agency. Arguments have been made that within the framework of transparency, there is a need to adjust to 'the growing diversity and modulate according to varying track records of higher educational institutions' (Agarwal 2009: 153). This indicates that the regulatory environment needs to encourage institutions of excellence to aspire to set still higher benchmarks while other institutions would be incentivised to improve standards. All universities do not have the same yardstick or aims and need not be tarred with the same brush. It is possible for a regulatory environment to accommodate and encourage a diversity of approaches for a variety of universities and allow more peer-reviewed systems of accountability and disclosure. Otherwise, in the name of uniformity and harmonisation, will have deadened and ossified systems that cannot innovate and have no incentive to better quality because they would just do enough to show adherence to a uniform regulatory floor on the surface at best. In the absence of quality talent, finances, and most importantly, a vision for excellence-inclusion-access, our finest universities would be able to only do so much and no more.

Comprehensiveness

Strategically sequenced, systemic measures need to be undertaken for development and not piecemeal ones. This seems to indicate the need for a new higher education policy that is comprehensive rather than ad-hoc stand-alone measures.

Heterogeneity and Diversity

There is a need to evolve from standardised, centralised approaches towards more innovative, decentralised and contextual approaches to respond to the needs of states and the diversity of requirements and aspirations across India. A diversity of approaches in institutional management and academic autonomy need to be recognised and celebrated, rather than prescribing standardised, centralised formulae.

Decentralisation

States deliver the bulk of the higher education finances and the majority of higher education institutions are also located in the states, where the relevant Concurrent List provisions also apply, which also makes it essential to involve and incentivise them. Decentralisation needs to be accompanied by effective coordination mechanisms, critically between academic peer communities on the one hand and between the central and state regulatory frameworks on the other. At the moment, there are few structures that enable a consistent policy dialogue on critical academic issues, across local-state and national scales.

Dynamism and Incentivisation

The aim should be to bring about dynamism into the entire system through systematic incentivisation in the allocation of public resources in centre and states in new, restructured and existing institutions, through linkages to outcomes rather than inputs. It is useful to facilitate a debate on how best outcomes can be understood, in a manner that does not take away academic and governance autonomy, and preserves the criticality of learning, research and knowledge production in universities.

Diversification

Since the bulk of future education budgets will deservedly go to elementary education, any case for 'expansion, inclusion and excellence' in higher education will be grossly inadequate without diversification of financial resources (as previously discussed) within a much more streamlined regulatory system that encourages open information-based competition and the flourishing of newer and qualitatively better private providers.

Intangibility

No sector development process will succeed without efforts, undertaken continuously and systematically, to actively engage with the 'softer' dimensions of human and knowledge resources. All institutional structural dimensions will be inadequate to revitalise the learning environment without rigorous emphasis on attracting and retaining talented faculty, including hiring and keeping the best Indian minds in India and drawing in minds from abroad; putting serious emphasis on educator training and development as an integral part of the learning system rather than in isolation; and undertaking measures to develop an appreciation of new learning methods, pedagogy as well as respecting the dignity of exploring questions of knowledge production and epistemology.

Openness and Experimentation

New technologies are changing the process of dissemination and construction of knowledge worldwide. It is essential to enable open, accessible and contemporary learning technologies that improve access (and supplement the teacher's pedagogic efforts) within contextual knowledge networks. The aim should be to enable continuous improvement, in developing benchmarks and reducing bureaucratic involvement in academic standard setting and enforcement.

Permeability

The development process should encourage new, innovative learning environments by recognising the power of mobility across boundaries between institutions, disciplines and technologies. Such a process should facilitate and not obstruct such cross-dialogue and exchange along multiple dimensions — domestic and international.

NEED FOR PRIVATE SECTOR INCENTIVES

If private investment is indeed considered necessary, the creation of an enabling environment to create high-quality universities will help stem the annual outflow of foreign exchange from India to support higher education abroad.[18] There is therefore a strong macroeconomic case for Ministry of Finance incentives to higher education initiatives (for all universities, private and public, and including those for private philanthropy) that will effectively stem this outflow and build domestic capacity of international quality. In particular, the following measures will be useful:

(a) Implicit disincentives in tax laws and trust laws need to be removed by:

    (i) allowing universities to invest in financial instruments of their choice (where rates of return can be high, and private professional fund managers can be employed as required);

    (ii) removing restrictions on the utilisation of income in any given time period and allowing the use of income from endowments to build up a corpus (currently, as previously discussed, private trusts have to spend 85 per cent of their income stream

from endowment in the same year, thereby seriously limiting options to raise corpus);

    (iii) making exceptions in income tax laws to encourage the creation of large endowments. A number of High Net-Worth Individuals (HNWIs) and corporates have made significant contributions towards higher education endowments to leading foreign universities. There is potential for higher education philanthropy in India that needs to be tapped into. For example, the Narayana Murthy Committee has recommended deductions to the extent of 300 per cent of such contributions (Planning Commission 2012).

(b) Sources of finance need to be diversified and innovative financial mechanisms explored. The proposed creation of the National Education Finance Corporation (NEFC) to address resource gaps (re-financing and direct financing of education infrastructure), credit guarantees, etc. needs to be explored in greater detail. The Narayana Murthy Committee has recommended the setting up of the Indian Corporate Higher Education Scholarship with a corpus of ₹10 billion contributed by the top 1,000 corporations in India (with matching grants by the government and tax exemptions up to 300 per cent). It has also recommended the creation of a National Educational Loan Fund of ₹1,000 billion to be set up by public sector banks.

(c) The 2011 Companies Act, 1956 Amendment Bill has mandated 2 per cent of Profit After Tax (PAT) as Corporate Social Responsibility for Public Sector Units. Some of this expenditure could go to higher education if the appropriate incentives and mechanisms are available.

(d) It is necessary to develop a comprehensive policy for PPP in higher education, especially on regulatory, institutional and investment issues. Some models could be developed that encourage large private investments in education with the central/state governments providing: (i) land and (ii) matching funds. Governance control may be exercised by a private board with government representation, subject to continuing review of standards. It is necessary to identify selected areas important for the nation (but where market demand is low) and provide value-added partnerships to prevent market failure, without bureaucratic or political controls.[19]

TOWARDS A NEW VISION FOR PRIVATE-SECTOR UNIVERSITY EDUCATION?

While all these policies are part of the external regulatory environment, it is critical for universities funded by the private sector to also look within. If there is a vision to create and run universities of excellence, of internationally competitive standards, there can be, at the very least, no room for malpractices or fraudulent behaviour. However, universities of excellence (whether public, private or PPP) are not built in a day and they need enabling and nourishing ecosystems within. The critical questions pertaining to the formation of an enabling academic and research environment within a university are therefore 'cultural', even as financial and regulatory considerations play their part. There are questions that need to be asked, explored, debated and made a part of the vision of the higher education policy. If the derision usually reserved for profiteers is to be avoided, universities that are privately funded also need to introspect. It is a particular crisis of confidence in the private sector in higher education that has impelled disparate narratives and perspectives on its role, and perhaps reflects itself perversely in the minutiae of regulatory detail and control. The academic and learning endeavour in universities, privately or publicly funded, calls for respecting academic autonomy, dignity, diversity, and heterogeneity. Where the discussion is largely centred around 'bogus universities' and malpractices, it has become generally difficult to engage in a dialogue on imaginative possibilities for universities.

Will private universities be predominantly governed by a vision that subordinates research and learning? Will the academic and learning enterprise be required to be less reflective, less organic, and less collegial than before? Will certain disciplines, especially in the Humanities, no longer be given the dignity they deserve or acknowledged for their indispensable role in the creation of human understanding and a liberal polity? Is the 'decline of the professoriate' or of academic collegiality inevitable with increasingly competitive and 'careerist' faculty, not just in private universities but also in the public ones? Isn't that a loss not just for universities but also for society? Is there at all a private philanthropy that allows minds to bloom and flourish — for their own sake and for the sake of learning — as essential preconditions to a liberal democratic society? Or will the constant pressure to meet operating and recurring capital expenses be so acute that the market will ultimately govern the university's aims? If public universities are overwhelmed by fiscal, bureaucratic, political, and other administrative pressures, why would private universities be any different?

There are historical precedents in India of genuine private philanthropy that created institutions of excellence. A 100 years ago, prominent universities of national repute — Vishwa Bharati, Aligarh Muslim University, the IISc and the Banaras Hindu University — were all created out of private philanthropic efforts. One might even argue that the continual challenge of meeting recurring capital and operating costs was one reason for their subsequent nationalisation.[20]

Universities are at their heart places for learning, whether publicly- or privately-funded. Such learning is also contextual, responding to the needs of the knowledge endeavour, and drawing from the immediacy of the socio-economic and cultural milieus. India's socio-economic realities will increasingly require the private sector to engage with critical social questions. They pertain to what university education can do to further social justice, the goals of the liberal constitutional democracy, deepen intellectual pursuit, and enable community engagement. These goals are part of the vision of what it means to be a university: the same university that also celebrates the 'adventure of ideas'. It is also a stereotype to assume that the 'celebration of ideas' is somewhat inconsistent with the 'application' of knowledge. These are rigid compartments that need stepping away from. The market requires immediate skills (which keep changing), but what is indispensable are basic perspectives, concepts, foundations, ideas about learning how to learn, how to think, how to ask questions, and perhaps more critically, understand the location of one's position within learning traditions as well as political, economic and culturally embedded contexts. All these aspects of higher education enable the development of thinking individuals, and creating such individuals is as much a part of the vision of higher education as the need to engage with the needs of a productive economy. It is a fallacy to assume beforehand that the twain shall never meet, even if they are assumed somehow to make 'strange bedfellows'![21]

A few issues that the private sector in university education can no longer afford to shy away from are discussed in this section:

(a) It is important to ensure academic autonomy, dignity, diversity and heterodoxy.[22] University spaces are different from the corporate industrial space (or spaces in a religious order, a political party, a non-governmental organisation [NGO], a government department, the armed forces, a private corporation, and so on) since heterodoxy is the very foundation of a university. Heterodoxy is not just a matter of different disciplines and ideologies but also of cultures and processes, which are more collegial and peer-driven.[23] Universities are supposed to encourage, respect and celebrate a plurality of ideas and practices.

Conversely, the more a university is subject to political and economic pressures, the less it will be able to fulfil its core responsibilities. Autonomy is therefore the very life-blood of the university and the people who comprise it.

The absence of heterodoxy and autonomy renders a university more susceptible to competing pressures (the State, political parties, private business, or a singular ideology) in a manner that questions its very existence.

Autonomy, intrinsic to the very idea of a university as a learning institution, therefore provides the legitimate basis for such heterodoxy.

The Kothari Commission report had shown vision in elaborating the concept of academic freedom (intrinsic to university autonomy) by highlighting that

a teacher cannot be ordered or required to teach something which goes against his conscience or conflicts of his conception of truth ... A teacher should be free to pursue and publish his studies and research; and speak and write about it and participate in debates on significant national and international issues. He should receive all facilities and encouragement in his work, teaching and research, even where his views and approach be in opposition to those of his seniors and the head of his department or faculty ... The universities have a major responsibility towards the promotion of an *intellectual climate* in the country which is conducive to the pursuit of scholarship and excellence, and which encourages criticism, ruthless and unsparing but informal and constructive. All this demands that teachers exercise their academic freedom in good measure, enthusiastically and wisely (NCERT 1970: 644; emphasis added).

More recently, Harsh V. Pant eloquently expressed the vision of a liberal education as one that 'encourages us to ask probing questions about the perplexities and challenges of human experience ... it is liberal education that produces a thinking citizen, the backbone of a democracy', while cautioning rather alarmingly that 'Indian Higher Education has all but abandoned the intellectual and moral principles that have traditionally informed and given substance to liberal education' (Pant 2008: 174).

(b) Autonomy and freedom from political, corporate and bureaucratic interference is often a direct function of the financial sustainability of the university. In universities funded by the private sector, it is critical to build large endowments and create policies that encourage such subsidies. In the absence of these, universities will be beset by questions of the long-run, of recurring operational costs and capital expenses for expansion and growth. A number of factors therefore have to work together: the regulatory environment needs to encourage large endowments; the private sector must show some vision to build universities for the long haul; and various supplemental arms of the university may well be engaged in forms of productive revenue generation, which can be ploughed back to the university's development without compromising on the not-for-profit status of the university and without detracting from its core learning and knowledge mission. Without a clear look at endowments (and

facilitative policies that enable these), as well as continuous revenue streams, questions of financial viability will continue to be locked into those of short-term sustainability, translated into quick results, limited to questions of fees, and at the worst, into malpractices and ethically questionable behaviour.

(c) It is important to address the challenge of social inclusion, especially with current disparities in GER rates among marginalised communities. It is expected that with the universalisation of secondary education in the future, increasing numbers of historically marginalised sections of the population will enter higher education. Enabling equity and social inclusion is a priority for the Government of India and higher education regulators. In practice this has translated into the provision of quotas in education to those from various disadvantaged backgrounds: economic, social and historical. Reservation (in the form of numerical quotas) exists for Scheduled Castes (SCs), Scheduled Tribes (STs) and Other Backward Classes (OBCs) in State-funded institutions. On 'needs-blind admissions' (recommended by the NKC), there is no clarity yet on any such policy.

The Supreme Court had earlier held that reservation in the form of state percentages in admission was impermissible in private unaided institutions.[24] However, in a more recent judgement not directly involving private educational institutions, three judges of the court left this particular matter an open question to be decided later. A single judge pronounced that such reservation is clearly constitutionally impermissible in private institutions.[25]

The private sector needs to come to terms with the goal of inclusive education and diversity as necessary and worthwhile, not just in instrumental terms but also in constitutive terms. They need to build on the autonomy currently provided to private unaided institutions in deciding on the means and manner of ensuring such inclusiveness through more comprehensive affirmative action schemes. There is no policy yet on Affirmative Action or on developing a Multi-Deprivation Index, which takes into account various dimensions of deprivation and exclusion such as caste, income, gender, region, social strata, residence, physical disability, religion, and so on.[26] A nuanced understanding of the multiple natures of deprivation and exclusion is necessary, which can be applied in the form of a Multi-Deprivation Index and further the cause of more inclusive education.

(d) Along with expansion and social equity is the critical need to ensure excellence in higher education. India's best institutions do not rank among the world's leaders, despite all the regulatory measures ostensibly carried out to ensure quality. The reasons are many. It takes a lot of time, investment, talent, and effort to set up and sustain universities of excellence that rank among the world's best and also fulfil India's multiple contextual needs, ideas, hopes, dreams, and aspirations. A regulatory framework needs to first acknowledge that such initiatives are within the realm of possibility first. Millions of young Indians do not have access to quality higher education, comparable to international standards. Only those who can afford it leave for foreign universities.

Large-scale private investment, particularly through a few 'trend-setting' institutions, will visibly demonstrate global best practices within the shortest possible timeframe, and thereby also help broaden the policy discourse into imagining possibilities. Some of these universities could also be engaged in developing solutions in critical and emerging areas of national development.

It is acknowledged that the best universities of the world have three defining characteristics:

(i) presence of a critical mass of top students and faculty in high concentrations of talent;

(ii) abundance of resources (including public funding, private endowments and other resources generated) and sustenance over a longer timeframe without intrusions on autonomy; and

(iii) appropriate governance, i.e., a very high degree of academic and managerial autonomy, which encourages competitiveness, unrestrained scientific inquiry, innovation, and creativity (Altbach and Salmi 2011; Salmi 2010). It will be worthwhile to explore how these conditions can be created in Indian institutions in order to fulfil critical national developmental goals as well as to reach globally competitive standards of quality.

(e) Community engagement is a crucial aspect (Planning Commission 2011a). The formal language of academic enquiry is not entirely familiar or conversant with the informal modes and languages of the community around which the university finds itself (see Becher and Trowler 2008: 161–64, 181–205). Universities in India and elsewhere have emerged as 'crucibles of modernity' (Guha 2008) as a result of a particular historical context. While these universities have played a significant part in the promotion of public reason and rights, the relationship between the university and the community is still somewhat tenuous at most times and ambivalent at best. Some of this ambivalence is a direct result of increasing specialisation within disciplines, where each discipline (and its sub-schools) has its own jargon, rendering engagement with the outside world (including those outside the university gates) incomprehensible (Frug 1999; Nandy 2006, 2008).[27]

Universities are spatially located within physical, social and political contexts. It is in the spirit of inclusion and learning to find meanings and methods of engaging better with the neighbourhoods around the university as well as the broader community. Pedagogic elements, evaluation patterns, incentives for students and faculty, are measures that universities could facilitate for better mutual interaction with community in a manner that does not detract from the learning mission.[28]

Whether it is a university funded by private or public hands, people will continue to be critical links. Dignity in learning and of learners (faculty and students) is worth preserving, also for its own sake. It is worth asking what people do, feel and think (and why), and what does such dignity in learning mean in the first place. This is, at its heart, a humanist enterprise and nothing should take the humanism away, by design or omission. Inherent in this enterprise are difficult questions on how the self is shaped, who an engaged citizen is, what 'cultivating humanity' requires, and what could be the various ways of learning in a university. Let answers keep coming and let difficult questions not go away (Nussbaum 1998).

Conclusion

The role of the private sector in university education will gradually acquire more significance with rising GER targets. The policy environment needs to encourage genuine private investment, within the framework of education as a not-for-profit activity, where revenue surpluses are ploughed back for development of the university. Various elements of the regulatory puzzle need to be unbundled for such policy facilitation. There is also a need for better visioning of basic regulatory principles, which can perhaps help anchor and inform the debate. At the heart of the university is a shared respect for academic endeavour, dignity of learning, along with the socio-economic and democratic values that a university must take care to nourish. This applies to the private sector as much as to the public, but particularly for the private sector as they shape their visions of a university. There is a clear need for institutional exemplars that can help demonstrate such a vision of private sector university education for public and social good. This will not only help allay some of the suspicions regarding private sector motivation but also initiate demonstrable first steps along a broader imagination of university education in general. It is necessary to renew the debate and introspect on imaginative possibilities of learning in universities.

NOTES

1. See also Planning Commission (2011b). The United States (US) and South Korea spend 3.1 per cent and 2.4 per cent of their GDP on higher education respectively (Planning Commission 2012).

2. *P. A. Inamdar v. State of Maharashtra* (2005) 6 SCC 537; *T. M. A. Pai Foundation v. State of Karnataka* (2002) 8 SCC 712.

3. See the Prohibition of Unfair Practices in Technical Educational Institutions, Medical Educational Institutions and Universities Bill, 2010 (particularly Clause 6).

4. *P. A. Inamdar v. State of Maharashtra* (2005) 6 SCC 537.

5. 'Co-ordination and determination of standards in institutions for higher education or research and scientific and technical institutions'. http://www.constitution.org/cons/india/shed07.htm (accessed 14 November 2012).

6. 'Education, including technical education, medical education and universities, subject to the provisions of entries 63, 64, 65 and 66 of List I; vocational and technical training of labour'. http://www.constitution.org/cons/india/shed07.htm (accessed 14 November 2012).

7. *Bharati Vidyapeeth (Deemed University) v. State of Maharashtra* (2004) 11 SCC 755; *State of Tamil Nadu v. Adhiyaman Educational and Research Institute* (1995) 4 SCC 104; *Prof. Yashpal & Anr v. State of Chhattisgarh & Ors* [Supreme Court, Writ Petition (Civil) No. 19 of 2004].

8. *State of Tamil Nadu v. Adhiyaman Educational and Research Institute* (1995) 4 SCC 104.

9. *Preeti Shrivastava (Dr.) v. State of Madhya Pradesh* (1999) 7 SCC 120; *Prof. Yashpal & Anr v. State of Chhattisgarh & Ors* [Supreme Court, Writ Petition (Civil) No. 19 of 2004].

10. *Prof. Yashpal & Anr v. State of Chhattisgarh & Ors* [Supreme Court, Writ Petition (Civil) No. 19 of 2004].

11. *Prof. Yashpal & Anr v. State of Chhattisgarh & Ors* [Supreme Court, Writ Petition (Civil) No. 19 of 2004].

12. 'Technical institutions' are subject to rigorous prior approval procedures not just to establish or change courses/programmes, but also to vary intake capacity, where the maximum intake is strictly prescribed by the AICTE. Further, rules of territorial jurisdiction circumscribe universities to limited geographical domains, making expansion efforts even more difficult.

13. The Indira Gandhi National Open University (IGNOU) could be considered the largest university in the world with over 2 million enrolled students; Delhi University with over 0.4 million students could be the largest regular university in India.

14. *T. M. A. Pai Foundation v. State of Karnataka* (2002) 8 SCC 712.

15. *P. A. Inamdar v. State of Maharashtra* (2005) 6 SCC 537.

16. See 'specific clauses' of the UGC Regulation — e.g., 'shall conform to relevant provisions of UGC Act, as amended, from time to time' (3.1); 'programme of study leading to a degree and post-graduate degree/diploma offered by a private university shall conform to relevant regulations/norms of the UGC or the concerned statutory body' (3.6); 'shall fulfill the minimum criteria ... as laid down ... by the UGC and [the statutory body]' (3.4) (UGC 2003).

17. *Prof. Yashpal & Anr v. State of Chhattisgarh & Ors* [Supreme Court, Writ Petition (Civil) No. 19 of 2004]; also *Bharati Vidyapeeth (Deemed University) v. State of Maharashtra* (2004) 11 SCC 755.

18. Devesh Kapur and Pratap Bhanu Mehta estimated that as much as $3.5 billion was spent by Indians in 'consuming education' abroad in 2005–06 alone, a 'staggering amount for a poor country whose own educational institutions are starved of resources' (Kapur and Mehta 2007: 127, 2008).

19. The K. B. Pawar Committee constituted by the UGC recommended four PPP models: *(a)* Basic Infrastructure (infrastructure investment by private sector, operations and management with annual payments by the government); *(b)* Outsourcing (infrastructure investment and operations and management by private sector with the government paying for specific services); *(c)* Equity/Hybrid (infrastructural investments shared, operations and management with the private sector); *(d)* Reserve Outsourcing (infrastructure investment by the government and operations and management by the private sector) (MHRD 2011).

20. See, for example, J. N. Tata's vision in creating the IISc in 1909, the creation and subsequent secularisation of the Banaras Hindu University (1915) and Aligarh Muslim University (1920) as also the role of Rabindranath Tagore in creating Vishwa Bharati University (1921) (Balaram 2009; Dar and Somaskandan 2007; Nizami 2009; Subbarayappa 1992). See also the prominent role played by Vikram Sarabhai in setting up the Indian Institute of Management (IIM), Ahmedabad.

21. A comment usually reserved with derision for politics, which is supposed to make strange bedfellows.

22. See André Béteille (2000), particularly, chapters on 'Intellectuals' (ibid.: 57–82) (quoting Gramsci: that 'all men are intellectuals, one could therefore say: but not all men in society have the function of intellectuals', further, 'there is a critical, creative and contemplative side to the mind of every human being, and no human being, whether scholar, poet or philosopher, is critical, creative or contemplative in every one of his activities' and the Gramscian categorisation of the 'traditional and organic' [Gramsci 2004: 57, 64–65]); 'A career in an Indian University', 'Universities as centres of learning and 'universities as institutions' (Béteille 2000). See Mehta (2007, 2009, 2010, 2011a, 2011b).

23. See Becher and Trowler (2008: 161–64, 181–205). 'Another anthropologist advocating "an ethnography of the disciplines" has sketched the outlines of a possible solution' (Geertz 1983, quoted in Becher and Trowler 2008: 205). 'The problem of integration of cultural life becomes one of making it possible for people inhabiting different worlds to have a genuine, and reciprocal impact, impact upon one another . . . and the first step is surely to accept the depth of the differences; the second is to understand what these differences are; and the third to construct some sort of vocabulary in which they can be formulated' (Becher and Trowler 2008: 205).

24. *P. A. Inamdar v. Maharashtra* (2005) 6 SCC 537.

25. *Ashoka Kumar Thakur v. Union of India* (2008) 6 SCC 1.

26. See NKC (2009), especially 'Recommendations' (ibid.: 21–162) and 'Note on Higher Education' (ibid.: 66–77).

27. '[I]t would be important from now on to know how to intertwine the love of the same and love of the other, faithfulness to self and becoming with the other ... cultural fertility would result from *listening* to the effects of mixing' (Irigaray 2002: 141).

28. See Prasad (1998), particularly, 'Why Art Education?' 'The educator who practises the experience of the other side and stands firm in it, experiences two things together, first that he is bound by otherness, and second that he receives grace by being bound to

the other ... the responsibility for this living soul [should point] him to that which seems impossible yet is somehow granted to us — to self-education. But self education, here as everywhere,

cannot take place through one's being concerned with oneself but only through one's being concerned, knowing what it means, with the world' (Buber 1947: 119–20, quoted in Prasad 1998).

References

Agarwal, Pawan. 2009. *Indian Higher Education: Envisioning the Future*. New Delhi: Sage Publications.

Altbach, Philip G. and Jamil Salmi (ed.). 2011. *The Road to Academic Excellence: The Making of World-Class Research Universities*. Washington, DC: World Bank.

Balaram, P. 2009. 'The Indian Institute of Science: Reflections on a Century', *Current Science*, 96(10): 1404–11.

Becher, Tony and Paul R Trowler (eds). 2008. *Academic Tribes and Territories*. Berkshire: McGraw-Hill.

Béteille, André. 2000. *Antinomies of Society: Essays on Ideologies and Institutions*. New Delhi: Oxford University Press.

Buber, Martin. 1947. *Between Man and Man*, trans. Ronald Gregor-Smith. London: Routledge and Kegan Paul.

Chopra, Ritika. 2011. 'UGC Puts Deemed University Tag in Freezer'. *India Today*, 31 December. http://indiatoday.intoday.in/story/ugc-puts-deemed-university-tag-in-freezer/1/166634.html (accessed 4 November 2012).

Dar, Shivanandan Lal and S. Somaskandan. 2007. *History of the Banaras Hindu University*. Varanasi: Banaras Hindu University.

Frug, Gerald E. 1999. *City Making: Building Communities without Building Walls*. Princeton: Princeton University Press.

Geertz, Clifford. 1983. *Local Knowledge*. New York: Basic Books.

Government of India (GoI). 2010a. 'The Educational Tribunals Bill, 2010'. http://www.prsindia.org/uploads/media/Educational%20Tribunals%20Bill%202010/Educational%20Tribunal%20Bill,%202010.pdf (accessed 14 November 2012).

———. 2010b. 'The Foreign Educational Institutions (Regulation of Entry and Operations) Bill, 2010'. http://www.prsindia.org/uploads/media/Foreign%20Educational%20Institutions%20Regulation/Foreign%20Educational%20Institutions%20Regulation%20of%20Entry%20and%20Operations%20Bill%20%202010.pdf (accessed 14 November 2012).

———. 2010c. 'The National Accreditation Regulatory Authority for Higher Educational Institutions Bill, 2010'. http://www.jeywin.com/wp-content/uploads/2010/05/National-Accreditation-Regulatory-Authority-for-Higher-Educational-Institutions-Bill-2010.pdf (accessed 14 November 2012).

———. 2010d. 'The Prohibition of Unfair Practices in Technical Educational Institutions, Medical Educational Institutions and Universities Bill, 2010'. http://www.barcouncilofindia.org/wp-content/uploads/2010/06/Prohibition-of-unfair-practices-in-Technical-Educational-Institutions-Medical-Educational-Institutions-and-University-Bill-2010.pdf (accessed 14 November 2012).

———. 2011. 'The Higher Education and Research Bill, 2011'. http://164.100.47.5/newcommittee/press_release/bill/Committee%20on%20HRD/high%20edu.pdf (accessed 15 November 2012).

———. 2012. 'The Universities for Research and Innovation Bill, 2012'. http://164.100.47.5/newcommittee/press_release/bill/Committee%20on%20HRD/Universities%20for%20Research%20and%20Innovation%20Bill,%202012.pdf (accessed 15 November 2012).

Gramsci, Antonio. 2004. *Social Theory*, ed. Charles Lemert. New Delhi: Rawat Publications.

Guha, Ramachandra. 2008. 'Crucibles of Modernity', *Beyond Degrees: IIC Quarterly*, 34(24).

Irigaray, Luce. 2002. *Between East and West*. New York: Columbia University Press.

Kapur, Devesh and Pratap Bhanu Mehta. 2007. 'Mortgaging the Future? Indian Higher Education', in Suman Bery, Barry Bosworth and Arvind Panagariya (eds), *India Policy Forum, 2007/08*, vol. 4, pp. 101–58. New Delhi: Sage Publications.

———. 2008. 'Mortgaging the Future', *Beyond Degrees: IIC Quarterly*, 34(24).

Mehta, Pratap Bhanu. 2007. 'Passing of the Professoriate'. *Indian Express*, 31 October.

———. 2009. 'Century of Forgetting'. *Indian Express*, 16 June.

———. 2010. 'Class Struggle'. *Indian Express*, 27 November.

———. 2011a. 'Questions Lit Up'. *Indian Express*, 26 October.

———. 2011b. 'The Multi-Individual Society', *Indian Express*, 9 February.

Ministry of Human Resource Development (MHRD). 2009. 'Report of the Committee to Advise on Renovation and Rejuvenation of Higher Education'. http://www.academics-india.com/Yashpal-committee-report.pdf (accessed 10 October 2012).

———. 2011. 'Consolidated Working Group Report of the Department of Higher Education for XII Five Year Plan on Higher Education, Technical Education and Private Sector Participation including PPP in Higher Education'. Department of Higher Education, Ministry of Human Resource Development, Government of India.

Nandy, Ashis. 2006. *Talking India*. New Delhi: Oxford University Press.

———. 2008. 'Modernity and the Sense of Loss', in *Does Culture Make a Difference? Progress and Development in India and its Implications for International Cooperation*, pp. 20–31. Calcutta: Seagull Books.

National Council of Educational Research and Training (NCERT). 1970. *Education and National Development: Report of the Education Commission, 1964–66 — Higher Education*. New Delhi: National Council of Educational Research And Training. http://www.teindia.nic.in/Files/Reports/CCR/KC/KC_V3.pdf (accessed 14 November 2012).

National Knowledge Commission (NKC). 2009. *Report to the Nation (2006–09)*. New Delhi: National Knowledge Commission, Government of India.

Nizami, Khaliq Ahmad. 2009. History of the Aligarh Muslim University. Delhi: Idarah-i Adabiyat-i-Delli.

Nussbaum, Martha C. 1998. *Cultivating Humanity: A Classical Defence of Reform in Liberal Education*. London: Harvard University Press.

Pant, Harsh V. 2008. 'In Defence of Liberal Education', *Beyond Degrees: IIC Quarterly*, 34(24).

Planning Commission. 2008. *Eleventh Five Year Plan 2007–2012*. New Delhi: Oxford University Press.

—————. 2011a. '12th Plan Sub-Committee on Strengthening of Community Engagement in Higher Educational Institutions in India'. Planning Commission, Government of India.

—————. 2011b. *Faster, Sustainable and More Inclusive Growth: An Approach to the Twelfth Five Year Plan*. New Delhi: Planning Commission, Government of India.

—————. 2012. 'Committee on Corporate Sector Participation in Higher Education (Chairperson N. R. Narayana Murthy)'. Planning Commission, Government of India.

Prasad, Devi. 1998. *Art: The Basis of Education*. New Delhi: National Book Trust.

Salmi, Jamil. 2010. 'Ten Common Errors in Building a New World-Class University'. World Bank.

Subbarayappa, B. V. 1992. *In Pursuit of Excellence: A History of the Indian Institute of Science*. New Delhi: Tata McGraw-Hill.

University Grants Commission (UGC). 2002. *The University Grants Commission Act, 1956 (As Modified up to the 20th December, 1985) and Rules and Regulations under the Act*. New Delhi: University Grants Commission. http://india.gov.in/allimpfrms/allacts/3334.pdf (accessed 14 November 2012).

—————. 2003. 'UGC (Establishment of and Maintenance of Standards in Private Universities) Regulations, 2003'. University Grants Commission, New Delhi.

—————. 2010. 'UGC (Institutions Deemed to be Universities) Regulations 2010'. University Grants Commission, New Delhi. http://www.ugc.ac.in/oldpdf/regulations/gazzeetenglish.pdf (accessed 14 November 2012).

—————. 2011. Inclusive and Qualitative Expansion of Higher Education — 12th Five-Year Plan (2012–17). New Delhi: University Grants Commission.

18 Skill Development in India
A Transformation in the Making

Dilip Chenoy

INTRODUCTION: THE SKILLS CHALLENGE

With the opening up of the economy and increase in exports, improving the productivity of the workforce is a key challenge for many corporations and entities in India. Further, as the Indian economy grows, a large number of skilled persons will be required to sustain this growth. Current studies indicate that net enrolment in vocational courses in India is about 5.5 million per year compared to 90 million in China and 11.3 million in the United States (US). A mere 2 per cent of Indian workers are formally skilled.

Significantly, the bulk of the labour force in India — about 93 per cent — who work in the unorganised sector are largely untouched by any kind of formal training. By way of comparison, 96 per cent of the workers in South Korea receive formal skills training. This is 80 per cent in Japan, 75 per cent in Germany and 68 per cent in the United Kingdom (UK).

According to a Boston Consulting Group (BCG) report prepared for the Confederation of Indian Industry (CII), India's workforce in 2006–07 numbered 484 million (Sinha et al. 2008). Out of this, 273 million were working in rural areas, primarily in agriculture, while 61 million were working in manufacturing and about 150 million in services. As per the BCG study, 40 per cent of the current workforce is illiterate and another 40 per cent is made up of school dropouts. Those who are vocationally-trained, diploma holders, graduates and above comprise a mere 10 per cent of the overall workforce, while those who have completed 12 years of schooling comprise another 10 per cent.

Software industry body National Association of Software and Services Companies (NASSCOM) says that of the 400,000-odd engineering graduates who pass out every year, only 20 per cent would meet the requirements of the Indian industry. The rest would have to go through rigorous training before businesses could find use for them.

Given this background, one would expect that firms would invest in in-service training. But the World Bank India Country Strategy 2009–2012 (World Bank 2010) indicates that in-service training is received by only 15 per cent of workers in the manufacturing sector, which is far below what is observed in many countries, with the inadequate availability of training capacity being one of the major reasons for this. So the first challenge is to increase the number of skilled persons in the workforce.

Yet this is far from easy. The 11th Five-Year Plan document mentioned that while 12.8 million people join the Indian workforce each year, the annual training capacity is less than half of that (GoI 2007). With one of the youngest populations in the world and projected to have 64 per cent of its likely population in the 15–59 age bracket by 2021 (GoI 2012), India is uniquely positioned to take advantage of this favourable demographic profile to take that giant leap from being a developing country to a developed one in a decade from now.

However, leveraging this 'demographic dividend' (the average age of an Indian would be 29 by 2020 compared to 37 in China and the US, and 45 in western Europe [GoI 2012]) is easier said than done on account of the poor level of skills possessed by the vast majority of those joining the workforce each year — a situation that has arisen owing to high rates of school dropouts, inadequate skills training capacity, a negative perception around skilling, and low employability of even those holding professional qualifications, such as degrees in different engineering disciplines. An additional issue is that these outcomes vary from state to state.

According to the *Economic Survey 2011–12* (ibid.), 63.5 million new entrants would be added to the working age group during the period 2011–16. The challenges are further enhanced by the studies by consulting firms IMaCS and Aon Hewitt that forecast an incremental shortfall of nearly 350 million people[1] by 2022 in 20 high-growth sectors of the Indian economy, the infrastructure sector and the unorganised segment.

NATIONAL POLICY ON SKILL DEVELOPMENT

Conscious of the vital role that skill development can play in the growth of a nation, the Prime Minister, in August 2008, outlined his vision for skill development in India. He stated that 'experts have estimated that India has the capacity to

TABLE 18.1   Incremental Skill Gap across Various Industries in India in 2022

Industry	Incremental requirement (in million)
Building and Construction Industry	33.0
Infrastructure Sector	103.02
Real Estate Services	14.0
Gems and Jewellery	4.6
Leather and Leather Goods	4.6
Organised Retail	17.3
Textiles and Clothing	26.2
Electronics and IT Hardware	3.3
Auto and Auto Components	35.0
IT and ITES	5.3
Banking, Financial Services and Insurance	4.2
Furniture and Furnishings	3.4
Tourism and Hospitality Services	3.6
Construction Material and Building Hardware	1.4
Chemicals and Pharmaceuticals	1.9
Food Processing	9.3
Healthcare	12.7
Transportation and Logistics	17.7
Media and Entertainment	3.0
Education and Skill Development Services	5.8
Select Informal Employment Sectors (Domestic Help, Beauticians, Security Guards)	37.6
Incremental	347

Sources: IMaCS reports 'Human Resource and Skill Gap Requirements (2022)', 2008; Aon Hewitt report 'Talent Projections and Skill Gap Analysis for the Infrastructure Sector (2022)', 2011, National Skill Development Corporation (NSDC).

create 500 million certified and skilled technicians by the year 2022' (PIB 2008).

The Prime Minister also outlined the institutional structure at the national level for coordinated action in the skills space. This consisted of the establishment of a National Council for Skill Development, chaired by the Prime Minister himself, at the apex to lay down the broad framework for this arena; a National Skill Development Coordination Board (NSDCB), coordinated by the Planning Commission to combine public and private prongs of action; and the setting up of a National Skill Development Corporation (NSDC) as a not-for-profit company through the Public–Private Partnership (PPP) route to catalyse private sector involvement in the skills space.

In March 2009, the Government announced a National Policy on Skill Development, laying down the framework within which it wanted skills-related training to be conducted. The Policy clarified the roles that different stakeholders — government, industry, trade unions, and civil society — would need to play for the creation of a skills ecosystem in India.

Making a departure from the past, the 2009 Skill Development Policy clearly specified that skills-related training should become outcome-focused and linked to jobs and employability. The Policy stated that access to training should be available to all, particularly those at the bottom of the pyramid. It said that the government should complement private sector initiatives in skill development and emphasised the need for short-term, industry-relevant courses.

Adding that infrastructure should be created for on-the-job training and apprenticeships encouraged through a possible change in legislation if required, it also stated that prevalent employment exchanges would be transformed into career guidance centres to channelise applicants to jobs, apprenticeships and training.

The Policy called for the establishment of an effective assessment and credible certification framework, publicising information on training institution outcomes to ensure greater transparency, and a greater role of state governments in the skilling initiative so that these combined measures could expand employment in the formal sector.

Significantly, the Policy talked of encouraging innovation in delivery such as using school infrastructure for skills training after school hours, ensuring greater participation of women and those living in rural India in vocational training programmes, and more PPPs in the skills space.

In January 2011, the Government appointed Mr S. Ramadorai, vice-chairman of India's biggest Information Technology (IT) software firm, Tata Consultancy Services (TCS), as Skills Advisor to the Prime Minister with the rank of a cabinet minister to provide an impetus to the skilling mission.

CURRENT SKILLS ARCHITECTURE AND LIMITATIONS

Seventeen Ministries of the Government of India, ranging from the Ministry of Labour and Employment to that of Human Resource Development and Food Processing Industries, are presently engaged in undertaking different training initiatives with the combined target of skilling 350 million people by 2022.

The NSDC was also set up to enable skills-related training through its private-sector partners with the intention of skilling 150 million people by 2022 to contribute to the prime minister's vision of skilling half-a-billion Indians.

Most of the formal skills-related training in the government apparatus happens through the Industrial Training Institutes (ITIs) and the Industrial Training Centres (ITCs), which come under the Ministry of Labour and Employment. The Ministry of Human Resource Development provides support to polytechnics for engineering disciplines. Many of the ITIs have now been brought under the PPP route with the private partner responsible for the management of the institution. The goal is to get all of 1,396 ITIs under the PPP mode. Through private sector participation, 400 other ITIs are being transformed into centres of excellence.

Informal skills-related training, including that in the traditional arts and crafts of India, is also supported through different government schemes. The Ministry of Textiles has a number of institutional partners to develop skills required in the textiles, apparel and handicraft sectors. The Ministry of Medium, Small and Micro Enterprises has programmes that run good-quality tool rooms and other training programmes through the Khadi and Village Industries Commission. The Ministry of Labour has developed the modular employable skills training scheme to enable vocational training providers to conduct short-term courses that are employment-linked.

All states have set up Skill Development Missions and some have even put together a strategy to equip millions of persons with skill over the next few years. Many PPP models have been put forth and bids invited to engage the private sector in skill development.

The National Open School system also runs a number of vocational training programmes. A number of community colleges — over 600 — have been approved by the Indira Gandhi National Open University (IGNOU) and other states. Many of these are run by the private sector. Some states are also approving the setting up of skills universities.

Many companies, too, conduct training programmes to meet the skilling requirements of their own workforce, or sometimes as part of their corporate social responsibility (CSR) initiatives. Non-governmental organisations (NGOs) also conduct skills-related training to address the needs of the segments they are working with. Clearly, there are multiple efforts and due to the nature of the PPP models, the efforts of the private sector are also linked to different schemes.

The Ministry of Labour and Employment has entrusted the National Council for Vocational Training (NCVT) to prescribe standards and curricula for the training imparted at ITIs and ITCs. States also play a part in this process through State Councils for Vocational Training (SCVTs). Steps are being under taken to strengthen the NCVT structure.

As part of the National Policy on Skill Development, 2009, the NSDC has been given the responsibility of setting up Sector Skill Councils (SSCs) to define standards for the segments they represent. The Ministry of Human Resource Development, in conjunction with the SSCs being set up by the NSDC, is launching the National Vocational Education Qualification Framework (NVEQF) to allow seamless migration from vocational to formal education. The All India Council for Technical Education (AICTE) has also launched a scheme under the NVEQF. Given that these efforts are parallel in nature, efforts are on to align them and bring about a uniform framework. This would be a key to the progress of skill development in future.

This framework for skill development, however, is not robust and has several limitations, which may be broadly categorised as:

(a) Institutional/scalability,
(b) Financial,
(c) Perceptional,
(d) Industry/Employer apathy, and
(e) Quality issues.

Although many ITIs are now managed by the private sector, which has resulted in some modification in course content at these institutions, the lack of scale means that not too many students benefited from this training. Lack of scale is also an issue with several vocational training centres run in the private sector. The year-on-year training capacity would have to rise to nearly 40–50 million incrementally over the next 10 years for India to achieve its target of skilling 500 million people by 2022.

The question of who pays for skill development is currently exercising the minds of many. It is clearly established that the poor are willing to pay for good quality products and services, including skill-training, as long as there is an outcome — job in the case of skill-training associated with it. Firms are not yet inclined to pay a placement fee for correctly skilled persons who could be productive on the job from the first day. In some other industries, the remuneration does not excite people enough to skill themselves and join a job. In some sectors, the challenge is much greater as people do not even join after a stint of free training.

The lack of a universal skill loan product is another big hindrance in the way of creating a skills ecosystem in the country. The current bank financing model, with its emphasis on collaterals or guarantees, acts as a big stumbling block for a number of people at the bottom of the pyramid who could have used the skill-training to improve their stations in life and contribute to the country's growth. As of now, the Central Bank of India is the only public sector lender active in this space, and there too, its intervention is limited to the partners of the NSDC. Although the declaration of a Credit Guarantee Fund in the Budget announced for 2012–13 is a positive development, it is still too early to comment on the impact it may have as the mechanism for its operations is still unclear. Even if the banks do aggressively start lending, there is a need for other Non-Banking Finance Companies (NBFCs) to enter this space.

Skill development also carries a negative perception in many quarters, with the prevalent notion being that skill-training courses are only meant for those who could not make it in the formal education system. Parents push their children to become graduates. This results in enrolments at vocational courses not taking place out of choice and also low enrolments at skilling centres. This, in turn, leads to a lower number of skilled people emerging out of these institutions. With no prestige or aspiration built into skilling and consequently people staying away from it, there is a huge skills gap created in diverse spheres, ranging all the way from plumbers and electricians, to nurses and teachers.

The problem in the way of evolving a skills culture has not been helped by the industry's own reluctance to encourage skilling by hiring skilled workers at all levels or creating an adequate salary differential between skilled and unskilled or semi-skilled workers so that people are encouraged to get themselves skilled. The industry has also been lukewarm in skilling its own workforce with the incidence of in-service skilling being one of the lowest in India. The industry, moreover, has not moved briskly on collectively addressing the problem of course curriculum at educational institutions/ vocational training centres not being in sync with its requirements. As part of the National Policy on Skill Development, 2009, though, the industry has been empowered to do this through the establishment of SSCs, which apart from defining the quality standard, can also take care of accreditation and certification issues.

Many skill development initiatives in the government and private space are not focused on employment and employability with the courses not keeping in mind the needs of the ultimate user — the industry or the employer. The stress on the supply side results in a quantity, quality and qualification mismatch. This causes disappointments to both the person wanting the job and the one giving it.

Many argue that the cause of skill development, moreover, has received a setback through select social schemes of the government, such as the Mahatma Gandhi National Employment Guarantee Act, that have had the impact of making rural people stay away from skill development initiatives. By being assured of a certain amount every year, a number of rural people have now started feeling they no longer need to make the extra effort to get themselves skilled as the money is already coming in. A case had been made out to introduce an element of skill in the scheme so that persons who are employed under it could use a part of the funds to attain a skill that could in the medium or long term enable them to earn a livelihood and not be dependent.

NATIONAL SKILL DEVELOPMENT CORPORATION — TRANSFORMING THE SKILLS LANDSCAPE

The deficiencies in the skills training framework prompted the Prime Minister's Council on Skill Development to come up with an innovative PPP in the form of the NSDC in 2008–09 to address the skills gap in India. The idea was to have a system that enabled the government provision of training to be delinked from the government financing of training; focused on output (demand) rather than input (supply); stressed on competencies and not specific skills; was flexible; based on periodic labour market surveys; and addressed the issues of affordability and accessibility.

A unique experiment in the skills arena, the NSDC was officially launched in October 2009 with a mandate to skill 150 million people by 2022 in 20 focus sectors identified by the government and the informal segment through a three-pronged approach revolving around creating, funding and enabling sustainable skills training initiatives in the private space.

Structured as a PPP with government-ownership restricted to 49 per cent of the equity capital, majority ownership of the NSDC rests with the private sector with the shareholdings equally dispersed among 10 chambers of commerce and sector-specific industry organisations (See Box 18.1).

The money for meeting its funding requirements though is made available to the NSDC through a trust called the National Skill Development Fund (NSDF). The NSDC acts as an investment manager for the NSDF, whose current corpus of ₹15 billion is slated to go up to ₹25 billion following the Finance Minister's announcement of a further infusion of ₹10 billion in 2012–13. Going forward, the NSDF may have to attract private funding (See Box 18.2).

A Section 25 Company, the NSDC is a board-managed enterprise, with its 13 directors (four from the government and nine seats held by private-sector shareholders) taking the final call on how best to structure the funding and

Box 18.1
NSDC Ownership Pattern

500 Million

Prime Minister's National Council
for Skill Development

Advisor to PM
on Skills

National Skill Development
Co-ordination Board

350 Million

Government
Initiatives

17 Central Ministries

150 Million

Private Sector
Initiatives

N·S·D·C
National
Skill Development
Corporation

NSDC Structure

NSDC is a Public–Private
Partnership created by the
Ministry of Finance
- 51 per cent stake by industry
- 49 per cent stake by GoI

Initial funding of ₹10 billion
received from the GoI and parked
with the NSDF for use by NSDC;
Curent total funding of ₹25 billion

Target skilling/up-skilling
150 million people by 2022
by fostering private sector
participation

Source: GoI (2009).

Note: Set up as a PPP by the Ministry of Finance, the NSDC is a Section 25 company with a paid-up equity capital of ₹100 million. The Government holds 49 per cent of the equity in NSDC while the private sector has 51 per cent shareholding. The private-sector shareholders of the NSDC include 10 business chambers and industry-specific associations, with each having 5.1 per cent shareholding. The private-sector shareholders of NSDC are the Federation of Indian Chambers of Commerce and Industry (FICCI), the Associated Chambers of Commerce and Industry of India (ASSOCHAM), the CII, the Gems and Jewellery Export Promotion Council (GJEPC), the NASSCOM, the Society of Indian Automobile Manufacturers (SIAM), the Confederation of Real Estate Developers Associations of India (CREDAI), the Confederation of Indian Textile Industry (CITI), the Council for Leather Exports (CLE), and the Retailers Association of India (RAI).

which proposals should be financially supported by the organisation.

Over the nearly two-and-a-half years that the NSDC has been operational, the Corporation has put in place a mechanism that would allow for the creation of large, for-profit skills training ventures linked to jobs and employability, with the onus on the skills provider to ensure the employment of at least 70 per cent of the people they trained.

From big corporates such as TVS, Future or NIIT to NGOs such as Pratham, or educational institutions like the Centurion Group of Odisha to social entrepreneurs, there has been a growing interest among organisations to align with the NSDC to start sustainable skill development ventures. Corporate groups have increasingly started seeing merit in setting up skilling ventures of their own or supporting the skills mission by hiring skilled workers at all levels. Enquiries on how organisations could associate with the NSDC have increased substantially, which in turn has resulted in more

proposals being submitted and approved for funding by the NSDC Board.

Importantly, again, the proposals for skill development have encompassed diverse spheres and different geographies. The pace should pick up in the near future. The challenge for the NSDC is to quickly get a capacity to skill 200–210 million people by 2022 in place. The system has to be built such that it caters for projects that do not reach full capacity or potential.

Several key lending institutions, including the World Bank and the Asian Development Bank, have also expressed interest in participating in the Indian skills development initiative through the NSDF. The challenge here, however, is that as a country India would have to decide how it would like to allocate the funds from these organisations.

The NSDC has developed a 10-year plan. Till September 2012, the NSDC Board had committed funds to 77 projects, of which 61 are pure-play training proposals and 16 are SSC

Box 18.2
NSDC Funding Process

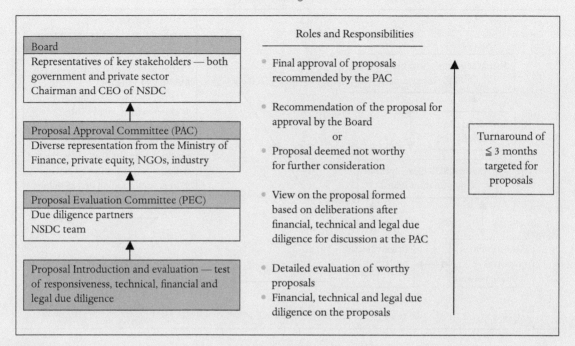

Source: GoI (2009).

NSDC assistance to its partners is provided in the form of soft loans, equity and grants, or even a combination of one or more financing options. Any organisation, including start-up ventures, having a scalable and sustainable business model that ensures the employability of the resources trained is eligible for funding by the NSDC. The amount of funding could extend up to 75 per cent of the project cost. Debt is offered at subsidised rates with other features like a moratorium built in depending on the nature of the project. Equity infusion by the NSDC is normally capped at 27 per cent of the total paid-up capital. Grant funding is considered only in select cases. The minimum ticket size of a training proposal that the NSDC normally insists on for the purpose of funding is 100,000 people over a 10-year span.

For the process of funding, the NSDC evaluates the 10-year business plan submitted by the prospective private partner, including NGOs, for its feasibility, sustainability and whether it meets its lending norms, and only then is a decision taken on whether the institution should be funded. Prospective NSDC partners also have to provide at least a 70 per cent employment guarantee for the students who would enroll in their centres to be eligible for funding by the NSDC. NSDC partner institutions have tie-ups with industry players and design courses keeping the requirements of the latter in mind. The certificates issued by the NSDC partners therefore have a good buy-in within the target industry segment. As mandated in the National Policy on Skill Development, 2009, the NSDC is also involved in constituting SSCs that would establish quality standards for the segments they represent. Funding for the establishment of SSCs in India is initially done by the NSDC. As it grows, each SSC can become a self-funded, for-profit organisation. The proposed SSCs would develop skill competency standards and qualifications, as well as standardise the affiliation and accreditation process. They would set up labor market information systems to assist in the planning and delivery of training, besides identifying skill development needs and preparing a catalogue of skill types. Promotion of academies of excellence and helping in executing train-the-trainers programmes also fall within the ambit of the SSCs. Once the SSCs are in place, an NSDC partner institution offering a course in that particular segment would have to get the curriculum ratified by the relevant SSC and also follow its assessment and certification procedure.

initiatives. As of August 2012, NSDC partners had trained 257,000 people across India and ensured jobs for over 194,000 of the young boys and girls who enrolled at their institutions to pursue skill development courses. In addition to this, NSDC Partners had also set up 4,030 physical and mobile training centres nationwide. Significantly, the capacity creation by NSDC partners has taken place not just in the bigger cities and towns, but also in remote and far-flung areas, small towns and villages.

Special skills training initiatives of the NSDC have been helping youth in restive parts of India, Jammu and Kashmir and the north-east to join the mainstream, and participate in and contribute to the process of economic growth. The NSDC has been able to get some of India's biggest corporate groups interested in the private sector-led skills training programme for graduates and post-graduates in Jammu and Kashmir. This initiative is targeted to be scaled up to 40,000 people being skilled and placed in jobs over a five-year span. We are seeking to reach out to more corporates to undertake projects under this initiative termed 'Udaan'. Incidentally, the Himayat programme run by the Ministry of Rural Development similarly is focused on the training and placement of youth who have not cleared Class XII.

In the north-east, nearly 200 people have already benefited from the Youth Employability Skill (YES) project for which the NSDC is partnering with the Ministry of Youth Affairs and Sports. This number would rise to 1,000 over the next few months.

Technology would play a crucial role in going forward, without the innovative use of which reaching the intended scale in a short duration would just not be possible. Technology for mobilisation — using the mobile phone, radio, social media, internet, television, movies, developing new online assessment tools, using modern-day technology such as haptics or other tools to develop computer- or tablet-based training curriculum or modules, digitised certificate banks, virtual employment exchanges — are all ecosystem interventions, and if done on a commercial basis, could be supported by the NSDC.

A transformation is taking place in the skills arena with a new breed of social entrepreneurs emerging in India.

By seeing its role as that of a social venture capital-cum-venture debit/development bank and putting its own skin in the game through patient capital, flexible financial terms and also a transparent and time-bound project approval, funding and monitoring framework, the NSDC has enabled its partners to make a business out of skills. A recent report by Kotak Institutional Equities has forecast that skill development can become a $20 billion business by 2022 (Kotak Institutional Equities Research 2011). Other reports have supported this market size.

Rather than being a pure-play financial institution though, the NSDC continues to focus on creating a supportive ecosystem for skill development. The emphasis is on creating a social market for skills and skill development. This is a tougher challenge than just funding entities to skill people.

To establish the demand for skill, the NSDC has been commissioning sectoral and state-specific skills gap studies. Through this initiative, the NSDC has been able to provide existing and prospective partners not only sectoral but district-level demand and supply perspectives for creating sustainable vocational training capacities. Skills gap studies are also being undertaken and commissioned for other critical sectors of the economy and ones holding promise. The NSDC has already completed skills gap studies for Odisha, the eight north-eastern states, and the infrastructure sector. Such studies are now being initiated for many other states. A sports skills gap study is also being done.

Through the incubation of the industry-led SSCs and development of Labour Market Information Systems, the NSDC has put in place the bedrock within which all skills training is to be conducted.

SSCs are employer-driven national partnership organisations that bring together all stakeholders — industry, labour and academia included — to achieve the common goal of creating a skilled workforce for the segments they represent. The SSCs develop skill competency standards and qualifications, as well as standardise the affiliation and accreditation process. They would put in place labour market information systems to assist in the planning and delivery of training, besides identifying skill development needs and preparing a catalogue of skill types. Promotion of academies of excellence and helping in executing train-the-trainer programmes would also fall within the ambit of the SSCs.

The NSDC has been actively engaged in fast-tracking the establishment of SSCs and integrating the courses being run by our training partners with the respective SSCs to facilitate accreditation, assessments, certification, and employment. Industry leadership is required to ensure that the Sector Councils function appropriately and the industry plays an active role. The challenge is to work collaboratively.

Many of the NSDC's partners such as NIIT, Future, Infrastructure Leasing & Financial Services Limited (IL&FS), for example, have embarked on large-scale training projects capable of training a minimum of 100,000 or more persons in 10 years either on their own or through consortiums and ensuring that the lack of trained people does not come in the way of the growth of Indian industry. This is not easy and requires new forms of working and partnerships.

At places, these organisations are even teaming up with ITIs to use the latter's spare infrastructure for running their courses in order to keep costs down and be in a position to start operations quickly. In other areas, school and other public infrastructure is being used. Training centres are being opened across the length and breadth of the country, including in areas affected by extremism.

The NSDC-funded institution, Gram Tarang, for instance, operates centres in the Naxal-affected belt of Odisha. Another NSDC Partner, IL&FS Education & Technology Services (ETS), proposes to start skill schools in some of the most backward areas of India so that the recipients of the training are in a position to get jobs or become self-employed.

Enterprises such as Empower Pragati are even training people to become housemaids or drivers and also helping them find gainful employment. Training organisations are setting up rural Business Process Outsourcing (BPO) services to employ persons trained by them and adding to the revenue streams. Companies are also coming up with innovative financing models whereby a part of the training costs of students are being taken care of by the potential employers of these trainees. Training firms are more often than not seeking potential trainees with employment letters from companies to mobilise students at their centres.

NGOs have also begun looking at sustainable models so that their programmes can benefit more people. Grants are no longer being seen as the only mode of raising funds for their activities. Going forward, government programmes could move towards scholarship- or voucher-based funding with the students having the choice of institution that they wish to attend.

Educational institutions too are either starting separate courses for skill development or establishing exclusive facilities for skills-related training. A new category of social entrepreneurs are slowly but surely transforming the space.

To counter a misconception around skills that it is only meant for those who could not make it in the formal education system, the NSDC has already started work on a communications campaign that would seek to glorify the pursuit of skills and explain to all stakeholders how a skilled workforce is absolutely essential for India to grow and prosper.

The proposed multi-lingual campaign will target all stakeholders — the prospective trainee, the society to which he/she belongs, corporates that would be hiring skilled workers, enterprises that would like to start sustainable skill development ventures, governments both at the Centre and states, and the media — to highlight the importance of skilling in a nation's advancement. It is not an easy task as many stakeholders have to be aligned to make it successful. Although seen by many as a panacea for filling the classroom, it would be dangerous to pin all hopes on the campaign alone. Training organisations have to build connections with the heart and soul of the many young people in the country and learn to tailor their offerings to fulfil their aspirations and also to meet the needs of the employer.

To create an aspiration for skills, the NSDC took on the responsibility of organising the Indian participation at the 2011 WorldSkills competition in London. A biennial event, WorldSkills is seen as a Skills Olympics and is designed to test the skills of people below the age of 23 in several disciplines, from car painting to IT software. India took part in 15 skills at the London WorldSkills event. The NSDC has already started preparing for the 2013 WorldSkills competition that would be held in Leipzig, Germany. The idea is to work towards creating standards conforming to international benchmarks.

CONCLUSION

Although the NSDC's interventions augur well for the cause of skills promotion, there is still no getting away from the fact that a lot more work needs to be done for the skills culture to take root in India. All the structural and financial interventions in the skills space would come to naught unless the industry sheds its reluctance to define what constitutes employability for a particular job role so that training programmes could be tailored to address this.

Each company within a particular industry often has its own yardstick for defining employability. Thus, for example, what Organisation A may describe as the basis for considering someone employable for a particular job role, Organisation B could have an entirely different perspective on it even if both enterprises are roughly of the same size and cater to similar kinds of customers.

With no uniform definitions of occupational standards for different job roles across industry segments, new entrants to the workforce in particular are often confused about where they stand on the employability scale, and are left completely at the mercy of Human Resource (HR) representatives of organisations to decide this for them.

Although the NSDC Board has approved funding of 16 SSCs till September 2012 (Agriculture, Auto, Banking, Financial Services and Insurance [BFSI], Electronics, Food Processing, Gems and Jewellery, Healthcare, IT, Logistics, Media and Entertainment, Plumbing, Private Security, Telecom, Retail, Leather and Rubber), getting a buy-in for the concept of a National Occupational Standard (NOS) is key. Even where the buy-in has taken place in a particular industry arena, getting it to fix a timeline for coming out with the occupational standards for as many job functions as possible has been pretty tough.

Skill development is a Chief Executive Officer (CEO) agenda. Industry leaders have to start taking ownership of driving the SSCs and the NOS exercise in their respective domains through greater involvement as without the occupational standards, accrediting system and certification in place, skill development would be reduced to just another futile exercise. Similarly, the various skill development programmes run by the different ministries and states could also align their requirements through the SSCs.

It is imperative to focus along the entire value chain of skill development, mobilisation to placement including post-placement support, and making this system scalable and sustainable. It is not a purely financial effort as it requires a great deal of understanding and social engineering as well. The skills landscape has to be transformed.

Unlike many developed countries, where skill development initiatives have been largely led by the government, the private sector in India has the opportunity to play a significant role in the country being able to produce job-ready and industry-ready professionals in large numbers.

Industry leaders here simply cannot afford to play a passive role in the skill development process and hope that the problem of skilled manpower would get sorted out all by itself, through government intervention or otherwise. Given the projected humongous shortfall of 347 million skilled people by 2022 in 20 key sectors of the economy and the infrastructure arena, the industry needs to wake up to the rude reality that a laidback approach to skilling on its part would only hasten its relegation to obscurity, and, in an extreme scenario, even put its own existence at risk.

For far too long, something as serious as skill development has been allowed to remain the exclusive preserve of either the HR, training or CSR cells of companies. Skill development is a CXO-level (executive-level) issue and deserves to be discussed in boardrooms.

The pace at which this transition happens would determine where India would stand 20 years hence — as just another fast-growing developing country or an influential member of the First World. CEOs have to lead and the time to act is now.

NOTE

1. IMaCS [ICRA Management Consulting Services Limited] Skill Gap Studies conducted for the National Skill Development Corporation (NSDC). http://www.nsdcindia.org/knowledge-bank/index.aspx (accessed 5 November 2012).

REFERENCES

Government of India (GoI). 2007. *Eleventh Five Year Plan 2007–12*. New Delhi: Oxford University Press.

———. 2009. 'National Policy on Skill Development'. Government of India.

———. 2012. *Economic Survey 2011–12*. New Delhi: Oxford University Press.

Kotak Institutional Equities Research. 2011. 'The Great Unskilled', *Game Changer*, 2(2), July.

Press Information Bureau (PIB). 2008. 'Prime Minister Writes to Chief Ministers Suggesting Use of Public Education Infrastructure for Skill Development'. Press Information Bureau, Government of India, 30 August.

Sinha, Janmejaya Kumar, James Abraham, and Rohit Vohra. 2008. *India's Demographic Dilemma: Talent Challenges for the Services Sector — [BCG Report]*. New Delhi: Confederation of Indian Industry and Boston Consulting Group.

World Bank. 2010. 'India Country Strategy (CAS) 2009–2012'. http://www.worldbank.org/en/news/2010/04/06/india-country-strategy (accessed 12 November 2012).

19 | Private Sector in Professional and Vocational Education

Manish Sabharwal and *Neeti Sharma*

THE SKILL DEFICIT

The last 20 years of economic reforms have demonstrated that growth is a necessary but not sufficient condition for sustained poverty reduction. Sustainable poverty reduction needs access to decent paying jobs. And access comes from the 3Es — Education, Employability and Employment. Our higher education system needs to deliver quantity, quality and inclusiveness. However, the current regulatory regime is sabotaging all the three requirements.

About 53 per cent of employed youth in India suffer some degree of skill deprivation, while only 8 per cent of youth are unemployed. Also about 57 per cent of India's youth bear some degree of un-employability. Thus, the 82.5 million unemployable youth fall into the following three skill-repair buckets:

(a) Last mile repair (<0.5 years): 5.3 million
(b) Interventional repair (0.5–1 year): 21.9 million
(c) Structural repair (1–2 years): 55.4 million

The last mile repair suggests simple training in certain basic business etiquettes, communication skills, soft skills, and certain generic skills which many of the educated people take for granted, be it even as simple as 'how to wear a tie'. This is exactly the kind of training which a candidate will get if he is given access to the workplace via apprenticeship programmes. The source of the problems lies in the mismatch between demand and supply; 90 per cent of employment opportunities require vocational skills but 90 per cent of our college/school output has only bookish knowledge. High dropout rates (57 per cent by Class VIII) are incentivised by the low returns of education; 75 per cent of school-finishers make less than ₹50,000 per year. The poor quality of skills/education shows up in low incomes rather than unemployment; 45 per cent of graduates make less than ₹75,000 per year. The situation is becoming more urgent because agriculture is unviable with 96 per cent of farm households having less than 2 hectare. Seventy per cent of our population and 56 per cent of our workforce produce 18 per cent of Gross Domestic Product (GDP). Demographics can be a dividend or a disaster because 300 million youth will enter the labour force by 2025. In fact 25 per cent of the world's workers in the next four years will be Indians. One can say that the country's 50 per cent self-employment rate does not reflect entrepreneurship but its failure to create non-farm jobs and skills. The skill-deficit hurts more than the infrastructure-deficit because it sabotages equality of opportunity and amplifies inequality while poor infrastructure maintains inequality (it hits the rich and the poor equally).

THE REFORM AGENDA

There are various reforms that can completely overhaul not only India's human capital ecosystem but its whole economy at a cost far lower than what the current policies entail. Broadly put, there are three buckets of reform:

(a) *Matching (Employment Reform)*: better matching of the available supply to the demand by removing the various market failures in India's employment/labour markets. This includes removing legislation that breeds unorganised employment, increasing the efficacy of within and across state infrastructure, such as employment exchanges to connect job-seekers with employers, and much else. These changes would be pivoted around a review of labour laws and labour infrastructure.

(b) *Mismatch (Employability Reform)*: fixing existing human capital for emerging requirements of a rapidly growing economy. This is particularly important for people already in the labour force in low productivity jobs or students who have finished formal education that did not give them the skills to get or keep a job.

(c) *Pipeline (Education Reform)*: re-orienting the education system to one that focuses on 'learning for earning'. The current education system has many issues around regulation, curriculum, teacher training, etc., that sabotage work-ready output.

Employment Reform

Of all the reforms, the reforms which connect supply to demand lead to the most instantaneous and perceptible impact on employment conditions in the country. This requires a combination of legal, regulatory as well as administrative reforms, given the issues with the current labour laws, discussed later. The labour laws are a minority rule since they value job preservation over job creation, and the organised sector is only 7 per cent of the total labour force. They amplify the capital and skill intensity of growth and investments. They also discriminate against labour market outsiders (less skilled, less educated, people from small towns, and women). Because a poor legal regime increases transaction costs and promotes corruption, over-legislation, non-harmonised and complicated laws create incentives for government functionaries to exploit. The next section discusses an immediate agenda to address the challenges from the labour laws.

(a) *Convert Employment Exchanges into Career Centres*: this would offer services such as Registration with a unique Candidate ID (this can get replaced once the Unique Identification Authority of India or UIDAI covers all citizens), Assessment, Counselling, Skill Development Programmes, Certifications, Apprenticeships, and Jobs. Public–Private Partnerships (PPPs) to bring in the best of the public and private sectors should be explored. The government-run Employment Exchanges are at District headquarters and almost everyone who needs a job in the district is aware of the Employment Exchange. On the other hand, a private organisation has access to industry and is better equipped at systems and processes, thereby being able to provide effective and timely services to both the industry as well as to the job-seeker. Karnataka's State Government has taken the initiative to 'upgrade' the Employment Exchanges to Human Resource Development Centres (HRDCs), bringing about a huge change in the number of job-seekers being given jobs through the erstwhile Employment Exchanges. Exchanges that earlier provided jobs to 50–60 candidates annually moved to providing jobs to over 2,000 job-seekers in the first year of its operations. The industry started viewing the Employment Exchanges as a medium to identify manpower for their requirements. See Box 19.1 for a case study of the upgrade of Employment Exchanges in Karnataka.

In the current context, Employment Exchanges are redundant. They do nothing but register job-seekers. However, most of these are situated in easily accessible locations, have decent infrastructure (though not properly kept) and a high awareness of the exchange. Instead of building new infrastructure, we should utilise the existing ones such that neither the public nor private institution have to make higher investments on hardware (infrastructure and other capital-intensive requirements), but divert the resources on enablers such as people, processes, technology, and output.

For every employee who earns till ₹10,000 per month, the employer needs to contribute a fixed percentage of wages in order to avail the social security benefits. Employees covered under the scheme are entitled to medical facilities for themselves as well as for their dependants at the Employees' State Insurance Corporation (ESIC) hospitals. Currently the employees and employers pay the funds without being able to avail the facilities, which also means that what the employee gets in hand is much lesser than what he could if he chose not to avail the ESIC facilities. Hence, this is important in the current context.

(b) *Create alternatives to the Employees' Provident Fund Organisation (EFPO) and Employer's State Insurance (ESI)*: ESIC is the country's premier social security organisation with 147 hospitals and more than 1,500 dispensaries catering to more than 14,000,000 insured persons and employing nearly 400,000 employers all over India. However, the customer experience of ESIC is rather poor. The facilities and quality of service at ESIC hospitals is way below the private hospitals and many times, employees are forced to go for private treatment at an extra cost despite mandatory payments made to ESIC. Instead of deducting a fee from the employee, a consideration should be to allow them to choose whether they want to pay ESI or buy alternate health financing and delivery. The poor service and value for money leads to evasion and breeds unorganised employment.

(c) *Review the philosophy and plumbing of labour laws that encourage the substitution of labour by capital and increase the skill intensity of employment.* There are three possible ways to consider this:

(i) Review the laws but leave out the sensitive ones such as Section VB of the Industrial Disputes Act and the Trade Union Act.

(ii) Separate Philosophy from Plumbing: Phase One of the review could focus on elimination, harmonisation and re-engineering. There is an urgent need to harmonise definitions and reduce the number of statutes (more than 45 statutes are directly associated with labour, and scores of others have some element related to labour issues). These need to be rewritten in simple language, harmonised with each other, and the redundant ones need to be eliminated.

(iii) Provide Apprenticeships to Job-seekers: Apprenticeships are a globally recognised vehicle for effective skill development because of the power of 'learning by doing' and 'learning while earning'. They enhance candidate résumé by giving them an opening balance of on-the-job experience and ensuring relevant training because of direct employer involvement. But India's apprenticeship regime is broken because it has only 0.3 million apprentices; smaller countries such as Germany and Japan have 6 and 10 million respectively.

The fundamental reason for the success of an apprenticeship programme is that it is based on a combination of formal education (in a classroom and online) and a programme

Box 19.1
Case Study on Public–Private Employment Exchange

Karnataka has over 34 Employment Exchanges to cater to the employment needs of the job-seekers and the employee needs of the organisations. However, this matching of demand and supply was not effective and the objectives of the Employment Exchanges were not being met. In 2009, the Karnataka Vocational Skills and Training Development Corporation (KVTSDC), Department of Employment and Training (DET) and Teamlease Services Pvt. Ltd. brainstormed to find possible solutions to the Employment and Employability problem in the State. Post multiple discussions and visits to District Employment Exchanges, the Human Resource Development Centre (HRDC) was conceptualised.

Objectives of HRDCs:
- To provide employability solutions to a wide range of job-seekers. These include:
  * Commerce, Science and Art graduates
  * School dropouts
  * 10th / 12th pass students
  * Skills upgradation of workers employed in various industries
  * ITI Tradesmen.
- To improve job-seekers' employability skills by optimally utilising the infrastructure available at the exchange.
- To provide Assessment and Counselling solutions to the job-seekers.
- To establish relationships with local industries and understand their manpower needs.
- To build industry and job-seeker linkages by providing periodic industry interaction to them.
- To empanel industry experts on the board of Employment Exchange and seek their guidance in improving their services.
- To build capacity for conduct of services such as assessments, training and placements.
- To bridge the skill gap of job-seekers by focusing on various trainings such as:
  * Employability
  * English Language
  * Information and Communication Technology
  * Sales Training
  * Customer Service Training
- To use technology platforms to deliver and monitor training programmes at the Exchange.
- To provide state-of-the-art infrastructure at the Exchange.
- To be able to automate and centralise industry and job-seeker databases for the use of all stakeholders (KVTSDC, TeamLease, Industry, Candidates)

The Model:
  * Partnership — to upgrade Employment Exchanges as HRDCs
  * Participants — KVTSDC, DET–Government of Karnataka, TeamLease Services

Responsibilities of the Government:
  * Infrastructure, provided and owned by the government
  * Branding Support
  * Operations Support
  * Recurring Costs

Responsibilities of Team Lease:
  * People, Processes, Technology, and Business Expertise
  * Manage day-to-day operations and be responsible for overall functioning of the centre
  * Deliver desired output for Registrations, Assessments, Counselling, Trainings, Placements, and Demand Generation

to gain field experience with workplace practice. During the formal educational phase, the candidate is provided training that is targeted at being effective on the workplace and during workplace phase of the programme, the candidate is actually put to work and required to be productive on the job. The skills developed in such an apprenticeship programme are therefore exactly what the industry (and the employer) needs. Further, the candidate leaves the apprenticeship programme ready to take on the responsibilities of the job from day one. This provides the necessary overlap between employability and employment, wherein, for job-ready employees. In order to make the apprenticeship programme viable, there are few changes that should be incorporated to the Apprentice Act of 1961. These are:

Stipend too Low	Stipend has now been set at the applicable minimum wage
Upper Age Limit	Nobody more than 35 years of age will be appointed
Lower Age Limit	Nobody less than 18 years of age will be appointed
Trade Definition	Instead of all MES trades, appoint apprentices in 22 high employment trades
Upper Tenure Limit	No apprentice should be appointed for a tenure of more than 24 months
Lower Tenure Limit	No apprentices should be appointed for a tenure of less than 3 months
Roll-Over Risk	No Apprentice after a 12-month combined tenure will be eligible for re-appointment
Government Collaboration	States and other central ministries (Urban Poverty, Rural Development, HRD, etc.) to create linkages and scale

Another consideration as part of this reform basket is to explore making labour a State subject. Given that a political logjam is holding labour reform at the Centre, it would make greater sense to move labour laws from the Concurrent list of the Constitution to the State list. This would also be in line with the spirit of decentralisation and give a chance to states to craft their labour habitat.

In India, all policies are developed by the Centre, however, implementation is in the hands of the State, thereby no one institute is responsible for the execution of the policy. If the labour laws are left in the hands of the state governments, instead of centralising at the national-level, many laws can be customised to suit the needs of the local industries and labour there on. This would be an important step towards employment reforms as that would enable all stakeholders — State, industry as well as the employee — to benefit from the reforms.

Employability Reform

This reform is about repairing supply for demand. This is particularly important for those who are already in low-productivity jobs in the workforce or students who have completed education but are unable to get a job. Training should have three values: (a) learning value, (b) signalling value, and (c) job value. Today our system fails in all three counts because of:

- No linkage of financing to outcomes.
- No separation of delivery from financing.
- No or ineffective assessment entry gates — any education/training institute would want its students to do their best, pass out with best divisions and get the best of jobs. This would only be possible if the trainees are selected by way of a pre-defined selection process and trained on the basis of his/her aptitude, behaviour and skills, instead of putting everyone in the same course. Employees should be selected by 'binning', that is, when a job-seeker walks in for a job one should be able to decide by answering few of the listed questions:
  1. What is it that the job seeker wants to do?
  2. Is he job-ready?
  3. If yes, for what kind of job?
  4. If no, why? What is the skill-gap? Which domain would he be a best fit for?
  5. Can we provide him employment without skills?
  6. What is the duration of training he would require before he becomes employable?
- Lack of credible exit gates for certification.[1]
- Lack of alignment, curriculum, assessment, certification, and jobs.
- Lack of technology usage for learning administration, teacher training and learning delivery.
- Lack of blended apprenticeships.

The following could be immediate agenda items under the employability reforms:

- Enforce the operating principles adopted by the Prime Ministers' Skill Council for all government-operated or funded skill programmes.
- Review the Apprentice Act of 1961 to explore 'learning by doing' and 'learning by earning'.
- The Apprenticeship Act should enable organisations to appoint apprentices across sectors and job profiles such that the job-seekers get the 'experience' required before actually getting into a job.
- Encourage and incentivise the setting up of State Skill Missions. All delivery systems are in the hands of the states.
- Formally make government financing available for delivery to government and private organisations, either through reimbursements or skill vouchers.

- Create a national framework and infrastructure for skill development that aligns occupation codes, entry gate assessment (an assessment to identify the knowledge, skills and behaviour that a job-seeker possesses) and exit gate certification.
- Converge all skill development programmes into the Modular Employment Schemes of the Ministry of Labour to make the curriculum relevant and courses shorter.
- Activate the National Skill Development Corporation (NSDC) that provides loans for skill development purposes; however, the challenge is for them to be able to manage this at a much larger scale with standardised monitoring mechanisms, ranking outputs of all partners, etc., to create project funding for corporate and individual ventures in skill development.
- Allow the 100-day job and resources of National Rural Employment Guarantee Act (NREGA) to be used for providing apprenticeships and funding for individual skill development. Instead of paying the beneficiaries directly (where there is the challenge on who eventually is a beneficiary and what amount of money reaches him/her), the funds can be used to provide skills to them and help them earn ₹100 on a consistent basis instead of just a limited period. Schemes such as NREGA solve an immediate problem of unemployment, but do not focus on developing long-term solutions to the problem of employability and unemployment. As a Chinese proverb goes, 'Give a man a fish and you feed him for a day. Teach a man to fish and you feed him for a lifetime'.
- Reduce information asymmetry by creating a framework to rank or rate skill development institutions.

Student Financing

While vocational skills are required for most job roles, there are many job-seekers who are unable to upgrade/develop their skills due to paucity of funds. Many state and central government ministries are working towards helping such trainees build their skills before entering the job market. The employer's financing of training for fresh recruits — as opposed to post-hiring training — is sabotaged by three risks:

(a) Learning risk: employers pay for the training but the candidate does not get a job.
(b) Productivity risk: employer pays for the training and the candidate gets a job, but is unable to do it.
(c) Attrition risk: employer pays for the training, the candidate gets a job, knows how to do it, but leaves.

These three holes in the bucket sabotage employer financing for new recruits who cannot pay for themselves. Hence, there is a need for skill vouchers, scholarships or collateral free vocational loans. The only financial models for employers that are completely aligned to their financial interest are stipends for apprentices (which allows a test drive) and reimbursements (are funds of student fees after a candidate has stayed with the employer for some time).

The skill voucher system enables a transparent, cashless transaction between the trainee and the training organisation. It is an instrument given to an individual to enable him to obtain skills-training from any accredited institute. Once the training is completed, the institute can redeem the voucher for cash. The skill voucher scheme is thus a mechanism to provide public funds for private delivery. This would also enable both the public as well as the private sector to track the deliverables for each skill development programme. Countries such as Kenya, Paraguay, Austria, Australia, El Salvador, and Peru have adopted this mechanism to provide skills-training to the job-seekers. A case study on the success of the model used in Kenya is provided in Box 19.2.

Third-party financiers such as microfinance or banks are unwilling to lend for vocational training unless a job is guaranteed, and guaranteeing a job may not be the right metric at the beginning. Banks also require collaterals from students and/or their parents. Those who need funding for skills development may not have any security to provide to the bank. Thus, students cannot depend on banks or other third-party financiers to aid their skills development.

The entry-level salaries in India for freshers at the bottom of the pyramid vary between ₹5,000 to ₹15,000. Given the difficulty in tracking individuals and high job mobility, collateral-free third-party financing requires training that leads to jobs, particularly those with a short payback period. The challenge currently faced by the training industry is that nobody wants to pay for training—job-seekers are only willing to pay for a job and corporate organisations for a trained resource. Government does pay for training but is yet to develop a transparent and scalable model to ensure right output at right cost. The emphasis on voucher system is due to the fact that it gives a right to the trainee to choose the training he/she wants and from which institute, and it also does not involve cash transactions, thereby making it less risky for the stakeholders. Banks and Mutual Funds Investments (MFIs) could provide training loans to the trainees; however, the risks for them are way too high going by the past data. If there is some kind of guarantee that the trainee would surely get employment post-training, this system would work well. Keeping the cost of loans to three or four times the exit salary (i.e., what the job-seeker will get after completion of training), with quality training that leads to jobs, is the key to finding sustainable models. Carrying forward the previous thought, all vocational trainings should lead to sustainable employment and the trainee should be able to repay the loan from his salary (without taking other

The Jua Kali Voucher programme in Kenya is one of the most successful Skills Voucher programmes in the world. Sponsored by the Government of Kenya, its main objectives are:

(a) Upgrade skills of 10 per cent of the Micro and Small Enterprise (MSE) manufacturing sector.
(b) Increase access of MSEs to technology, marketing information and infrastructure.
(c) Improve the policy and institutional environment.

The programme is aimed at expanding the market for a broad range of training and other business development services, by catalysing the demand-side for such services rather than through supply-side interventions. MSEs could purchase vouchers that entitle them to get training for their owners or workers at 10–30 per cent of the value of the voucher. These could be redeemed to obtain training from any of the registered training providers. The providers are diverse and include master crafts(wo)men, private training institutions, technology and financial institutions, consulting firms and individual trainers or consultants, apart from public sector institutions.

An important role is played by the allocation agencies, Jua Kali associations, NGOs and others, who coordinate with the players in the MSE sector and facilitate implementation of the scheme. The role of these allocation agencies is to:

(a) publicise the scheme among potential beneficiaries,
(b) assist MSEs in filling in the voucher applications, and
(c) provide counselling to MSEs in selecting the most suitable and relevant type of training.

In compensation for these services, the allocation agencies received 3 per cent of the voucher value from the Government of Kenya. The pilot phase of the voucher scheme took place in the cities of Nairobi and Machakos, and covered the following sectors: textiles, woodwork, metalwork, motor vehicle mechanics, and food processing.

A tracer study of the pilot phase found that:

(a) The prime beneficiaries of the programme were private training providers, some of whom earned up to KSh. 2 million through the vouchers.
(b) Public training providers generally did not gain as much from the scheme as they were not able to market themselves as well as the private training providers, and did not have the resources to conduct many training courses before redemption of the vouchers.

Some of the positive impacts noted in the training providers included increased incomes, better networking, development of new training programmes, and an increase in training resources and staff. Many of the allocation agencies were Jua Kali associations, which gained from increased income, new office space and equipment, extra publicity, networking and sponsoring of some of their members to participate in trainings or exhibitions. Interestingly, the study found that while the MSEs in the control group saw their average sales decrease by 2 per cent, which could be attributed to the deteriorating economic situation, the MSEs which participated in the training voucher programme saw their average sales increase by more than double: from KSh. 8,342 to KSh. 18,235 per month. The study showed that the beneficiaries performed better than the control group on almost all variables studied.

Source: CCS (2010).

loans) over a period of few months. As a standard calculation, the cost of training should not exceed more than 3 or 4 times the exit salary. Following is an example of a trainee undergoing a programme on retail sales: his salary would be approximately ₹7,000, which means his training course fee should be in the range of ₹20,000–25,000. While quality is a challenge across the board, innovation in low-cost delivery (expenditure is largely incurred on trainers, marketing and infrastructure) is possible with well-designed government partnerships.

The launch of the Credit Guarantee Fund (funds that would be provided to banks who offer loans for skills-training) and exempting vocational training institutions from service tax will make skills-training affordable in India.

Private Sector in Vocational Training

India has a significant demographic dividend in the age group of 15–59 years due to its large and growing population. The vast working-age population is currently estimated to be more than 600 million and can make a significant contribution to the country's growth if made productive.

The vocational training infrastructure in India mainly consists of government Industrial Training Institutes (ITIs) and Industrial Training Centres (ITCs), and is vastly inadequate to meet the varied skill requirement of the industry. Ninety per cent of the jobs today require freshers just out of schools/colleges to possess 90 per cent knowledge and 10 per cent skills; this is because most of them do not receive any kind of formal or informal vocational skills-training within the Indian education system. This leaves a large gap to be filled, and the private sector can play a key role in developing vocational skills. However, the private players face many challenges in developing a scalable model for vocational training. Private training providers are unable to set up adequate training facilities due to the lack of access to credit and financing of initial investments.

Another area of concern for private training providers is the level of government bureaucracy they have to face in order to register their training institution, and attain accreditation and certification of their courses, thereby rendering many institutions unaccredited. Private players also face the problem of finding skilled trainers. Besides, attracting job-seekers to classrooms for training is also difficult as there is very little prestige attached to vocational training. Another challenge faced by private training providers is 'Who pays for the training'? High attrition makes employers unwilling to pay for training for candidates; though they are willing to pay for trained ones. Candidates, on the other hand, are unwilling to pay for training but are ready to do so for a job. Third-party financiers such as microfinance or banks are reluctant to lend for vocational training unless a job is guaranteed. The government wants to pay for the outcomes but has not figured out how to do that effectively, efficiently or honestly. Training companies are unable to fill up classrooms because the many students who need skills or 'repair' cannot afford their courses.

Quality of Vocational Training Providers

The need for skills development in India is humongous and it would take many organisations to work together to start filling this gap. However, quality cannot be compromised for quantity.

Employability is a bigger challenge than Employment. Private training organisations should map industry requirements and provide training to job-seekers who match these needs and ensure that they become employable. Every skills development programme should lead to an apprenticeship and/or a job, failing which the intent of providing skills is lost. Job roles need to be identified and defined, according to which trainings should be planned. The right fitment of a job-seeker's knowledge and skills to the job role is extremely important, or he/she will not be productive and thereby attrition would increase. Assessing a job-seeker before he/she either takes up a skills development programme or a job would enable training organisations to find a better match. There are many assessing companies that provide skills assessments; however private training organisations can build their own assessments to identify a job-seeker's knowledge, skills and behaviour.

One way is mapping job roles to sectors and industries to provide a better fitment. A top–down approach to plan the same is depicted in Figure 19.1. The mapping helps develop an Ideal Candidate Profile (ICP) which in turn is vertically matched to a job profile, a sub-function, function, industry, and sector. An example of mapping a Customer Support Executive in a Telecom industry is depicted in Figure 19.2. These tools will enable private training companies to provide better skills and make the trainees effectively employable.

FIGURE 19.1   Mapping Job Roles

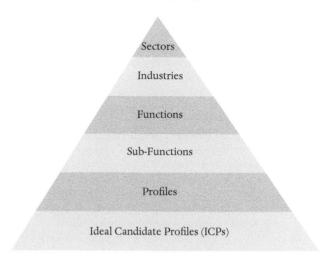

FIGURE 19.2   Mapping a Customer Support Executive in a Telecom industry

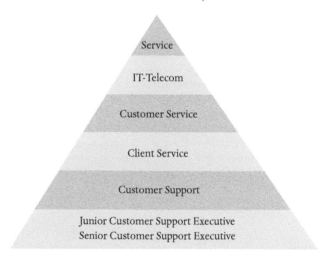

The industry ought to participate more by offering practical training programmes to students. The universities also need to take bold decisions, such as opting for credit-based, continuous and comprehensive evaluation at the undergraduate level of studies. This will ensure suitable opportunities for students to improve their performance.

The NSDC was set up as part of a National Skills Development Mission to narrow the existing gap between demand and supply of skills. Many private training organisations are joining hands with NSDC to become a part of their objective of providing skills to 150 million people in focused sectors (such as Construction, Manufacturing, Engineering, Telecommunication, Retail, Security, and others) of India by 2022, and identifying roles on the basis of industry requirement. The partnership with NSDC provides the financial support that most private training organisations need at start up as well as work with Sector Skills Councils to provide focused skills development. On the other hand, NSDC gets an implementation partner who can scale up and provide skills-training to job-seekers.

Education Reform

This reform is about preparing supply for demand. The broad principles for a better educational regime have to do with improved regulation of quality, aligned incentives and the creation of an ecosystem where preparation is in line with the requirements. This will only be possible in a decentralised environment that encourages the entry of a range of educational and vocational training options.

Elementary Education (Classes I–VIII)

The approach would need to move from enrolment to timely completion of elementary education by 15 years of age. Encouraging competition in elementary education is one method of ensuring greater responsibility. One such desirable move would be giving greater choice to the consumer — a voucher-based approach that will create options and competition by allowing parents to use government resources to pay for schools of their choice. Incentives and answerability in elementary education is another critical component. There is a need to create a performance management system for government-paid teachers — rewards and punishments for attendance and learning outcomes.

Secondary (Classes IX–X) and Higher Secondary (Classes XI–XII)

The balance between knowledge and vocational content is hard to achieve but the current school system is low on vocational content and high on knowledge. This needs to be changed. Vocational education can be provided within the school or outside with appropriate transfer of credits. It is important to recognise that different models for paying for education can be followed simultaneously. These include:

(a) Government paying subsidies towards vocational education instituted through a voucher system.

(b) Educational loan to the underprivileged for vocational education in the formal sector to be repaid directly by the individual families.

(c) Employer paying educational loan to be repaid through salary deductions from the future employees who then repays the creditor.

Tertiary Education

This component requires the improvement of regulation, easier entry, as well as rewarding performance of good quality providers. There is a need to create an Education Regulatory Authority for Higher Education that will substitute current institutions such as All India Council of Technical Education (AICTE) and University Grants Commision (UGC). Likewise, decentralisation, greater autonomy and governance reforms for institutions are required. One could also look to create a broad-based voucher programme — as mentioned earlier, a voucher system is a transparent mechanisms of providing vocational skills to the trainees. Along with this, various other ways of providing private sector funding would be:

- Corporate funding through their Corporate Social Responsibilty (CSR) activities.
- Corporate funding and deducting through salaries.
- Funding institutions providing loans with quick paybacks (short loans and short repayment cycles), would lead to better and tighter control, thereby reducing the risks of non-payments.

There is a need to shift policy framework from accreditation and regulation of capacity to measuring and publicising outcomes and quality.

CONCLUSION

Urgent action on the three reform buckets of employment, employability and education is the need of the hour. Failing this, translating the demographic opportunity into dividend will be a tall order. For long, skill-training has taken a back seat in India's educational system. It is time that this be rectified and training made an integral aspect of employability for India's growing young population.

NOTE

1. Post undergoing training on any skill, the job-seeker should be ready to meet the industry requirements, i.e., he or she should be job-ready. Exit gates for certification are a way of assessment at the end of the training programme, which will assess the skill a job-seeker has gained over the period of skill-training and whether the person is job-ready.

Select References

Centre for Civil Society (CCS). (2010). 'Skill Vouchers: Global Experiences and Lessons for India'. ViewPoint 9, Centre for Civil Society. http://ccs.in/ccindia/pdf/viewpoint9.pdf (accessed 23 November 2012).

National Knowledge Commission (NKC). 2006–09. *Report to the Nation*. New Delhi: Government of India.

National Skill Development Initiative. March 2009.

Planning Commission. 2008a. 'Education', in *Eleventh Five Year Plan (2007–12): Social Sector*, vol. 2 Chapter 1. New Delhi: Oxford University Press.

————. 2008b. 'Skill Development and Training', in *Eleventh Five Year Plan (2007–12): Inclusive Growth*, vol. 1 Chapter 5. New Delhi: Oxford University Press.

TeamLease. 2007. 'India Labour Report 2007: The Youth Unemployment Crisis'. TeamLease Services.

————. 2008. 'India Labour Report 2008: The Right to Rise; Making India's Labour Markets Inclusive'. TeamLease Services.

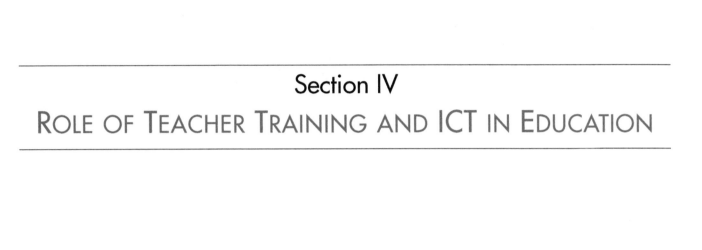

Section IV
ROLE OF TEACHER TRAINING AND ICT IN EDUCATION

20

Positioning Teachers in the Emerging Education Landscape of Contemporary India

Poonam Batra

THE CHANGING CONTEXT OF ELEMENTARY EDUCATION IN INDIA

Rapid strides taken in the area of school education in India since the 1990s have led to a significant rise in overall literacy, school enrolment, infrastructure, and the political priority to universalise elementary education. Yet, dramatic regional and gender disparities in education are closing very slowly. Though elementary school enrolment rates increased considerably and the rate of out-of-school children has declined to a mere 4 per cent (ASER 2010), the dropout rate is reported to be as high as 49 per cent and is likely to increase as a result of the global financial crisis (Prabhu 2009). Huge investments in building new schools closer to homes have had little impact on the teaching–learning environment and learner-achievement. In many schools, the school curriculum is often ideologically contested; the burden of non-comprehension continues to be inhuman and teachers across the country continue to be disempowered with the increasing informalisation of their employment.[1] This spreading malaise has led to major gaps in the quality of state schools, leading to the mushrooming of unregulated private schools across the country (De et al. 2003, 2005; Srivastava 2007; Streuli et al. 2011), caused by state policy failure to fill the immense quality gap in school education.[2] The National University of Educational Planning and Administration (NUEPA) data indicates that about 80 per cent of elementary school enrolment continues to be in state-funded schools, only a small proportion of which are privately managed (2010). Yet, over 16 per cent of rural children go to private schools (ASER 2006: 14). This trend is reported to be growing (Desai et al. 2009). In comparison, 'even now, in most OECD countries, only about 10 per cent of students attend private primary schools' (Jha 2005: 3683). Hence, in spite of the massive public investment by the

Government of India into Universalisation of Elementary Education (UEE) and two years into the Free and Compulsory Education (Right to Education [RTE]) Act (GoI 2009a), the sharp decline in the share of public school enrolment is a serious public policy question which underlies the need to respond to a rapidly changing educational context.

Much water has flowed under the bridge since Myron Weiner's (1991) scathing criticism of India's educational performance and policy in the early 1990s. The two key constraints identified by Weiner were: the lack of faith of educators and officials in education as an equaliser, or an instrument for developing shared attitudes and social characteristics; and the reported low regard that teachers have for teaching and their lack of faith in the ability of students to think independently.[3] While much of Weiner's pessimism about India's educational performance has been overtaken by facts,[4] these two constraints still remain as critical challenges to the structural reform of the state-led educational revolution in India. Within this, the most serious unaddressed issue is the critical role of the teacher.

EDUCATIONAL REFORM IN POST-INDEPENDENCE INDIA

One of the outcomes of the incomplete Indian political settlement of 1947–50 and the Nehruvian emphasis on higher education, science and technology as instruments for economic transformation was that the ordinary village school was relegated to a minor role in the momentous nation-building years of the 1950s (GoI 1949). Educational institutions at the capstone of the system, especially the Indian Institutes of Technology (IITs) and the Indian Institutes of Management (IIMs), were given this role. After Mahatma Gandhi's assassination in 1948, the contrarian voices within Indian polity and society which perceived school education as being central to social transformation and the creation of a modern, secular society were slowly stilled by the alliance of an upper-caste-dominated polity and a reluctant bureaucracy (Sri Aurobindo 1924; Azad 1956). Thus the well-established colonial system of education, even though challenged by Rabindranath Tagore and Gandhi, became the default mainstream instrument to educate India.

Education however, and the school teacher in particular, was seen for a time, at least in the popular Indian imagination, as a key agent of personal transformation and a bulwark against feudal and communitarian interests.[5] This can be seen as an attempt to revive the popular image of the pre-colonial village school master, who enjoyed the political and social space to exercise agency in terms of curricula content and pedagogic approach, an image alluded to by Krishna Kumar (2005) as well. The school teacher under the colonial regime was reduced to a state agent and became at best the 'meek dictator' of a classroom that had been severed of all links with the social and political lives of its learners.

India waited until the mid-1960s before a penetrating and holistic analysis of the challenges facing the education sector was presented by the Education Commission chaired by Prof. D. S. Kothari (GoI 1966). Meanwhile, the number of illiterates rose from 294 million in 1951 to 376 million in 1971; an absolute increase of 82 million illiterates,[6] few years after the first post-Independence education policy was unveiled (GoI 1968).

The Education Commission (1964–66) identified three significant interventions, which if implemented could have made for dramatic educational and social change in the 1970s. These were: the common school system, the introduction of integrated courses of general and professional teacher education in universities, and the increase of educational expenditure at double the then rates of economic growth leading to an estimated investment of 6 per cent of the Gross Domestic Product (GDP) in the education sector. The political and economic instability of the late-1960s, and the sheer lack of political will in addressing key concerns and pragmatic proposals that were presented in the Kothari document, can be regarded as the more important reasons for India's inability to implement its constitutional commitment of universal education.

One of the worst impacts of this neglect has been the complete marginalisation of the school teacher from the core agenda of political, social and educational development. It laid the seeds for intellectually isolating schools from sites of knowledge generation such as universities, institutes of higher education and research. Thus, concerns of school education, including curriculum and pedagogic studies, have till today not captured the imagination of young researchers. The 1970s were a largely lost decade for Indian

education, punctuated by the national Emergency (1975–77) and a period of political experimentation and uncertainty.

A new generation of political leaders in the 1980s saw education as a critical element in building 21st-century India. The National Policy on Education (NPE) (GoI 1986) and the National Curriculum for Elementary and Secondary Education: A Framework (or National Curriculum Framework/ NCF) (NCERT 1988) mark a watershed in educational reform that created a number of educational institutions catering to the assimilation of the growing rural elite (Navodaya Vidyalayas) and schemes for mass education (Operation Blackboard) which sought to provide minimal facilities to schools. District Institutes of Education and Training (DIETs) were established for the first time and Institutes of Advanced Studies were set up to deal with the backlog of untrained teachers (GoI 1987). In a major policy shift, a parallel non-formal system of education for the marginalised was established to reach those who remained outside the ambit of the formal system. In spite of considerable political rhetoric, education was not yet seen as a priority sector for public investment or one in which international presence was welcome.

Although the NPE brought ideas associated with child-centred education and social change into the policy discourse, many of the innovations of the 1980s were initiated outside the state-system. For instance, Eklavya[7] (with systemic support) demonstrated the effectiveness of the strategy to work intensely with government school teachers through curriculum and textbooks. In the mid-1980s a National Commission on Teachers was set up to examine the critical relationship between the teacher and the society (GoI 1985). It brought into focus the critical need to view the teacher as being central to the process of change in school education, in particular noting that 'if schoolteachers are expected to bring about a revolution in their approach to teaching...the same revolution must precede and find a place in the College of Education' (ibid.: 52). Despite the fact that this report spelt out several pragmatic solutions for the stagnating teacher education sector, it was ignored until very recently during a review of the Curriculum Framework for Teacher Education suggesting radical reforms in the education of teachers, including lengthening the duration of pre-service teacher education and providing professional development and on-site support to teacher practitioners.[8]

Greater international donor presence, forced by the external debt crisis of the early-1990s, catalysed a further shift in educational policy and performance. While the importance of education in facilitating change and development in society (Drèze and Sen 1995, 2002) and the need for scaling up public investment in education came to the fore, the primary focus of large-scale education interventions continued to be the provision of physical access to schools and arresting of dropout rates. The World Bank-funded District Primary Education Programme (DPEP) created some opportunities for textbook and pedagogical renewal and led to isolated attempts at transforming the capacity and role of teachers. As a result, over 1995–2003 there was acceleration in educational reform in some states, as reform-oriented state political leaders sought to improve Human Development Indices.

Nevertheless, both the bureaucracy and the political class continued to be paralysed by the volume of resources required to fund a systemic revamp of the educational system, despite credible financial estimates provided by the Tapas Majumdar Committee that dispelled major fears with regard to the economic viability of the implementation of RTE (GoI 1998). The increasing resignation of policy-makers to the declining capacity and credibility of the public education system, perceived resource constraints, and international and national pressures to achieve high enrolment and literacy rates in short periods of time led the government to choose 'economically viable' but 'sub-optimal' options, thus compromising quality.[9] Short-term policy measures such as developing a cadre of under-qualified teachers emerged from the widely-held view that elementary school teachers require minimal investment in terms of professional development and personal support.

Multiple gaps in government investments and school reform led many communities and parents to prefer private over government schools even in rural areas. This provided opportunities for the private sector to fill gaps in provisioning. The private sector expanded in states where the government system is most dysfunctional. For instance, the sector is very large in the states of Uttar Pradesh, Bihar and Rajasthan, which also have the largest number of out-of-school children. Studies indicate that Uttar Pradesh has the second highest distribution of private school enrolments in elementary education in the country at 57 per cent (Panchamukhi and Mehrotra 2005).

The wide proliferation of these private schools has perpetuated the myth that they offer a more sound curriculum and pedagogy than government schools.[10] In many states, a clearly discernable trend is that, with the exception of the poor and the socially disadvantaged, there has been a steady movement out of government schools into these often worse private schools. An attitude of despondent resignation towards the state school system, reflected in policy documents (starting with the NPE [GoI 1986]), resulted in the large-scale expansion of the Education Guarantee Scheme (EGS)[11] and EGS-like schemes (characterised by under-qualified and under-paid para-teachers) as the only means of schooling facilities for the poorest of communities (Jha and Jhingran 2005: 301). This trend continued despite the expansion of resources for school education during United Progressive Alliance (UPA) I governance.

The period starting from the mid-1990s also saw the first systematic experiments to re-orient state education policy and practice on ideological grounds. Political parties, enabled by various allied and 'front' educational organisations in education, especially in the backward and difficult areas were at the forefront of these initiatives. These, in turn, led to a series of systemic efforts to rewrite the national policy framework and curriculum to accommodate these perspectives (NCERT 2000). Seen by many as a retrogressive step, this led to passionate ideological debates over the rewriting of history texts. Yet, most school teachers were disempowered to join in these intense public debates and hence marginalised from a discourse that ought to be their central concern.

Thus the early 21st century saw significant shifts in public policy and the debate on school education in India after the introduction of the RTE Bill (2005) on UEE,[12] a sector-wide attempt to 'de-saffronise'[13] the curriculum and a massive fiscal commitment to funding UEE in the form of an educational cess, which was introduced in the 2004 national budget. A political consensus around the need to universalise elementary education appeared to have emerged, but the frame within which this ought to be pursued remains a contested space between academia, the bureaucracy and politicians. The millions of school teachers in the country are still, however, largely marginal in this discussion.

This paper argues that any significant change in the learning environment of our state schools is seriously jeopardised unless we change the central reality of teachers and teacher development.

CHALLENGES OF UNIVERSALISING ELEMENTARY EDUCATION IN CONTEMPORARY INDIA

It is in this context that a wide range of challenges that remain, in forging an appropriate trajectory for UEE in India, need to be examined. While there is a considerable decline in the overall percentage of out-of-school children, research shows that this group has mainly comprised girls, children belonging to disadvantageous social groups such as Dalits, Scheduled Tribes (STs), Muslims, and in some areas Other Backward Castes (OBCs) (Jha and Jhingran 2005; Majumdar 2009). Uttar Pradesh, Bihar, Rajasthan, Madhya Pradesh, and West Bengal account for 69 per cent of the out-of-school children (GoI 2007). It is evident that deprivation of any kind is linked intimately and negatively with the school participation of children.

Gaps in Teacher Recruitment

Expansion in the number of teachers has been abysmally slow compared to the number of children enrolling for education. Researchers have observed that teacher recruitment in most states remained frozen for many years, leading to sub-optimal solutions such as hiring para-teachers to override fiscal constraints (Govinda and Josephine 2005; Mehrotra 2006). Limited attention to the need for teacher recruitment is evident in the proportion of single- or two-teacher schools. Recent District Information System for Education (DISE) data (NUEPA 2010) reveals that the percentage of single-teacher schools continues to be high in Madhya Pradesh (14 per cent), Odisha (12 per cent), Rajasthan (16 per cent), and Assam (11 per cent). The most marginalised communities in specific blocks of these states indicate a much higher percentage of single-teacher schools as compared to well-developed blocks within the same district (Rana 2006). This could also be a result of 'mainstreaming' non-formal arrangements into 'regular' schools. While this is set to change with the provisions of the RTE, two anomalies in the Act that are likely to maintain status-quo in schooling processes are: the provision of a pupil–teacher ratio (PTR) of 40:1 based on school as a unit rather than ensuring one teacher per class; and the studied silence on defining who is to be regarded as a teacher (see Batra 2009a).

DISE data indicates that the percentage distribution of contractual teachers to total teachers is particularly high in Chhattisgarh (40 per cent), Jharkhand (56 per cent), Odisha (41 per cent), Uttar Pradesh (37 per cent), and Jammu and Kashmir (31 per cent), with the national average at over 15 per cent. The overall trend is one of increase in the number of contractual teachers with pressures to recruit a large teaching workforce to meet RTE obligations. The Ministry of Human Resource Development (MHRD) Report of RTE (GoI 2011) estimates figures as high as 75 per cent teachers without professional qualification in the north-eastern states, 61 per cent in Assam and 51 to 30 per cent in states of Bihar, Jharkhand, West Bengal, Chhattisgarh, Uttar Pradesh, and Odisha. These are identified as states with grossly inadequate teacher education capacity. Many of these have sought exemption from fulfilling their legally binding teacher qualification norms while recruiting the required number of teachers.[14] The expectation is that states will make arrangements to upgrade the qualifications of these large cadres of untrained teachers while in service through the use of the distance mode within stipulated timeframes. This dilution will have serious long-term consequences as it will weaken the teacher cadre, further ensuring poor learning outcomes. Bihar is the second state to follow Madhya Pradesh in removing the cadre of primary school teachers.

Poor Institutional Capacity

There were a total of 7,300 teacher training institutes approved by the NCTE in 2007.[15] Of these, 51 per cent are engaged with the training of secondary school teachers

and 43 per cent train elementary level school teachers. Of the total 0.5 million potential seats for pre-service teacher education that these institutes offer, 0.3 million (64 per cent) are for the training of secondary level teachers and 0.1 million (34 per cent) for the elementary level, to cater to 27 per cent of the students belonging to the secondary level and 73 per cent to the primary level. Of these, a mere 40,000 seats are in the DIETs. This implies that mushrooming sub-standard teacher training institutes are expected to fill the unfilled demand of 0.1 million (79 per cent) elementary school teachers. There would be a considerable rise in these figures given another quantum jump in the number of teacher education institutes since 2007. Another important fact is that only 20,000 of the 0.3 million secondary level seats approved by the NCTE are university-based.

Recent estimates prepared by NUEPA and MHRD show that the implementation of RTE would require the appointment of 0.5 million additional teachers over and above the existing vacancies of 0.5 million (GoI 2009b). Teacher vacancies are concentrated in the states of West Bengal, Bihar, Odisha, Chhattisgarh and Rajasthan, with Uttar Pradesh alone having over 0.1 million vacant positions. Data indicates larger number of vacancies at the upper primary school level than the primary school level.

Many states do not have DIETs as per the number of districts in that state. These include Bihar, Madhya Pradesh, Odisha, West Bengal, and Uttarakhand. It is therefore not surprising that these states are also high on teacher deficits. The GoI Report (2011) of the Committee on the implementation of RTE has identified Assam, Bihar, Chhattisgarh, Jharkhand, Odisha, Uttar Pradesh, and West Bengal, apart from the north-eastern states, as states with grossly inadequate institutional capacity to educate teachers. This means that while over 80 per cent of new teachers are being prepared in private institutions mushroomed over the last decade, the rest are poorly prepared through inadequate training in public institutions that have outdated curricula and pedagogic approaches. Private institutions too are of poor quality as these remain largely unregulated as a consequence of a weak regulatory framework. A quick appraisal of private teacher education institutes in and around the city of Delhi alone suggests inadequate faculty specialisations, a pre-service curriculum frozen in time and an exclusive reliance on sub-standard guidebooks as sources of reading.[16] The Justice Verma Commission recommended in its report that 86 per cent (249) of the 291 private institutions inspected by the Commission in Maharashtra did not qualify to be recognised as teacher education institutions for conducting the DEd programme (GoI 2012).

Massive increase in the number of private teacher training institutions has also created an imbalance in favour of urban areas in the spread of teacher training facilities.

This has adversely affected access of marginalised groups to teacher education in the relatively more rural and remote areas. Data reveals that many districts that have a lower 'intake ratio'[17] in most of the states are those having SC and ST populations of more than 25 per cent. States that have a surplus of teachers also have lower intake ratios in districts with SC and ST populations of over 25 per cent. These include Kerala, Gujarat, Punjab, and Uttarakhand.[18]

Gaps in Teacher Educators

Recruitment and career policy for faculty at DIETs and State Councils of Educational Reseacrh and Training (SCERTs) is yet another challenge. Mukhopadhyay et al. report that

Very few states have direct recruitment and career policy for personnel staffing the key academic institutions at the state level — the SCERT, DSERT and the DIETs. There is mobility between the administrative and academic positions and as a result there is continuous tendency to move into administrative positions from academic positions based on the greater power/authority associated with administrative posts. This in turn implies that academic institutions such as DIETs often function as 'transit lounge' for functionaries and devalue any effort to build institutional capabilities (2009: 7–8).

This often implies a shortage of staff in these institutions.

It has been reported that in several states there is a shortage of faculty in the DIETs which directly impacts the quality of the pre-service programmes (NCTE 2010). The National Council of Educational Research and Training (NCERT) report indicates that about 44 per cent DIETs in the northern region, 58 per cent in north-eastern region, 33 per cent in the eastern region, 44 per cent in the western region, and 67 per cent in the southern region have about 50 per cent academic posts vacant (2009: 19). Specific norms for recruitment of faculty in the DIETs are also left unclear.

WHAT EXPLAINS THESE GAPS?

Three distinct reasons could explain why India's national system of education has not measured up to the expectations of the common person. First, there has been a paucity of resources allocated for school education, even though every political party promises to remedy the situation in its election manifesto. This has changed since India's economic growth remained stable despite the recent economic crises. Second, limited attention has hitherto been given towards building institutions and institutional capacity to educate teachers, provide academic leadership and support school reform. While over 80 per cent of elementary stage children attend state schools, approximately 85 per cent teacher training institutions are in the private sector. As indicated

earlier, the ills that plague the state institutes of teacher training — paucity of faculty, outdated curriculum and substandard reading materials — plague the private institutes as well. This breaks the myth that 'private' indicates quality and efficiency in the sector of teacher education.

This has resulted in much of the available public resources (through the Sarva Shiksha Abhiyan or SSA) being spent on 'motivating' poorly qualified and poorly equipped teachers through piece-meal in-service training without addressing the real needs of the classroom practitioner. Ramachandran et al. (2005, 2008) report a stark mismatch between the concerns of teachers inside the classroom and the content of the training programmes. Teachers feel that training is a ritual, often characterised by sporadic lectures without relating to the needs of the classroom.

Third, there is the issue of a supposed missing link — the school curriculum was rediscovered almost simultaneously in the 1990s by three sets of agencies: educational NGOs, large donor agencies and political ideologues of various persuasions. The political and sectarian outcomes of their interventions have been subject to a contentious debate in the recent past. Educational issues related to curriculum, text material and pedagogy have been publicly debated for the first time since Independence,[19] an issue dealt with later in this paper. Also for the first time, various 'independent' stakeholders, including civil society and university professionals have pitched in to work towards reform of textbooks and the curriculum. The most recent example of this is the rewriting of school textbooks post-NCF, 2005.

It is becoming more than evident that even though improving infrastructure and access, providing mid-day meals and the much referred to 'detoxification' of the school curriculum are critical elements of school reform, a concerted focus on quality is a pre-requisite for achieving UEE. Quality education is centred on a quality curriculum, improving the teaching–learning environment in the classroom to bring every child into the fold of education; appropriate and adequate preparation of and incentives for teachers; a positive learning milieu for children (including proper nutrition), a psychologically conducive and pedagogically sound environment along with family and social support. This is a challenge even for some of our best private schools in metropolitan cities.

More important, the emerging 'corporatised' understanding of quality, viewed in terms of learning guarantee, teacher accountability and the scientific management of education, is antithetical to the understanding of quality seen as being integral to the concept and process of education. Yet it is this hope of a creative engagement with quality teaching–learning opportunities that brings tens of millions of children to school every day and leads millions of others to drop out in its absence. The conventional policy position on quality education in India is that a professionally educated cadre of school teachers is too expensive for a poor country to afford.[20] Nothing can be further from the truth. India's lack of attention to its school system, professional education of teachers and their socio-economic status is one of the major reasons it lags behind China, most of the Association of Southeast Asian Nations (ASEAN) countries and even some of its South Asian neighbours on the Human Development Index, and consequently on long-term economic performance (Goldman et al., cited in Dickson et al. 2009; Haq 1995). This lack of attention created many vacuous spaces that attracted international trends and perceived national imperatives to determine the current trajectories of educational reform in India.

EDUCATIONAL REFORM IN CONTEMPORARY INDIA: IMPACT OF INTERNATIONAL TRENDS

The opening up of India's education sector, first to donor funding, then to international researchers, managerial and technical collaboration, and finally to public–private partnerships since the 1990s, has brought into play a number of institutional interests, forces and debates from the international arena. Some of these debates and experiences have been useful in providing an impetus to a few elements of India's educational reform. However, the wide divergence between the socio-economic, cultural and institutional conditions of South Asia, many Organisation for Economic Co-operation and Development (OECD) countries and even China, has created a number of stark policy contradictions in India due to the unthinking application of processes and experiences from very different contexts. Some of these are examined in the following section.

Education has been the site of significant reform in many OECD economies since the 1980s. Two parallel discourses have typically characterised post-1980 school reform. First, the voice of the academia beginning with the New Sociology, followed by the post-modernist discourse has brought into question the processes of curriculum design, selection of knowledge and pedagogic approaches. While the early sociological theorists made explicit the relationship between educational knowledge, social control and cultural reproduction (Apple 1982; Bourdieu and Passeron 1977), the more recent post-modernist and post-structuralist discourse serves to challenge the very idea of knowledge (Ball 1993; Middleton 1995; Moore and Muller 1999; Weiner 1994). Second, the post-Thatcher and Reagan era has seen the emergence of a neoliberal economic and social engineering-oriented policy discourse. This is largely centred on concerns of national competitiveness in a globalising world. Economic efficiency and the linked educational framework

of improved learner assessment, accountability and effectiveness, much of which derives from the discredited behaviourist traditions of educational psychology of the 1950s and 1960s are central to this discourse. Scholars observe that 81 per cent of economically developed countries and 51 per cent of economically developing countries have been using national assessments since 2006. Some examples are: the Southern African Consortium for the Measurement of Educational Quality, the Latin American Association for the Assessment of the Quality of Education and other industry-based assessments emanating from the financial world (Kamens and McNeely 2010, cited in Soudien 2011). India too has been focusing on national assessments,[21] Programme for International Student Assessment (PISA) being the most recent international partner.

An increased emphasis on educational standards, teacher accountability, effectiveness, efficiency and 'quality' in India therefore needs to be viewed against the backdrop of an era of increased marketisation of public services in the OECD nations, as argued by Praveen Jha (2005). Neoliberal policies in India since the early 1990s led to the increasing engagement of the corporate sector in education and the concern especially for the Information Technology (IT) and services sector in terms of its future competitiveness. The success of the neoliberal growth model during the second wave (2000s) led to a deeper penetration of market-based reforms in the education sector and the redefinition of education as a deliverable (Batra 2011). Teacher accountability, learning guarantee programmes, learning achievement levels and school management, driven by the corporate sector thus became significant constituents of the quality discourse.[22] Within this framework, educational research has become increasingly policy-driven, focused on evaluation and learner assessment rather than oriented around multiple interpretations of social and classroom reality.

Research funded by international aid agencies have fostered a discourse around aspects of teacher absenteeism (Kremer et al. 2004), teacher motivation and accountability (Ramachandran et al. 2005), rather than around the veracity of professional partaking to develop qualified practitioners. With limited access to culture and context-sensitive educational perspectives and research in India, the corporate sector has found easy comfort in the policy and management-oriented discourse. An important feature of this increased engagement by the corporate and management sector is an emphasis on the 'rhetoric' of democracy, and notions of community participation and empowerment, set within the broader context of a learning society. This is in contradiction with both the experience of the everyday classroom and the preferred set of simple instruments used by these agencies to enable complex education-linked empowerment processes in a fundamentally unequal society. This has resulted in declaring prematurely many well-meaning interventions as successful and the 'war on illiteracy' easily won even before they develop critical momentum.[23]

Private educational initiatives of curriculum development and transaction are now being advocated as 'cost-effective market solutions'. Attempts are being made to 'disaggregate complex (pedagogic) processes into simple, routine and standardised tasks'. Scholars have argued how such attempts are designed for the less-skilled workers (read para-teachers), with the desired reduction in costs and a simultaneous increase of volume and output (cited in Nambissan 2010: 734). Several private initiatives across India are 'producing' meticulously designed 'lesson plans' and other 'teacher-proof' materials for use by a cadre of school teachers that are hired with or without pre-service qualification to merely implement and enhance learner performance. The recent Central Board of Secondary Education (CBSE) decision to 'relieve' school teachers of the 'onerous' task of setting question papers is indicative of the process of 'de-skilling' them; substituting it with 'para-skilling'.

Pressures to recruit a large teaching workforce to meet RTE obligations have led the Indian state to once again seek comfort in convenient solutions that 'equip' teachers to 'deliver' education for which theory is not necessary, nor the design of meaningful 'learning experiences'. The more recent legal requirement of qualifying a Teacher Eligibility Test (TET) is a case in point. Instituted in 2011, the TET is an essential criterion for teacher recruitment over and above a professional degree in teacher education. Abysmally low rates of qualifying the test (5–15 per cent) in the past two years of its conduct,[24] has demonstrated the poor quality of pre-service teacher education programmes (both private and state-led) and the poor subject-knowledge of candidates reflecting the poor quality of general education.

Although the TET proves to be a significant criterion for selecting teachers, a word of caution is needed. The fear that teacher education institutes may end up becoming teaching shops for qualifying the TET may not be unfounded. If this were to be, no serious attempts would then be made to revamp teacher education. It would therefore be important to strategise the use of TET to augment teacher quality *along with* serious attempts at reforming pre-service education and continued professional development of teachers. Else, it is likely to dilute and even abandon any attempts to redesign pre-service teacher education, thus sustaining the culture of producing 'test materials' and 'teaching shops' for profit.

While on the surface there appears to be a policy consensus on many of these questions, there continues to be tension between contemporary policy imperatives and the lived reality of school education in India. Issues of teacher education, new curricula and the (re)definition of knowledge, funding and school management, the system of inspection and learner assessment, and notions of accountability to the customer and free choice, which are implicit in proposals such as the 'voucher system',[25] have remained areas of contention and conflict. Subjects of equality and social justice appear to have been relegated to the periphery of contemporary educational priorities in India.

It is argued that even though concerns of equity in education are intimately tied with questions of aims of education, the two have become increasingly disconnected in the prevalent policy discourse. This is especially worrying as the link between school education and universities in India continues to be fragile and still a site of struggle.

REAFFIRMING THE SOCIAL TRANSFORMATION AGENDA

Alongside the policy discourse which perceives education as a mere deliverable to be closely monitored and controlled, education has enjoyed a resurrection as a vital agent of social change in contemporary India. The ongoing debate on social transformation and the nature of citizenship and national development in India provides new opportunities and fertile ground to establish the link between theory and practice. An important contemporary example is the rich debate on curriculum and curriculum reform, and its relationship with the agency of the child and teacher that has emerged. Scholars have raised questions of multiple childhoods and the need to address social contexts of learning while designing curricula (Anveshi 2003; Balagopalan 2008; Vasantha 2004) and the criticality of transforming the state of teacher education in India (Batra 2006, 2009b).

The NCF (2005) has established a concrete link between the ongoing debate on UEE and curriculum renewal to the agency of the child and has reiterated the close relationship between school and society. With this articulation emerges a renewed interest in an education that can empower children, their parents, and communities to change their lives in a way and at a pace that is meaningful to them.

India is also in a unique moment when social movements and civil society initiatives have culminated in several progressive legislations such as the Right to Information Act, 2005 (GoI 2005) and the RTE Act, 2009 (GoI 2009a). This comes at a time when education is being positioned as central to the national project of creating a more equitable and just society. The educational discourse through the NCF, 2005, and National Curriculum Framework for Teacher Education (NCFTE) has articulated major epistemological shifts in imagining the nation where constructs of local knowledge, active citizenship, diversity, and inclusion attempt to redefine curriculum and establish teaching as social practice (NCTE 2009).

However, two parallel strands of thought can be discerned within the current policy discourse in India: the neoliberal frame of standardisation, teacher accountability and learning outcomes; and the academic-led perspective on school curriculum (NCERT 2005) and teacher education curriculum (NCTE 2009) that regard education as critical for social transformation. Given the RTE, the policy imperative is to bring both into the fold of education. However, the agenda, driven by economic imperatives is to create knowledge workers for a service economy, not an active citizenry. In this frame the pedagogic enterprise is to 'teach to test' and the central thrust of pedagogic practice is one of control and outcomes. This is coupled with an evasion of any serious engagement with the professional development and concerns of teachers.

These strikingly different assertions reflect a fundamental shift in thinking about education, its purposes and role in a democratic society. The policy–practice interface thus remains unexamined. Several issues, long debated, are now being positioned as 'forced choices'. These include: the conflict between private and public schooling arrangements; diversification and selectivity of the teacher workforce; multiple locations as the site for teacher preparation: private and public; long duration pre-service teacher education *vs* short-term measures of in-service training and the contradictions of simultaneous regulation and deregulation. The challenge is to resist making 'forced choices'; instead, invoke various political, social and educational means to widen the democratic space for developing informed practitioners who can assert their right to educate all children.

This is a huge challenge given that most school teachers across the country being under-trained, mis-qualified and under-compensated are de-motivated instruments of a mechanical system of education that was initially conceived as a support to a colonial regime. Dominated by upper castes and forward sections of society the system strengthens the status quo on questions of caste, community and gender asymmetry (Batra 2005).

Moreover, school teaching in India has declined to the status of a least favoured profession in the last three decades. It has largely become a last resort of educated unemployed youth, part-time business people and young women seeking to find a part-time socially acceptable profession. Yet, the massive demand for teachers in both government and private schools almost guarantees a job to most participants of the better teacher education programmes. In practice, however, this has been recognised more as a 'fall-back option' than a preferred career choice. Government- and NGO-led educational school reforms have paid little attention to this reality and continue their focus on improving access to schooling and building a more convivial teaching–learning environment.

RECONCEPTUALISING TEACHER EDUCATION

There exist across India, several examples of radical innovations in school education that have concertedly focused on the curriculum and the teacher. The Bachelor of Elementary Education (BElEd) Programme is a robust example of radical innovation in the nature and structure of the pre-service education of elementary school teachers. Emerged as the first professional degree programme for elementary school teachers offered by an Indian Central University, the BElEd programme design took the bold step of opting for a federal (versus a centralised) model of management in which the programme was offered and managed by a number of undergraduate colleges, supported and guided by the Maulana Azad Centre for Elementary and Social Education (MACESE) at the Department of Education, University of Delhi. This model has enabled a rapid scale-up of the programme in response to demand from students and schools; and lower operational costs due to the sharing of infrastructure and participation of faculty from existing arts and science departments in undergraduate colleges. Establishing an active link between elementary and higher education has been a fundamental achievement of this programme.

This linkage not only enables the expansion of an integrated professional pre-service training process at a relatively low cost, but helps build a cadre of elementary school educators who can assist in the rejuvenation of the existing national district-level elementary school-support infrastructure, i.e., DIETs. The bilingual nature of the programme has generated new channels of knowledge creation in national languages and the opportunity of reflective practice among linked network of schools and teachers participating in its 'practicum' component. This holds significant potential for curriculum development and closing the gap between educational practice and pedagogical theory.

The programme's success lies in its ability to bring together faculty from various disciplines, especially outside the conventional boundaries of the field of education to develop a functional curriculum that responds to current social, educational and economic changes. The establishment of a federal structure between colleges and a university department has helped to develop robust institutional mechanisms by which expansion and replication is pragmatic and financially viable. This 'undergraduate college model' has been found to have many benefits including the wider institutional involvement of the university; psychological space for interdisciplinary, peer and faculty interaction; breaking down the insular approach to teacher education; and drawing upon existing academic resources in colleges and lowering the fixed and operating costs.

The partnership model of the internship programme allows for consistent university interaction with government schools, thereby creating space and mechanisms for academic support to school teachers. This model has prompted several initiatives by colleges including opening a public discourse on elementary education, developing modules for in-service and pre-service training and generating context-based body of knowledge in elementary education.[26] The federal structures developed provide collective academic supervision over course implementation, norms and regulations. In keeping with the vision of partnership of the school internship model, the interns establish a resource centre in each of the internship schools. This centre helps to create a structural space within the school for innovation and holds the promise of setting innovative processes in motion among regular teachers of these schools. In addition, the resources developed can be collated for wider dissemination.

The creation of structural spaces within teacher education institutions and the convergence of institutional linkages provide the opportunity to bridge the divide created between the school curriculum and the teacher. The conviction that teachers can be educated to engage with issues of social change by being exposed to egalitarian methods of teaching–learning has been demonstrated for almost two decades via this alternative vision of teacher education. The NCFTE and the subsequent model syllabi draw upon the experiences of the BElEd to provide a set of robust ideas that states can use as a frame to revamp teacher education programmes.

RECLAIMING THE EDUCATIONAL AGENDA: FUTURE TRAJECTORIES

It is evident that the problems of the teacher education sector are manifold, ranging from a huge undersupply of professionally trained teachers to the need for radical shifts in curriculum and pedagogic approaches to teacher preparation. This clearly cannot be met over the next decade by the private sector which has primarily promoted the proliferation of sub-standard institutions across the country, facilitated by a weak regulatory regime provided by NCTE.

The response to this mix of policy and supply failure needs to be addressed as a priority through carefully formulated short- and long-term strategies. The former would include rationalisation and redeployment of teachers at the district, block and cluster levels. However several structural mechanisms will need to be put in place to enable a radical transformation of the teacher education sector. The first step will be to relocate the education of teachers in the higher education system, with four-year integrated programmes in undergraduate colleges, two-year programmes after

graduation in universities and research-based programmes in centres of excellence. The 12th Five-Year Plan proposes to forge the critical link between university and school education based on the experience of multiple successful initiatives across the country. These range from the BElEd of University of Delhi, to the textbook-creation initiative of NCERT and the dual mode MA (Elementary Education) Programme of the Tata Institute of Social Sciences, which are now recognised as international benchmarks.

Under the 12th Plan, Schools of Education are being established in select universities and institutes of higher education to help develop education as an interdisciplinary enterprise. These Schools of Education are envisaged to include several centres that would undertake in-depth work in neglected areas of school education. This includes concerted research and material development in areas of curriculum studies, pedagogic studies, assessment, and policy studies apart from their core function of educating teachers and teacher educators.

The NCFTE includes a model syllabus (NCTE 2011) for teacher education for the first time in independent India. It is hoped that this will close the gap between the education of teachers and learners — the missing link that the quality debate has failed to connect. Enabling this connection via regulation, reform and upgradation of teacher education institutions could be the critical differentiating factor between performing and non-performing states over this decade (Batra 2011). It is expected that the NCFTE will provide the necessary vision and space for a convergence between the school curriculum and the education of teachers. There is need to institutionalise the ideas articulated in the NCFTE to revitalise teacher education, by enabling a confluence between schools, the system of teacher education and higher education.

The challenge lies in an appropriate institutional response to enable the concrete realisation of this new vision through the current and future Five-Year Plans. This includes the proactive regulation of both public and private teacher education services to ensure that India's elementary education quality deficit can be addressed in a decade or less. A proposed inter-university centre (12th Plan) at the national level can help coordinate between the university-based Schools of Education in terms of academic content: redesigning of teacher education curricula, developing curriculum materials (offline and online), including commissioning of materials in regional languages through the specific state-based institutions such as SCERTs. The mandate of this centre would be to provide a separate yet integrated focus on elementary and secondary levels of school education.

Apart from strengthening and re-structuring existing institutions, and revamping the content and pedagogy of teacher education programmes along the lines suggested in NCFTE and the model syllabi, there is need to establish new institutional arrangements that will ensure breaking the isolation of elementary school teacher development and practice. This would include re-prioritising the role and functions of DIETs and their relationship with SCERTs. A concrete suggestion is to upgrade DIETs to the status of undergraduate colleges in a phased manner. The mere upgradation of DIETs to undergraduate colleges, however, may not be the answer. A set of guidelines[27] to this effect will need to be formulated and support mechanisms provided for their implementation. Systemic linkages will also need to be forged between existing institutes such as the DIETs, SCERTs and universities in order to redesign programmes of teacher education and professional support.

The other critical link is between the DIETs and Block and Cluster Resource Centres (BRC and CRC). The establishment of the DIET–BRC–CRC structure has been the most significant institutional development in elementary education over the past decade. There is need to build capacities of these institutions based on support from universities and other institutes of higher education. Through instituted mechanisms of fellowships, faculty exchange and research programmes, the DIET faculty can be supported to assume a mentoring role for the coordinators of BRCs and CRCs. Block and district resource centre capacities will need to be augmented and facilitated to strengthen cluster-level processes.

An interdisciplinary platform for teacher education, educational research and practice will need to be established through new structures that make provision for widening the base for the intake of teacher educators and trainees. This can be done through a focus on entry at the +2 and undergraduate levels and lateral disciplinary entry in courses on education, especially in areas of critical current deficit in both number and quality in the social sciences, sciences, mathematics, and languages. Specialised national institutes of excellence (such as Indian Institute of Science, Homi Bhabha Centre for Science Education and the Indian Institutes of Management) can be drawn upon to help fill some of these critical areas and school leadership and management, which are increasingly being taken over by the private sector. Interdisciplinary postgraduate programmes of study with specialisation in curriculum studies, pedagogic studies

and assessment need to be developed so that university students can opt for credit courses in these areas, based in their parent departments. This would help develop a cadre of professionals — curriculum developers, pedagogues in sciences, social sciences, languages, and mathematics; to facilitate students to engage with critical areas of applied study and, thereby in time, create a body of knowledge relevant to the Indian context.

The long-term goal envisaged would be to move away from standalone institutions of teacher education and to increase the State's active involvement in the process. It is imperative to bring private institutes under regulation, to set up adequate systems of periodic curriculum review and close monitoring. It would therefore be essential to extend the benefits, quality and regulation of university/public teacher education interventions to private institutions on a cost-sharing basis.

This paper argues that the operational linkage between a more socially inclusive and humane India pivots around the most neglected element of India's education system — the teacher. Luis Armando Gandin's analysis of the reforms in Porto Alegre in Brazil demonstrates how the growth and acceptance of critically democratic educational policies and practices have been possible because of the active participation of critically reflexive teachers (2006, cited in Apple 2011).

Developing the agency of teachers necessarily requires a series of structural reforms, beginning with the institution of mechanisms to draw linkages between schools and centres of higher education. The availability of finances via the national educational cess, the promised strengthening of national educational infrastructure through the RTE and the commitment to increased rural employment opportunities provide a unique opportunity to create hundreds of thousands of jobs for adequately trained and motivated school teachers. This is effectively the beginning of an 'employment guarantee' scheme for millions of educated unemployed youth who aspire to enter into the formal economy. Multiple innovative interventions at scale across India have demonstrated this as a challenging but sure route to realising the immense human potential of the largest youth population in the world, thereby helping transform both India's economy and society.

NOTES

1. Parveen Jha (2005) and Poonam Batra (2005) have argued how the swelling number of para-teachers across many states has diluted the teaching profession. Batra (2005) also argues how systemic constraints (including the increasing cadres of para-teachers) and processes of conventional teacher education circumscribe teachers' thinking and capacities, widen gaps

between the teacher and school curriculum, leading to their disempowerment.

2. An educator's perspective of quality includes all that is inherent to the process of education: physical and social access, sound learning environment and curriculum and an inclusive teaching community. More recently, quality is seen largely in terms of

'learning outcomes'. It has become a new 'silver bullet' of Indian education among many political leaders of all hues, apart from intellectuals and bureaucrats of various persuasions. An actionable framework to link investments and other educational inputs to outputs and outcomes is weakly articulated except by special interest groups: the World Bank, Pratham, IT Fortune 500 corporation-funded organisations.

3. Reported in the field studies by Tata Institute of Social Sciences (TISS), 1968, cited in Myron Weiner (1991).

4. *Census 2011* places India's overall literacy rate at 74 per cent with a rise of 9.2 per cent. Gender disparity continues to remain even though the gap has narrowed.

5. Popular Hindi films of early post-Independence era, such as *Sujata* and *Jagriti,* portrayed education as central and teachers as important characters and agents of change in their plots.

6. See 'Recent Literacy Trends in India', Occasional Paper No. 1 of 1987, Registrar General and Census Commissioner, 1987, cited in Myron Weiner (1991).

7. A non-governmental organisation (NGO), Eklavya is a centre for school innovation, action and research set up in Madhya Pradesh, a state in central India, in 1982. In India, several NGOs have played a key role in experimenting with new ideas in school education and have also contributed to the current educational discourse.

8. A National Curriculum Framework for Teacher Education was approved by the National Council for Teacher Education (NCTE) in 2009 after several attempted drafts (NCTE 2009).

9. Parveen Jha observes that 'it is during the 1990s after the launch of the World Bank — supported DPEP that the country has seen a phenomenal rise in the number of para-teachers' (2005: 3684) Jha observed that, approximately 400,000 para-teachers in regular and alternative schools exist across the country as per the Seventh All India Educational Survey, NCERT (2002). Current estimates would be much larger.

10. There is an active lobby for private 'for-profit' schools that celebrates how the poor in India are educating themselves despite a 'dysfunctional' state system of education. See Tooley (2009).

11. EGS started as a learning centre, or an alternative to the formal school, in Madhya Pradesh under the DPEP. It had become a model for many states to emulate because of its cost-effectiveness in meeting the goal of universalisation. People from within the communities are appointed as para-teachers on remuneration as low as ₹1,000 a month.

12. The Right to Free and Compulsory Education was enacted only in 2009 after a long struggle (GoI 2009a).

13. The NCF has attempted to lift the curriculum discourse out of ideological frames to include a thrust on concerns of the learner and pedagogical approach (NCERT 2005).

14. See *Gazette of India* notification, New Delhi, 25 August 2010 for teacher qualifications; and notice of the GoI, F No. 1-15/2010 EE 4, dated 8 November 2010 for guidelines under section 35(1) of the RTE Act, 2009.

15. Based on NCTE data accessed in 2007 (Batra 2009b), current estimates put the figure of NCTE-approved teacher education institutes at 14,704 as on March 2011 with an intake of around 1.1 million students.

16. Preliminary findings of an ongoing study by the Regional Resource Centre for Elementary Education, CIE, University of Delhi.

17. 'Intake ratio' pertains to the number of students that can be enrolled for training to be teachers. With few institutions or no institutions existing in a district, intake ratios are likely to be low or nil. See NCTE (2010).

18. Analysed on the basis of NCTE data (ibid.) on demand and supply juxtaposed with data of districts with SC/ST populations of over 25 per cent, obtained from GoI (2010).

19. The NCFSE was much debated (NCERT 2000). Many of the controversial issues with regard to the saffronisation of the curriculum, centred on the writing of history textbooks, came to the public domain for the first time, thus increasing the number and participation of various stakeholders in school education.

20. While acknowledging the substantial rise in the remuneration of school teachers as a positive move, Amartya Sen cautioned that 'the very big increases in recent years have also made school education vastly more expensive, making it much harder to offer regular school education to those who are still excluded from it' (2002: 3). Also see Mehrotra and Buckland for a detailed analysis of strategies for managing teacher costs, 'by employing unqualified personnel and still achieve good quality learning' (2001: 4578).

21. Education Initiatives and Annual Status of Education Reports (ASER) are examples of private initiatives of learning achievement surveys.

22. The Learning Guarantee Programme, Achievement Surveys and now Teacher Education are focused programmes of corporate houses in India.

23. The Read India Programme of Pratham and the Learning Guarantee Programme of Azim Premji Foundation are examples of this kind.

24. Percentage of candidates qualifying for the State TET has been as low as five in Bihar and 15 in Central Teacher Eligibility Test or CTET (organised by the CBSE).

25. The voucher system was recommended in India's 11th Five-Year Plan (2007–12) as a feature that would enable democratisation of the issue of 'school choice' for the poor. Small private initiatives have been underway to institute the mechanism of vouchers, for example, the School Choice Campaign by the Centre for Civil Society in New Delhi. For more details, see http://www.ccsindia.org/ccsindia/edu-policy.asp (accessed 29 October 2012).

26. A large number of BElEd graduates and teacher educators have participated in initiatives of textbook writing both at the state and national levels and in programmes of teacher education curriculum renewal.

27. Guidelines for Restructuring and Revitalisation of DIETs in the 12th Five-Year Plan, MHRD Draft, February 2012.

References

Annual Status of Education Report (ASER). 2006. *Annual Status of Education Report (Rural) 2006*. Mumbai: Pratham Resource Centre.

—————. 2010. *Annual Status of Education Report (Rural) 2010*. Mumbai: Pratham Resource Centre.

Anveshi. 2003. 'Curricular Transaction in Selected Government Schools in Andhra Pradesh'. Unpublished Report submitted to Sir Ratan Tata Trust, Mumbai.

Apple, Michael W. 1982. *Cultural and Economic Reproduction in Education: Essays on Class, Ideology, and the State*. London: Routledge.

—————. 2011. 'Global Crises, Social Justice, and Teacher Education', *Journal of Teacher Education*, 62(2): 222–34.

Azad, Maulana Abul Kalam. 1956. *Speeches of Maulana Azad 1947–1955*. New Delhi: Publications Division, Ministry of Information and Broadcasting, Government of India.

Ball, Stephen J. 1993. 'Education Markets, Choice and Social Class: The Market as a Class Strategy in the UK and USA', *British Journal of Sociology of Education*, 14(1): 3–19.

Balagopalan, Sarada. 2008. 'Memories of Tomorrow: Children, Labour, and the Panacea of Formal Schooling', *Journal of History of Childhood and Youth*, 1(2): 267–85.

Batra, Poonam. 2005. 'Voice and Agency of Teachers: The Missing Link in the National Curriculum Framework 2005', *Economic and Political Weekly*, 40(40): 4347–56.

—————. 2006. 'Building on the National Curriculum Framework to Enable the Agency of Teachers', *Contemporary Education Dialogue*, 4(1).

—————. 2009a. 'Teacher Empowerment: The Education Entitlement-Social Transformation Traverse', *Contemporary Education Dialogue*, 6(2): 121–56.

—————. 2009b. 'Reclaiming the Space for Teachers to Address the UEE Teaching–Learning Quality Deficit'. Theme Paper for the Mid-term Review of EFA, published by NUEPA, September.

—————. 2011. 'Teaching the Teacher'. *Indian Express*, 4 July.

Bourdieu, Pierre and Jean Claude Passeron. 1977. *Reproduction in Education, Society and Culture*. London: Sage Publications.

De, Anuradha, Claire Norohna and Meera Samson. 2003. 'Private Schools for Less Privileged: Some Insights from a Case Study', *Economic and Political Weekly*, 37(52): 5230–36.

—————. 2005. 'The New Private Schools', in Rukmini Banerji and Sharmi Surianarain (eds), *City Children, City Schools: Challenges of Universalising Elementary Education in Urban India*, pp. 95–113. New Delhi: United Nations Educational, Scientific and Cultural Organization and Pratham Resource Centre.

Desai, Sonalde, Amaresh Dubey, Reeve Vanneman, and Rukmini Banerji. 2009. 'Private Schooling in India: A New Educational Landscape', in Suman Bery, Barry Bosworth and Arvind Panagariya (eds), *India Policy Forum 2008–09*, pp. 1–58. New Delhi: Sage Publications.

Dickson, Janet R., Barry Hughes and Mohammod T. Irfan. 2009. *Patterns of Potential Human Progress: Enhancing Global Education*. Denver: Pardee Centre for International Futures.

Drèze, Jean and Amartya Sen. 1995. *India Economic Development and Social Opportunity*. New Delhi: Oxford University Press.

—————. 2002 [1996]. *India: Development and Participation*. New York: Oxford University Press.

Government of India (GoI). 1949. *Report of the University Education Commission: December 1948–August 1949*. New Delhi: Manager of Publications, Government of India Press.

—————. 1966. *Education and National Development: Report of the Education Commission, 1964–66*. New Delhi: Ministry of Education, Government of India Press.

—————. 1968. *National Policy on Education, 1968*. New Delhi: Ministry of Education, Government of India.

—————. 1985. *The Teacher and Society: Report of the National Commission on Teachers-I (1983–85)*. New Delhi: Ministry of Human Resource Development, Government of India.

—————. 1986. *National Policy on Education, 1986*. New Delhi: Ministry of Human Resource Development, Government of India.

—————. 1987. *Centrally Sponsored Scheme of Teacher Education*. New Delhi: Educational Consultants India Ltd.

—————. 1998. 'Report of the Group of Experts on the Financial Resource Requirements for Operationalizing the Proposed Constitutional Amendment Bill Making the Right to Free and Compulsory Education up to 14 years of age a Fundamental Right'. Tapas Majumdar Committee Report, Department of Education. New Delhi: Ministry of Human Resource Development, Government of India.

—————. 2005. 'Right to Information Act, 2005'. *Gazette of India*, 21 June.

—————. 2007. 'Report of Working Group on Elementary Education and Literacy for the 11th Five Year Plan'. Planning Commission, Government of India.

—————. 2009a. 'Right of Children to Free and Compulsory Education Act, 2009'. *Gazette of India*, 27 August.

—————. 2009b. 'SSA-RTE Report'. Anil Bordia Committee, Ministry of Human Resource Development, Government of India.

—————. 2010. 'Report of the Committee on Implementation of the Right of Children to Free and Compulsory Education Act, 2009'.

—————. 2011. 'The Right to Free and Compulsory Education Act, 2009: The 1st Year'. Department of School Education and Literacy, Ministry of Human Resource Development, Government of India.

—————. 2012. 'Vision of Teacher Education in India: Quality and Regulatory Perspective — Report of the High Powered Commission on Teacher Education Constituted by the Hon'ble Supreme Court of India', vol. 2, August. New Delhi: Ministry of Human Resource Development, Government of India.

Govinda, R. and Y. Josephine. 2005. 'Para-Teachers in India: A Review', *Contemporary Education Dialogue*, 2(2): 193–224.

Haq, Mahbub ul. 1995. *Reflections on Human Development*. New York: Oxford University Press.

Jha, Parveen. 2005. 'Withering Commitments and Weakening Progress: State and Education in the Era of Neo-Liberal Reforms', *Economic and Political Weekly*, 40(33): 3677–84.

Jha, Jyotsna and Dhir Jhingran. 2005. *Elementary Education for the Poorest and Other Deprived Groups: The Real Challenge of Universalisation*. New Delhi: Manohar Publishers.

Kumar, Krishna. 2005 [1991]. *Political Agenda of Education: A Study of Colonialist and Nationalist Ideas*. New Delhi: Sage Publications.

Kremer, Michael, Nazmul Chaudhury, F. Halsey Rogers, Karthik Muralidharan, and Jeffrey Hammer. 2004. 'Teacher Absence in India: A Snapshot', *Journal of the European Economic Association*, 3(2/3): 658–67.

Majumdar, Manabi. 2009. *Universal Elementary Education: Pursuit of Equity with Quality*. New Delhi: National University of Educational Planning and Administration.

Mehrotra, Santosh. 2006. 'What Ails the Educationally Backward States? The Challenges of Public Finance, Private Provision and Household Costs', in *The Economics of Elementary Education in India: The Challenge of Public Finance, Private Provision and Household Costs*, pp. 11–53. New Delhi: Sage Publications.

Mehrotra, Santosh and Peter Buckland. 2001. 'Managing School Teacher Costs for Access and Quality in Developing Countries: A Comparative Analysis', *Economic and Political Weekly*, 8–14 December, 36(49): 4567–79.

Middleton, Sue. 1995. 'Doing Feminist Educational Theory: A Post-Modernist Perspective', *Gender and Education*, 7(1): 87–100.

Moore, Rob and Johan Muller. 1999. 'The Discourse of "Voice and the Problem of Knowledge and Identity in the Sociology of Education', *British Journal of Sociology of Education*, 20(2): 189–206.

Mukhopadhyay Rahul, N. Ramkumar and A. R. Vasavi. 2009. *Management of Elementary Education Structures and Strategies*. New Delhi: National University of Educational Planning and Administration.

Nambissan, Geetha (2010) The Global Economic Crisis, Poverty and Education: a perspective from India, *Journal of Education Policy*, 24 (6), 729–37.

National Council of Educational Research and Training (NCERT). 1988. *National Curriculum for Elementary and Secondary Education: A Framework*. New Delhi: National Council of Educational Research and Training.

—————. 2000. *National Curriculum Framework for School Education*. New Delhi: National Council of Educational Research and Training.

—————. 2002. *Seventh All India Educational Survey*. New Delhi: National Council of Educational Research and Training.

—————. 2005. *National Curriculum Framework 2005*. New Delhi: National Council of Educational Research and Training.

—————. 2009. *Comprehensive Evaluation of Centrally Sponsored Scheme on Restructuring and Reorganisation of Teacher Education: A Report*. New Delhi: National Council of Educational Research and Training.

National Council for Teacher Education (NCTE). 2009. *National Curriculum Framework for Teacher Education: Towards Preparing Professional and Humane Teacher*. New Delhi: National Council for Teacher Education.

—————. 2010. *Demand and Supply Estimates of School Teachers and Teacher Educators (2007–08 to 2016–17), All States*. New Delhi: National Council for Teacher Education.

—————. 2011. 'Re-Envisioned Two-Year Elementary Teacher Education Programme'. NCTE Review Committee, National Council for Teacher Education, 12 May.

National University of Educational Planning and Administration (NUEPA). 2010. 'District Information System for Education (DISE)'. National University of Educational Planning and Administration.

Panchamukhi, P. R. and Santosh K. Mehrotra. 2005. 'Assessing Public and Private Provision of Elementary Education in India', in Santosh Mehrotra, P. R. Panchamukhi, Ranjana Srivastava and Ravi Srivastava (eds), *Universalising Elementary Education in India: Uncaging the 'Tiger' Economy*, pp. 229–90. New Delhi: Oxford University Press.

Prabhu, K. Seeta. 2009. 'Impact of Financial Crisis on India's March to MDGs', in Rajiv Kumar, Bibek Debroy, Jayati Ghosh, Vijay Mahajan and K. Seeta Prabhu (eds), *Global Financial Crisis: Impact on India's Poor — Some Initial Perspectives*, pp. 45–54. New Delhi: United Nations Development Programme. http://www.rrojasdatabank.info/crisisdb/FinalFCPIndia.pdf (accessed 31 October 2012).

Ramachandran, Vimala, Madhumita Pal, Sharada Jain, Sunil Shekar, and Jitendra Sharma. 2005. *Teacher Motivation in India*. New Delhi: Educational Resource Unit.

Ramachandran, Vimala, Suman Bhattacharjea and K. M. Sheshagiri. 2008. *Primary School Teachers: The Twists and Turns of Everyday Practice*. New Delhi: Educational Resource Unit.

Rana, Kumar. 2006. 'Mid-Day Meal and Primary Education: Prospects and Challenges in West Bengal'. Paper presented at the seminar on 'Education and Inequality in Andhra Pradesh and West Bengal', Centre for Studies in Social Science, 21–22 September, Hyderabad.

Sen, Amartya. 2002. 'Introduction', in Samantak Das (ed.), *The Delivery of Primary Education: A Study in West Bengal*. Delhi: TLM Books in association with Pratichi (India) Trust.

Soudien, Crain. 2011. 'Building Quality in Education: Are International Standards Helpful?' *Contemporary Education Dialogue*, 8(2): 183–201.

Sri Aurobindo. 1924. *A System of National Education*. Calcutta: Arya Publishing House.

Srivastava, Prachi. 2007. Low-Fee Private Schooling: Challenging an Era of Education for All and Quality Provision?' in Gajendra K. Verma, Christopher R. Bagley and Madan Mohan Jha (eds), *International Perspectives on Educational Diversity and Inclusion: Studies from America, Europe and India*, pp. 138–61. London: Routledge.

Streuli, Natalie, Uma Vennam and Martin Woodhead. 2011. 'Increasing Choice or Inequality? Pathways through Early Education in Andhra Pradesh, India'. Working Paper no. 58, Studies in Early Childhood Transitions, Bernard van Leer Foundation.

Tooley, James. 2009. *The Beautiful Tree: A Personal Journey into How the World's Poorest People are Educating Themselves*. Washington, DC: Cato Institute.

Vasantha, D. 2004. 'Childhood, Work and Schooling: Some Reflections', *Contemporary Education Dialogue*, 2(1): 5–29.

Weiner, Myron. 1991. *The Child and the State in India: Child Labour and Educational Policy in Comparative Perspective*. New Delhi: Oxford University Press.

Weiner, Gaby. 1994. *Feminisms in Education: An Introduction*. Buckingham: Open University Press.

21

Educational Technology

Relevance and Possibilities for Education in India

Manish Upadhyay and *Amitava Maitra*

SOLVING QUALITY WITH SCALE PROBLEMS IN EDUCATION THROUGH TECHNOLOGY

The central argument of this chapter is that without the aid of Educational Technology (EduTech),[1] the Right to Education (RTE) will remain either unrealised or will only result in a mediocre education quality. An exactly similar fate will befall vocational training and higher education as without the intervention of EduTech, quality education on a large scale — which is the crying need of India — it is just not possible.

It's perhaps best to address the predictable cynicism that surrounds EduTech at the outset, and in many cases, justifiably so. But opponents and detractors are missing a crucial point here. Arguing that EduTech does not, or rather cannot, make a significant difference is perhaps akin to a Luddite arguing against the introduction of printed books during Johannes Gutenberg's time. Just as print technology revolutionised the phenomenon of information and knowledge dissemination, so can EduTech. But just as bad textbooks and curriculum can wreak havoc, similarly the mere insertion of EduTech without proper thought and design will at best make no difference and at worst have a negative impact on the quality of education. Puritans may well argue that print technology, which allows relatively cheap production and distribution of textbooks, should have a rightful place in the list of EduTech. However, for the purpose of this chapter it has been excluded owing to the fact that it's now universally embedded in all systems though its content and production quality in many a case is perhaps far from ideal.

THE EDUCATIONAL TECHNOLOGY FRAMEWORK

The critical parts that go missing in any discussion on EduTech are the crucial interrelationships and involvement of various entities, such as stakeholders, content, pedagogy, technologies, and the development model — comprising the cyclical iterations of Analysis, Design, Development, Implementation and Evaluation (ADDIE). Any discourse on this topic will be diluted without a holistic view of them all in an integrated manner. The interrelationships are explained through Figure 21.1.

Analysis, Design, Development, Implementation and Evaluation Model

Before any discussion of EduTech, we shall begin with a description of a generic instructional systems design model — the ADDIE model (Figure 21.1, I–V). ADDIE stands for the phases of Analysis, Design, Development, Implementation, and Evaluation (See Box 21.1). Although implementations differ, most models are variants of this model. It is important to note that the ADDIE model is independent of the educational technology insofar as the advocacy of any one or multiple technologies are involved. ADDIE defines the process of development of teaching and learning materials, irrespective of the delivery platforms and technologies involved. In fact, the model can be used in the application of any kind of technology or intervention. For example, if a model of using *Aadhar* Identity Document (ID) cards is conceived to monitor teacher attendance, the development of the model should go through all the stages in the ADDIE model.

The application of the ADDIE model in the sphere of EduTech has suffered from two crucial lacunae. The first is that monitoring and evaluation have been very weak. Most projects commissioned by the government or even those implemented in the private education space have had no rigorous programme management and evaluation, resulting in a plethora of problems — from crossing budgeted costs and timelines to being completely off in terms of outcome

FIGURE 21.1   The Educational Technology Framework

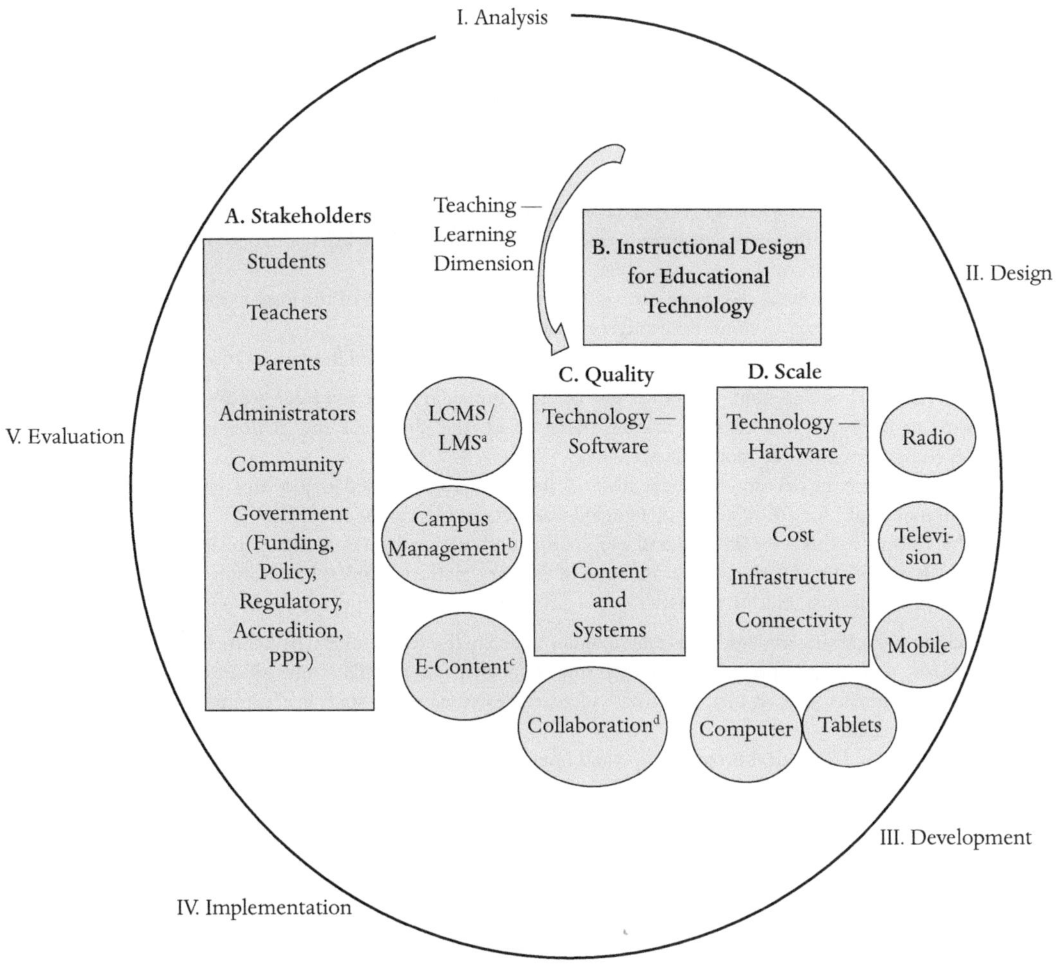

Sources: The authors' depiction of the EduTech paradigm. For the ADDIE model used in the chapter, see Branch (2010).

Note: All definitions provided in this note are from Kaplan-Leiserson (n.d.).

[a] LCMS: Learning Content Management System. LMS: 'Infrastructure platform through which learning content is delivered and managed. A combination of software tools perform a variety of functions related to online and offline training administration and performance management'.

[b] Campus Management/ILS (Integrated Learning System): 'A complete software, hardware and network system used for instruction. In addition to providing the curriculum and lessons organised by level, an ILS usually includes a number of tools such as assessments, record keeping, report writing, and user information files that help to identify learning needs, monitor progress, and maintain student records'.

[c] Multimedia: 'Encompasses interactive text, images, sound, and colour. Multimedia can be anything from a simple PowerPoint slide show to a complex interactive simulation'.

[d] Collaboration or Collaborative Learning/Online Community-Based Learning: 'Meeting place for learners on the Internet designed to facilitate interaction and collaboration among people who share common interests and needs'.

achievement. And as a consequence, the ADDIE model in almost all cases has not gone through the repeated iterations needed to refine the solutions conceived so as to make them better and more effective. The second flow is that though given the large upfront costs involved, it is necessary to look at rapid proto-typing and continuous piloting, beta testing and other modes of ongoing evaluation for sustainable

deployments of EduTech. However, as a norm these steps are never taken.

Evaluation: A Crucial but Missing Piece in Most Implementations of the ADDIE Model

As Figure 21.1 indicates, the ADDIE model is an iterative model. It recognises that a single attempt may not suffice

Box 21.1
The ADDIE Model

Analysis: This stage answers the 'What' question: as in what are the key problems that need to be solved?

This includes:

(a) Instructional Goals: What are the general goals for the learner?

(b) Learning Outcomes: How will you know if the learners have met these goals? What changes in performance, knowledge, attitudes, and skills will be observable and measurable?

(c) Task Analysis: What are the steps the learner is expected to follow to accomplish a specific task?

(d) Learner Characteristics: What prior knowledge do learners have? What are their learning goals and motivation for engaging with the instruction?

(e) Learning Environment: What physical classroom constraints may affect the design of the instruction?

(f) Constraints: Evaluating the delivery options, time and costs associated.

(g) Project Management: What time, resource and staff constraints affect the successful implementation of the project?

Design: This stage answers the 'How' question — how the problems identified in the design stage are going to be solved. This includes:

(a) Delivery Platforms to be used: This involves making decisions on the choice of the platform — print, radio, television (TV), CD/ DVD-ROM, computers, internet, mobile devices, etc.

(b) Instructional Strategies: Here the decision is to be made regarding which specific pedagogies are to be used and how they are going to be implemented. For example, for a K-12 audience a guided discovery model can be used.

(c) Media and Graphic Design: At this stage the look and feel, colour combination, layout, usability and interfaces are defined and finalised.

(d) Technical Design: Design-related decisions about the type of delivery platform, content authoring and production, content distribution, and reporting-related factors, etc. are finalised.

Development: The teaching and learning materials are created or developed in the actual format of delivery in this stage. This phase includes:

(a) Detailed Storyboards: Storyboards provide frame-by-frame (page-by-page) details about all aspects of instructional, media and technology. Thus, all elements such as text, graphics, video are described along with instructions on interactivity and how all the elements are to be integrated.

(b) Creation of Media Assets and Technical Programming and Integration: Based on the storyboards, individual media assets are created and the overall output is programmed and integrated.

(c) Development is followed by rigorous testing and debugging.

Implementation: During implementation, teaching/learning intervention is actually rolled out:

(a) Materials are delivered or distributed to the teacher and student groups.

(b) Programmes to prepare the trainers/teachers are rolled out keeping in mind the specifics of the intervention. It's important that the trainer and teacher programmes also go through the complete ADDIE model.

(c) The programme-rollout timetable is established.

(d) The courses are scheduled, learners enrolled, and on-site and off-site classrooms reserved.

(e) Arrangement is made for the printer to deliver course workbooks to the class site.

(f) It is ensured all hardware and software is ready.

Evaluation: During this phase the efficacy of the teaching/learning intervention is tested against the objectives or parameters set in the analysis stage. It includes looking at the following parameters:

(a) Likeability: Whether learners like the programme/enjoy it.

(b) Attainment of Learning Outcomes: Whether learners achieve the learning objectives set.

(c) Change of Behaviour: Whether the learners show a change in behaviour, exhibit skills or attitudes as intended in the analysis stage.

(d) Cost-Benefit Analysis: Whether the benefits justify the cost incurred.

Note: Parts taken from https://wikis.uit.tufts.edu/(accessed 16 November 2012).

and successive iterations or cycles may be needed to attain the intended goals. Thus, the results of evaluation are inputs for the analysis stage of the next cycle and these iterations need to go on till the goals are attained. Since educational technology interventions are very often costly in terms of upfront costs, rapid prototyping and pilot testing should be introduced throughout the cycle to measure efficacy on a continuous basis rather than in one shot at the end, as previously mentioned.

The 11th Five-Year Plan (2007–12) of the Government of India allocated ₹50 billion for expenditure on Information and Communication Technology (ICT) in schools across India. The funding was supposed to cover everything, from digital infrastructure in classrooms and labs, high-speed network and internet connectivity, and digital content for students and teachers, to teacher training on ICT skills. Even if we assume that all the money allocated was legitimately spent, the ₹50 billion question remains: How effective has it been? Has it translated into better teaching and improved student outcomes? Has it made a real, tangible and measureable difference?

Since ICT for education is a long-term investment, it follows that evaluation must also be long term, measuring all the factors and outcomes stemming from goals set: from an increase in students' knowledge and skills and an increase in teachers' pedagogical skills to positive changes in students' behaviours and attitudes. The fact is, however, that there is little specific evaluation of ICT for education to speak of.

As far as international comparisons are concerned, the Programme for International Student Assessment (PISA) of the Organisation for Economic Co-operation and Development (OECD) also shows that Indian education standards lag far behind global standards. There is little research to show that ICT interventions in schools actually improve student performance the world over. In a country like India, where many of our schools are in shambles and the number of quality government schools and colleges is inadequate, resources have to be spent judiciously and the interventions we put in place must be evaluated with rigour. Any serious evaluation of ICT for education should include a longitudinal study with comparisons of student performance data between the intervention group and a statistically similar control group.

PISA's rich treasure trove of data and studies has thrown up some startling conclusions (Sweet and Meates 2004). First, rather than ICT interventions alone in schools, it is the successful integration of ICT in a robust educational strategy that pays dividends. ICT interventions in isolation have a negligible impact on student learning and performance. Second, the successful use of ICT at home by the student is a better predictor of performance than use at schools. Third, and perhaps most critically, there is a significant digital gap between students who successfully use ICT at home and achieve high academic outcomes and those students who cannot. It may be that those students who perform well academically have the skills and strategies required to use ICT and digital resources available on the internet to increase their achievement levels. Further research can perhaps help identify and define these skills and strategies so that the same can be taught to other students to help them perform well academically too.

In India, where the penetration of ICT and internet at home lags far behind the developed world and even behind rapidly developing countries like China, we need to evaluate the effectiveness of ICT interventions for all key stakeholders, parents, students, school leaders, and teachers. So far there is little information and data on use of ICT in education to carry out comprehensive evaluation (See Box 21.2). Following are some ideas on using technology to ensure reliable methods of evaluation:

(a) Student assessments could be carried out via devices like mobiles phones, computers or fixed-line telephones using interactive voice response, with the data from these collected, collated and analysed to evaluate student outcomes as well as project, school and teacher performance; assessments could include questionnaires to capture data on demographics and ICT usage at school and home in order to identify correlations between student outcomes, project, school and teacher performance, and demographics and ICT usage,

(b) There could be internet portals where educators, education technology experts, student, and parents can leave feedback on school, teacher and ICT project performance, which can provide necessary information to be aggregated and analysed.

(c) Since the commercial production of ICT solutions and digital content in India has not evolved sufficiently to make market competition alone generate quality, and because most educational institutions and their personnel lack the wherewithal to reliably evaluate ICT products and services, accreditation or certification bodies should be established to regulate and audit ICT products and services in terms of quality and appropriateness for education. Whether the 12th Five-Year Plan will have an emphasis on evaluation of ICT for education remains to be seen, but without it investments in ICT for education make little sense.

Box 21.2
Right to Information (RTI) Applications on Evaluation of ICT in Education Investment by Government of India

We filed RTIs with the following departments within the Ministry of Human Resource Development (MHRD):
- Department of Higher Education — Technology Enabled Learning (TEL) division
- Department of Higher Education — Technical Section-II
- Department of School Education and Literacy
- Department of School Education and Literacy — School-5 Section

The reply from the Department of School Education and Literacy — School-5 Section states that evaluation studies/data exist for only four states: Kerala, Meghalaya, Punjab and Sikkim. These evaluations cover only 100 schools across these states.

Stakeholders[2]

Students

Though students have been the prime focus of most EduTech interventions, most of these interventions have been misguided. As users their views count the most and therefore the design of all solutions must essentially revolve around them. But this has hardly been taken into account. Instead, the malaise of the traditional educational system, where curricula and content has been rammed down the throat of students without taking into account the aspirations and needs, has simply permeated into the realm of ICT for Education too — where they have been at the receiving end of insufficient, non-working hardware and inappropriate content that seldom engages or teaches effectively. The design of content would therefore have to be student-centric: be it content used by the teacher in the classroom as a teaching aid or that used by the student to learn on his/her own in a self-paced manner.

The other big issue that needs to be examined in detail is equipping the student with the meta-skill of using ICT — both by way of further increasing ICT skills and also by way of using ICT to gain mastery over various subjects. Without these, investments in ICT are bound to go waste. Technology systems should also be designed so that they can both take student feedback directly and also indirectly through the data collected and analysed by learning management systems. Ultimately we have to recognise that quality and accountability can only be driven through the involvement of students.

Teachers

Research indicates that ICT can play a role in various ways to benefit teachers. Just as ICT skills are both a means and an end in the case of students (Figure 21.2), it is necessary to build these skills in teachers too. Teachers need these skills to be able to teach them to students. ICT can also play a vital role in equipping teachers with modern pedagogic practices and skills as well as updating and increasing their knowledge of the subjects they teach. Intelligent usage of associated systems such as those of assessment and school management/governance can also reduce the burden on teachers by automating various tasks or reducing the effort therein significantly.

Research also indicates that teachers should figure as the first priority in a country such as India. A cascading approach towards the deployment of ICT is needed where it should first be used to enhance the skills of teachers, and then in the classroom so that it can be used to teach more effectively; only then should ICT be implemented for students to learn on their own in a self-paced manner.

Parents

Perhaps no other stakeholder is as committed to the cause of quality education as the parents of a child. Yet very little has been done to empower this group and give them a say, though the RTE does attempt to do something about it. Technology if implemented well can play a role here too. For example, school management systems can be programmed to send details of student attendance, school performance, etc., to mobile phones of parents. To further overcome problems of digital divides and literacy among parents, Interactive Voice Response System- (IVRS-) enabled systems can help parents proctor summative assessments of children, delivered through phones, to form an independent check or audit on the quality of education delivered to the student.

Administrators

Technology systems can do a lot to decrease the time spent on the administration of educational institutions as well as making it more efficient. Campus management software can

FIGURE 21.2   Categories for ICT in Teacher Training

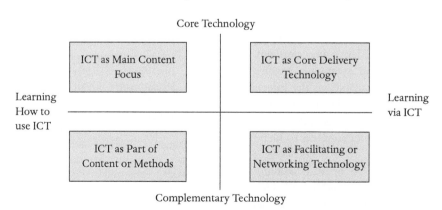

Source: Adapted from Jung (2005).

help in automating and streamlining all functions — from payroll, class scheduling, library management, attendance management to student assessments and reporting.

Governments: Central and State

Though education is now at last coming into the ambit of regulations and guidelines, ICT for education has unfortunately not yet come under the scanner. As a result, lots of players are able to dump badly-designed hardware and software and get away with it. There is clearly a need for government regulatory bodies to form standards, guidelines and then accredit/audit private suppliers of ICT for education solution providers, something which the Central Advisory Board of Education (CABE) has taken cognisance of.

Communities

The advent of the internet has made it possible for communities of people to work together for a common purpose even though they might be separated geographically. Communities of academicians, researchers and teachers can collaborate online for the development of curricula and content. Teachers may further collaborate to share best practices and knowledge and students can collaborate to learn from each other. In a country as vast as India, where a one-shoe-fits-all solution will never work and where localisation is so necessary for proving meaningful contexts to students, online collaboration among curricula management bodies and teachers can make it possible for central bodies to lay down the foundation, author the core content and yet devolve the responsibility of localising content to communities downstream.

Instructional Design for Educational Technology[3]

Technology cannot Compensate for Bad Instructional Design

For the development of any teaching or learning material, sound instructional design is must. Simply put, there is no substitute for good teaching and learning strategies. This basic fact has nothing to do with the kind of educational technology used. In fact, quite tragically, as mentioned in the beginning, the myth being perpetuated by many a vested interest that just by implanting some technology — most commonly computers in computer labs or in the classroom — the quality of teaching and learning will be magically enhanced! Similarly it can't be stated that just the creation of animations, videos or other multimedia or digital content will automatically result in effective learning.

Dialogue, Structure and Learner Autonomy

One of the cornerstones of good teaching is personalised attention and learning customised for the individual student,

through intensive two-way interactions and query resolutions. Michael Moore's model (developed in 1972 at University of Wisconsin-Madison [see Figure 21.3]) articulated three aspects of transactional distance in distance education which are applicable to ICT in education as well:

(a) dialogue, which looks at the one-on-one interaction between the teacher and students as well as among students;

(b) structure, which addresses the curriculum and learning objectives; and

(c) learner autonomy, which looks at the degree of freedom and time given to the individual student to work on her own till mastery is attained. Modern EduTech such as student response systems in the classroom can increase the level of dialogue even in cases where the Pupil–Teacher Ratio (PTR) is skewed. Similarly, in online learning two-way audio-video conferencing channels can address this aspect. Well-designed electronic content can likewise allow the individual learner to diagnose and remediate his/her problems as well as allow him/her to explore areas that he/she is interested in depth, thus enabling greater learner autonomy.

Keeping Technology in Mind while Designing a Programme

Any technology has a set of positives and negatives associated with it. Therefore, it is critical to use the best instructional strategies keeping in mind the specific technologies

FIGURE 21.3   Michael Moore's Model

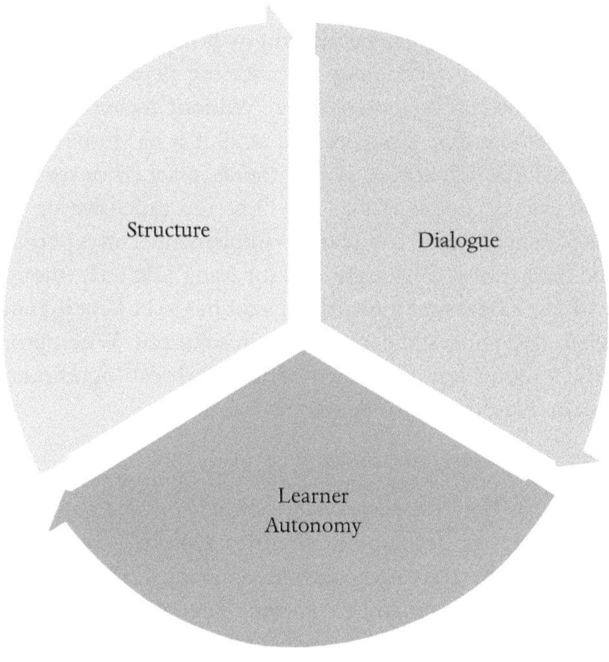

Source: Falloon (2010).

involved and how they are to be used. For example, while using non-interactive technologies (one-way dissemination) like print, radio and TV, good instructional design should ensure that after the presentation of the material, students reflect upon, question and explore concepts in the classroom and beyond. On the other hand, while using interactive technologies (two-way) such as computers, tablets and mobiles, the instructional design of the content should ensure discovery and exploratory modes of learning through simulations, quizzes, etc., and not reduce it to a 'show and tell' mode, thus not utilising the strengths of these interactive technologies.

Modern educational technology can allow equitable access to world-class interactive, engaging content that allows the learner to explore, research and assimilate learning — a paradigm far removed from the rote-learning-based systems that exist now.

Quality and Scale: How Technology can Act as an Enabler?[4]

Any programme or solution when implemented can only be viewed in an integrated manner, and thus the distinctions between all components blur — at least in the eyes of the end users. However, for the purpose of explication, the parts are being delineated so as to allow a nuanced view. Broadly, hardware can be looked at as delivery platforms and thus as an enabler of scale, and software can be looked at as an enabler of quality. To explain these components well, they have been taken as different entities. To use the analogy of the print medium, printing technology — the production process that can use technology to 'create' the text — can be thought of as the scale factor, and the text that the student finally gets to read can be thought of as the quality factor.

The use of technology permits the deployment of a programme on a massive scale. Without technology this is something that is not feasible at all if it has to be implemented through armies of well-trained teachers or trainers. And even if it is workable, it will be too expensive or will take an inordinately long time to implement. This is perhaps the most compelling argument for using EduTech, though with the caveat that the quality factor has to be kept in mind when designing and deploying such solutions. When properly designed and implemented, EduTech can significantly enhance the quality of delivery of education.

Hardware, Cost, Infrastructure and Connectivity[5]

There has been an all-pervading belief in India as well as perhaps other developing countries that ICT necessarily equals computers. As a consequence, many a computer lays gathering dust in many a computer lab. Without ensuring that there is adequate infrastructure such as electricity, that teachers and students are skilled at using ICT and that

there are resources to maintain and service hardware and systems, investing blindly in computers is a total wastage of money.

Research indicates that EduTech works only when it's both strategically and tactically integrated into the educational systems. Also, the last-mile connectivity and the cost of such connectivity have to be factored into any solution deployed. So, for example, it might be a good idea to give students low-cost tablets, but the move would be futile without giving them economical access to the internet. Therefore, investments must be made in providing free or inexpensive wi-fi zones in educational institutions and at community centres in rural and semi-urban settings where students can go to get access to the internet.

There is no doubt that in ideal conditions a combination of interactive whiteboards, tablets and computer labs with good content can make a huge difference. But in a place like India this utopian thought fails on many counts, the main reasons being lack of infrastructure: electricity, internet penetration, bandwidth availability, and most of all, lack of awareness and ability to use technologies by both teachers and students. Even if these problems were somehow to be solved, India just does not have the financial resources to implement such solutions in a uniform way across all schools through the length and breadth of the country.

It is in this light that we have to take a fresh look at the application of EduTech in classrooms across India. To create an impact we have to look at harnessing technologies that have existed for a long while, with which people are already quite conversant and do not suffer the biggest danger that confronts emerging technologies — huge hype followed by either obsolescence or a fade-away effect.

EduTech can be looked at as a continuum. At one end is the print medium, then the purely audio (radio) to audio-video (TV) and then on to interactive technologies such as computers and tablets. The furthest end of the continuum can be thought of as a combination that uses the internet to allow users to interact and collaborate with each other. While the latter in the continuum should perhaps be the eventual goal, for now a middle path comprising mostly components from the former and few from the latter (see Box 21.3) — wherever the luxury permits — represents the rational hope for making goals set in the RTE law realistic and attainable.

Software: Content[6]

In the end, as the oft-repeated cliché goes, content is the king. Be it the content of a train-the-teacher programme or teaching aids used in the classroom or learning materials that a student uses to learn on his/her own, it is the content and how it is used that makes the difference. As discussed

Box 21.3
Examples of Good Educational Technology

Radio-Based: As a device it can operate even without electricity and can run efficiently on simple batteries. A good model to emulate involves the integration of radio in the classroom, keeping interactivity as the central goal. Known as Interactive Radio Instruction (IRI), it has tremendous scope in developing nations such as India. As part of the dot-EDU India Technology Tools for Teaching and Training (T4) project funded by the United States Agency for International Development (USAID), Education Development Center (EDC) uses IRI for improving the quality of education at the elementary level in seven states in India — Bihar, Chhattisgarh, Jharkhand, Karnataka, Madhya Pradesh, Rajasthan, and Delhi.

Another well-known example is 'English is Fun' — a radio-based English teaching programme that has been a huge hit in Bihar. In all the 38 districts of the state, 7 million students attending 65,000 primary schools have access to a 122-episode English learning programme through radio sets. The state government has given ₹1,000 ($25) to every primary school to purchase a radio set. While sceptics might balk at the logistics of integrating radio in day-to-day teaching because of the organisation of scheduling, we believe that this problem can be solved by recording such programmes and delivering them through MP3 players connected with speakers so that they can be used again and again and built into the operational schedules of the school or the teachers.

TV-Based: Unlike print and radio or purely audio-based technologies, TV can through video bring lessons to life and provide a real-life immersive learning environment. In Mexico a very successful TV-based project called *Telesecundaria* has had a significant impact on student learning (Wolff et al. n.d.). Launched in far-flung areas where the population is less than 2,500 and where finding trained teachers was very tough, TV-based content was used to teach school children by teachers who were close to and trusted by the community.

In Brazil a project called *Telcurso* involving TV-based teaching was successfully used to target young adults who had dropped out of school so that they could learn on their own and appear for certification exams (ibid.). TV has a proven track record even within India where it has been successfully used for distance education though once again the quality of content has been in many cases quite mediocre. Just as in the case of live radio, scheduling-related logistics can be sorted out by storing the Audio-Visual (AV) programmes in DVDs or in hard disks so that DVD players or hard disk-based MP4 players can be used to show the content in a classroom.

Movie-Based: Same Language Subtitling (SLS) by PlanetRead is simply the idea of subtitling the lyrics of existing film songs (or music videos) on TV, in the 'same' language that they are sung in. SLS is delivering regular reading practice to 150 million weak-readers in India.

Tablets-Based: A portable tablet-based English Learning Lab by English Edge is a great example. It is a trolley that comes with centralised charging, an in-built Wi-Fi device and can house up to 40 tablets loaded with English language content. There is no investment needed for physical space for a classroom/lab and an institute can run a complete day's class without any interruption, even in the absence of electricity. The trolley (with tablets) moves to the place of learning and converts the classroom into an interactive, activity-based learning environment enabled by high-quality user-generated video recording through the tablets' camera and teacher-led video analysis of group activities, like role-plays, group discussions and presentations. Depending on the tablets, the cost of the Lab ranges from ₹10 to ₹70 per student per month. The cost includes teacher training and support costs. The product is currently made for and sold in India.

Mobile-Based: BBC Janala is a nine-year English in Action project in Bangladesh, which capitalises on teachers' familiarity with mobile phones by developing a set of engaging interactive materials uploaded onto Secure Digital (SD) cards in locally available $30 Nokia phones. An authentic classroom video of Bangladeshi teachers teaching their own students and using the government textbook is 'sandwiched' between that of a video mentor who introduces each video clip, asks questions, checks understanding and encourages reflection, aided by the use of Short Message Service (SMS) and regular monthly group meetings. Calls made to the BBC Janala service cost 50 per cent less than the standard call rates and SMSs are charged at 75 per cent of the normal service rates to the users.

Collaboration-Centric: Agropedia, spearheaded by the Indian Institute of Technology (IIT),Kanpur, is trying to create a kind of Facebook for Agriculture, where experts from across India can easily communicate with each other. Another good example is the collaborative community-based game — 'Farmville' (a Facebook application) — which is a simulation environment that mimics real-life farming practices (Srinivas 2012).

Enabling Literacy through Solar-Powered Projector: The Kinkajou Projector is a solar-powered projector designed by Design that Matters. The projector improves and expands access to education by transforming night-time learning environments in rural, non-electrified settings. The pilots have been run for night-time literacy classes in Mali, Africa.

previously, technology can only help in ensuring that the solution reaches a large number of users rapidly with relatively low net costs.

Given the complexities of creation of interactive, multimedia digital content, defining what is good or appropriate is a challenge. This is best solved using a robust evaluation framework where long-term learner performance has to be measured with respect to defined learner outcomes to gauge the efficacy of the content. Surveys can also reveal how the target audience enjoys the learning experience. In addition to the efficacy parameter, the correctness and appropriateness has to be gauged and audited by a panel of multi-disciplinary experts (subject matter, instructional, media, and technical experts).

While some technologies allow interactivity by definition, such as in computer and mobile devices, in those such as radio and television, the interactive elements that are lacking have to be built into the teaching learning experience through well-designed lesson plans, which elicit student responses and integrate them into meaningful learning experiences.

Technology-deployed content has many advantages:

(a) It can have audio, audio-video and even high-quality static graphics as a bare minimum and highly-interactive digital content, allowing peer-based collaboration and participation at the upper end of the spectrum.

(b) Once made, the cost of replication is minimum as is the ease of distribution if the set-up has been well thought-of.

(c) High-quality content made by leading experts will become available to large populations who otherwise would have had no chance of accessing such content.

(d) Learners, no matter who they are — teachers or students — can learn from each other and collaborate to learn together.

Software: Systems[7]

The focus of ICT interventions has been very clearly content. Yet without an equal emphasis on systems very negligible impact can be made. As discussed previously in the chapter, campus management can help streamline the administration and governance of educational institutions. Learning management systems can help track, manage and analyse student and teacher performances. Content management systems can help manage repositories of content and also help in the collaborative and online creation of digital content. Similarly, assessment systems can help in the creation and implementation of evaluations with corresponding reports and analytics.

RELEVANCE OF EDUCATIONAL TECHNOLOGY TO SCHOOL, VOCATIONAL AND HIGHER EDUCATION

School

In school education, EduTech can have a huge impact in training teachers both in ICT skills as well as in subject knowledge. A clear roadmap has to exist however in terms of the priorities of investment.

Phase I

The first priority should obviously be to use EduTech to rapidly grow the number of master trainers, who in turn can then use scaled technological models to train both pre-service and in-service teachers in modern pedagogy and subject knowledge.

Phase II

The next step should be to train teachers in ICT skills. It must be noted that hitherto ICT skills have been wrongly interpreted to mean basic computer operation skills. ICT skills should encompass the ability to use hardware, software tools and techniques to both teach students and update their own knowledge.

Phase III

As a next step, ICT should be integrated into the teaching and learning experience in the classroom and not sequestered into computer lab compartments. And till the dream of equipping and integrating modern EduTech, such as interactive whiteboards, clickers, etc., into each and every classroom is realised, it makes sense to empower students by coming up with models where low-cost EduTech devices can be provided with free or economical access to good content.

Vocational

What plagues the school education sector perhaps affects the vocational education as much if not more — the availability of skilled trainers, who are not only capable in the vocations that they will teach but also in training or teaching skills. Once again, without creating models where educational technology can optimise training time by creating self-paced and self-driven learning, developing a pool of skilled trainers will remain an unattainable objective.

Unlike K-12[8] and the higher education domains, vocational learning does not have a rich base of existing material. Using technological systems such as internet-based content authoring and management systems, domain experts in vocational training can collaborate to quickly create repositories of new digital content. These high-quality repositories can then be made available to teachers in vocational training institutes as teaching aids and to students as learning resources. Content authoring and management systems can furthermore make the translation of content into local languages and the localisation and customisation of content for specific local needs much easier and more manageable, thus making a good Return on Investment (ROI) case. Like all other domains, vocational skills are also no longer untouched by technology. In an era of constant evolution, these need to be upgraded, plus most need ICT skills embedded in them. Therefore, EduTech is needed to facilitate the learning of students in vocational streams and also subsequently to keep upgrading their skills after they come out of formal educational systems. EduTech can also play a critical role in assessing and automating the certification of the massive number of students expected in the vocational streams. In certain content areas where hands-on experience is either relatively expensive to give or has safety concerns, the use of simulations, videos and other such e-assets creates a compelling case for the use of educational technology. Some of the industries where simulations can be best used are chemical and heavy industries.

Internet-enabled social networking tools can allow communities of mentors, entrepreneurs, employers, and trainees to come together on a common collaboration platform, allowing for apprenticeships and employment opportunities.

Higher Education

The need for EduTech is perhaps easiest to establish in the higher education sector. Fast-changing knowledge and skills, rapid obsolescence, super-specialisation, the inter-disciplinary nature of teaching/learning, the research-based learning required, and the inherent embedding of technology in higher education tend to make the use of EduTech an obvious one. Once again, the fact that there are very few teachers or specialists skilled in certain disciplines makes the case for a model where EduTech becomes indispensable. Also, since higher education needs research and collaboration, sometimes across geographies, technological platforms can play a pivotal role.

The Massive Open Online Course (MOOC) has emerged as new paradigm in higher education where several universities have collaborated to provide free world-class learning materials and platforms for interaction. Notable examples include Coursera[9] seeded by the Universities of Princeton, Stanford, Michigan, and Pennsylvania; and EdX,[10] which is a joint partnership between the Massachusetts Institute of Technology (MIT) and Harvard University.

The Ministry of Human Resource Development (MHRD) has proposed a 'meta university', which would be a collaborative platform for a network of universities to come together and offer courses in a variety of disciplines, allowing students and teachers to access and share teaching materials, scholarly publications, research work, scientific works in progress, virtual experiments, etc. In fact, India's first meta university is expected to start its functioning from January 2013. The Cluster Innovation Centre and Institute of Life Long Learning as well as the Centre for Education will conduct the course in the University of Delhi. Models such as the MOOC address the economics of higher education by ensuring access to quality content without the trappings of high tuition fees.

EDUCATION TECHNOLOGY: COST COMPONENTS

Analogue Media

There is always an upfront cost related to the development of educational materials, which varies according to the richness, quality and extent of interactivity of the media. For example, an hour of pure audio content can vary from ₹10,000 to ₹25,000 per hour of output. Then there is a cost of broadcast (cost varies depending on terrestrial to community radio types of broadcast), and finally, cost of execution in the IRI type of intervention wherein infrastructure (physical space, radio set, speaker), teacher costs and PTR would need to be taken into consideration. In case of TV-based interventions there is a huge multiple (to the radio cost) due to the video nature of media. Distribution mechanism can be non-broadcasting-based such as through audio cassettes etc., but here there is a significant distribution cost.

Digital Media

In digital media there are two major upfront cost components: one, the richness of media and second, the amount of interactivity. Depending on these two parameters the cost may vary from ₹30,000 to ₹200,000 for a learning hour output. The replication and distribution cost in a digital setup is very minimal as compared to analogue distribution. However, given the fact that digital setup requires the presence of some hardware for learners and teachers the cost of execution is higher than the analogue model. However, certain services like student performance reports and tracking — the cost per student can be very low in comparison.

Evolution of Business Models

Historically, business models began with per user subscription-based ones for access to content. While this model is still the most prevalent, new models are emerging that are based on cheap/free access to content supported by advertisement- or services-based (certification, etc.) revenue streams. For e.g., Udacity[11] which offers MOOCs plans to make monies by offering a list of students with proven skills to potential recruiters and collecting a fee in return.

POLICY ISSUES IN THE DEPLOYMENT OF EDUCATION TECHNOLOGY IN INDIA

Integration of Education Technology into the Educational Policy Framework

Simply from a mindset perspective, all EduTech initiatives and policy-making have been disparate, isolated from the overall education policy framework.[12] This has resulted in silo-based thinking and implementation where there are technologists who only think technology without a basic knowledge of pedagogy, and conversely educationists who have no background in technology and end up diluting or sabotaging initiatives either through wilful acts of commission or acts of omission. A classic example of this exists in the way EduTech programmes are implemented in schools via the lab model. In this, 'computer teachers' or technicians oversee the administration of content (assuming there is subject-specific content apart from pure EduTech use-related content) and most other teachers have nothing to do with this model thus resulting in both a lack of ownership as well as ensuring that EduTech never gets integrated into day-to-day teaching. To create an impact, EduTech has to be incorporated into the entire supply chain of policy-making, administration and delivery of education. And this has to begin from the top: requiring intra-ministry coordination in the Ministry of Human Resource Development (MHRD) as well as inter-ministerial coordination with the Ministries of Communication and Information Technology.

The Importance of Monitoring and Evaluation

Monitoring and evaluation by independent bodies has to be factored into the implementation of all Educational Technology projects. Clear and measurable outcomes have to be devised and mechanisms for measuring them transparently deployed.

The Distinction between Basic Computer Operation Skills and Integration of Educational Technology into Teaching and Learning

Up till now the emphasis has been on equipping educational institutions with rudimentary hardware without much thought about assimilation into day-to-day teaching. The focus thus has to shift to equipping teachers and administrators with the skills to use content and systems to administer and teach effectively. This is especially true for teachers who need to be trained in using technology and existing content and tools as well as collaborating within their community to create new content and repurpose existing content. The need to fill the yawning gap in terms of recruiting new teachers can be a blessing in disguise as new recruits can be pre-taught new technology-enabled pedagogies and thus hit the ground running.

Problems with PPP and BOOT Models in Educational Technology Programmes

In the absence of evaluation and the resulting lack of accountability, Public–Private Partnership (PPP) and *Build–Own–Operate–Transfer* (BOOT) models have resulted in the 'dumping' of hardware, which has rapidly gone obsolete with it being put to little or no use. Content produced by providers have suffered from bad instructional design and have by and large been page-turners (linear and non-interactive content) supporting a 'tell mode' of delivery where information is delivered in a one-way manner without getting the learner to reflect and think. This goes against the very standards set by the National Curriculum Framework that seeks to promote critical thinking and higher-order thinking skills. Given this scenario, bodies like the National Council of Educational Research and Training (NCERT) and the various State Councils of Educational Research and Training (SCERTs) have to lay down stringent standards and guidelines and have to have powers of oversight over the acquisition and use of software and systems. In the long term, India should move toward using open-source content and software, which can be reused and repurposed without paying additional licensing costs. With education being a concurrent subject in India, the central government through

---

Box 21.4
BOOT vs Kerala Model: An Extract from the 59th Meeting (2012) of CABE

In some cases, states have allowed the BOOT agency to define its own syllabi and use invalidated e-content, delivered using inappropriate methodologies, thereby defeating the spirit of the National Curriculum Framework. The BOOT agencies deploy instructors to manage the system, which results in its dissociation from the rest of the school programme. Teachers in the school are not a part of the ICT programme process, barring a few isolated individual cases. They perceive the ICT inputs as external to their curriculum. Kerala has developed its own ICT curriculum with the active involvement of its teachers woven around Free Open Source Software (FOSS), demonstrating a heightened sense of ownership, the consequent sense of achievement and improved integration of ICT into the regular curriculum on a sustainable basis.

The Kerala experience has helped individual schools to take charge of the programme. The hardware is directly procured and managed through a strong service-level agreement and penalties. The entire process of development of curriculum and digital resources for all school subjects is taken up collaboratively by teacher groups supported by experts. The ICT curriculum is woven around a variety of FOSS applications, which extends the range and scope of learning experiences of students and teachers. Teachers manage the ICT curriculum as well as the IT infrastructure. These practices have demonstrated a heightened sense of ownership and achievement. There is a significant integration of ICT into the regular curriculum.

Source: MHRD (2012).

its nodal agencies can create a digital-based teaching and learning framework and create a central repository of core content. State governments through their nodal agencies can then modify the same as per local needs.

Capacity-Building through Setting up Courses in Educational Technology

There are hardly any educational programmes in Instructional Design or EduTech in India. It requires a different mindset and skill-set to design technology-enabled learning programmes. This entails not only the understanding of technology but also how technologies can be leveraged in the classroom and in learner-directed, self-paced modes to help promote deeper and better learning. Bachelors- and Masters-level degrees in education offered by most universities in India do not cover instructional technologies in depth and detail and thus separate courses in Instructional Technology are needed. Two institutions that offer some parts of these curricula are Shreemati Nathibai Damodar Thackersey (SNDT) Women's University and Symbiosis. As a result, there are very few skilled practitioners who have a background and experience in using technology-enabled pedagogy to build meaningful programmes. The government has to close this gap by setting up such programmes in institutes of repute so that this shortfall is addressed in the next few years.

Creating an Ecosystem to Catalyse the Development of Educational Technology in India

The troika of academic institutions, government bodies and the private sector has to form a thriving interdependent ecosystem to create low-cost, indigenously-made EduTech solutions that work well at a local level. There is undoubtedly a huge market in India for high-quality and low-cost technology-enabled educational content and services. However, as discussed earlier in the chapter, this market though huge, is unregulated, badly organised and thus the offered products and services are lacking in quality. To address these issues, academic institutions can play the lead role in research and development; the government can create policies and provide seed funding, and educational technology infrastructure such as ICT equipment and bandwidth availability at cheap rates at the grassroots level; and the private sector can provide entrepreneurs, more investments and thus develop cost-effective solutions.

With such a model it will be possible for the private sector to innovate and provide high quality, economical content and services with the costs of initial research and development being borne by the government and implementation left to state agencies and private players.

Relevance of Educational Technology to the Debate on the MDG and the MLG

Millennium Development Goal (MDG) vs Millennium Learning Goal (MLG)

One of the eight goals defined by the Millennium Summit of the United Nations in 2000, through the Millennium Development Goals (MDGs) was the achievement of universal primary education by the year 2015. The setting of this goal has led to the increase in enrolments in schools in most developing countries, as has also been the case in India. But as mentioned previously, study after study, from the Annual Status of Education Reports (ASERs) to the PISA, indicates that children lack both literacy and numeracy skills even though they might have completed primary schooling. Three World Bank economists, Deon Filmer, Amer Hasan and Lant Pritchett (2006) have proposed that 'the current education MDG' — a universal completion of primary education with nebulous definitions of quality — 'be replaced by a Millennium Learning Goal (MLG)', where the success of the goal is defined by the rigorous measurement of learning outcomes (Barrett 2009: 3).

The Definitions of Quality

This has stirred a debate on what constitutes quality and whether it can be measured by standard pan-country, internationally valid assessment mechanisms. The United Nations Children's Fund (UNICEF) framework defines five dimensions:
(a) what learners bring to learning;
(b) learning environments;
(c) content;
(d) processes; and
(e) outcomes.

Therefore, will a fixation with outcomes be a true measure of learning? What about the first, third and fourth inputs? Also, since the focus of most forms of assessment have mostly been cognitive skills, what about affective skills and attitudes and behaviours that lead to the overall development of children into responsible citizens. What about the larger social goals of education such as establishing gender equality, fostering tolerance, upholding democratic values? How can these 'outcomes' be measured in standardised tests? Also, can the very assumption behind a standard test being culturally and contextually neutral be a meaningful one?

Where does Educational Technology Come in?

It is our belief that not only are these questions pertinent but also that EduTech is very relevant to these and will be indispensable in answering some, if not all, of them. While we do agree that assessments that are not contextualised and meaningful for students defeat their very purpose, we are of the firm opinion that proper assessments will always remain a cornerstone of education — not only in terms of measuring outcomes but also in increasing the quality of education through analyses of assessment data. In our view, EduTech will be indispensable in this regard in the long run. A technology-enabled assessment system can help deliver contextualised, significant assessments at the grassroot levels while adhering to one cogent framework based on common standards. While we do agree that it's impossible to directly measure learning outcomes in non-cognitive domains, the deployment of technology-enabled games, scenario-based learning and simulations can at least indirectly measure the efficacy of teaching and learning interventions in this regard. Furthermore, integration of such data with e-governance systems can subsequently be used for impact studies by comparing experimental and control groups and seeing whether 'education' translates to changes in behaviour in real life.

Various studies, including the data coming out of PISA, have shown that the socio-economic status of households is a very good predictor of achievements as measured through standard assessments. There is no disputing and wishing away of the fact that the resources that children have access to and the attitudes fostered and atmosphere provided to them have a lot to do with the financial wherewithal and social standing of the families they come from. We believe that EduTech can play a great role here in levelling the playing field by giving access to high-quality digital content to all students irrespective of their backgrounds. However, we recognise the difficulty of implementing such ideas and as we have elaborated earlier, such moves will have little or no impact without inculcating in students the skills to use such resources.

Lastly, we agree that the other dimensions of learning (apart from outcomes) are also very critical in the process of learning. While giving students resources to learn from can help in the first dimension — 'what learners bring to learning' — the dimensions of learning environments, content and processes have to be continuously monitored so that evaluation and further improvement can happen. Learning content has been the primary focus of EduTech initiatives and thus it is really beyond debate whether EduTech can help in this area. It undoubtedly can but we think that there is a huge role for EduTech in the other two dimensions as

well. By implementing and embedding technology in the classroom, quality of teaching can be monitored and evaluated through various learning and teaching management systems. And while human intervention is undoubtedly indispensable for monitoring of processes, the data that is gathered through such endeavours can only be processed meaningfully through technology-driven data gathering and analysis tools.

CONCLUSION

There is no doubt that educational technology can and must play a pivotal role in delivering quality in the realms of school, vocational and higher education. But for this to happen, a structured systems development model like the ADDIE has to be followed. Furthermore, it has to be ensured that there are repeated iterations of the ADDIE cycle rather than a single one. These should continue till the evaluation stage confirms that all objectives defined in the analysis have been attained. There should be a strong emphasis on monitoring and evaluation. We have to get away from the thinking that educational technology means computer labs and computer education, and a judicious mix of old and new technologies must be used to ensure that goals and outcomes are attained. Software systems that help in the governance and administration of educational institutions must also get adequate attention. The government should ensure that ICT for education is completely integrated into MHRD policy-making and implementation. It has to leverage technology to rapidly repurpose content and localise it at the most granular level possible — state, district, and so on. It has to ensure that it uses a *cascading approach* where policy-makers, personnel from ministries and regulatory bodies, and teachers are first trained and equipped in ICT before students can reap the benefits. The government must ensure the creation of technology-enabled quality content, systems and assessment and build low-cost delivery systems in partnership with the private sector. While many of these points have been articulated in policy-making, implementation and execution has to be ensured.

While it will be very naive to assert that technology is the only answer to the problem of providing quality education for all, it will be equally foolish to state that it's not a necessary part of the answer.

NOTES

1. In this chapter, while we by and large prefer the term 'Educational Technology' we shall use 'ICT in Education' interchangeably with EduTech.

2. Please see Figure 21.1, A.
3. See Figure 21.1, B.
4. See Figure 21.1, C–D.

5. See Figure 21.1, D.
6. See Figure 21.1, C.
7. See Figure 21.1, C.
8. 'K-12', a term used in education and educational technology, is a short form for school grades prior to college — kindergarten (K) and I to the XII grade.

9. http://www.coursera.org/ (accessed 17 November 2012).
10. http://www.edxonline.org (accessed 17 November 2012).
11. http://www.udacity.com/ (accessed 17 November 2012).
12. EduTech is often referred to as 'ICT' in Education in government and international policy documents.

REFERENCES

Barrett, Angeline M. 2009. 'The Education Millenium Development Goal beyond 2015: Prospects for Quality and Learners'. EdQual Working Paper no. 13, University of Bristol and Department for International Development.

Branch, Robert Maribe. 2010. *Instructional Design: The ADDIE Approach.* Boston, MA: Springer Science+Business Media, LLC.

Falloon, Garry. 2010. 'Making the Connection: Moore's Theory of Transactional Distance and Its Relevance to the Use of a Virtual Classroom in Postgraduate Online Teacher Education', *Journal of Research on Technology in Education,* 43(3): 187–209.

Filmer, Deon, Amer Hasan and Lant Pritchett. 2006. 'A Millennium Learning Goal: Measuring Real Progress in Education'. Working Paper no. 97, Center for Global Development and World Bank.

Jung, Insung. 2005. 'ICT-Pedagogy Integration in Teacher Training: Application Cases Worldwide', *Educational Technology & Society,* 8(2): 94–101.

Ministry of Human Resource Development (MHRD). 2012. 'Agenda Items and Background Notes'. Fifty Ninth Meeting of the Central Advisory Board of Education, Ministry of Human Resource Development, Government of India, 6 June, New Delhi. http://mhrd.gov.in/sites/upload_files/mhrd/files/59 THCABEAGENDANOTES.pdf (accessed 16 November 2012).

Srinivas, Nidhi Nath. 2012. 'Bringing Farmville to Life: Social Media Empowers Farmers'. *Economic Times,* 24 May.

Sweet, Richard and Alina Meates. 2004. 'ICT and Low Achievers: What does Pisa Tell us?', in Andrea Kárpáti (ed.), *Promoting Equity Through ICT in Education: Projects, Problems, Prospects,* pp. 13–54. Budapest: Organisation for Economic Co-operation and Development and Hungarian Ministry of Education. http://www.oecd.org/dataoecd/29/29/33680762.pdf (accessed 16 November 2012).

Wolff, Laurence, Claudio de Moura Castro, Juan Carlos Navarro, and Norma García 2002. 'Television for Secondary Education: Experience of Mexico and Brazil', in Wadi D. Haddad and Alexandra Draxler (eds), *Technologies for Education: Potentials, Parameters and Prospects,* pp. 144–52. Paris: United Nations Educational, Scientific and Cultural Organization. http://www.ictinedtoolkit.org/usere/library/tech_for_ed_chapters/10.pdf (accessed 16 November 2012).

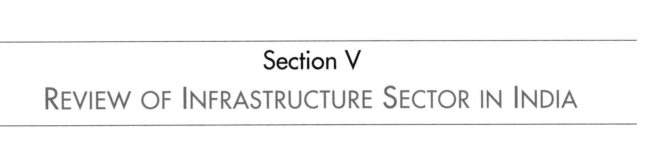

Section V
REVIEW OF INFRASTRUCTURE SECTOR IN INDIA

The Infrastructure Sector in India 2012

Megha Maniar

The Indian infrastructure sector continues its sluggish journey in 2012, marked by poor macroeconomic forces, policy gridlock and political instability. Delays in land acquisition and environmental clearances continue to be key areas of concern, while the poor enforcement of contracts, ineffective monitoring and high input costs are also factors that are hindering growth. Nonetheless, some areas have witnessed progress. The telecom sector saw the emergence of the National Telecom Policy, a cohesive document covering a broad range of communication services. In both civil aviation and power sectors, the Government of India has approved foreign investment of 49 per cent, bringing relief to the heavily leveraged public and private companies. However, several events in the infrastructure sector have been disappointing this year — the telecom sector dealt with the fallout of the 2G scam, the power sector witnessed the coal scam and the grid collapse, the roads and urban sectors saw the poor private participation, and the civil aviation sector witnessed the poor financial health of the airport and airline operators.

The end of the 11th Five-Year Plan saw India missing targets in infrastructure development in sectors such as railways, ports, electricity, and airports, while investing beyond the budgeted investment in others — the roads and telecom sectors (Table 1). Overall, ₹19.45 trillion was invested in Indian infrastructure between fiscal years 2007–08 and 2011–12, 95 per cent of the projected ₹20.56 trillion.

The 12th Five-Year Plan projects the total investment in infrastructure during the period to be ₹51.46 trillion, with 47 per cent contributed by private participation and 53 per cent by the central and state governments. Table 2 shows the breakup of these investments across various infrastructure sectors.

This chapter addresses the achievements, policy developments and problems faced by various sectors during the calendar year 2012. Physical and financial progress are tracked in these crucial sectors, along with the introduction of new policies and participation of the private sector.

TELECOMMUNICATIONS

By October 2012, the wireless subscriber base in India had increased to 938 million, consisting of 596 million urban

TABLE 1   11th Five-Year Plan Investment in Infrastructure (at 2006–07 prices)

Sector	Projected Investment (₹ in trillion)	Actual Investment (₹ in trillion)	Actual Investment as Proportion of Projected Investment (in per cent)
Electricity	6.66	6.35	95
Roads	3.14	3.62	115
Telecommunications	2.58	3.36	130
Railways	2.62	1.95	75
Ports	0.88	0.35	40
Airports	0.31	0.29	95
Others*	4.37	3.53	81
Total	20.56	19.45	95

Source: High Level Committee on Financing Infrastructure (2012).

Note: *Others include irrigation, water supply and sanitation, storage, and oil and gas pipelines.

TABLE 2 12th Five-Year Plan Investment Projections in Infrastructure (at 2011–12 prices)

Sector	Projected Investment (₹ in trillions)	Project Investment as Proportion of Total Investment (in per cent)
Electricity	18.48	36
Roads	9.20	18
Telecommunications	8.84	17
Railways	4.57	9
Ports	1.61	3
Airports	0.71	1
Others*	8.05	16
Total	51.46	100

Source: High Level Committee on Financing Infrastructure (2012).

Note: *Others include Mass Rapid Transit System (MRTS), irrigation, water and sanitation, storage, and oil and gas pipelines.

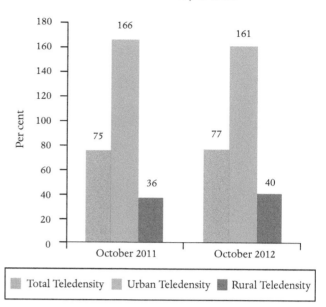

FIGURE 1 Teledensity in India

Source: TRAI (2011, 2012).

and 342 million rural subscribers. The number of wireline subscribers continued to decrease, with only 3.3 per cent of all telecom subscriptions belonging to wireline services. This decline can be attributed to the relative affordability of wireless connections and the convenience with which they can be obtained. Overall telephone density or teledensity had increased from 75 per cent in October 2011 to 77 per cent in October 2012, while urban and rural teledensity had reached 161 per cent and 40 per cent, respectively. Urban teledensity levels have fallen due to the recent cancellation of 2G licenses, while rural teledensity has increased steadily. The urban and rural teledensity levels in India demonstrate the stark contrast between urban and rural communication levels, which continues to be a major concern (Figure 1).

The New Telecom Policy (NTP) was approved by the Indian Cabinet in May 2012, more than a year after its expected launch. This policy aims 'to provide secure, reliable, affordable and high quality telecommunication services' to all citizens (Department of Electronics and Information Technology 2012). The Department of Telecommunications (DoT) seeks to enhance the Unified Access Services (UAS) license regime through this policy, allowing operators to provide all telecom services (including internet telephony, cable television, radio broadcasting, and all other wireline or wireless media) under one license. As opposed to the earlier licence fee of 6–10 per cent of gross revenue (depending on the telecom circle and type of service), the NTP stipulates a uniform fee of 8 per cent of annual gross revenue starting from 2013. Each license will be allocated for 10 years instead of the current tenure of 20 years. Telecom spectrum, previously available in combination with the license, can now be acquired separately. Spectrum sharing between telecom

firms within the same frequency in a telecom circle will be permissible in 2G networks but not in 3G networks. Merger and Acquisition (M&A) activity is currently allowed if the merger results in a combined network market share of 35 per cent; however, this may be extended to 60 per cent, pending the approval of the Telecom Regulatory Authority of India (TRAI). Mobile Number Portability (MNP) will be implemented under the concept of 'one nation, one license', allowing customers to use the same number across the country without paying roaming charges. The policy plans to increase rural teledensity to 70 per cent by 2017, and 100 per cent by 2020. Broadband services shall be provided at affordable rates by 2015, and cross 600 million connections by 2020. Research and Development (R&D) will be promoted in telecom equipment production to meet domestic and international demands. Finally, in order to meet the international standards of telecommunications, it will be a priority to change to cloud computing and the new Internet Protocol version 6 (IPv6) by 2020. Cloud computing uses the internet and central remote servers to maintain, store and share data, and the IPv6 is a global internet policy which accommodates for the growing number of internet users and widening communication networks, by increasing the number of available IP addresses (Table 3 provides a summary of the NTP).

The Interim Report of the High Level Committee on Financing Infrastructure pushed for an increase in external commercial borrowings for 2G licenses, and suggested that rural telephone connections could be subsided with the help of the Universal Service Obligation Fund (USOF).

TABLE 3   Summary of National Telecom Policy 2012

Item	Target
License Fee	8 per cent of annual gross revenue
License Tenure	To be extended to 10 years
Spectrum	Spectrum to be paid for separately Spectrum sharing now permitted on 2G but not on 3G
M&A	Allowed up to 35 per cent of resultant revenue market share, while awaiting TRAI recommendation before extending up to 60 per cent
MNP	No roaming charges across the country
Rural Teledensity	By 2017, should reach 70 per cent, and 100 per cent by 2020
Broadband Connectivity	600 million boadband connections should exist by 2020
Future Implementations	Effectively use cloud computing and IPv6 by 2020

Source: Department of Electronics and Information Technology (2012).

The Committee also stipulated that if the Foreign Direct Investment (FDI) limit in the sector was increased, safeguards should be implemented to protect domestic interests.

Growth in broadband services has slowed down recently. Despite the target of reaching 20 million subscribers by 2010, as envisaged in the Broadband Policy of 2004, the number of broadband subscribers had only reached 15.08 million in October 2012. TRAI issued guidelines for a National Broadband Policy in 2010 and proposed the establishment of a nation-wide broadband network which would connect all areas with populations of 500 people or more. This plan aims to increase the number of subscribers to 75 million in 2012 and 154 million by 2014. Based on this, the DoT has been working on a National Broadband Plan but no concrete steps have been taken. The National Optical Fibre Network (NOFN) project, approved and launched in November 2011, will continue to expand broadband services to about 250,000 gram panchayats by 2014. By providing connectivity to these public institutions, the network will facilitate governance, education, health, and commerce at the grassroots level. Requiring an investment of ₹200 billion over two years, NOFN will be funded by the USOF and executed by a special purpose vehicle — Bharat Broadband Network Ltd (BBNL). BBNL should be operational by November 2013.

The Rural Wireline Broadband Policy was launched in 2009 under Bharat Nirman, funded and managed by USOF. Facilitated by Bharat Sanchar Nigam Limited (BSNL), 900,000 broadband connections need to be provided to individuals and government institutions in rural areas by 2014. By March 2012, about 350,000 connections had been provided. In 2009, the scheme had budgeted ₹15 billion to be disbursed over the following five years. It seems that while financing may not be a major concern (currently, USOF has a balance of ₹220 billion available for disbursement), the inefficiencies in planning and execution may force extending the scheme.

The investigation into the 2G scam continued in 2012. The Central Bureau of Investigation (CBI) has levied charges against several private telecom companies and various associated government officials. In February 2012, the Supreme Court cancelled 122 UAS licenses which had been allotted at 2001-market prices in 2008. Several telecom corporations were subjected to the cancellation of all UAS licenses and their spectrum allocation withdrawn (see Table 4).

With inputs from the deliberations of the Empowered Group of Ministers (EGoM) appointed to determine the 2G spectrum pricing, the DoT has set the spectrum price at ₹140 billion for the 5 MHz pan-India license for Global System for Mobile (GSM) Communications operators while the spectrum for Code Division Multiple Access (CDMA) operators has been priced at ₹182 billion. Following this, the Supreme Court ordered that the new 2G auctions should be completed by 11 January 2013. If the Ministry does not conform to this order, the court will initiate contempt proceedings against it. It is vital for this auction to be conducted in an efficient and precise manner in order to rebuild confidence in the telecom market.

The MNP was launched in February 2012 and is seen to be a major gain for customers, but can result in major losses for telecom providers. At the beginning of 2012, 32.8 million subscribers had subscribed to the MNP facility, but by October 2012 the number had increased to 69.78 million. Considering that many of these customers are long-term users, telecom operators may suffer from lower profits due to the loss of future gains expected from such users. To offset this, operators may increase subscription charges in the long term, causing harm to subscribers.

While the 3G spectrum auction was successfully conducted in 2011, the roll out of the network will require one–three years. The Ministry of Communications and Information Technology states that the roll out will ensure that 3G services can be accessed in remote areas where broadband networks have not yet arrived due to high infrastructure investment. Currently, more than 5,000 cities have 3G services available with the establishment of 80,000 Base Transceiver Stations (BTSs) to facilitate the 3G services between the network and the user. Figure 2 exhibits the 3G coverage of various telecom companies across Indian states. However, 3G services have not been well-received by consumers and the slow returns on their investments are

TABLE 4   Cancellation of 2G Licence in Telecom Companies

Company	Licenses Issued Post-January 2008	Spectrum Held (MHz)	Affected Users (in million)	Comments
Videocon	21	88.0	5.4	Licences cancelled and spectrum withdrawn
Loop Telecom	21	88.0	3.2	Licences cancelled and spectrum withdrawn
Uninor (Unitech)	22	92.4	36.3	Licences cancelled and spectrum withdrawn; Norwegian company Telenor exited its joint venture with Unitech following cancellation of licences
Sistema Shyam	21	52.5	12.6	Licences cancelled and spectrum withdrawn
Etisalat	15	66.0	1.7	Licences cancelled and spectrum withdrawn; not participating in 2G auction
STel	6	26.4	3.5	Licences cancelled and spectrum withdrawn
Idea Cellular	13	52.8	6.7	13 circle licences cancelled and spectrum withdrawn
TTSL	3	7.5	0.2	3 CDMA licences cancelled and spectrum withdrawn
Total	122	473.6	69.6	

Source: IDFC (2012), Indian Infrastructure (2012).

FIGURE 2   3G Network Coverage in Indian States

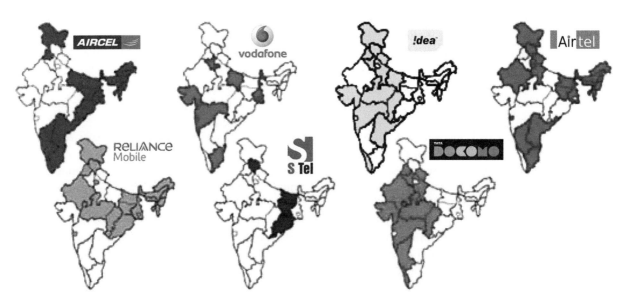

Source: Biswas (2010).
Note: Maps not to scale. Used with permission from TelecomTalk.info.

preventing operators from further expanding their services in Tier II and III cities and other states.

After the Broadband Wireless Access (BWA) or 4G spectrum auctions were completed in 2011, Bharati Airtel was the first to launch its services in Kolkata, Bangalore and Pune, and is also expected to do so in Punjab in the coming months. Additionally, by acquiring a 49 per cent stake in Qualcomm Asia Pacific in May 2012, Bharati Airtel will also be able to offer services in Qualcomm's telecom circles,

viz., Delhi, Mumbai, Haryana, and Kerala by 2014. Reliance Infotel, the only firm to have a pan-India BWA license, is finalising plans to commence services towards the end of the year, while Aircel, holding licenses in eight circles, will be launching their BWA services by December 2012. After winning licenses for Madhya Pradesh and Chhattisgarh, Augere Wireless is planning to sell its stake in the 4G spectrum because of regulatory uncertainty and funding concerns. Figure 3 exhibits the geographic distribution of

FIGURE 3   4G Network Coverage in Indian States

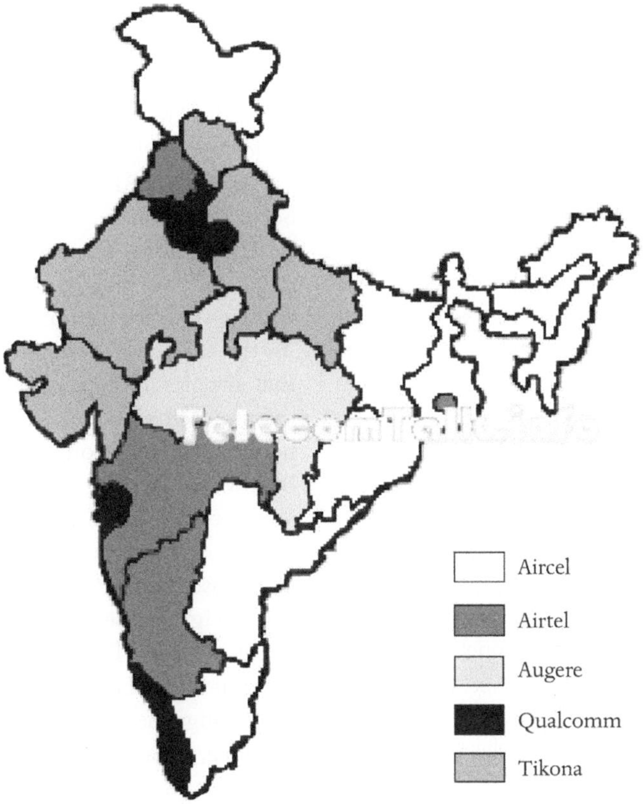

Aircel
Airtel
Augere
Qualcomm
Tikona

Source: Biswas (2012).
Note: Map not to scale. Used with permission from TelecomTalk.info.

4G operators excluding Reliance Infotel. Since the BWA network does not require much physical infrastructure, these services should greatly increase internet accessibility across the nation if regulations remain liberal in order to incentivise private investment. The DoT has asked 4G operators to expedite the roll out of their services.

TRANSPORT

Civil Aviation

The civil aviation sector has seen turmoil throughout the year, and it appears that recovery will be slow. Almost all private carriers are currently reporting losses, while some are facing insolvency. In relative terms, low-cost carriers have performed better than full-service ones. Most of the problems are being attributed to the overextension of loans taken for purchase of aircraft, working capital loans, and increasing aviation fuel costs which make up to 35–40 per cent of operating costs. The Airport Authority of India

(AAI) has approved 14 greenfield projects at a combined investment of ₹300 billion, and has received proposals for seven similar projects. However, land acquisition and environmental clearances are major hindrances for these ventures. Projects in Tier II and III are on the fence since they may not guarantee sufficient revenue to offset costs, even in the long term. The Task Force set up by the Committee on Infrastructure recommends the upgradation of 35 nonmetro airports and the expansion of air terminals in 27 nonmetro airports.

The merger of Air India and Indian Airlines in 2007 resulted in massive unsolved human resource issues. Air India prepared a Comprehensive Turnaround Plan (CAP) which was approved in April 2012. This systematically charts the financial restructuring and operational turnaround process. The Crew Management System (CRS) will ensure operational safety, optimally utilise crew and meet regulatory requirements by replacing the ineffective manual system. The Financial Restructuring Plan (FRP) aims to alleviate Air India's debt obligation while the airline's operations can be improved. After the plan was approved by the Government of India, ₹29 billion was injected into the entity for the payment of salaries, fuel and taxes between April and August 2012; ₹105 billion will be converted to long-term debt with tenure of 10–15 years, while ₹74 billion will be repaid through non-convertible debentures with government guarantees. Recent developments have indicated that Air India will be selling or leasing some of its domestic and international properties for additional fund raising. The Dharmadhikari Committee was set up to form recommendations on the human resource issues which will arise from the Air India merger and its report was submitted on 31 Jan 2012. A committee made up of Air India officials was set up in June 2012 to implement the Dharmadhikari Committee report (Table 5).

TABLE 5   Dharmadhikari Committee Report

Recommendations
1.   Instilling inter se seniority among employees of Indian Airlines and Air India (except for pilots and engineers who will be given line seniority based on type of aircraft assigned, and cabin crew will be provided uniform seniority).
2.   Promotions should be based on seniority and merit, but for the next two years the Rota-Quota system should be implemented. This system draws on maintaining a fixed quota for a particular position, and the rotational component states that the next eligible candidate be considered.
3.   The Postal Life Insurance (PLI) system is a violation of the Department of Public Enterprises' guidelines and should be replaced by another incentive system.
4.   Pay should be a product of the profit earned by the company and target achievement. A committee comprising airline officials was formed to implement these stipulations.
5.   Transfer the Maintenance, Repair and Overhaul business into a separte entity. Subjected to the new regulations and global standards, it will be supported financially by Air India and is projected to be a profit-making body by 2017.

Source: Dharmadhikari Committee (2012).

A number of fundamental changes have occurred within this year. The FDI limit has been increased to 49 per cent, to the comfort of some struggling airlines who view the move as a relief to their debt-laden finances, while others fear the possibility of foreign oligopoly and takeovers. However, FDI improvements will not be successful without infrastructure and regulatory reforms. The creation of an independent regulatory body — the Civil Aviation Authority — has been proposed. Its objectives are to facilitate a safety monitoring system, economic regulation, consumer protection and environment regulation. The entity is being formed to circumvent the problems the Directorate General of Civil Aviation (DGCA) faces in human resource management, and to respond to these problems. Concurrently, the

Ministry has decided to remove the Airport Development Fee (ADF) in Delhi and Mumbai airports, effective from January 2013. While removing the ADF lessens the financial burden on passengers, it will also reduce the airports' corpuses by ₹42 billion in Mumbai and ₹11.8 billion in Delhi. To bridge this funding loss, the Ministry suggests that the majority stakeholders in both airports should raise further capital while AAI should infuse equity in the projects (IDFC Securities 2012).

The National Transport Policy Development Committee (NTPDC) working group reports for each of the sector includes policy recommendations on transportation sectors for the 12th Five-Year Plan. In civil aviation, it recommends that airports in metro cities should be expanded, and in the cases of Mumbai and New Delhi, a second airport should be created. The Committee also emphasises the creation of low-cost airports with development of regional airlines. While prices are to be regulated, it is necessary to ensure that predatory pricing does not occur, while competition is not discouraged. Finally, the group suggests setting up an Air Navigation Services Corporation for the management of air traffic. The Interim Report of the High Level Committee on Financing Infrastructure (2012) recommends expediting the award of the airport projects in Navi Mumbai, Goa, Kannur, and Chandigarh as Public–Private Partnerships (PPPs). The group also recommends using the PPP framework to manage Chennai and Kolkata airports, and for the development and operation of air- and city-side facilities at 15 non-metro airports.

The aviation carbon footprint report, released by the Directorate General of Civil Aviation (DGCA) in July 2012, determined that Indian airlines emitted 12.7 million tonnes of CO_2 in 2012, an increase by 6 per cent from 2011. Indian Airlines emitted 1 per cent of the total carbon emission in the country, much lower than the 2 per cent emitted on average by airlines across the globe. The DGCA pledged to sustainably expand aviation in the country and implement proactive measures to reduce the national carbon footprint (2012).

Ports

The maritime sector has experienced tepid growth in India primarily because of project delays and adverse global economic conditions. The performance of major ports has dragged and most of the traffic growth in the sector has been driven by the minor ports; while traffic at major ports decreased from 570 million tonnes (MT) to 560 MT, minor ports saw traffic increase from 315 MT to 370 MT during the fiscal year 2012. By April 2012, port capacity had crossed 1,200 MT, having increased by 100 MT from the previous year. While the optimal capacity utilisation of ports should stand at 70 per cent, major ports face 90 per cent capacity utilisation implying traffic congestion and high berth occupancy. The Draft 12th Five-Year Plan envisages an increase in India's share of world trade from 0.8 per cent to 1.5 per cent, requiring an increase in the current port capacity. In the present fiscal year, the Ministry of Shipping (MoS) has facilitated the creation of 245 MT of capacity in major ports through PPPs, and allowed the investment of ₹145 billion across 42 projects.

In April 2012, three major PPP capacity-expansion projects had been awarded in Navi Mumbai, Kandla and Visakhapatnam, with a total investment of ₹80 billion to create a capacity of 79 MT per annum; incidentally, all three ports handled most of the traffic in the country between April and August 2012. The approvals for these projects had been completed within three months, which is seen as some of the fastest approvals in the port sector and the government hopes to continue this trend. Nonetheless, private interest for port projects seems to be waning. In Navi Mumbai's Jawaharlal Nehru Port Trust (JNPT), only one company bid for the construction of a container terminal, whereas in Visakhapatnam private firms are unwilling to bid due to liquidity concerns. At the same time, multiple projects in Maharashtra, Tamil Nadu and Kerala have been terminated after the cancellation of Memorandums of Understanding (MoUs) and unrealistic bids offered by private firms.

Currently, the sector faces crippling issues in PPP projects. These include delays in obtaining clearances, heavy litigation during the tendering process, the lack of supporting infrastructure at terminals such as container freight stations, and difficulties with land acquisition. Some policy measures have been instilled to simplify this process. In September 2012, the Cabinet Committee of Infrastructure allowed the MoS to approve PPP projects valued at less than ₹500 million without the consent of the Cabinet; previously, the limit was ₹300 million. This was done to hasten the approval process and prevent cost overruns. Additionally, in August, land transfer norms were relaxed for government land, whereby land may be freely transferred without Cabinet approval for state-run entities.

Recently, private terminal operators at major ports have criticised the Tariff Authority for Major Ports (TAMP) for setting tariffs that are forcing them to scale down operations. According to the 2008 guidelines, tariffs are fixed at the maximum capacity, thereby capping profits and inadvertently, dis-incentivising efficiency. Through current legislation, tariff setting occurs for 30 years and no corrective mechanism is in place since future conditions are difficult to anticipate. This is under review by the Mumbai High Court. At the same time, the Ports Regulatory Authority Bill of 2011, hoping to establish regulatory bodies for setting tariffs for both central and state ports, is also pending approval.

If passed, TAMP would be replaced by a new entity which would regulate both major and non-major ports.

The NTDPC interim report recommends that the 12th Five-Year Plan should incorporate measures to reverse the shortfall in investments in major ports and improving productivity (2012). The Committee argues that port trusts should be transformed into statutory landlord port authorities, while terminal operations are transferred to public sector corporations. One comprehensive law should be introduced for major and minor ports to enable the previously mentioned transformation and provide them with autonomy. Competition should be encouraged in this sector as well; tariffs should be set through market forces, and as competition grows the TAMP should be restructured to better manage the ports. Coastal shipping should be encouraged by setting up coastal terminals, providing road and rail connectivity to the terminals, and fiscal incentives to transporters of cargo from road or rail to ships. Finally, ties should be forged between bordering countries for inland water transport and to encourage investment in these inter-country linkages.

The interim report of the High Level Committee on Financing Infrastructure outlines broad changes in most areas of the sector (2012). The Committee suggests that the MoS should expedite the awarding process under the PPP framework, encourage the creation of private ports in co-ordination with state governments, deregulate port tariffs, implement a plan to reduce the dwell time by modernising processes and technologies, and hasten capital dredging activities with the help of private participation.

Railways

The Indian Railways earned ₹586.5 billion between April and September 2012, increasing its revenues by about 20 per cent from ₹489.64 billion earned during the same period in 2011. The 12th Five-Year Plan maintains a focus on capacity-building, modernisation and safety in railways, and estimates a budget of ₹7,197 billion for the sector, of which ₹800 billion is expected to be invested by the private sector. PPP investment in the 12th Five-Year Plan is likely to be in the high speed corridor between Mumbai and Ahmedabad, the elevated rail corridor in Mumbai, redevelopment of stations, logistics parks, freight terminals and corridors, port connectivity projects, manufacturing units, and energy projects. The increased demand and sub-par quality of railways has led to plans to modernise 19,000 km of railway lines over the next five years.

In the report of the High Level Safety Review Committee, released in February 2012, the Committee argues to keep safety as the topmost concern of the railways, despite the fall in number of train accidents. The Committee advises the Ministry of Railways (MoR) to implement an advanced signalling system on the 19,000-km trunk route through a special purpose vehicle (SPV) costing ₹200 billion and to eliminate all level crossings across the country costing ₹500 billion, over the next five years. All new coaches should be built with the Linke Hofmann Bush (LHB) design, replacing the Integral Coach Factory (ICF) design in order to ensure safety. Also, the maintenance of safety-related infrastructure should be firmly implemented, which would cost ₹200 billion, and is to be funded through various mechanisms including a safety tax on passengers, a road tax, deferred dividend, and a matching grant by the central government (2012).

The Expert Group on Modernisation of Indian Railways also released their report in February 2012 and made various recommendations on the modernisation of Indian railways. These include modernising existing rail tracks, strengthening 11,250 km of bridges, modernising 100 major stations, developing stations and terminals in PPP mode, manufacturing of coaches and high speed railway lines, and construction of freight corridors covering 6,200 km, over the next 10 years. The total investment of ₹5.6 trillion can be raised through the monetisation of assets, private participation, and funds generated by the railways.

The NTDPC interim report (2012) points out that MoR does not have a cogent long-term policy on capacity expansion and must focus on creating such guidelines. In order to act as a commercial body, the Railway Board should be reorganised, including its accounting policies which should conform to standard business practices. Also, the 12th Five-Year Plan should look into setting up a tariff regulatory body, which is present in other transportation sectors.

The interim report of the High Level Committee on Financing Infrastructure (2012) encourages the MoR to make a number of changes in order to generate funds for projects and encourage private investment. They recommend the rationalisation of fares to gather funds for the upgradation and modernisation of railways. To encourage private investment, they believe the Ministry should use the PPP framework in major development projects. Also, they recommend that the Commercial Railways Board be restructured to stimulate growth and investment.

The MoR made two major policy decisions this year. In June 2012, the private freight terminal policy was altered by separating the revenue sharing clause from the wholesale price index. Through this modification new terminals will share the revenue after five years, and existing terminals will do so after two years. In January 2012, a draft Policy for Private Participation in Rail Connectivity and Capacity Augmentation Projects was released with an objective of replacing the Railways' Infrastructure for Industry Initiative Policy and Rail Connectivity to Coal and Iron Ore Mines Policy (MoR 2012). This policy contains six models for private participation based on the type of project and outlines an active role for state governments in the development and implementation of these projects.

After the cabinet approved the leasing of railway land, the Rail Land Development Authority (RLDA) invited bids for the commercial use of land. Sixty new multi-functional complexes and eight standalone sites have been made available, and parties can bid either on a one-time lease premium or annual lease rent. This came after a performance audit was conducted on land management in the Indian Railways by the Comptroller and Auditor General (CAG), which advised RLDA to strengthen the organisation of land management, maintain records, prevent land encroachment, expedite land acquisition, and augment income with the leasing of railway land for commercial development.

Roads

By September 2012, the total length of the road network was 3.31 million km. The National Highway Development Program (NHDP) being implemented by the National Highways Authority of India (NHAI) had achieved 17,372 km of four-lane national highways (by October 2012) out of the total 48,254 km covered under the NHDP (NHAI 2012). Under the Pradhan Mantri Gram Sadak Yojana (PMGSY) about 55 per cent of all rural settlements had been connected by 214,758 km of new roads and 142,528 km of improved roads by June 2012. During the fiscal year 2011–12, NHAI constructed roads at the rate of 6.16 km per day, while the State Public Work Departments and Border Roads Organisation completed 4.23 km per day. The average road length constructed, however, falls well short of the targeted 20 km per day. Given that the road freight volumes have grown by 9.08 per cent and vehicles have grown by 10.76 per cent, it is important to achieve the 20 km per day target.

The digitalisation of Regional Transport Offices (RTOs) and national and state databases have been a major accomplishment towards achieving total connectivity between RTOs and the computerisation of records. The National Permit Scheme, launched in 2010 to facilitate the movement of cargo between states, has largely been successful and popular among transport companies. The Cabinet Committee on Infrastructure recently approved the Engineering, Procurement and Construction model for two-lane highways. This model specifies design and performance standards while allowing construction companies to innovate and quicken road construction. Additionally, a concession model has been approved for the operation, maintenance and transfer (OMT) of projects, making the contractor responsible for the OMT of projects for four to nine years.

The Indian government entered into two major bilateral agreements for the exchange of knowledge in the road sector. A Memorandum of Cooperation (MoC) was signed between Japan and India, allowing for cross-exchange of information on capacity-building and technology in road construction. India and Canada signed an MoU for the transfer of knowledge on infrastructure development, and road operations and maintenance.

Ministry of Road Transport and Highways (MoRTH) is planning to use natural rubber modified bitumen in road construction and maintenance, in order to improve the durability of roads. The Ministry will also implement an electronic toll collection system based on radio frequency identification to improve the efficiency of toll collection. Each vehicle will be fitted with a radio frequency identification tag, automatically crediting the tag account while transferring the toll from the bank. Pilot programmes have been initiated on the Delhi–Chandigarh highway. The MoRTH hopes to expand this programme to the entire national highway network by 2014.

The NTDPC interim report (2012) recommends that MoRTH should mandate all state highways to be two-lane by the end of the 12th Five-Year Plan. Tolls can only be justified if some 'enhanced service' is provided, thus, any highway with less than four lanes should not be taxed. A data centre should be established to collect data on traffic flows, road conditions and accidents. Emphasis should be placed on design standards for road, capacity-building of central, state and local agencies, and skill-building relevant to the road sector in educational institutions (Table 6).

The interim report of the High Level Committee on Financing Infrastructure (2012) proposes streamlining the awarding process by specifying and measuring against monthly/quarterly targets, updating the award progress on the public domain, reducing time and cost overruns by using the Engineering, Procurement and Construction (EPC) model in low-traffic density projects, and restructuring the NHAI to reduce implementation and management delays.

The road sector has seen some unfortunate setbacks this year. By March 2012, 95 projects handled by NHAI, and 126 projects through the state public work departments had been delayed. These have occurred because of tedious land acquisition and environment clearance procedures, poor contractor performances, and law and order. PPPs, a touted step in infrastructure development in India, are seen to be a disappointment this year in the road sector. While investments in PPP projects were valued at ₹1,800 billion in June 2012, an increase from ₹1,300 billion in June 2011, private participation may be winding down. Between April and September 2012, NHAI only awarded six projects, resulting in the construction of 560 km at a total cost of ₹49 billion. A recent IIT-Chennai study on time and cost overruns in road construction projects in India demonstrates that while PPP road projects take less time to complete, they have significantly higher costs than non-PPP projects (Thillai and Govind 2012). Furthermore, several construction companies are facing financial constraints in their road projects because of the aggressive auctions that hiked up bids, and high interest rates on loans coupled with stringent collateral mandates.

TABLE 6   Policy Recommendations for Road Sector from NTDPC's Interim Report

Target Area	Policy Suggestions
NHDP	• Clarify financial tools for funding. • Change policy to target heavy road construction according to traffic flows. • Impose tolls only when 'enhanced services' are provided.
State Highways	• Mandate each state to create state highway development plan; prioritise plans on the basis of traffic flows and demand and ensure each highway has two lanes.
Expressways	• Create more elevated entry points to expressways for increased rural accessibility.
Rural Roads	• Increase fuel cess in proportion to fuel price hikes. • Existing PMGSY projects to be completed and upgradation of network to occur in the next 10–15 years.
Design Standards	• Generate new design standards while studying road capacity and traffic flows.
Capacity-building and R&D	• Invest in capacity-building in engineering and designing of roads, and skill-building of workers and contractors. • Create professional institution to set design standards and conduct research in road sector.
Road Safety	• Using recommendations made in the Sundar Committee on Road Safety and Traffic Management (2007) Report, invest in building road safety capacity.
Road Transport	• Incorporate recommendations made by Sundar Committee on amending the Motor Vehicles Act 1988.
Data Centre	• Set up a road data centre to enhance data collection on cargo and passenger flows, historical flows on roads and road performance.

Source: National Transport Development Policy Committee (2012).

POWER

Despite the jarring disappointments brought to the power sector this year in the form of the coal scam, the only notable step taken by the government is towards the financial restructuring of power distribution companies. By September 2012, total generation capacity stood at about 208,000 MW, having increased by 15,000 MW since the beginning of the calendar year (Central Electricity Authority 2012). A majority of the capacity enhancement occurred in coal-based thermal plants, followed by marginal increases in gas-based thermal and renewable energy generation (Table 7).

TABLE 7   Installed Capacity of Power in India

Type of Energy	MW
Thermal	138,806
Coal	118,703
Gas	18,903
Diesel	1,199
Nuclear	4,780
Renewable	64,289
Hydro	39,291
Other	24,998
Total	207,875

Source: Central Electricity Authority (2012).

By September 2012, 558,240 villages had been provided electricity, i.e., 87 per cent of all Indian villages. Under the Rajiv Gandhi Grameen Vidyutikaran Yojana (RGGVY) or the Scheme for Rural Electricity Infrastructure and Household Electrification, 105,000 (of the targeted 110,000) villages had been provided with electricity, while free electricity connections had been given to 19.5 million Below Poverty Line (BPL) households (by April 2012). According to the 18th Electric Power Survey Report (2011), by the end of the 12th Five-Year Plan, the estimated peak demand will be 196,398 MW while the country's energy requirement will stand at 1,348,515 billion unit (BU). To facilitate meeting these requirements, the working group for the 12th Five-Year Plan proposes increasing the installed power capacity by about 76,000 MW, through public and private entities (Table 8), at an investment of 13.73 million in generation, transmission and distribution.

To encourage private participation in the creation of electricity infrastructure, tariff-based competitive bidding would be implemented for the provision of transmission services, as against the cost plus method, from January 2013 onwards. However, it may be noted that this process has already been used for the generation of electricity, where developers are going back on the tariffs quoted in the bidding process for mega projects, citing higher coal costs. Thermal power

TABLE 8   12th Five-Year Plan Working Group Projections for Capacity Addition

Developers	Hydro	Thermal	Nuclear	Capacity Addition (MW)
Central	5,632	11,426	2,800	19,858
State	1,456	12,340	0	13,796
Private	2,116	40,015	0	42,131
Total	9,204	63,781	2,800	75,785

Source: Press Information Bureau (2012).

TABLE 9   Proposed Budget for Power Sector in 12th Five-Year Plan

Energy Sub-Sectors	Proposed Budget (₹ in billion)
Generation	6,386
Transmission	1,800
Distribution	3,062
Others	2,477
Total	13,726

Source: Press Information Bureau (2012).

plant developers are scrapping their development plans or delaying work on their projects. More recently, the Cabinet Committee on Economic Affairs approved the foreign investment limit of 49 per cent on investment in generation, transmission and distribution companies, which caps FDI at 26 per cent and Foreign Institutional Investor (FII) at 23 per cent. The Electricity Act stipulates that all consumers with loads greater than 1 MW should be considered open access consumers, relieving state regulators of their jurisdiction on them. Despite mandating state governments and distribution companies to implement this policy, it has not been enacted; the central government is deliberating on how to resolve this situation. The interim report of the High Level Committee on Financing Infrastructure (2012) recommends establishing PPPs in the distribution sector and adding incentives such as viability gap funding. The Committee also suggests that coal should be imported in the short term but PPPs should be allowed in coal production for the long term; State Electricity Regulatory Commissions (SERCs) should establish the wheeling charge and open access surcharge but not regulate tariffs; and 25 per cent of the central discretionary allocation should be made available for direct sale to open access customers, in order to facilitate competition.

Fundamental problems in the sector include concerns which extend to all infrastructure sectors — land acquisition and environmental clearances. Obtaining land for power plants is increasingly difficult due to lengthy and complicated clearance systems. Environmental clearances take one–two years, when the allowed timeframe is seven–ten months. Between April 2009 and September 2012, 854 projects in mining, thermal and hydropower plants had filed for environmental clearances, of which only 76 have been processed and approved.

The domestic coal supply in India has reached abysmal levels, with 35 thermal power plants having less than seven days of coal reserves. Due to the overdependence on thermal power, the low quality and supply of domestic coal and Coal India Limited's (CIL) inability to meet supply agreements, India has increased its coal imports over the years. However, uncertainty lingers due to price hikes in Indonesia and Australia, the largest coal exporting countries to India. In attempts to lessen the burden on private and public developers, steam coal has been exempted from import duties. Additionally, CIL's board has agreed to the modified fuel supply agreements (FSAs), with 80 per cent supply commitment through which CIL will supply 65 per cent of domestic coal and 15 per cent imported coal on a cost plus basis. The original FSAs were modified in terms of the penalty, moratorium on penalty and force majeure clauses. Due to these input concerns, it has become even more important to improve the efficiency of the power plants. Between April and September 2012, the Plant Load Factor (PLF) of all coal-based thermal power plants in India was 68.51 per cent, implying low capacity utilisation on average. It is necessary to improve the capacity utilisation by renovating or modernising equipment, especially because of the high average and peak shortages and the lack of short-term alternative power sources.

The thermal power sector has been tainted with the coal scam, which has implicated large private companies, bureaucrats and politicians. The inter-ministerial group on coal recommended de-allocating 10 coal blocks and forfeiting the bank guarantees of several accused companies, after unearthing the controversy surrounding the allocation of 57 coal blocks in September 2012. The CAG reported losses of ₹10.52 billion to the government due to the low bids received for the coal block allocations, resulting in ₹1.86 trillion in benefits to participants. The CAG report added that the government had delayed the bidding and instead allotted the blocks between 2004 and 2009 (CAG of India 2012). The CBI has launched its investigation into five companies for misrepresenting net worth and experience when they obtained the coal blocks.

Gas-based thermal power plants have been performing quite poorly, given the limited supply in liquefied natural gas (LNG). The required gas for stations is 85.89 million metric standard cubic metre per day (mmscmd), while the actual availability is 48.44 mmscmd. The domestic gas production has fallen steeply and widened the demand and supply gap. The depreciation of the Rupee and the international market competitive demand, have added on the costs of gas imports. Nonetheless, the stagnant domestic supply prompts India to import a large amount of LNG despite the higher costs. While 25 mmscmd of gas can be sourced from Indian fields, about a 100 mmscmd will be required to fulfil the demand in 2014–15.

In light of the Fukushima disaster in Japan, protests against nuclear power have gained momentum in India. In fact, appeals have been filed in the Supreme Court to stay the commissioning of new nuclear projects, in states such as Tamil Nadu. Meanwhile, the liability clause in the Civil Liability for Nuclear Damage Rule, 2011, has been altered, with expectations of extending the five-year time limit for nuclear operators seeking damages from foreign suppliers, if a nuclear accident occurred.

Stagnant policy-making may prevent progress and expansion in the renewable sector. It appears that total renewable energy capacity addition may not even reach 1,500 MW this year, let alone meeting the target of having 15 per cent of renewable power on the grid by 2020, unless significant policy moves are made. After April 2012, renewable energy power plants have not been eligible for accelerated depreciation benefits and generation-based incentives. However, the Ministry of New and Renewable Energy (MNRE) may bring them back in the 12th Five-Year Plan, since it has caused a drop in capacity addition. In February 2012, the CERC launched the Terms and Conditions for Tariff Determination from Renewable Energy Sources Regulations, effective from April 2012 (CERC 2012). The tariffs fixed for all renewable energy sectors were lower than those in previous years. A major problem with this policy has been that the Renewable Power Obligations (RPOs) have not been enforced by the SERCs, causing poor energy generation. A few SERCs are even allowing the carryover of RPOs from the previous financial year, further aggravating the problem. Also the delays in the approval process for transmission companies have caused higher transaction costs for developers. Renewable Energy Certificates (RECs), which are traded on the Indian Energy Exchange, have a year-long annual compliance period, resulting in low trading volumes. Unless this period is shortened, the renewable energy sector will continue to suffer through the weakness of the REC instrument.

The installed generation capacity of solar power has crossed 1 GW, with a majority of these power plants being grid-connected. The Jawaharlal Nehru National Solar Mission (JNNSM), by which solar projects are set up by developers on build, own and operate basis, have added 201 MW of power. The bidding for first phase, second round, of the scheme had resulted in low tariffs due to falling prices of solar modules. Currently, Gujarat is the largest solar power producer with 680 MW of installed capacity and plans for 600 MW across 10 districts (KPMG 2012).

Since the beginning of the year, India has added only 750 MW in wind capacity, in comparison to 3,500 MW during the same period last year. Some states have asked wind power plants to close operations because of cheaper alternative power options, even though the central government mandates the sale of renewable energy. This comes at the cost of consumers, who are cut off from power supply because states are unwilling to pay for the wind energy. To add to this, state utility companies have asked for a portion of the REC revenue and increased transmission charges on wind power plants to encourage the former practice.

By the end of August 2012, the transmission network in India was made up of 275,530 circuit km of 220 kV of high voltage, and 425,866 of transformer capacity for 220 kV levels. The world's highest voltage test line station of 1,200 kV has been commissioned in Madhya Pradesh. Recent developments in this area included awarding two ultra mega transmission projects to Powergrid, while RInfra has set up plans for 220 km of 440 kV double circuit transmission line in Maharashtra.

Following the grid collapse in July 2012, which affected 20 states and 600 million consumers, the Ministry of Power (MoP) has proposed various alternatives including an islanding scheme for Delhi to prevent the reoccurrence of such situations. The poor financial state of the distribution companies prompted the MoP to once again develop a financial restructuring plan. It may be noted that the previous effort of cleaning up the balance sheets of the State Electricity Boards, in 2001, was not very successful. According to the present plan, state governments will take over 50 per cent of the short-term liabilities and convert them to bonds, and the remainder will be restructured by banks, by extending the moratorium on the principal and giving better terms for repayment. This assistance will be granted on the condition that the distribution companies carry out operational and financial reforms including rationalising tariffs, balancing high tension and low tension loads, extending metering to all consumers, and curtailing unauthorised electricity consumption.

New guidelines for the short-term procurement of electricity have been formulated to promote competition and reduce power purchase costs. This will reduce short-term charges for distribution companies, which are the largest component of the costs for distribution companies and are completely transferred to the customers. Through this plan, bidding companies will quote prices for a year as opposed to previous statute of 25 years. A new Perform, Achieve and Trade (PAT) scheme has also been brought out to incentivise energy efficiency by providing the option for energy-intensive industries to trade additional energy-saving certificates on energy exchanges. Furthermore, the MoP is implementing the Re-structured Accelerated Power Development & Reforms Programme (R-APDRP) across states, which is expected to reduce aggregate technical and commercial (AT&C) losses to the extent of 15 per cent.

The Case I and Case II standard bidding documents (SBDs) for power procurement were released in February 2012. Since then, revisions have included changes related to the volatility of fuel prices and a provision for pass through to consumers. Draft SBDs have also been designed for Ultra Mega Power Projects (UMPPs) to enable a stringent bidding process, higher performance guarantees and tougher eligibility norms.

URBAN INFRASTRUCTURE

India's urban population increased from 286 million in 2001 to 377 million in 2011, and accounts for 37 per cent of the total population. The total number of towns has also increased over the decade to 7,935, a 54 per cent increase from 2001. The low capacity of Urban Local Bodies (ULBs), limited financial resources and multiple clearance channels, have led to a mismatch in the demand and supply of urban services and development. While PPPs have been popular in solid waste management and sewage treatment plants, they have been scarce in urban transport due to high construction costs, capital requirements and long project tenures.

The first phase of the Jawaharlal Nehru National Urban Renewal Mission (JNNURM) was launched in December 2005, with the intention of promoting urban sector reforms, and enhancing urban infrastructure and facilities. Collating funds from the central and state governments, and ULBs, this programme works through the Ministry of Urban Development (MUD) and the Ministry of Housing and Poverty Alleviation (MHUPA). Under MUD, ₹480 billion were allocated to two sub-programmes, i.e., the Urban Infrastructure and Governance, and Urban Infrastructure Development Scheme for Small and Medium Towns (UIDSSMT), while MHUPA directed ₹22 billion to two programmes, i.e., Basic Services to the Urban Poor and Integrated Housing and Slum Development Programme, over the entire five-year period. The tenure of JNNURM first phase was extended up to March 2014, to ensure the completion of urban sector reforms and ongoing projects. The second phase of JNNURM, with an increased central allocation of 0.35 per cent of the Gross Domestic Product (GDP) as opposed to 0.1 per cent of the GDP in the first phase, will focus on small cities and towns. It will enhance the capacities of *nagar palikas* and *nagar panchayats*, while improving revenue generation of ULBs, implement reforms effectively, employ alternate financing methods, and enhance land management. As the first policy programme to solely focus on urban India, JNNURM has made some improvements in urban development. However, urban sector reforms have not been implemented by the states and ULBs, though these developments were supposed to have been contingent on them.

The UIDSSMT has relaxed its stipulations of basing the release of funds on urban reforms. Compared to its previous preconditions of the completion of urban reforms prior to the release of funds, the second instalments of funds are subjected to the completion of four of six mandatory reforms. If even these relaxed norms are not met, states may provide funds which can be reimbursed if reforms are completed later. However, these conditions are exempted for the north-eastern states and Jammu and Kashmir.

Various ministries have come up with important legislations to tackle other urban issues. The National Water Policy draft was released in January 2012, outlining the need for a strong institutional framework on water usage, by concentrating on levying effective water tariffs, promoting private participation in water service provision, launching periodic water supply audits, and promoting sustainable water usage (Ministry of Water Resources 2012). The draft was revised later in the year, to emphasise decentralised and water conservation-focused sanitation systems. The E-wastes (Management and Handling) Rules were implemented in May 2012 and formalised the role of electronic waste recyclers. These rules will prompt electronics producers to channel their e-waste to formal recyclers, as well as increase the number of recycling units by motivating informal recyclers to enter the formal market. For effective implementation of the policy, monitoring and regulation must be enforced.

CONCLUSION

India's infrastructure needs the government's renewed attention to restart an almost stagnant economy. It is imperative to strengthen the regulatory and governance processes to ensure smooth transition to a sustainable higher economic growth trajectory. It is not only important to find solutions to infrastructure project impediments, but also critical to find the right balance between growth and environmental concerns. Finally, de-politicisation and ensuring operations on efficient and commercial principles is critical for realising the targets of the 12th Five-Year Plan.

REFERENCES

18th Electric Power Survey Committee. 2011. 'Agenda for 3rd Meeting of 18th Electric Power Survey Committee'. Ministry of Power, Government of India. http://www.cea.nic.in/reports/planning/dmlf/venue_agenda_3rd_meeting.pdf (accessed 21 November 2012).

Biswas, Rudradeep. 2010. 'Is Your Favourite Operator Offering 3G/BWA in Your Circle? Check It Out'. *Telecomtalk.info*, 27 October. http://telecomtalk.info/is-your-favourite-operator-offering-3g-bwa-in-your-circle/45748/ (accessed 19 November 2012).

————. 2012. 'Way to 4G: Reliance Infotel is Busy to Finalize Vendors'. *Telecomtalk.info*. http://telecomtalk.info/4g-reliance-infotel-busy-finalize-vendors/100144/ (accessed 21 November 2012).

Central Electricity Regulatory Commission (CERC). 2012. 'Terms and Conditions for Tariff Determination from Renewable Energy Sources'. Central Electricity Regulatory Commission, Government of India. http://www.cercind.gov.in/regulation/RE_Amend.html (accessed 19 November 2012).

Central Electricity Authority. 2012. 'Monthly Review of Power Sector Reports: September 2012'. Ministry of Power, Government of India. http://www.cea.nic.in/executive_summary.html (accessed 21 November 2012).

Committee on Road Safety and Traffic Management. 2007. 'Report of the Committee on Road Safety and Traffic Management'. Ministry of Road Transport, Government of India, February. http://morth.nic.in/writereaddata/linkimages/SL_Road_Safety_sundar_report4006852610.pdf (accessed 21 November 2012).

Comptroller and Auditor General (CAG) of India. 2012. 'Report No. -7 of 2012-13 for the period ended March 2012 - Performance Audit of Allocation of Coal Blocks and Augmentation of Coal Production (Ministry of Coal)'. http://saiindia.gov.in/english/home/Our_Products/Audit_Report/Government_Wise/union_audit/recent_reports/union_performance/2012_2013/Commercial/Report_No_7/Report_No_7.html (accessed 19 November 2012).

Dharmadhikari Committee. 2012. 'Report of Expert Committee on HR Issues of Merged Air India'. Ministry of Civil Aviation, Government of India, 31 January. http://www.civilaviation.gov.in/MocaEx/content/conn/MyTutorialContent/path/Contribution%20Folders/REPORTS/Dharmadhikari%20Committee%20Report.pdf (accessed 19 November 2012).

Department of Electronics and Information Technology. 2012. 'National Telecom Policy – 2012'. Ministry of Communications and Information Technology, Government of India. http://deity.gov.in/sites/upload_files/dit/files/National%20Telecom%20Policy%20(2012)%20(480%20KB).pdf (accessed 19 November 2012).

Directorate General of Civil Aviation (DGCA). 2012. 'The Carbon Footprint of Indian Aviation 2011'. Government of India, 10 July. http://dgca.nic.in/env/Carbon%20Footprint%20Report%202011.pdf (accessed 19 November 2012).

Expert Group for Modernisation of Indian Railways. 2012. 'Report of the Expert Group for Modernisation of Indian Railways'. Ministry of Railways, Government of India, February. http://www.indianrailways.gov.in/railwayboard/uploads/

directorate/infra/downloads/Main_Report_Vol_I.pdf (accessed 19 November 2012).

High Level Committee on Financing Infrastructure. 2012. 'Interim Report'. Secretariat for Infrastructure, Planning Commission, August. http://infrastructure.gov.in/pdf/Interim_Report.pdf (accessed 19 November 2012).

High Level Safety Review Committee. 2012. 'Report of High Level Safety Review Committee'. Ministry of Railways, Government of India, February. http://irsme.nic.in/files/FINAL-BOOK-HLSRC_latest-17-02-2012.pdf (accessed 19 November 2012).

Infrastructure Development Finance Company (IDFC) Limited. 2012. 'Growing Steadily: Annual Report 2011–12'. IDFC. http://www.idfc.com/pdf/IDFC_15AR_Shareholder_2011_12.pdf (accessed 19 November 2012).

Infrastructure Development Finance Company (IDFC) Securities. 2012. 'Govt. Plans to Abolish ADF at Delhi and Mumbai Airports', *Event Update*, 16 October. Mumbai: IDFC Limited.

Indian Infrastructure. 2012. *Indian Infrastructure*, 15(1). New Delhi: India Infrastructure Publishing Private Ltd.

KPMG. 2012. 'The Rising Sun: A Point of View on the Solar Energy Sector in India'. KPMG, September. http://www.indiaenvironmentportal.org.in/files/file/Rising-Sun-2-kpmg-sep-12.pdf (accessed 19 November 2012).

Ministry of Water Resources. 2012. 'Draft National Water Policy 2012'. Ministry of Water Resources, Government of India. http://mowr.gov.in/writereaddata/linkimages/DraftNWP2012_English9353289094.pdf (accessed 19 November 2012).

National Highways Authority of India (NHAI). 2012. '150th MIS report for period ending August 30th, 2012'. Ministry of Road Transport and Highways. http://www.nhai.org/rmenujune2012.asp (accessed 19 November 2012).

Ministry of Railways (MoR). 2012. 'Draft Policy for Private Participation in Rail Connectivity and Capacity Augmentation Projects'. Ministry of Railways, Government of India. http://www.indianrailways.gov.in/railwayboard/uploads/directorate/infra/downloads/draft%20policy%20letter.pdf (accessed 21 November 2012).

National Transport Development Policy Committee (NTDPC). 2012. 'Interim Report'. Planning Commission, Government of India, April. http://transportpolicy.gov.in/NTDPCWEB/Home/InterimReport_NTDPC_2012.pdf?MOD=AJPERES&CACHEID=1eec7c804538e11a8a5cdf9490b39db2 (accessed 19 November 2012).

Press Information Bureau. 2012. 'Press Releases'. Press Information Bureau, Government of India. http://www.pib.nic.in/newsite/pmreleases.aspx?mincode=3 (accessed 19 November 2012).

Telecom Regulatory Authority of India (TRAI). 2011. 'Press Release: Highlights on Telecom Subscription Data as on 31st August, 2011'. Telecom Regulatory Authority of India, Government of India, 20 October. http://www.trai.gov.in/WriteReadData/PressRealease/Document/Press_Release_Aug-11_2.pdf (accessed 19 November 2012).

———. 2012. 'Press Release: Highlights on Telecom Subscription Data as on 31st August 2012'. Telecom Regulatory Authority of India, Government of India, 9 October. http://www.trai.gov.in/WriteReadData/PressRealease/Document/PR-TSD-Aug12.pdf (accessed 19 November 2012).

Thillai, Rajan A. and Gopinath Govind. 2012. 'PPPs for Roads, a Costly Affair'. *The Hindu Business Line*, 27 June. http://www.thehindubusinessline.com/opinion/article3577157.ece (accessed 19 November 2012).

Contributors

Yamini Aiyar is Director of Accountability Initiative (AI) at the Centre for Policy Research, New Delhi. Set up in 2008, AI is a research group that works to promote accountability for service delivery by developing innovative, people-friendly models for tracking the implementation of key social sector government programmes, and undertaking policy research on the effectiveness of different accountability experiments underway in India.

Rukmini Banerji is Director at Pratham and Annual Status of Education Report (ASER) Centre, New Delhi. Along with her colleagues, she has worked to build large-scale programmes to help children go to school and learn well. This is done via partnerships with state governments and with village communities. Today, Pratham is active in 250 districts out of a total of about 600 districts in India and in over 30 cities. She is also a leading member of the team that designs and implements the ASER, which is the largest annual study ever done by Indian citizens to monitor the status of elementary schooling and basic learning in the country. Each year over 700,000 children are assessed in basic reading skills and arithmetic to see if they are in school and are learning satisfactorily. In the seven years since it was initiated, the ASER effort has been widely recognised for its innovative use of citizens' participation.

Sambit Basu is Director (Policy Group) at IDFC Limited since 2008. He is a senior member of the team engaged in research on infrastructure policy and regulations. Although specialising in the energy sector, he has worked in other areas of infrastructure policy. He edits and manages IDFC Limited's flagship annual publication, the *India Infrastructure Report*, a thematic report on contemporary infrastructure issues. Previously, he has worked with Rio Tinto (a global mining company) as an analyst and economist; PricewaterhouseCoopers Ltd and Crisil Advisory Services Ltd. as management consultant; and ICRA Ltd as economist. He was also associated with the Administrative Staff College of India on a key World Bank assignment. After graduating from Presidency College, Calcutta, he completed his MA, MPhil and PhD in economics from the Centre for Economic Studies and Planning, Jawaharlal Nehru University, New Delhi.

Poonam Batra is Professor of Education at the Maulana Azad Centre for Elementary and Social Education, Central Institute of Education, University of Delhi. Major areas of her professional focus include public policy in education, curriculum and pedagogy, social psychology of education, teacher education, and gender studies. Awarded the Jawaharlal Nehru Fellowship in 2008 for undertaking research in teacher education and social change, she has been on several Government of India committees, including the Planning Commission Working Group on Teacher Education, the NAC-RTE Task Force on Teachers and the Justice Verma Commission on Teacher Education constituted by the Supreme Court of India. Her published work — covering a range of issues in elementary education and public policy — includes *Social Science Learning in Schools: Perspective and Challenges* (2010).

Suzana Andrade Brinkmann works as an education consultant with United Nations Children's Fund (UNICEF) India, New Delhi, and was earlier with the Ministry of Human Resource Development, advising on how to improve the quality of government teachers, teacher training, curriculum and assessment systems across India. She is committed to bringing transformation among teachers and school systems, for promoting a more equitable and just society, and has worked at the grassroots level to help set up Gyanankur Schools in Pune to provide low-cost quality education to underprivileged children. She is currently pursuing a PhD in Education from London University's Institute of Education, researching how Indian teachers' cultural beliefs affect their teaching practices, and how effective teacher training programmes can alter both teachers' beliefs and practices.

Saumen Chattopadhyay is Associate Professor at the Zakir Husain Centre for Educational Studies, School of Social Sciences, Jawaharlal Nehru University, New Delhi since 2004. He completed his PhD on black economy in India from the Centre for Economic Studies and Planning, Jawaharlal Nehru University, New Delhi. Previously, he worked at the National Institute of Public Finance and Policy (NIPFP), New Delhi (1995–2004). His research areas include public finance, specialising in the areas of state finances, tax evasion and tax compliance; and economics of education, focusing on policy-making in higher education. He has presented papers at several conferences, and involved in many projects — funded and collaborative — in the areas of taxation and education. He has authored *Macroeconomic Disequilibrium and the Black Economy: The Indian Context* (2012) and *Education and Economics: Disciplinary Evolution and Policy Discourse* (2012).

Dilip Chenoy is currently Chief Executive Officer and Managing Director of the National Skill Development Corporation (NSDC), New Delhi. The NSDC is a Public–Private Partnership (PPP) mandated to skill 150 million people in India by 2022 in 20 high-growth sectors and the unorganised segment by fostering private sector investment in training and skill development. Prior to joining the NSDC, he was Director General of the advocacy group for the automobile industry in India, Society of Indian Automobile Manufacturers (SIAM). He represented SIAM on various Government Committees as well as on the board of NSDC and the Steering Committee of the International Motorcycle Manufacturers Association. Before SIAM, he had been Deputy Director General at the Confederation of Indian Industry (CII), responsible for the Industry Sectors and Associations Council (ASCON). He was part of the research team that worked on the competitiveness of the Indian industry.

Sonalde Desai holds a joint appointment as Professor of Sociology at University of Maryland and Senior Fellow at National Council of Applied Economic Research, New Delhi. She is a demographer whose work deals primarily with social inequalities in developing countries with a particular focus on gender and class inequalities. She studies inequalities in education, employment and maternal and child health outcomes by locating them within the political economy of the region. While much of her research focuses on India, she has also engaged in comparative studies across Asia, Latin America and Sub-Saharan Africa. She has published articles in journals including the *Economic and Political Weekly*, *American Sociological Review*, *Demography*, *Population and Development Review*, and *Feminist Studies* and is the author of *Human Development in India: Challenges for a Society in Transition* (2010). She holds a PhD from Stanford University.

Amlanjyoti Goswami is Head, Legal and Regulation at the Indian Institute for Human Settlements, New Delhi, and holds an LLM degree from Harvard Law School, and an LLB from the University of Delhi, where he received the university gold medal. His research interests include urban law, politics and governance, land acquisition and land use, law and politics, law and policy for higher education in India, epistemology, cultural narratives, and the uses and discontents of modernity. Previously, he served as an advocate at

the chambers of Harish Salve (Senior Advocate, Supreme Court of India) and in the law firm, Amarchand Mangaldas; and as research associate to Prof. James Gustave Speth at Yale University on international environmental law. At the National Knowledge Commission, he worked on cross-cutting policy linkages in higher education, legal education, entrepreneurship, innovation, knowledge access, and aspects of folklore. He is an Inlaks scholar and an Asia 21 Fellow.

Annie Koshi is Principal of St Mary's School, New Delhi, and is pursuing a PhD on 'The Discourse of Education: Re-examining the Concept of Inclusion via the Narratives of School Children and the Indian State' at the Department of Humanities and Social Sciences at the Indian Institute of Technology (IIT), New Delhi. She has trained in Testing and Evaluation as part of the CBSE ELT Project at the College of St Mark and St John, Plymouth. A devoted social worker, she actively advocates the cause of the disabled and has worked towards introducing an inclusive education system where physically, mentally, emotionally, and financially-challenged children study in the mainstream, a school where 'difference' is accepted and celebrated. She is on the Board of trustees, Pratham Delhi Education Initiative, is a member of the Executive Committee, Dil Se, Centre for Equity Studies; the Committee of the Central Advisory Board of Education on the subject of extension of the Right of Children to Free and Compulsory Education Act, 2009 to pre-school education and secondary education; and is also on the Board of Directors of Karuna Vihar, Dehradun. She received the prestigious National Award for Teachers, conferred by the Ministry of Human Resource Development, Government of India, in the year 2004 and has been felicitated by the National Literacy Mission for her leadership in the field of literacy. She has also received many award for her contributions in the fields of education, art and culture.

Toby Linden joined the World Bank's South Asia Human Development Unit as a Lead Education Specialist in January 2011, and moved to New Delhi in July 2011. Before joining the India team, he was on secondment from the Bank to serve as Director of the Roma Education Fund, an international NGO working to improve the educational outcomes of Roma (Gypsies), the poorest minority in Europe. Other positions in his 14 years with the World Bank include working in the Country Office in Bosnia and as part of the analytical and research unit of the Education Network. His publications in the education sector include the World Bank's first book on lifelong learning and papers in secondary and higher education.

M. R. Madhavan is Co-founder of PRS Legislative Research, New Delhi, which was established in 2005. PRS is a non-profit, independent research initiative that seeks to strengthen the legislative process by making it better informed, more transparent and participatory. Before starting PRS, he was Principal and Senior Strategist for the Asia region for Bank of America in Singapore. He is a Fellow (doctorate) from Indian Institute of Management (IIM), Calcutta, and holds an MBA and a BTech degree from IIM, Calcutta and Indian Institute of Technology (IIT) Madras respectively. He was recently selected as a Chevening Gurukul Scholar by the London School of Economics.

Amitava Maitra is Head, Content at OKS Education Pvt Ltd, New Delhi, and has more than 16 years of experience in the e-learning industry, covering both custom content development as well as product development. He has worked in various roles ranging from pre-sales to design, development and delivery of learning solutions. His experience includes six years in managing projects 'on-site', with international exposure and the opportunity to work with people from different nationalities and cultures. He is passionate about the transforming role that learning design and technology can play in the domains of training and education. He is currently designing learning products that can be delivered on low-cost mobile devices and tablets so as to make quality mathematics and science education available to a large number of school students throughout India.

Megha Maniar is associated with the IDFC Policy Group in Mumbai where she primarily works on projects related to urban infrastructure. She holds a Bachelor of Arts (BA) in Economics from Claremont McKenna College, where she wrote her senior-year thesis on the demand for affordable rental housing in India.

Luis Miranda founded IDFC Private Equity in 2002 and retired in 2010 to focus on not-for-profits, and is currently Chairman, Board of Advisors, Centre for Civil Society, New Delhi. He is a trustee of the Society for Nutrition Education and Health Action, Mumbai; Senior Advisor at Global Environment Fund India; Director at SilverNeedle Hospitality, GMR Sports, Samhita Social Ventures and CSIR Tech; Advisor at Manipal Education and Medical Group; and a member of the Institute of Chartered Accountants of India. He is also a member of the Global Advisory Board of the Booth School of Business, University of Chicago and the Advisory Board of St. Xavier's College, Mumbai.

Shobhini Mukerji is Executive Director of Jameel Poverty Action Lab (J-PAL) South Asia at the Institute for Financial Management and Research, Chennai. She oversees the research, policy, training activities, and financial and administrative functions of the organisation, and is a principal investigator on a randomised evaluation of an education project that looks at interventions to improve learning levels of children in government schools in India. She has experience in managing large-scale assessments, training and capacity-building, data management and analysis. She has previously been employed with Pratham, a major education initiative in India, and has worked on research projects with the Commonwealth Education Fund (CEF-UK), United Nations Development Programme (UNDP) and UNICEF. She holds an MSc degree in Social Research Methods from the London School of Economics with a focus on Social Policy and Statistics.

Anit N. Mukherjee is Associate Professor at the National Institute of Public Finance and Policy, New Delhi, and he specialises in the analysis of public expenditure in education, health and social protection. His research focuses on the design, implementation and impact of publicly-funded programmes such as universal elementary education and universal health coverage, rural employment and social security. Combining policy research with field-level survey, he has created a network of research institutions, NGOs and community groups to better understand the process and determinants of successful policy reform. He advises several national and international institutions including Unique Identification Authority of India, ASER Centre, Accountability Initiative, Commonwealth Secretariat, and various United Nations organisations such as UNDP, UNICEF and the Joint United Nations Programme on HIV/AIDS (UNAIDS). He has a PhD in Economics from the University of Tsukuba, Japan, and an MA from Jawaharlal Nehru University, New Delhi.

Geetha B. Nambissan is Professor of Sociology of Education at the Zakir Husain Centre for Educational Studies, Jawaharlal Nehru University, New Delhi. Her areas of specialisation are exclusion, inclusion and the education of marginal groups in India and educational policy. Her current work focuses on the middle classes and educational advantage, and the social and educational implications of private schools for the poor. She has published widely in these areas. She is co-editor of *Child Labour and the Right to Education in South Asia: Needs Versus Rights?* (2003) and *Education and Social Justice in the Era of Globalisation: Perspectives from India and the UK* (2011). She is on the editorial board of Contemporary Education Dialogue and the advisory board of the Journal of Education Policy. She is also President (2013–14) of the Comparative Education Society of India.

Emon Nandi is a doctoral student at the Zakir Husain Centre for Educational Studies (ZHCES), Jawaharlal Nehru University, New Delhi. She works primarily on economics of education and her current research is on quality of education and its impact on economic growth and development. She is a recipient of the Indian Council of Social Science Research (ICSSR) doctoral scholarship, and has presented her research at many international and national conferences. She will present her latest work at the forthcoming 36th Indian Social Science Congress in Bhubaneswar (2012).

Manish Sabharwal is Chairman and Co-founder of Team-Lease Services Pvt Ltd, Bangalore, which is today among India's largest private-sector employers. He also co-founded IndiaLife Hewitt, ICap India and India InsureRisk Management. Awarded the Forbes India Leadership Award — Entrepreneur with Social Impact recently, he is an MBA from the Wharton School, University of Pennsylvania, member of the PMO's Skill Council, and the visionary and guiding light behind TeamLease Indian Institute of Job Training (IIJT).

Kaushiki Sanyal is Senior Analyst, heading the social sector team at PRS Legislative Research, New Delhi. She has consulted with the World Bank on a project related to the regulatory challenges faced by private engineering institutions in India. Previously, she was Senior Researcher at Capital IQ (a subsidiary of Standard & Poor's) where her primary responsibility was to track business intelligence data on the Capital IQ platform for investment banks and private equity firms. She earned her PhD in International Relations, and MPhil and MA degrees in Political Science from Jawaharlal Nehru University, New Delhi.

Chanchal Chand Sarkar is an Indian Economic Service (IES) Officer and is currently working as Deputy Secretary, Department of Expenditure, Ministry of Finance, Government of India, New Delhi. Prior to his present assignment, he has worked with the Ministry of Commerce and Industry, Government of India and has taken part in many bilateral and multilateral trade negotiations on behalf of the government, both in India and abroad. He has written on trade-related issues.

Parth J. Shah is Founder-President of Centre for Civil Society, New Delhi, a public policy think tank for community and market-based solutions within the framework of rule of law, subsidiarity and competitive markets. He holds a PhD in Economics and focuses his research and advocacy work on economic freedom, school choice, property right approaches for the environment, and good governance. Previously, he has taught Economics at the University of Michigan, and has published several academic articles and opinion pieces in the areas of development economics, education reform and business cycle theory.

Neeti Sharma is Vice-President and co-founder of Team-Lease Services Pvt Ltd, Bangalore, and currently manages the PPPs with various state and central government initiatives in the areas of employability and employment. With over 20 years of experience in the domains of outsourcing including employment and employability, customer relationship, operations, training, profit centre management and international business development, her current focus is to set up self-sustaining employability and employment models with various networks of centres that profile, assess, train, and certify job-seekers across profiles and cities or towns, linking various stakeholders such as the government, educational institutes, NGOs and training centres, catering to manpower requirements across sectors. She has been involved in various initiatives to increase the employability of tribal, rural and urban youth in various states. She holds an MSc in Economics and Statistics and an MA in Marketing Management from Symbiosis Institute of Management, Pune.

Satadru Sikdar is Research Associate at the National Institute of Public Finance and Policy, New Delhi, specialising in the analysis of public expenditure in education and social protection. He is pursuing a PhD from the Centre for Economic Studies and Planning, Jawaharlal Nehru University, New Delhi.

Sandhya Subramanian is Strategy Analyst with Manipal Global Education Services (MaGE), Bangalore. An MBA from Great Lakes Institute of Management, Chennai, she has been working with the company for more than two years. Prior to this, she worked as a Business Analyst with HCL Technologies. At MaGE, Sandhya works as part of the Strategy team primarily looking at business opportunities in the education space.

Anand Sudarshan is an education sector veteran and is currently a director at MaGE, Bangalore. Till July, he was Vice-Chairman and Managing Director of MaGE, where over the last six-plus years he successfully led the rapid transformation of MaGE into a major enterprise with a multi-country footprint. Prior to this, he was a part of the InfoTech industry for about 14 years, predominantly in an entrepreneurial role. He is a Charter Member of The Indus Entrepreneurs (TiE), a life-member of the Computer Society of India, and an active member of the World Economic Forum. He is involved in collaborating and building partnerships with universities in India and the United States and has special interest in areas of technology-driven education, and newer didactic and pedagogic models.

Sybil Thomas is currently Associate Professor of Education at the Department of Education, University of Mumbai. Prior to her current assignment, she was teaching at the Somaiya College of Education and has also worked with the Department of Adult and Continuing Education University of Mumbai. She has an MA in English Literature, and an MEd and PhD in Education. As a postgraduate teacher, she has taught various subjects such as Advanced Philosophy of Education, Advanced Educational Psychology, Educational Technology and Research Methodology. She has published several research papers in academic journals in gender studies, management of education and educational psychology. She has also presented papers at various conferences, and authored two books. Apart from her teaching and research endeavours, she is also keenly involved in Extension Work. She has designed various extension projects and is working in different community-based projects.

Amit Thorat is Associate Fellow at the National Council of Applied Economic Research (NCAER), New Delhi. Previously, he has worked at the International Food Policy Research Institute, New Delhi, and the National Centre for Agricultural Economics and Policy Research, New Delhi. He has a PhD in Economics from Jawaharlal Nehru University, New Delhi. His work has been around issues of income, assets, education, skills and health inequality across social, ethnic and religious groups as well as gender, and has included understanding patterns of diversification of crop production and food consumption over time as well as systems of collective farming in India.

Manish Upadhyay is Co-founder and Chief Evangelist of LIQVID, New Delhi — which recently received funding from Soft Bank International, a Japan-based $3-billion fund — and has over 17 years of experience in the eLearning/EduTech industry. He has earlier worked with NIIT and Lionbridge Technologies and has exposure in working across all types of eLearning projects. His previous key assignments include helping shape the Smart Schools project for the Ministry of Education, Malaysia and running the Offshore Development Center (ODC) for Pearson. In LIQVID, amongst other products, he recently architected a pioneering tablets-based portable English Language Lab, which has won the Aegis Graham Bell Awards, 2012.

N. V. Varghese is currently Head of Governance and Management in Education at the International Institute for Educational Planning (IIEP/UNESCO), Paris. He is the Secretary General of the International Working Group on Education (IWGE) and is the Editor General of the 'Fundamentals of Educational Planning' series of the Institute. Prior to joining IIEP, he was Professor and Head of Educational Planning at the National Institute of Educational Planning and Administration (NIEPA), New Delhi and was the focal point of the Asian Network of Training and Research Institutions in Educational Planning (ANTRIEP). His recent publications include *Higher Education Reforms: Institutional Restructuring in Asia* (2009), *Financing Education: Redesigning National Strategies and the Global Aid Architecture* (with Lene Buchert, 2011), and *Directions in Educational Planning: International Experiences and Perspectives* (with Mark Bray, 2011).

Wilima Wadhwa is Director of the ASER Centre, New Delhi. She has been associated with the ASER since its inception in 2005 and is responsible for its sample design and processing and analysis data. She earned her MA degrees in Economics from the University of Delhi and University of California, and her PhD in Economics from the University of California. She has published extensively and teaches Econometrics and Development Economics at the University of California, Irvine, and the Indian Statistical Institute, New Delhi. She has also been a member of various government committees, including the Committee on the Methodology of the BPL Census, Ministry of Rural Development; and the Working Group for the Revision of Wholesale Price Index Numbers, Ministry of Commerce and Industry, Government of India.

Michael Walton is Lecturer in Public Policy at the Kennedy School of Government, Harvard University, and Visiting Fellow at the Centre for Policy Research, New Delhi. He was VKRV Rao Chair Professor at the Institute for Social and Economic Change, Bangalore (2008–09), and Visiting Professor at the Delhi School of Economics in 2008. He previously worked with the World Bank, on Brazil, Indonesia, Mexico, and Zimbabwe; as Director of the 1995 World Development Report (WDR) on labour; Chief Economist for East Asia; Director for Poverty Reduction and Co-Director of the 2006 WDR on Equity. Other major publications include edited books on culture and public action and on equity and growth in Mexico. His current research is mainly on India, education, inequality, the political economy of cities, corporate behaviour and the politics of state–society and state–business interactions. He has an MPhil in Economics from University of Oxford.

T - #0113 - 230425 - C305 - 276/216/16 - PB - 9780415837217 - Gloss Lamination